HUMAN RIGHTS

The 1998 Act and The European Convention

AUSTRALIA
LBC Information Services—Sydney

CANADA and USA
Carswell—Toronto

NEW ZEALAND
Brooker's—Auckland

SINGAPORE and MALAYSIA
Sweet & Maxwell Asia
Singapore and Kuala Lumpur

HUMAN RIGHTS

THE 1998 ACT AND THE EUROPEAN CONVENTION

"A field day for crackpots, a pain in the neck for judges and a gold mine for lawyers."
(H.L. Debates, November 3, 1997, col. 1269.)

Stephen Grosz

MA (Cantab), Licencié spécial en droit européen (Brussels), Solicitor

Jack Beatson Q.C.

Rouse Ball Professor of English Law, Director of the Centre for Public Law,
University of Cambridge

Peter Duffy Q.C.

MA LLB (Cantab), Licencié spécial en droit européen (Brussels)

With additional material by:

Tim Eicke

LLB (Hons) (Dundee), Barrister, Joint Editor of the European Human Rights
Reports

Conor Gearty

BCL (NUI), LLB, Ph.D. (Cantab), Barrister, Professor of Human Rights Law,
University of London

Marie Demetriou

BA, BCL (Oxon), Barrister

LONDON
SWEET & MAXWELL
2000

Published in 2000 by
Sweet & Maxwell Limited of
100 Avenue Road,
London NW3 3PF
(http://www.smlawpub.co.uk)

Reprinted 2000

Phototypeset by LBJ Typesetting Ltd of Kingsclere
Printed and bound in Great Britain by
MPG Books Ltd, Bodmin, Cornwall

Index prepared by Indexing Specialists, Hove

No natural forests were destroyed
to make this product; only farmed
timber was used and re-planted.

ISBN 0 421 630 604

A CIP catalogue record for this book is
available from the British Library

To Vivienne, Clare, Sarah and Helen,
and to the memory of Peter;
to Teddy Grosz
and to the memory of Miriam Beatson

Foreword

An important aspect of the reorientation of the United Kingdom's constitution towards a culture of human rights is that it draws upon not one but two new sources of law. One is the pervasive Human Rights Act 1998; the other is the overarching European Convention on Human Rights. The two will be largely but by no means entirely coextensive.

This book, usefully divided between the two elements, shows why. The Act is neither a mere vehicle for the Convention nor an ordinary Act of Parliament. It is a statute in the nature of a fundamental law, permeating the whole of the common law and equity, all public administration and delegated legislation, with the Convention's values, and stopping short only where Parliament has unequivocally legislated to the contrary. This scheme, accompanied by the original device of the declaration of incompatibility, ingeniously respects both the Convention and the sovereignty of Parliament. But because it is a domestic statute, it opens the door to a wealth of jurisprudence and experience from other Commonwealth, common law and European jurisdictions, as well as from the Strasbourg Court itself, in its interpretation and application.

It is through this rich prism that the Convention, in its turn, will be read and applied in our courts: not as a monochrome exercise in textual interpretation and the application of received authority, but as a kaleidoscopic pattern combining the symmetry of law with the variety of experience. We may not simply reach down answers from the Strasbourg shelf: in every case the question will remain what is the impact of the Convention on our law and our public administration.

This is why it is a mistake to imagine that a case can be conducted under the Human Rights Act 1998 by simply looking up a relevant article and any decisions of the European Court of Human Rights relating to it. To this exercise—to which Part II of the book is directed—must be added an understanding of the nature of the Act and of the world of human rights jurisprudence of which the United Kingdom is now a part—the indispensable subject of Part I.

It is to the practising and academic profession that the courts will be looking for assistance in this task. The Judicial Studies Board is ensuring that all judges have a basic understanding of the Act and the Convention, but this will be of little use unless the professions play a corresponding role. It is important that legal education should not be treating human rights as a bolt-on to existing disciplines, and that practitioners should not start by regarding human rights points as the last resort in a difficult case. If this happens, judges will be encouraged to regard the Act as no more than an advocate's port in a forensic storm. Good points will be lost in the hail of bad ones. If on the other hand the Act and Convention are used with care and discrimination as a source of viable points backed by educated arguments, the bench and the profession will learn together, and the new culture which Parliament has set out to create will begin to take shape.

This volume is a major contribution to a major task. It deserves wide use, both as preparation for the new system and as a handbook for working within it. Of its authors, all of whom enjoy great distinction in the field, it is right to make special mention of Peter Duffy, whose early death has robbed human rights law of one of its best and brightest exponents.

Stephen Sedley
Royal Courts of Justice

Preface

The Human Rights Act 1998 has been the catalyst for many books. The idea for this one was Peter Duffy's. He brought the three of us together and his enthusiasm for the project continued even after he fell ill. Although he did not live to see its completion, he is not merely an author in a formal sense. The Article by Article commentary on the European Convention in Part II is largely based on his drafts, which we have revised and brought up to date. Readers with eagle eyes will detect that some of the material on the 1998 Act in Part I is based on his annotation to the Act for Current Law Statutes; and we have also drawn on his other writings and lectures on the effect of the Act and the Convention. We dedicate this book to his memory and hope that it measures up to his high standards.

We had two distinct aims in putting this book together. First, to explain how the 1998 Act will operate in practice, its constitutional status, and how it fits into the existing body of our statutory and common law. This is done in Part 1. We consider the impact of the strong interpretative obligation in the Act directing courts to give effect to legislation in a way that is compatible with the rights contained in the European Convention of Human Rights "so far as it is possible to do so", using practical examples of how this may be done by the courts. Where appropriate we refer to decisions concerning European Community law and from Commonwealth jurisdictions. We also examine the scope of the obligation on public authorities to comply with Convention rights, and whether, and if so how, the Convention rights may have a horizontal effect. The remedies under the Act; judicial review, damages, and the novel provisions for declarations of incompatibility and "fast track" remedial orders are dealt with in chapters 3 and 6. Part I also considers the impact of the Convention on judicial review and the review of discretion, and the restrictive "victim" test of standing imposed for human rights cases, and how it will operate alongside the more liberal approach used in other judicial review cases. Dealing with a new Act as yet untested in the courts, even one so heavily analysed by lawyer Parliamentarians during its legislative passage, presents challenges. We have sought to identify areas of dispute, to present the arguments in a balanced way with the assistance of the government's *Pepper v. Hart* statements in Parliament, and to suggest a way forward.

Our aim in Part II is different. Here, after a section dealing with the Convention principles, we have sought to present the jurisprudence of the Strasbourg Commission and Court in an accessible and clear way to United Kingdom lawyers, especially those coming to it for the first time. It was never our intention to provide an exhaustive treatment dealing with every Convention issue. Instead we hope that we have provided an introduction to the approach which the Convention demands: it will be seen that in most instances courts and tribunals will reach the same conclusions as they did before the entry into force of the Act. What may change is the language and reasoning which lead to those conclusions.

This book is a joint enterprise (one achieved primarily with the aid of e–mail and the telephone). We are particularly grateful to Tim Eicke, who helped to update the commentary on Articles 5 and 6 and checked some of the proofs; to Conor Gearty, who is responsible for Chapter 7 of Part I on Devolution, and to Marie Demetritou for additional material on the relationship between the Convention and E.C. law and on the Strasbourg case law on its "victim" test of standing. We are also grateful to many friends who read and commented on parts of the book; in particular to Robin Lewis and Judith Beale, who read and commented on large parts of the book and wrestled with the octopus which was the authors' combined prose; to colleagues at Bindmans who allowed Stephen time off to write; and to the staff of the Squire Law Library, Cambridge for their valuable help. We are also grateful to the editorial team at Sweet & Maxwell for their support throughout, their patience and for producing the book with astonishing speed. Company policy precludes us from identifying those who have been particularly supportive, but they know who they are. In particular we would like to thank Sweet and Maxwell for taking on the task of preparing the tables and index.

We have taken account of decisions and other materials that were available to us on August 1, 1999. We have also been able to include some more recent material at the proof stage, in particular there is a brief treatment of the decision of the Court of Human Rights in *Smith & Grady v. United Kingdom* in Chapter 5 and in the commentary on Articles 3, 8 and 13, and of the decisions of the House of Lords in *R. v. D.P.P., ex parte Kebeline* and *Fitzpatrick v. Sterling Housing Association* in Chapter 3.

J.B.
S.G.
November 15, 1999

Table of Contents

Part I: The Human Rights Act 1998

Chapter 1: The status of the European Convention of Human Rights in United Kingdom Law

Chapter 2: The status of the jurisprudence of the Strasbourg Court and institutions in United Kingdom Law

Chapter 3: Impact of the Act on legislation

Chapter 4: The scope of protection given by the Act

Part III: Appendices

Table of Cases

TABLE OF CASES BEFORE THE EUROPEAN COURT OF HUMAN RIGHTS

TABLE OF CASES BEFORE THE EUROPEAN COMMISSION OF HUMAN RIGHTS

Table of Cases before the European Court of Justice

TABLE OF STATUTES

Table of Foreign Enactments

Australia

Canada

Hong Kong

Nambia

New Zealand

South Africa

United States

TABLE OF STATUTORY INSTRUMENTS

TABLE OF INTERNATIONAL TREATIES AND CONVENTIONS

TABLE OF EUROPEAN COMMUNITY TREATIES

PART I: THE HUMAN RIGHTS ACT 1998

CHAPTER 1

The status of the European Convention of Human Rights in United Kingdom law

1–01 This chapter is concerned with the analytical framework of, and background to, the Human Rights Act (HRA) 1998. It considers the status of the Convention before and after enactment of the HRA, the HRA's rejection of full incorporation in favour of a different approach, survival of previous authority concerning the Convention, and the indirect incorporation of the Convention via E.C. law. While of theoretical importance, the issues canvassed here are unlikely to come before the courts in a run of the mill human rights' case.

1. THE STATUS OF THE CONVENTION AT COMMON LAW PRIOR TO THE HRA

1–02 Treaty obligations binding on the United Kingdom under international law can only be directly enforced as law within the United Kingdom if they are given legislative effect[1] either by statute, or by subordinate legislation. Such subordinate legislation may be made pursuant to a specific Act passed in consequence of the treaty or a more general enabling Act.[2] The process of giving legislative effect to an international treaty or convention is called incorporation. But the rule that only incorporated treaty obligations can be enforced as law does not mean that unincorporated treaties are without effect. The principles of statutory interpretation include a presumption that Parliament intends to comply with the United Kingdom's obligations in international law, so any ambiguity in the statutory language is resolved by preferring the meaning that is consistent with the treaty obligations.[3]

---

[1] *The Parlement Belge* (1879) 4 P.D. 129, 154 (1880) 5 P.D. 197; *Walker v. Baird* [1892] A.C. 491; *J.H. Rayner (Mincing Lane) Ltd v. DTI, Maclaine Watson v. DTI, Re International Tin Council* [1990] 2 A.C. 418, 476, 499–500 (Lord Templeman and Lord Oliver); [1989] Ch. 72, 163–164, 207, 239 Kerr, Nourse and Ralph Gibson L.JJ.). In the context of the ECHR, see *R. v. Chief Immigration Officer, Heathrow Airport, ex parte Salamat Bibi* [1976] 1 W.L.R. 979, 984–985; *Rantzen v. Mirror Group Newspapers* [1994] Q.B. 670, 690. See also Bennion, *Statutory Interpretation* (3rd ed.), pp. 523–524; Brownlie, *Principles of International Law* (4th ed.), p. 47 *et seq.*
[2] *e.g.* the International Organisations (Immunities & Privileges) Act 1950 and the International Organisations Act 1968.
[3] *Salomon v. CCE* [1967] 2 Q.B. 116; *R. v. Home Secretary, ex parte Brind* [1991] A.C. 696. *Cf. Garland v. British Rail Engineering* [1983] 2 A.C. 751, 771 which takes a broader approach to "ambiguity". See also *Post Office v. Estuary Radio* [1968] 2 Q.B. 740 (construction of Order in Council); *Wilson Smithett*

Before the enactment of the HRA, this presumption applied to the European Convention of Human Rights (ECHR), even where the legislation in question was not intended to incorporate any Convention provision into national law.[4] The force of the presumption depends on the meaning of "ambiguity". In the context of the Convention, it has been held to mean "open to two or more different constructions"[5] rather than, more widely, "reasonably capable" of bearing a meaning consistent with the Convention.[6] It has also been said that the common law should be interpreted, so far as possible, so as to conform with the principles of the Convention.[7] This includes the principles upon which a judicial discretion, for example to grant injunctive or declaratory relief, is to be exercised, and the quantum of damages.[8] There was no duty upon a public body to take account of the principles of the Convention in the exercise of its powers, because, it was said, this would "inevitably result in incorporating the Convention into English domestic law by the back door".[9] However, it was permissible for a public body exercising an administrative power to take Convention principles into account[10] and if it did, its decision would be vitiated by any misdirection about the effect of the Convention.[11] In any event, where the exercise of discretion affected fundamental human rights there was a more intensive form of review, albeit of a *Wednesbury* sort, where the court subjected the decision to "anxious scrutiny".[12] Furthermore, where a European Community institution had exercised its legislative powers within the

---

& *Cope v. Teruzzi* [1976] 1 Q.B. 683; *The Jade, The Eischersheim* [1976] 1 W.L.R. 430 (HL); *Pan American World Airways Inc. v. Dept. Trade* [1976] 1 Lloyd's R. 257; *James Buchanan & Co. Ltd v. Babco* [1978] A.C. 141; *Fothergill v. Monarch Airlines Ltd* [1981] A.C. 251; *Gatoil v. Arkwright-Boston Mfg Mutual Ins. Co.* [1985] A.C. 255; *Alcom v. Republic of Columbia* [1984] A.C. 580, 592 *et seq.*; *J.H. Rayner (Mincing Lane) Ltd v. DTI, Maclaine Watson v. DTI, Re International Tin Council* [1990] 2 A.C. 418, 500 [1989] Ch. 72, 165; Lord Browne-Wilkinson [1992] P.L. 406.

[4] *R. v. Miah* [1974] 1 W.L.R. 692, 694; *R. v. Home Secretary, ex parte Phansopkar* [1976] Q.B. 606, 626; *A-G v. BBC* [1981] A.C. 303, 352; *R. v. Home Secretary, ex parte Wynne* [1992] Q.B. 406, 427; *Champion v. Chief Constable of Gwent Constabulary* [1990] 1 W.L.R. 1, 14; *R. v. Home Secretary, ex parte Brind* [1991] A.C. 696, 747–748 (taking a narrow view of "ambiguity"). See further, Duffy (1980) 29 I.C.L.Q. 585, 590 *et seq.*; Hunt, *Using Human Rights Law in English Courts* (1996) esp. Ch. 1.

[5] *R. v. Home Secretary, ex parte Brind* [1991] A.C. 696, 761.

[6] *Garland v. British Rail Engineering Ltd* [1983] 2 A.C. 751, 771 (though note there was more than one possible construction there) and see cases cited in n. 3 above.

[7] *Raymond v. Honey* [1983] 1 A.C. 1; *A-G v. Guardian Newspapers Ltd* [1987] 1 W.L.R. 1248; *A-G v. Times Newspapers Ltd* [1990] 1 A.C. 109; *Derbyshire CC v. Times Newspapers Ltd* [1992] Q.B. 770, 812, 830 (aff'd on other grounds: [1993] A.C. 534). See also *R. v. Home Secretary, ex parte McQuillan* [1995] 4 All E.R. 400; *R. v. Khan* [1996] 3 All E.R. 289. But *cf. Malone v. Met Police Commissioner* [1979] Ch. 344; *Kaye v. Robertson* [1991] F.S.R. 62. In some cases it has been concluded that a particular rule of "the common law . . . is consistent with the obligations assumed" under the ECHR: *A-G v. Times Newspapers Ltd* [1990] 1 A.C. 109, 283–284; *Derbyshire CC v. Times Newspapers Ltd* [1993] A.C. 534, 551; *R. v. Home Secretary, ex parte Norney* (1995) 7 Admin. L.R. 861, 871. For an example of inconsistency, see *Gleaves v. Deakin* [1980] A.C. 477, 482–484 (Lord Diplock).

[8] *Rantzen v. MGN* [1993] 4 All E.R. 975, 994; *John v. MGN* [1996] 2 All E.R. 35 (jury awards).

[9] *R. v. Home Secretary, ex parte Brind* [1991] A.C. 696, 761–762 (Lord Ackner). *Cf.* Lord Templeman, *ibid.* at 750–751.

[10] *R. v. Home Secretary, ex parte Zibirila-Alassini* [1991] Imm. A.R. 367; *R. v. Home Secretary, ex parte Sinclair* [1992] Imm. A.R. 293, 300; *R. v. Home Secretary, ex parte Chahal* [1993] Imm. A.R. 362, 380; *R. v. Home Secretary, ex parte Khan* [1998] Imm. A.R. 106. See also *Minister for Immigration and Ethnic Affairs v. Teoh* (1995) 128 A.L.R. 353, 360, 363, 365, 371 (High Court of Australia); *Tavita v. Minister of Immigration* [1994] 2 N.Z.L.R. 257; Hunt, *Using Human Rights Law in English Courts* (1996) 230 *et seq. Cf. Chundawadra v. Immigration Appeal Tribunal* [1988] Imm. A.R. 161, 173.

[11] *R. v. Secretary of State for the Home Department, ex parte Launder* [1997] 1 W.L.R. 839, 867C (Lord Hope of Craighead); *R. v. Director of Public Prosecutions, ex parte Kebeline & ors* [1999] 3 W.L.R. 175. (Divisional Court).

[12] *Budcaycay v. Secretary of State for the Home Department* [1987] A.C. 514; *R. v. Secretary of State for the Home Department, ex parte Brind* [1991] 1 A.C. 517; *R. v. Ministry of Defence, ex parte Smith* [1996] Q.B. 517; *R. v. Lord Saville of Newdigate and Others, ex parte A and Others*, The Times, July 29, 1999, 149 N.L.J. 965, 1201.

scope of E.C. law, the Convention's principles were likely to constitute general principles of E.C. law and, as such, to have had effect in U.K. law.[13] In *R. v. Secretary of State for the Home Department, ex parte McQuillan*, Sedley J. stated that "the principles and standards set out in the Convention can certainly be a matter of which the law of this country now takes notice in setting its own standards" and that "once it is accepted that the standards articulated in the Convention are standards which both march with those of the common law and inform the jurisprudence of the European Union, it becomes unreal and potentially unjust to continue to develop English public law without reference to them".[14]

1–03 Between 1964 and July 1999 the Convention, though unincorporated, was referred to in over 650 English cases.[15] Lord Bingham C.J. has summarised the ways in which the Convention has influenced domestic proceedings as follows.[16] First, where a United Kingdom statute is capable of two interpretations, one consistent with the Convention and one inconsistent, the courts will presume that Parliament intended to legislate in conformity with the Convention. Secondly, if the common law is uncertain, unclear or incomplete, the courts have to declare what the law is, and will do so, wherever possible, so as to conform with the Convention. Thirdly, in construing a domestic statute enacted to fulfil a Convention obligation, the courts will ordinarily assume that it succeeds Fourthly, where the courts have a discretion to exercise, they seek to act in a way which does not violate the Convention. Fifthly, when the courts must decide what British public policy demands, international obligations enshrined in the Convention may provide guidance. Sixthly, on matters covered by the law of the European Community, the Convention may have effect as part of the general principles of Community law. [17]

2. THE APPROACH OF THE HRA

1–04 Section 1 of the HRA has the following purposes:

(a) to define the "Convention rights" to which the Act applies;

(b) to give effect to the Convention rights;

(c) to set out the limitations, derogations and reservations which circumscribe the application of the Convention Rights; and

(d) to enable the Secretary of State to add to the catalogue of Convention rights.

A. The definition and scope of "Convention rights"

1–05 Section 1(1) provides that "Convention rights" means:

(a) Articles 2 to 12 and 14 of the Convention;

(b) Articles 1 to 3 of the First Protocol; and

---

[13] See below para. 1–18.
[14] [1995] 4 All E.R. 400, 422–423.
[15] For a list of cases until December 1996 see Hunt, *Using Human Rights Law in English Courts* (1996) Appendix 1.
[16] *Hansard*, H.L. Vol. 574, July 3, 1996, col. 1466. See further Beloff & Mountfield [1996] E.H.R.L.R. 467.
[17] *e.g.* Case 222/84 *Johnston v. Chief Constable of the RUC* [1986] E.C.R. 1651. See para. 1–18 below.

(c) Articles 1 and 2 of the Sixth Protocol.

The text of these articles is set out at pages 391–395. Articles 1 and 13 are not included in section 1(1), an omission which provoked much debate during the passage of the Bill, and requires explanation. Section 1(1) of the HRA also omits any reference to the Fourth and Seventh Protocols to the Convention, which contain additional substantive rights.[18] Convention rights are to be read with Articles 16 to 18 of the Convention.[19]

1–06   Turning to the omitted Articles, Article 1 provides that:

"The High Contracting Parties shall secure to everyone within their jurisdiction the rights and freedoms defined in section 1 of this Convention."

Article 1 of the Convention contains the states' mutual undertaking to give effect to the Convention within their jurisdiction.[20] It also sets out the jurisdictional and personal scope of the obligation on states to secure the rights and freedoms under the Convention ("To everyone within their jurisdiction"). However, the Strasbourg institutions have also referred to this provision, coupled with the substantive provisions of section 1, to impose not only negative obligations, to refrain from interfering with Convention rights, but also certain positive obligations on states to protect an individual's enjoyment of Convention rights from interference by other individuals.[21]

The inter-state obligation is unnecessary for the purposes of the HRA, which is designed to carry it out. Similarly, Article 1 is not needed to define the jurisdictional scope of the HRA, although by virtue of section 2 of the Act account can be taken of the case law under Article 1 in determining any question relating to a Convention right; nor is the omission of Article 1 intended to limit the scope of positive obligations which the substantive Articles of the Convention impose on states. The overriding purpose of the HRA is to "bring home" the Convention rights, *i.e.* to enable those within the United Kingdom jurisdiction to enforce before national courts and tribunals rights of the same ambit as they could enforce before the Strasbourg institutions.[22] By imposing an obligation to respect Convention rights on the public authorities for whom it would be held responsible in Strasbourg, the Government is effectively securing enjoyment of those rights, and inclusion of Article 1 is unnecessary.

Article 13 provides that:

"Everyone whose rights and freedoms as set forth in this Convention are violated shall have an effective remedy before a national authority notwithstand-

---

[18] The White Paper, Rights Brought Home, Cm. 3782, paras 4.11–4.12 and 4.14–4.16 explain this as follows. Protocol. 4: there are potential conflicts between Protocol. 4 and domestic law concerning categories of British nationality which must be maintained. Protocol. 7: although its provisions reflect principles already inherent in our law, some domestic law provisions (*e.g.* property rights of spouses) cannot be interpreted compatibly with the Protocol. The government intends to bring forward legislation to remove these and when it does so, the United Kingdom will ratify the Protocol.
[19] See p. 404.
[20] States may enforce this undertaking against each other by application to the Commission/Court: see Article 33, formerly Article 24, of the Convention.
[21] *X & Y v. Netherlands* (1986) 8 E.H.R.R. 235, para. 23 (Article 8); *Plattform 'Ärtzte für das Leben' v. Austria* (1991) 13 E.H.R.R. 204, para. 32 (Article 11). See further below, para. C0–05, pp. 164–165.
[22] See the White Paper, Rights Brought Home, Cm. 3782, paras 1.14 and 1.18–1.19.

ing that the violation has been committed by persons acting in an official capacity."

As will be seen later,[23] Article 13 has received a fairly restrictive interpretation. Together with Articles 1, 34[24] and 35,[25] it plays an important part in the structure of responsibility and enforcement which the Convention establishes. This structure is threefold. First, there is an obligation on the state to secure the enjoyment of the Convention rights. Secondly, the state is required to provide an effective remedy, and thirdly there is the opportunity to make an application to Strasbourg complaining of violation of one's rights under the Convention. The requirement that an applicant should exhaust domestic remedies before seeking redress in Strasbourg is a corollary of the state's obligation to make effective remedies available.

1–07 Seen in this perspective, there is nothing sinister about the omission of Article 13 from the catalogue of Convention rights given effect by the HRA. The HRA itself, and in particular sections 6 to 8,[26] set out the remedies which an individual may claim in proceedings involving Convention rights. Attempts were made during the passage of the Bill to include Article 13. The Government maintained that it was unnecessary, because section 8 gave courts the widest possible scope to provide effective remedies, and inclusion of the Article might confuse or mislead courts into developing new remedies which they have no power to grant.[27] Those seeking to include the provision claimed that its absence might lead courts to believe that their power to grant remedies was more circumscribed than it should be. But it is clear that in deciding questions concerning Convention rights, including questions of remedy, courts and tribunals must take account of *all* Convention case law, including that relating to Article 13.[28] This may be of particular importance in relation to proceedings under the HRA alleging that a judicial act amounts to a contravention of a Convention right. Such proceedings may be brought only by appeal or judicial review, or in such other forum as may be prescribed by rules.[29] In deciding whether to grant permission to appeal or to move for judicial review, the court or tribunal in question will need to take account of what the Strasbourg institutions have said about the requirements of the right to an effective remedy under Article 13.[30]

1–08 There may nonetheless be cases where a national court or tribunal is unable to furnish an effective remedy because the legislation governing its powers clearly prevents it from doing so.[31] The absence of an effective procedure for investigation, for example in relation to an allegation that death or injury was

---

[23] See paras C13–01—C13–07. See also paras 6–12—6–14.
[24] The right of individual petition to the Court; formerly Article 25, which provided the same right in respect of the Commission.
[25] The requirement to exhaust all domestic remedies before exercising the right of individual petition; formerly Article 26.
[26] See pp. 381–383.
[27] Although neither Ministers nor the Lord Chancellor could give an example. See, for example, *Hansard*, H.C., May 20, 1998, col. 979 (Home Secretary, Committee Stage); *Hansard* H.L., November 18, 1997, col. 475 (Lord Chancellor, Committee Stage).
[28] See below, paras C13–01 *et seq.*, and para. 5–40.
[29] Section 9(1), see further below, para. 6–03.
[30] *Vilvarajah v. United Kingdom* (1991) 14 E.H.R.R. 248; see also *R. v. Secretary of State for the Home Department, ex parte Launder* [1997] 1 W.L.R. 839 (HL).
[31] *Chahal v. United Kingdom* November 15, 1996, R.J.D., 1996-II, No. 22; 23 E.H.R.R. 413. See further below, paras 3–43—3–48.

caused by ill-treatment in custody, may also amount to an independent breach of Article 13[32] while not giving rise to a breach of a Convention right under the Act. Although such cases may be rare, in the light of the experience in the Stephen Lawrence case,[33] the Act's failure to deal with them is a regrettable omission.

B.   The effect of Convention rights

1–09   Section 1(2) provides that the Convention rights "are to have effect for the purposes of this Act subject to any designated derogation or reservation . . . ". It is this provision which brings the Convention rights into national law, although, as discussed below, it does not adopt the normal method for incorporating international treaties into domestic law, namely by enacting that the relevant treaty or Convention is to have the force of law.[34] This difference is significant and is fundamental to the whole structure of the HRA. It does not incorporate the Convention rights wholesale into national law, nor is it intended to do so. As is clear from the Long Title, the purpose of the HRA is to "give further effect" to Convention rights. The Articles of the Convention and the First and Sixth Protocols set out in Schedule 1 are not part of our law; they do not create rights beyond the confines of the Act save to the extent that they will influence the development of the common law.[35] Pre-existing primary legislation is not impliedly repealed by the HRA if inconsistent with a Convention right[36]; incompatible subordinate legislation may be quashed or declared invalid only if the parent statute does not require the incompatibility. The HRA creates a self-contained statutory scheme within which Convention rights will apply and be given effect, without limiting the pre-existing common law jurisprudence relating to the effect of the Convention.

C.   Indirect and incomplete incorporation

1–10   The approach of the HRA differs markedly from the methods normally used to give effect to international treaties in the domestic law of the United Kingdom. It constitutes a new, incomplete and indirect form of incorporation[37] in which, although U.K. courts are empowered to apply the Convention and its jurisprudence, and there is a strong presumption of the conformity of U.K. law to the law of the Convention, the Convention itself is not fully part of our domestic law. We shall see that the HRA's technique of giving "further effect" to the Convention is by the creation of a rule of interpretation and the enactment of a public law wrong. While the HRA has a special status above that of ordinary statutes, it is not a fully-fledged constitutional instrument. The Articles and the First and Sixth Protocols set out in Schedule 1 to the Act are not made part of domestic law, and there is no attempt to entrench the rights set out in the Articles contained in Schedule 1 to the Act. The constitutional reasons for this approach and its consequences are discussed below.

1–11   The White Paper stated that incorporation of the Convention was "necessary"[38] and that the Government had a manifesto commitment to introduce

---

[32] See, for example, *Aksoy v. Turkey* December 18, 1996, R.J.D., 1996–IV, No. 26; 23 E.H.R.R. 553.

[33] "The Stephen Lawrence Inquiry" Cm. 4262–I (1999).

[34] For examples and for the effect of this formulation, see below, para. 1–12 and, on the incorporation of E.C. law, see below, paras 1–18, n. 70 and para. 1–23.

[35] See below, paras 1–14, 1–15, 4–53—4–59.

[36] Although it is subject to the interpretative obligation and may be the subject of a declaration of incompatibility, see below, paras 3–01, 3–06 and 3–43.

[37] See Mr John Bercow, MP, *Hansard*, H.C. Vol. 306, February 16, 1998, col. 816.

[38] Para. 1.4. See also paras 1.14 and 2.1 (will "give them further effect directly in our domestic law").

legislation to incorporate the Convention.[39] The Prime Minister's Introduction stated that the new rights were "based on bringing the European Convention . . . into U.K. law". The debates on the Bill also have statements that its intention is to incorporate the Convention into domestic law.[40] The Lord Chancellor stated that the technique adopted in the HRA "will prove a strong form of incorporation".[41] But the language of the HRA itself, and indeed the explanations given by both the Lord Chancellor and the Home Secretary show that, from a technical legal point of view, it is an incomplete form of incorporation. As well as the use of a restrictive formula—section 1(2) provides that the Convention rights are "to have effect for the purposes of this Act"—other elements reinforce the conclusion that something short of wholesale incorporation is intended. The Long Title to the Act states that its purpose is, *inter alia*, "to give further effect to" the rights and freedoms guaranteed under the ECHR. The courts are not bound to follow the jurisprudence of the Strasbourg Court and decisions and opinions of the Commission: by section 2(1) they must simply *"take account"* of them; and section 3(1) provides that *"so far as possible to do so,* primary legislation and subordinate legislation *must* be read and given effect in a way which is compatible with the Convention rights" (emphasis added). By section 6, "it is unlawful for a public authority to act in a way which is incompatible with a Convention right" unless, as the result of the provisions of primary legislation, it could not have acted differently. As a consequence, where a public authority is exercising a discretionary power, it must take account of and act in accordance with Convention rights and the principles of the Convention, unless the exercise is pursuant to a statutory provision which cannot be read or given effect in a way which is compatible with the Convention rights.

The HRA stops at the point where complete incorporation would impinge upon parliamentary sovereignty: legislation is not to be distorted to make it comply with the Convention. If it is not possible to give it a consistent interpretation, the will of Parliament prevails over Convention rights, leaving it to Parliament and the executive to remedy the inconsistency. If such legislation requires a public authority to violate a Convention right, it is not acting unlawfully.

3. THE EFFECT OF THE HRA

A. Convention rights are not part of substantive domestic law under the HRA

1–12   Where an incorporating statute states that the relevant treaty or Convention is to have the force of law,[42] its effect is to give the treaty provisions "direct

---

[39] *ibid.* p. 2.

[40] Second Reading HL, November 3, 1997 (Lord Kingsland) cols 1264 ("subsume into the law of the land") and 1325; Lord Bingham C.J. 1245; Lord Windlesham: 1282. HL Committee Stage November 27, 1997: Earl Russell ("to receive another system of law . . . into our domestic law"). HC Second Reading February 16, 1998 Home Secretary col. 770 ("The effect of non-incorporation on the British people is a practical one"). See also *e.g.* cols 372, 774, 784, 819, 830, 833, 843, 846, 850, 857 and see HC Committee May 20, 1998, cols 978 (Home Secretary), 983 and 1044.

[41] Second Reading HL, November 3, 1997, col. 1227; Committee November 18, 1997 cols 512, 515; Report HL January 19, 1998, col. 1266 (Lord Chancellor). See also third Reading February 2, 1998, col. 840 (the dispute as to the meaning of the word "incorporation" is "theological").

[42] See for example the Carriage of Goods by Sea Act 1971, s. 1(2) providing that the Hague-Visby Rules "as set out in the Schedule to this Act, shall have the force of law". See also the Carriage of Goods by Air Acts 1932 and 1966 (on which see *Corocraft Ltd v. Pan American Airways* [1969] 1 Q.B. 616;

effect in England".[43] While it has been stated that this means the treaty provisions are to be treated as if they were part of directly enacted statute law and are "given the coercive effect of law",[44] the question whether the treaty provisions are to be regarded as mandatory depends upon its precise terms: "what its effect is depends on the meaning of the Convention".[45]

1–13   The HRA does not contain a "force of law" provision, and in the Second Reading debate in the House of Commons the Home Secretary stated that "the Bill does not create new substantive rights, but it makes the existing Convention rights more immediate and relevant".[46] In the House of Lords the Lord Chancellor stated that, under the HRA, "the Convention rights will not . . . become part of our substantive domestic law".[47] He went on to explain the rationale for this approach in the following passage:

> "The provisions of clause 3 operate on an interpretative basis and require legislation to be construed in accordance with the Convention rights so far as it is possible to do so. That interpretative provision interacts with the obligations put upon public authorities in accordance with the generous definition of 'public authority' in the bill. As we will explain in more detail when we come to the relevant clauses, this provides an effective way of giving effect to the Convention rights and avoids constitutional and other difficulties which would arise if we made those rights part of domestic law.
>
> The scheme of the Bill . . . is to make provision so as to respect the sovereignty of Parliament for the continuing force and effect of legislation held by the courts by way of a declaration of incompatibility to be incompatible with the Convention rights. If those Convention rights were themselves to constitute provisions of domestic United Kingdom law there would be obvious scope for confusion when the courts were obliged to give effect to legislation that predated the coming into force of the Human Rights Bill. That might give rise to the doctrine of implied repeal. That is a doctrine that can have no application because of the express terms of Clause 3."[48]

By contrast Lord Browne-Wilkinson took the view that the purpose of the Bill "is to make enforceable in English law known rights under the covenant which are

---

Fothergill v. Monarch Airlines [1981] 1 A.C. 251); Merchant Shipping Act 1979, s. 17 (now s. 185(1) of the 1995 Act) (on which see *Caltex Singapore Pte v. BP Shipping Ltd* [1996] 1 Lloyd's Rep. 286, 297); Contracts Applicable Law Act 1990, s. 2(1). This may be so even where the treaty is only implemented in part: see Bretton Woods Agreement Act 1945 (on which see *Wilson Smithett & Cope v. Teruzzi* [1976] 1 Q.B. 683, 711).

[43] *Caltex Singapore Pte v. BP Shipping Ltd* [1996] 1 Lloyd's Rep. 286, 297.

[44] *The Hollandia* [1982] Q.B. 872, 883, 885 (Lord Denning M.R. and Sir Sebag Shaw); [1983] A.C. 565, 572 (Lord Diplock with whom all agreed).

[45] *Caltex Singapore Pte v. BP Shipping Ltd* [1996] 1 Lloyd's Rep. 286, 297 (Convention on Limitation of Liability for Maritime Claims 1976). *Cf.* the Conventions incorporated by the Carriage of Goods by Sea Act 1971 and those incorporated by the Merchant Shipping Act 1979 and the Contracts Applicable Law Act 1990, see above, n. 42. For the special case of the European Communities Act 1972, see para. 1–18, n. 70 below.

[46] Second Reading, February 16, 1998, col. 771.

[47] He further emphasised this point when he stated "I have to make this point absolutely plain. The European Convention on Human Rights under this Bill is not made part of our law. The Bill gives the European Convention on Human Rights a special relationship . . . but it does not make the Convention directly justiciable as it would be if it were expressly made part of our law. I want there to be no ambiguity about that." Report HL, January 29, 1998, col. 421. See also January 19, 1998, col. 1261.

[48] HL Committee Stage, November 18, 1997, col. 508–509. See also col. 522 and October 23, 1997, col. 825.

currently in force in Strasbourg"[49]; and in *Barrett v. London Borough of Enfield,*[50] he said that " . . . under the Human Rights Act 1998 Article 6 will shortly become part of English law". Lord Bingham, in *R. v. D.P.P., ex parte Kebilene,*[51] appeared to agree, describing the status of the Convention as "prospective" law, and indicating that when the HRA is in force it will be "binding" law. We shall see that the only area in which it can be argued that the Convention rights are fully, although indirectly, incorporated into U.K. law is where they have been imported via E.C. law; *i.e.* within the E.C.'s area of competence.[52] In principle the limited nature of the incorporation effected by the HRA means that the pre-existing jurisprudence concerning the effect of the Convention on statutory interpretation may still be relevant. But the common law requirement of "two-meaning" ambiguity[53] and the strength of the interpretative direction contained in section 3[54] mean that it is unlikely to be of practical importance save in an exceptional case.

B.　A new form of common law

1-14　The result of not incorporating the Convention rights is to make them, in effect, a new form of common (*i.e.* non-statutory) law. They are not paramount, and will be over-ridden by any clearly incompatible statutory provisions, both existing and future. The Lord Chancellor stated that "the only practical difference between the full incorporation of the Convention rights into our domestic law and the actual effect of the [HRA]"[55] is that the Government had sought to give the Convention a vertical rather than a horizontal effect. It had "sought to protect the human rights of individuals against the abuse of power by the state, broadly defined, rather than to protect them against each other" by making "the Convention rights themselves directly a part of our domestic law in the same way that, for example, the civil wrongs of negligence, trespass or libel are part of our domestic law".[56] His view that this was the only practical difference from full incorporation is based on the strength of the presumption of compatibility of U.K. statutes with Convention rights contained in section 3 of the HRA.

The effect of Convention rights under the HRA will not differ from full incorporation where there is no question of incompatibility with a specific statutory provision, or where executive rather than legislative power is involved. In such cases for all practical purposes the Convention rights are part of domestic law. This is because section 6 makes it unlawful for a public authority to act in a way which is incompatible with a Convention right, and it follows that a public authority exercising a discretionary power must respect Convention rights and the principles of the Convention. Any victim of a breach can bring proceedings against the authority under section 7, and seek the broad range of remedies, including damages, made available by section 8. Even in such cases, the Convention rights are a floor below which standards may not fall: the HRA does not prevent U.K. legislation or common law according greater protection to human rights than is required by the Convention, so long as it does not thereby infringe the conflicting right of another person.[57]

---

[49] HL Committee Stage, November 18, 1997, col. 498.
[50] [1999] 3 W.L.R 79, 85; [1999] 3 All E.R. 193, 200. Lord Nolan and Lord Steyn agreed.
[51] [1999] 3 W.L.R. 175.
[52] *e.g.* Case 222/84 *Johnston v. Chief Constable of the RUC* [1986] E.C.R. 1651. See below, paras 1–19—1–22.
[53] See above, para. 1–02.
[54] See below, para. 3–01.
[55] HL Third Reading February 5, 1998, col. 840.
[56] *ibid.*
[57] See below, para. 2–06.

1–15   The size of any gap between the effect of the HRA and full incorporation turns on the extent to which the courts can maintain the Lord Chancellor's sharp distinction between abuses by public authorities which will give rise to a remedy (vertical effect) and abuses by others for which there is no direct remedy (no horizontal effect). We shall see that, because courts and tribunals are themselves "public authorities"[58] with a duty to act compatibly with Convention rights, it may not be entirely possible to maintain this distinction. To the extent that it is blurred by according the Convention rights some horizontal effect, possibly only of an indirect nature through their influence on the rules of private law,[59] the effect of the HRA may be greater than the Lord Chancellor envisaged.[60] This will be of particular importance where the Convention imposes on public authorities positive obligations to prevent interference with rights by other individuals.[61]

Where, however, an issue of compatibility of specific legislation with the Convention rights arises, an assessment of the practical difference between the approach of the HRA and full incorporation, also depends upon other factors. First, and most importantly, it depends upon how strong the presumption of compatibility turns out to be when tested in the courts.[62] In relation to existing legislation, unless that presumption is a strong one, the approach of the HRA will be significantly less effective than giving the rights the force of law. This is because prior legislation inconsistent with fully incorporated Convention rights would have been impliedly repealed, whereas under the HRA's approach, it will be for Parliament to decide whether to remove any incompatibility either by primary legislation or by the "fast track" procedure under section 10. If a decision is taken not to remove the incompatibility, the person whose Convention rights are thereby rendered unenforceable in domestic courts will, as before the enactment of the HRA, have to institute proceedings in the Strasbourg Court. The extent of any practical difference from full incorporation of Convention rights will also depend on the extent to which individuals' remedies even against the state turn out to be limited by the omission of Articles 1 and 13 from the "Convention rights" specified by the HRA.[63]

4.   Limitations, derogations and reservations

1–16   Section 1(2) also limits the domestic effect of the Convention by reference to "any designated derogation or reservation". Reservations may be made in accordance with Article 57[64] at the time of signing or ratifying the Convention or

---

[58] Section 6(3)(a).

[59] See below, paras 4–53—4–59. Any such blurring is likely to enhance the effective scope of the Convention rights.

[60] But *cf.* remarks by him at earlier stages which appear to anticipate some indirect horizontal effect. See also section 12, below, para. 4–61, the effect of which would be unduly limited if Article 10 of the Convention were not afforded some measure of horizontal effect.

[61] See below, para. C0–06.

[62] See Ch. 3 below. As to the common law presumption that statutes will not infringe fundamental rights, see *Marcel v. Commissioner of Police for the Metropolis* [1992] Ch. 225; *R. v. Lord Chancellor, ex parte Witham* [1998] Q.B. 575; *R. v. Secretary of State for the Home Department, ex parte T & V* [1998] A.C. 407. Compare *R. v. Brentwood CC, ex parte Peck* [1998] E.M.L.R. 697 (CA); *R. v. Secretary of State for the Home Department, ex parte Simms and O'Brien* [1999] 3 W.L.R. 328 (HL), where Lord Steyn described this presumption as being of general application operating as a constitutional principle which there comes into play even in the absence of an ambiguity: see further below, para. 3.12.

[63] See paras 6–12—6–14 below.

[64] Formerly Article 64.

any of its Protocols.[65] Derogations may be made under Article 15 "in time of war or other public emergency threatening the life of the nation". At the present time, one derogation and one reservation exist in respect of the United Kingdom. The derogation,[66] which was made in 1988, concerns the length of detention of suspected terrorists and followed the judgment of the Court in the case of *Brogan & ors v. United Kingdom*.[67] The reservation[68] was made in 1952 and seeks to limit the effect of the second sentence of Article 2 of the First Protocol, which obliges a state to respect the rights of parents to ensure education and teaching in conformity with their own religious and philosophical convictions.[69]

5. ADDITION OF NEW CONVENTION RIGHTS

1–17 Where the United Kingdom has ratified a Protocol or signed it with a view to ratification, the Secretary of State may by order "make such amendments to [the] Act as he considers appropriate to reflect the effect, in relation to the United Kingdom, of a Protocol" under section 1(4) of the HRA. But by section 19(6) no amendment may come into force before the Protocol concerned has been ratified and is in force in relation to the United Kingdom.

6. INDIRECT DOMESTIC INCORPORATION OF CONVENTION RIGHTS VIA E.C. LAW

1–18 E.C. law provides an important method whereby the terms of the ECHR and the rights it confers may be invoked before a national court where the issue falls within the scope of E.C. law. This is because, within its scope, Community law takes precedence over inconsistent national law,[70] and it is well-established that respect for fundamental rights including the Convention rights "forms an integral part of the general principles of Community law protected by the Court of Justice".[71] This principle has now been given legislative force by Article 6(2) of the Treaty of European Union, which provides that "the Union shall respect fundamental rights as guaranteed by the European Convention for the Protection of Fundamental Rights and Freedoms . . . and as they result from the constitutional traditions common to the Member States as general principles of Community law".[72]

In developing this aspect of the general principles of Community law, the ECJ has been guided by the constitutional traditions common to the Member States,

---

[65] see below, p. 409.

[66] The full text is set out in Part I of Schedule 3 to the HRA.

[67] (1989) 11 E.H.R.R. 117. See below, para. C5–54.

[68] The full text is set out in Part II of Schedule 3 to the HRA. See below at p. 397.

[69] See p. 398.

[70] *ibid.* The European Communities Act 1972, s. 2 gives legal effect to this within the U.K. For judicial acceptance of this, see *R. v. Secretary of State for Transport, ex parte Factortame Ltd* [1990] 2 A.C. 85; *R. v. Secretary of State for Employment, ex parte EOC* [1995] 1 A.C. 1; *R. v. Secretary of State for the Environment, ex parte Seymour-Smith* [1995] I.R.L.R. 464. See further below.

[71] Case 11/70 *Internationale Handelsgesellschaft v. Einfuhr- und Vorratsstelle Getreide* [1970] E.C.R. 1125, 1134. See Joint Declaration of Community Institutions of April 5, 1977 O.J. 1977, C–103/1. See generally Tridimas, *The General Principles of E.C. Law* (1999) pp. 236–243; Craig & de Burca, *E.C. Law* (2nd ed.) pp. 299–347.

[72] The Treaty of Amsterdam made this provision justiciable by amending TEU Article 46 to bring Article 6(2) within the ECJ's jurisdiction.

including international treaties of which they are signatories,[73] and in this process the ECHR, although not directly enforceable, has been particularly important[74] because all Member States are party to it. There are many references to it in the case law of the ECJ, in particular to Articles 6, 8, 10 and 13. Accordingly, "through the jurisprudence of the European Court of Justice the principles, though not the text of the Convention, now inform the law of the European Union".[75] As such, the principles underlying the Convention must be given effect in U.K. courts, in considering both the legislative and administrative acts of the Community itself, and U.K. legislation or administrative decisions adopted under Community law or to take advantage of such derogations as Community provisions allow.

1–19   The general principles of E.C. law, including the Convention rights, apply to any matter which is within the legislative scope of Community law and in respect of which the Community has exercised its legislative competence.[76] The interpretative obligation in section 3 of the HRA does not apply to provisions of E.C. law,[77] but it does not need to, since the ECJ has held that Community measures must be interpreted in the light of the Convention[78] and in principle annulled if they are incompatible.[79] However, the Convention principles are not absolute and may be subjected to restrictions, provided that those restrictions correspond to legitimate Community interests and are not disproportionate.[80]

The ECJ has also held that in certain circumstances the acts of the Member States are reviewable for conformity with the Convention rights, albeit as part of the general principles of E.C. law rather than directly. This will be so where the Member State is applying treaty provisions or implementing E.C. legislation.[81] The act of a Member State derogating from an E.C. right, in reliance on a Community measure permitting such derogation, is also subject to review for conformity with the Convention.[82] But even though an issue is connected with Community law, for

---

[73] Case 4/73 *Nold v. Commission* [1974] E.C.R. 491, para. 13.

[74] Case 44/79 *Hauer v. Land Rheinland-Pfalz* [1979] E.C.R. 3727, paras 17–19. It was first referred to in Case C36/75 *Rutili v. Minister of Interior* [1975] E.C.R. 1219.

[75] *R. v. Home Secretary, ex parte McQuillan* [1995] 4 All E.R. 400, 422 (Sedley J.).

[76] On fundamental rights as a source of competence, see Case C–13/94 *P v. S & Cornwall CC* [1996] E.C.R. I–2143 (but *cf.* Case C–249/96 *Grant v. SW Trains* [1998] E.C.R. I–621); Opinion 2/94 *Accession by E.C. to ECHR* [1996] E.C.R. I–1759; *R. v. Home Secretary, ex parte Adams* [1995] All E.R. (E.C.) 177 (but *cf.* Case C–299/95 *Kremzoh v. Austrian Republic* [1997] E.C.R. I–2629).

[77] They do not fall within the definitions of "primary legislation" or "subordinate legislation" in s. 22(1).

[78] Case 44/79 *Hauer v. Land Rheinland-Pfalz* [1979] E.C.R. 3727.

[79] Case 155/79 *AM & S Europe Ltd v. Commission* [1982] E.C.R. 1575; Case 85/87 *Dow Benelux NV v. Commission* [1989] E.C.R. 3137; *Hoecht AG v. Commission* [1989] E.C.R. 2859; Case 100/88 *Oyowe & Traore v. Commission* [1989] E.C.R. 4285; Case C–404/92P *X v. Commission* [1994] E.C.R. I–4737; C–49/88 *Al-Jubail Fertilizer Co. v. Council* [1991] E.C.R. I–3187. See also Case C–193 194/87 *Maurissen v. Court of Auditors* [1990] E.C.R. I–117 (reference to fundamental rights).

[80] Case 5/88 *Wachauf v. Germany* [1989] E.C.R. 2609, 2639. Member States must apply the rights "as far as possible": *ibid.*

[81] Case 63/83 *R. v. Kent Kirk* [1984] E.C.R. 2689; Case 222/84 *Johnston v. Chief Constable of the RUC* [1986] E.C.R. 1651; Cases 201 & 202/85 *Klensch v. Secretaire d'Etat a l'Agriculture et la Viticulture* [1986] E.C.R. 3477; Case 222/86 *UNECTEF v. Heylens* [1987] E.C.R. 4097; Case 249/86 *Commission v. Germany* [1989] E.C.R. 1263; Case 5/88 *Wachauf v. Germany* [1989] E.C.R. 2609; Cases C–65 & 110/95 *R. v. Home Secretary, ex parte Shingara* [1997] E.C.R. I–3341 (paras 74 *et seq.*).

[82] Case C–36/75 *Rutili v. Minister of Interior* [1975] E.C.R. 1219; Case C–260/89 (express provision in Treaty for derogation); *ERT v. Dimotiki Etairia Pliroforissis* [1991] E.C.R. I–2925. The reasoning in *ERT* and Case C–368/95 *Vereinigte Familiapress Zeitungsverlags etc v. Heinrich Bauer Verlag* [1997] E.C.R. I–3689 suggest that the position should be similar where the justification for the derogation is in the jurisprudence of the ECJ, but *cf.* Cases 60 &61/84 *Cinetheque v. Fed. Nat. des Cinemas Francais* [1985] E.C.R. 2609; AG Gullman in Case C–2/92; *R. v. MAFF, ex parte Bostock* [1994] I–E.C.R. 955, 971.

instance because it may affect the common market, if it lies outside the scope of Community competence and is within the sole jurisdiction of the national legislator, an act of a Member State is not reviewable for conformity with the general principles of E.C. law.[83] It is therefore important to determine what falls within the scope of E.C. law, a matter upon which there is some uncertainty because the approach of the ECJ shows that it is a developing concept. It is not enough that a measure operates in the same field as a Community measure or is interdependent with a Community regime. According to the present state of the case law it would appear to be necessary for the national measure to be adopted under powers conferred or duties imposed by Community law.[84] In such a case "domestic law is a vehicle for a measure whose legality falls to be tested according to the law of the Community"[85] including Convention rights.

1–20   There are, however, signs that the ECJ might take a broader approach. In *Konstantinidis*,[86] Advocate-General Jacobs considered whether Article 8 of the Convention could be used to challenge a state measure in Germany requiring the applicant to spell his name in a particular way when transliterated from the Greek alphabet. The only link between the application of the measure to the applicant and Community law was that, by living in Germany, the Greek applicant was exercising his right to freedom of establishment under Article 52 (now 43) of the Treaty. The Advocate General was prepared to countenance this possibility, stating that:

> "In my opinion, a Community national who goes to another Member State as a worker or self-employed person under Articles 48, 52 or 59 of the Treaty, is entitled not just to pursue his trade or profession and to enjoy the same living and working conditions as nationals of the host State; he is in addition entitled to assume that, wherever he goes to earn his living in the European Community, he will be treated in accordance with a common code of fundamental values, in particular those laid down in the European Convention on Human Rights."

Further support for a broader interpretation of the scope of Community law may be derived from the *Phil Collins* case[87] in which the ECJ was prepared to find that action taken by Germany was contrary to the principle of equal treatment enshrined by Article 6 of the Treaty, even though the measures in question were not taken pursuant to any provision of Community law.

1–21   Despite some initial support for a broad approach,[88] the U.K. courts have proceeded cautiously in determining whether or not acts of public bodies are within the scope of Community law so as to attract the application of the general principles, including the Convention. Thus, in *R. v. MAFF, ex parte First City Trading*,[89] Laws J. had to consider whether an aid package adopted by MAFF

---

[83] Cases 60 & 61/84 *Cinetheque v. Fed. Nat. des Cinemas Francais* [1985] E.C.R. 2609 (within the jurisdiction of the natonal legislator); Case 12/86 *Demirel v. Stadt Swabisch Gmund* [1987] E.C.R. 3719 (outside the scope of Community law).

[84] Case C–2/92 *R. v. MAFF, ex parte Bostock* [1994] I E.C.R. 955. See also Case C–144/95 *Maurin* [1996] E.C.R. I–[1045/2909]; Case C–299/95 *Kremzoh v. Austrian Republic* [1997] E.C.R. I–2629.

[85] *R. v. MAFF, ex parte First City Traders* [1997] 1 C.M.L.R. 250, 269 (Laws J.).

[86] Case C–168/91 *Konstantinidis* [1993] E.C.R. I–1191.

[87] Cases C–92/92 and C–326/92 *Phil Collins* [1993] E.C.R. I–5145.

[88] *R. v. MAFF, ex parte Hamble Fisheries* [1995] 4 All E.R. 714.

[89] [1997] 1 C.M.L.R. 250. See also *R. v. International Stock Exchange, ex parte Else* [1993] 1 All E.R. 420, 425; *R. v. MAFF, ex parte Hamble Fisheries* [1995] 4 All E.R. 714.

following the beef ban imposed by the European Commission fell to be assessed in accordance with the general principles of Community law. He held that it did not. The general principles would only have applied to the aid package if it had constituted a measure taken pursuant to Community law either as implementing a Community provision or as operating under a derogation from Community law. Although the package had been occasioned by a Commission decision and made reference to Community law, Community law did not require it and the Government did not have to rely on any Community provision in order to implement it. Laws J. distinguished the *Phil Collins* case, holding that it concerned the field of application of a Treaty provision which he considered to be broader than that of the general principles. He stated that "[w]here action is taken, albeit under domestic law, which falls within the scope of the Treaty's application, then of course the Court has the power and duty to require that the Treaty be adhered to. But no more: precisely because the fundamental principles elaborated by the Court of Justice are not vouchsafed by the Treaty, there is no legal space for their application to any [domestic] measure or decision taken *otherwise than in pursuance of treaty rights or obligations*".[90] Where, however, a domestic measure is adopted *pursuant* to Community law "the internal law of the Court of Justice applies" and to the extent that a domestic decision is taken "so as to implement Community law, or must necessarily rely on it" the decision of the Member State is subject to the Community's internal law and "its legality falls to be tested according to the law of the Community"[91] including Convention rights.[92]

1-22   Where the Convention rights are applicable in this way, U.K. courts should determine their meaning and effect in accordance with any relevant decision of the ECJ.[93] If there is any doubt as to the application of those Convention rights, the courts could seek a reference to the ECJ under Article 234 (formerly 177) of the Treaty. If the applicant is asking the court to quash a provision of Community law (as opposed to domestic action taken pursuant to Community law) then a reference to the ECJ must be made as it is the only court that has jurisdiction to declare a Community act invalid.[94]

As Convention rights are given effect via E.C. law, differences may arise between the decisions of the ECJ and of the Strasbourg Court as to the interpretation of the Convention. A number of contrasting decisions show that the possibility of inconsistency is not merely theoretical,[95] particularly since it is not possible for the

---

[90] [1997] 1 C.M.L.R. 250 at 268–269 (emphasis added).

[91] *ibid.*

[92] The approach in the *First City Trading* case was endorsed by the Divisional Court in *R. v. Customs and Excise, ex parte Lunn Poly* [1998] Eu.L.R. 438. See also *Booker Acquaculture Ltd v. Secretary of State for Scotland, The Times*, September 24, 1998.

[93] European Communities Act 1972, s. 3. For the position of the ECJ see, *e.g.* Cases C–74/95 and 129/95 *Criminal Proceedings against X* [1996] E.C.R. I–6609. On the scope of review in such cases, see below. The ECJ is not bound by previous decisions (*e.g.* Cases 267/91 & 268/91 *Keck v. Mithouard* [1993] 1 E.C.R. 609). On the effect of a ruling on a national court, see Anderson, *References to the ECJ*, pp. 307–315.

[94] Case 314/85 *Firma Foto-Frost v. Hauptzollamt Lubeck-Ost* [1987] E.C.R. 4199. On interim relief see Cases C–143/88 & 92/89 *Zuckerfabrik Suderdithmarschen AG v. Hauptzollamt Itzehoe* [1991] E.C.R. I–415; Case C–465/93 *Atlanta Fruchthandelsgesellschaft mbH v. Bundesamt fur Ernahrung und Forst-wirtschaft* [1995] E.C.R. I–3761.

[95] See, *e.g.* the contrasts between (1) Cases 46/87 and 227/88 *Hoechst AG v. Commission* [1989] E.C.R. 2859 (ECJ.) and *Niemietz v. Germany* (1992) 16 E.H.R.R. 97 (Article 8) (2) Case 374/87 *Orkem v. Commission* [1989] E.C.R. 3283 and *Funke v. France* (1992) 16 E.H.R.R. 297 (Article 6), and (3) the opinion of Advocate-General Van Gerven in Case C–159/90 *S.P.U.C. v. Grogan* [1991] E.C.R. I–4685 (E.C.J.) and *Open Door Counselling and Dublin Well Woman Centre v. Ireland* (1992) 15 E.H.R.R. 244 (Article 10). See further Tridimas, *The General Principles of E.C. Law* (1999) pp. 237–241; Craig & de Burca, *E.C. Law* (2nd ed) pp. 345–346.

ECJ to refer a question to the Strasbourg Court, and the Community is not a party to the Convention and indeed lacks the competence to become one.[96] Craig and de Burca have argued[97] that the risk of such inconsistency is reduced by the fact that the ECJ is likely to defer to the Strasbourg Court[98] and in any event may be likely to leave it to national courts to decide whether a particular measure is compatible with fundamental rights unless it is specifically asked for a ruling on that point. But in the event of an inconsistency, a U.K. court would be obliged to follow the ECJ rather than the Strasbourg Court because of the overriding nature of E.C. law and the express direction in section 3(1) of the European Communities Act 1972 to determine the meaning and effect of the Community provisions and any qualifying national measures in accordance with any relevant decision of the ECJ. Once an inconsistency is revealed, it is not "possible" to comply with the interpretative obligation under section 3 of the 1998 Act in a way which is fully compatible with the Convention rights without derogating from the supremacy of Community law which is achieved by section 2 of the 1972 Act.[99] While compatible interpretation may be possible from a linguistic point of view, the court's duty, derived from the supremacy of Community law, makes it a legal impossibility. A practical way around this would be for a court which is considering an issue upon which it believes there is an inconsistency to refer the issue to the ECJ under Article 234 (the former Article 177).

1–23   Where E.C. law requires the acts of a Member State to conform to the Convention, the Convention rights may have greater efficacy than they will have under the HRA. First, those rights (including the right to an effective remedy in Article 13, to which the HRA does not give express effect) are, by virtue of section 2(1) of the European Communities Act 1972, "given legal effect" and "shall" be "enforced" in the U.K. They are fully incorporated, albeit by a circuitous route, and are part of our domestic law. Secondly, where a Convention right applies as part of E.C. law, it may override a statutory provision which is inconsistent with it.[1]

---

[96] See *Opinion 2/94 on Accession of the Community to the ECHR* [1996] E.C.R. I–1759. See further *The Human Rights Opinion of the ECJ and its Constitutional Implications* (Cambridge University CELS, Occasional Paper No. 1.

[97] *E.C. Law* (2nd ed.), p. 346, citing Case C–260/89 *ERT v. DEP* [1991] E.C.R. I–2925 and Case C–368/95 *Vereingte Familiapress Zeitungsverlags v. Heinrich Bauer Verlag* [1997] 3 C.M.L.R. 1329 and, as an example of the ECJ making a ruling when specifically asked, Case C–23/93 *TV10 SA v. Commissariaat voor de Media* [1994] E.C.R. I–4795, paras 11, 23–26.

[98] Cases 46/87 and 227/88 *Hoechst AG v. Commission* [1989] E.C.R. 2859; Case 374/87 *Orkem v. Commission* [1989] E.C.R. 3283, esp 3350. See also Case C–13/94 *P v. S and Cornwall CC* [1996] E.C.R. I–2143, para. 16; Case C–249/96 *Grant v. South West Trains Ltd* [1998] E.C.R. I–621.

[99] See below. See Mr Robert Mclennan, M.P., *Hansard*, H.C. Vol. 306, February 16, 1998, col. 809.

[1] *R. v. Secretary of State for Transport, ex parte Factortame Ltd* [1990] 2 A.C. 85; *R. v. Secretary of State for Employment, ex parte EOC* [1995] 1 A.C. 1. *Cf. Garland v. British Rail Engineering* [1983] 2 A.C. 751, 771 (distinguishing "inconsistency" and "deliberate derogation"). For examples of the disapplication of domestic statutory provisions in favour of the fundamental right to an effective remedy deriving from Community law, see Case 222/84 *Johnston v. Chief Constable of the Royal Ulster Constabulary* [1986] E.C.R. 1651; *Marshall v. Southampton & S.W. Hampshire AHA (No. 2)* [1993] I.C.R. 893.

The status of the jurisprudence of the Strasbourg Court and institutions in United Kingdom law

1. INTRODUCTION

2–01 Section 2(1) of the HRA provides that a court or tribunal determining a question which has arisen under the Act in connection with a Convention right "must take into account" the decisions and opinions of the Strasbourg Court, Commission and Committee of Ministers, whenever made, so far as, in its opinion, they are "relevant to the proceedings in which that question has arisen".[1] This is a weaker direction than that in section 3(1) of the European Communities Act 1972 which requires "any question as to the meaning or effect of any of the Treaties, or as to the validity, meaning or effect of any Community instrument" to "be treated as a question of law" and, if not referred to the ECJ, to "be for determination as such in accordance with the principles laid down by and any relevant decision of the European Court . . . ". The Strasbourg jurisprudence, unlike that of the ECJ, does not therefore bind a U.K. court. It is only persuasive.

The case law to be taken into account is not only that relating to the Convention rights to which section 1(1) refers, *i.e.* those set out in Schedule 1 to the HRA. A national court will have to take account of the case law relating to Article 1 and Article 13 in certain circumstances. It will have to take account of the Article 1 jurisprudence when considering the ambit of its own duty as a public authority[2] not to do an act which is incompatible with a Convention right, since the court is a body for which the state is responsible before the Strasbourg institutions. It will have to take account of the jurisprudence relating to Article 13 when determining the remedy to be given in the exercise of its powers under section 8 of the HRA.[3]

2–02 The status of the case law relating to the concept of "victim" under Article 34,[4] and to the remedial notion of "just satisfaction" under Article 41[5] may well also be stronger.[6] Section 7(1) of the HRA provides that only an actual or

---

[1] See HRA, s. 2(2), as to the manner in such decisions and opinions are to be brought before the Court or tribunal and below, para. 2–17, as to the weight to be given to decisions of Committees of Ministers.
[2] Under HRA, s. 6(3)(b), on which see below, paras 4–15—4–17.
[3] See Lord Irvine L.C., *Hansard*, H.L., November 18, 1997, col. 477 " . . . the courts may have regard to Article 13. In particular they may wish to do so when considering the very ample provisions of Clause 8(1) . . . ".
[4] Formerly Article 25.
[5] Formerly Article 50.
[6] See HRA, s. 8(3) and 8(4). The caselaw is discussed below, paras 4–26 *et seq*.

potential victim may bring proceedings in respect of an act made unlawful under section 6; and section 7(3) provides that only a victim will have sufficient interest for the purpose of making an application for judicial review in respect of such an act.[7] Section 7(7) provides that "a person is a victim of an unlawful act only if he would be a victim for the purposes of Article 34 of the Convention if proceedings were brought in the European Court in respect of that act". The effect of these provisions appears to be to incorporate into domestic law the concept of victim, as it is interpreted by the Strasbourg institutions. Indeed, in the Convention system, determination of victim status falls within the sole competence of the Strasbourg institutions, representing as it does an essential foundation of their jurisdiction. As to remedies, section 8(3) of the HRA directs the court not to award damages in respect of unlawful acts "unless it is satisfied that the award is necessary to afford just satisfaction to the person in whose favour it is made"; and section 8(4) further directs the court to "take into account the principles applied by the European Court of Human Rights in relation to the award of compensation under Article 41".[8] "Just satisfaction" is not a term familiar to domestic law, and again it would appear that the enactment of the concept into domestic law imports the case law which gives it meaning.[9]

Although Schedule 1 to the Act contains only the English text of the Articles enshrining Convention rights, the concluding paragraph of the Convention itself provides that the French text is equally authentic. The Strasbourg institutions have regard to both texts when determining the scope and meaning of the provisions of the Convention, and national courts will have to adopt this approach where appropriate.[10]

2. JURISPRUDENCE SHOULD BE PERSUASIVE BUT NOT BINDING

2–03   There are good reasons for stipulating that (with these possible exceptions) the Strasbourg jurisprudence should be only persuasive rather than assigning to it the binding effect given to the jurisprudence of the ECJ. The ECHR system recognises that it is possible to satisfy the Convention's requirements and give effect to the Convention rights in a number of ways, particularly where societal values are still in an uncrystallised state,[11] whereas the European Community system strives towards harmonisation. The Convention case law is a minimum, which contracting states may wish to exceed. Further, national courts have much easier access to the ECJ through the preliminary ruling procedure under Article 234 (formerly Article 177) of the E.C. Treaty, enabling the ECJ to give guidance. By contrast, Strasbourg is dependent on an individual victim making an application, which he can do only

---

[7] As to proceedings in respect of unlawful acts, see below, paras 4–25 et seq.

[8] As to remedies, see below, Ch. 6.

[9] On the effect of incorporating a treaty concept into domestic law, see above, para. 1–13. nn. 43 and 44.

[10] See, for example *Niemietz v. Germany* (1992) 16 E.H.R.R. 97, para. 31, in which the court relied upon the broader connotation of the word *"domicile"* in the French text of Article 8(1) in order to conclude that the right to respect for the "home" extended to a professional person's office: see below, para. C8–12. Similarly, the court's insistence that Article 6(1) applies only to a "dispute" about civil rights and obligations derives from the presence of the word *"contestation"* in the French text. The English text does not refer to the need for a dispute: see, for example, *W v. United Kingdom* (1988) 10 E.H.R.R. 29, para. 73. On the reconciliation of different meanings, see further *Wemhoff v. FR Germany* (1968) 1 E.H.R.R. 55; *James v. United Kingdom* (1986) 8 E.H.R.R. 123; *Brogan v. United Kingdom* (1988) 11 E.H.R.R. 117; Vienna Convention, Article 33(1): see below, para. 2–09.

[11] See, *e.g. Dudgeon v. United Kingdom* (1981) 4 E.H.R.R. 149.

on completion of all domestic proceedings. In addition to these structural factors, there are considerations deriving from the Strasbourg institutions' approach to their own case law, in particular the doctrines of "living instrument" and "margin of appreciation", which we now consider.

A.   Convention a "living instrument" requiring "dynamic" interpretation

2–04   The court and the Commission have stated that the Convention is "a living instrument" which must be given a "dynamic" interpretation in the light of conditions prevailing at the time a matter falls to be considered.[12] It follows that judgments given some years ago, in particular on moral issues, may no longer be a reliable guide to the approach to be given today.[13] This makes it wholly inappropriate to treat all Strasbourg case law as binding authority.[14] A U.K. court would be bound where the ECHR was not, although in the interests of legal certainty and the orderly development of the Convention case law the Strasbourg Court "usually follows and applies its own precedents".[15] Lord Browne-Wilkinson stated that he saw "no reason that we should fetter ourselves . . . in dealing with a jurisprudence that is by definition a shifting one".[16] It should, however, be noted that the jurisprudence of the ECJ is similarly a shifting one but nonetheless section 3 of the European Communities Act 1972 provides a stronger direction. In that context our courts have recognised,[17] as does the ECJ (although often covertly)[18] that the interpretation of the Treaty provisions can change to match the development of the Communities and Community institutions. A similar approach can be seen in the pre-HRA jurisprudence involving human rights. Thus, in *R. v. Ministry of Defence, ex parte Smith*, the Master of the Rolls stated[19] that the lawfulness of the discharge of homosexual servicemen was to be judged as at the date of their discharge, and indicated that "a belief which represented unquestioned orthodoxy in year X may become questionable by year Y and unsustainable by year Z".[20]

B.   Inapplicability of "margin of appreciation"

2–05   A more serious objection to requiring a U.K. court to follow the Strasbourg jurisprudence, is that it might also have to apply the doctrine of "margin

---

[12] *Tyrer v. U.K.* (1978) 2 E.H.R.R. 1; *Marckx v. Belgium* (1979) 2 E.H.R.R. 330; *Dudgeon v. U.K.* (1981) 4 E.H.R.R. 149; *Soering v. U.K.* (1989) 11 E.H.R.R. 439. See also *Sutherland v. U.K.* [1998] E.H.R.R. 117. But this only extends to the interpretation of rights included in the Convention and does not permit the introduction of new rights: *Johnston v. Ireland* (1986) 9 E.H.R.R. 203; *Feldebrugge v. Netherlands* (1986) 8 E.H.R.R. 425 (joint dissenting opinion); Harris, O'Boyle & Warbrick, *Law of the E.C.H.R.* (1995), p. 8; Mahoney (1990) 11 H.R.L.J. 57, 62–68. See also below, para. C0–08.
[13] See, to similar effect, Sir Thomas Bingham M.R. in *R. v. Ministry of Defence, ex parte Smith* [1996] Q.B. 517, 554 quoted below.
[14] Other implications of this are discussed below.
[15] *e.g. Cossey v. U.K.* (1990) 13 E.H.R.R. 622; *Sheffield and Horsham v. United Kingdom* (1998) 27 E.H.R.R. 163.
[16] *Hansard*, H.L. Vol. 584, January 18, 1998, col. 1269.
[17] *Henn & Darby v. DPP* [1981] A.C. 850, 905.
[18] Case C–358/89 *Extramet v. Council of Ministers* [1991] E.C.R I–2501; Cases C–267 & 268/91 *Keck & Mithouard* [1993] E.C.R I–6097. Examples of departure from earlier jurisprudence are the ECJ's gradual broadening of the doctrine of direct effect (*cf.* Case 43/75 *Defrenne v. Sabena* [1976] E.C.R 91; Case 4/74 *Van Duyn v. Home Office* [1974] E.C.R 1337 and Case 26/62 *Van Gend en Loos v. Nederlandse Administratre der Belastingen* [1963] E.C.R 10 and the qualification in the *Keck* case of the earlier case law on Article 30. For more overt departure from earlier case law, see, *e.g.* Case C–10/89 *CNL Sucal v. Hag GF AG* [1990] E.C.R I–3711 ("*Hag II*"); Case C–308/93 *Cabanis-Issarte* [1996] 2 C.M.L.R. 729.
[19] [1996] Q.B. 517, 554. See also 563 (Henry L.J.).
[20] [1996] Q.B. 517, 554.

of appreciation" in the same way as the Strasbourg Court. The Strasbourg institutions exercise an understandable degree of restraint when judging the compatibility of national measures with the Convention, and as a result, in a number of cases they have found no violation on the basis that the state enjoys a "margin of appreciation". This doctrine is considered further in Part II of this book,[21] but it is necessary to say something about it here. The margin of appreciation is an area of freedom of action within which the Strasbourg institutions will not interfere with the state's judgment. Its principal use is in relation to a state's justification for interference with a Convention right, for example what is "necessary in a democratic society"[22] under Articles 8–11 or "in the public interest"[23] or as to compensation terms[24] under Article 1 of the First Protocol; what is a "public emergency" and what measures are "strictly required by the exigencies of the situation" within the meaning of Article 15.[25] The court has also applied the margin when assessing what constitutes objective and reasonable justification for a difference of treatment under Article 14;[26] and when establishing the ambit of positive obligations[27] or inherent obligations such as access to courts.[28] The scope of the margin of appreciation varies according to the importance of the right in issue, the seriousness of the interference, the degree to which the issue is one on which a consensus exists among the parties to the Convention and the extent to which the matter may be the subject of national variation. The principal justification for the doctrine of margin of appreciation, as explained in *Handyside v. United Kingdom*, is that "state authorities are in principle in a better position than the international judge to give an opinion on the exact content of"[29] restrictions on Convention rights and their necessity, and the subsidiary role of the Convention in protecting human rights.[30] In view of this, a transposition of the doctrine to the domestic context would be wholly inappropriate.[31] In 1995, in *R. v. Ministry of Defence, ex parte Smith*, members of the Court of Appeal expressed the view that if the Convention had then been part of U.K. law, the primary judgment on a human rights issue would be for U.K. judges, whereas at that time the court's constitutional role was to exercise a secondary or reviewing judgment.[32] While U.K.

---

[21] See below, para. C0–17.
[22] *Olssson v. Sweden* (No. 1) (1989) 11 E.H.R.R. 259, para. 72.
[23] *Hentrich v. France* (1994) 18 E.H.R.R. 440.
[24] *James & ors v. United Kingdom* (1986) 8 E.H.R.R. 123, para. 54; *Lithgow v. United Kingdom* (1986) 8 E.H.R.R. 329, para. 122.
[25] *Ireland v. United Kingdom* 2 E.H.R.R. 25, para. 207 of the judgment.
[26] *Rasmussen v. Denmark* (1985) 7 E.H.R.R. 371, para. 40 of the judgment.
[27] *Abdulaziz, Cabales and Balkandali v. United Kingdom* (1987) 7 E.H.R.R. 471, para. 67 of the judgment. See also below, paras C0–04 *et seq.*
[28] See, *e.g. Stubbings v. United Kingdom* (1997) 23 E.H.R.R. 213.
[29] *Handyside v. U.K.* (1976) 1 E.H.R.R. 737, para. 49; *Brannigan & McBride v. U.K.* (1993) 7 E.H.R.R. 539.
[30] Harris, O'Boyle & Warbrick, *Law of the ECHR* (1995), p. 14.
[31] See Laws [1998] P.L. 254, 258; Marshall, *Constitutional Reform in the U.K.: Practice and Principles* (1998), p. 82. See also Feldman & Stevens [1997] P.L. 615, 621; Mahoney (1998) 19 H.R.L.J. 1, 3. But *cf.* Harris, O'Boyle & Warbrick, *Law of the ECHR* (1995), p. 14; Van Dijk & van Hoof, *Theory and Practice of the ECHR* (2nd ed.), p. 685; Jacobs & White, *The ECHR* (2nd ed.), p. 37 for the view that the margin of appreciation doctrine is rooted in national case-law concerning judicial review of government action. See also Schokkenbroek (1998) 19 H.R.L.J. 30. Van Dijk & van Hoof (p. 604) consider that even at the international level this uncertain doctrine is "to be compared to a spreading disease"; and see Lord Irvine of Lairg L.C. [1998] P.L. 221, 235, n. 66. See further Lavender [1997] E.H.R.L.R. 380; Pannick [1998] P.L. 545, 548.
[32] [1996] Q.B. 541, 564. Compare Simon Brown L.J. in the Divisional Court, in which at p. 541 he suggested that such primary review would be subject to "a limited margin of appreciation" and see below, para. 5–40.

courts exercising a reviewing or supervisory jurisdiction will act with restraint in reviewing the actions of public bodies, particularly in relation to policy issues such as complex economic matters,[33] national security[34] and the conduct of diplomatic relations,[35] it does not and should not follow that the "margin" they allow to a public body will be determined in the same way as that allowed by the ECHR. This has been recognised by the Divisional Court. In *R. v. Stafford JJ., ex parte Imbert*, Buxton L.J. stated that "[t]he application of the doctrine of the margin of appreciation would appear to be solely a matter for the Strasbourg Court" and "[t]he English judge cannot therefore himself apply or have recourse to the doctrine of the margin of appreciation as implemented by the Strasbourg Court. He must, however, recognise the impact of that doctrine upon the Strasbourg Court's analysis of the meaning and implications of the broad terms of the Convention provisions . . . ".[36]

The inapplicability of the margin of appreciation doctrine does not mean that the court will have to re-take all executive and legislative policy decisions. The extent of intervention will depend upon the seriousness of the right at issue, the degree of interference and the extent to which the court is capable of substituting its own view of the matter.[37]

C.   A U.K. court may give greater protection to human rights than the Strasbourg Court

2–06   Thirdly, the "take into account" requirement in section 2 of the HRA enables a U.K. court to go further than the Strasbourg institutions. Unlike the case law relating to the European Union, there is no imperative that parties to the Convention should adopt a uniform approach, only that they should not fall below an irreducible minimum, which will be maintained by the Strasbourg institutions. It is therefore open to national courts to develop a domestic jurisprudence under the Convention which may be more generous to applicants than that dispensed in Strasbourg, while remaining broadly consistent with it.[38] While this may be relevant in considering the scope of application of the substantive rights, initially, at least, it is likely that this greater generosity will be shown when determining the ambit of the exceptions to the rights, the requirements of a democratic society and the application of the principle of proportionality.

2–07   This aspect of the HRA was emphasised during the parliamentary progress of the Bill: the Act is designed to ensure the enjoyment of the Convention

---

[33] *R. v. Secretary of State for the Environment, ex parte Nottinghamshire CC* [1986] A.C. 240, 247; *R. v. Secretary of State for the Environment, ex parte Hammersmith & Fulham LBC* [1991] 1 A.C. 521, 593.
[34] *CCSU v. Minister for the Civil Service* [1985] A.C. 374, 402; *R. v. Home Secretary, ex parte Cheblak* [1991] 1 W.L.R. 890, 904.
[35] *CCSU v. Minister for the Civil Service* [1985] A.C. 374, 398, 418; *ex parte Molyneaux* [1986] 1 W.L.R. 331, 336.
[36] [1999] 2 Cr.App.R. 276. See also *R. v. DPP, ex parte Kebeline*, October 28, 1999 (Lord Hope). But the varying ways of satisfying Article 6 adopted in different Member States reflect the different national procedures rather than a variable concept of fairness. We suggest that Buxton L.J. is in error to the extent that he suggests that the margin of appreciation "recognises that the detailed content of at least some Convention obligations is more appropriately determined in the light of national conditions". The margin of appreciation relates not to the definition of a cat, but to the manner of its skinning. For an E.C. parallel, see Case 14/83 *Von Colson & Kamann v. Land Nordrhein-Westfalen* [1984] E.C.R. 1891.
[37] See *R. v. Secretary of State for the Home Department, ex parte Simms & O'Brien* [1999] 3 W.L.R. 328, in which Lord Steyn states that the approach of judicial deference to the views of prison authorities is at variance with the pressing social need test in *Silver v. United Kingdom* and inconsistent with the variable review test in *Ex parte Smith*. These issues are considered in more detail below in Chap. 5.
[38] This appears to have been the Government's intention: see *Rights Brought Home*, para. 2.5.

rights as a minimum. It was and would be open to domestic law to provide greater protection than that given by the Convention.[39] The Home Secretary stated that the legislation "will guarantee to everyone the means to enforce a set of basic civil and political rights, establishing a floor below which standards will not be allowed to fall"[40] and that "[t]hrough incorporation we are giving a profound margin of appreciation to British courts to interpret the convention in accordance with British jurisprudence as well as European jurisprudence".[41] The Lord Chancellor considered that our "courts must be free to develop human rights jurisprudence by taking into account European judgments and decisions, but they must also be free to distinguish them and to move out in new directions in relation to the whole area of human rights law".[42] The HRA permits U.K. courts to depart from existing Strasbourg decisions and the Lord Chancellor stated that "upon occasion it might be appropriate to do so, and it is possible that [U.K. courts] might give a successful lead to Strasbourg".[43]

D. International law and other considerations

2–08 As a matter of international law the United Kingdom is only obliged to abide by the final judgment of the ECHR in cases to which it is party.[44] It would therefore be inappropriate to require U.K. courts to follow cases concerned with the legality of laws and practices which are not those of the U.K. or any part of it.[45] Finally, the Lord Chancellor stated that "to make the courts bound by Strasbourg decisions could . . . result in the [HRA] being confusing if not internally inconsistent when the courts are faced with incompatible legislation".[46]

3. UNITED KINGDOM COURTS ARE GENERALLY UNLIKELY TO DEPART FROM STRASBOURG JURISPRUDENCE

2–09 Although the Strasbourg case law is only of persuasive authority, courts will be slow to depart from it, save in limited circumstances, which are discussed below. First, section 6 of the HRA provides that it is unlawful for a public authority (which includes a court or tribunal[47]) to act in a way which is incompatible with a Convention right, and the Strasbourg jurisprudence, particularly judgments of the Strasbourg Court, will be the best indicator of incompatibility.

Secondly, the approach of U.K. courts to provisions of E.C. law shows they have accepted that the interpretation of provisions which lay down general principles in

---

[39] It was to prevent this that the Opposition moved an amendment in the Lords which would have made the Strasbourg court's decisions binding: see *Hansard*, H.L. Vol. 584, January 19, 1998, col. 1268. But in the House of Commons a different approach was taken: an amendment was moved which would have lowered the requirement by enabling (by the word "may") a court to have regard to the Strasburg jurisprudence rather than requiring it to (by the word "must"): *Hansard*, H.C. Vol. 313, June 3, 1998, col. 388.

[40] *Hansard*, H.C., February 16, 1998, col. 769 (Second Reading). See also the Lord Chancellor *Hansard*, H.L. Vol. 1711, November 18, 1997, cols 514–515.

[41] *ibid.*

[42] *Hansard*, H.L. Vol. 1712, November 24, 1997, col. 835. See also *Hansard*, H.L. Vol. 584, January 19, 1998, col. 1271 and *Hansard*, H.L., January 29, 1998, col. 387.

[43] *Hansard*, H.L. Vol. 1711, November 18, 1997, col. 514.

[44] ECHR, Article 46(1). See Lord Lester of Herne Hill *Hansard*, H.L. Vol. 1711, November 18, 1997, col. 512; *Hansard*, H.L. Vol. 584, January 19, 1998, cols 1268–1269.

[45] *Hansard*, H.L. Vol. 1711, November 18, 1997, col. 514 (Lord Chancellor).

[46] *Hansard*, H.L. Vol. 1711, November 18, 1997, col. 514.

[47] s. 6(3)(a).

broad terms differs from that appropriate for the more detailed and precise approach used in U.K. legislation;[48] and that "the choice between alternative [interpretations] may turn not on purely legal considerations, but on a broader view of what the orderly development of the Community requires."[49] The consideration of legal harmony is particularly important where the court has to compare texts in different languages, all being equally authentic.[50] Subject to one caveat, it is likely that national courts will adopt a similar approach to the Convention, which is similarly dynamic, has authentic texts in English and French,[51] and in respect of which, in part because of its dynamic nature, it is less appropriate to use *travaux préparatoires*.[52] The caveat is that, as indicated above, it will be possible and may be desirable for a U.K. court to give greater protection to the Convention rights than is required by the Strasbourg institutions, particularly because it will not be appropriate to transpose the Strasbourg doctrine of margin of appreciation to the domestic adjudication.[53]

4.   CIRCUMSTANCES IN WHICH THE STRASBOURG JURISPRUDENCE MAY NOT BE FOLLOWED

2–10   It will be possible to depart from the Strasbourg jurisprudence in order to give more protection to the Convention rights, but only very exceptionally—when incompatible primary legislation so requires—will it be necessary to do so in order to give less protection. When therefore is a U.K. court likely to depart from the Strasbourg jurisprudence? First, it will not be permitted to give full effect to the jurisprudence where, notwithstanding the interpretative direction in section 3 of the HRA, U.K. legislation is incompatible with the Convention right under consideration.[54] In that case, however, the court will have to apply the Strasbourg case law in order to conclude that there is incompatibility. Secondly, for the reasons given above,[55] it should be willing to depart from a Strasbourg decision where a finding that there has been no infringement of the Convention rests on the application of the "margin of appreciation" or the ambit of the exceptions to Convention rights, the requirements of a democratic society or the application of the principle of proportionality. Thirdly, there is the dynamic nature of the interpretation of the Convention. Since "the interpretation of the convention rights develops over the years" "[c]ircumstances may . . . arise in which a judgment given

---

[48] *Bulmer v. Bollinger* [1974] Ch. 401, 425. See also the Privy Council decisions interpreting Commonwealth constitutional instruments: below, para. 3–13, n. 69.

[49] *Customs & Excise Comms v. ApS Samex* [1983] 1 All E.R. 1042, 1056 (Bingham J.). See also *R. v. Stock Exchange, ex parte Else* [1993] 2 W.L.R. 70, 76.

[50] *ibid.*

[51] ECHR Article 59. On the reconciliation of different meanings, see *Wemhoff v. FR Germany* (1968) 1 E.H.R.R. 55; *James v. U.K.* (1986) 8 E.H.R.R. 123; *Brogan v. U.K.* (1988) 11 E.H.R.R. 117; Vienna Convention, Article 33(1).

[52] *i.e.* the drafts of the Convention and the minutes of inter-ministerial discussions leading to the adoption of the final text. See *Johnston v. Ireland* (1986) 9 E.H.R.R. 203; *Cruz Varas v. Sweden* (1991) 14 E.H.R.R. 1; *Sigurjonsson v. Iceland* (1993) 16 E.H.R.R. 462.

[53] For a recent example of a Strasbourg case which the U.K. courts are unlikely to follow, see *Janowski v. Poland* (Application No. 25716/94) judgment of January 21, 1999: the applicant was fined for the offence of insulting a civil servant during and in connection with the carrying out his official duties—he had called two municipal guards "dumb" and "oafs" while they unlawfully were trying to move on two street traders. The Court held that the interference with his right to freedom of expression was justified for the prevention of disorder. See the dissenting opinion of Judge Sir Nicholas Bratza.

[54] See below paras 3–01, 3–43 and 3–48.

[55] See above, para. 2–05.

by the European Court of Human Rights decades ago contains pronouncements which it would not be appropriate to apply to the letter in the circumstances of today in a particular set of circumstances affecting this country".[56] For this reason, in general, the older a decision is, the less reliable a guide it is as to the interpretation of the Convention today. There can, for example, be evolution in what is regarded as "degrading treatment" under Article 3, an interference with privacy which is proportionate and "necessary in a democratic society" under Article 8, and interference with "respect for family life" or "respect for private life" under Article 8.[57] As indicated above, the approach of domestic courts in the context of E.C. law suggests that they are unlikely to have difficulty with this. In particular it has been recognised that the interpretation of the E.C. Treaty can change to match the development of the Communities and Community institutions.[58]

2–11   As in the case of the interpretation of the E.C. Treaty by the ECJ,[59] the Strasbourg institutions favour a purposive approach to interpretation.[60] Thus, one has to look to the system and objectives of the Convention, as well as to the spirit, general scheme and wording of a particular provision.[61] The aim is to achieve the objectives of the Convention effectively. In the *Golder* case a majority of the Court adopted the Commission's submission that "the over-riding function of this Convention is to protect the rights of the individual and not to lay down as between states mutual obligations which are to be restrictively interpreted . . . On the contrary, the role of the Convention and the function of its interpretation is to make the protection of the individual effective".[62] Elsewhere, the Court has said that "the Convention is intended to guarantee not rights that are theoretical or illusory but rights that are practical and effective".[63] Nevertheless, words may be given their ordinary meaning[64] even when this produces a restrictive interpreta-tion.[65] Where words have technical meanings in national systems an "independent" or "autonomous" convention meaning is given to them in order to promote uniformity.[66] But where a common tradition of constitutional law and legal tradition can be found it will be influential in the interpretation of the Convention by the Strasbourg institutions. So, for example, national law standards have been relevant in deciding on the scope of the right to respect for family life in Article 8(1), or the right to a trial within a reasonable time in Article 6(1).[67]

---

[56] The Lord Chancellor; *Hansard*, H.L. Vol 584, January 19, 1998, col. 1271.
[57] For an application of this approach, see *Sheffield and Horsham v. United Kingdom* (1999) 27 E.H.R.R. 163. The judgment is based substantially on the Court's deference to the State's margin of appreciation. See further C8–07.
[58] *Henn & Darby v. DPP* [1981] A.C. 850, 905.
[59] Case 6/72 *Continental Can* [1973] E.C.R 215, 243. See generally, Brown & Kennedy, *The Court of Justice of the European Communities* (4th ed., 1994), Ch. 14; Collins, *European Community Law in the U.K.* (4th ed., 1990), pp. 130–134; Bennion, *Statutory Interpretation,* (3rd ed. 1997), pp. 998–1000.
[60] See generally Harris, O'Boyle & Warbrick, *Law of the ECHR* (1995) pp. 5–19; Jacobs & White, *The ECHR* (2nd ed.), Ch. 3. On the principle of proportionality, see below, paras 5–13—5–15 On the margin of appreciation see above, para. 2–05 and below, para. C0–17.
[61] *Wemhoff v. FR Germany* (1968) 1 E.H.R.R. 55; *Golder v. U.K.* (1975) 1 E.H.R.R. 524. See also *Airey v. Ireland* (1979) 2 E.H.R.R. 305; *Artico v. Italy* (1979) 3 E.H.R.R. 1; *Soering v. U.K.* (1989) 11 E.H.R.R. 439.
[62] *Golder v. U.K.* (1975) 1 E.H.R.R. 524 (9:3 majority).
[63] *Artico v. Italy* (1981) 3 E.H.R.R. 1.
[64] *e.g Johnston v. Ireland* (1987) 9 E.H.R.R. 203.
[65] *Wemhoff v. FR Germany* (1968) 1 E.H.R.R. 55. cf. *Pretto v. Italy* (1983) 6 E.H.R.R. 182.
[66] *Engel v. Netherlands* (1976) 1 E.H.R.R. 647 ("criminal charge"); *Konig v. FR Germany* (1978) 2 E.H.R.R. 170 ("civil right").
[67] *Marckx v. Belgium* (1979) E.H.R.R. 330; *Brogan v. U.K.* (1988) 11 E.H.R.R. 117. See further Harris, O'Boyle & Warbrick, *Law of the ECHR* (1995) pp. 9–11; Jacobs & White, *The ECHR* (2nd ed.), pp. 32–33.

5.   Understanding the Strasbourg jurisprudence

2-12   Finally, although section 2(1) of the HRA lumps together all the Strasbourg jurisprudence, varying weight will be given to the different classes of decision made by the Convention institutions, according to their place in Convention procedure.

Applications may be made to Strasbourg by state parties (but only against other states)[68] or by individuals claiming to be victims of a violation.[69] Before entry into force of the 11th Protocol, the (now defunct) Commission received all applications. It first considered whether the application was admissible, *i.e.*, in the case of an individual petition, whether it was made against a party who had accepted the right of individual petition, in respect of a time and territory covered by that acceptance, and not manifestly ill-founded or an abuse of the right of petition.[70] In the case of all applications from individuals, it would also consider whether all domestic remedies had been exhausted and the application had been brought within six months of the date of the final domestic decision.[71] Having considered these matters, the Commission would make a *decision* on the *admissibility* of the application. If it declared an application admissible, then unless it could achieve friendly settlement of the case, the Commission would prepare a *Report* setting out the facts and stating its *opinion* as to whether the facts it had found disclosed a breach of the Convention.[72] The Report would be transmitted to the Committee of Ministers of the Council of Europe and, if the case was not referred to the Court, the Committee would reach a *decision* as to whether the Convention had been violated, a decision which the states undertook to regard as binding on them.[73] Alternatively, the Commission or a state party could refer the case to the Court,[74] for final *judgment*[75], and the states undertook to be bound by any decision of the Court to which they were parties.[76]

2-13   With effect from 1 November 1998, the 11th Protocol to the Convention has abolished the Commission and replaced it with a unitary Court. The Court now receives all applications and Chambers[77] or committees[78] of the Court decide whether they are admissible.[79] Unless (a) a friendly settlement is reached,[80] or (b) the Chamber relinquishes jurisdiction in favour of the Grand Chamber,[81] the Chamber will hear the case and give *judgment*.[82] The judgment of the Chamber will

---

[68] Article 33, formerly Article 24. See further below, para. 3–09.
[69] Article 34, formerly Article 25.
[70] Article 27 of the unamended Convention. See now Article 35.
[71] Article 26 of the unamended Convention. See now Article 35.
[72] Article 31 of the unamended Convention.
[73] Article 32 of the unamended Convention.
[74] Article 48 of the unamended Convention.
[75] Article 52 of the unamended Convention.
[76] Article 53 of the unamended Convention.
[77] Article 27(1) of the Convention as amended provides that the Court shall sit in committees of three judges, in Chambers of seven judges and in a Grand Chamber of 17 judges.
[78] Committees may declare an individual application inadmissible by a unanimous vote: Article 28 of the Convention as amended. Otherwise, admissibility decisions are taken by Chambers.
[79] Article 35 of the Convention as amended.
[80] Article 39 of the Convention as amended.
[81] Unless a party objects, a Chamber may, at any time before it has rendered its judgment, relinquish jurisdiction in any case which "raises a serious question affecting the interpretation of the Convention or the protocols thereto, or where the resolution of a question before the Chamber might have a result inconsistent with a judgment previously delivered by the Court".
[82] Within a period of three months from the date of the judgment of the Chamber, any party to the case may, in exceptional cases, request that the case be referred to the Grand Chamber. Such requests are determined by a panel of five judges of the Grand Chamber, which "shall accept the request if the case raises a serious question affecting the interpretation or application of the Convention or the protocols thereto, or a serious issue of general importance": Article 43 of the amended Convention.

be final unless following judgment the case is referred to the Grand Chamber.[83] If the Grand Chamber accepts the case,[84] its judgment in the case will be final.[85] In either case, states undertake to abide by the final judgment of the Court in any case to which they are parties.[86] In addition, the Court may give advisory opinions.[87]

From this summary, it will be seen that Strasbourg generates the following classes of case law:

2–14 Decisions on admissibility, taken by the Commission or by committees or Chambers of the new Court:. Although Commission decisions on admissibility are reasoned, the volume of cases with which the Commission had to deal means that the quality of those resulting in findings of inadmissibility varies considerably. The bulk of applications were declared ∕ inadmissible without even requiring any observations from the proposed respondent government, and such cases in particular were usually written in relatively summary form. But much of the case law on the concept of "victim" is to be found in Commission admissibility decisions; and such decisions also provide an overview of matters which fall within or outside the scope of the substantive articles of the Convention. Moreover, when the Commission declared an application admissible, it did not express any view of the merits beyond reciting that the case raised serious issues under the Convention. By contrast, where a Commission held an application inadmissible as being manifestly ill-founded, its decision might well contain useful material about the ambit of Convention rights. The admissibility decisions produced by the new Court to date appear to follow the same format as those of the Commission. Admissibility decisions are expressed to be unanimous or by a majority, although they do not contain dissenting opinions.

2–15 Opinions of the Commission on the merits of an application:. As noted above, if the Commission did not achieve a friendly settlement of an application, it would ascertain the facts and its report would set out its opinion on the merits of the application. Separate or dissenting opinions would also be included. Although a Commission opinion was not binding on the parties, it was produced after considering full argument and it carried considerable jurisprudential weight, particularly in cases which were not referred to the Court.[88] A domestic court will be bound to prefer a finding of violation by the Court to a Commission finding of no violation in the same case. Indeed, the domestic court's duty as a public authority will often make it unlawful to depart from a Court finding of violation. However, it was much more common for the Commission's opinion of violation to be overturned by the Court.[89] In such cases, as the obligation of the domestic court

---

[83] Article 44(2) of the Convention as amended.
[84] The Grand Chamber will not include any of the judges of the Chamber which heard the case other than the President of the Chamber and the judge who sat in respect of the State Party concerned.
[85] Article 44(1) of the Convention as amended.
[86] Article 46(1) of the Convention as amended.
[87] Article 47 of the Convention as amended.
[88] Where a case was not referred to the Court, the Committee of Ministers took the final decision as to violation.
[89] See, for example, *Stubbings & Others v. United Kingdom* October 22, 1996, R.J.D., 1996–IV, No. 18; 23 E.H.R.R. 213, concerning limitation in child abuse proceedings, in which the Commission was of the unanimous opinion that Articles 14 and 6(1) had been violated whereas the Court decided by eight votes to two that there had been no violation: see below, para. C14–18. Compare the position in *McCann, Farrell & Savage v. United Kingdom* (1996) 21 E.H.R.R. 97 (the "Death on the Rock" case), where the Commission found no violation by 11 votes to six, whereas the Court found a violation by 10 votes to nine. However, they were largely in agreement as to the principles to be applied, although there was extensive disagreement as to their application to the case: see below, para. C2–14.

is only to "take into account" the Strasbourg case law, it may well be more convinced by the reasoning of the Commission than that of the Court (or, indeed, by the reasoning of the minority of the Court than by that of the majority). In addition, in controversial cases, an overwhelming Commission majority in favour of violation, when added to a substantial minority opinion in the same direction in the Court, may well show that a majority of Strasbourg judicial opinion favoured a finding that there had been a violation in a particular case. While such head-counting is not normally appropriate, it should be borne in mind that many former members of the Commission have now been appointed to the Court, so that the distinction between Commission opinions and Court judgments may be blurred. Again there may be cases in which the Court has found no violation but where the domestic court or tribunal will be more persuaded by the reasoned opinion of one of the dissenters.[90]

2–16 Judgments of the Court:. The judgments of the old Court were, in theory at least, all of equal weight. Inevitably judgments given by the plenary Court carry more authority than those of a Chamber.[91] Judgments of the Grand Chamber of the new Court take precedence over those of the Chambers. Nonetheless, a domestic court may be persuaded to prefer a Chamber's more expansive approach to the scope of Convention rights or the ambit of exceptions even if it has been overruled by a judgment of the Grand Chamber. This more flexible approach to the case law is a proper reflection of the national court's freedom to develop a body of human rights law which is more generous than that of the Strasbourg institutions.

2–17 Decisions of the Committee of Ministers:. Decisions of the Committee of Ministers are the fruit of discussion, in closed session, between the representatives of the Member States of the Council of Europe, which include the respondent government. The applicant has no right to address the Committee, nor is he made aware of any communications or submissions made by the respondent. The Committee does not give reasons for its decisions. It is hard to see how any juridical significance can attach to the Committee's pronouncements or, indeed, how a Committee finding of no violation[92] could sensibly be held to cast doubt on a Commission opinion of violation. The weight to be given to decisions of the Committee of Ministers as a result of section 2(1)(d) of the HRA is therefore minimal.

2–18 Advisory opinions of the Court:. The reference in section 2(1)(a) of the HRA to advisory opinions of the Court may safely be ignored altogether. Although the Convention empowers the Court to give such opinions,[93] Article 47(2) of the amended Convention provides that such opinions "shall not deal with any question relating to the content or scope of the rights or freedoms defined in Section 1 of the Convention and the protocols thereto, or with any other question which the Court

---

[90] For an example see the dissenting opinion of Judge Sir Nicolas Bratza joined by Judge Rozakis *Janowski v. Poland* (Application No. 25716/94) judgment of January 21, 1999. The Court held by 12 votes to five that there had been no violation of Article 10 of the Convention.

[91] Rule 48 of the Rules of the old Court enabled a chamber to relinquish jurisdiction in favour of the plenary Court in any case which "raise[d] a serious question affecting interpretation of the Convention". See now Article 30 of the amended Convention.

[92] Or a failure to reach any decision by the prescribed majority, as happened in *East African Asians v. United Kingdom* (1973) 3 E.H.R.R. 76, 102–103.

[93] Article 47(1) of the Convention as amended; formerly Article 1(1) of the Second Protocol.

or the Committee of Ministers might have to consider in consequence of any such proceedings as could be instituted in accordance with the Convention".[94] Consequently, the Court has never given and is never likely to give an advisory opinion.

2–19 In summary, the categories of Strasbourg jurisprudence most likely to assist U.K. courts are: judgments of the old and the new Court; Commission reports on the merits; and admissibility decisions in so far as they concern the concept of a 'victim' and the ambit of Convention rights.

---

[94] Formerly Article 1(2) of the second Protocol.

CHAPTER 3

Impact of the Act on legislation

1. INTRODUCTION: THE INTERPRETATIVE OBLIGATION

3–01 Section 3 of the HRA provides that primary and subordinate legislation,[1] whenever enacted, must be read and given effect, "so far as it is possible to do so", in a way which is compatible with the Convention rights. It also provides that this interpretative obligation does not affect the validity, continuing operation or enforcement of any incompatible primary legislation, or of any incompatible subordinate legislation if primary legislation prevents the removal of the incompatibility.[2] If it is not possible to give effect to the obligation in a way which is compatible with Convention rights a competent court must consider whether to make a declaration of incompatibility. This obligation applies to all courts and tribunals in all proceedings at every level, but in contrast with the obligation in section 2, it is also addressed to anyone else who has to give effect to or enforce legislation. The interpretative obligation is of the most important aspects of the Act and arguably the one which will have the most effect in practice.

This chapter considers the provisions of section 3, the way in which the HRA reconciles giving further effect to Convention rights with the doctrine of parliamentary sovereignty, and the approach of the HRA to interpretation of pre-existing legislation and future legislation. The effectiveness of its attempt to protect fundamental rights by an "ordinary" non-entrenched statute, and reliance on interpretative instructions and (in the case of government-sponsored legislation enacted after the HRA) ministerial statements that the provisions of a Bill are compatible with the Convention rights will be assessed by considering the approach of the courts to the interpretation of legislation affected by European Community law, and the experience of other common law jurisdictions.

3–02 A number of possible models were considered for giving effect to the Convention rights.[3] These included:

(a) entrenchment with courts having the power not to enforce any statute or statutory instrument which infringed the Convention rights (but, as with the European Communities Act 1972, leaving open the possibility of express repeal of the HRA);

(b) a more limited form of entrenchment which would operate save where future legislation expressly provides that it should apply notwithstanding the HRA (the solution in the Canadian Bill of Rights 1960 and the Charter of Rights 1982); and

---

[1] On the meaning of this see below, para. 3–03 and HRA, s. 21(1), below, pp. 389–390. It does not include E.U. legislation which is directly applicable or which has direct effect in the U.K.

[2] On the approach to subordinate legislation, see below, para. 3–42.

[3] See generally Constitution Unit, *Human Rights Legislation* (1996) pp. 30–40.

(c) a purely interpretative approach by which Parliament would be deterred from diverging from the Convention rights but the traditions of parliamentary sovereignty would be respected (the approach of the New Zealand Bill of Rights 1990). In this instance the courts would not have power to refuse to enforce statutes that, on their proper interpretation, are clearly incompatible with the Convention rights.

The government rejected any form of entrenchment, favouring an interpretative approach similar to that adopted in New Zealand.[4] But even so, as will be seen, this form of incorporation will involve "a modified form of judicial review of statutes".[5]

2. SCOPE OF SECTION 3

A. Primary and subordinate legislation

3–03   The interpretative obligation applies to all legislation whenever enacted. Primary legislation means[6] any public general Act, local personal Act and private Act, as well as a Measure of the Church Assembly and a Measure of the General Synod of the Church of England. It also includes Orders in Council made under section 38(1)(a) of the Northern Ireland Constitution Act 1973 and an Order in Council made under the exercise of the Royal Prerogative,[7] and subordinate legislation made for the purpose of bringing into force or amending primary legislation.[8] Subordinate legislation includes Acts of the Scottish Parliament and the (former) Parliament of Northern Ireland and Measures of the Northern Ireland Assembly.[9]

B. The interpretative obligation and ministerial statements of compatibility

3–04   So far as future government-sponsored legislation is concerned, the interpretative obligation is underpinned by the obligation on a Minister of the Crown in charge of Bill to make a statement to Parliament about the compatibility of the Bill with the Convention before its Second Reading.[10] He must either make a statement that in his view the provisions of the Bill are compatible (known as a "statement of compatibility") or he must state that the government wishes to proceed with the Bill although no such statement can be made.[11] The formula adopted to date is brief and uninformative, *i.e.*:

---

[4] *Hansard*, H.C., February 16, 1998, cols 771–772 (Home Secretary), cols 806, 842; *Hansard*, H.C., May 20, 1998, col. 978.
[5] Lord Hoffmann in *Matadeen v. Pointu* [1999] 1 A.C. 98, 110. See also *R. v. Secretary of State for the Home Department, ex parte Simms & O'Brien* [1999] 3 W.L.R. 328, 341; Hoffmann (1999) 62 M.L.R. 1.
[6] s. 22(1).
[7] for example the Queen's Regulations governing the armed forces.
[8] For example s. 5 of the European Communities Act 1972 and s. 10 of the Human Rights Act. A commencement order might conceivably infringe Article 7, which prohibits retrospective criminal legislation.
[9] s. 21(1). On the power to disapply Acts of the Scottish Parliament and the Northern Ireland Assembly, see Scotland Act 1998, s. 29(2)(d), Northern Ireland Act 1998, s. 6(2)(c). Legislation of the Welsh Assembly will be subordinate legislation only, within the meaning of HRA, s. 21(1)(f).
[10] HRA, s. 19. This provision came into force on November 24, 1998: Human Rights Act 1998 (Commencement) Order 1998, S.I. 1998 No. 2882.
[11] No similar obligation applies to Private Members' Bills. Where the Bill is directly assisted by the Government, however, the Minister responsible for the policy should, as a matter of good practice, express the Government's views on compatibility with the Convention rights during the Second Reading debate: written answer by Lord Burlison, *Hansard*, H.L., May 5, 1999, W.A. 92.

"EUROPEAN CONVENTION ON HUMAN RIGHTS–The [*relevant minister*] has made the following statement under section 19(1)(a) of the Human Rights Act 1998: In my view the provisions of the [*name of Bill*] are compatible with the Convention Rights."

No reasons are given where a statement is made: reasons are thought to disclose legal advice which is regarded as confidential. If no statement is made, this is explained on the ground that Convention issues are frequently complex and a debate in Parliament provides the best forum for the ministers to explain their thinking.[12] The present practice is to make a statement of compatibility only if legal advice indicates that it is more likely than not that the provisions of the Bill will stand up to challenge on Convention grounds before the domestic courts and the ECHR in Strasbourg.[13] Where legal advice is that on balance the provisions of the Bill would not survive such a challenge, a Minister will not be advised to make a statement of compatibility.[14] Assuming a statement of compatibility has been made, in principle it will be difficult to adopt an interpretation which is incompatible with Convention rights.[15] However, even in the absence of such a statement, the interpretative obligation will remain.

3. CONSISTENCY OF HRA WITH PARLIAMENTARY SOVEREIGNTY

3–05   The Lord Chancellor described the design of the HRA as intended to maximise "the position of human rights without trespassing on parliamentary sovereignty"[16] and to be "consistent with the sovereignty of Parliament as traditionally understood".[17] Lord Hoffmann has said that the HRA will not detract from the power of Parliament, if it chooses, to legislate contrary to fundamental principles

---

[12] *Hansard*, H.L., May 19, 1999, W.A. 35 (Lord Williams of Mostyn). But note the position where draft legislation is prepared and considered by Parliament. The Joint Committee on Financial Services and Markets gave extensive consideration to compliance with the Convention and the Treasury's legal advisers (Sydney Kentridge Q.C. and James Eadie) gave evidence to the Committee: Second Report, HC 465 1998–99, May 27, 1999, Minutes of Evidence, pp. 4–14. See also First Report, HC 328–I 1998–99, April 27, 1999, para. 16 and Annexes C and D (legal opinions prepared on the instructions of the British Bankers Association, the London Investment Banking Association, the Futures and Options Association and several firms of city solicitors), reproduced in Cambridge Centre for Public Law, *The Human Rights Act and the Criminal and Regulatory Process* (Hart, 1999).

[13] A statement may be made even where a court has stated that a provision is incompatible with the Convention provided the government has appealed against the decision and is advised that the appeal is more likely than not to succeed. See the unusual circumstances in which it was discovered that ss. 16A–16D and Sched. 6A of the Prevention of Terrorism (Temporary Provisions) Act 1989 had erroneously been allowed to lapse after the Divisional Court in *R. v. DPP, ex parte Kebeline* [1999] 3 W.L.R. 175 had stated that ss. 16A and 16B were incompatible with the presumption of innocence in Article 6(2) of the Convention: *Hansard*, H.C. Vol. 333, June 23, 1999, col. 1172 (Home Secretary), June 24, 1999, cols 1382 *et seq.* esp. 1388–1389 (Home Secretary). See below, paras 3–14 and 3–18 for the House of Lord's decision.

[14] *Hansard*, H.L., May 5, 1999, col. W.A. 93. This will be so even where valid arguments can be advanced against any anticipated challenge but it is thought that these arguments would not ultimately succeed before the courts.

[15] But *cf.* the position where a court has already expressed a view on the matter (see n. 13 above) before the statement is made or where the precise ground on which incompatibility is based is shown not to have been considered at the time the statement is made.

[16] *Hansard*, H.L., November 3, 1997, col. 1229.

[17] (November 18, 1997, col. 522). See also February 5, 1998, col. 839 ("The sovereignty of Parliament should not be disturbed"); *Hansard*, H.C. Vol. 306, cols 771–772, 774 (Home Secretary). See further White Paper, "Rights Brought Home", Cm. 3782 (1997) paras 2.9–2.15.

of human rights;[18] but, as will be seen,[19] it cannot do so by general or ambiguous words: "it must squarely confront what it is doing and accept the political cost".[20]

Under the doctrine of parliamentary sovereignty which emerged after the constitutional settlement of 1688 and was placed by Dicey at the centre of his account of the British constitution, the courts recognise no legal limit to the legislative power of the Queen in Parliament.[21] Save in relation to E.C. law where the doctrine has been modified,[22] and notwithstanding a number of practical limitations on the power of Parliament, the doctrine remains a fundamental principle of the U.K.'s constitution. At the same time, it has been subjected to powerful criticism[23] and is likely to be increasingly scrutinised as European integration develops. As traditionally understood, sovereignty is said to be "illimitable, perpetual, and indivisible" with the consequence that it is not possible to entrench legislation so as to prevent its repeal.[24]

A. The doctrine of implied repeal

3–06   Legislation may be repealed impliedly as well as expressly, notably when its provisions are inconsistent with those of a later statute. Thus in *Ellen Street Estates v. Ministry of Health* Maugham L.J. stated that:

> " . . . [A]ccording to our constitution . . . it is impossible for Parliament to enact that in a subsequent statute dealing with the same subject-matter there can be no implied repeal. If in a subsequent Act Parliament chooses to make it plain that the earlier statute is being to some extent repealed, effect must be given to that intention just because it is the will of Parliament."[25]

Those designing the HRA were concerned to circumvent the operation of the doctrine of implied repeal for constitutional reasons. The Lord Chancellor stated that the Government did "not wish to incorporate the Convention rights, and then, in reliance on the doctrine of implied repeal, allow the courts to strike down Acts of Parliament".[26] The solution adopted was to "give further effect" to the Convention

---

[18] *R. v. Secretary of State for the Home Department, ex parte Simms & O'Brien* [1999] 3 W.L.R. 328.
[19] para. 3.2.4, below.
[20] *R. v. Secretary of State for the Home Department, ex parte Simms & O'Brien* [1999] 3 W.L.R. 328 (Lord Hoffmann).
[21] *Cheney v. Conn* [1968] 1 W.L.R. 242 at 247; *Blackburn v. AG* [1971] 1 W.L.R. 1041; *Madzimbamutu v. Lardner-Burke* [1969] 1 A.C. 645 at 723.
[22] *R. v. Secretary of State for Transport, ex parte Factortame (No. 2)* [1990] 2 A.C. 85 on which see Craig (1991) 11 Y.B. Eur. L. 221; Wade (1996) 112 L.Q.R. 568; Eekalaar (1997) 113 L.Q.R. 185; Allan (1997) 13 L.Q.R. 443.
[23] Notably by Jennings *The Law and the Constitution* (5th ed., 1967), Chap. 4; Heuston, *Essays on Constitutional Law* (2nd ed., 1964), Chap. 1; Marshall, *Constitutional Theory* (1971), Chap. 3. On Commonwealth support for the suggestion that Parliament may make it more difficult to legislate by requiring the use of a particular "manner and form" for certain changes, see *Bribery Commission v. Rannasinghe* [1965] A.C. 172; *Liyanage v. R* [1967] 1 A.C. 259; *A-G New South Wales v. Trethowan* [1932] A.C. 526; *Minister of the Interior v. Harris* [1952] 1 T.L.R. 1245; *R. v. Mercure* [1988] 1 S.C.R. 234.
[24] HL Select Committee on a Bill of Rights (1977/78) HL 176; but note the debate as to whether, while unable to bind itself as to substance, Parliament can bind itself as to the "manner and form" of legislation. The U.K. and Privy Council authorities are inconclusive. For arguments favouring such a limit see Jennings, *The Law and the Constitution* (5th ed., 1967) p. 149; Heuston, *Essays in Constitutional Law* (2nd ed.), p. 6 *et seq. cf.* Wade [1955] C.L.J. 172. In Canada the limit applies: *R. v. Mercure* [1988] 1 S.C.R. 234; Hogg, *Constitutional Law of Canada* (3rd ed., 1992), pp. 309–314.
[25] [1934] K.B. 590, 597. See also *Vauxhall Estates Ltd v. Liverpool Corp.* [1932] 1 K.B. 733. See generally *R. v. Davis* (1783) 1 Leach. 271; *GW Railway Co. v. Cheltenham Extension Railway Co.* (1884) 9 App. Cas. 787, 809; *R. v. Halliday* [1917] A.C. 260, 305; Bennion, *Statutory Interpretation*, sect. 87; *Driedger on the Construction of Statutes* (3rd ed., 1994), pp. 188–190.
[26] *Hansard*, H.L., November 18, 1997, col. 522. See also col. 509.

rights rather than incorporating them.[27] There were also technical reasons for excluding the doctrine. In the following sections we consider first the effect *on* the HRA of legislation enacted after it and secondly the effect *of* the HRA on legislation enacted before it.

B. Legislation enacted after the HRA

3–07   The courts have been reluctant to apply the doctrine of implied repeal to modern statutes drafted in detail and with precision,[28] and to statutes which, like the HRA, are constitutionally significant.[29] Moreover, it has been held that section 2 of the European Communities Act 1972 and the E.C. rights incorporated by it into U.K. law were not impliedly repealed by subsequent inconsistent domestic legislation.[30] Nevertheless, there was a danger that the HRA itself, or certain parts of it, would be held to be impliedly repealed by subsequent legislation found to be inconsistent with it.[31] This could have been avoided only by according the HRA a measure of entrenchment against subsequent legislation. Entrenchment would have raised political difficulties, and would have been inconsistent with the Diceyan notion of parliamentary sovereignty described earlier.

C. Legislation enacted before the HRA

3–08   There is a presumption against implied repeal where the later enactment is, like the HRA, a general one covering circumstances for which specific provision was made in the earlier Act.[32] But notwithstanding both this presumption and the strength of the interpretative direction in section 3 (considered below), if the HRA had given the Convention rights the force of law in domestic courts, existing legislation held to be inconsistent with them would have been impliedly repealed.[33] Although, in the case of legislation enacted before the HRA, the exclusion of the doctrine of implied repeal allows the legislature, rather than the courts, to have the final say on any incompatibility, the application of the doctrine in this context would not conflict with parliamentary sovereignty. This is because the use of the HRA to override earlier legislation would, in principle, itself have been a manifestation of Parliament's sovereignty.[34]

3–09   But the application of the doctrine of implied repeal to legislation enacted before the HRA is open to other objections. First, there is doubt whether the earlier

---

[27] See above, paras 1–12 and 1–13.
[28] *Jennings v. United States* [1982] 1 A.C. 624, 643–644; Bennion, *Statutory Interpretation*, p. 226. See also *Re Marr* [1990] 2 All E.R. 880, 885.
[29] *Re the Earl of Antrim and others' Petition* [1967] 1 A.C. 691, 724. See also Canadian cases which, however, proceed on the "constitutional" nature of the Bill of Rights: *Singh v. Minister of Employment and Immigration* [1985] 1 S.C.R. 177; *Ford v. Quebec, Devine v. Quebec* [1988] 2 S.C.R. 712, 790.
[30] *R. v. Secretary of State for Transport, ex parte Factortame* [1990] 2 A.C. 85.
[31] Commonwealth examples of the implied repeal of unentrenched constitutional legislation include *McCawley v. R* [1920] A.C. 691 and *Kariapper v. Wijesinha* [1968] A.C. 717, 742–743. See further *Halsbury's Laws of England*, para. 1301.
[32] *Generalia specialibus non derogant* (a general provision does not derogate from a general one): *R. v. Home Secretary, ex parte Hickey (No. 1)* [1995] 1 All E.R. 479, 487 (applying Bennion, *Statutory Interpretation*, sect. 88); *Patterson v. Finneyley Internal Drainage Bd* [1970] 2 Q.B. 33, 38–39; *Re B.C. Teachers' Federation* (1985) 23 D.L.R. (4th) 161 (British Columbia).
[33] *R. v. Drybones* [1970] S.C.R. 282 (Canada: previous inconsistent statute rendered "inoperative" by Bill of Rights Act 1960, s. 2 *quaere* whether by "ordinary" operation of implied repeal or by the constitutional nature of Bill of Rights); *Winnipeg School Division No. 1 v. Craton* [1985] 2 S.C.R. 150.
[34] See *Hansard*, H.L., November 18, 1997, col. 523 (Lord Simon of Glaisdale); January 19, 1998, cols 1291 (Lord Lester of Herne Hill Q.C.), 1293 (Lord Ackner).

provision is in fact treated as repealed for all purposes by an implied repeal or, more likely, as merely inoperative.[35] If the earlier Act is only inoperative, although suspended, it does not cease to be law and would again become operative if the later Act were repealed or amended so as to remove the inconsistency. Secondly, the application of implied repeal leads to a problem of transparency; it means that the body of statute law in force at a given time is less easy to ascertain.[36] Thirdly, the application of implied repeal would mean that if an English court interprets the Convention more favourably to a citizen than the Strasbourg Court (which is in principle possible),[37] the relevant pre-HRA English legislation would be rendered ineffective without the possibility of a remedy for the government or public body, because the government or public body cannot take the issue to the Strasbourg Court.[38]

Lord Lester of Herne Hill Q.C. stated that he found nothing in the Bill to prevent the courts, where appropriate, from applying the doctrine of implied repeal to existing legislation.[39] But the Lord Chancellor stated that the doctrine "can have no application because of the express words of [section] 3", which imposes the interpretative obligation. He added that it was "not relevant" to cite the doctrine of implied repeal because the Convention rights would not, by the HRA, "become part of our domestic law, and will therefore not supersede existing legislation".[40] This analysis is correct. Any conflict would be between statutory provisions and Convention rights which do not have "the force of law" in the United Kingdom. The doctrine of implied repeal applies to resolve conflicts between laws enacted by the same legislative body and not between a law and an instrument of lesser effect.[41]

4. APPROACH TO INTERPRETATION

A. Introduction

3–10   The White Paper stated that the provisions of what is now section 3 go "far beyond" the pre-HRA rule which enabled the courts to take the Convention into account in resolving any ambiguity in a legislative provision: "[t]he courts will be required to interpret legislation so as to uphold the Convention rights unless the legislation itself is so clearly incompatible with the Convention that it is impossible to do so".[42] Section 3 itself provides that the statute "*must* be read and given effect" in a way which is compatible with Convention rights "*so far as it is possible to do so*".[43]

---

[35] See above, n. 33. See generally *Driedger on the Construction of Statutes* (3rd ed., 1994), pp. 493–496, noting, at p. 493, that the U.K. cases are divided.

[36] *Driedger on the Construction of Statutes*, pp. 495–496.

[37] See above paras 2–06 and 2–07.

[38] The Government resisted attempts to introduce such a right on the ground that, under the HRA's scheme, if the Government thought the U.K. court had gone too far or at any rate further than the Strasbourg Court would, because the courts are limited to making a declaration of incompatibility, it could decline to take any remedial action and leave the citizen to petition the Strasbourg Court for relief.

[39] *Hansard*, H.L., November 18, 1997, col. 521.

[40] *ibid.*, cols 509, 522. See also *Hansard*, H.L., January 19, 1998, col. 1293 (Lord Donaldson), implied repeal only works where there are two alternative and inconsistent sets of rights, liabilities or procedures, but on the HRA's approach there is only inconsistency but no alternative set of rights liabilities or procedures with which to replace the earlier and inconsistent regime.

[41] *cf.* the analogous position in a federation where it is a conception of "federal paramountcy" rather than implied repeal which resolves conflict: US Constitution Article 6., cl. 2; Australian Constitution, s. 109; Hogg, *Constitutional Law of Canada* (3rd ed., 1992), pp. 418–419.

[42] "Rights Brought Home", Cm. 3782 (1997), para. 2.7.

[43] Emphasis added.

The question is *how* far beyond the pre-HRA rule this authorises the courts to go. Unquestionably they must be enabled at least to ask whether the statute is "reasonably capable" of hearing a meaning that is consistent with the Convention, *i.e.* to apply the *Garland* test[44] rejected by *Brind's* requirement[45] that the statute being scrutinised must be "open to two or more different constructions" before any recourse might be had to the Convention. If this is all that section 3 did, the sole effect of the HRA's limited form of incorporation would be to reverse the decision in *Brind* on when it is permissible to have regard to an international Convention, a decision that some considered took an unnecessarily narrow approach to the existing cases.[46] But in fact the "emphatic direction"[47] contained in section 3 will have a more far-reaching effect and in this context will lead to a wider departure from the rules of construction generally applied by English courts. This view is supported by the approach of the New Zealand courts to the equivalent interpretative direction in section 6 of the New Zealand Bill of Rights Act 1990, which provides that "whenever an enactment can be given a meaning that is consistent with the rights and freedoms contained in this Bill of Rights, that meaning shall be preferred to any other meaning".[48]

B. The general approach to statutory construction in the United Kingdom

(1) "Ordinary" meaning

3–11 The starting point of the normal English approach to statutory construction[49] is the "plain" or "ordinary" meaning rule. There is a presumption that parliamentary intention is primarily determined by the text and that a provision is *prima facie* to be given its literal meaning,[50] taking into account its context. Although there is increasing use of a purposive approach to construction,[51] the traditional formulation of the rules is that only when the ordinary meaning leads to something unjust, anomalous, or contradictory,[52] or is ambiguous, can the courts say that Parliament intended a secondary meaning to be given to the provision. In determining this secondary meaning the courts take into account a large number of interpretative criteria, in particular the need to give effect to the statutory purpose[53] aided by recourse to the legislative history, including parliamentary debates under the rule in *Pepper v. Hart*,[54] and common law presumptions. The presumption that municipal law should conform to international law has been discussed above.[55] Other

---

[44] *Garland v. British Rail Engineering* [1983] 2 A.C. 751, 771. Note that the Commons rejected an opposition amendment designed to limit the interpretative obligation by substituting the word "reasonable" for the word "possible"; *Hansard*, H.C., June 3, 1998, col. 415 *et seq.*

[45] *R. v. Home Secretary, ex parte Brind* [1991] A.C. 696, 761.

[46] Browne-Wilkinson [1992] P.L. 406; De Smith, Woolf & Jowell *Judicial Review of Administrative Action* (5th ed.), p. 325; Hunt, *Using Human Rights Law in English Courts* (1996).

[47] See also Lord Cooke in *R. v. DPP, ex parte Kebeline*, October 28, 1999 and *Police v. Smith & Heremini* [1994] 2 N.Z.L.R. 306, 313 (Cooke P).

[48] See below, paras 3–14, 3–24, 3–30, 3–34 and 3–39 for examples of the New Zealand courts' approach.

[49] See generally Bennion, *Statutory Interpretation* (3rd ed.), pp. 423–545.

[50] *Barrell v. Fordree* [1932] A.C. 676, 682; *Duport Steels Ltd v. Sirs* [1980] 1 W.L.R. 142, 157.

[51] *e.g. Carter v. Bradbeer* [1975] 1 W.L.R. 1204, 1206; *IRC v. McGurkian* [1997] 1 W.L.R. 991, 999.

[52] A literal meaning which is not in accordance with the statutory purpose can be seen as leading to one of these consequences.

[53] Bennion, *Statutory Interpretation* (3rd ed.), pp. 740–742. See also *ibid.* p. 749: "the British doctrine of purposive construction is more literalist than the European variety, and permits a secondary construction only in comparatively rare cases".

[54] [1993] A.C. 593.

[55] See above, para. 1–02.

presumptions relevant in the present context include those that penal statutes be construed strictly,[56] presumptions against retrospectivity,[57] against interference with personal liberty,[58] or with access to the courts[59] and due process, and other common law rights[60] and freedoms, including freedom of speech[61] and freedom of association.[62] It should be noted that it is only at the second stage, where the court considers the statutory provision to be ambiguous or obscure, or where its literal meaning leads to an absurdity, that recourse can be had to parliamentary debates.

(2) The principle of legality

3–12 More recently, recognition has been given to a broader principle, which does not depend on statutory ambiguity. This is "the principle of legality" under which long-standing principles of constitutional and administrative law are assumed by the courts to have been taken for granted by Parliament.[63] In the present context this means that fundamental rights cannot be overridden by general words in statutes and subordinate legislation. Otherwise, as Lord Hoffmann stated:[64]

> "there is too great a risk that the full implications of [the] unqualified meaning [of statutory words] may have passed unnoticed in the democratic process. In the absence of express language or necessary implication to the contrary, the courts therefore presume that that even the most general words were intended to be subject to the basic rights of the individual. In this way the courts of the United Kingdom, though acknowledging the sovereignty of Parliament, apply principles of constitutionality little different from those which exist in countries where the power of the legislature is expressly limited by a constitutional document."

It is perhaps in this sense that one should understand the characterisation of the individual's right of access to justice, as a "constitutional right" which is given particularly strong protection by the courts.[65]

---

[56] e.g. Cutter v. Eagle Star [1998] 4 All E.R. 417, 425. See generally Bennion, Statutory Interpretation (3rd. ed.).

[57] L'Office Cherifen des Phosphates v. Yamashinnihon SS Co. Ltd [1994] 1 A.C. 486, 525; In the context of criminal law, see Case 63/83 R. v. Kirk [1985] 1 All E.R. 453, 462.

[58] Collins v. Wilcock [1984] 1 W.L.R. 1172, 1177; R. v. Home Secretary, ex parte Khawaja [1984] A.C. 74; R. v. Hallstrom, ex parte W (No. 2) [1986] Q.B. 1090, 1104; R. v. Home Secretary, ex parte Muboyayi [1992] Q.B. 244, 254; cf. R. v. Bournewood Community & Mental Health NHS Trust, ex parte L [1998] 3 W.L.R. 107 (common law doctrine of necessity justified treatment and care of person lacking capacity).

[59] R. v. Secretary of State for the Home Department, ex parte Leech [1994] Q.B. 198; R. v. Lord Chancellor ex parte Witham [1998] Q.B. 575.

[60] Mixnams v. Chertsey UDC [1965] A.C. 735(freedom of contract); Marcel v. Commissioner of Police [1992] Ch. 225; Morris v. Beardmore [1981] A.C. 446; Entick v. Carrington (1765) 19 St. Tr. 1030; R. v. Wilkes (1770) 4 Burr. 2527; R. v. Bournewood Community & Mental Health NHS Trust, ex parte L [1998] 3 W.L.R. 107.

[61] R. v. Leveller [1979] A.C. 440, 465; R. v. Central Independent Television [1994] 3 All E.R. 641, 652–653; A.G. v. BBC [1981] A.C. 303; A.G. v. Times Newspapers Ltd [1974] A.C. 273; A.G. v. Times Newspapers Ltd [1992] 1 A.C. 191; Gleaves v. Deakin [1980] A.C. 477; Derbyshire CC v. Times Newspapers Ltd [1993] A.C. 534.

[62] Beatty v. Gillbanks (1882) 9 Q.B.D. 308, 313; UKAPE v. ACAS [1979] 1 W.L.R. 570.

[63] R. v. Secretary of State for the Homes Department, ex parte Pierson [1998] A.C. 539, 573–575, 587–590; General Mediterranean Holidays SA v. Patel [1999] 3 All E.R. 673; Bell & Engle (eds), Cross, Statutory Interpretation (3rd ed.), pp. 165–166.

[64] R. v. Secretary of State for the Home Department, ex parte Simms & O'Brien [1999] 3 W.L.R. 328, 341 (Lord Hoffmann). See also, ibid., p. 340 (Lord Steyn).

[65] R. v. Secretary of State for the Home Department, ex parte Leech [1994] Q.B. 198; R. v. Lord Chancellor ex parte Witham [1998] Q.B. 575. But cf. R. v. Lord Chancellor, ex parte Lightfoot [1999] 2 W.L.R. 1126 (access to a statutory bankruptcy scheme is not a "constitutional right").

C. The direction to read and give effect to legislation in a way which is compatible with the Convention rights so far as it is possible to do so

3-13   Section 3's use of the phrase *"so far as it is possible to do so"* is intended to make clear that the courts must do everything possible to interpret legislation in such a way as to be compatible with Convention rights.[66] Statutes must be read in accordance with the Convention unless it is clearly impossible to do so. Experience with European Community law has shown the lengths to which the courts have been prepared to go in order to find that national law does not conflict with European norms.[67] Moreover, the Privy Council treats "a constitutional instrument" as *sui generis* calling for principles of interpretation of its own" suitable to give to individuals the full measure of the fundamental rights and freedoms[68] and avoiding what has been called the "austerity of tabulated legalism". This "broad and generous" approach will apply to the interpretation of the HRA, including the word "possible" in section 3, and to the provisions of the Convention itself.[69] But it does not necessarily apply to the potentially incompatible statutes since the vast majority of them are not constitutional statutes, let alone constitutional instruments. If it does not, reliance will have to be placed solely on the direction in section 3.

3-14   We consider that it is permissible to have regard to the direction in section 3 in the initial construction of the statutory provision which it is argued is incompatible.[70] In one of the early cases on the similar New Zealand provision it was said that the statutory provision requiring compatible interpretation was "unlikely to be available except where there is ambiguity or uncertainty".[71] But it has also been said that the court is required to interpret the other enactment in two distinct steps and at two distinct levels. "The first involves the question whether the other enactment can reasonably be given a meaning consistent with the Bill of Rights and the second question whether in the end it *should* be given that meaning".[72] The first stage is concerned with unequivocal inconsistency and the second with more refined aspects where there is room for the interpretation to be influenced by the Bill of Rights and other sources. This is a more restrictive approach than was envisaged by the Lord Chancellor. In his Tom Sargant Memorial lecture he said that "it will not be necessary to find an ambiguity"[73] before courts have recourse to the Convention and the Strasbourg jurisprudence and that, whereas hitherto they were not enforcing

---

[66] For a comprehensive study of the use of interpretative techniques in this field, see Hunt, *Using Human Rights Law in English Courts* (1997). See also Lester [1998] E.H.R.L. Rev. 665; Irvine [1999] E.H.R.L. Rev. 350 (Sieghart Memorial Lecture).

[67] See below, paras 3–26—3–28.

[68] *Minister of Home Affairs v. Fisher* [1980] A.C. 319, 328–329; *Thornhill v. A.G. Trinidad & Tobago* [1981] A.C. 61, 69; *Jobe v. A.G. Gambia* [1984] A.C. 689, 700; *Vasquez v. The Queen* [1994] 1 W.L.R. 1304, 1313; *Matadeen v. Pointu* [1999] A.C. 98, 108; *A.G. of Hong Kong v. Lee Kwong-kut* [1993] A.C. 951, 966; *Huntley v. A.G. for Jamaica* [1995] 2 A.C. 1, 12; *US v. Cretoni* [1989] 1 S.C.R. 1469, 1480.

[69] Laws [1998] P.L. 254, 264.

[70] Gardner & Wickremasinghe, in Dickson (ed.), *Human Rights and the European Convention* (1997), p. 98.

[71] *Knight v. CIR* [1991] 2 N.Z.L.R. 30, 43 (Hardie Boys J.). See also *Ministry of Transport v. Noort* [1992] 3 N.Z.L.R. 260, 272 (Cooke P).

[72] *Herewini v. MOT* (1992) 9 C.R.N.Z. 307, 323.

[73] [1998] P.L. 221, 228. Though extensively referred to in the Parliamentary debates by Lord Lester of Herne Hill Q.C. (*Hansard*, H.L. Vol. 584, January 19, 1998, cols 1291–1292), a strict interpretation of the rule in *Pepper v. Hart* [1993] A.C. 593 would mean that it will not be possible to call this in aid of the construction of s. 3 because the *Parliamentary* statement was not made by or on behalf of the Minister promoting the Bill. But in any case the Lord Chancellor, in a damage limitation exercise, thought that not much authority would be added to whatever authority his extra-judicial observations had if he were to repeat them in the House: *ibid.*, col. 1294.

the Convention when they used it, under the HRA they would be.[74] Since primary and secondary legislation "must" "so far as it is possible to do so" be "read and given effect in a way which is compatible with the Convention rights",[75] the Convention and its jurisprudence are relevant in the initial construction of the statute. In other words, they are relevant to the identification of possible incompatibility which must then be resolved if possible by removing it. Again, the principle of legality, discussed above,[76] applies regardless of whether the statute is ambiguous. It has been said that "reading and giving effect" is a broad process and is "not so much a question of interpretation or construction of language but of assessment or characterisation or proper description of the relevant legislative provision when placed alongside the relevant right or rights in the Convention".[77] Consequently, it appears that under section 3 the Convention is relevant both to identifying an incompatibility, and to resolving it, an approach which gains support from the speeches in *R. v. DPP, ex parte Kebeline*,[77a] concerning the meaning of section 16A of the Prevention of Terrorism (Temporary Provisons) Act 1989. Section 16A provides that it is a defence for a person charged with possession of articles, in themselves innocuous, for terrorist purposes, to prove that the articles were not in his "possession" or, if they were, that they were not possessed for "terrorist purposes". Although the natural and ordinary meaning of the section is that it imposes the persuasive burden of proof on the defendant and is therefore incompatible with the presumption of innocence in Article 6(2), it was suggested that a "possible" and compatible interpretation under the strong interpretative direction in HRA, section 3 might be that section 16A imposes only an evidential burden of proof on the defendant.

D. Guidance from the legislative history of the HRA

3–15 What guidance is obtained from what was said during the consideration of the HRA by Parliament? The Government, worried about giving *Pepper v. Hart* hostages to fortune,[78] said little on the precise effect of section 3 on the existing rules of construction. The Lord Chancellor made a number of statements about section 3. He stated that the HRA "rests upon giving the strongest jurisdiction possible to the judges to interpret Acts of Parliament so as to make them, whenever possible, compatible with the Convention"[79]; that the Government wanted the courts "to strive to find an interpretation of legislation which is consistent with Convention rights and only in the last resort to conclude that the legislation is simply incompatible with them"; that "the word 'possible' is the plainest means . . . for simply asking the courts to find the construction consistent with the intentions of Parliament and the wording of legislation which is nearest to the Convention rights"; and that, at least in the case of statutes enacted after the U.K.'s ratification of the

---

[74] [1998] P.L. 221, 227.

[75] HRA, s. 3.

[76] See para. 3–12.

[77] Marshall [1998] P.L. 167, 169. He concludes that the section 3 requirement that the legislation is if possible found to be "compatible" suggests a "startling paradox" because "the more faithfully the courts follow the injunction . . . the less effect the Convention will have". But this appears to assume that indirect effect via interpretation does not count and neglects the potential for re-examining existing interpretations of provisions as well as the need not to give such provisions a technical construction: see *Huntley v. A.G. for Jamaica* [1995] 2 A.C. 1, 12; *A.G. of Hong Kong v. Lee Kwong-kut* [1993] A.C. 951, 975; Lester [1998] E.H.R.L. Rev. 665, 671–672.

[77a] H.L. October 28, 1999. See further below, para. 3–18, n. 90.

[78] The many references to *Pepper v. Hart* [1993] A.C. 593 in the debates on the HRA reflect the role played by lawyer-Parliamentarians.

[79] *Hansard*, H.L. Debs, November 24, 1997, col. 795.

Convention, Parliament "must be deemed to have intended its statutes to be compatible with the Convention . . . and that courts should hold that the deemed general intention has not been carried successfully into effect only where it is impossible to construe a statute as having that effect".[80]

3-16 The Home Secretary also stated that the Government wanted the courts "to strive" to find an interpretation of legislation consistent with Convention rights "so far as the plain words of the legislation allow" and only "in the last resort" to conclude that the legislation is simply incompatible with them.[81] While the HRA would allow recourse to the Convention in more cases than had previously been the case, he was not convinced by Opposition fears that the terms of what is now section 3 would mean that the courts would be required to give a strained meaning to language. He did not think that the courts would "contort the meaning of words until they lose their meaning altogether"[82] because he considered that their task (in which they were well versed) would be to say what the law means where it was not clear or where its application in particular circumstances was not clear. After expressly referring to *Pepper v. Hart*, he stated that it was not the Government's "intention that the courts, in applying . . . [section 3], . . . should contort the meaning of words to produce implausible or incredible meanings".[83]

3-17 Although the Government's stated desire that the courts "strive" to find compatibility and should only find incompatibility "in the last resort" supports Lord Lester of Herne Hill's view that the HRA will "profoundly affect Statutory interpretation"[84] some of what the Home Secretary said suggests a less radical shift. Lord Cooke of Thorndon, who in his former role as President of the New Zealand Court of Appeal made a significant contribution to the interpretion of the equivalent New Zealand provision, has described it as a "strong adjuration" and an "emphatic direction",[85] and stated that section 3(1) "definitely goes further than the existing common law rules of statutory interpretation, because it enjoins a search for possible meanings as distinct from the the meaning–which has been the traditional approach in the matter of statutory interpretation in the courts".[86] Lord Simon of Glaisdale stated that what is now section 3 "departs from the ordinary rules of construction, and . . . does so rightly".[87]

The legislative history of the HRA underlines the nature of this shift. During the Commons Committee stage, the Opposition unsuccessfully moved an amendment to qualify section 3(1) so that courts should interpret legislation in a manner compatible with Convention rights so far as it is "reasonable" to do so and in a manner which reflected the intentions of Parliament, rather than so far as is "possible" to do so.[88]

---

[80] *Hansard*, H.L.Debs, November 18, 1997, col. 535. See also col. 547.
[81] *Hansard*, H.L. Debs, June 3, 1998, cols 421–422. He did not dissent from Mr Hogg M.P.'s suggestion (*ibid.*, col. 424) that the courts' working assumption should be that when Parliament has addressed an issue involving Convention rights it has not derogated from those rights.
[82] *Hansard*, H.C., June 3, 1998, cols 421–422.
[83] *ibid.*
[84] "The impact of the Human Rights Act on Public Law" in *Constitutional Reform in the U.K.: Practice and Principles* (Cambridge Centre for Public Law, 1998), p. 106. See also Lester [1998] E.H.R.L. Rev. 663.
[85] *R. v. DPP, ex parte Kebeline*, October 28, 1999 and *Police v. Smith & Heremini* [1994] 2 N.Z.L.R. 306, 313.
[86] *Hansard*, H.L., November 18, 1997, col. 533.
[87] *ibid.*, col. 536.
[88] See *Hansard*, H.C., June 3, 1998, col. 415. A linked amendment, which was also rejected, sought to oblige the courts, when interpreting legislation, to have full regard to the margin of appreciation which the Strasbourg jurisprudence allows to states.

E. The meaning of "incompatible"

3–18 Where it is impossible to comply with both the requirements of a U.K. statute and those of the Convention, there will be incompatibility with the Convention rights. One form of incompatibility arises where there is express contradiction between statute and the Convention rights so that compliance with one necessarily involves non-compliance with the other.[89] The two will be inconsistent. Where the Convention right in question is unqualified (for example those in Articles 2, 3, 5(2) and 6(2)) a comparison of the texts may well reveal a prima facie contradiction. So, in *R. v. DPP, ex parte Kebeline*, the Divisional Court considered that on the natural and ordinary construction of section 16A of the Prevention of Terrorism (Temporary Provisions) Act 1989, summarised above at para. 3–14 was incompatible with the presumption of innocence required by Article 6(2). As indicated above, the House of Lords, taking account of what Lord Steyn described as the "strong interpretative obligation" in HRA, section 3, considered the incompatibility was arguable but less clear.[90]

But the texts alone will not be determinative, although on the traditional English approach there is a reluctance to depart from the ordinary meaning of the words used by Parliament if it is "plain" from the text. Where the Convention right in question is qualified (for example, Article 6's exceptions to the right to a public hearing and interference with the right to privacy authorised by Article 8(2)), a comparison of the texts is less likely to indicate contradiction. In such cases, the contradiction may arise from the operation of the U.K. statute. On one view of the law which is considered below,[91] incompatibility may also arise where it is shown that the intention behind the earlier provision (rather than its text) was inconsistent with the Convention rights. There is no such incompatibility where the U.K. statute gives more extensive protection to human rights than the ECHR[92] because it is possible to comply with both the more stringent requirements of the particular statute and the Convention rights, which are the minimum required.

3–19 The position is similar where the protection is not specifically mentioned on the face of the Convention. This can be illustrated by an example involving the right not to incriminate oneself, a right which, although said to be at the heart of the notion of a fair procedure under Article 6, is not mentioned in Article 6.[93] Section 434 of the Companies Act 1985 gives inspectors compulsory powers to question,[94] among others, directors of companies. Section 434(5) provides that "an answer given by a person to a question put to him in exercise of powers conferred by this section . . . *may* be used in evidence against him".[95] In *R. v. Saunders* Lord Taylor C.J. stated that "Parliament has, in this context, overridden the principle against self-incrimination" and added, after referring to pending proceedings in Strasbourg, " . . .

---

[89] See *Smith v. Queen* [1960] S.C.R. 776, 800; *Bank of Montreal v. Hall* [1990] 1 S.C.R. 121 (determining inconsistency in the context of the scope of federal and provincial statutory authority in Canada).

[90] October 28, 1999. The decision of the Divisional Court ([1999] 3 W.L.R. 175, 190, 201) was reversed primarily because of the statutory (Supreme Court Act 1981, s. 29(3) and common law restrictions on judicial review of a decision affecting the conduct of a trial on indictment and the need to discourage satellite litigation. For another aspect of this case, see above, para 3–05, n. 13.

[91] See paras 3–24 and 3–31.

[92] See above, para. 2–06 and below, para. 3–21.

[93] *Saunders v. United Kingdom* December 17, 1996 R.J.D., 1996–VI, No. 24; 23 E.H.R.R. 313, para. 68.

[94] By s. 436(2) inspectors are empowered to certify a refusal to answer to the court which (s. 436(2)(3)) may punish the individual as if he had been guilty of a contempt.

[95] Emphasis added.

our domestic law . . . is unambiguous. Parliament has made its intentions quite clear in section 434(5)".[96] The section seems clearly incompatible with the Article 6 right not to incriminate oneself, as was confirmed by the Strasbourg Count's subsequent decision that the use of evidence obtained under such compulsory powers in a criminal trial violates the right to a fair trial.[97] It is, however, possible that this pre-HRA interpretation of the section 434 could be reconsidered in the light of the interpretative direction in section 3 of the HRA.[98]

3–20   The test of express contradiction is easiest to apply where a statute imposes duties; but it is also applicable where the relevant statute is facilitative and contains permissive rules. For example, in *Secretary of State for Defence v. Guardian Newspapers Ltd*[99] the court was concerned with the relationship between section 10 of the Contempt of Court Act 1981, which prohibits a court from requiring a person to disclose the source of information in a publication for which he or she is responsible, and section 3 of the Torts (Interference with Goods) Act 1977, which empowers a court to order property to be handed over to its owner. In that case returning a document in the possession of the newspaper might have identified the person who had leaked information to it. The statutory prohibition on disclosure in section 10 was inconsistent with the statutory power to order delivery in section 3, and the inconsistency was resolved by giving primacy to the later statute.[1] Since the Convention rights are not fully part of domestic law such a result based on the doctrine of implied repeal would be excluded by the structure of the HRA. However, the direction under HRA section 3 will enable a court to achieve the same result in most cases.[2]

3–21   The mere fact that the specific statute covers the same field as that governed by a provision of the Convention does not, however, mean that it is incompatible with the Convention rights. First, it might specify more extensive protection and, for

---

[96] [1996] 1 Cr. App. R. 463, 475, 477. See to the same effect *R. v. Staines & Morrisey* [1997] 2 Cr. App. R. 426. Evidence obtained compulsorily may, however, be used in civil proceedings for the disqualification of a company director: *R. v. Secretary of State for Trade and Industry, ex parte McCormick*, *The Times*, February 10, 1998.

[97] *Saunders v. United Kingdom* December 17, 1996, R.J.D., 1996–VI, No. 24; 23 E.H.R.R. 313.

[98] See below, para. 3–29, but note that the matter is unlikely to arise since the Government has stated (a) self-incriminating evidence obtained under such statutory provisions will not be used in criminal prosecutions unless the defendant himself introduces the evidence, or else the charge against the defendant relates to his failure to supply information required of him as required by law (*e.g.* under Banking Act 1987, s. 94 and Criminal Justice Act 1987, s. 2(14)): Attorney-General's guidelines to prosecutors set out in (1998) 148 N.L.J. 208; and (b) it intends to bring forward legislation to ensure that domestic law is fully compatible with the U.K.'s obligations under the Convention: HC Debs, February 4, 1998, WA 640. Similar powers to compel information which may be used in subsequent criminal proceedings exist in the planning and environmental protection field: see, *e.g.*, s. 171C of the Town and Country Planning Act 1990; ss. 23(1)(g) and 71(3) of the Environmental Protection Act 1990; s. 110 of the Environment Act 1995; s. 202(4) of the Water Resources Act 1991; s. 203(4) of the Water Industry Act 1991. As to the obligation to provide information see *R. v. Hertfordshire County Council, ex parte Green* [1998] Env. L.R. 153 (CA) (now pending before the House of Lords); as to the admissibility of answers given under compulsion under s. 78 of the Police and Criminal Evidence Act 1984, see *R. v. Staines & Morrisey* [1997] 2 Cr. App. R. 426.

[99] [1985] A.C. 339. For examples of such literal inconsistency in the context of human rights see *Winnipeg School etc v. Croton* [1985] 2 S.C.R. 150; *TV3 Network Services v. R* [1993] 3 N.Z.L.R. 421; *Temese v. Police* (1992) 9 C.R.N.Z. 425.

[1] It was held that the prohibition in s. 10 was not subject to an implied exception so as to maintain the power in s. 3, which was, accordingly "read down" by excluding one kind of property–property which might identify the source of information–from its scope.

[2] See *Goodwin v. United Kingdom* March 27, 1996, R.J.D., 1996–II, No. 7; 22 E.H.R.R. 123 and *Camelot v. Centaur Communications* [1999] Q.B. 124, CA.

the reason given above, this is not incompatible. It is possible to obey both by obeying the more stringent.[3] Where a statute appears to specify a lower degree of protection than the Convention requires, for instance by according a public authority wide discretion, it will be possible to "read down" the broad discretion by implying in the Convention rights.[4] Only where there is an irreconcilable textual contradiction will it be impossible to read the statute in a way which is compatible with the Convention rights. The court will also be faced with a dilemma where it appears from the legislative history of the enactment that its purpose or effect is to abridge or abrogate Convention rights. Resolution of that dilemma will depend upon the approach which the court adopts to section 3, reinforced where appropriate by section 19 and the common law presumptions as to statutory interpretation, in particular the principle of legality.[5] These matters are considered in the next sections.

F. Post-HRA legislation

3–22 In the case of post-HRA legislation the ministerial statements that are required by section 19 for all public Bills will be of fundamental importance.[6] The Minister in charge of a Bill must, before its Second Reading, make a written statement to the effect either "that in his view the provisions of the Bill are compatible with the Convention rights" or "that although he is unable to make a statement of compatibility the government nevertheless wishes to proceed with the Bill". These statements are only the view of the Minister, and as such do not bind the court, nor are they legitimate aids to the construction of the resulting statute. But if they are repeated during parliamentary consideration of the Bill, as they will be, ministerial statements of compatibility will be strong evidence of parliamentary intent. Together with the common law presumption that domestic legislation conforms to international obligations, and the other presumptions against the interference with common law rights and freedoms,[7] it is likely that a statement of compatibility will create a strong presumption of compatibility with the Convention rights. As the Lord Chancellor indicated, in such cases Parliament "must be deemed to have intended its statutes to be compatible with the Convention".[8] It follows from this that for post-HRA legislation the only cases in which there is a significant danger that a court will be unable to hold that a provision is compatible with the Convention rights are where: (a) there is a clear and irreconcilable textual inconsistency with the Convention rights on the face of the particular statute, or (b) the government has indicated that it wishes to proceed with a Bill although it cannot make a statement of compatibility, because it takes the view that the Bill either is or may be inconsistent with the Convention rights.[9] In case (b), while the interpretative direction in section 3 will apply, the presumption of compatibility will undoubtedly be weaker.

---

[3] *O'Grady v. Sparling* [1960] A.C. 304 (PC).
[4] See below para. 3–33.
[5] Considered above, in para. 3–12.
[6] See above, para. 3–04. As to Private Members' Bills which are directly assisted by the Government, see written answer by Lord Burlison, *Hansard*, H.L., May 5, 1999, col. W.A. 92, *ibid.*, n. 11 above.
[7] See above, para. 3–11.
[8] *Hansard*, H.L., November 18, 1997, col. 535. *cf.* the unusual circumstances concerning legislation to re-enact ss. 16A–16D and Sched. 6A of the Prevention of Terrorism (Temporary Provisions) Act 1989 after the Divisional Court in *R. v. DPP, ex parte Kebeline* [1999] 3 W.L.R. 175 had stated that sections 16A and 16B were incompatible with Article 6(2) of the Convention: *Hansard*, H.C. Vol. 333, June 23, 1999, col. 1172 (Home Secretary), June 24, 1999, cols 1382 *et seq.* esp. 1388–1389 (Home Secretary) and see above, paras 3–04 and 3–14.
[9] In deciding whether to make a statement of compatibility, ministers " . . . will consider whether it is more likely than not that the provisions of the Bill will stand up to challenge on Convention grounds before the domestic courts and the European Court of Human Rights in Strasbourg. A Minister should not be advised to make a statement of compatibility where legal advice is that on balance the provisions of the Bill would not survive such a challenge": *Hansard*, H.L., May 5, 1999, W.A. 93.

G.   Pre-HRA legislation

3–23   So far as pre-HRA legislation is concerned, it appears from Commonwealth authority that a distinction may be made between legislation enacted before and after the U.K. ratified the ECHR and the relevant protocol.[10] The strong interpretative aid afforded by the procedure under section 19 of the HRA is not available in the case of post-ratification legislation. However, the common law presumption that domestic legislation conforms with international obligations, and the other presumptions against the interference with common law rights and freedoms will apply,[11] reinforced by the strong direction in section 3 of the HRA which, at a minimum, removes the "two meanings" requirement laid down in *Brind*.

3–24   In the case of pre-ratification legislation, the only specific guide to the court is the direction in section 3, although the common law presumptions against interference with common law rights and freedoms may be of assistance. In these cases, however, Commonwealth authority indicates that incompatibility may arise not only from textual inconsistency but from the intention behind the earlier provision. If the intention was broader than the provision's literal words, and if that intention (as revealed from all the pre-legislative materials, including the parliamentary debates under the rule in *Pepper v. Hart*[12]) is inconsistent with the Convention rights, the provision will be incompatible with them.[13] In such a case, there appears to be a clash between the requirements of the HRA and the actual intention of Parliament. We suggest, however, that the stronger direction in section 3 will enable a court to hold that where the literal meaning of the text is compatible with the Convention rights, no regard should he had to the evidence of a contrary legislative intention. Use of a literal approach to interpretation would make it "possible" to find compatibility, and it is therefore strongly arguable that a court "must" adopt such an interpretation. The contrary argument is that the literal approach would involve a departure from the modern trend to give statutes a purposive construction. Moreover, even in the context of constitutional interpretation, "legislative purpose is a function of the intention of those who draft and enact legislation, and not any shifting variable".[14] *Quilter v. Attorney-General*,[15] a decision of the New Zealand Court of Appeal, provides an example of this. In that case the court was considering whether the word marriage in the New Zealand Marriage Act 1955 could be interpreted as including same-sex partnership in the light of the New Zealand Bill of Rights Act guarantee of freedom from discrimination on the grounds of sexual orientation and the interpretative direction, similar to that in section 3 of the HRA, contained in section 6 of the Bill of Rights Act.[16] It examined the legislative intention at the time of the original

---

[10] The United Kingdom ratified the Convention on March 8, 1951, the First Protocol on November 3, 1952 and the Sixth Protocol on January 27, 1999.

[11] See above, para. 3–11.

[12] [1993] A.C. 593.

[13] For N.Z. examples see *Birch v. Minister of Transport* (1992) 9 C.R.N.Z. 83; *Reille v. Police* [1993] 1 N.Z.L.R. 587; *Quilter v. A.G.* [1998] 1 N.Z.L.R. 523. For Canadian examples, see *R. v. Big M Drug Mart* [1985] 1 S.C.R. 295; *R. v. Edwards Books and Art Ltd* [1986] 2 S.C.R. 713.

[14] *R. v. Big M Drug Mart* [1985] 1 S.C.R. 295, 335 (Canada; purpose of Lords Day Act); *Birch v. Minister of Transport* (1992) 9 C.R.N.Z. 83; *Reille v. Police* [1993] 1 N.Z.L.R. 587 (pre-Bill of Rights Act provision stating that statutory provision giving the right to elect trial by jury "shall not apply").

[15] [1998] 1 N.Z.L.R. 523, on which see Butler [1998] P.L. 396.

[16] For a similar issue in English law, see *Fitzpatrick v. Sterling Housing Association Ltd* [1998] Ch. 304 (CA), October 28, 1999 (HL) ("living with the original tenant as his wife or her husband": para. 2(1) of Pt I of Sched. 1 to the Rent Act 1977). See also *Attorney-General for Ontario v. M & H*, (1999) 171 D.L.R. (4th) 577. Supreme Court of Canada.

enactment,[17] in the light of the "well-established common law background" against which the Marriage Act was passed, and in the light of the provisions of other statutes and regulations. In the light of these, it held that, notwithstanding the interpretative direction in section 6 of the Bill of Rights Act, the word "marriage" could not be interpreted as including same-sex partnerships.

Nevertheless, the logic of the direction in section 3 is that the court should apply the HRA in priority to the rule in *Pepper v. Hart*. On this view, the count should first ask itself what is the natural and ordinary meaning of the words. If the meaning is clear, it should be applied unless it is incompatible with a Convention right without recourse to the legislative history. If the meaning is unclear, the court should look at the possible meanings of the statutory provision, *i.e.* those which the language is capable of bearing without undue distortion, and adopt the one which is compatible with Convention rights. Only if more than one compatible meaning is available would it be necessary to resort to *Hansard* or other materials in order to ascertain which of the compatible meanings most closely accords with the legislative intention.

H. Provisions implementing E.C. obligations

3–25 The relationship between E.U. law and the Act may also give rise to difficult questions. The definition of legislation in section 21(1) of the HRA does not include provisions of E.U. law which are directly applicable[18] or which have direct effect, such as certain provisions of the Treaty or of directives. However, provisions of national law adopted to give effect to obligations under Community law will be caught by the interpretative obligation. Subordinate legislation amending primary legislation[19] will itself be treated in the same way as primary legislation. But other subordinate legislation implementing Community obligations is to be regarded as subordinate legislation for the purposes of the Act. In terms of the hierarchy of norms, Community law will prevail. The duty under the European Communities Act is to interpret and apply national law subject to and in accordance with Community law. This national law will include the Human Rights Act, so that in the event of a conflict, Community law will take precedence.[20] However, Community law itself contains a guarantee of fundamental rights,[21] so that in most cases the presumption of respect for fundamental rights should apply. In cases of apparent conflict between domestic law and fundamental rights, a court or tribunal can refer questions to the Court of Justice of the European Communities for a preliminary ruling.[22]

I. Guidance on interpretation from cases concerned with E.C. law

3–26 The U.K. courts' approach to inconsistency between Community law and U.K. law provides the best guidance about their likely approach to the question of

---

[17] Although Tipping J. [1988] N.Z.L.R. 523 at 581, indicated that had post-Bill of Rights statutes shown a shift in the meaning of marriage, that would support the case of a reinterpretation of the Marriage Act to accord with the shift.

[18] *i.e.* the provisions of Regulations, see E.C. Treaty Article 249, formerly 189.

[19] European Communities Act 1972, s. 2(4). See, for example, the Equal Pay (Amendment Regulations) 1983, S.I. 1983 No. 1794 amending the Equal Pay Act 1970 to include equal value.

[20] See Case 4/73 *Nold v. Commission* [1974] E.C.R. 491; Case 11/70 *Internationale Handelsgesellschaft v. Einfuhr-und Vorratstelle fur Getreide und Futtermittel* [1970] E.C.R. 1125; *R. v. Secretary of State for Transport, ex parte Factortame Ltd (No. 2)* [1991] A.C. 604. This is also relevant in the context of declarations of incompatibility, see below, para. 3–47.

[21] Article 6(2) of the Treaty of European Union, as amended by the Treaty of Amsterdam. See further above, para. 1.6.

[22] See E.C. Treaty, Article 234, formerly 177.

incompatibility between a U.K. statute and a Convention right. The approach used in E.C. cases has already been influential in other contexts not involving E.C. law, and this "spillover" effect may occur here too.[23]

There is of course an important difference between the two contexts since E.C. law is fully incorporated into U.K. law and the European Communities Act 1972 provides that Community law is to prevail in the case of any conflict.[24] Moreover, whereas the European Communities Act 1972 directs that the meaning and effect of national law are to be determined in accordance with any relevant decision of the ECJ,[25] the HRA[26] provides only that a court "must take into account" any relevant Strasbourg case law.[27] But, in broad terms, the interpretative direction is similar and the approach of U.K. courts in E.C. cases is likely to be helpful in developing the law under section 3 of the HRA. The cases show a willingness to use directly effective European law in the initial interpretation of a U.K. statute[28] which, it has been said, must be construed as far as possible in the light of E.C. law.[29] An important distinction is, however, drawn between legislation designed to implement E.C. law and other legislation. We shall see that in the present state of the authorities courts will more readily find a conforming interpretation where the legislation is designed to implement E.C. law.

In the case of legislation implementing E.C. law, the courts will endeavour to give a meaning that conforms to E.C. law.[30] In *Pickstone v. Freemans plc* Lord Oliver said that notwithstanding the general reluctance to depart from the ordinary meaning of the words of a statute, statutes implementing European Community law were in a special category:

" . . . a construction which permits the section to operate as a proper fulfilment of the U.K.'s obligation under the Treaty involves not so much doing violence to the language of the section as filling a gap by an implication which arises, not from the words used, but from the manifest purpose of the Act and the mischief it was intended to remedy."[31]

3-27 The *Pickstone* case and *Litster v. Forth Dry Dock & Engineering* are examples of refusal to give effect to the clear literal meaning of the U.K. legislation because to do so would entail non-conformity with E.C. law, and of the use of purposive construction to do so. This approach is adopted even where at the time of introduction U.K. implementing legislation conforms to an understanding of E.C. law

---

[23] *M v. Home Office* [1994] 1 A.C. 377 (spilling over from Cases C–43 and C48/93 *Brasserie du Pecheur v. Germany* and Case 48/93 *R. v. Secretary of State for Transport, ex parte Factortame Ltd* [1996] E.C.R. I–1029) and *Woolwich Building Society v. Inland Revenue Commissioners* [1994] A.C. 70 (spilling over inter alia from Case 199/82 *Amministrazione della Finanze dello Stato v. San Giorgio* [1983] E.C.R. 3595). See further Jacobs [1999] P.L. 232.
[24] ss. 2(1) and 2(4).
[25] s. 3(1).
[26] s. 2(1) of the HRA.
[27] See above, Ch. 2.
[28] *Garland v. BR Engineering Ltd* [1983] A.C. 751, 771 (but note this was in the context of a provision which had more than one possible meaning). See also *Snoxell v. Vauxhall Motors Ltd* [1978] Q.B. 11; *Macarthys v. Smith* [1978] 1 W.L.R. 849, 851. *Quaere* whether this was because of the primacy accorded to European law or on a wider principle: see Hunt, *Using Human Rights Law in English Courts* (1996) pp. 81–82.
[29] *MRS Environment Services Ltd v. Marsh* [1997] 1 All E.R. 92, 94 (Phillips L.J.).
[30] *Pickstone v. Freemans plc* [1989] A.C. 66; *Litster v. Forth Dry Dock & Engineering* [1990] 1 A.C. 546.
[31] [1989] A.C. 66 [125]. See also *ibid.*, pp. 111, 122–123.

which a later decision of the ECJ reveals to be too narrow. Such examples are of relevance to post-HRA statutes where there has been a section 19 statement of compatibility, and to pre-HRA statutes which were designed to implement obligations under the Convention, perhaps as the result of a decision of the Strasbourg Court.

The section 19 statement should make up for the fact that the section 3 direction is weaker than that in the European Communities Act. In the case of legislation implementing E.C. law, in the light of the *Factortame* litigation, it is arguable that only a positive statement in an Act of Parliament that a provision is intended to contravene an obligation under E.C. law would justify a non-conforming interpretation of the U.K. legislation.[32] But in the case of Convention rights, the weaker interpretative direction in the HRA means that something less than an express positive statement—for example a section 19(1)(b) statement of inability to make a statement of compatibility or having to give the statutory words an unduly distorting meaning—would probably suffice. However, the section 3 direction as to interpretation remains even in the absence of a section 19 statement of compatibility.

3–28   Where the U.K. statute is not implementing E.C. law, in the current state of the authorities, there is less willingness to depart from the ordinary English approach to interpretation. In particular it was held in *Duke v. GEC Reliance Ltd*[33] and *Finnegan v. Clowney Youth Training Programme Ltd*[34] that the court should not give an interpretation which distorts the meaning of the statute in order to achieve conformity with E.C. law. There are also statements that the U.K. legislation should be interpreted as at the time the statute was passed rather than in the light of the current state of E.C. law,[35] *i.e.* a dynamic interpretation appears to be rejected. These decisions have been criticised,[36] and, in their context, the development of E.C. jurisprudence in particular by the decision of the ECJ in *Marleasing*[37] means that it is not possible to adhere to the distinction between legislation implementing E.C. law and other legislation. But there is no analogue in the case of the HRA. There is no external source with authority to instruct English courts to reject non-conforming interpretations[38] and to restrain the reluctance of English courts to depart from "the traditional conception of their role as seekers of an historical intention when interpreting national legislation, and as upholders of; the interests of legal certainty".[39] Indeed the whole structure of section 3, the provisions for declarations of incompatibility under section 4 and for remedial action in section 10 and Schedule 3 are strong indications of a different approach. So, although the interpretative direction applies to legislation "whenever enacted", there is a danger that the approach indicated in *Duke* and *Finnegan* may be applied to pre-HRA statutes which do not specifically implement Convention rights. A similar limit applies to the New Zealand equivalent to section 3 of the HRA. Compatibility can only be found if it is possible to do so without a "strained" or "unnatural" interpretation.[40]

---

[32] *R. v. Secretary of State for Transport, ex parte Factortame Ltd (No. 2)* [1991] A.C. 604 and see Lord Diplock in *Garland v. British Rail Engineering Ltd* [1983] 2 A.C. 751.
[33] [1988] A.C. 618, 641.
[34] [1990] 2 A.C. 407, 414–416 (the fact that the relevant Northern Ireland regulations were made *after* the E.C. Directive did not affect the issue).
[35] *Duke v. GEC Reliance Ltd* [1988] A.C. 618, 638.
[36] *e.g.* by Arnull [1988] P.L. 313.
[37] Case C–106/89 *Marleasing SA v. La Commercial Internacionale de Alimentation SA* [1990] E.C.R I–4135. See also Case 14/83 *Von Colson v. Land Nordrhein-Westfalen* [1984] E.C.R 1891.
[38] On the status of ECHR cases, see above, Ch. 2.
[39] Hunt, *Using Human Rights Law in English Courts* (1996), p. 115 describing the approaches in *Duke* and *Finnegan*. On the need for a construction that updates its meaning, see below, para. 3–31.
[40] See below, para. 3–39, and in particular *Ministry of Transport v. Noort* [1992] 3 N.Z.L.R. 260, 272; *Simpson v. Attorney-General N* [1994] 3 N.Z.L.R. 667, 674.

J. Reconsidering the interpretation of a statutory provision

3–29 Since section 3 contains a new interpretative direction which did not apply to statutory interpretation before enactment of the HRA, it will require the reconsideration of the interpretations laid down by pre-HRA decisions. It will entitle, and indeed oblige, a court to depart from a binding decision concerning the interpretation of a statutory provision where that interpretation is inconsistent with Convention. Section 6 of the New Zealand Bill of Rights has been said to justify overruling a long-standing and settled interpretation of a statutory provision. In *Flicklinger v. Crown Colony of Hong Kong*,[41] although the bare text of the provision in issue appeared wide enough to permit an unsuccessful applicant in habeas corpus proceedings to appeal, its statutory context and legislative history had led to earlier decisions that there was no such appeal. The Court of Appeal stated that it saw "force in the argument that, to give full effect to the rights . . . , [the statutory provision] . . . should now receive a wider interpretation than has prevailed hitherto".[42] In New Zealand it has been stated that such reinterpretation is more likely where statutes enacted after the Bill of Rights show a shift in the meaning of the relevant terms and concepts.[43]

3–30 We have mentioned the position of statutory provisions, such as section 434(5) of the Companies Act 1985, providing that information obtained from an individual by the exercise of compulsory powers "may be used in evidence against him".[44] Although it has been said[45] that Parliament has made its intentions quite clear in such provisions, they may be given a narrower interpretation in the light of section 3 in order to achieve compatibility with the Article 6 rights of those charged with criminal offences.[46–47] So, for example, although some may regard this as a strained meaning,[48] they could be reinterpreted as only authorising the use of non-incriminating evidence.

K. A contemporary construction

3–31 The interpretative direction will also reinforce the common law presumption that Parliament intends the court to apply–particularly to provisions expressing a dynamic concept, such as what constitutes "prejudice", "unfairness", or "family"–a construction which allows for changes since the legislation was initially framed.[49]

---

[41] [1991] 1 N.Z.L.R. 439.

[42] [1991] 1 N.Z.L.R. 439, 441.

[43] *Quilter v. Attorney-General* [1998] 1 N.Z.L.R. 523, 579 (Tipping J.); *Fitzpatrick v. Sterling Housing Association*, October 28, 1999 (HL).

[44] See above, para. 3–19. See also Companies Act 1985, ss. 443, 446(3), 447(8), Insurance Companies Act 1982, ss. 43(5), 44(5), Insolvency Act 1986, s. 433, Financial Services Act 1986, s. 94(3), 105(5), 177(6), Banking Act 1987, s. 41(10), Criminal Justice Act 1987, s. 2(8), Companies Act 1989, s. 83(6).

[45] *R. v. Saunders* [1996] 1 Cr. App. R. 463, 475, 477.

[46–47] It is unlikely that they will come before the courts again in view of the Attorney-General's guidelines to prosecutors not to use such evidence (see above, para. 3–19, n. 98) and the Government's intention to promote rectifying legislation: *Hansard*, H.C., February 4, 1998, W.A. 640. However, a similar issue may arise under provisions relating to other areas such as planning or environmental protection. See n. 95.

[48] On the limits of what is possible under s. 3, see below, para. 3.39.

[49] See Bennion, *Statutory Interpretation*, pp. 616, 618 ("the ongoing Act resembles a vessel launched on some one-way voyage from the old world to the new. The vessel is not going to return; nor are its passengers. On arrival in the present, they deploy their native endowments under conditions originally unguessed at") approved in *R. v. Hammersmith & Fulham LBC, ex parte M* (1997) 30 H.L.R. 10; Dworkin, *Law's Empire* (1986), p. 348 ("The judge interprets not just the statute's text but its life, the process that begins before it becomes law and extends far beyond that moment. His (the judge's) interpretation changes as the story develops"); Beatson [1997] C.L.J. 291, 302–303.

This means that in its application on any date the language of the Act, though necessarily embedded in its own time, is nevertheless to be construed in accordance with the need to treat it as current law.[50] So, for example, when in 1925 the Land Registration Act gave a person "in actual occupation" of property an overriding interest, the balance of authority suggested that a wife residing with her husband was not "in actual occupation" where the husband alone was the legal owner of the property". But by the beginning of the 1980s the social and legal status of husband and wife had changed and it was held that the wife was "in actual occupation" and entitled to the statutory protection.[51]

Where the common law presumption does not permit the reconsideration of the construction of a statutory provision, the interpretative obligation in section 3 may do so. For example, a majority of the Court of Appeal[52] held that "living with the original tenant as his wife or her husband" in paragraph 2(1) of Part I of Schedule 1 to the Rent Act 1977 does not include those in a same-sex relationship. This might have been incompatible with the claimant's right under the Convention to enjoyment of property, or right to respect for private and family life and home, read with the right not to be discriminated against on the ground of sexual orientation. If so it would have been necessary to consider whether it is "possible" to give the provision a different meaning but the House of Lords decision that a same sex partner may be a member of the tenant's "family" means that the issue is unlikely to arise.

L. Interpretation of general powers

3–32 We have seen that "the principle of legality",[53] under which the courts assume that Parliament has taken for granted long-standing principles of constitutional and administrative law, means that fundamental rights cannot be overridden by general words in statutes and subordinate legislation. Where Convention rights are in play, this principle is fortified by the direction in section 3 that "so far as it is possible to do so", statutory powers must be construed as having to be exercised in accordance with the Convention principles of necessity, pressing social need and proportionality.[54] We now consider a number of overlapping aspects of this.

(1) "Reading down" broadly phrased statutory powers to ensure conformity with Convention rights

3–33 The direction in section 3 will mean that broadly phrased discretionary powers contained in a statute will be interpreted as subject to the Convention rights and to the approach used in construing those rights. For example, section 10(3) of the Broadcasting Act 1990 empowers the Home Secretary to direct broadcasters to refrain from broadcasting "any matter".[55] In accordance with the interpretative obligation, this power is now impliedly limited by reference to the criteria set out in Article 10 of the Convention. The Home Secretary may only give a direction where it is necessary in a democratic society for the protection of one of the interests specified

---

[50] Bennion, *op cit.*, p. 616 *et seq.*
[51] *Williams & Glyns Bank v. Boland* [1981] A.C. 487, 502 (Lord Wilberforce).
[52] *Fitzpatrick v. Sterling Housing Association Ltd* [1998] Ch. 304, and see H.L., October 28, 1999. See also *Quilter v. Att.-Gen.* [1998] 1 N.Z.L.R. 523.
[53] See above, para. 3.12.
[54] On the use of these principles in judicial review proceedings, see below, Chapter 5. On the Strasbourg jurisprudence, see below, paras 5–08 *et seq.* and C0–12 *et seq.*
[55] *R. v. Home Secretary, ex parte Brind* [1991] A.C. 696 concerned the previous provision, Broadcasting Act 1981, s. 29(3).

in Article 10(2) and the direction responds to a pressing social need. Further, the giving of a direction must be proportionate to that need.[56] A direction outside these parameters would be *ultra vires*.

3–34   This approach is similar to that of the English courts when determining the width of a power which, if given its literal meaning would interfere with the exercise of common law rights[57] and fundamental human rights.[58] The decision of the House of Lords in *R. v. Secretary of State for the Home Department, ex p. Simms & O'Brien*,[59] in which the principle of legality was invoked, is a striking example. The Prison Rules provided that visits to prisoners by journalists in their professional capacity should in general not be allowed, and that, "where, exceptionally a journalist . . . is permitted to visit an inmate . . . he or she will be required to give a written undertaking that . . . any material obtained at the interview will not be used for professional purposes except as permitted by the governor". The House of Lords held that the rules did not empower the Home Secretary to impose a total restriction on prisoners' freedom of expression where no undertaking had been given. Applying the principle of legality,[60] it held that on their true construction, the rules did not authorise a ban on interviews with prisoners who wished to persuade journalists to investigate the safety of their convictions and to publicise their findings in an effort to gain access to justice.[61] Another useful example is provided by a decision concerning the New Zealand Bills of Rights' guarantee of the right to "be secure against unreasonable search or seizure". A statutory provision authorising searches for drugs without warrant was held, in the light of this guarantee, not to authorise a search without warrant in circumstances where the police could have obtained a search warrant.[62] These cases are examples of the judicial "reading down" of broad statutory terms by reference to the fundamental rights. A limitation was in effect grafted onto the statutory provisions or administrative rules.

(2)   The requirements of the rule of law

3–35   In some cases it is helpful to consider the general principle from another viewpoint. Any interference with Convention rights must be "prescribed by law"[63] or "in accordance with the law",[64] or "lawful".[65] This means not only that such interference must be lawful in accordance with domestic law, but also that the law must be adequately accessible and foreseeable and that there must be adequate safeguards–both substantive and procedural–against abuse.[66] The law itself must lay down the conditions and procedures justifying the interference.[67] General powers, for

---

[56] *Observer & Guardian v. United Kingdom* (1991) 14 E.H.R.R. 153.
[57] *Chertsey v. Mixnams* [1965] A.C. 735; *Padfield v. Minister of Agriculture* [1968] A.C. 997 (freedom of contract); *Congreve v. Home Office* [1976] Q.B. 629 (freedom from taxation). See above, para. 3.4.2.
[58] *R. v. Home Secretary, ex parte Khawaja* [1984] A.C. 74; *R. v. Halliday* [1917] A.C. 260 (deprivation of liberty); *Raymond v. Honey* [1983] A.C. 1 (access to legal advice); *R. v. Lord Chancellor's Dept., ex parte Witham* [1998] Q.B. 575 (access to the courts).
[59] [1999] 3 W.L.R. 328 (HL); see also *R. v. DPP, ex parte Kebeline*, above, para. 3–14.
[60] On which, see above, para. 3–12.
[61] Such "reading down" may not always be possible. *cf. R. v. Secretary of State for the Home Department, ex parte Leech* [1994] Q.B. 198, 207–208; *General Mediterranean Holdings SA v. Patel* [1999] 3 All E.R. 673, see below, para. 3–40.
[62] *R. v. Laugalis* (1993) 10 C.R.N.Z. 350. See also *TVNZ Ltd v. Attorney-General* [1995] 2 N.Z.L.R. 641, 646; *R. v. Sparrow* (1990) 70 D.L.R. 4d 385 (Canada).
[63] Articles 9(2) and 10(2).
[64] Article 8(2).
[65] Article 5.
[66] As to the Convention requirements of the Rule of Law, see below, paras 5–09, C0–10 and C0–11.
[67] *Klass v. Germany* (1983) 2 E.H.R.R. 214, para. 50; *Silver & others v. United Kingdom* (1983) 5 E.H.R.R. 347.

example "to do anything . . . which is calculated to facilitate, or is conducive or incidental to . . . " the discharge of other specific statutory functions[68] will be insufficient for this purpose. Thus, section 111 of the Local Government Act 1972 will now have to be interpreted as not empowering local authorities to maintain and publish video footage recorded from CCTV cameras, because it contains no safeguards at all concerning the retention and publication of such material.[69] Other general powers to interfere with Convention rights may have procedural guarantees read into them, for example to comply with the requirements of Articles 6 or 8.[70]

(3) Implication of Convention rights as relevant considerations

3–36 The propriety of the purposes for which a public authority may exercise a statutory discretion, and the relevance or irrelevance of the factors it can take into account, are determined primarily by reference to the statutory framework within which the decision is made.[71] Again, "the principle of legality"[72] is of assistance. That principle means that the impact of an exercise of discretion on Convention rights will always be a relevant consideration and this in turn may require reconsideration of statutory powers. For example, in the past the test of what is a material purpose in planning terms has been whether a planning purpose is served, and a planning purpose is one that relates to the character of the use of the land. But it is possible that the personal circumstances of an occupier, personal hardship, and the effect of a planning decision on, for example, gypsies and travellers, will have to be given a greater role than the subsidiary one they are given at present.[73]

(4) Presumption of non-discrimination in the exercise of powers

3–37 Where a statutory power touches a Convention right, so far as it is possible to do so it will be interpreted as not authorising an exercise of the power which is discriminatory.[74] So, for example, in *Wheeler v. Leicester CC*[75] the Council, which had statutory power to grant permission for the use of its land, refused permission to a rugby club which would not condemn a tour of South Africa in which three of its members had participated. The House of Lords quashed the decision on conventional *Wednesbury* grounds. Browne-Wilkinson L.J. had taken a broader approach in the Court of Appeal, stating that the Council should not be allowed to exercise its discretionary powers so as to discriminate against those whose expressed views were not unlawful or unreasonable but merely differed from the Council's policy. He

---

[68] See s. 111 of the Local Government Act 1972.
[69] See *R. v. Brentwood Borough Council, ex parte Peck* [1998] E.M.L.R. 697 (Harrison J. and CA). See also *Westminster City Council v. Bleinheim Leisure, The Times,* February 24, 1999 (Brooke L.J.).
[70] These guarantees may include, for example, an opportunity to be heard (*W v. United Kingdom* (1988) 10 E.H.R.R. 29; *Johansen v. Norway* August 7, 1996, R.J.D., 1996–IV, No. 13; 23 E.H.R.R. 33) or to be given reasons for a decision (*H v. Belgium* (1988) 10 E.H.R.R. 339). See also *Stefan v. GMC* [1999] 1 W.L.R. 1299, in which the Privy Council considered that they were unable to find in the General Medical Council Health Comittee (Procedure) Rules an implied obligation on the Health Committee of the General Medical Council to give reasons for its decisions. Their Lordships found that a common law duty arose in the circumstances of the case.
[71] See *Padfield v. Minister of Agriculture, Fisheries & Food* [1968] A.C. 997; *Bristol DC v. Clark* [1975] 1 W.L.R. 1443, 1451; *Congreave v. Home Office* [1976] Q.B. 629, 658; *R. v. Liverpool University, ex parte Caesar Gordon* [1991] 1 Q.B. 124, 131. See also De Smith, Woolf & Jowell, *Judicial Review of Administrative Action* (5th ed.), para. 6–087 *et seq.*
[72] See above, paras 3–12 and 3.34.
[73] We are grateful to Hunt, *Using Human Rights Law in English Courts* (1997), p. 322 for this example. See *Westminster City Council v. Great Portland Estates* [1985] A.C. 661, 670.
[74] On the Article 14 prohibition of discrimination, see below, paras C14–01 *et seq.*
[75] [1985] A.C. 1054.

considered that this would undermine the constitutional right to freedom of speech and conscience which exists in the absence of express legislative provision to the contrary. Section 3 is likely to mean that, in such a case, Browne-Wilkinson L.J.'s broader view will prevail. Apart from cases involving freedom of expression and conscience, the presumption of non-discrimination may be relevant in cases involving the right to respect for family and private life, such as the age of consent for sexual activity, the status of those born outside marriage, and the position of those wishing to emigrate to the United Kingdom. The presumption will place on public authorities the onus of justifying any difference of treatment of people placed in analogous circumstances.[76]

(5) Interpretation of terms capable of more than one meaning

3–38 Expressions which are capable of more than one meaning should be interpreted in a way which will ensure that Convention rights are respected, particularly where they express a dynamic concept, such as what constitutes "unfairness" or "family".[77] A recent example of an updating construction is the decision of the House of Lords[78] that, in today's circumstances, a same sex partner may be a member of a tenant's "family" for the purposes of the Rent Act 1977, although not the tenant's "wife" or "husband".

M. Limits

3–39 Experience in New Zealand suggests that there may limits to what is possible under section 3.[79] First, although one New Zealand decision[80] suggests that the text may be looked at in isolation from its context and legislative history to identify a meaning consistent with the Bill of Rights, other cases have held that a pre-Bill of Rights statutory provision prevails if it is inconsistent with the Bill of Rights.[81] Such incompatibility can, as noted above, be found not only where there is textual inconsistency,[82] but also where it is shown that the intention behind the earlier provision was broader than its words and that intention is inconsistent with the Bill of Rights.[83] In the United Kingdom the fact that the Convention rights were first relevant as part of the U.K.'s international obligations is likely to mean that it will be more difficult to establish this second form of inconsistency, i.e. inconsistency of intention. This is because, at least in respect of statutes enacted after the United Kingdom ratified the ECHR or the First and Sixth Protocols, there is a common law presumption that domestic legislation was intended to conform with its international

---

[76] See, for example *Stubbings v. United Kingdom* October 22, 1996, R.J.D., 1996–IV, No. 18; 23 E.H.R.R. 213. See further below, paras C14–18 *et seq.*

[77] On the need for updating constructions in such cases, see above, para. 3.31. See also Ward L.J.'s dissenting judgment in *Fitzpatrick v. Sterling Housing Association Ltd* [1998] Ch. 304, 324 *et seq.*

[78] *Fitzpatrick v. Sterling Housing Association Ltd* October 28, 1999. See also *Quilter v. Att.-Gen.* [1998] 1 N.Z.L.R. 523, above, para. 3–24.

[79] Rishworth in Huscroft & Rishworth (eds) *Rights and Freedoms* (Brooker's, 1995), pp. 94–99; Taggart in Cambridge Centre for Public Law, *Constitutional Reform in the U.K.: Practice and Principles* (1998) pp. 93–97.

[80] *Flicklinger v. Crown Colony of Hong Kong* [1991] 1 N.Z.L.R. 439.

[81] *TV3 Network Services v. R* [1993] 3 N.Z.L.R. 421; *Temese v. Police* (1992) 9 C.R.N.Z. 425.

[82] See *R. v. Secretary of State for the Home Department, ex parte Leech* [1994] Q.B. 198, 207–208: r. 33(3) of the Prison Rules permitting censorship of prisoners' letters held *ultra vires* to the extent that it purported to apply to correspondence with legal advisers. Although the language of rule 33(3) was general and might therefore have been "read down" by application of the presumption principle of legality discussed above at 3.4.11(a), this was inconsistent with r. 37A.

[83] See Rishworth in *Huscroft & Rishworth (eds), Rights and Freedoms* (Brooker's, 1995), p. 96.

obligations.[84] has been said that the New Zealand interpretative direction does not authorise the Court to legislate. Even if a meaning is theoretically possible, it must be rejected if it is clearly contrary to what Parliament intended".[85] As we have said, however,[86] the logic of the direction in section 3 is that the Court should apply the HRA in priority to the rule in *Pepper v. Hart*. If the meaning of a provision is clear, a court may decide to apply it without recourse to the legislative history, unless that meaning it is incompatible with a Convention right.

3–40   Secondly, the preference for consistency (in HRA terms compatibility) with the rights and freedoms in the Bill of Rights "can only come into play" where the enactment can "reasonably" or "properly" be given such a meaning.[87] It is clear from the New Zealand jurisprudence that a "strained" or "unnatural" interpretation is not enough.[88] It has been said that "properly" means "by a legitimate process of construction".[89] While the legislative history of section 3, and the statements by the Lord Chancellor and the Home Secretary[90] suggest that U.K. courts are intended to adopt a broader approach than that adopted in New Zealand, recent House of Lords' authority indicates the likely limits of consistent interpretation. In *Clarke v. Kato* the House of Lords had to decide whether a car park qualified as a "road" within section 192 of the Road Traffic Act 1988, an issue which involved consideration of three European Directives on the approximation of the laws of Member States relating to insurance against civil liability in respect of the use of motor vehicles. Lord Clyde accepted that it might be "perfectly proper to adopt even a strained construction to enable the object and purpose of legislation to be fulfilled". He continued, however, that "it cannot be taken to the length of applying unnatural meanings to familiar words or of so stretching the language that its former shape is transformed into something which is not only significantly different but has a name of its own."[91] He considered that this "must be particularly so where the [statutory] language has no ambiguity or uncertainty about it".[92]

N.   Conclusion: the overall approach

3–41   The overriding effect of the HRA's interpretative obligation will be, wherever possible, to place limitations on provisions which directly interfere, or permit interference, with Convention rights. Section 3 is likely to lead to the following inquiry in the case of primary legislation.

Where the natural and ordinary meaning of the words of a provision give rise to no incompatibility they will be adopted. If, however, consideration of the Convention jurisprudence shows that an incompatibility would result from the natural and ordinary meaning, the court must ask whether it is "possible" to find an interpreta-

---

[84] *Hansard*, H.L. Debs, November 18, 1997, col. 535 (Lord Chancellor).
[85] *Quilter v. Att.-Gen.* [1998] 1 N.Z.L.R. 523, 542.
[86] Para. 3–24.
[87] See, *mutatis mutandis*, *Matadeen v. Pointu* [1999] 1 A.C. 98, 108 (the generous approach used in the interpretation of constitutions does not "release judges from the task of interpreting the statutory language and enable them to give free reign . . ." approving Kentridge A.J. in *State v. Zuma* 1995 (4) B.C.L.R. 401, 412 ("if the language used by the lawgiver is ignored in favour of a general resort to 'values' the result is not interpretation but divination").
[88] *Ministry of Transport v. Noort* [1992] 3 N.Z.L.R. 260, 272; *Simpson v. AG NZ* [1994] 3 N.Z.L.R. 667, 674; *R. v. Phillips* [1991] 3 N.Z.L.R. 175, 177.
[89] *Quilter v. Att.-Gen.* [1998] 1 N.Z.L.R. 523, 581.
[90] See above, paras 3–15—3.17.
[91] Such as a car park rather than a road.
[92] [1998] 1 W.L.R. 1647, 1655 (HL).

tion which would remove that incompatibility. The approach to be used may permit the departure from the clear literal meaning by the use of a purposive construction of the potentially incompatible statute.[93] Although it remains uncertain whether legislative intention will be determined strictly in the light of the state of the law at the time of the enactment of the relevant statute, the approach taken in the E.C. cases suggests that there may be some flexibility: courts have adopted interpretations which have achieved conformity with later interpretations of E.C. law by the ECJ. But while it will apparently be possible to adopt a "strained" construction in order to achieve compatibility,[94] is unlikely that an "unnatural" construction will be permissible. Where compatible interpretation is not possible, the court will have to consider making a declaration of incompatibility. Section 3(2)(a) provides that the interpretative obligation does not affect the validity, continuing operation or enforcement of any incompatible primary legislation. This provision is perhaps unnecessary, since on its face section 3(1) contains no power or duty which would have such an effect.

3–42   In the case of subordinate legislation made under a rule making power in primary legislation, the process is similar, save that it is also necessary to inquire into the compatibility of the primary legislation with the Convention. Section 3(2)(b) provides that section 3 does not affect its validity, continuing operation or enforcement ". . . if (disregarding any, possibility of revocation) primary legislation prevents removal of the incompatibility". Where the subordinate legislation can be interpreted compatibly, it should be so interpreted unless the primary legislation prevents the adoption of such interpretation.[95] Where the subordinate legislation cannot be interpreted compatibly, there are two possibilities. First, if the primary legislation can, by the application of section 3, be interpreted so as not to require rules made under it to be incompatible, it will have to be so interpreted and the incompatible subordinate legislation will be *ultra vires*. In such a case, section 3 requires an interpretation of the power which does not *allow* the making of incompatible rules. The subordinate legislation should therefore be declared invalid or quashed.[96] Secondly, if the primary legislation cannot be interpreted so as to prohibit the making of incompatible rules under it, effect must be given to the subordinate legislation, and again the court will have to consider making a declaration of incompatibility of both primary and secondary legislation.

5.   DECLARATIONS OF INCOMPATIBILITY

A.   Introduction

3–43   Courts have no power to strike down or disapply legislative provisions which are incompatible with Convention rights, except when applying the *ultra vires*

---

[93] *R. v. DPP, ex parte Kebeline*, October 28, 1999, above, para. 3–14. But *cf.* Lord Clyde in *Clarke v. Kato* [1998] 1 W.L.R. 1647, 1655, above, para. 3–40.

[94] *ibid.*

[95] See the application of the presumption principle of legality, *e.g.* in *R. v. Secretary of State for the Home Department, ex parte Simms & O'Brien* [1999] 3 W.L.R. 328, above, paras 3.12 and 3.34.

[96] A result expressly contemplated by the terms of s. 10(4). See below, para. 4–44. An amendment to prevent the courts striking down incompatible subordinate legislation was defeated: *Hansard*, H.C., June 3, 1998, col. 426 *et seq.* esp. col. 433 (Parliamentary Secretary, Lord Chancellor's Department). A declaration is the appropriate remedy for statutory instruments: *R. v. Secretary of State for Social Security, ex parte Joint Council for the Welfare of Immigrants* [1997] 1 W.L.R. 275; *R. v. Lord Chancellor, ex parte Witham* [1998] Q.B. 575. In other cases, a declaration or an order of *certiorari* may be appropriate; and see further s. 10(4). On the meaning of primary and subordinate legislation under the HRA, see above, para. 3–03

rule in respect of subordinate legislation,[97] and in respect of primary legislation of the devolved Assemblies.[98] However, certain higher courts are given power to declare that a provision is incompatible with a Convention right. In practice, it is likely that such declarations will be rare, applying only to cases in which a court is unable to remove any incompatibility by interpretation, or by operation of the *ultra vires* rule for subordinate legislation.

B. Which courts

3–44 Not every court is given the power to make a declaration of incompatibility. Such a declaration may be made only by:

(a) the House of Lords;

(b) the Judicial Committee of the Privy Council;

(c) the Courts-Martial Appeal Court;

(d) in Scotland, the High Court of Justiciary sitting otherwise than as a trial court or the Court of Session;

(e) in England and Wales and Northern Ireland, the High Court or the Court of Appeal.

Other courts have no such power. Although they are bound by the interpretative obligation, if a legislative provision is incapable of consistent interpretation they cannot make such a declaration.[99] But this does not mean that an inferior court should refrain from expressing its opinion about the compatibility of a statutory provision. Such an inquiry will not be entirely hypothetical and therefore inadmissible.[1] Indeed it may be considered essential since the court must first identify a potential incompatibility before determining whether it can interpret it away; in order to carry out its section 3 duty, the court must know what is or would be compatible. Even if the inferior court is not able to make a declaration, its opinion may well be useful to an appellate court determining compatibility, particularly in proceedings before specialised tribunals dealing with areas of law with which the higher courts may not be readily familiar.[2] This may be so particularly where questions of proportionality or necessity in a democratic society arise[3] before the fact-finding tribunal, even though its conclusions on those issues cannot affect its disposition of the case before it.

C. Which proceedings

3–45 The power to make a declaration of incompatibility arises in *any* proceedings in which a court determines whether a legislative provision is incompatible with

---

[97] See above, para. 3–42.

[98] See Scotland Act 1998, s. 29(2)(d); Northern Ireland Act 1998, s. 6(2)(c) and below, Ch. 7.

[99] However, such courts could apply the *ultra vires* rule to provisions of subordinate legislation: see above, para. 3–42 and, by analogy, *Chief Adjudication Officer v. Foster* [1993] A.C. 754; *Boddington v. British Transport Police* [1998] 2 W.L.R. 639.

[1] In *R. v. Ministry of Defence, ex parte Smith* [1996] Q.B. 517, 564, before the enactment of the HRA, Henry L.J. questioned the utility of a debate in our U.K. courts as to the likely fate of a policy if tested in the European Court of Human Rights. *cf.* now *Barrett v. London Borough of Enfield* [1999] 3 W.L.R. 79, 84–85.

[2] See Lord Bridge in *Chief Adjudication Officer v. Foster* [1993] A.C. 754, 767. See also *Ex parte Waldron* [1986] Q.B. 824 at 852; *R. v. Ministry of Agriculture, Fisheries and Food, ex parte Dairy Trade Association Ltd* [1995] C.O.D. 3. On alternative remedies, see further below, para. 3–47, n. 23.

[3] See below, paras 5–13 *et seq.*

a Convention right.[4] This includes proceedings between two private parties, in which no "public authority"[5] is involved. So, for example, it would apply to proceedings between a private landlord and a tenant concerning the enfranchisement of a long leasehold house,[6] or between a journalist and a private party seeking disclosure of the journalists source of information alleged to be confidential.[7]

D. Which legislation

3–46   A declaration of incompatibility may be made in relation to provisions of primary legislation and provisions of "subordinate legislation made in the exercise of a power conferred by primary legislation".[8] In addition to Acts of Parliament, primary legislation includes Measures of the Church Assembly, Measures of the General Synod of the Church of England, and certain Orders in Council, including an Order in Council made under the Royal Prerogative, an Order in Council amending an Act of Parliament,[9] and an order or other instrument made under primary legislation which operates to bring into force a provision of primary legislation or which amends primary legislation.[10]

The power to make a declaration may be exercised in respect of a provision of primary legislation if the court is satisfied that it is incompatible with a Convention right.[11] In relation to subordinate legislation, the court must in addition be "that (disregarding any possibility of revocation) the primary legislation concerned prevents removal of the incompatibility".[12] The words in parenthesis enjoin the court to disregard the possibility that a Minister might revoke the provision of primary legislation by making a remedial order.[13] Thus, where subordinate legislation cannot be interpreted compatibly, the court must consider whether the rule-making power in the "parent" legislation requires the making of an incompatible rule. If it does not, the court may declare the subordinate provision *ultra vires* and unlawful. If the incompatible subordinate provision is so required, either expressly or by unavoidable implication, the court must consider whether to make a declaration of incompatibility.

E. A power not a duty

3–47   Sections 4(2) and (4) provide that if the court is satisfied of the relevant incompatibility, it "may" make a declaration; but it is not obliged to do so. The Act gives no guidance as to the circumstances in which a court might make or decline to make a declaration.[14] The remedial provisions of section 8(1) have no application in this context. The section empowers a court, in proceedings arising out of an unlawful act of a public authority, to "grant such relief or remedy, or make such order, within

---

[4] Ss. 4(1) & (3).
[5] As to public authorities see s. 6 and below, paras 4–02—4–20. As to the "horizontal" effect of the HRA see below, paras 4–45 *et seq.*
[6] See *James & others v. United Kingdom* [1986] 8 E.H.R.R. 123.
[7] *X v. Morgan Grampian* [1991] 1 A.C. 1; *Michael O'Mara Books Ltd v. Express Newspapers plc and others* [1999] F.S.R. 49 [1998] E.M.L.R. 383; *Camelot v. Centaur Communications* [1998] I.R.L.R. 80, CA.
[8] s. 4(3).
[9] For example under s. 2(4) of the European Communities Act 1972.
[10] As to the application to legislation of the devolved assemblies, see below, Ch. 7.
[11] s. 4(2). As to the meaning of "incompatible", see above, paras 3–18 *et seq.*
[12] s. 4(3)(b).
[13] See s. 10, below, paras 6–23 *et seq.*
[14] See De Smith, Woolf & Jowell, *Judicial Review of Administrative Action* (5th ed.), paras 20–001 *et seq.*; Sir Thomas Bingham [1991] P.L. 64 (discretion to refuse relief in judicial review).

its powers, as it considers just and appropriate".[15] However, a public authority does not act unlawfully where it acts under a provision of irremediably incompatible primary legislation, or if it is acting so as to give effect to or enforce irremediably incompatible provisions of; or made under, primary legislation.[16] In such cases, therefore, the declaration of incompatibility will be the only "relief" which a court can give to an individual who is prejudiced by incompatible legislation. Although such a declaration is not binding on the parties to the proceedings before it,[17] the court should be slow to refuse to make one in the exercise of its discretion, in particular given the possibility that remedial action might follow. As the intention of the Act is to enable the applicant to make his case before the domestic courts without resort to Strasbourg, those courts should seek to afford, to the extent allowed by the Act, at least such relief as the applicant could expect in Strasbourg. Refusing to make a declaration might in practice compel the applicant to pursue his case in Strasbourg, which would be contrary to the primary intention of "bringing rights home". A declaration of incompatibility[18] will prompt Parliament and the Government to consider what legislative amendments are necessary, and will enable Ministers to use the "fast track" procedure for taking remedial action.[19] It is therefore undesirable that a national court should refuse to make a declaration, forcing on the applicant the expense and delay of pursuing both domestic appeals and proceedings before the ECHR.[20] The Lord Chancellor explained the discretion during the Committee stage of the Bill, indicating that he would expect that once a court had found a legislative provision to be incompatible it would declare that incompatibility. But the Government wished to leave the court a discretion not to do so in the circumstances of a particular case:

" . . . there might be an alternative statutory appeal route which the court might think it preferable to follow, or there might be any other procedure which the court in its discretion thought the applicant should exhaust before seeking a declaration which would then put Parliament under pressure to follow a remedial route."[21]

Once a matter is before the court it is, however, difficult to see why it might want to decline to make a declaration of incompatibility. The High Court[22] is the only court of original jurisdiction with power to make such a declaration. The presence of an alternative remedy may well mean that it will not allow an application for judicial review to proceed.[23] If it does allow an application, even though there is an

---

[15] See further below, paras 6–11 et seq.
[16] Ss. section 6(2), below, para. 4–21.
[17] See s. 4(6) and below, para. 3–48.
[18] And an equivalent finding by the Strasbourg Court.
[19] s. 10 and Sched. 2, see below, paras 6–23 et seq.
[20] To similar effect see Lester [1998] E.H.R.L.R. 663, 672.
[21] Hansard, H.L., November 18, 1997, col. 546.
[22] The High Court of Justiciary in Scotland, HRA, s. 4(5)(d).
[23] As to the circumstances in which an application for judicial review may be entertained in spite of the availability of alternative remedies, see Wade & Forsyth, Administrative Law (7th ed), pp. 721–726; De Smith, Woolf & Jowell, Judicial Review of Administrative Action (5th ed.), paras 17–025 et seq. and 20–018 et seq. Beatson, "Prematurity & Ripeness for Review" in Forsyth & Hare (eds), The Golden Metwand and the Crooked Cord (1998), pp. 229–235. The Law Commission, Administrative Law: Judicial Review and Statutory Appeals, Law Com. No. 226 (1994), noted (paras 3.24–3.26) that there was widespread support for a requirement that an applicant exhaust an alternative remedy only where the alternative remedy was an "adequate" one, and concluded (paras 5.31–5.35) that appeals to courts, tribunals and statutory appeals to ministers should normally have to be exhausted before either an application for judicial review is allowed to proceed or a remedy is granted.

alternative appeal procedure, it is hard to see why it should then decline to make a declaration of incompatibility. It is not clear what sort of "other procedure" the Lord Chancellor had in mind; nor is the reference to "pressure" easy to understand. The Government is under no obligation to use the remedial route—indeed the circumstances in which it may do so are closely circumscribed[24]—but if no declaration is made it will have no power to do so at all unless or until the Strasbourg Court makes a finding in proceedings against the United Kingdom.[25]

F. The effect of a declaration

3-48   Like a compatible interpretation under section 3, a declaration of incompatibility does not affect the validity, continuing operation or enforcement of the provision in respect of which it is given.[26] Moreover, it is not binding on the parties to the proceedings in which it is made. Its only effect is to prompt parliamentary consideration of legislative amendment and, in appropriate cases, to empower a Minister of the Crown, or the Queen in Council, to make a remedial order[27] amending or repealing the legislation to remove the incompatibility. Such an order may be made so as to have retrospective effect[28] and may make different provision for different cases.[29] The Act creates no obligation to legislate in any form to remove an incompatible provision of legislation. The Government's view was that the imposition of such an obligation would be tantamount to empowering the court, through the medium of declarations of incompatibility, to require changes in legislation, which power was considered inconsistent with parliamentary sovereignty.[30] However, in practice, governments in the past have introduced legislation to give effect to decisions of the ECHR where they considered it necessary to do so. It is likely that a similar practice will apply to declarations by domestic courts, save that a government could decline to give effect to a domestic judgment which it does not accept in order to await a decision of the Strasbourg Court.

If legislation is not amended following a declaration of incompatibility, or if no redress is provided to the relevant party in the proceedings in which the declaration was made, the person concerned may still make an application to the Strasbourg Court under Article 34[31] of the Convention. However, if he has an arguable case that the legislative provision in issue is capable of compatible interpretation, he will need to exhaust domestic remedies by seeking to appeal against the court's rejection of that contention.

G. Procedural issues

3-49   The Crown is entitled to notice in any case in which a court is considering making a declaration of incompatibility, and a Minister of the Crown or a member of

---

[24] See below, para. 6–24.

[25] s. 10(1)(b), see below, para. 6–25.

[26] s. 6(a).

[27] s. 10, see below, paras 6–24—6–27. Note, however, that the power to take remedial action does not apply to a Measure of the Church Assembly or of the General Synod of the Church of England: s. 10(6).

[28] Sched. 2, para. 1(1)(b).

[29] Sched. 2, para. 1(1)(d). As to remedial orders, see further below, paras 6–24 et seq.

[30] Hansard, H.L. Debs, November 27, 1997, col. 1139. The Lord Chancellor stated " . . . we expect that the Government and Parliament will in all cases almost certainly be prompted to change the law following a declaration. However, we think that it is preferable, in order to underpin parliamentary sovereignty, to leave this on a discretionary basis. The decision whether to seek a remedial order is a matter for government to decide on a case-by-case basis. It would be wrong for a declaration automatically to lead to a remedial order. It would in effect be tantamount to giving the courts power to strike down Acts of Parliament if there were an obligation in all cases to bring remedial orders forward".

[31] Formerly Article 25.

the Scottish Executive is entitled, by giving notice at any time during the proceedings, to be joined as a party to the proceedings.[32] The Minister may nominate another person to be joined, for example a regulator of public utilities, the Director General of Fair Trading or the General Synod of the Church of England.[33] As the Home Office Minister made clear when introducing the Minister's power to nominate another person, the purpose of the power is not to join the party as partisan in the case:

> "We want to make sure that all the arguments which need to be put are put before the court, and information which be relevant should be made available to the court."[34]

No other person has a right to intervene in the proceedings, although the court may well consider it useful in such cases to entertain submissions from "public interest interveners" with specialist knowledge or interest in the area under consideration in the case before it.[35] Interventions of this nature are now a common feature of proceedings before the ECHR,[36] particularly in cases originating in the United Kingdom.[37]

In criminal proceedings,[38] other than in Scotland, a person who has been made a party may, with leave,[39] to appeal to the House of Lords against any declaration of incompatibility made in the proceedings.[40]

3–50 There remains a question as to how a court should dispose of a case if it has made a declaration of incompatibility. As the declaration is not binding on the parties to the proceedings in which it is made, it cannot affect the result. A court may be infringing a litigant's Convention rights if it grants relief to his opponent in accordance with a legislative provision which it has declared to be incompatible with the Convention. While it will not be acting unlawfully under section 6(1),[41] a court will nonetheless want to exercise its powers in a way which is likely to give the greatest effect to Convention rights. Sir William Wade has suggested[42] that in such

---

[32] ss. 5(1) and (2). Rules of court will provide for the giving of notice in each case.

[33] See *Hansard*, H.C., June 17, 1998, cols 391–392 (Home Office Minister of State).

[34] *ibid.*, col. 397.

[35] JUSTICE/Public Law Project, *A Matter of Public Interest—Report of a working party on third party interventions* (1996). See also *R. v. Ministry of Defence, ex parte Smith* [1996] Q.B. 517, 564E–F (Henry L.J.). Public interest intervention may be particularly important given the limitations on standing in s. 7 of the Act: see below, paras 4–25, 4–33 and 4–34. On the Government's view that the possibility of third party interventions by non-governmental organisations meant that there was no need to broaden the standing provisions, see the statement of the Lord Chancellor, *Hansard*, H.L., November 24, 1997, col. 833, quoted below at para. 4–38.

[36] Article 36(2) of the Convention makes provision for the President of the Court to permit third parties to submit written comments or take part in hearings "in the interest of the proper administration of justice".

[37] See for example *Chahal v. United Kingdom* November 15, 1996, R.J.D. 1996–II No. 22. 23 E.H.R.R. 413 (Amnesty International, Joint Council for the Welfare of Immigrants, JUSTICE, Liberty and the AIRE Centre) *Young, James & Webster v. United Kingdom* 4 E.H.R.R. 38 (Trades Union Congress), *Ashingdane v. United Kingdom* (1985) 7 E.H.R.R. 528 (MIND), *Soering v. United Kingdom* (1989) 11 E.H.R.R. 439 (Amnesty International), *Lingens v. Austria* (1986) 8 E.H.R.R. 103 (Article 19), *Malone v. United Kingdom* (1985) 7 E.H.R.R. 14 (Union of Communication Workers).

[38] Including proceedings before the Courts-Martial Appeal Court: s. 5(5)(a).

[39] Granted either by the court making the declaration of incompatibility or by the House of Lords: s. 5(5)(b).

[40] s. 5(4).

[41] See s. 6(2)(b). As to unlawful acts, see below, paras 6–03—6—05.

[42] "The United Kingdom's Bill of Rights", in Cambridge Centre for Public Law (ed.), *Constitutional Reform in the United Kingdom: Practice and Principles* (1998) p. 67.

cases, the court should grant a stay of execution while the Minister considers whether to make a remedial order, and whether it should be retrospective. A difficulty with this suggestion, and with alternative of adjourning the proceedings after making the declaration but before deciding what other relief or remedy to grant, is that a Minister may make a remedial order only once all rights of appeal have been exercised, lost or formally abandoned.[43] This difficulty might be avoided if the question of compatibility were dealt with as a preliminary issue.[44] Once a declaration had been made and all appeals dealt with, the Minister would have an opportunity to make a remedial order, following which the court could consider its effect on the proceedings.[45] A further difficulty, however, arises from Sir William Wade's suggestion that the determination of civil rights by ministerial order is itself a violation of Article 6(1) of the Convention.[46]

3–51 If the court does not deal with the question of compatibility as a preliminary issue, it will also have to consider what order for costs it should make following a declaration of incompatibility. In proceedings in Strasbourg, an applicant who has secured a finding of a violation will normally be awarded his costs even if he obtains no other redress. In domestic proceedings, at least where public authorities are concerned, a court which has made a declaration that a legislative provision is incompatible with a litigant's Convention rights must nonetheless give judgment to his opponent. It would be adding insult to injury to order the unsuccessful litigant to pay costs which, on the court's own view of the legal merits, he will have to go to Strasbourg to recover. In those circumstances the court should use its discretion at least to award costs to the litigant whose Convention rights have been violated by incompatible legislation, at least where the opposing party is a public authority. In proceedings which do not involve a public authority the issue will not be so easy to resolve. In many cases, however, a Minister will have been joined as a party and the justice of the case may well require that he pay the loser's costs and the winner's (or that he indemnify the loser in respect of the costs of the winner). By adopting the approach to costs advocated in this paragraph, the court will be going as far as it can to give to the litigant the remedy which would be available to him in Strasbourg.

---

[43] s. 10(1)(a).

[44] *Hansard*, H.L., November 27, 1997, col. 1158, where the Lord Chancellor said that it was a matter for the court's discretion to decide whether to adjudicate on a Convention point as a preliminary issue or as part of its final judgment.

[45] The Lord Chancellor may have contemplated such a possibility when stating (*Hansard*, H.L., November 27, 1997, col. 1108) that, should it be thought necessary, it would be possible for a remedial order affecting the legislation to take effect from a date earlier than that on which the order was made. Such an order would "not of itself provide a direct remedy to individuals affected by the legislation which has been retrospectively amended; but, *following the order, it may be open to them to seek such a remedy*" (emphasis added).

[46] See Wade, *loc. cit.* This suggestion is considered at para. 6–30. On remedial orders generally, see below, paras 6–24 *et seq.*

CHAPTER 4

The scope of protection given by the Act

1 INTRODUCTION

4–01 Section 6 makes it unlawful for a public authority to act[1] in a way which is incompatible with a Convention right.[2] The broad effect of the provision is to create a new public law wrong. In judicial review proceedings, this will mean that infringement of a Convention right will be a question of illegality rather than of irrationality. The Act does not create criminal offences[3]; and a person's reliance on a Convention right does not restrict any other right or freedom conferred on him or her by or under any law having effect in any part of the United Kingdom; nor does it restrict any existing rights of action.[4]

The HRA is primarily designed to give Convention rights a "vertical" effect, i.e. to protect the rights of citizens against encroachment by the state and public bodies. It is clear from section 6 that individuals will be able to rely on Convention rights against public authorities and those exercising functions of a public nature.[5] This will be so both in proceedings initiated by the individual, whether by way of judicial review or otherwise, and as a defence in proceedings initiated by a public authority or a person exercising functions of a public nature.[6] Although the position is less clear, for the reasons developed below[7], the Convention rights will also have some "horizontal" effect.[8] This means that in some circumstances individuals will be able to rely on them (although less directly) in proceedings against another private person or entity.[9] This chapter first examines the vertical effect of the HRA. It considers which bodies are public authorities, which acts are covered and who is entitled to bring proceedings under the HRA. It then considers whether the HRA has any "horizontal" effect and the extent to which the Convention rights are likely to apply to relations between individuals. It also deals with the special provision which the Act has made for freedom of expression and freedom of religion.

---

[1] An "act" of a public authority includes a failure to act, but failure to introduce legislation is excluded: s. 6(6). See below para. 4–23.
[2] s. 6(1).
[3] s. 7(8).
[4] s. 11.
[5] HRA, s. 6(3)(b).
[6] See paras 6–06 *et seq.*
[7] See below paras 4–45 *et seq.*
[8] See generally Clapham, *Human Rights in the Private Sphere* (1993), Chap. 4, 6; Dremczewski, *European Human Rights Convention in Domestic* Law (1997), Chap. 8. See also Tribe, *Constitutional Law* (2nd ed. (1985) pp. 350–353, Chap. 18 (United States); Hogg, *Constitutional Law of Canada* (3rd ed., 1992, Chap. 34.2; Hanks, *Constitutional Law in Australia* (3rd ed., 1996), pp. 15–16, 495–498; Casey, *Constitutional Law of Ireland* (2nd ed., 1992) pp. 378–379; Joseph, *Constitutional and Administrative Law in New Zealand* (1992), p. 856.
[9] See further, Hunt [1998] P.L. 423, 427 *et seq.*; Bamforth [1999] C.L.J. 159.

2. PUBLIC AUTHORITIES: WHO IS REQUIRED TO ACT COMPATIBLY WITH CONVENTION RIGHTS?

4–02   The obligation to act in a manner that is compatible with Convention rights is imposed on any "public authority", a term which the HRA draws very broadly.[10] In order to achieve the purpose of "bringing rights home", the Act is intended to impose the obligation to act in accordance with the Convention on any body for which the government of the United Kingdom might find itself responsible in Strasbourg. The HRA contains no closed definition of a "public authority". What section 6 does is to provide expressly that the term "includes" a court or tribunal and any person "certain of whose functions are functions of a public nature". In the case of hybrid bodies with a mixture of public and private functions, only the former functions are brought within the scope of section 6. The breadth of the Act's reach is deliberate, as the Lord Chancellor made clear during the Committee Stage of the Bill:

> "In developing our proposals in Clause 6 we have opted for a wide-ranging definition of public authority. We have created a correspondingly wide liability. That is because we want to provide as much protection as possible for the rights of the individual against the misuse of power by the state within the framework of a Bill which preserves parliamentary sovereignty."[11]

The Lord Chancellor also described this approach as "a very ample definition" and "a wide interpretation".[12] The Government intended to "provide as wide a protection as possible for the human rights of individuals against an abuse of those rights"[13] and to do this by a principle rather than a list of bodies.[14] The Home Secretary stated that what was wanted was "a realistic and modern definition of the state so as to provide correspondingly wide protection against an abuse of rights".[15] Accordingly liability under the HRA was designed to go beyond "the narrow category of central and local government and the police–the organisations that represent a minimalist view of the state" and to extend to those bodies in respect of whose actions the U.K. government is answerable in Strasbourg.[16]

4–03   The intention was to distinguish three categories: "organisations which might be termed "obvious" public authorities, all of whose functions are public",[17] "organisations with a mix of public and private functions", and "organisations with no public functions", the last of which fall outside the scope of section 6.[18] The HRA is intended to cover three categories of public authority (1) "obvious" public authorities, i.e. public authorities properly so called; (2) courts or tribunals;[19] and

---

[10] See White Paper, "*Rights Brought Home*" Cm. 3782 (1997), para. 2.2.

[11] *Hansard*, H.L., November 24, 1997, col. 808.

[12] Hansard, H.L. Vol. 583, col. 475 and *Hansard*, H.L. Vol. 584, col. 1262. See also White Paper, para. 2.2.

[13] *Hansard*, H.L. Vol 584, col. 1262 (Lord Chancellor).

[14] Hansard, H.L. Vol. 583, col. 796 (Lord Chancellor). *cf*. the different approach in the context of Freedom of Information, *Your Right To Know* Cm. 3818 (1997) and Sched. 1 to the draft Freedom of Information Bill 1999.

[15] *Hansard*, H.C. Vol. 314, col. 406.

[16] *ibid*. 406–408.

[17] Note the jurisprudence relating to judicial review suggests that, for that purpose, there are no such bodies: see the contract/employment cases, below para. 4–09 n. 58.

[18] *Hansard*, H.C. Vol. 314, cols 410–411 (Home Secretary). See also *Hansard*, H.L. Vol. 583, col. 796 (Lord Chancellor).

[19] s. 6(3)(a). The Act limits the proceedings which may be brought in respect of the acts of courts and tribunals and the remedies available for their unlawful acts: see s. 9 and below paras 6–18 *et seq*.

(3) any person certain of whose functions are of a public nature.[20] "Obvious" public authorities, such as central government and the police, are to be "caught in respect of everything they do".[21] But this is not apparent on the face of the HRA and indeed is not clearly reflected in the drafting of section 6. It is, however, made clear by section 6(5) that bodies which are public in certain respects but not in others will not be subject to section 6 if the particular act is of a private nature.[22]

English law has hitherto primarily[23] considered the distinction between the public and the private in the context of the scope of applications for judicial review and the supervisory jurisdiction of the High Court. Courts have considered when proceedings must be by way of judicial review and when they cannot be by reference to the concepts of "public bodies" and "public functions". The Government anticipated that the jurisprudence relating to judicial review would be drawn upon in determining what is a public authority under HRA section 6. The Home Secretary described this jurisprudence as the "most valuable asset that we have to hand".[24]

4-04   The law on the scope of judicial review cannot, however, be determinative. First, it will be necessary for the English courts to take into account the Strasbourg jurisprudence which identifies the bodies whose actions engage the responsibility of the state for the purposes of the Convention, which, as we shall see, differs from the judicial review criteria in material respects. That jurisprudence also makes clear that the Convention's reach is determined by reference to "autonomous"[25] concepts of Convention law and not by the manner in which national law classifies bodies or their acts. Secondly, notwithstanding the Home Secretary's statement that "the concepts are reasonably clear", the way English courts have drawn the distinction between "public" and "private" for the purpose of judicial review produced a complicated and not altogether consistent body of cases, using a variety of tests. Thirdly, as will be seen, not all the acts of "obvious" public authorities are treated as "public" for the purposes of judicial review. In contrast, the HRA will apply to *all* their acts. Nevertheless, the case law on the judicial review jurisdiction is instructive.

A.   The "public/private" distinction in the context of the application for judicial review

4-05   This is not the place for a full consideration of the way the courts have determined whether a matter is "public" for the purposes of the application for judicial review,[26] but a brief account is instructive in view of the absence of a definition in the HRA. Broadly, two questions are asked; first is the proposed respondent a "public body", and secondly, is the claim a "public law" claim concerning a "public" function.

---

[20] s. 6(3)(b).
[21] *Hansard*, H.C., February 18, 1998, col. 775 (Home Secretary).
[22] *Hansard*, H.L. Vol. 584, col. 1232 (Lord Chancellor).
[23] But not exclusively, see *D v. N.S.P.C.C.* [1978] A.C. 171.
[24] *Hansard*, H.C. Vol. 314, col. 409 (Home Secretary); *Hansard*, H.L. Vol. 582, November 3, 1997, col. 1310 Lord Williams of Mostyn, *Hansard*, H.L. Vol. 583, col. 811 (Lord Chancellor).
[25] See below, paras 4–14, C0–07.
[26] For fuller consideration of the case law on the identification of public functions and public law see Craig, *Administrative Law* (4th ed., 1999), pp. 767–783; Wade & Forsyth, *Administrative Law* (7th ed., 1994) pp. 680–695; De Smith, Woolf & Jowell, *Judicial Review of Administrative Action* (5th ed., 1995), pp. 167 *et seq.*; Beatson (1987) 102 LQR 34. See also Law Com. 226 (1994) Part III.

(1) Is the proposed respondent a "public body"?

4–06 This question is sometimes framed as asking whether its functions involve a "public" element. The courts have developed two tests in this context; "source" based tests, and "functional" tests. "Source" based tests look to the source of a body's power. Thus, the courts ask whether a body's power is derived from statute,[27] or from the prerogative.[28] Atkin L.J.'s classic test for the scope of the remedy of *certiorari* in *R. v. Electricity Commissioners, ex parte London Electricity Joint Committee Co.*[29] asks whether the body has "legal authority to determine questions affecting the rights of subjects".

"Functional" tests, on the other hand, look at the nature of the power exercised by the body. The functional questions asked include the extent to which the body is institutionally or structurally controlled by government,[30] whether it exercises *de facto* non-consensual power, and whether there was a government decision that a particular sphere should be dealt with by a self-regulatory body. If there was such a government decision, several other factors are also relevant. First, is the body supported by a framework of statutory powers and penalties whenever non-statutory powers or penalties prove insufficient? Secondly, do E.C. requirements call for statutory provisions?[31] Thirdly, is the power the body exercises "governmental in nature"? Fourthly, would this power be exercised by government (or by another governmental body) if this body did not do so.[32]

4–07 Where the source of a body's power is statutory or prerogative this will generally be a decisive factor in deciding that it is "public".[33] Where it is neither, it may nevertheless qualify as "public" where the functional tests are satisfied. It is clear that central and local government and inferior courts and tribunals, the police, immigration officers, prisons, health authorities, NHS Trusts, the Legal Services Commission,[34] the Criminal Injuries Compensation Board,[35] executive agencies and statutory regulatory bodies such as the Broadcasting Complaints Commission,[36] and the Independent Television Commission,[37] are "public" bodies and amenable to judicial review. As is shown below, in the context of the HRA they will be considered "public authorities" by virtue of the source of their power, without needing to apply the functional test which section 6(5) propounds.

Apart from these "core" cases, a number of examples can be given of bodies that have been held to be "public" bodies for the purposes of the judicial review

---

[27] *R. v. Deputy Governor of Parkhurst Prison, ex parte Leech* [1988] A.C. 533, 561.

[28] *R. v. Criminal Injuries Compensation Bd., ex parte Lain* [1967] 2 Q.B. 864; *C.C.S.U. v. Minister for the Civil Service* (the "GCHQ" case) [1985] A.C. 374.

[29] [1924] 1 K.B. 171, 205.

[30] See the cases on the incidence of privilege under the Crown Proceedings Act 1947, *e.g. Tamlin v. Hannaford* [1950] 1 K.B. 18; *BBC v. Johns* [1965] Ch. 32.

[31] *R. v. Take-Over Panel, ex parte Datafin* [1987] Q.B. 815.

[32] *R. v. Take-Over Panel, ex parte Datafin* [1987] Q.B. 815; *R. v. Advertising Standards Authority, ex parte Insurance Service plc* (1990) 2 Admin. L.R. 77; *R. v. Disciplinary Committee of the Jockey Club, ex parte Aga Khan* [1993] 1 W.L.R. 909; *R. v. Disciplinary Committee of the Jockey Club, ex parte Massingberg-Mundy* [1993] 2 All E.R. 207.

[33] *R. v. Take-Over Panel, ex parte Datafin* [1987] Q.B. 815, 847. But note that, for judicial review purposes, this will not be so where the "claim" is not a "public law" claim: see below. For examples of "obvious" public authorities, see below, para. 4–13.

[34] *R. v. Legal Aid Board, ex parte Bateman* [1992] 1 W.L.R. 711; *R. v. Legal Aid Board, ex parte Donn & Co.* [1996] 3 All E.R. 1.

[35] *R. v. Criminal Injuries Compensation Bd., ex parte Lain* [1967] 2 Q.B. 864. For a recent example, see *R. v. Criminal Injuries Compensation Bd., ex parte A* [1998] Q.B. 659.

[36] *R. v. Broadcasting Complaints Commission, ex parte Owen* [1985] Q.B. 1153.

[37] *R. v. Independent Television Commission, ex parte TSW Broadcasting Ltd, The Times,* March 30, 1992.

jurisdiction. Professional bodies such as the General Medical Council,[38] the Institute of Accountants,[39] the Law Society[40], and the Bar Council,[41] the last of which did not at the time possess statutory powers, have qualified because of the *de facto* powers they have over practitioners and those wishing to become practitioners. Other bodies which have qualified include the regulatory bodies such as those recognised under the Financial Services Act 1986,[42] the Stock Exchange,[43] the Take-over Panel,[44] the Advertising Standards Authority,[45] the Association of the British Pharmaceutical Industry,[46] university visitors,[47] and a railway company in the exercise of its regulatory functions.[48] For the HRA such bodies would fall within section 6(3)(b) since only "certain" of their functions are functions of a public nature. Accordingly, by section 6(5), in relation to a particular act, such a body is not a "public authority" if the nature of the act is private.

4–08   The following bodies have been held not to be amenable to judicial review. The first group consists of sporting bodies such as the National Greyhound Racing Club,[49] the Jockey Club,[50] and the Football Association.[51] Secondly, the courts have shown great reluctance to become involved in the affairs of religious authorities, and have held that they are not amenable to judicial review,[52] although the position of the Established Church, the Church of England, should in principle fall into a different category. Finally, certain dispute resolution bodies and other regulatory bodies have been held not to qualify, the Insurance Ombudsman's Bureau being a notable example of this category.[53] In these cases, in particular *Ex p. Aga Khan*, involving the Jockey Club, the courts have emphasised the non-governmental nature of the bodies rather than (as some of the cases in the former category, such as *Ex p. Datafin*, had done) the *de facto* power they exercise. Although it has not been decided whether the Press Complaints Commission is amenable to judicial review,[54] it was widely assumed in the debates on the HRA

---

[38] *R. v. GMC, ex parte Colman* [1990] 1 All E.R. 489.
[39] *Andreou v. ICA* [1998] 1 All E.R. 14 (private law claim struck out).
[40] *R. v. The Law Society, ex parte Mortgage Express* [1978] A.C. 247; *R. v. The Law Society, ex parte Reigate Projects* [1993] 1 W.L.R. 1531. See also *R. v. Solicitors Complaints Bureau, ex parte Singh & Choudry* (1995) 7 Admin. L.R. 249.
[41] *R. v. General Council of the Bar, ex parte Percival* [1991] 2 Q.B. 212.
[42] *R. v. Lautro, ex parte Ross* [1993] Q.B. 17; *R. v. Personal Investment Authority and PIA Ombudsman, ex parte Burns-Anderson Network plc* (1998) 10 Admin. L.R. 57.
[43] *R. v. ISE of the U.K. and Ireland, ex parte Else* [1993] Q.B. 534.
[44] *R. v. Take-Over Panel, ex parte Datafin* [1987] Q.B. 815.
[45] *R. v. Advertising Standards Authority, ex parte Insurance Service plc* (1990) 2 Admin. L.R. 77.
[46] *R. v. Code of Practice Committee, ex parte Professional Counselling Aids Ltd* (1991) 3 Admin. L.R. 697.
[47] *R. v. Hull University Prison Visitor, ex parte Page* [1993] A.C. 682.
[48] *R. v. GW Trains, ex parte Frederick* [1998] C.O.D. 239 and see Lord Williams: *Hansard*, H.L. Vol. 582, November 3, 1997, col. 1310. See also the example given by the Home Secretary (*Hansard*, H.C., col. 409) of a commercial security company operating a privatised prison.
[49] *Law's case* [1983] 1 W.L.R. 1302.
[50] *R. v. Disciplinary Committee of the Jockey Club, ex parte Aga Khan* [1993] 1 W.L.R. 909.
[51] *R. v. Football Assoc., ex parte Football League* [1993] 2 All E.R. 833.
[52] *R. v. Chief Rabbi, ex parte Wachmann* [1992] 1 W.L.R. 1036; *R. v. Imam of Bury Park, ex parte Sulaiman Ali* [1992] C.O.D. 132. Compare the ECtHR in *Holy Monasteries v. Greece* (1995) 20 E.H.R.R. 1 (the monasteries do not exercise governmental powers and cannot be classed as governmental organisations). See also *Hauanemi v. Sweden* (1996) 22 E.H.R.R. C.D. 155: see below, para. P1/1–17.
[53] *R. v. Insurance Ombudsman Bureau, ex parte Aegon Life Assurance Ltd*, *The Times* January 7, 1994; [1994] C.L.C. 88. See also *R. v. Panel of the Federation of Communication Services Ltd, ex parte Kubis* [1998] C.O.D. 5. But if they are underpinned by statute they will qualify: *R. v. Personal Investment Authority and PIA Ombudsman, ex parte Burns-Anderson Network plc* (1998) 10 Admin. L.R. 57.
[54] *R. v. PCC, ex parte Stewart-Brady* (1996) 9 Admin L.R. 274 [1997] E.M.L.R. 185.

that it would qualify as a body "certain of whose functions are functions of a public nature" within section 6(3)(b).[55]

(2) Is the claim a "public law" claim concerning a "public" function?

4-09   In the context of judicial review but, as will be seen, not in the application of the HRA,[56] a qualification has to be made to the statement that the statutory or prerogative source of a body's power will generally be decisive in deciding that it is "public" for the purposes of the judicial review procedure. Even in such cases it must be asked whether the claim is a "public law" claim. If there is a contractual relationship between the individual and the body, or if the source of its power over the individual is "contractual", it is unlikely that the function will be sufficiently "public" to come within the ambit of the judicial review procedure.[57] Even if the body whose act or decision is to be challenged is clearly a "public" body, the claim must be "public" to be litigated under the public law procedure. Judicial review is considered to be an inappropriate means of challenging a public authority when that authority is acting as a private contracting party.[58] Furthermore, individuals affected by the decision of a public body may be held not to have a public law claim against that body where they have a contractual, tortious or restitutionary claim (a "private" law claim) against a third party in respect of that decision.[59] Traditionally judicial review has also not been thought appropriate for "commercial" or "managerial" decisions.[60]

B. Public authorities properly so called: the difference between the HRA and judicial review

4-10   The second question, is the claim a "public law" one concerning a "public function", shows that, so far as judicial review is concerned, even an "obvious" public authority is not caught in respect of everything it does. Since section 6 does not specify which bodies are "public" in respect of all their functions and acts, some may argue that if not all of the functions of a body are "public", it must be a body "certain of whose functions are of a public nature" within section 6(3)(b). Therefore, by section 6(5), it is only a public body (and required to act in accordance with Convention rights) in respect of its "public" acts.

The argument in effect seeks to apply the "public law claim" limit in domestic law to the determination of the meaning of "public authority" for the purpose of section 6 of the HRA. The judicial review cases which apply the limit would be said to show that, even in the core category of "obvious" public authorities, it is not

---

[55] See Hansard, H.L. Vol. 583, November 24, 1997, cols 771–774, 783–787, 796 (Lord Chancellor). Hansard, H.C., February 16, 1998, col. 778; Hansard, H.C. Vol. 316, June 17, 1998, col. 414 (Home Secretary). See further below, para. 4–68 (HRA, s. 12).
[56] See below, para. 4.2.2.
[57] R. v. Disciplinary Committee of the Jockey Club, ex parte Aga Khan [1993] 1 W.L.R. 909; R. v. Insurance Ombudsman Bureau, ex parte Aegon Life Assurance Ltd, The Times January 7, 1994 [1994] C.L.C. 88.
[58] R. v. East Berkshire Health Authority, ex parte Walsh [1985] Q.B. 152 (dismissal of nurse); R. v. Derby CC, ex parte Noble [1990] I.C.R. 808 (dismissal of police surgeon); McLaren v. Home Office [1990] I.C.R. 824 (conditions of appointment of prison officer); R. v. Lord Chancellor, ex parte Hibbit & Saunders [1993] C.O.D. 326 (court shorthand services).
[59] R. v. Secretary of State for Employment, ex parte Equal Opportunities Commission [1995] 1 A.C. 1; Case C–167/97 R. v. Secretary of State for Employment, ex parte Seymour-Smith [1997] 1 W.L.R. 473.
[60] R. v. National Coal Board, ex parte NUM [1986] I.C.R. 791, 795 but see now Mercury Ltd v. Electricity Corp. [1994] 1 W.L.R. 521 (termination of contractual arrangements reviewable but probably only for fraud, corruption or bad faith).

possible (notwithstanding what the Lord Chancellor and the Home Secretary said about the scope of the HRA) to conclude that all their functions are public. If so, some activities and functions of central and local government, such as those characterised as "contractual", "commercial" or "managerial" would not be "public". It would follow from sections 6(3)(b) and 6(5) that section 6 would only apply to those of its acts which are of a public character.

4–11 Both textual and other considerations mean this result is unlikely. Considering the matter first from a purely textual point of view, it is to be noted that section 6(3) does not in fact furnish an exhaustive definition (or indeed any definition) of public authorities. Section 6(1) refers to a public authority without defining it and section 6(3) specifies what the term "includes"; but the "obvious" core public authorities fall within neither paragraph (a) nor paragraph (b). The first issue for the court is therefore whether a body is a "public authority" according to the ordinary understanding of that expression. Central and local government and the police would be so regarded without question. Moreover, as a matter of construction, the functional test of a public authority in section 6(5) comes into play only in respect of bodies within section 6(3)(b), i.e. which are not "obvious" public authorities according to the ordinary sense of the expression.

There are also a number of broader reasons for concluding that the domestic qualification of the concept of what is "public" is unlikely to be appropriate in the context of section 6 of the HRA. First, as we shall see, the Strasbourg jurisprudence shows that the mere fact that a relationship is contractual is not conclusive and that protection has been afforded to employment in the public service.[61] The availability of this protection in principle has often been undermined in practice by the deference shown to national bodies by the Strasbourg Court as part of the application of the doctrine of margin of appreciation.[62] But this does not affect the scope of the Convention concept of bodies that count as "the state". For the reasons given above,[63] the doctrine of margin of appreciation should not be transposed to the domestic context.

4–12 Secondly, as noted above, it is clear that the intention behind the treatment of the concept of "public authority" in section 6 was to replicate the Strasbourg concept of the state. Indirect support for this position can also be garnered from the decisions of the ECJ and the House of Lords in *Foster v. British Gas*,[64] albeit in the different context of what bodies are directly bound by the equality provisions in a European Community Directive. The ECJ had held that all organs of the administration, including decentralised authorities were bound. Those engaged in commercial activities were included, as were bodies exercising a

---

[61] *Lombardo v. Italy* (1992) (judge) 18 E.H.R.R. 205; *Scuderi v. Italy* (1993) 19 E.H.R.R. 187 (civil servant); *Darnell v. U.K.* (1993) 18 E.H.R.R. 205 (health service employee); *Muti v. Italy* (1994) Series A, No. 281–C. See also *C v. U.K.* (1987) 54 D.R. 162 (state school janitor). But claims concerning public employment have also been held to fall outside the scope of the Convention's protection, particularly where they are really claims of access to such employment and in the context of Article 6: see Harris, O'Boyle & Warbrick, *Law of the ECHR* (1995), pp. 182, 362, 381, 410. As to the application of Article 10 of the Convention to civil service employment generally see below, para. C10–23.
[62] See Clapham, *Human Rights in the Private Sphere* (1993), p. 222.
[63] See above, para. 2–05.
[64] Case 188/89 [1990] E.C.R. I–3313; [1991] 2 A.C. 306. See also Case 152/84 *Marshall v. Southampton & SW Hampshire HA* [1986] E.C.R. 723; *Fratelli Costanzo v. Commune di Milano* [1989] E.C.R. 1839; *Kampelmann v. Landschaftverband Westfalen-Lippe* [1998] I.R.L.R. 333.

function that had previously been undertaken by a state body, but which, as a result of a governmental decision (and legislation), had been privatised.[65]

Thirdly, there are the clear *Pepper v. Hart* statements by the Lord Chancellor and the Home Secretary,[66] of which perhaps the following is the clearest:

> " . . . we could not directly replicate in the Bill the definition of public authorities used by Strasbourg because, of course, the respondent to any application in the Strasbourg Court is the United Kingdom, as the state. We have therefore tried to do the best we can in terms of replication by taking into account whether the body is sufficiently public to engage the responsibility of the state . . . As we are dealing with public functions and with an evolving situation, we believe that the test must relate to the substance and nature of the act, not to the form and legal personality."[67]

4–13   Accordingly, the bodies within the core category[68] such as central and local government and inferior courts and tribunals, the police, immigration service, prisons, health authorities, NHS Trusts, the Legal Services Commission, the Criminal Injuries Compensation Board, the Parliamentary Commissioner, Local Government Ombudsmen, the Crown Prosecution Service, the Legal Services Ombudsman, the Data Protection Registrar, the Security Services and Interception of Communications Commissioners, the Planning Inspectorate, English Heritage, executive agencies and statutory regulatory bodies are obliged to act in a manner which is compatible with Convention rights in relation to *all* their activities, whether they are public or private in nature. For example, section 6 will apply to employment in the public service,[69] the keeping of employment files,[70] interception of employees' communications,[71] religious discrimination in employment,[72] and regulation of employees' political activities.[73] It is not, however, clear whether other bodies fall within this core category.[74]

There may be other differences between the location of the "public" and the "private" divide in a domestic context not involving human rights and one in which, as a result of the HRA, the Strasbourg approach must be applied. So, for example, it has been held that only state schools are amenable to the judicial review jurisdiction; other schools "fall fairly and squarely into the private sector" and the relationship between the pupils and the school is founded on contract.[75] But it has

---

[65] See for example Case 249/96 *Grant v. South West Trains* [1998] I.C.R. 428. In the context of the Convention, see *Powell & Rayner v. U.K.* (1990) 12 E.H.R.R. 355; *Baggs v. U.K.* (1987) 44 D.R. 13, 52 D.R. 29 (Heathrow Airport).

[66] See above, para. 4–02.

[67] *Hansard*, H.C. Vol. 314, cols 409–410.

[68] See above, paras 4–03, 4–07.

[69] See above, para. 4–11.

[70] See, *mutatis mutandis*, *Leander v. Sweden* (1987) 9 E.H.R.R. 433.

[71] *Halford v. United Kingdom* (1997) 24 E.H.R.R. 523.

[72] *Kalac v. Turkey* July 1, 1997 R.J.D., 1997–IV, No. 41; 27 E.H.R.R. 552.

[73] *Ahmed v. United Kingdom* judgment of September 2, 1998. *Rekvennyi v. Hungary* (Application No. 25390/94) May 20, 1999.

[74] See above, para. 4–07 for examples not within the core category. Lord Williams of Mostyn stated (*Hansard*, H.L. Vol. 583, November 3, 1997, cols 1309–1310) that, while the matter was for courts to decide as the jurisprudence develops, the Government anticipated that the BBC would be a public authority and that Channel 4 might be one but that private television stations might not be. For examples of judicial review proceedings against the BBC, see *R. v. BBC, ex parte Lavelle* [1983] 1 W.L.R. 23; *R. v. BBC, ex parte Quintavelle* (1998) 10 Admin. L.R. 425; *R. v. British Broadcasting Company and Another, ex parte Referendum Party* [1997] E.M.L.R. 605.

[75] *R. v. Fernhill Manor School, ex parte Brown* (1993) 5 Admin. L.R. 175. See Bamforth [1998] P.L. 572. For other examples of applications for judicial review which have not succeeded because the body or the issue was not considered "public" see above, para. 4–08.

been held that the U.K. government can be liable for the violation of human rights in the disciplinary systems of independent schools since they co-exist with a system of public education and since the Convention right to education is guaranteed to pupils in all schools.[76] The development of the Strasbourg jurisprudence on bodies for which the state is responsible has been further affected by the existence of positive duties on Member States to secure protection of Convention rights. Where the Strasbourg institutions hold that the Convention imposes a positive duty on the state to protect individuals against violations of Convention rights by other individuals, it is not necessary to decide whether the body that infringed the right in question was a "public authority". Thus, in the *Young, James & Webster* case concerning dismissal of workers for refusing to join a union in a closed shop,[77] it was not necessary to decide whether the employer, the nationalised British Rail, was a "public authority" for which the state is responsible.[78]

4–14 Finally it should be emphasised that the Strasbourg institutions have insisted upon giving an "autonomous" meaning of Convention terms,[79] asserting that the reach of the Convention is not to be limited by the application of domestic law concepts. Although the characterisation in national law is a relevant factor, it will not be conclusive, since otherwise the scope of application of the Convention could differ from one state to the other depending on the whims of domestic law. The location of the distinction between "public" and "private" may itself fall to be determined by Strasbourg in appropriate cases. Thus in *Chassagnou & ors v. France,*[80] the applicants submitted that their freedom of association had been violated because by law they had against their will been made automatic members of an approved municipal hunters' association, which the law did not permit them to leave. The court rejected the Government's argument that the associations were public law bodies and accordingly outside the scope of Article 11. According to the court it was not a question of whether French law classified them as public or private law bodies, but whether they were associations for the purposes of Article 11:

> "If Contracting States were able, at their discretion, by classifying an association as 'public' or 'para-administrative', to remove it from the scope of Article 11, that would give them such latitude that it might lead to results incompatible with the object and purpose of the Convention, which is to protect rights that are not theoretical or illusory but practical and effective . . . The term "association" therefore possesses an autonomous meaning; the classification in national law has only relative value and constitutes no more than a starting-point."[81]

---

[76] *Y v. U.K.* (1992) 17 E.H.R.R. 233, *Edwards v. U.K.* (1992) 15 E.H.R.R. 417, *Costello-Roberts v. U.K.* (1993) (corporal punishment).
[77] June 26, 1981, Series A, No. 44; 4 E.H.R.R. 38.
[78] See below, paras 4–49, C0–16 in respect of positive duties.
[79] *Ringeisen v. Austria* (1971) 1 E.H.R.R. 455 and *Konig v. FRG* (1978) 2 E.H.R.R. 170 ("civil right" in Article 6); *Engel v. Netherlands* (1976) 1 E.H.R.R. 647 ("criminal charge" in Article 6); *Deweer v. Belgium* (1980) 2 E.H.R.R. 439 and *Funke v. France* (1993) 16 E.H.R.R. 297 ("accused" in Article 6); In *Welch v. United Kingdom* (1995) 20 E.H.R.R. 247 ("penalty" in Article 7); *Matos e Silva LDA & ors v. Portugal* September 16, 1996, R.J.D., 1996–IV, No. 14; (1997) 24 E.H.R.R. 573 ("possessions" in Article 1 of the First Protocol).
[80] Judgment of April 29, 1999. See below, para. C0–07 on "autonomous concepts".
[81] para. 100 of the judgment.

The converse proposition also holds good. The Convention will not be excluded by the mere fact that national law classifies a body as one governed by private law.

C. Court and tribunals

4–15 By section 6(3)(b) of the HRA, "public authority" includes a court or tribunal and, as with public authorities properly so called, the Act applies to anything done by a court or tribunal. The duty to act compatibly with Convention rights will apply not only to judicial acts, but also to listing and other administrative functions of the court, such as dealings with court funds, issuing of proceedings and applications, correspondence, and the employment of court staff. The duty will apply in any proceedings, including those between private parties.[82] For the purposes of discussion, the obligations arising from the judicial acts of courts and tribunals can be classified as those which are addressed directly to the courts and those which arise indirectly.

(1) Obligations placed directly on courts and tribunals

4–16 Certain articles of the Convention are directed specifically at the activities of the courts. Direct obligations may be regarded as those where the order of the court, or the procedure it adopts, may amount to a violation of Convention rights.

Courts and tribunals which adjudicate on "civil rights or obligations" will be bound by the guarantees of fair trial and access to courts contained in Article 6(1) of the Convention.[83] These guarantees apply to all proceedings relating to civil rights or obligations, whether both parties are private or one party is a public authority. So, as a general rule hearings must be public and judgments must be pronounced publicly. The approach of Article 6 is reflected in Rule 39.2(2) and (3) of the Civil Procedure Rules. A hearing may take place in private only when the specific circumstances set out in Article 6 are satisfied.[84] In the case of small claims, formerly often dealt with by county court arbitration in chambers, this has resulted in a significant change.[85] When a hearing is held in private what happened is not confidential and information about the proceedings can be made public when requested, and the judgment should be so made available.[86] A court determining criminal charges, including courts-martial,[87] will in addition be bound to respect the minimum guarantees of criminal procedure contained in Articles 6(2) and (3).[88] Courts with powers to order detention, or bail or other release from detention, or to review the lawfulness of detention, will be bound to apply the provisions of Article 5. Any court or tribunal dealing with Convention rights must also take

---

[82] *Hansard*, H.L. Vol. 583, November 24, 1997, col. 783 (Lord Chancellor).

[83] For a commentary on Article 6, see below, paras C6–02 *et seq.*

[84] *i.e.* that a private hearing is required in the interest of morals, public order or national security, the interests of juveniles, the protection of the private life of the parties, or "to the extent strictly necessary in the opinion of the court in special circumstances where publicity would prejudice the interests of justice". Rule 39.2(3) sets out the Article 6 exceptions and also specifically includes cases in which there is information relating to personal financial matters, hearings without notice where it would be unjust to the respondent for the hearing to be public, and uncontentious matters in the administration of estates or trusts. The Practice Direction (39P.D.–001) fleshes out the exceptions.

[85] See CPR, Pt 27 and 27P.D.–001 para. 4.1(1) (hearing in public unless parties agree, a ground in r. 39.2(3) applies, or the hearing takes place other than at the court). See also *Scarth v. United Kingdom*, Application No. 33745/96, judgment of July 22, 1999: holding of county court arbitration proceedings in private violated right to a public hearing under Article 6(1).

[86] *Hodgson v. Imperial Tobacco* [1998] 2 All E.R. 673, esp. 684–687.

[87] *Findlay v. United Kingdom*, February 25, 1997, R.J.D., 1997–I, No. 30.

[88] See below, paras C6–81—C6–108.

account of the obligation under Article 13 to provide an effective remedy, even though that Article is not listed among the Convention rights in Schedule 1 to the Act.[89]

(2) General and indirect obligations which also bind courts

4–17 An order of a court may itself violate a Convention right, even in proceedings where no public authority is involved. For example, a judgment or award in defamation proceedings may raise an issue of freedom of expression under Article 10 of the Convention[90]; an order that a journalist disclose the source of his or her information, even though made at the instance of another private litigant, may also amount to a violation of Article 10[91]; as may the grant of an injunction restraining publication[92]; or the grant of an order banning exhibition of a film[93]; the making of an *Anton Piller* order order (now known as a search order[94]) may raise property issues under Article 1 of the First Protocol[95]; orders of the court in family matters may deprive a party of his or her right to respect for family life under Article 8[96]; or in a property dispute, an order may deprive a person of property rights to which the Convention entitles him or her.[97]

In the examples given in the previous paragraph, the order of the court itself interferes with the enjoyment of a Convention right. The injunction restraining publication, or the damages award in the libel proceedings, prevents or impedes the exercise of the right of freedom of expression; likewise the disclosure order. However, where the Convention also imposes a positive obligation to secure respect of certain rights, a court's failure to grant relief to an individual against interference with the right by a another private party may itself amount to a violation of the Convention right in issue.[98] This is of particular importance in relation to interferences with private and family life,[99] and in relation to the right to life; although it may arise also in other circumstances.[1] In these limited circumstances, therefore, the court's liability under section 6(1) will be engaged if it fails to grant a remedy to an individual, even though the "primary" violation of his rights has been suffered at the hands of another individual.

We consider below[2] the argument that section 6(3) subjects courts and tribunals to the section 6(1) duty not to act in a way which is incompatible with a

---

[89] See above, para. 1–06; below paras C3–01 *et seq.*

[90] *Lingens v. Austria* (1986) 8 E.H.R.R. 103, *Tolstoy Miloslavsky v. U.K.* (1995) 20 E.H.R.R. 442. See also *Rantzen v. Mirror Group Newspapers* [1994] Q.B. 670; *Reynolds v. Times Newspapers Ltd and ors.* [1998] 3 W.L.R. 675, petition allowed [1999] 1 W.L.R. 478.

[91] *X v. Morgan Grampian* [1991] 1 A.C. 1; *Michael O'Mara Books Ltd v. Express Newspapers plc and others* [1999] F.S.R. 49 [1998] E.M.L.R. 383; *Camelot v. Centaur Communications* [1998] I.R.L.R. 80, CA. *Goodwin v. United Kingdom*, March 27, 1996, R.J.D.; 1996–II, No. 7; 22 E.H.R.R. 123. On orders to disclose privileged documents, see *General Mediterranean Holdings SA v. Patel* [1999] 3 All E.R. 673.

[92] *Sunday Times v. United Kingdom* (1979) 2 E.H.R.R. 245; *Observer & Guardian v. United Kingdom* (1991) 14 E.H.R.R. 153.

[93] *Otto Preminger Institut v. Austria* (1994) 19 E.H.R.R. 34.

[94] C.P.R. 25.1(h).

[95] *Chappell v. United Kingdom* (1990) 12 E.H.R.R. 1.

[96] For example, care and custody of children. See below, paras C8–23—C8–30 and *McMichael v. U.K.* (1995) 20 E.H.R.R. 205; *Hendricks v. Netherlands* (1982) 29 D.R. 5 (private proceedings).

[97] For example forfeiture of an entitlement to rent (*Mellacher v. Austria* (1983) 12 E.H.R.R. 391) or to exercise a profession (*Von Marle v. Netherlands* (1986) 8 E.H.R.R. 343). See further below, para. P1/1–12.

[98] See, for example, *X & Y v. Netherlands* (1985) 8 E.H.R.R. 235; *Marckx v. Belgium* (1979) 2 E.H.R.R. 330. See below, paras C0–06, C0–16.

[99] As to the relationship between privacy and freedom of expression, see below, s. 12, paras 4–61 *et seq.*

[1] See, for example, *Young, James and Webster v. United Kingdom* (1981) 4 E.H.R.R. 38; *Plattform 'Artzte fur das Leben'* (1991) 13 E.H.R.R. 204, para. 32.

[2] See paras 4–45 *et seq.*

Convention right in *all* proceedings, whether the defendant is a public authority or a private person; i.e. impliedly to require *direct* horizontal effect to be given to Convention rights is considered below.

D.   Other persons exercising functions of a public nature

4-18   The obligation to respect Convention rights is also imposed on any person certain of whose functions are of a public nature; but such a person is not a public authority if the nature of the particular act in issue is private.[3] It is this class of public authority which occupied much time during the passage of the Bill. Critics considered that the expression was too vague to be workable, and suggested that the provision be limited, for example by publication of a list of bodies to be regarded as public authorities. As discussed above, the intention of the broad approach is to ensure that the Act covers bodies for which the government would be responsible under the Convention before the Strasbourg institutions. Only in this way can Convention rights be "brought home", in the sense that individuals will be able to obtain remedies before national courts and tribunals rather than having to apply to Strasbourg. The Strasbourg case law on state responsibility will therefore be of considerable importance.[4]

4-19   The case law relating to amenability to judicial review, discussed above,[5] will also play a large part in determining what are functions of a public nature for the purposes of the Act. The position was explained in the following way by the parliamentary Under-Secretary of State to the Home Office, Lord Williams of Mostyn, during the Bill's Second Reading in the House of Lords:

> "The noble and learned Lord, Lord Simon of Glaisdale asked what would or would not be a public body. He rightly conjectured that we would anticipate the BBC being a public authority and that Channel 4 might well be a public authority, but that other commercial organisations, such as private television stations, might well not be public authorities. I stress that this is a matter for the courts to decide as the jurisprudence develops. Some authorities plainly exercise wholly public functions; others do not. There is no difficulty here . . . Perhaps I may cite Railtrack as a simple example. It is the statutory safety regulator, but equally it carries out private functions of property development or property acquisition. It is perfectly easy for the judiciary, which is as well accustomed as is ours to questions of judicial review, to resolve such problems. It is a mistake to think that we are hobbling authorities because they are now private whereas they used to be public utilities. The point is not the label or description; it is the function. I hope that I have made that plain."[6]

This class of public authority will include professional bodies such as the Law Society,[7] the Bar Council[8] and the General Medical Council[9] which exercise

---

[3] s. 6(5).
[4] See above, Ch. 2, paras 4–11—4–12. The case law of the Court of Justice of the European Communities on what constitutes the "State" for the purpose of the application of the doctrine of direct effect of directives may also be of assistance. See for example *Foster v. British Gas plc* [1991] 1 A.C. 1; *Fratelli Costanzo v. Commune di Milano* [1989] E.C.R. 1839; *Kampelmann v. Landschaftverband Westfalen-Lippe* [1998] I.R.L.R. 333.
[5] See paras 4–06—4–09.
[6] *Hansard*, H.L., November 3, 1997, cols. 1309–1310.
[7] *R. v. The Law Society, ex parte Mortgage Express* [1978] A.C. 247; *R. v. The Law Society, ex parte Reigate Projects* [1993] 1 W.L.R. 1531. See also *R. v. Solicitors Complaints Bureau, ex parte Singh & Choudry* (1995) 7 Admin. L.R. 249.
[8] *R. v. General Council of the Bar, ex parte Percival* [1991] 2 Q.B. 212. See also *R. v. Visitors to Lincoln's Inn, ex parte Calder* [1994] Q.B. 1.
[9] *R. v. GMC, ex parte Colman* [1990] 1 All E.R. 489.

regulatory and disciplinary functions; private commercial organisations exercising public functions such as security companies operating privatised prisons, private schools,[10] a railway company in the exercise of its regulatory functions[11], industry based ombudsmen, university visitors[12], regulatory bodies such as the City Panel on Takeovers and Mergers,[13] those recognised under the Financial Services Act 1986,[14] the Stock Exchange,[15] the Association of the British Pharmaceutical Industry,[16] the Press Complaints Commission,[17] the Advertising Standards Authority[18] and other media or commercial regulators.[19]

4–20   A person or body in this class falls within section 6(3)(b) of the HRA since only "certain" of its functions are functions of a public nature. Accordingly, by section 6(5), in relation to a particular act, such a person or body is not a "public authority" if the nature of the act is private. It is obliged to comply with the Convention only in respect of the exercise of its public functions. When it is acting in a private capacity, for example as an employer, a commercial enterprise or a representative of a profession[20] it is not treated as a public authority.

E.   Excluded acts of public authorities

(1)   Statutory requirement

4–21   The HRA excludes two classes of acts of public authorities from the ambit of the new wrong; (1) acts done pursuant to a statutory requirement; and (2) failure to legislate. By section 6(2) of the HRA, a public authority is not liable for doing an act which is incompatible with a Convention right if:

> "(a) as a result of one or more provisions of primary legislation, the authority could not have acted differently; or
> (b) in the case of one or more provisions of, or made under, primary legislation which cannot be read or given effect in a way which is compatible with the Convention rights, the authority was acting so as to give effect to or enforce those provisions."

The application of the first part of the exception is relatively straightforward. Having established that the act of a public authority is *prima facie* incompatible with a Convention right, one must next look at any provisions of primary legislation under which the authority purported to act. Interpreting those provisions compatibly with Convention rights, so far as it is possible to do so,[21] it must

---

[10] *Costello-Roberts v. United Kingdom* (1995) 19 E.H.R.R. 112.
[11] Lord Williams of Mostyn, *loc. cit.* n. 69 above.
[12] *R. v. Hull University Visitor, ex parte Page* [1993] A.C. 682.
[13] *R. v. Panel on Takeovers and Mergers, ex parte Datafin plc* [1987] Q.B. 815, (CA).
[14] *R. v. Lautro, ex parte Ross* [1993] Q.B. 17.
[15] *R. v. ISE of the U.K. and Ireland, ex parte Else* [1993] Q.B. 534.
[16] *R. v. Code of Practice Committee, ex parte Professional Counselling Aids Ltd* (1991) 3 Admin. L.R. 697.
[17] *R. v. Press Complaints Commission, ex parte Stewart-Brady* [1997] E.M.L.R. 185 (1996) 9 Admin. L.R. 274 (CA). The court left open the question whether the PCC was amenable to judicial review. However, the preponderance of opinion during the passage of the Bill was that it would be a public authority: see discussion of s. 12, below, para. 4–68.
[18] *R. v. Advertising Standards Authority, ex parte Insurance Service plc* (1990) 2 Admin. L.R. 77 (DC).
[19] See Lord Lester, *Hansard*, H.L., November 24, 1997, col. 775.
[20] See above, paras 4–09, 4–11.
[21] s. 3(1), and see above, Ch. 3.

be asked whether the authority could have acted differently. Where a compatible interpretation is possible, it will be possible to conclude that the provision did not require the authority to contravene Convention rights, that it could have acted differently, and consequently its act will be unlawful. The court should adopt an approach similar to that adopted in respect of section 41(1)(b) of the Race Relations Act 1976, which provides a defence to an act done "in pursuance of any instrument made under or any enactment by a Minister of the Crown". In *Hampson v. Department of Education & Science*,[22] the House of Lords held that this protected only acts done in the *necessary* performance of an express obligation in the instrument and did not extend to acts done in the exercise of a power or discretion conferred by the instrument. Lord Lowry, with whom their Lordships agreed, was influenced by a submission that an enactment *requiring* racial discrimination could be subject to parliamentary scrutiny, whereas if what is done is not *necessary* to comply with the statutory requirement, there is no valid reason why it should not have to be justified before an industrial tribunal. A similar argument of policy clearly applies to the scrutiny of statutory requirements and powers in relation to the HRA.

4-22   Where the legislation cannot be interpreted in this way, it might be argued that the answer to the question whether the authority could have acted differently in the circumstances may depend on whether primary legislation imposed a duty or merely conferred a power. If it imposes a duty to act, the authority is obliged to act in the manner dictated by primary legislation and could not have acted differently.[23] If the legislation merely confers a power,[24] however, it might be contended that the authority could have acted differently, by refraining from exercising the power at all. There are two objections to this argument. First, a refusal ever to exercise a power in principle constitutes an improper fetter on discretion.[25] Secondly, if *any* exercise of the power would involve a breach of Convention rights, the position is covered by the second part of the exception in section 6(2)(b), to which we now turn.

The purpose of section 6(2)(b) is to enable incompatible primary legislation to remain fully effective. It makes clear that so long as the primary legislation remains in force, a public authority is not obliged to neutralise that legislation by treating it as a dead letter. It does this by protecting an authority where it is acting so as to "give effect to or enforce" (i) one or more provisions of primary legislation; or (ii) one or more provisions made under primary legislation, in either case where the primary legislation cannot be read or given effect in a way which is compatible with Convention rights. In such a case, it will not be possible to interpret the subordinate provisions compatibly with the Convention, nor can incompatible provisions of subordinate legislation be declared *ultra vires* or quashed. Either course would be tantamount to striking down the primary legislation under which

---

[22] [1990] I.R.L.R. 302.
[23] See above, paras 3–18 *et seq.*.
[24] For example powers to search property (Police and Criminal Evidence Act 1984, ss. 18, 32), to release prisoners before the completion of their sentence (Criminal Justice Act 1991, Pt II, as amended by the Crime and Disorder Act 1998), to admit or remove non-citizens (Immigration Act 1971, ss. 3, 5, Asylum and Immigration Appeals Act 1996, Sched. 2, para. 1(2)), to restrict the freedom of movement of citizens (Prevention of Terrorism (Temporary Provisions) Act 1989, s. 5, considered in *R. v. Secretary of State for the Home Department, ex parte McQuillan* [1995] 4 All E.R. 400.
[25] *R. v. Secretary of State for the Home Department, ex parte Fire Brigades Union* [1995] 2 A.C. 513; *William Cory & Son Ltd v. City of London Corp.* [1951] 2 K.B. 475.

the subordinate provisions were adopted which, as we have seen, is contrary to the general scheme of the HRA embodied in sections 3(2)(b) and (c) and 4(6)(a).[26] Accordingly, the statutory requirement stands and the authority is not acting unlawfully. But where provisions of primary legislation can be interpreted compatibly with Convention rights, an authority acts unlawfully if it seeks to give effect to or enforce those provisions in an incompatible manner. Similarly, provisions made under such legislation must be interpreted compatibly or, if that is not possible, quashed or declared *ultra vires*: in either such case, an authority will be acting without lawful authority and unlawfully if it acts in a manner which is incompatible with Convention rights.[27]

(2) Failure to legislate

4–23   Although an unlawful "act" includes a failure to act, section 6(6) of the HRA provides that it does not include a failure to introduce, or lay before Parliament, a proposal for legislation; or to make any primary legislation or a remedial order.

This exclusion is intended to prevent the courts adjudicating directly upon the issue whether primary legislation should be enacted, an issue which is constitutionally reserved to Parliament and the government. Under the scheme of the Act, a higher court can draw Parliament's attention to a legislative incompatibility with a Convention right by making a declaration of incompatibility.[28] However, it cannot strike down or disapply incompatible legislation (other than *ultra vires* subordinate legislation)and it would therefore be inconsistent with the statutory scheme to make a Minister liable for a failure to introduce legislation (whether by a proposal for primary legislation or by remedial order) to remove an incompatibility.[29]

During the Committee Stage of the Bill in the House of Lords, Lord Ackner[30] drew attention to cases where a state is under a positive obligation to protect Convention rights, so that the absence of legislation could itself amount to a violation.[31] The Lord Chancellor responded in the following terms:

---

[26] This is not so where removal of the incompatibility is not prevented by statute: see s. 10(4), dealing with the making of remedial orders, which expressly contemplates that subordinate legislation may be quashed, or declared invalid by reason of incompatibility with a Convention right. As to remedial orders generally, see below, paras 6–23 et seq.

[27] The legal effect of subordinate legislation which is declared invalid (*e.g. DPP v. Hutchinson* [1990] 2 A.C. 783; *Boddington v. British Transport Police* [1998] 2 W.L.R. 639) raises difficult questions (Forsyth, [1998] P.L. 364, De Smith, Woolf & Jowell, *Judicial Review of Administrative Action* (5th ed.), paras 5–044–5–056) which we do not ignore. However, the HRA appears to favour the view that such legislation would be ineffective to provide lawful justification: see, for example ss. 6(2)(b) (in relation to subordinate legislation made under primary legislation which can be read compatibly with Convention rights) and 10(4). Indeed the contrary argument would run counter to the scheme of the Convention itself, which requires, for example, that restrictions on certain rights must be "in accordance with the law" or "prescribed by law" (Articles 8, 9, 10 and 11), and that arrest and detention must be "lawful" (Article 5). These requirements include compliance with domestic law. See further *Percy & another v. Hall* [1997] Q.B. 924, CA, in which the court concluded that an action for false imprisonment did not lie in respect of arrest pursuant to byelaws which were subsequently held to be invalid. This decision will have to be reconsidered in the light of the HRA. See also *R. v. Governor of Brockhill Prison, ex parte Evans* [1999] 2 W.L.R. 103.

[28] ss. 4(2) and (4); see above, para. 3–47.

[29] Compare the position of E.C. legislation: *R. v. Secretary of State for Employment, ex parte Equal Opportunities Commission* [1995] 1 A.C. 1. *R. v. Secretary of State for Transport, ex parte Factortame (No. 2)* [1991] 1 A.C. 603; *(No. 3)* [1992] 2 Q.B. 680; *(No. 4)* [1996] Q.B. 404.

[30] *Hansard*, H.L., November 24, 1997, col. 813.

[31] See, for example, *X & Y v. Netherlands* (1985) 8 E.H.R.R. 235 and *A v. United Kingdom* (1998) 2 F.L.R. 959; *Marckx v. Belgium* (1979) 2 E.H.R.R. 330; *Plattform 'Ärzte für das Leben' v. Austria* (1991) 13 E.H.R.R. 204.

"If a person believes that his Convention rights have been violated as a result of action by a public authority which is not governed by legislation the right course is for him to bring legal proceedings against the authority under Clause 7 of the Bill or to rely on his Convention rights in any other legal proceedings to which he and the authority are a party. If the court finds in his favour it will be able to grant whatever remedy is within its jurisdiction and appears just and appropriate. The fact that there is no specific legislation for the court to declare incompatible with the Convention does not affect the ability of the person concerned to obtain a remedy. The absence of legislation means that there is no legislative warrant for acts in breach of the Convention.[32] The Minister, however . . . is protected by Clause 6(6) from any claim that he is in breach by failing to bring forward legislation. That is part of the scheme of the Bill to underpin parliamentary sovereignty.

Further, the purpose of a declaration of incompatibility is to allow the courts to make a public statement that they cannot interpret legislation in a way which is incompatible [sic] with Convention rights. It is just not possible to do so. This provides a trigger for the power to make a remedial order in Clause 10. Because the Bill protects public authorities which are acting so as to give effect to primary legislation, even if the action is incompatible with Convention rights, there is nothing that the courts can do to provide a remedy to the person affected by their actions. That is why the power to make a declaration of incompatibility is needed in these cases. There is no corresponding need to make a declaration of incompatibility in cases where the problem is an absence of legislation, because there is nothing to stop the courts providing a remedy in those cases. There is no legislative bar or block on the courts doing so."[33]

4-24 This explanation does not answer Lord Ackner's point that there may be cases in which a failure to legislate will itself violate the Convention where the state has a positive obligation to secure the enjoyment of Convention rights against the acts of persons other than public authorities.[34] Moreover, the Lord Chancellor's position set out above is difficult to reconcile with what he said on Second Reading:

"In my opinion, the court is not obliged to remedy the failure by legislating via the common law either where a Convention right is infringed by incompatible legislation or where, because of the absence of legislation–say, privacy legislation–a Convention right is left unprotected. In my view, the courts may not act as legislators and grant new remedies for infringement of Convention rights *unless the common law itself enables them to develop new rights or remedies.* I believe that the true view is that the courts will be able to adapt and develop the common law by relying on existing domestic principles in the law of trespass, nuisance, copyright, confidence and the like, to fashion a common law right to privacy . . . They may have regard to the Convention in developing the common law, as they do today and . . . it is right that they should."[35]

The courts are likely to accept this invitation, and in such cases a court will probably do all that it can in the performance of its duty as public authority to

---

[32] *i.e.* no defence is available to the authority under s. 6(2).
[33] *Hansard*, H.L., November 24, 1997, cols. 814–815.
[34] *Marckx v. Belgium* (1979) 2 E.H.R.R. 330; *X & Y v. Netherlands* (1985) 8 E.H.R.R. 235; *A v. U.K.*, *The Times*, October 1, 1998 See below, paras C0–05, CO–16.
[35] *Hansard*, H.L., November 3, 1997, col.785, emphasis added.

adapt the common law to provide remedies to individuals against other individuals.[36]

A failure to introduce in, or lay before Parliament, a proposal for primary legislation is not reviewable in the courts on general principle.[37] Moreover, by section 6(6), failure to make a remedial order does not constitute an unlawful act under section 6(1). However, although Orders in Council made under the Prerogative are treated as primary legislation under the Act,[38] the courts have reviewed the use of the Royal Prerogative to legislate.[39] It is in principle possible for failure to make a remedial order to be reviewable on general public law grounds although it is not an unlawful act under section 6(1). But save in an extreme case a challenge is unlikely to succeed. Apart from the general structure of the HRA and the reluctance of the courts to review broad policy questions, it is possible that a failure to make a remedial order will be treated as in the same category as failure to legislate.

3. WHO MAY BRING PROCEEDINGS IN RESPECT OF UNLAWFUL ACTS OF PUBLIC AUTHORITIES: THE "VICTIM" REQUIREMENT

4–25 Where it is alleged that a public authority has acted in a way which is made unlawful by section 6(1) of the HRA, only a person who claims that he or she is or would be a victim of the unlawful act in question may bring a claim against a public authority under section 7.[40] Similarly, if the proceedings are by an application for judicial review, only an actual or potential victim of the act is to be taken to have a sufficient interest[41] under RSC, Order 53, rule 3(7). A person is a victim of an unlawful act only if he would be a victim for the purposes of Article 34, formerly Article 25, of the Convention.[42] The Commission and Court have emphasised that the conditions governing individual applications under Article 34 are not necessarily the same as national criteria relating to *locus standi*.[43] It is clear that the requirement of victim status is in most respects narrower than the general test of "sufficient interest" on an application for judicial review. In particular, it is likely to exclude non-governmental organisations who are able to bring "public interest" challenges by way of an application for judicial review in respect of non-HRA issues. But the fact that victim status will include potential victims, for example members of a class of person who are likely to be affected by legislation which has not yet been applied to them,[44] may mean that relief for infringement of Convention rights will be available in circumstances in which an application for judicial review in respect of non-HRA issues will not.[45]

---

[36] See further below, paras 4–53 *et seq.*

[37] See *R. v. Secretary of State for Employment, ex parte Equal Opportunities Commission* [1995] 1 A.C. 1.

[38] s. 21(1).

[39] *R. v. Secretary of State for the Home Department, ex parte Fire Brigades Union* [1995] 2 A.C. 513.

[40] s. 7(1).

[41] s. 7(3). s. 7(4) applies the identical rule to the requirement of title and interest in proceedings by way of petition for judicial review in Scotland. An attempt to amend the HRA by the substitution of the "sufficient interest" test for raising s. 6(1) points in judicial review proceedings failed: *Hansard*, H.L. Vol. 585, February 5, 1998, cols. 805–812.

[42] s. 7(7). See above, para. 2–02 on the effect of the Strasbourg case law on "victim". For a detailed commentary on the "victim" requirement, see Harris, O'Boyle and Warbrick, *The Law of the European Convention on Human Rights* (1995), pp. 632–638.

[43] *e.g. Norris v. Ireland* (1988) 13 E.H.R.R. 186, para. 31, App. 25052/94; *Andronicou v. Cyprus* (1995) 20 E.H.R.R. C.D. 105 (admissibility decision).

[44] See further below, para. 4–26.

[45] See further below, para. 4–31.

This section examines the Strasbourg case law on the meaning of victim, which, unlike other case law, is arguably incorporated into domestic law by section 7(7) of the Act.[46] This case law is then compared with the domestic rules on standing in order to identify the differences. Finally, the policy arguments for and against a limitation on standing are examined and in the light of these considerations the proper extent of the limitation is considered.

A. The Strasbourg case law on "victim"

4-26   The Strasbourg "victim" case law is similar to the domestic "sufficiency of interest" test in denying standing to people who have only an abstract general interest in an alleged infringement of the Convention. The Court of Human Rights has repeatedly stated that no *actio popularis* or right to bring proceedings about the law in abstract exists under the former Article 25 of the Convention, now Article 34, and, although associations can be 'victims' if their rights have been infringed,[47] governmental organisations cannot be.[48] The Court has, however, equally stressed the need, in a human rights context, to construe standing flexibly and effectively.[49] For example, the Court stated that the existence of a law permitting covert telephone tapping "by itself violates the rights of the individual if the individual is directly affected by the law in the absence of any specific measure of implementation",[50] or "if [he] run[s] the risk of being directly affected by it."[51] Individuals have been permitted to complain about laws which have not yet been applied to them in cases concerning, among other matters, the criminalisation of homosexual conduct in private between consenting adult males,[52] legislation discriminating against children born out of wedlock,[53] legislation preventing unmarried people from adopting children,[54] constitutional provisions preventing police officers from engaging in political activities,[55] and the consequences for certain family relationships of the unavailability of divorce in Ireland.[56] Women of child bearing age have been accorded standing to challenge restrictions on access to information about abortion,[57] fathers have been accorded standing to challenge abortion laws,[58] and the families of deceased victims to complain on the deceased's behalf as well as their own.[59]

---

[46] See above, para. 2–02.

[47] For example, it is clearly established that a trade union may bring a complaint for a breach of Article 11 of the Convention: *National Union of Belgian Police v. Belgium* (1975) 1 E.H.R.R. 578. See also *Council of Civil Service Unions v. U.K.* (1987) 50 D.R. 228.

[48] Article 34 only provides for applications by a "non-governmental organisation". See *Ayuntamiento de M v. Spain* (1991) 68 D. & R. 209.

[49] In *Loizidou v. Turkey* (1995) 20 E.H.R.R. 99, the ECHR Court expressly held that the "living instrument" approach was not confined to the substantive Convention provisions but also applies to procedural provisions, including Article 25 (para. 71, at p. 133); it added that: " . . . the object and purpose of the Convention as an instrument for the protection of human beings require that its provisions be interpreted and applied so as to make its safeguards practical and effective" (para. 72, *ibid.*).

[50] *Klass v. Germany* (1978) 2 E.H.R.R. 214, para. 33.

[51] *Marckx v. Belgium* (1979) 2 E.H.R.R. 330, para. 27.

[52] *Dudgeon v. United Kingdom* (1981) 4 E.H.R.R. 149; *Norris v. Ireland* (1991) 13 E.H.R.R. 186.

[53] *Marckx v. Belgium* (1979) 2 E.H.R.R. 330.

[54] App No. 31924/96 *Di Lazzaro v. Italy*.

[55] App No. 25390/94 *Rekvenyi v. Hungary*, judgment of May 20, 1999.

[56] *Johnston v. Ireland* (1987) 9 E.H.R.R. 203.

[57] *Open Door Counselling and Dublin Well Woman v. Ireland* (1993) 15 E.H.R.R. 244.

[58] *Paton v. U.K.* (1980) 3 E.H.R.R. 409.

[59] *McCann, Farrell & Savage v. United Kingdom* (1996) 21 E.H.R.R. 97; *Osman v. United Kingdom* (1996) 22 E.H.R.R. C.D. 137 [1999] 1 F.L.R. 193; *Andronicou & Constantinou v. Cyprus* (1997) 25 E.H.R.R. 491.

4–27   Notwithstanding these examples of a broad approach to the concept of "victim", it is important to note that the Strasbourg case law about "victims" has its inconsistencies and complexities. For example, the Commission's decision in *App. No. 10039/82 Leigh and Others v. United Kingdom*[60] takes a narrower approach than the cases mentioned in the previous paragraph. A journalist and two newspapers alleged that their right to receive and impart information had been interfered with by the House of Lords'[61] decision that a solicitor had acted in contempt of court when she allowed the first applicant to inspect confidential documents which had been read out in a public hearing. They claimed that their sources of information had been adversely affected because recipients of documents disclosed on discovery which had been read out in court would be unwilling to permit inspection of such documents. The Commission, however, considered that:

> "the concept of 'victim' in Article 25(1) [now Article 34] may not be interpreted so broadly as to encompass every newspaper or journalist in the United Kingdom who might conceivably be affected by the decision of the House of Lords. The form of detriment must be of a less indirect and remote nature."

Accordingly, the important issue of access to information, by the very journalist who was involved in the case in question, did not receive examination; he was denied standing.[62] The case must be contrasted with *Open Door Counselling and Dublin Well Woman v. Ireland*.[63] The Commission and Court considered that a Supreme Court injunction restraining some of the applicants from providing information about abortions abroad to pregnant women directly affected two other applicants who, although not pregnant, were of child-bearing age. The more personal nature of the individual interests at stake in the second case must be held to account for the different outcome on the victim issue.

B.   Effect of redress at national level

4–28   The Convention organs have repeatedly held that "the question of the existence of prejudice is not a matter for Article 34 which, in its use of the word 'victim', denotes 'the person directly affected by the act or the omission which is in issue'."[64] There exist, however, cases where the applicants were not held to be "victims" for the purposes of what is now Article 34 because the harm they had suffered had already been remedied at the national level.

Donnelly and six others v. United Kingdom,[65] concerned ill-treatment in custody. The Commission considered that some of the applicants could not claim to be victims of acts in violation of Article 3 because they had, by using the local remedies available, received and accepted compensation. Again, in *App. No. 9320/81 v. Germany*,[66] the Commission, concluded that a favourable judicial settlement of the applicant's action for damages had remedied any prejudice

---

[60] (1984) 38 D. & R. 74.
[61] *Home Office v. Harman* [1983] 1 A.C. 280.
[62] Compare the approach in *R. v. Felixstowe JJ., ex parte Leigh* [1987] Q.B. 582 in which the same journalist successfully challenged the refusal of a magistrate to identify herself.
[63] (1993) 15 E.H.R.R. 244.
[64] *Marckx v. Belgium* (1979) 2 E.H.R.R. 330, para. 27; *Prager & Oberschlick v. Austria* (1995) 21 E.H.R.R. 1; *Groppera Radio AG v. Switzerland* (1990) 12 E.H.R.R. 321.
[65] App. Nos. 5577–5583/72, 4 D. & R. 4.
[66] 36 D. & R. 24.

resulting from possible violations of his right to a fair hearing within a reasonable time.[67] However, the compensation awarded must be attributable to the violation of the Convention alleged by the applicant. Thus, an applicant who was detained in police custody on a particular charge and then acquitted following trial was compensated by the deduction of the time he had spent in custody from the prison sentence imposed upon him in other criminal proceedings. The Commission held that this deduction of time was attributable to the applicant's acquittal rather than to any finding that the detention was unlawful. It therefore followed that the applicant had not been deprived of his status as a victim.[68]

4-29 According to the Commission's established case law, national measures redressing the harm suffered must be accompanied by an acknowledgement that the prospective applicant's rights had been violated. There are, however, several indications in the case law that this requirement will be applied with some flexibility. In *App. No. 9320/81 v. Germany*, for example, although it was not expressly mentioned in the settlement that the substantial payment of interest which the applicant had received also represented compensation for the length of the proceedings, the Commission considered that "it would appear that the length of the proceedings was, in fact, one element of relevance for the agreement of the interest to be paid".

Measures mitigating the effects of the alleged violation, which do not provide full redress, cannot deprive an applicant of his status as a victim and capacity to bring proceedings. Thus, a measure putting an end to an alleged violation was held not to deprive the applicant of the status of victim because the authorities had not acknowledged any breach of the Convention (indeed they had contested its existence before the Court) or afforded redress for it.[69] In *Inze v. Austria*,[70] for example, the Convention organs considered that a judicial settlement concluded between the applicant and his half-brother did not redress his complaints about legislation which discriminated against children born outside marriage. The applicant had obtained by virtue of the settlement a piece of land from his mother's estate. However, since the law had deprived him, as a result of his illegitimate birth, of the possibility of taking over the whole of his mother's farm, he had been in a weak position in the settlement negotiations and had accepted the settlement as the lesser of two evils. Moreover, although the judicial settlement had alleviated the financial consequences of the discriminatory legislation, the Government had neither acknowledged that the inheritance law breached the applicant's Convention rights nor offered any redress itself. *Gaskin v. United Kingdom*[71] is to similar effect. The applicant had complained of the continuing refusal of the local authority to allow him access to the file relating to the period which he spent in care. The

---

[67] See also App 203339/92 *Tsovolas v. Greece* where the Commission held that a Presidential Pardon granted to the applicant with a formal declaration that he had been the victim of a "blatant miscarriage of justice" did intend "in the most explicit terms, to eradicate the stigma attached to the applicant as a result of his conviction and that it did formally make appropriate and sufficient redress for the violations of Article 6" which had allegedly occurred.

[68] App No. 31464/96 *Douiyeb v. Netherlands*.

[69] *Nsona v. Netherlands Reports* November 28, 1996, R.J.D., 1996–V, No. 23. See further, *Ludi v. Switzerland*; 15 E.H.R.R. 173 (1992), *Guillemin v. France* February 21, 1997 R.J.D., 1997–I, No. 29; 25 E.H.R.R. 435, *Amuur v. France* June 10, 1996, R.J.D., 1996–III, No. 10, para. 36; 22 E.H.R.R. 533, *Balmer-Schafroth v. Switzerland* August 26, 1997, R.J.D., 1997–IV, No. 43, para. 32; (1998) 25 E.H.R.R. 598; App. No. 25052/94, *Andronicou v. Cyprus* (1995) 20 E.H.R.R. C.D. 105 (admissibility decision).

[70] (1988) 10 E.H.R.R. 394.

[71] App. No. 10454/83, 45 D. & R. 91; See the judgment of the court (1990) 12 E.H.R.R. 36.

Commission considered that, although he had had access to his file for three days, his grievances could not have been redressed, given his unsatisfactory mental condition, his insufficient education and the volume of the records. Again, in *Bowman v. United Kingdom*,[72] the applicant was able to complain to Strasbourg about the restriction on expenditure on electoral publications by an unauthorised person, although her conviction under section 75(1) and (5) of the Representation of the People Act 1983 had been quashed as the prosecution had been brought out of time. The statute had been invoked against her and the prosecution was a strong indication that unless she modified her behaviour at future elections, she could expect to be prosecuted again.

C. Comparing the "victim" requirement with the "sufficient interest" test in judicial review

(1) Standing in relation to purely domestic law issues

4–30 By section 31(3) of the Supreme Court Act 1981 and RSC Order 53, rule 3(7) the applicant must have "a sufficient interest in the matter to which the application relates". At the initial stage when permission to move for judicial review is sought, standing operates only to weed out hopeless applications by "busy-bodies and mischief makers". In *R. v. IRC, ex parte National Federation of Self-Employed*[73] the House of Lords held that at the substantive hearing sufficiency of interest depends on consideration of the full legal and factual context, i.e. the nature of the power or duty involved and the illegality alleged. The importance of the statutory context should not be overlooked. Thus, Lord Fraser said that the correct approach is "to look at the statute . . . and to see whether it gives any express or implied right to persons in the position of the applicant to complain of the alleged unlawful act or omission."[74] Standing should not be considered separately from the substance or merits of the application, for instance as a preliminary issue.[75] However, it is sometimes considered separately at the full hearing, and the Court of Appeal has stated that it is an issue that goes to the jurisdiction of the court.[76]

(2) "Sufficient interest": claimants whose rights are infringed or who are or will in fact be affected

4–31 Claimants whose private rights are infringed, who suffer identifiable damage, over and above that suffered by the public at large, from the administrative action, or who have a financial stake in the outcome, will usually have standing. For instance, the interest of competitors, challenging decisions concerning their commercial rivals, has sufficed, particularly where the issue raised is of discriminatory

---

[72] (1998) 26 E.H.R.R. 1.
[73] [1982] A.C. 617.
[74] *ibid.* at p. 646C–D (Lord Fraser).
[75] In *R. v. Sec. State for Transport, ex parte Presvac Engineering Ltd* (1992) 4 Admin L. R. 121, the Court of Appeal suggested that the test as to standing used at the full hearing really formed part of the exercise of the court's discretion whether to grant relief. See also *R. v. Monopolies and Mergers Commission, ex parte Argyll Group Plc.* [1986] 1 W.L.R. 763, 774. If so, arguably the practical effect of linking standing to the factual and legal context is virtually to eliminate from the full hearing a discrete test of standing, in the sense of a test of entitlement to raise and argue the issue because of a sufficient connection with it. If this is correct, the only true test of standing is the one applied at the leave stage.
[76] *R. v. Sec. State for Social Services, ex parte CPAG* [1990] 2 Q.B. 540, 556E.

treatment.[77] The infringement of rights or special damage are not necessary and the interest of those who are in fact adversely affected by a decision has also been recognised. Where the members of a group are affected by a decision, the group will probably have standing to bring judicial review proceedings.[78]

A person who claims to be potentially affected may, as we have seen,[79] qualify as a "victim" for Convention purposes. In principle the position is the same in a purely domestic application for judicial review provided the administrative act to be challenged has an actual or threatened legal effect: there is no general bar on premature applications[80] although prematurity has precluded the review of preliminary and interlocutory decisions.[81]

4–32   Where the statutory power or duty concerns, or is owed to, an individual, or to a narrow range of individuals, an application by a person outside the designated category may fail for want of standing even where he or she is affected. Thus, it is possible that only a person who has been dismissed, or has had a licence revoked, will have sufficient interest to challenge the decision.[82] The position of an applicant who is not affected by a decision which has not been challenged by the person affected is even weaker.[83] In this respect the requirement that an applicant have "sufficient interest" may be narrower than the Strasbourg "victim" test. Although there are references to the individual having to be "directly affected",[84] and, as we have noted, there are differences of approach in the case law, *Open Door Counselling and Dublin Well Woman v. Ireland*[85] shows one can be a victim even though others are more affected.

But, save in this respect, the "sufficient interest" test is likely to be broader than the requirement that a claimant be a "victim". Thus, a public authority, such as a local authority,[86] is likely to have standing to bring judicial review proceedings but, as has been noted, will not qualify as a "victim".[87]

---

[77] R. v. Thames Magistrates' Court, ex parte Greenbaum (1957) 55 L.G.R. 129 (grant of market pitch); R. v. Att.-Gen., ex parte ICI plc [1987] 1 C.M.L.R. 588 (taxpayer's challenge to method used to value rival's profits).

[78] R. v. Chief Adjudication Officer, ex parte Bland, The Times, February 6, 1985 (reduction of benefits to striking miners); Royal College of Nursing of the U.K. v. DHSS [1981] A.C. 800 [1981] 1 All E.R. 545, 551; (advice that it was lawful for nurses to carry out abortion where prescribed by a doctor who remained in charge).

[79] See above, para. 4–26.

[80] Wade & Forsyth, Administrative Law (7th ed.), p. 629. For the suggestion that this has impeded the rational development of the circumstances in which the supervisory jurisdiction will be exercised in difficult cases, such as those concerned with advice, recommendations and other non-legally binding acts, and hypothetical issues, see Beatson in Forsyth & Hare (eds), The Golden Metwand and the Crooked Cord (1998), p. 221 et seq.

[81] R. v. Chief Constable of the Merseyside Police, ex parte Merrill [1989] 1 W.L.R. 1077 at 1088; R. v. Inland Revenue Commissioners, ex parte Ulster Bank Ltd [1997] S.T.C. 636; R. v. Association of Futures Brokers and Dealers Ltd, ex parte Mordens Ltd (1991) 3 Admin L.R. 254; R. v. Wells Street Stipendiary Magistrate, ex parte Seillon [1978] 1 W.L.R. 1002 at 1008. cf. Laws J. in R. v. Broadcasting Complaints Commission, ex parte B.B.C. (1994) 6 Admin L.R. 714 at 717–718.

[82] Durayappah v. Fernando [1967] 2 A.C. 337 (as explained in Hoffmann-La Roche & Co. AG v. Secretary of State for Trade and Industry [1975] A.C. 295); R. v. Lautro, ex parte Ross [1993] Q.B. 17 (CA).

[83] R. v. Legal Aid Board, ex parte Bateman [1992] 1 W.L.R. 711.

[84] Klass v. Germany (1978) 2 E.H.R.R. 214 at 33; Marckx v. Belgium (1979) 2 E.H.R.R. 330 at 27.

[85] (1993) 15 E.H.R.R. 244, see above, para. 4–29.

[86] R. v. Secretary of State for Transport, ex parte Richmond LBC [1994] 1 W.L.R. 74 (No. 4) [1996] 1 W.L.R. 1005; R. v. Chichester JJ, ex parte Chichester DC (1990) 60 p. & C.R. 342; R. v. Secretary of State for the Environment, ex parte Hammersmith & Fulham LBC [1991] 1 A.C. 52; R. v. Secretary of State for Employment, ex parte Equal Opportunities Commission [1995] 1 A.C. 1. See also Cook v. Southend BC [1990] 2 Q.B. 1; Nottinghamshire CC v. Secretary of State for the Environment [1986] A.C. 240.

[87] See above, para. 4–26. Article 34 only provides for applications by a "non-governmental organisation".

(3) "Sufficient interest" in challenges by taxpayers and public interest groups

4–33　There are other situations where the impact of a decision on an individual is not substantial, or no more substantial than it is on other citizens but standing has been accorded. In such cases it is the nature of the individual's interest in the matter, or the public interest, rather than the fact that she or he has been affected, that is important. Unlike private law claims, "the true nature of the court's role in public law cases . . . is not to determine the rights of individual applicants but to ensure that public bodies do not exceed or abuse their powers."[88] With this consideration in mind, the rules on standing have developed in such a way that pressure groups[89] and non-governmental public bodies[90] now play an important role in bringing public interest cases before the judicial review courts. So, for example, in *R. v. HM Treasury, ex parte Smedley*[91] a taxpayer was accorded standing to challenge a Government undertaking to pay contributions to the E.C. Again, the interest of ratepayers may suffice even where the alleged breach of duty has no demonstrable effect on them.[92]

The position of challenges by such public interest groups constitutes perhaps the most significant difference between the "sufficient interest" test and the victim test in section 7(3). Often the public in general or a wide section of it is affected. In determining whether to allow a "public interest" challenge in a purely domestic application for judicial review, the court takes account of a number of factors. These include the importance of maintaining the rule of law; the importance of the issue raised by the application; the likely absence of any other "responsible" challenger; the nature of the breach of duty against which relief is sought; and the expertise and experience of the applicant body.[93] It will also consider the allocation of scarce judicial resources and the concern that in the determination of issues the courts should have the benefit of the conflicting points of view of those most directly affected by them. These are matters going to the "justiciability" of an issue.

4–34　By providing that *only* a victim will have a sufficient interest, rather than automatically according standing to victims, section 7(3) of the HRA may preclude a public interest group from mounting a challenge based on the infringement of fundamental rights. A public interest group may have standing only to plead the

---

[88] JUSTICE/Public Law Project, *A Matter of Public Interest—Report of a working party on third party interventions* (1996), p. 3. In its 1994 Report, *Administrative Law: Judicial Review and Statutory Appeals* (Law Com. No. 226), the Law Commission stated (para. 2.5): "The public interest in the vindication of the rule of law underpins the very existence of the prerogative jurisdiction and its supervisory role over inferior courts and decision-makers." This distinctive, constitutional function of the High Court's supervisory jurisdiction gives rise to an essential difference between judicial review and ordinary private litigation, noted by the Commission at para. 2.1 of its Report: "Judicial review often involves values and policy interests, which must be balanced against and may transcend the individual interests which are normally the subject of litigation between private citizens.".

[89] *R. v. Secretary of State for Social Services, ex parte CPAG* [1990] 2 Q.B. 540 at 556G *per* Woolf L.J.; *R. v. HMI Pollution, ex parte Greenpeace* [1994] 1 W.L.R. 570; *R. v. Foreign Secretary, ex parte World Development Movement* [1995] 1 W.L.R. 386, 392–396, 403; *R. v. Secretary of State for the Home Department, ex parte Immigration Law Practitioners Association* [1997] Imm. A.R. 189. *cf.* the narrower approach in *R. v. Secretary of State for the Environment, ex parte Rose Theatre Trust* [1990] 1 Q.B. 504.

[90] *R. v. Secretary of State Employment, ex parte Equal Opportunities Comm.* [1995] 1 A.C. 1.

[91] [1985] Q.B. 657. See also *R. v. Secretary of State for Foreign and Commonwealth Affairs, ex parte Rees Mogg* [1994] Q.B. 552.

[92] *Arsenal FC v. Ende* [1979] A.C. 1.

[93] *R. v. Secretary of State for Foreign and Commonwealth Affairs, ex parte World Development Movement Ltd* [1995] 1 W.L.R. 386, at 395H. The relevant cases are drawn together in the judgment of Rose L.J. See also *R. v. HMI Pollution, ex parte Greenpeace* [1994] 1 W.L.R. 570.

points in the case which do not involve fundamental rights except, as will be seen, insofar as a common law or an E.C. basis can be found for its submissions. Such an outcome would reintroduce the legal technicalities which it was the purpose of the 1977 reforms of RSC Order 53 to remove and which Lord Diplock described as outdated in 1982.[94]

To take one example, in 1996, the Court of Appeal allowed an appeal by the Joint Council for the Welfare of Immigrants (JCWI) and declared unlawful regulations which drastically restricted access to benefits by asylum seekers and which, according to Simon Brown L.J., rendered the rights of appeal accorded to genuine asylum seekers "nugatory". He continued:

> "Either that, or the Regulations necessarily contemplate for some a life so destitute that to my mind no civilised nation can tolerate it. So basic are the human rights here at issue that it cannot be necessary to resort to the European Convention on Human Rights to take note of their violation."[95]

The Convention had not been incorporated at the time but Simon Brown L.J. (with whom Waite L.J. agreed) felt able to give effect to such fundamental rights in that case through the common law and to hold that the Regulations were "so uncompromisingly draconian in effect that they must be held to be *ultra vires*".[96] What would the position be under the HRA? Article 6(1) of the Convention protects the right of access to a court and Article 3 proscribes "inhuman or degrading treatment". Could section 7(3) be read as preventing a public interest body such as JCWI from bringing proceedings concerning issues that can be classified as Convention violations but of which the public interest group itself is not the victim? There is a risk that, whatever the position may have been before enactment, section 7(3) will be interpreted as a statutory removal of standing from public interest groups disabling them from making appropriate, important human rights challenges. On facts such as those in the JCWI case, the consequence might be that JCWI could advance the common law arguments concerning access to justice and inhuman or degrading treatment but not the equivalent protections under the Convention.

D. Standing in relation to E.C. law issues

4–35 Consideration of the requirements of E.C. law in cases that come before national courts reveals further difficulties which the "victim" restriction in section 7(3) may produce. Where a Community measure is implemented or applied by the United Kingdom, a person with "sufficient interest" under section 31(3) and RSC, Order 53, rule 3(7) may challenge the national measure or decision in an English court. If the validity of the Community measure or the conformity of the national measure with Community law is in issue, the national court may refer the matter to

---

[94] "It would, in my view, be a grave lacuna in our system of public law if a pressure group, like the federation, or even a single public-spirited taxpayer, were prevented by outdated technical rules of locus standi from bringing the matter to the attention of the court to vindicate the rule of law and get the unlawful conduct stopped": R. v. *Inland Revenue Commissioners, ex parte National Federation of Self-Employed* [1982] A.C. 617 at 644E.
[95] R. v. *SS for Social Security, ex parte JCWI* [1997] 1 W.L.R. 275 at 292F.
[96] *ibid.* at 293B.

the ECJ for a preliminary ruling under Article 234, formerly Article 177, of the TEU.[97]

Limitations or restrictions on directly effective E.C. rights must be compatible with E.C. law, including the general principles of E.C. law. As we have seen, the settled case law of the ECJ establishes that one of those general principles is that E.C. institutions and Member States must respect fundamental human rights as set out, particularly, in the Convention.[98] The statutory basis for applying the Convention in E.C. cases is section 2(1) and section 3(1) of the European Communities Act (ECA) 1972 and not the HRA.[99] Accordingly, an applicant alleging breach of E.C. law must satisfy only the normal "sufficient interest" test even if the breach of E.C. law depends on a Convention point. The standing requirement for such a challenge will therefore differ from the section 7(3), victim only, test applicable in purely domestic (*i.e.* non-E.C. judicial reviews with a human rights point (unless, perhaps, the point can be derived from the common law[1]). As the learned editors of De Smith, Woolf & Jowell's *Judicial Review of Administrative Action* have observed, however:

> "there is little to commend the development of a dual-track system of public law litigation in the U.K., with one set of procedures and remedies applying to Community law matters and another to purely domestic issues. Reconciling these differences will be a key challenge in the coming years."[2]

4–36 This challenge is particularly pressing where, for example, the same statutory provision or administrative decision may have an E.C. context when applied to person or a company from another E.C. Member State or even to a British registered company, owned by a parent company from another Member State, but will have no E.C. dimension when applied to a British citizen or a British registered and British owned company. Further, the impracticality risks being compounded since the test of standing may change if ownership of a company changes from British to that of another E.C. Member State or vice versa.

---

[97] Such indirect challenge of a Community decision is permitted even though the individual could not have challenged it directly in the ECJ because the decision was neither addressed to him nor was of "direct and individual concern" to him as is required for a direct challenge by Article 230, formerly 173, of the TEU: see, *e.g.* Case 55/72 *Gesellschaft für Getreidehandel v. EVGF* [1973] E.C.R. 15. Where a person has standing to make a direct challenge but fails to do so, an Article 234 reference may not be possible: Case C–188/92 *TWD v. Bundesminister für Wirtschaft* [1994] E.C.R. I–833; Case 241/95 *R. v. Intervention Board, for Agricultural Produce, ex parte Accrington Beef Co.* [1996] E.C.R. I-6699. See further Hartley, *The Foundations of E.C. Law* (4th ed.), pp. 404–406; De Smith, Woolf & Jowell, *Judicial Review of Administrative Action* (5th ed.), para. 21–066.

[98] See above, paras 1–18 *et seq.* In Case C–260/89 *ERT v. DEP* [1991] E.C.R. I–2925, for example, the ECJ stated that when: "rules do fall within the scope of Community law, and reference is made to the Court for a preliminary ruling, it must provide all the criteria of interpretation needed by the national court to determine *whether those rules are compatible with the fundamental rights the observance of which the Court ensures and which derive in particular from the European Convention on Human Rights.* In particular, when a Member State relies on the combined provisions of Articles 56 and 66 in order to justify rules which are likely to obstruct the exercise of the freedom to provide services, such justification, provided by Community law, *must be interpreted in the light of general principles of law and in particular of fundamental rights.* Thus, the national rules in question can fall under the exceptions provided by the combined provisions of Articles 56 and 66 only if they are compatible with the fundamental rights the observance of which is ensured by the Court" (paras 42 and 43 of the judgment, emphasis added).

[99] See above, paras 1–18, 1–23.

[1] See above.

[2] (5th ed.), p. 613, para. IV–007. See also Advocate-General Francis Jacobs, "Public Law—The Impact of Europe" [1999] P.L. 232, 242, and see, *e.g.. M v. Home Office* [1994] 1 A.C. 377, 406–407 (Lord Woolf); *Woolwich Equitable B.S. v. I.R.C.* [1993] A.C. 70, 177 (Lord Goff); *R. v. Secretary of State for Transport, ex parte Factortame (No.1)*, Case C–213/89 [1990] E.C.R. I–2433.

E. Arguments for and against limiting standing to "victims"

4–37   There is nothing objectionable about providing that a private law claim alleging a violation of Convention rights should be brought only by a victim. In such a case, the claimant is almost invariably seeking an individual remedy for breach of a personal right. But public law and judicial review often involve values and policy interests which must be balanced against, and may transcend, individual interests. In particular there is the importance of vindicating the rule of law, so that public bodies take lawful decisions and are prevented from relying on invalid decisions.[3] Once the character of public law is recognised, it is difficult to understand the policy behind having a more restrictive test of standing than that under section 31(3) of the Supreme Court Act 1981 and RSC, Order 53, rule 3(7).

The Government's intention appears to have been largely to exclude public interest challenges. In Committee the Lord Chancellor stated:

> "The standing rule which the Bill proposes in relation to Convention cases *simpliciter* is identical to that operated at Strasbourg . . . It would not, however, prevent the acceptance by the courts in this country of non-governmental organisational briefs here any more than it does in Strasbourg . . . So it appears to me, as at present advised, that the natural position to take is to adopt the victim test as applied by Strasbourg when a complaint is made of a denial of Convention rights, recognising that our courts will be ready to permit *amicus* written briefs from non-governmental organisations, that is to say briefs, but not to treat them as full parties."[4]

4–38   There is, of course, a difference between, on the one hand, ensuring that *as a minimum* all those who claim to be victims of violations of Convention rights are considered to have sufficient interest and, on the other, stipulating that *only* victims have sufficient interest. The Bill's purpose appears to be the latter, although the Lord Chancellor was at pains to explain that potential victims would also be included:

> "I also point out that Clause 7, consistently with the position in Strasbourg, also treats as victims those who are faced with the threat of a public authority proposing to act in a way which would be unlawful under Clause 6(1). So potential victims are included. Interest groups will similarly be able to assist potential victims to bring challenges to action which is threatened before it is actually carried out . . . Clause 13(2)[5] also makes clear that the Bill does not affect the existing ability of anyone with a sufficient interest to seek judicial review on non-Convention grounds. The sole and narrow point is whether the domestic English judicial review test of standing should apply where an application for judicial review is made on grounds other than Convention grounds."[6]

On Third Reading, the Lord Chancellor explained that it was the Government's intention to mirror the approach to standing taken by the Strasbourg institutions.

---

[3] Law Commission, *Administrative Law: Judicial Review and Statutory Appeals* (Law Com. No. 226, 1994), paras 2.1, 2.3. See also *R. v. Inland Revenue Commissioners, ex parte National Federation of Self-Employed* [1982] A.C. 617, 644, 652.

[4] *Hansard*, H.L., November 24, 1997, cols. 832–833.

[5] Now s. 11(a).

[6] *Hansard*, H.L., November 24, 1997, col. 830.

He referred to the expansive approach to the test adopted by the Strasbourg Court and continued:

> "I acknowledge that as a consequence, and despite the flexibility of the Strasbourg test, a narrower test will apply for bringing applications on Convention grounds than in applications for judicial review on other grounds. But I venture to think that interest groups will plainly be able to provide assistance to victims who bring cases under the Bill, including, as I mentioned in Committee, the filing of *amicus* briefs. Interest groups themselves will be able to bring cases directly when they are victims of an unlawful act. I do not believe that different tests for Convention and non-Convention cases will cause any difficulties for the courts or prevent interest groups providing assistance to victims of unlawful acts."[7]

4–39   During the Committee stage in the House of Commons, the Opposition introduced an amendment which would extend standing to a person who "can demonstrate that he is acting on behalf of a victim or potential victim of an unlawful act".[8] The Minister of State confirmed[9] that the provision on standing was not intended to prevent certain types of applicant from bringing proceedings. Thus, it was not intended to prevent: (a) members of a deportee's family from complaining about a deportation order under Article 8 of the Convention; (b) guardians *ad litem* or others who could normally undertake cases from doing so; or, (c) the family of a dead victim bringing a case about the right to life under Article 2. He also confirmed that public interest groups might properly be invited to submit *amicus* briefs, adding that:

> "Our courts will develop their own jurisprudence on the issue, taking account of Strasbourg cases and the Strasbourg jurisprudence. As a government, our aim is to grant access to victims. It is not to create opportunities to allow interest groups from SPUC to Liberty . . . to venture into frolics of their own in the courts. The aim is to confer access to rights, not to license interest groups to clog up the courts with test cases, which will delay victims' access to the courts."[10]

4–40   This candid statement is the closest any minister came to explaining the policy behind the provision rather than simply describing its effect. But although in many cases public interest challenges can be brought by an individual who has standing, and often this will be desirable, because of the limited availability of legal aid[11] and the costs rules, there will be some cases where an individual applicant cannot be found. This may happen where a large number of people are affected but cases are settled as they arise, leaving the general issue of lawfulness undecided. It may also happen where the amount of money at stake does not justify the grant of legal aid, as currently in some social security cases;[12] or where a challenge would be premature because an individual has not yet been affected. This last problem may

---

[7] *Hansard*, H.L., February 3, 1998, col. 810.
[8] *Hansard*, H.C., November 24, 1997, col. 1058.
[9] *Loc. cit.*, col. 1086.
[10] *ibid.*
[11] See the criteria on legal aid funding in s. 8 of the Access to Justice Act 1999 and the funding code, currently in draft.
[12] See the facts in *R. v. Secretary of State for Social Services, ex parte C.P.A.G.* [1990] 2 Q.B. 540.

not always be resolved by the inclusion of the words "would be" a victim in section 7(3) because it may not be known at the time proceedings are instituted that a person would be affected by a potential violation of human rights. For example, a migrant may wish to bring proceedings to establish that some aspect of immigration law or practice infringes his Convention rights. An immigrant who has, say, applied for leave to remain in the United Kingdom, will have a right of appeal against a refusal. Such an appeal may, if successful, mean that, in Strasbourg terms, the immigrant is not a "victim" because he has obtained redress at the national level. If, therefore, the immigrant wishes to bring proceedings under the HRA, it will not be known until the application for leave to remain is refused, whether an appeal will be necessary, let alone successful. We have also drawn attention to the technical (and, as it seems to us, pointless) complexities of standing which are likely to arise in relation to a challenge which a public interest litigant seeks to bring on both Convention and non-Convention grounds.

4–41   It is not apparent what advantages there are to a narrower test for standing under the HRA than in ordinary judicial review proceedings. No particular virtue attaches to replication of the Strasbourg test. Indeed, that test was designed specifically for the purpose of regulating individual access to an international tribunal in what was, at the time of its creation, a novel procedure. It was never intended to apply to standing in domestic proceedings and it is not appropriate for that purpose. If the perceived harm is that numerous unmeritorious applications will be brought, the court has the necessary tools to control this risk through the discretion concerning sufficiency of interest, or by refusing permission to launch the application, and, of course, by the exercise of discretion over the grant of any relief. In appropriate cases the court's use of its discretion on costs can also be used to deter such applications.

F.   The scope of the limitation in section 7 properly understood

4–42   Given both the policy considerations in favour of wider rules of standing, and the technical inconvenience and anomalies which arise from a dual track system of access,[13] the courts may well view the attempt to limit standing in HRA cases with some scepticism. To this scepticism must be added the courts' traditional reluctance to cut down rights of access to the courts in the absence of an express, and clear, statutory direction to do so.[14]

In view of these factors, we consider that the courts are likely to confine the effect of section 7(3) as closely as the language and structure of the Act allow, and that the limits of the restriction may have been overstated. It should apply *only*

---

[13] Harlow and Rawlings have likened the classical judicial review model to a drainpipe "narrow, inflexible lengths of tubing joined by rigid collars", and reference is also made to "motorway" and "funnel" models of access: *Pressure Through Law* (Routledge, London, 1992). On this analysis the victim requirement represents either the pipette or the contra-flow model.

[14] In *R. v. Lord Chancellor ex parte Witham* [1997] Q.B. 575, Laws J. stated that the "constitutional right" of access to justice cannot be abrogated "unless specifically so permitted by Parliament" (at 585G–H). Laws J. considered what language would be needed to make plain Parliament's intent so to abrogate this constitutional right and stated: " . . . for my part, I find great difficulty in conceiving a form of words capable of making it plain beyond doubt to the statute's reader that the provision in question prevents him from going to court (for that is what would be required) save in a case where that is expressly stated" (at 586A). See also *Pyx Granite Co. Ltd v. Ministry of Housing and Local Government* [1960] A.C. 260; *Commissioners of Customs and Excise v. Cure & Deeley Ltd* [1962] 1 Q.B. 340; *Anisminic Ltd v. Foreign Compensation Commission* [1969] 2 A.C. 147; *Raymond v. Honey* [1983] 1 A.C. 1, 14.

where a person is claiming under section 7 that he is a victim of an act of a public authority made unlawful under section 6(1) and seeking a remedy under section 8 or 9. On principle, standing in all other cases remains unaffected, as is made explicit in section 11(b) of the Act, which provides that a person's reliance on a Convention right "does not restrict . . . his right to make any claim or bring any proceedings which he could make or bring apart from sections 7 to 9". The limitation in section 7 does not therefore affect applications based on common law and probably not those in English courts based on an infringement of E.C. law. It will also not affect the rights of public interest groups or others with a sufficient interest—such as a public authority directed to enforce or give effect to legislation which it considers incompatible with Convention rights—to seek relief based on other provisions of the Act, including interpretative declarations, the quashing of unnecessarily incompatible subordinate legislation or the making of a declaration of incompatibility. Applications of this nature are grounded not on the duty contained in section 6 but on the interpretative obligation contained in section 3, which applies in all cases, and to which the restrictions on standing do not apply.

4–43 For example, suppose a Secretary of State gives a local authority or a health authority a direction under one of his default powers,[15] and the authority, which is not a "victim" in Strasbourg terms,[16] considers that carrying out the direction would be incompatible with a Convention right. Section 7 cannot in our view prevent the authority from applying for judicial review of the Secretary of State's direction where the local authority is not seeking a remedy under the HRA but is simply relying on the interpretative obligation contained in section 3. If it is so precluded it would be placed in an impossible position. It would have either to comply with the direction (and risk exposing itself to liability under section 6 at the suit of a victim), or to defy the direction and face enforcement proceedings in which, as a non-victim, it would not be able to defend by relying on the Convention.

As we have seen,[17] section 3 requires that, so far as it is possible to do so, legislation must be read and given effect in a way which is compatible with Convention rights. The court has a power to grant a declaration of public rights even where there is no decision which could be the subject of a prerogative order.[18] It remains open to a body or group with a sufficient interest in the subject-matter of particular legislation to seek an advisory declaration as to the proper meaning of a provision of primary or subordinate legislation; or to contend in the alternative that a competing meaning would be incompatible with Convention rights.[19]

---

[15] *Nottinghamshire CC v. Secretary of State for the Environment* [1986] A.C. 240; *Secretary of State for Education v. Tameside MBC* [1977] A.C. 1014.

[16] See above, para. 4–26.

[17] See above, Ch. 3.

[18] *R. v. Secretary of State for Employment, ex parte Equal Opportunities Commission* [1995] 1 A.C. 1, in particular 27 (Lord Keith) and 36 (Lord Browne-Wilkinson).

[19] On advisory declarations see Law Commission, *Administrative Law: Judicial Review and Statutory Appeals* (Law Com. No. 226, 1994), paras 8.9–8.14. See also De Smith, Woolf & Jowell, *Judicial Review of Administrative Action* (5th ed.), paras 20–017 and 20–018, distinguishing a "hypothetical" question, "which needs to be answered for a real practical purpose, although there may not be an immediate situation on which the decision will have practical effect" from an "academic" question, "which need not be answered for any visible practical purpose, although an answer would satisfy academic curiosity, for example by clarifying a difficult area of law". The "real practical purpose" of a declaration in the public interest cases discussed here would be the avoidance of breaches of Convention rights and the bringing of legislative incompatibility to Parliament's attention. See *R. v. Secretary of State for the Home Department, ex parte Salem* [1999] 2 W.L.R. 483 (HL): where there is an issue involving a public authority as to a question of public law, the House of Lords has discretion to hear the appeal, even if the outcome will no longer directly affect the rights and obligations of the parties. See further, Beatson in Forsyth & Hare (eds), *The Golden Metwand and the Crooked Cord* (1998), pp. 243–251.

4–44 The Government also made clear during the passage of the Bill that it did not intend to restrict the power of the courts to strike down subordinate legislation where it is *ultra vires*. During the Committee Stage of the Bill in the Commons, the Home Secretary said:

> " . . . the courts already have power to strike down subordinate legislation . . . If they feel that a statutory instrument has been introduced in a way that is *ultra vires* the primary legislation, they can do so. When we discussed the matter in detail in the Cabinet Ministerial Sub-Committee on Incorporation of the European Convention on Human Rights, it seemed to us that, as that power was already there, it would be very odd not to continue to allow courts to strike down subordinate legislation if it was incompatible with the Bill."[20]

The requirement in section 7 that only a victim has standing to bring proceedings does not therefore prevent all proceedings by interest groups. An interest group could argue (a) that on its proper construction, in accordance with the Convention, a provision of subordinate legislation does not authorise breaches of Convention rights; (b) that if it does, the rule-making power in the statute, construed in accordance with the Convention, does not authorise the making of that subordinate legislation, which is therefore *ultra vires*;[21] or (c) that if the rule-making does authorise the making of such rules, it ought to be declared incompatible with a Convention right under section 4.[22] Such proceedings may *indirectly* entail an allegation that a public authority has acted or proposes to act in a way which is incompatible with a Convention right. However, the primary ground on which relief is sought relates to the proper interpretation of a statute and the Convention rights and the rule of law that a public body must act within its powers. These are not claims under section 6, nor does the applicant seek a remedy under sections 7 to 9.

To hold that any such claim is in substance a claim that a public authority has acted or proposes to act in breach of the Convention would unduly restrict the existing powers of the court to make declarations and the operation of the rule against *ultra vires* acts. It would also limit the saving for existing rights of action in section 11(b): in effect section 6 would limit an interest group, claiming that an act is *ultra vires*, to arguing its case on the pre-existing rules of statutory construction without reference to section 3 of the Act. Such an anomalous result was not intended.

4. Private Individuals and Bodies

4–45 The extent to which the HRA leaves open the possibility of direct horizontal application, i.e. as between private parties, was a matter of considerable debate during its parliamentary passage. Concern was expressed (mainly by media interests) that the HRA would enable the courts to develop a general tort of infringement of privacy based on ECHR Article 8 and that this would weaken the freedom of the press.[23] This provoked several (not always consistent) explanations

---

[20] *Hansard*, H.C., June 24, 1998, col. 1128.

[21] See, *mutatis mutandis, R. v. Secretary of State for Social Security, ex parte Joint Council for the Welfare of Immigrants* [1997] 1 W.L.R. 275 (CA).

[22] See, *mutatis mutandis, R. v. Secretary of State for Employment, ex parte Equal Opportunities Commission* [1995] 1 A.C. 1.

[23] *Hansard*, H.L., November 24, 1997, col. 771–779; *Hansard*, H.C. Vol. 314, February 16, 1998, cols 791–794; June 17, 1998, cols 399–405, 411, 413 *et seq*. These concerns led to the introduction of what is now s. 12, on which see below, paras 4–61 *et seq*. and *Hansard*, H.C. Vol. 306, February 16, 1998, col. 860; *Hansard*, H.C. Vol. 315, July 2, 1998, cols 535 *et seq*.

by Government Ministers as to how they anticipated the Convention rights might be relevant in an action between private parties.[24]

The argument in favour of horizontal effect is primarily, although not exclusively, based on section 6(3), which provides that a court or tribunal is a "public authority". It has been argued that the effect of this is to subject courts and tribunals to the section 6(1) duty not to act in a way which is incompatible with a Convention right in *all* proceedings, whether the defendant is a public authority or a private person. On this view section 6(3) impliedly requires *direct* horizontal effect to be given to Convention rights.[25] Sections 12 and 13 of the HRA may appear to provide some support for this. These provisions apply where a court is considering whether to grant any relief which, if granted, might affect the Convention right of freedom of expression, and where a court's determination might affect the exercise by a religious organisation of the Convention right to freedom of thought, conscience and religion. The support for direct horizontal effect might be thought to follow from the fact that those provisions are not limited to cases to which a public authority is a party.[26]

4–46 It is, however, clear from the structure of the HRA and from what was said during its parliamentary passage[27] that section 6(3) does not have such a wide-ranging effect. It has been suggested that section 6(3) "means only that the courts *in their own sphere* must give effect to such fundamental rights as the right to a fair trial; and to more particular rights such as a right to an interpreter".[28] This is not horizontal effect, in that it regulates the rights which an individual can assert against the court, rather than his rights against another individual party before the court. That it is proper not to give section 6(3) the widest possible meaning is shown by the structure of section 6. The duty to act consistently with Convention rights is imposed on public authorities, and section 6 clearly shows that it was not intended to include private individuals and entities within its ambit. This is, for example, shown by the treatment of persons or entities only certain of whose functions are of a public nature. By section 6(5), such a person or entity will be a public authority and subject to the obligation to act compatibly with Convention rights in respect of acts whose nature is public but not in respect of acts whose nature is private.[29] Nor do sections 12 and 13 support *direct* horizontal effect of Convention rights either in general or in the particular case of Articles 9 and 10. First, all they do is replace the section 2 "take into account" formula by a stronger but not conclusive "have particular regard" formula.[30] Secondly, they do not affect section 6.

---

[24] See *e.g. Hansard*, H.L. Vol. 583, November 24, 1997, col. 783 *et seq.* 811 *Hansard*, H.C. Vol. 306, February 16, 1998, cols 776–777.

[25] HWR Wade, in *Constitutional Reform in the U.K.: Practice and Principles* (Cambridge Centre for Public Law, 1998), p. 63; [1998] E.H.R.L.R. 522. Hunt's suggested intermediate position ([1998] P.L. 423, 426) "in which the norms protecting fundamental rights apply to all law, whatever its nature", is in practice likely to be very close to Wade's. See also, Leigh, [1999] 48 I.C.L.Q. 57.

[26] *Hansard*, H.C. Vol. 315, July 2, 1998, col. 536 (Home Secretary).

[27] *e.g.* LC HL Third Reading, February 5, 1998, col. 840; HL Second Reading, November 3, 1997, cols 1231–1232.

[29] Kentridge, in *Constitutional Reform in the U.K.: Practice and Principles* (Cambridge Centre for Public Law, 1998), p. 70, emphasis added. But *cf.* his view in *Du Plessis v. De Klerk* 1996 (3) S.A. 850, 877–8 that provisions (*e.g.* that in the Namibian Constitution, Article 5) that rights are to be upheld by the judiciary, which are similar to HRA, s. 6(3) do support wider than purely vertical application and may equate the judgment of a court with state action, so that their absence from the South African Constitution was a strong pointer to the rights under it only having direct vertical effect.

[29] Interestingly, however, the subsection does not provide that the Act "does not apply" to such acts, but rather that "a person is not a public authority" in relation to them.

[30] See below, paras 4–65 *et seq.*

Accordingly, save for those cases (discussed below) in which states and thus the courts have a positive duty to secure an individual's Convention rights against interference by other private persons or entities, it is unlikely that there will be *direct* horizontal effect. But even apart from the fair trial obligations referred to above, there is likely to be a substantial *indirect* horizontal effect in the manner in which courts and tribunals dispose of proceedings between private parties. Although the extent is difficult to predict with confidence, it is likely to arise in the following circumstances:

A. Interpretation of primary or secondary legislation

4–47 The first of these circumstances is where the proceedings involve the interpretation of primary or secondary legislation. Section 3(1) of the HRA provides that statutes are to be read and given effect in a way which is compatible with the Convention rights "so far as it is possible to do so".[31] So, statutory protection of privacy or confidentiality in a particular context would have to be construed "so far as it is possible to do so" to ensure compatibility with the right to freedom of expression in proceedings where all parties are private individuals or entities. A court would have to give a compatible construction to statutory provisions limiting the freedom of employees to belong or not to belong to a trade union and thus limiting the freedom of association in Article 11, even though the question of its interpretation arose in proceedings between private parties. Again, a court might be required to give a compatible interpretation to a statutory provision governing family succession to a protected or statutory tenancy which on its face appeared to exclude same-sex partners.[32] It is important to distinguish "private activity and laws that regulate private activity".[33] The Convention rights are relevant in the application of such laws. So, if a party to private litigation founds a claim or a defence on a legislative provision, its compatibility with the Convention rights is an issue, which may properly be raised, and the court will strive to interpret the provision so as to produce compatibility.

B. Court orders and the exercise of judicial discretion

4–48 We have noted that in some circumstances the order of the court, albeit made in proceedings between private parties, may itself interfere with a party's substantive rights.[34] Although mediated through the court's obligation not to act incompatibly with an individual's Convention rights, the consequence may be to modify the rights of the other party to the litigation. The case law under the Convention abounds with examples, of which a handful will serve to illustrate the point. Thus, the grant to a claimant of an injunction restraining publication of a defamatory article or of a breach of confidence may amount to a breach of the defendant's freedom to impart information under Article 10;[35] as may the making of an excessive award of damages in defamation proceedings,[36] and other injunc-

---

[31] See above, Ch. 3.
[32] See para. 2(1) of Pt I of Sched. 1 to the Rent Act 1977 and *Fitzpatrick v. Sterling Housing Association Ltd* [1998] Ch. 304, (CA), October 28, 1999 (HL). See also *Attorney General for Ontario v. M & H*, (1999) 171 D.L.R. (4th) 577, Supreme Court of Canada.
[33] *Vriend v. Alberta* [1998] 1 S.C.R. 493, 535 (Cory and Iacobucci JJ.).
[34] See above, para. 4–17.
[35] *Sunday Times v. United Kingdom* 2 E.H.R.R. 245; *The Observer and The Guardian v. United Kingdom* (1992) 14 E.H.R.R. 153 and *Sunday Times v. United Kingdom (No. 2)* (1992) 14 E.H.R.R. 229.
[36] *Tolstoy Miloslavsky v. United Kingdom* (1995) 20 E.H.R.R. 442; see also *Rantzen v. Mirror Group Newspapers* [1994] Q.B. 670.

tions may also affect freedom to receive information.[37] Again, the making of an *Anton Piller* order (now known as a search order[38]) may interfere with a person's right to respect for his or her private life or home;[39] and the grant or refusal, or suspension of an order for possession may interfere with the rights of the landlord or the tenant.[40] Finally, an order determining contested custody proceedings will interfere with the right to respect for family life of one or other of the parties to the proceedings.[41] As noted above, these cases are different from the positive obligation cases, considered below. This is because they involve the interference with the Convention right by the court's own act or omission. The positive obligation cases involve the interference with a Convention right by another private party's act which the court fails to remedy. In giving effect to one party's Convention right, the court may be modifying the rights of the opposing party.

C. Positive duties on states to secure an individual's Convention rights against interference by others

4–49   In certain circumstances the Strasbourg institutions impose positive duties on states' parties to the Convention to secure an individual's Convention rights against interference by other persons or entities.[42] This has occurred particularly in relation to the prohibition of torture and inhuman or degrading treatment (Article 3), the right to liberty and security (Article 5), the right to respect for private and family life (Article 8), and the right to freedom of peaceful assembly and to freedom of association (Article 11). Where it is held that there is such a positive duty, a state that is party to the Convention is obliged to ensure a practical and effective system for the protection of the right in question. In some cases this will include "the adoption of measures designed to secure respect for [the right] even in the sphere of the relations of individuals between themselves".[43]

An English court which is confronted with a situation in which the Convention imposes such positive duties will have to decide whether it is able to protect the right in question and, if so, whether it should. Save where prevented from so doing by irreconcilably incompatible U.K. legislation[44] and/or where the incompatibility of U.K. law can only be remedied by the enactment of legislation,[45] the court should in principle protect the individual's Convention rights against such interference by other private persons. That would be consistent with the aim of the

---

[37] *Open Door Counselling and Dublin Well Woman v. Ireland* (1993) 15 E.H.R.R. 244.
[38] C.P.R. 25.1(h).
[39] *Chappell v. United Kingdom* (1990) 12 E.H.R.R. 1.
[40] *Spadea & Scalabrino v. Italy* (1995) 21 E.H.R.R. 482; *Scollo v. Italy* (1996) 22 E.H.R.R. 514.
[41] *Hoffmann v. Austria* [1994] 17 E.H.R.R. 293.
[42] See commentary on individual articles, below, para. C0–05.
[43] *X and Y v. The Netherlands* (1985) 8 E.H.R.R. 235 (Article 8). See also *Marckx v. Belgium* (1979), 2 E.H.R.R. 330; *B v. France* (1993) 16 E.H.R.R. 1; *Guerra v. Italy* (1998) 26 E.H.R.R. 357; *Whiteside v. United Kingdom* (1994) 18 E.H.R.R. C.D. 126 On Article 2, see *Mrs W v. U.K.* (1983) D. & R. 10; *Mrs W v. Ireland* (1983) 32 D. & R. 211; *McCann v. U.K.* (1996) 21 E.H.R.R. 97; *Osman v. United Kingdom* (1996) 22 E.H.R.R. C.D. 137 (Report of the Commission), but see now the judgment of the court dated October 28, 1998. On Article 3, see *A v. U.K.* [1998] E.H.R.L.R. 688. On Article 11, see *Young, James and Webster v. U.K.* (1981) 4 E.H.R.R. 38; *Plattform Arzte fur das Leben v. Austria* (1988) 13 E.H.R.R. 204; *Gustafsson v. Sweden*, April 25, 1996, R.J.D., 1996–II, No. 9; 22 E.H.R.R. 409; on Article 6 see *Airey v. Ireland* 2 E.H.R.R. 305 On Article 9, see *Dubowska & Skup v. Poland* (1997) 23 E.H.R.R. C.D. 204.
[44] HRA, ss. 4(2), 6(2). See above, paras 3–18, 3–39—3–40.
[45] HRA, s. 6(6) provides that while a failure to act by a public authority (including a court) which produces incompatibility with a Convention right is unlawful, this is not the case where the failure is to introduce in or lay before Parliament a proposal for legislation or to make any primary legislation or remedial order. See further Pt II below.

HRA of "bringing rights home"[46] and with the requirement in section 2(1) of the HRA that the court "take into account" the Strasbourg jurisprudence, which imposes the positive duty.[47] Moreover, the court is an organ of the state for which the United Kingdom is responsible under the Convention regime[48] and is by section 6(3) of the HRA a "public authority" and therefore under a duty not to act in a way which is incompatible with a Convention right.[49] Section 6(3) does not, for the reasons given above, create direct horizontal effect in all cases involving Convention rights. But in those cases in which the state and its organs (including the court) are under a positive duty to secure an individual's Convention rights against interference by other persons or entities, it is clearly arguable that it must do so save where precluded by the terms of the HRA.

4–50 The HRA's only impediment to the enforcement of Convention rights is the doctrine of parliamentary sovereignty.[50] A distinction must be drawn between incompatibility which can only be remedied by legislation, and incompatibility which can be removed by the development of common law doctrine and remedies. Absent legislation which is incompatible with the Convention rights or the inability of the court to remedy the incompatibility by the development of common law doctrine,[51] protection should be afforded in cases where the state and thus the court is under a positive duty. If the right is not protected, it will not have been "brought home" and an application to Strasbourg is likely to succeed.

There are, however, counter-arguments. The first is the argument from legal certainty. Beyond the decided cases, it is not always easy to predict when a positive duty will be imposed by the Strasbourg institutions. Clapham points out that the policy questions regarding violations by private individuals have been developed in the context of specific Articles[52] and the guidelines he suggests[53] are very broad and open-textured. The Court itself has stated that, where Article 8 is concerned, positive obligations are imposed where it has found "a direct and immediate link between the measures sought by the applicant and the latter's private and/or family life",[54] but beyond that its guidance has been limited. Even where the Strasbourg Court has imposed a positive duty upon another state party in a particular context, the extent of the duty may be unclear, and legal position in the United Kingdom may not amount to a violation.[55] Although this may well lead to a period of

---

[46] White Paper, Cm 3782. See above, para. 1–06.

[47] See above, Ch. 2.

[48] For examples of the actions of U.K. courts being challenged in Strasbourg see *The Observer and The Guardian v. U.K.* (1992) 14 E.H.R.R. 153; *Sunday Times (No. 2)* (1992) 14 E.H.R.R. 229; *Stubbings v. United Kingdom*, October 22, 1996, R.J.D., 1996–IV, No. 18; 23 E.H.R.R. 213; *SW v. United Kingdom* (1996) 21 E.H.R.R. 363; *Goodwin v. United Kingdom*, March 27, 1996, R.J.D., 1996–II, No. 7; 22 E.H.R.R. 123; *Chahal v. United Kingdom* (1997), November 15, 1996, R.J.D. 1996–II, No. 22; 23 E.H.R.R. 413.

[49] By s. 7(6)(b) "legal proceedings" include an appeal against the decision of a court or tribunal. On appeal a victim may rely on a failure by the lower court or tribunal to comply with its duty under s. 6(1) to give effect to positive rights: see s. 9(1).

[50] See above, paras 1–14, 3–05.

[51] See below, paras 4–56 *et seq.*, for suggestions as to the limits of such ability.

[52] *Human Rights in the Private Sphere* (1993), p. 240.

[53] *ibid.* pp. 196, 240. There may be a positive duty where the aim of the right in question is to protect the individual's dignity but not where is it to protect democracy, and the violation of human rights would probably not have occurred "but for" the absence of state action.

[54] *Botta v. Italy*, February 20, 1998; 26 E.H.R.R. 241, para. 34 (no positive obligation to furnish disabled access to bathing facilities.

[55] Compare, in relation to transsexuals, *Cossey v. U.K.* (1991) 13 E.H.R.R. 622, *B v. France* (1993) 16 E.H.R.R. 1 and *Sheffield & Horsham v. United Kingdom* (1997) 27 E.H.R.R. 163.

uncertainty while the courts identify the circumstances in which the Convention imposes on them a positive obligation to furnish a remedy, any such uncertainty already exists by reason of the activities of the Strasbourg Court. Domestic courts should not consider it a reason not to act compatibly with Convention rights.

4–51 The second objection relies upon the consequences of the positive obligation for the victim's opponent. It will be objected that in Strasbourg it is the state, not the individual, that is liable. Holding the individual liable would be to do more than "bringing rights home": full protection of a litigant's Convention rights would make an individual opponent liable in an English court where he or she could not be liable in Strasbourg, or would deprive him or her of rights which was understood that he or she enjoyed under domestic law. According to this approach, moreover, there is a strong reason of substance for not imposing such liability, or effecting such a deprivation. This is that where the Strasbourg Court holds the United Kingdom to be under a positive duty, any subsequent remedial legislation is not retrospective.[56] By contrast retrospective effect is the normal consequence of a judgment which makes new law or overrules a previous decision.[57] However, in positive obligation cases, failure to provide a remedy against another individual is the very thing for which Strasbourg holds the state liable. The right to such a remedy is one of the rights which is being "brought home". As to the objection based on retrospective judicial legislation, the individual is in no worse position than he would be had the domestic court revised or developed a new common law doctrine in a non-Convention area to take account of changed circumstances,[58] or overruled a previous interpretation of a statute governing relations between individuals in order to give effect to a Convention right.

The third objection relies on the structure of the Act itself. The HRA has not removed the right to take proceedings before the Strasbourg Court. This will still be necessary in cases of incompatible legislation where no remedial action is taken. The express exclusion of failure to legislate from the category of unlawful acts[59] suggests that the HRA itself contemplates that recourse to Strasbourg is the appropriate remedy for the individual where the Strasbourg case law on positive obligations reveals a lacuna. The question of when it is appropriate for courts to develop the common law raises fundamental questions.[60] But the mere fact that, at the international level, a Member State is under a positive duty to secure the Convention rights of individuals against other individuals does not *per se* justify the development of common law doctrine to remove inconsistency. It is suggested that this argument attaches too much importance to retention of the right of individual petition.

4–52 Fourthly, it may be suggested that the express terms of the HRA preclude horizontal effect. Section 6(1) of the Act imposes the duty to act compatibly with

---

[56] In the case of the creation of a criminal offence it cannot be retrospective (ECHR Article 7(1)) unless the act was criminal according to the general principles of law recognised by civilised nations (Article 7(2)).

[57] *DPP v. Shaw* [1962] A.C. 220; *Knuller v. DPP* [1973] A.C. 435; *R. v. R. (Rape: marital exemption)* [1992] 1 A.C. 599; *Woolwich Equitable BS v. IRC* [1993] 1 A.C. 70; *Kleinwort Benson v. Lincoln CC* [1998] 3 W.L.R. 1095.

[58] See the cases cited at n. 57 above.

[59] s. 6(6).

[60] The failure to incorporate Article 13 is not of significance in this context because of the remedies in HRA, ss. 6–8; see further below, paras 4–56 *et seq.*

Convention rights on "public authorities", but not on private parties. Although section 2(1) requires a court to take account of the Strasbourg case law, it may be argued that section 6 limits the effect which can be given to it. But this argument should not prevail. First, the national court itself is a public authority. By failing to give a right horizontal effect, the court itself is acting in a manner which is incompatible with its positive obligation arising from section 6 and the Convention. Secondly, where there is a positive duty, the policy of "bringing rights home" should affect the weight which a court gives to the Convention right and the Strasbourg jurisprudence when it takes them into account under section 2(1).

D. Convention rights as a tool for the development of the common law

4–53   The third situation in which Convention rights will have some horizontal effect is as a tool for the development of the common law. This was done by the Court of Appeal in *Derbyshire CC v. Times Newspapers Ltd*[61] and may have been done by the House of Lords[62] notwithstanding what their Lordships said.[63] Other examples have been given above.[64] Strictly speaking this form of horizontal effect is not a consequence of incorporation since the *Derbyshire* case is one of many examples of its occurrence before the enactment of the HRA. But it is likely that, although the HRA creates no presumption of compatibility between common law and Convention rights (as it does in the case of statutes as a result of section 2), the HRA will make courts more willing to use the Convention in this way. In the context of the South African Constitution, Kentridge JA (drawing on Canadian and German law) described this form of horizontal effect as indirect. He stated that while a fundamental right may override a rule of public law, "it is said to 'influence' rather than to override the rules of private law".[65] An example of this influence is provided by *Barrett v. Enfield LBC*.[66] The House of Lords held that a damages claim against a local authority for personal injury arising out of negligence should not be struck out. Lord Browne-Wilkinson, with whom Lord Nolan and Lord Steyn agreed, took account of the decision of the Strasbourg Court in *Osman v. United Kingdom* as to the scope of Article 6 in concluding that Barrett's case should be allowed to proceed to trial.

4–54   During the parliamentary consideration of the HRA it was widely thought that Article 8 might be used by the courts to create a general tort to protect privacy, as occurred in the United States.[67] The Lord Chancellor stated that any such development would not be the courts enforcing the Convention but developing the

---

[61] [1992] Q.B. 770.

[62] [1993] A.C. 534.

[63] The suggestion that the Convention and Article 10 in fact played an important, if spectral role, is supported by the summary of the argument for the newspaper, and the reliance by the Court on United States and Commonwealth cases involving constitutional provisions protecting freedom of speech: *City of Chicago v. Tribune Co.* 307 Ill. 595 (1923); *New York Times v. Sullivan* 376 U.S. 254 (1964); *Hector v. AG. of Antigua and Barbadua* [1990] 2 A.C. 312. See also *Die Spoorbond v. South African Railways* [1946] A.D. 999. For more overt reliance on the Convention's jurisprudence on Article 10, see *R. v. Secretary of State for the Home Department, ex parte Simms & O'Brien* [1999] 3 W.L.R. 328 especially Lord Steyn.

[64] See para. 1–02, n. 7.

[65] *Du Plessis v. De Klerk* 1996 (3) S.A. 850, 874.

[66] [1999] 3 W.L.R. 79, 84–85. See also *Gibson v. Chief Constable of Strathclyde Police, The Times*, May 11, 1999; *Reynolds v. Times Newspapers Ltd.*, October 28, 1999 (HL).

[67] See, *e.g. Pavesich v. New England Life Insurance Co.* 50 S.E. 68 (1905). See also the First Restatement of Torts, §867.

common law;[68] and sections 12 and 13 of the HRA, which were inserted to meet fears about the erosion of press and religious freedom, only require the courts to "have particular regard to the importance of" the Convention rights of freedom of expression and religion.[69] While this suggests some horizontal effect, it also implies that it is only to be what has been termed indirect effect. It has, however, been argued that the effect of section 6(3), while not creating direct horizontal effect, goes "considerably further in the direction of horizontality" than the Canadian and South African approaches.[70] This is because it places the courts "under an unequivocal duty to act compatibly with Convention rights" and will in some cases "require them actively to modify or develop the common law in order to achieve such compatibility". However, such development may be slow, as it is likely, at least in the early stages of the development of HRA jurisprudence, that the courts will adhere to their traditional incremental approach to the judicial development of the common law.

4–55   In the light of this discussion, the effect of the HRA on individuals will largely depend upon an identification at first, the compass of the term "public authority" and, secondly, the limits to the use of the Convention rights as a tool for the development of the common law. The broader the circumstances in which it is legitimate to use it in this way, the less the distinction in practice (if not in theory) between direct and indirect horizontal effect.[71] The "public authority" question has been considered above. The question of limitations upon the development of the common law is dealt with in the next section.

E.   The limits to the use of the Convention rights as a tool for the development of the common law

4–56   In Canada and South Africa it has been recognised that the fact that a Bill of Rights does not directly apply to the common law in private proceedings does not mean that it is not relevant in such cases. Thus, in *Retail Wholesale & Department Store Union v. Dolphin Delivery*[72] McIntyre J. said that the issue of the direct applicability of the Canadian Charter of Rights was "a distinct issue from the question whether the judiciary ought to apply and develop the principles of the common law in a manner consistent with the fundamental rights enshrined in the [Charter]". He stated that "the answer to this question must be in the affirmative". The South African Constitutional Court[73] has adopted a similar position, and, even before the enactment of the HRA, there were statements in the cases that the common law should be *interpreted*, so far as possible, with a predilection that it

---

[68] *Hansard*, H.L. Vol. 583, November 24, 1997, col. 784. See also *Hansard*, H.C. Vol. 306, cols 776–777; *Hansard*, H.C. Vol. 314, cols 411, 414. For signs of such a development at common law irrespective of the HRA, see *Khorasandijan v. Bush* [1993] Q.B. 727; *Hellewell v. Chief Constable of Derbyshire* [1995] 4 All E.R. 473, 476. *cf. Kaye v. Robertson* [1991] F.S.R. 62; Leigh, (1999) 48 I.C.L.Q. 57.

[69] ss. 12(4), 13(1). See further below, paras 4–60 *et seq.*

[70] Hunt [1998] P.L. 423, 441.

[71] For this reason the approach of Hunt [1998] P.L. 423, 441–442 , who rejects direct horizontal application, but argues that the effect of s. 6(3) is that norms protecting fundamental rights apply to all law so that a generous approach to the development of the common law is required, may in practice amount to the same thing.

[72] [1986] 2 S.C.R. 573 (Supreme Court of Canada). See also *Hill v. Church of Scientology of Toronto* [1995] 2 S.C.R. 1130, 1170–1171. For commentary, see Hogg, *Constitutional Law of Canada* (3rd ed. pp. 842, 845–847.

[73] *Du Plessis v. De Klerk* 1996 (3) S.A. 850.

should conform with the principles of the Convention.[74] We have noted the argument that the effect of section 6(3) of the HRA is to impose a duty actively to consider modifying the common law to achieve compatibility with Convention rights. We also noted the suggestions made during the parliamentary passage of the HRA that one example of such development might well be a tort of invasion of privacy. But can any further guidance be given as to when the courts are likely to modify the common law to make it more consistent with the fundamental values enshrined in the Convention?

4-57   There are a number of factors that will affect the willingness of a court, normally the court of last resort, to develop the common law. First, there is the status of the particular common law rule that is under consideration. Has it been criticised in purely common law terms, as were the rules precluding the recovery of payments made in response to *ultra vires* demands for tax,[75] and payments made under a mistake of law?[76] Is it based on a public policy which no longer requires it?[77] Can it be seen as fundamental or inextricably linked to other important rules, as some but not all consider the doctrine of privity of contract to be?[78] If the rule is deeply embedded so that any modification will have a ripple effect on other rules or require consequential changes, it is likely that the view will be that any change should be by legislation rather than by modifying common law doctrine. Secondly, the likelihood of judicial development will be reduced where the common law rule has been modified by statute, as in the case of the payment of interest in respect of damages.[79] Thirdly, judges are likely to be reluctant to respond when asked to devise a common law solution to a complex social and ethical problem.[80] Nevertheless, they may have to. A number of the significant developments that have taken place recently show that important questions have remained unresolved in our common law system and which Parliament has been either unable or unwilling[81] to resolve. For example, until 1989 there was no English authority on the question of whether medical treatment can lawfully be given to a person who is disabled by mental incapacity from consenting to it, a situation described by Lord

---

[74] See above, para. 1–02, in particular n. 7.

[75] *Woolwich Equitable BS v. IRC* [1993] 1 A.C. 70. Until then, in the absence of an agreement to repay, there was only an entitlement to recover money paid where, broadly speaking, the payment had been made under a mistake of fact or as a result of coercion amounting to duress, or where a right of recovery had been explicitly created by statute.

[76] *Kleinwort Benson v. Birmingham* [1998] 3 W.L.R. 1095.

[77] *Thai Trading Co. v. Taylor* [1998] 2 W.L.R. 893 (contingency fee agreements). One reason (901) the Court considered the policy against maintenance and champerty needed to be considered afresh was because of the policy in making access to justice readily accessible to persons of modest means, a factor perhaps sharpened (albeit silently) by the Court's awareness of the impact of the proposed withdrawal of legal aid in many cases. While the Divisional Court in *Hughes v. Kingston upon Hull City Council* (*The Times*, December 9, 1998) declined to follow *Thai Trading* as having been decided *per incuriam*, its principle is enshrined in legislation: see Access to Justice Act 1999, s. 27.

[78] *cf.* the majority and the minority in *Trident General Insurance Co. Ltd v. McNeice Bros Pty Ltd* (1988) 165 C.L.R. 107 (High Court of Australia). See also Lord Reid's view in *Tomlinson (Hauliers) Ltd v. Hepburn* [1966] A.C. 451, 470–471.

[79] *e.g. President of India v. La Pintada Cie Nav. S.A. (No. 2)* [1985] A.C. 104.

[80] See, *e.g.* Lord Browne-Wilkinson and Lord Mustill in *Airedale NHS Trust v. Bland* [1993] A.C. 789, 885, 891; see also Lord Mustill and Lord Slynn in *R. v. Brown* [1994] 1 A.C. 212 and *Laskey, Jaggard & Brown v. United Kingdom* (1997) 24 E.H.R.R. 39.

[81] Lord Goff thought this would be the position in respect of *ultra vires* receipts of tax, "however compelling the principle of justice", favouring recovery: *Woolwich Equitable BS v. IRC* [1993] A.C. 70, 176.

Goff as "startling";[82] and again, the failure of the common law to elaborate a general duty to give reasons is a candidate for change.[83]

4–58 But beyond this it is difficult to predict the response to a submission that a common law rule should be modified or developed. In part it will depend on the view taken of the judicial role, particularly in what, in the context of the HRA, is a constitutional matter. The difficulty is illustrated in Lord Goff's speech in the *Woolwich* case. The Crown had argued that the development of the common law to provide for a restitutionary remedy to citizens who had paid tax in response to an unlawful demand by a public authority would overstep the boundary the courts traditionally set for themselves, separating the legitimate development of the law by the judges from legislation. Lord Goff responded as follows:

" . . . although I am well aware of the existence of that boundary, I am never quite sure where to find it. Its position seems to vary from case to case. Indeed were it as firmly and clearly drawn as some of our mentors would wish, I cannot help feeling that a number of leading cases in [the House of Lords] would never have been decided in the way they were."[84]

He considered that, on that approach, the minority view would have prevailed in *Donoghue v. Stevenson*, the modern law of judicial review would never have developed, and *Mareva* injunctions (now known as "freezing injunctions"[85]) would have never seen the light of day.

But examples of the vitality of the common law can be given. These days judges are less impressed by the view that once seemed to be gaining favour that major developments, even in areas hitherto the preserve of the common law should, in future, be achieved by legislation.[86] For example, in 1991 the House of Lords held that the rule that a husband cannot be criminally liable for raping his wife no longer forms part of the law of England, recognising for the first time that rape within marriage is a crime.[87] In 1993 the House had to grapple with fundamental questions concerning the scope of the principle of the sanctity of life. In the tragic *Bland* case it held, for the first time, that doctors responsible for the treatment of a patient in a persistent vegetative state were not under a duty to provide medical treatment, including artificial feeding.[88] Of less dramatic impact but of fundamental significance to the law of obligations, in 1991 it also recognised the principle of

---

[82] *Re F (Mental Patient: Sterilisation)* [1990] A.C. 1, 72 (Lord Goff of Chievely). See also *R. v. Bournewood Community & Mental Health NHS Trust, ex parte L* [1998] 3 W.L.R. 107.

[83] As the Privy Council recognised in *Stefan v. General Medical Council*, [1999] 1 W.L.R. 1293. See also *R. v. Civil Service Appeal Board, ex parte Cunningham* [1992] I.C.R. 816; *R. v. Secretary of State for the Home Department, ex parte Doody & ors* [1991] A.C. 531.

[84] [1993] 1 A.C. 70, 173.

[85] C.P.R. 25.1(f).

[86] *Myers v. DPP* [1965] A.C. 1001, 1021; *Beswick v. Beswick* [1968] A.C. 58, 72, 85; *President of India v. La Pintada Cie Navegacion S.A. (No. 2)* [1985] A.C. 104, 111–112; *National Westminster Bank plc v. Morgan* [1985] A.C. 686, 708. But even when this was fashionable there were striking exceptions: *Rookes v. Barnard* [1968] A.C. 1129.

[87] *R. v. R. (Rape: Marital exemption)* [1992] 1 A.C. 599. This development of the law was approved by the ECtHR in *SW v. United Kingdom* (1996) 21 E.H.R.R. 363, which unanimously dismissed a challenge under Article 7 of the Convention (retrospective criminal legisation). Indeed, the Court implied at para. 44 of its judgment that criminalisation of such conduct was required by virtue of Articles 3 and/or 8 of the Convention: see below, para. C7–03. For another example concerning criminal law and evidence, see *R. v. Kearley* [1992] 2 A.C. 228, 345 (willingness to develop the rules governing the admissibility of hearsay evidence).

[88] *Airedale NHS Trust v. Bland* [1993] A.C. 789.

unjust enrichment as the unifying principle underlying liabilities to make restitution of benefits gained by the defendant at the claimant's expense.[89]

4-59 This vitality is especially apparent in cases concerning the relationship of the citizen and the state, in particular the development of a system of administrative law based on the power of the court to review the legality of administrative action. It has recently been held, albeit with a European Community catalyst, that coercive orders can be made against government ministers[90] and a citizen who makes a payment in response to an unlawful demand for tax is entitled to the repayment of the money irrespective of whether the payment was mistaken or made under coercion.[91] As in the rape in marriage case, the House consciously "reformulated" the law and "reinterpreted" principles. In particular, what holds for Community law is likely to spill over into purely domestic cases, as the courts will not willingly countenance distinctions in common law protections of fundamental rights which arise not from any difference of principle but from the simple question whether the actor is a public authority or not; or whether the substance is a matter within Community competence or not.[92]

These examples, particularly those in the area of public law with its constitutional dimension, suggest that the traditional incremental approach to the development of the common law need not be a significant barrier to the alignment of common law doctrine and Convention rights. The enactment of the HRA means that courts are likely to go beyond their existing predilection that the common law should be interpreted so far as possible to conform with the principles of the Convention.

5. FREEDOM OF EXPRESSION AND FREEDOM OF RELIGION

4-60 During the passage of the Act media interests and religious groups expressed concerns about its effect on their activities. The press and broadcasters were concerned that the HRA might lead to interference with freedom of the press, which is protected by Article 10 of the Convention, and about the possible creation of a right to privacy modelled on Article 8 of the Convention. Religious groups were concerned that the HRA might lead to interference with matters of doctrine, for example by requiring churches to marry homosexual couples, or the decisions of church courts. Although sections 12 and 13 of the HRA were inserted to meet these concerns, they are unlikely to make any practical difference.[93] In the case of the media, the Convention itself requires any rights to privacy to be balanced

---

[89] *Lipkin Gorman (a firm) v. Karpnale Ltd* [1991] A.C. 548.

[90] *R. v. Secretary of State for Transport, ex parte Factortame Ltd (No. 2)* [1991] 1 A.C. 603; *M v. Home Office* [1994] 1 A.C. 377. A citizen is also in principle entitled to an interim remedy preserving the status quo until the final determination of the matter. See further Advocate-General Jacobs, [1999] P.L. 232.

[91] *Woolwich Equitable Building Society v. IRC* [1993] 1 A.C. 70.

[92] See Sedley J. in *R. v. Secretary of State for the Home Department, ex parte McQuillan* [1995] 4 All E.R. 400, 422G–J. See also *M v. Home Office* [1994] 1 A.C. 377, 406–407 (Lord Woolf); *Woolwich Equitable B.S. v. I.R.C.* [1993] A.C. 70, 177 (Lord Goff).

[93] This was also the view of Edward Garnier M.P., who said of the section that "With all the diffidence at my command, I suggest that the new clause adds nothing in practice, except perhaps the imposition of an obligation on the court to express a view about the ultimate merits of an application before trial": HC Debs, July 5, 1998, col. 551.

against the right to freedom of expression,[94] and in the case of religions, much of what churches do is, in the context of the HRA, "essentially private in nature".[95]

A. Freedom of expression

4–61 Section 12 applies if a court[96] is considering whether to grant any relief[97] which, if granted, might affect the exercise of the Convention right to freedom of expression. Freedom of expression is protected by Article 10 of the Convention, and includes the right to "impart information and ideas without interference by public authority", subject to limitations "prescribed by law" and "necessary in a democratic society". Unlike section 13, section 12 is not limited to questions "arising under" the HRA: it applies to any relief touching upon freedom of expression. Nor is it limited to cases to which a public authority is a party[98]; and thus gives support to the proposition that this Convention right is enforceable in purely private proceedings; i.e. direct horizontal effect.[99] English law already reflects freedom of expression in a number of areas where relief is granted, for example in relation to the availability of injunctions to restrain the publication of allegedly defamatory material,[1] the level of damages in defamation proceedings,[2] the disclosure of sources[3] and control of access to the media.[4] Section 12(1) draws on this tradition, and generalises it so as to make it clear that it applies whenever freedom of expression is in issue, regardless of the formal characterisation of the issue. This meets a particular concern that any right to privacy developed as a result of Article 8 of the Convention should not unduly interfere with the freedom of the press. The reference in section 12(1) to any relief which "might" (as opposed to "would") affect the exercise of freedom of expression is a further indication of the importance which the Act ascribes to this right. Section 12(2) deals with grant of any such relief in the absence of the respondent. Section 12(3) deals specifically with interim injunctions. Section 12(4) propounds a general rule, applicable to all relief in this area, and a special rule applicable to "journalistic, literary or artistic material".[5]

---

[94] See below, paras 4–65 et seq.. The Government took this view: *Hansard*, H.C. Vol. 315, July 2, 1998, col. 543 (Home Secretary). See *Hansard*, H.C. Vol. 306, February 16, 1998 cols. 775–777; *Hansard*, H.L. Vol. 582, November 3, 1997, col. 1229, *Hansard*, H.L. Vol. 583, November 24, 1997, cols 771–774, 783–787 (Lord Chancellor); *Hansard*, H.L. Vol. 583, November 3, 1997, cols 1309–1310 (Lord Williams of Mostyn). For a recent example of the balance, see *Fressoz and Roire v. France* Application No. 29183/95 January 21, 1999.

[95] *Hansard*, H.C. Vol. 312, May 20, 1998, cols 1015–1018 (Home Secretary), 1036, 1066 (Secretary of State for Scotland). See also *Hansard*, H.C. Vol. 317, October 21, 1998, col. 1368.

[96] By HRA, s. 12(5) this includes a tribunal, as defined in s. 21.

[97] Other than in criminal proceedings, s. 12(5). These were said to be excluded so as not to affect practice on reporting restrictions in such proceedings: *Hansard*, H.C. Vol. 315, July 2, 1998, col. 540 (Home Secretary).

[98] See Jack Straw M.P., *Hansard*, H.C., July 2, 1998, col. 536.

[99] On the ways in which the HRA may have horizontal effect, see above, paras 4–47 et seq.

[1] See below.

[2] *Rantzen v. Mirror Group Newspapers* [1994] Q.B. 670; *Reynolds v. Times Newspapers Ltd.*, October 28, 1999 (HL).

[3] *Camelot v. Centaur Communications* [1999] Q.B. 124, CA.

[4] *R. v. Secretary of State for the Home Department, ex parte Simms & O'Brien* [1999] 3 W.L.R. 328.

[5] The expression is also used in s. 32 (1)(a) of the Data Protection Act 1998 (exemption from the data protection principles and ss. 7, 10, 12 and 14(1)–(3) of the Act). See also ss. 8–13 and ss. 13–14 of the Police and Criminal Evidence Act 1984 (special provision in respect of "journalistic material" in relation search and seizure and production orders).

B.   Freedom of expression and injunctive relief

(1)   The grant of relief in the absence of the respondent

4–62   Section 12(2) meets a particular concern among the media, about "gagging" orders sought without notice to the respondent shortly before publication. It provides:

> "(a) if the person against whom the application for relief is made is neither present nor represented, no such relief is to be granted unless the court is satisfied
> (b) that the applicant has taken all practicable steps to notify the respondent; or that there are compelling reasons why the respondent should not be notified."

The Civil Procedure Rules already require that an interim remedy should be granted without notice only if "the matter is urgent" or "it is otherwise necessary to do so in the interests of justice".[6] In practice notice should be given to the proposed respondent if it is possible to do so, save in exceptional circumstances (such as where notice would be likely to lead to a disreputable respondent taking steps to pre-empt the order before it can be made or in cases raising issues of national security).[7] Since subsection (2) now embodies these rules of practice in statutory form, an applicant for an injunction (who owes a duty of full and frank disclosure on an application made without notice) should include in evidence a statement of the steps that have been taken to notify the respondent, or of the "compelling reasons" why such notification is inappropriate. This requirement would appear to go to jurisdiction, and failure to comply with it is not a mere irregularity under the rules of court.

(2)   Interim injunctions generally[8]

4–63   Section 12(3) deals more generally with the principles on which interim injunctions may be granted. It provides that:

> "No such relief[9] is to be granted so as to restrain publication before trial unless the court is satisfied that the applicant is likely to establish that publication should not be allowed."

In general, an applicant for such an injunction need only show that there is a "serious question to be tried" in order to engage the court's discretion to grant an injunction.[10] That standard, however, has never applied where an injunction is sought to restrain publication of allegedly defamatory material.[11] According to

---

[6] Civil Procedure Rule 25.2(1). CPR, 25 is broader than RSC, Ord. 29, r. 1(2) where "urgency" was required in all cases. However, it is doubtful whether any change in the former practice was intended: see Civil Procedure, CPR 25.2.4.
[7] *Hansard*, H.C., July 2, 1998, col. 536 (Home Secretary).
[8] The Strasbourg case law on prior restraints is considered below at paras C10–16—C10–12. See in particular *The Observer and The Guardian v. U.K.* (1992) 14 E.H.R.R. 153 and *Sunday Times v. U.K. (No. 2)* (1992) 14 E.H.R.R. 229.
[9] *i.e.* relief which, if granted, might affect the exercise of the Convention right to freedom of expression.
[10] *American Cyanamid Co. v. Ethicon Ltd* [1975] A.C. 396.
[11] *Bestabell Paints Ltd v. Bigg* [1975] F.S.R. 421.

Bonnard v. Perryman, "[t]he importance of leaving free speech unfettered is a strong reason in cases of libel for dealing most cautiously and warily with the granting of interim injunctions."[12] Thus, the statement complained of must be clearly defamatory;[13] and no injunction is granted where the respondent states that he is prepared to justify the defamatory statement,[14] unless the statement is plainly a lie. A similar approach has been taken to other defences, such as privilege[15] and fair comment.[16]

The effect of section 12 is to apply this cautious approach—requiring an applicant to show that on balance his claim is likely to succeed—to all cases where an injunction is sought that would restrain publication before trial. This is necessary because there is authority that the ordinary *American Cyanamid* standard applies outside the libel field,[17] (although in practice the courts have shown considerable restraint as a matter of discretion in granting interlocutory injunctions restraining publication in such cases).[18] Thus, the position outside the libel field is unsettled. The application of any special principle in the area of breach of confidence that is likely to form the basis of any development of a privacy tort is also controversial.

4–64   What change, if any, does section 12 make to the established principles applicable to the grant of injunctions to restrain publication? First, it makes it clear that the rule requiring more than merely a serious question to be tried is a jurisdictional rule: without proof that an applicant is "likely" to succeed at trial, no injunction is to be granted. In this respect the Act may go beyond the common law, where the rule in *Bonnard v. Perryman* operates as an aspect of the court's discretion.[19] Secondly, as stated above, it makes clear that the cautious approach is required in all cases where freedom of expression is in issue, not simply in defamation cases. Thirdly, it is arguable that in order to discharge the burden of showing that he is likely to succeed at trial, the applicant must positively adduce evidence that will enable the court to assess the likelihood of there being an available defence. For example, he ought at least to depose to the fact that an alleged libel is untrue.

In some respects, however, section 12 may provide less protection than the common law. For instance, it is generally sufficient to preclude the grant of an interlocutory injunction that the respondent avers an intention to justify a defamatory statement, and that the statement is not "plainly untrue". The Act may not go so far, since it can be "likely" that a statement is untrue without it being "plainly" untrue. In so far as additional protection is offered at common law, section 12 does not supersede that protection, but, as is shown by section 11 of the HRA,[20] leaves it intact.

(3)   The balance between freedom of expression and other rights

4–65   Section 12(4) provides that:

---

[12] *Bonnard v. Perryman* [1891] 2 Ch. 269 *per* Lord Coleridge at 284. On the Article 10 jurisprudence on this, see below, para. C10–16 and *Observer & Guardian v. U.K.* (1994) 14 E.H.R.R. 153, 191.
[13] *Coulson v. Coulson* [1887] 3 T.L.R. 846 (CA).
[14] *Bonnard v. Perryman,* above.
[15] *Harakas v. Baltic Mercantile and Shipping Exchange Ltd* [1982] 1 W.L.R. 958.
[16] *Fraser v. Evans* [1969] 1 Q.B. 349, *per* Lord Denning MR at 360.
[17] Albeit that freedom of expression is brought into the balance when deciding as a matter of discretion whether to grant an injunction: *Gulf Oil (G.B.) Ltd v. Page* [1987] Ch. 327 (CA) (conspiracy to injure).
[18] *Femis-Bank (Anguilla) Ltd v. Lazar* [1991] 2 All E.R. 865.
[19] *Holley v. Smyth* [1998] Q.B. 726, *per* Auld L.J. at 743.
[20] By s. 11 "A person's reliance on a Convention right does not restrict–(a) any other right or freedom conferred on him by or under any law having effect in any part of the United Kingdom".

"The court must have particular regard to the importance of the Convention right to freedom of expression and, where the proceedings relate to material which the respondent claims, or which appears to the court, to be journalistic, literary or artistic material (or to conduct connected with such material), to:

    (a) the extent to which:

        (i) the material has, or is about to, become available to the public, or

        (ii) it is, or would be, in the public interest for the material to be published;

    (b) any relevant privacy code."

Section 12(4) anticipates the possible development of a privacy tort.[21] The first part of the subsection is a general rule which directs a court to have particular regard to the importance of freedom of expression when it is considering whether to grant any relief which might affect the exercise of that freedom. The second part is especially directed at the exercise of discretion to grant an injunction to restrain publication of material which is alleged to breach the applicant's right of privacy.

4–66 The requirement that "the court must have particular regard to the importance of the Convention right to freedom of expression" is not intended to alter the Convention, under which freedom of expression is not an absolute right. Rather, it is a direction to the court to lean in favour of freedom of expression, in particular in cases concerning the freedom of the press to publish material on matters of public interest. This part of section 12(4) echoes the case law of the Strasbourg Court[22] to the effect that the press have the task of imparting information and ideas on matters of public interest and the public also has a right to receive them; and that an interference with the exercise of press freedom cannot be compatible with Article 10 of the Convention unless it is justified by an overriding requirement in the public interest.[23] But Article 10 will not invariably "trump" Article 8.[24]

The second rule in subsection (4) differs from subsections (1)–(3), because it does not apply to all cases where freedom of expression is in issue. It is concerned to protect "journalistic, literary or artistic material".[25] "Conduct connected with such material" was said to be intended to cover cases where it is believed there is a story but it has not yet been written,[26] *i.e.* investigation for the purposes of preparing a story will be covered.[27] It appears that the mere claim by the respondent that

---

[21] For signs of such a development at common law, see *Khorasandijan v. Bush* [1993] Q.B. 727; *Hellewell v. Chief Constable of Derbyshire* [1995] 4 All E.R. 473, 476. *cf. Kaye v. Robertson* [1991] F.S.R. 62. On the impact of the HRA on this, see above, paras 4–53 *et seq.* See further Grosz & Braithwaite, "Privacy and the Human Rights Act" in *A Practitioner's Guide to the Impact of the Human Rights Act 1998*, Hunt & Singh (eds.).

[22] The case law relating to Article 10 is considered below, C10–01 *et seq.*

[23] See *Fressoz & Roire v. France*, Application No. 29183/95, judgment of January 21, 1999.

[24] See, however, the *dictum* of Hoffmann L.J. in *R. v. Central Television plc.* "It cannot be too strongly emphasised that outside the established exceptions (or any new ones which Parliament may enact in accordance with its obligations under the Convention) there is no question of balancing freedom of speech against other interest. It is the trump card": [1994] 3 All E.R. 641 at 652.

[25] The expression is also used in the exemptions contained in s.32 (1)(a) of the Data Protection Act 1998 (exemption from the data protection principles and ss. 7, 10, 12 and 14(1)–(3) of the Act). See also Police and Criminal Evidence Act 1984, s. 14 and Sched. 1 (production of journalistic material).

[26] *Hansard*, H.C. Vol. 315, July 2, 1998, col. 540 (Home Secretary).

[27] *Goodwin v. U.K.* March 27, 1996, R.J.D., 1996–II, No. 7; 22 E.H.R.R. 123, 143. See below, para. C10–34.

material falls within that category is sufficient. The court is apparently not permitted to go behind the respondent's claim, no matter how far-fetched and unreasonable; although there must come a point where a claim is so absurd as to lead to the inference that it is not made honestly and in good faith. In these exceptional circumstances the court would be justified in disregarding it. And when the court comes to apply subsection (4) the weight to be given to each of the factors mentioned will quite properly be coloured by the court's own assessment of the nature of the material in question. Subsection (4) also requires the court to consider the matters in paragraphs (a) and (b) of its own motion, for example where it arises in proceedings in which the respondent is not represented.

4–67 In connection with injunctions to protect confidential information the court is also directed to have particular regard to the extent to which the material has, or is about to become, available to the public.[28] The fact that information has already been made public is naturally a relevant factor. In *Attorney-General v. Guardian Newspapers Ltd (No. 2)*[29] the House of Lords declined to accept that imminent publication by a third party would have prevented the grant of an injunction to restrain publication by the respondent.[30] In equating prior publication with *imminent* publication where the grant of an interlocutory injunction is in issue, the Act, therefore, breaks new ground.

The court is further required to have particular regard to the extent to which "it is, or would be, in the public interest for the material to be published".[31] Again, the law of confidentiality already recognises that "public interest" may operate both as a defence and as a reason not to exercise the equitable jurisdiction to restrain publication.[32] In this respect, therefore, the Act recognises and generalises the common law position.

4–68 Finally, by section 12(4)(b), the court is directed to have regard to "any relevant privacy code". "Privacy code" is undefined. It clearly includes codes produced by regulatory and self-regulatory bodies which qualify as public author-ities for the purposes of section 6 of the HRA.[33] The Court of Appeal, and the preponderance of opinion during the passage of the HRA, assumed that the Press Complaints Commission is amenable to judicial review and thus qualifies as a public authority.[34] It is suggested that in any event codes produced by such self-regulatory bodies as the Press Complaints Commission, the Broadcasting Standards Council or the Independent Television Commission clearly qualify.[35] It is also possible that the

---

[28] Section 12(4)(a)(i).
[29] [1990] 1 A.C. 109.
[30] *ibid., per* Lord Keith at 261, per Lord Goff at p. 292.
[31] s. 12(4)(a)(ii).
[32] See, *e.g., Attorney-General v. Guardian Newspapers (No. 2)* [1990] 1 A.C. 109; *Price Waterhouse v. BCCI* [1992] B.C.L.C. 583. On the need for a "pressing social need", see *Sunday Times Ltd v. U.K. (No. 2)* (1991) 14 E.H.R.R. 229, para. 50; *Goodwin v. United Kingdom*, March 27, 1996, R.J.D., 1996–II, No. 7; 22 E.H.R.R. 123, para. 39.
[33] See above, paras 4–02 *et seq.*
[34] But *R. v. PCC, ex parte Stewart-Brady* (1996) 9 Admin L.R. 274 [1997] E.M.L.R. 185 did not decide the point. On which regulatory bodies are likely to be "public authorities" and directly subject to the duty in HRA, s. 6, see above, paras 4–07, 4–10—4–14. On views expressed about the status of the PCC, see *Hansard*, H.L. Vol. 583, November 24, 1997, cols 771–774, 783–787, 796 (Lord Chancellor) *Hansard*, H.C., February 16, 1998, col. 778; *Hansard*, H.C. Vol. 316, June 17, 1998, col. 414 (Home Secretary).
[35] *Hansard*, H.C. Vol. 315, July 2, 1998, cols 538–539.

principles contained in a privacy code may render it "relevant" even though the media organisation is not itself subject to the code. But it also appears to have been intended that purely private codes, such as those that might be developed by a particular newspaper or broadcasting body for internal use, would be encompassed.[36] The weight to be attached to any such code must vary depending on its provenance and content; more weight is bound to be attached to general public codes developed by independent organisations than to potentially self-serving internal documents. Some might think it odd, in any event, that codes produced by private organisations without statutory authority, which may not even be publicly available, should affect the rights of third parties.

C. Religious bodies and freedom of thought, conscience and religion

4–69   Section 13(1) of the HRA provides that "[I]f a court's determination of any question arising under this Act might affect the exercise by a religious organisation (itself or its members collectively) of the Convention right to freedom of thought, conscience and religion, it must have particular regard to the importance of that right". This section was inserted to meet concerns expressed by religious groups that the Act might lead to interference with matters of doctrine, for example by requiring churches to marry homosexual couples. It only applies to questions arising under the HRA and is therefore narrower than section 12.

The requirement to have "particular regard to the importance" of the right of freedom of thought, conscience, and religion embodied in Article 9 of the Convention should not be regarded as derogating from or altering the Convention. At most it is a direction to U.K. courts, within the margin of appreciation which the court affords to states, to pay particular attention to those freedoms. This is consistent with the approach in *Wingrove v. U.K.*[37] where the Strasbourg Court indicated that Article 9 should be taken into account in assessing restrictions on the freedom of expression designed to prevent insult to religious feelings. But the Article 9 right is not to be treated as inevitably trumping other rights under the Convention. If, having had regard to Article 9, a court decides that its importance is outweighed by another right in a particular case, then that other right will take precedence.

4–70   Indeed, if section 13 were to single out "religious" organisations for special treatment, it would probably be inconsistent with the Convention. Article 14 precludes any discrimination in the enjoyment of the Convention's rights and freedoms "on any ground such as . . . religion, political or other opinion . . .".[38] It is hard to see what justification there can be for treating the right to freedom of thought, conscience and religion as more important when it is claimed by a "religious" organisation than when it is claimed by some other organisation of conscience. Consistently with section 3 of the HRA, then, section 13 should not be treated as conferring special protection on theistic organisations. Read in this way, section 13 adds very little to the Act: it simply reinforces the message that courts, as public authorities, are bound to respect the Convention.[39]

D. Ecclesiastical courts and tribunals

4–71   Section 13 applies to the determination of "courts" and "tribunals". A tribunal is defined as "any tribunal in which legal proceedings may be brought".

---

[36] *Hansard*, H.C. Vol. 315, July 2, 1998, cols 539–540.

[37] November 25, 1996, R.J.D., 1996–V, No. 23; 24 E.H.R.R 1. See further, below, para. C10–28.

[38] See below, paras C14–01 *et seq.*

[39] See *Hansard*, H.C. Vol. 312, May 20, 1998, col. 1015, *Hansard*, H.C. Vol. 317, October 21, 1998, col. 1368.

The question whether ecclesiastical "courts" fall within section 13 depends upon whether they are "public authorities" and whether the proceedings in them are "legal" proceedings.

E. The Church of England

4–72 The courts of the Established Church, the Church of England, exercise jurisdiction either under the Ecclesiatical Jurisdiction Measure 1963 or the Benefices Act 1898.[40] They are regulated by Measures which have the effect of Acts of Parliament. They have the right to compel the attendance of witnesses and the production of documents.[41] They have "legal authority to determine questions affecting the rights of subjects" and satisfy Atkin L.J.'s classic test for the amenability of bodies to *certiorari*.[42] As such they are public authorities: the state sanctions their carrying out these judicial functions, and they form, for that reason, part of its fabric. It is this that is the justification for the exercise by the Court of its judicial review jurisdiction over the courts of the established church.[43] Since section 13 is limited to questions arising "under" the HRA, and these bodies are "public authorities", it will apply to them.

F. Unestablished churches and other religions

4–73 The position of other ecclesiastical tribunals, for example those of unestablished or disestablished churches, the Jewish Beth Din, or the Muslim Sharia court, is different. They do not carry out their functions on behalf of the state and are not public authorities for the purposes of judicial review[44] or the HRA. During the parliamentary passage of the HRA, it was said that the Scottish churches do not adjudicate on citizens' legal rights or obligations, either statutory or at common law. This would appear to be true of all unestablished religions.[45] On this basis, even if section 13 has an application beyond bodies which are public authorities for the purposes of section 6, it does not apply to tribunals of unestablished religions since they do not have power to affect citizens' *legal* rights or obligations and do not fall within the term "tribunal" in section 13(2), as defined in section 21 of the HRA.

---

[40] See further 14 *Halsbury's Laws of England*, paras 1272 *et seq.*
[41] *Hansard*, H.L. Vol. 585, February 5, 1998, col. 794; *Hansard*, H.C. Vol. 312, May 20, 1998, cols 1064–1066.
[42] *R. v. Electricity Commissioners, ex parte London Electricity Joint Committee Co.* [1924] 1 K.B. 171, 205. On the scope of the judicial review jurisdiction, see further above, para. 4–05.
[43] *R. v. Chancellor of St Edmundsbury and Ipswich Diocese, ex parte White* [1948] 1 K.B. 195; *R. v. Chancellor of the Chichester Consistory Court, ex parte News Group Newspapers* (unreported) June 27, 1991.
[44] *R. v. Chief Rabbi of United Hebrew Congregations, ex parte Wachmann* [1992] 1 W.L.R. 1036; *Ali v. Imam of Bury Park*, May 12, 1993; *R. v. London Beth Din (Court of the Chief Rabbi) ex parte Bloom*, November 18, 1997; *R. v. Provincial Court of the Church in Wales, ex parte Williams*, October 23, 1998.
[45] Save where, and to the extent that, a specific statute provides otherwise. On solemnisation and registration of marriages, see 14 *Halsbury's Laws of England*, paras 1398, 1411, 1420, 1430. On the slaughter of animals and birds by Jews and Muslims, see Slaughter of Poultry Act 1967, s. 1(2); Slaughterhouses Act 1974, s. 36(3), Sched. 1.

CHAPTER 5

The impact of the Convention on judicial review and the review of discretion

1. INTRODUCTION

5-01   Enactment of the HRA will lead to significant changes in the approach of English courts to the review of administrative acts and subordinate legislation which impinge upon a Convention right. Until recently the combination of very open-textured principles of judicial review and a relatively unstructured and opaque discretion at the remedial stage has made for a rather fragile set of public law "rights". This is so despite the undoubted advances made since the landmark decisions of the 1960s,[1] in particular the "anxious scrutiny" to which administrative decisions concerning human rights are now subjected.[2] The greater willingness to adopt a "rights" based approach to judicial review seen in recent cases,[3] often with the aid of common law presumptions,[4] will become more important when the HRA comes into force. The court's duty as a public authority, under section 6(1), to act in a manner which is compatible with Convention rights, will add statutory force to common law doctrine. This is likely to require a greater articulation of the principle by courts than has generally been seen.[5] In the longer term the Strasbourg jurisprudence may have a "spill-over" effect on the approach of courts exercising the judicial review jurisdiction in the same way as the Luxembourg jurisprudence

---

[1] *Ridge v. Baldwin* [1964] A.C. 40; *R. v. Criminal Injuries Compensation Board, ex parte Lain* [1967] 2 Q.B. 864; *Anisminic v. F.C.C.* [1969] 2 A.C. 147.

[2] *Bugdaycay v. Secretary of State for the Home Department* [1987] A.C. 514; *R. v. Secretary of State for the Home Department, ex parte Brind* [1991] 1 A.C. 696, 748–749; *R. v. Ministry of Defence, ex parte Smith* [1996] Q.B. 517.

[3] *R. v. Secretary of State for Foreign and Commonwealth Affairs, ex parte Everett* [1989] Q.B. 811; *R. v. Secretary of State for the Home Department, ex parte McQuillan* [1994] 4 All E.R. 400 (freedom of movement); *R. v. Maidstone Crown Court, ex parte Clark* [1995] 1 W.L.R. 831 (right to bail); *R. v. Lord Chancellor, ex parte Witham* [1998] Q.B. 575 (access to justice); *R. v. Secretary of State for the Home Department, ex parte Simms & O'Brien* [1999] 3 W.L.R. 328 (access to justice); *R. v. Lord Saville of Newdigate and Others, ex parte A and Others* (DC) *The Times*, July 29, 1999, 149 N.L.J. 965, 1201 (right to life). On statutory rights see *R. v. Secretary of State for Social Security, ex parte JCWI* [1997] 1 W.L.R. 275, 292. For other examples see Fordham, *Judicial Review Handbook* (2nd ed.), pp. 128 *et seq.* See also Browne-Wilkinson [1992] P.L. 397; Laws [1993] P.L. 59.

[4] See above, paras 1–02, 3–11—3–12.

[5] *R. v. Ministry of Defence, ex parte Smith* [1996] Q.B. 517, at 541 (*per* Simon Brown L.J. and Sir Thomas Bingham M.R.). See Hunt *Using Human Rights Law in English Courts* (1997) pp. 211 *et seq.* and pp. 319 *et seq.* But *cf.* Bratza in Gardner (ed.), *Aspects of the Incorporation of the European Convention on Human Rights into Domestic Law* (1993), p. 65; McCrudden & Chambers, *Individual Rights and the Law in Britain* (1994) p. 575. For examples of such articulation, see *R. v. Secretary of State for the Home Department, ex parte McQuillan* [1994] 4 All E.R. 400; *R. v. Broadcasting Complaints Commission, ex parte BBC* (1994) 6 Admin. L.R. 714.

has had an effect in contexts in which E.C. or E.U. law is not applicable.[6] But initially the effect will probably be confined to cases in which Convention rights are or are likely to be affected.

5–02 Even where Convention rights are in play some things will not change. For the most part, the role of the court will remain that of a reviewing court exercising a supervisory rather than an appellate jurisdiction, although the supervision is likely to become more extensive. So also, courts are likely to remain disinclined to exercise close scrutiny over complex and polycentric economic issues or sensitive socio-moral questions, or areas of decision depending largely on administrative expediency, specialised technical issues or questions of policy. But other things will change. For example, *Wednesbury* "unreasonableness" will probably evolve into a number of more concrete principles including proportionality, legal certainty, consistency and non-discrimination.[7] The principles of consistency and non-discrimination may be the vehicles for the development of the substantive protection of legitimate expectations in appropriate cases. Laws L.J. has said that the challenge is to develop the common law as "part of a *continuum* with everything that has gone before" and not as "an alien add-on", because the principles of freedom and fairness which the ECHR enshrines are the very principles respected by the common law.[8] It is indeed important to do this and, again in Laws L.J's words, "to modernize the common law according to the methods of the common law" so as to achieve a good "fit" between the old and the new. But while significant aspects of existing administrative law may survive scrutiny by the standards of the Convention, regarding the role of the Convention rights as giving new focus and emphasis to principles respected by the common law should not be seen as a way of minimising the extent of the changes that will be necessary.

5–03 In this chapter we examine the effect which the HRA will have on judicial review of administrative action. In order to do so, we first set out in outline the questions which the Strasbourg Court asks when reviewing national measures or defining the extent of states' positive obligations arising from the Convention rights. This is likely to be of assistance to an English court in view of the obligation in section 2 of the HRA to take account of the Strasbourg case law. We will then consider how that analytical structure will impact upon the process of judicial review.

The Strasbourg Court first enquires whether an administrative decision or legislative measure has interfered with a Convention right. This question has to be answered bearing in mind the need to construe the Convention broadly in order to give it practical effectiveness.[9] In many areas there exists a body of case law that will assist in this process of interpretation. This issue is mentioned briefly in this chapter but is primarily dealt with in the commentary on the Strasbourg case law.[10]

---

[6] *M v. Home Office* [1994] 1 A.C. 377 (spilling over from Cases C–43 and C48/93 *Brasserie du Pecheur v. Germany* and Case 48/93 *R. v. Secretary of State for Transport, ex parte Factortame Ltd* [1996] E.C.R. I–1029) and *Woolwich Building Society v. Inland Revenue Commissioners* [1994] A.C. 70 (spilling over *inter alia* from Case 199/82 *Amministrazione della Finanze dello Stato v. San Giorgio* [1983] E.C.R. 3595). See also Jacobs [1999] P.L. 232 and note the discussion concerning interpretation above, para. 3–26.
[7] This was anticipated in Jowell & Lester's important critique of *Wednesbury* "unreasonableness"; [1987] P. L. 368.
[8] *The Human Rights Act and the Criminal Justice and Regulatory Process* (Cambridge Centre for Public Law, 1999), p. xiii.
[9] *e.g. Artico v. Italy* (1980) 3 E.H.R.R. 1, para. 33.
[10] See below, Part II.

5–04   Where an administrative decision has interfered with a Convention right, the court asks whether the interference is justified. While some forms of interference are never, or almost never, justified,[11] in many cases some restriction on rights is justifiable. Characteristically, to be justified a restriction must be:

(a) "lawful";

(b) intended to pursue a legitimate aim;

(c) "necessary in a democratic society"; and

(d) non-discriminatory.

We shall see that similar issues arise when determining the existence and extent of a state's positive obligation to protect or "respect" Convention rights. Determination of these questions, whether in relation to positive or negative obligations, raises a difficult issue for our courts. On what basis should they approach the task of evaluating the justification for an interference with a Convention right or the propriety of the balance which the public authority has struck? In assessing the lawfulness and proportionality of domestic measures, the Strasbourg institutions have attached considerable importance to the availability of adequate judicial safeguards against abuse.[12] Provision of those safeguards is therefore an inherent part of ensuring that an interference is justified and that a fair balance is struck.

5–05   Questions about the necessary degree of intervention required arise particularly acutely where an administrative decision involves the "determination of a civil right" within the meaning of Article 6(1) of the Convention.[13] In such a case our courts will also have to work out the practical implications of the "right to a fair hearing by an independent and impartial tribunal" in Article 6, i.e. implicitly the "right to a court",[14] and of the guarantees inherent in the notion of a "court".[15] In particular, must there be access to a court with full jurisdiction to determine all aspects of the issue (i.e. factual matters as well as questions of law)?

The final section of this chapter deals with the sort of evidence that will be needed in cases where there has been interference with a Convention right. Even where Article 6 does not require a court to substitute its own findings of fact, the requirements that the interference must be justified according to Convention principles, and those of a fair trial are likely to mean that a wider range of evidence will have to be before the court.

2. HAS THE ADMINISTRATIVE DECISION INTERFERED WITH A CONVENTION RIGHT?

5–06   In considering whether there has been interference with a Convention right, the court must bear in mind the need to construe the Convention broadly. As

---

[11] See below, paras C2–15 et seq., C3–03, C4–03, C7–02.
[12] See, for example, *Buckley v. United Kingdom* (1997) 23 E.H.R.R. 101, paras 81–84. See further paras 5–24 et seq., 5–33 et seq., C6–46 et seq., C13–11 et seq.
[13] As well as Article 6 (right to a court), other provisions may also require effective access to a remedy: see Article 5 (judicial review of detention), and Article 13 (right to an effective remedy before a national authority when a Convention violation is claimed—need not be a court). The need for (judicial) safeguards may also be implied in the requirements of lawfulness or proportionality: see below, paras 5–09, 5–13.
[14] *Golder v. United Kingdom* (1975) 1 E.H.R.R. 524.
[15] *De Wilde, Ooms and Versyp v. Belgium* (the 'Vagrancy Case') (1971) 1 E.H.R.R. 373, para. 78. See also *Sanchez-Reisse v. Switzerland* (1987) 9 E.H.R.R. 71; and see further II–5.073.

with any treaty, the Convention is to be interpreted "in good faith in accordance with the ordinary meaning to be given to the terms of the treaty in their context and in the light of its object and purpose".[16] However, these general principles must themselves be applied with sensitivity to the fact that the Convention is far from being a typical international treaty.

5–07   The Strasbourg Court has frequently stressed the importance of giving full weight to the object and purpose of the Convention.[17] It has declined invitations to construe the rights guaranteed by the Convention narrowly, regarding such an approach as insufficient to "realise the aim and achieve the object" of the Convention.[18] Thus, the court considers that "the object and purpose of the Convention as an instrument for the protection of individual human beings require that its provisions be interpreted so as to make its safeguards practical and effective".[19] In many areas there exists a body of case law that will assist in this process of interpretation. This is considered in the commentary on the Convention in Part II.[20] The fact that the Convention is a "living instrument" which must be given a dynamic interpretation has been noted.[21] This dynamic interpretation and of the prohibition of discrimination in the enjoyment of Convention rights have been vehicles for expansion of the scope and content of the rights. The commentary on the Strasbourg case law[22] also gives examples of this. The most notable ones concern access to the court[23] and, in the context of discrimination, the status of the children born outside marriage and of homosexuals.[24] This is not to say, of course, that the court aims to corral state action within unrealistic bounds. Interferences with rights may often be justified, and the "living instrument" approach means that, like the scope of the rights, the ambit of the permitted exceptions will also vary over time. In delimiting the rights themselves, however, the court prefers to take a broad approach in order to secure that the Convention is effective. The broader the scope of the rights, the greater the extent to which interference with them is subjected to judicial scrutiny. The legitimacy of each interference with those rights is then separately considered, on its own merits. It should not be forgotten, however, that not all administrative acts affect human rights.[25]

3.   JUSTIFICATION: THE PROPER APPROACH TO THE REVIEW OF INTERFERENCES WITH CONVENTION RIGHTS AND THE IDENTIFICATION OF POSITIVE OBLIGATIONS

5–08   We now turn to the approach to be adopted in considering whether an interference with a Convention right is justified or a positive obligation arises. As

---

[16] Vienna Convention on the Law of Treaties, Article 31.
[17] *Brogan v. United Kingdom* (1989) 11 E.H.R.R. 117, para. 58; *Gropppera Radio A.G. v. Switzerland* (1990) 12 E.H.R.R. 321, para. 61; *Van der Mussele v. Belgium* (1984) 6 E.H.R.R. 163, para. 49.
[18] See *Wemhoff v. Germany* (1968) 1 E.H.R.R. 55, para. 8.
[19] *Loizidou v. Turkey* (1995) 20 E.H.R.R. 99, para. 72. See also *Artico v. Italy* (1980) 3 E.H.R.R. 1, para. 33.
[20] See below, p. 162 *et seq.*
[21] See above, paras 2–04, 2–10 and below, C0–08.
[22] See below, paras C0–08, C8–16, C8–32, C8–34—C8–37.
[23] *Golder v. U.K.* (1975) 1 E.H.R.R. 524. See also *Airey v. Ireland* (1979) 2 E.H.R.R. 305.
[24] *Marckx v. Belgium* (1979) 2 E.H.R.R. 330, para. 41; *Sutherland v. U.K.* [1998] E.H.R.L.R. 117. *cf. Sheffield & Horsham v. United Kingdom* (1999) 27 E.H.R.R. 163.
[25] For examples of administrative acts which do not affect human rights, see below, paras 5–27, C6–18.

noted above, some forms of interference may never, or almost never, be justified under the Convention.[26] But, in many cases some restriction on rights is justifiable. Characteristically, as also noted above, under the Strasbourg jurisprudence such restrictions have to meet four criteria: (a) they must be lawful; (b) they must be intended to pursue a legitimate aim; (c) they must be "necessary in a democratic society"; and (d) they must not be discriminatory. Although the Convention only expressly requires that these issues be addressed in relation to "interferences", the court has held that:

> "(i)n determining whether or not a positive obligation exists, regard must be had to the fair balance that has to be struck between the general interest of the community and the interests of the individuals . . . In striking this balance the aims mentioned in the second paragraph of Article 8 may be of a certain relevance . . ."[27]

A. Restrictions must be "lawful" or "prescribed by law"[28]

5–09 Where Convention rights are in issue, the requirement that restrictions must be "lawful" or "prescribed by law" represents a reversal of the traditional common law principle applied by Megarry V.-C. in *Malone v. Metropolitan Police Commissioner*[29] that certain public authorities are permitted to do anything that is not proscribed. On the contrary, interference with Convention rights is *prima facie* unlawful and must be specifically authorised by law. In many cases, of course, this effects no change to English law, for it is an established constitutional principle that where a common law right is infringed, specific legal authority must be found.[30] However, the Convention extends this principle to those rights (e.g., privacy) which have not been specifically protected by the common law.[31] Moreover, "lawfulness" involves more than merely formal authorisation. It requires that "the law must indicate the scope of any such discretion conferred on the competent authorities and the manner of its exercise with sufficient clarity, having regard to the legitimate aim of the measure in question, to give the individual adequate protection against arbitrary interference".[32] This tendency, too, finds echoes in existing constitutional practice. It embodies Dicey's first conception of the rule of law as "the absolute supremacy or predominance of regular law as opposed to the

---

[26] These include the prohibitions of torture, inhuman and degrading punishment (Article 3), of slavery (Article 4(1)), and of retroactive criminal offences (Article 7) are absolute. Other provisions are subject to strictly limited derogation only. For example, in time of war or grave public emergency a State may, under Article 15, derogate from the right to life, but only in respect of deaths resulting from "lawful acts of war". See further below, paras C2–15 *et seq.*, C3–03, C4–03, C7–02.

[27] *Rees v. United Kingdom* (1987) 9 E.H.R.R. 56, para. 37. See also *B v. France* (1993) 16 E.H.R.R. 1, para. 44. As to positive obligations, see further below, para. C0–06; above, para. 4–49.

[28] See Commentary, below, para. C0–10.

[29] [1979] Ch. 244 (no common law right to be free of telephone tapping).

[30] *Entick v. Carrington* (1765) 2 Wils. 275. See also the cases on the common law presumptions, particularly the principle of legality, considered above, para. 3–12.

[31] As to the effect of the Convention on privacy see Grosz and Braithwaite, "Privacy and the Human Rights Act", in Hunt & Singh (eds), *A Practitioner's Guide to the Impact of the Human Rights Act* (1999).

[32] *Malone v. U.K.* (1985) 7 E.H.R.R. 14, para. 68. In E.C. law it is the similar principle of legal certainty that enables the protection of substantive legitimate expectations (Case 120/86 *Mulder I* [1988] E.C.R. 2321; Tridimas, *The General Principles of E.C. Law* (1999) Chap. 5) but under the Convention such protection may be more likely to be achieved where the principle of non-discrimination applies, see below, para. 5–23. English law has not yet clearly accepted substantive protection: De Smith, Woolf & Jowell, *Judicial Review of Administrative Action* (5th ed.), paras 8–037 *et seq.* 13–026 *et seq.*

influence of arbitrary power, [which] excludes the existence of arbitrariness",[33] a concept reflected in administrative law's strong presumption against "unfettered" discretion.[34]

5-10   The extent of the match between this approach and the European notion of lawfulness may be illustrated by reference to the Strasbourg Court's judgments in *Hentrich v. France* and in *Halford v. United Kingdom*. In the former the court held to be unlawful a pre-emption procedure operated by the revenue authorities in cases of alleged sale at undervalue, on the basis that it "operated arbitrarily and selectively and was scarcely foreseeable, and it was not attended by basic procedural guarantees".[35] And in the latter it held that the interception of telephone calls from the applicant's office violated her Article 8 right to privacy because it was subject to no legal regulation.[36]

Courts in the United Kingdom will have to satisfy themselves that any restriction on Convention rights is "lawful". Yet although the significance of lawfulness was recognised by Brooke L.J. in his concurring judgment in *Westminster City Council v. Blenheim Leisure (Restaurants) Limited and others*,[37] the courts appear to have made no reference to the principle in other recent cases in which the Convention has been considered. A prominent example is *R. v. Chief Constable of the North Wales Police & others, ex parte Thorpe*,[38] which concerned the lawfulness of police disclosure of information about the criminal record and whereabouts of convicted sex offenders who had been released after serving their sentences. The argument turned on the justifiability of the disclosure rather than its lawfulness. Although the parties could not identify any statutory authority which governed disclosure, the Court of Appeal appears to have concluded that publication of the disclosure policy of the respondent police force would have been sufficient to comply with the requirement that interference with private life must be "in accordance with the law".[39] It must, however, be open to question whether this total absence of statutory regulation complies with this requirement.[40]

B.   A legitimate aim:

5-11   Any interference must pursue a legitimate aim. There will not usually be any doubt about this. It has been very rare indeed for the Strasbourg Court not to be satisfied that a legitimate aim is in play, and it is understandably wary of suggestions that the purpose advanced by the state is not advanced in good faith, or that there was some ulterior motive. Argument usually focuses on the question of whether the purpose, legitimate in itself, is sufficient to justify the particular

---

[33] *The Law of the Constitution* (10th ed., Macmillan, 1959), p. 202.
[34] *Padfield v. Minister of Agriculture, Fisheries and Food* [1968] A.C. 997.
[35] (1994) 18 E.H.R.R. 440, para. 42. See further below, para. C0-11.
[36] (1997) 24 E.H.R.R. 523.
[37] *The Times*, February 24, 1999, although the judgment of Brooke L.J. is not reported.
[38] [1999] Q.B. 396 considered by Barber, [1998] P.L. 19.
[39] *ibid.*, 322C. See also *Woolgar v. Chief Constable of Sussex Police and Another*, [1999] 3 All E.R. 604, CA (police disclosure to regulatory body of information obtained during interview with suspect); *MS v. Sweden* (74/1996/693/885) judgment of August 27, 1997 (communication, without the patient's consent, of personal and confidential medical data by one public authority to another).
[40] See *Malone v. United Kingdom* (1985) 7 E.H.R.R. 14; *Silver v. United Kingdom* (1983) 5 E.H.R.R. 347; *Leander v. Sweden* (1987) 9 E.H.R.R. 433; *Halford v. U.K.* (1997) 24 E.H.R.R. 523. See also *R. v. Brentwood Borough Council, ex parte Peck* [1998] E.M.L.R. 697 (Harrison J. and CA: dissemination by local authority of CCTV recordings authorised by s.111 of the Local Government Act 1972), considered above, para. 3-35.

restriction in issue: a question addressed by the third and fourth criteria which are considered below.

C.   The interference must be "necessary in a democratic society":

5–12   The meaning of "necessary" is considered below at paragraphs C0–13 and C0–14. Its application by the Strasbourg institutions has involved the important principles of proportionality and the margin of appreciation.

D.   Proportionality:

5–13   Proportionality means that an interference with a Convention right must not only pursue a legitimate aim.[41] It must also correspond to a "pressing social need",[42] and the means used to achieve the aim must be proportionate to the aim sought to be achieved.[43] If it is not proportionate, it is not "necessary" and the justification fails.[44] Thus the Convention recognises that in many fields neither the *prima facie* rights of the individual nor the legitimate objectives of the state and of society as a whole can take absolute priority. What is required is a "fair balance" between the demands of the general interest of the community and the requirements of the protection of the individual's rights.[45] The end which the administrative decision seeks to achieve is balanced against the means applied to do so. An alternative formulation, emphasising that the test is one of "necessity", is that, where the end can be achieved in more than one way, the one that is least harmful to Convention rights should be chosen.[46] A similar test of fair balance is applied when determining whether the state owes individuals an obligation to adopt positive measures to secure the enjoyment of a Convention right or to protect the individual from interference with that right by third parties.[47]

E.   Examples:

5–14   The proportionality requirement aims to ensure that the balance struck is fair.[48] This will depend on the particular circumstances. So, for example, an interference with Convention rights is likely to be more difficult to justify if it contradicts an undertaking by a public authority or its previous policy or practice.[49] Again, legislation which retrospectively validated regulations held invalid and

---

[41] See generally Ellis (ed.), *The Principle of Proportionality in the Laws of Europe* (1999), pp. 23 (McBride) and 117 (Feldman); Harris, O'Boyle & Warbrick, *Law of the ECHR* (1995), pp. 11–12, 300. On the principle in E.C. law, see below, para. 5–15 and on its relationship to *Wednesbury* unreasonableness, see below, para. 5–19.

[42] *Informationsverein Lentia v. Austria* (1993) 17 E.H.R.R. 93.

[43] *Handyside v. U.K.* (1976) 1 E.H.R.R. 737, para. 49; *Vogt v. Germany* (1996) 21 E.H.R.R. 205; *Otto-Preminger Institute v. Austria* (1994) 19 E.H.R.R. 34.

[44] Harris, O'Boyle & Warbrick, *Law of the ECHR* (1995), p. 300; Feldman in Ellis (ed.), *The Principle of Proportionality in the Laws of Europe* (1999), p. 123.

[45] See, *e.g. National Provincial Building Society & ors v. United Kingdom* (1998) 25 E.H.R.R. 127, para. 80; *Sporring & Lönnroth v. Sweden* (1982); 5 E.H.R.R. 35; *Lithgow v. U.K.* (1986) 8 E.H.R.R. 329, para. 120.

[46] *Marckx v. Belgium* (1979) 2 E.H.R.R. 330, para. 40.

[47] *Rees v. United Kingdom* (1987) 9 E.H.R.R. 56, para. 37. See also *B v. France* (1993) 16 E.H.R.R. 1, para. 44. As to positive obligations, see below, para. C0–06.

[48] See further C0–14.

[49] See the approach in *R. v. Ministry of Agriculture, Fisheries & Food, ex parte Hamble Fisheries* [1995] 2 All E.R. 714 (on substantive legitimate expectations) which is likely, see *R. v. North and East Devon H.A., ex parte Coughlan, The Times*, July 20, 1999, and below, para. 5–23, n. 4, to prevail where Convention rights are at issue. See further above, para. 5–09, n. 32 (E.C. law) and below, para. 5–23 (non-discrimination).

deprived certain building societies of the right to restitution of tax paid under the regulations did not upset this balance. There was a "compelling public interest to ensure that private entities do not enjoy the benefit of a windfall in a changeover to a new tax payment regime and do not deny the Exchequer revenue simply on account of inadvertent defects in the enabling tax legislation".[50] Again, the privilege of company inspectors against liability in defamation was a legitimate interference with the right of access to the courts in view of the interest of the state in supervising and regulating the operation of companies.[51] But a claim of entitlement to censor prisoners' mail to legal advisers where it was suspected that it contained unlawful enclosures was disproportionate.[52] The public interest could be satisfied by a narrower rule allowing inspection only on reasonable suspicion. Again, an injunction preventing the publication of information about pending litigation was disproportionate to the aim of maintaining the authority of the judiciary.[53] In another case, the court found that France had violated its positive obligation to "respect" the applicant's private life by failing to give official recognition to her new sexual identity following gender reassignment surgery.[54] The French system could have permitted annotation of the applicant's new gender on her birth certificate; the authorities had refused to allow her to change her forename; and because her former sex was indicated on her official documents she experienced considerable difficulties in social and professional integration.[55]

F. European Community law:

5–15 Guidance can also be obtained from the application of the principle of proportionality in E.C. law.[56] In that context a standard formula, similar to that in the Strasbourg jurisprudence, has been used by the ECJ to establish whether a decision or a provision is consistent with the principle of proportionality. First there is a test of appropriateness or suitability: are the means employed reasonably likely to achieve the objective sought? Secondly, are the means employed necessary for the attainment of the objective? At this stage competing interests are weighed; the importance of the objective, whether there is a less restrictive way of achieving it, and whether the measure in issue imposes an excessive burden on the individual.[57] A distinction, however, must be drawn between cases in which proportionality is applied as a ground of review of *Community* acts, and where it is applied to determine the compatibility with the Treaty of *national* measures which

---

[50] *National and Provincial Building Society & ors v. United Kingdom*, October 23, 1997, R.J.D. 1997–VII, No. 55; 25 E.H.R.R. 127, para. 81. See also *Lithgow v. U.K.* (1986) 8 E.H.R.R. 329, para. 120.
[51] *Fayed v. U.K.* (1997) 18 E.H.R.R. 393.
[52] *Campbell v. U.K.* (1992), 15 E.H.R.R. 137, para. 48.
[53] *Sunday Times v. U.K.* (1979); 2 E.H.R.R. 245, para. 67.
[54] *B v. France* (1993) 16 E.H.R.R. 1.
[55] Compare *Rees v. United Kingdom* (1987) 9 E.H.R.R. 56; *Cossey v. United Kingdom* (1991) 13 E.H.R.R. 622. See further *X, Y & Z v. United Kingdom* (1997) 24 E.H.R.R. 143 (refusal to register post-operative transsexual as father of child born to partner by artificial insemination by donor: balance of the right to respect for private and family life with interest of the community as a whole in maintaining a coherent system of family law).
[56] For a detailed study see Tridimas, *The General Principles of E.C. Law* (1999), Chaps 3–4. See also Schwartze, *European Administrative Law* (1992), Chap. 5. On the consideration of E.C. proportionality by English courts, see below, para. 5–23, n. 4.
[57] *e.g.* Case 66/82 *Fromancais v. Forma* [1983] E.C.R. 395, para. 8; Case C–331/88 *Fedesa* [1990] E.C.R. I–4023. There is some support for a three stage test in which "necessity" is considered separately from "excessive burden" (the strict sense of proportionality): de Burca (1993) 13 Y.E.L. 105, 113; Case C–331/88 *Fedesa, op cit* at 4051 (Mischo A.G.); Case C–159/90 *SPUC v. Grogan* [1991] E.C.R. I–4685 (van Gerven A.G.), but in practice the ECJ does not separate these tests: Tridimas, *op cit.*, p. 92.

interfere with fundamental freedoms. In the first type of case, given the discretion of the Community's legislative organs, the ECJ will not strike down a measure unless it is found to be "manifestly inappropriate" to achieve its objectives[58] although a more rigorous test is used in the case of administrative acts. In the second type of case the ECJ (or a national court applying E.C. law) scrutinises national measures more rigorously. A national measure which affects the fundamental freedoms of the Treaty will be found incompatible with Community law unless it is "necessary" to achieve a legitimate aim and that aim cannot be achieved by a less restrictive alternative.[59] Considerations of justiciability also have a role in E.C. cases. Thus, the more severely a measure affects private interests, the stricter the standard of review[60] and the more technical or policy-based the subject, the more reluctant the court is to intervene.[61]

G. The "margin of appreciation" and relative expertise:

5–16   The second important principle used by the Strasbourg Court is the "margin of appreciation". The principal justification for the doctrine, as explained in *Handyside v. United Kingdom*, is that "state authorities are in principle in a better position than the international judge to give an opinion on the exact content of"[62] restrictions on Convention rights (for instance to assess the degree to which morality might require a prohibition on obscene expression) and their necessity. The Strasbourg institutions play only a subsidiary role in protecting human rights.[63] The "margin of appreciation" is a degree of latitude or deference accorded to national authorities, including national courts, by the Strasbourg Court in recognition of this relative advantage. It also reflects a recognition by Strasbourg that national authorities, in particular the courts, may have had the benefit of direct contact with the parties and witnesses and are in a better position to assess questions of justification. For those reasons, the court is reluctant to substitute its own view for that of the domestic authorities.[64] However, the "margin" is not a blank cheque; it is ultimately for the Strasbourg Court, in every case, to set the limits within which states may act. Moreover, those limits depend on context, and vary depending on matters such as the importance of the right at stake, the

---

[58] Case C–331/88 *Fedesa* [1990] E.C.R. I–4023, para. 30. See also Case 59/83 *Biovilac v. EEC* [1984] E.C.R 4057, para. 17; Case C–280/93 *Germany v. Council (Bananas)* [1994] E.C.R. I–4973, paras 89–98. But note that there are varying degrees of scrutiny in different contexts: Tridimas, *op cit.*, pp. 95 *et seq.* 122–123.

[59] Case 36/75 *Rutili v. French Minister of the Interior* [1975] E.C.R. 1219; Joined Cases C–267 & C–268/91 *Keck* [1993] E.C.R. I–6097; *Stoke-on-Trent CC & Norwich CC v. B & Q plc* [1992] E.C.R. I–6635, para. 15 [1993] A.C. 900, 947. See further Tridimas, *op cit.*, pp. 124 *et seq.*

[60] *e.g.* Case 240/78 *Atalanta v. Produktschap voor Vee en Vless* [1979] E.C.R. 2137; Case 181/84 *Man (Sugar) v. IBAP* [1985] E.C.R. 2889 (penalties); Case 36/75 *Rutili v. French Minister of the Interior* [1975] E.C.R. 1219; Case 170/78 *Commission v. U.K.* [1980] E.C.R. 417 (national measures restricting free movement of workers and goods).

[61] *e.g.* Case C–331/88 *Fedesa* [1990] E.C.R. I–4023, para. 14 (market regulation measures under the Common Agricultural Policy); Case 240/84 *NTN Toyo v. Council* [1987] E.C.R. 1809; Case 255/84 *Nachi Fujukoshi v. Council* [1987] E.C.R. 1861; Case 260/84 *Minebea v. Council* [1987] E.C.R. 1975 (anti-dumping measures), criticised by Eggar (1993) 18 E.L. Rev. 367. But *cf.* Cases T 163 & T 165–94 *Koyo Seiko v. Council* [1995] E.C.R. II–1381, aff'd [1998] E.C.R. I–401 (anti-dumping) and Case C–24/90 *Werner Faust* [1991] E.C.R. I–85; Casse C–25/90 *Wunsche I* [1991] E.C.R. I–4939; Case C–296/94 *Pietch v. Hauptzollamt Hamburg-Waltershof* [1996] E.C.R. I–33409 (strict approach to Commission protective measures concerning trade with non-E.C. states).

[62] *Handyside v. U.K.* (1976) 1 E.H.R.R. 737, para. 49; *Brannigan & McBride v. U.K.* (1994) 17 E.H.R.R. 539.

[63] Harris, O'Boyle & Warbrick, *Law of the ECHR* (1995), p. 14.

[64] See, for example, in the care field, *Johansen v. Norway* (1997) 23 E.H.R.R. 33, para. 64.

particular purpose pursued by the state, and the degree to which practice varies among Convention states. As suggested above,[65] transposition of this doctrine of margin of appreciation to the domestic context would be wholly inappropriate. Indeed, far from foreclosing the issue of justification, a Strasbourg finding that a restriction comes within the state's margin of appreciation places on the national court (and other authorities) a duty to assess for itself the necessity and proportionality of that restriction.[66]

H. Justiciability:

5–17　National courts are much closer to national values and problems than the international tribunal in Strasbourg. In consequence it will usually be inappropriate for them to accord public authorities the degree of deference exhibited by the Strasbourg Court. This is not to say, however, that the consideration which underlies the doctrine of margin of appreciation is irrelevant in cases before U.K. courts. The doctrine is founded on a concern to establish the proper limits of the judicial function and the extent to which an issue is justiciable. This concern is manifestly relevant in our courts in the context of the scope of the judicial review jurisdiction[67] and will remain relevant in the exercise of the powers under the HRA. As with the question of fact-finding,[68] there is no clear-cut answer to the question when the judicial review court should substitute its own view of the justification of an interference. Lord Hoffmann has stated that "[d]emocracy requires both the recognition of the decision-making power of the elected organs of the state over a large range of issues and the protection of certain fundamental rights of the individual against infringement even by majority decision. There are no hard and fast rules to tell judges how these two elements of a democracy are to be reconciled and they have to tread a delicate line which avoids the extremes of populism on the one hand and judicial over-activism on the other".[69] But it is possible to identify some considerations from the Strasbourg jurisprudence on margin of appreciation which will help, by analogy, to elaborate the applicable principles. In the national context, however, to avoid confusion with the Strasbourg doctrine, it would be preferable to refer to this aspect of the issue as a question of "justiciability" rather than the "margin of appreciation".

5–18　Considerations of relative expertise in relation to a particular issue and the degree to which a matter is justiciable, which at present affect the effective scope of judicial review in our courts, will continue to be important factors. A court is clearly less well placed to substitute its views on issues which are technical or specialised than it is, for example, to scrutinise the fairness of a procedure.[70]

---

[65] See above, para. 2–05.

[66] See for example, *Stubbings v. United Kingdom*, October 22, 1996, R.J.D., 1996–IV, No. 18; 23 E.H.R.R. 213, where the Commission unanimously found the inflexible limitation on actions for intentional trespass to the person to be disproportionate whereas the Court found it to be proportionate. See also *Stubbings v. Webb* [1993] A.C. 232, where the House of Lords and the Court of Appeal differed as to the interpretation of the Limitation Act 1980.

[67] See *R. v. IRC, ex parte Rossminster* [1980] A.C. 952, 1001, 1027 (limits of judicial function); *R. v. Criminal Injuries Compensation Board, ex parte P* [1995] 1 W.L.R. 895 and the cases cited below, para. 5–18.

[68] See below, paras 5–28—5–29 *et seq.*

[69] In Ellis (ed.), *The Principle of Proportionality in the Laws of Europe* (1999), p. 110. See his approach in *Stoke-on-Trent CC v. B & Q plc* [1991] Ch. 48, 61–65 but note the disapproval in the ECJ proceedings by Advocate-General Van Gerven: Joined Cases C–306/88, C304/90, and C169/91 *Stoke-on-Trent CC & Norwich CC v. B & Q plc* [1992] E.C.R. I–6635, para. 35 [1993] A.C. 900, 945B–D.

[70] See, *e.g. R. v. DPP, ex parte Kebeline* [1999] 3 W.L.R. 175.

Decisions in fields which are necessarily secret[71] or, we suggest, involving foreign policy or diplomatic considerations,[72] may be subject to a lesser degree of intervention. Likewise courts are unlikely to adopt a high level of intervention in decisions involving a considerable degree of general policy content, in particular social and economic issues,[73] including the allocation of inadequate resources to competing demands,[74] or the determination of tax policy,[75] or general immigration policy.[76] By contrast, the court will be better placed where the interests involved are those of the individual, or the competing interests of different individuals.[77] The nature and importance of the right at stake and the degree of interference with it will also be factors. So, for example, interference with political speech[78] will be scrutinised more closely than regulation of commercial speech.[79] We have seen that considerations of justiciability also play a part in determining the intensity of review on the ground of proportionality under E.C. Law.[80]

I.   Proportionality and *Wednesbury* unreasonableness[81]

5–19   The traditional English approach to the review of discretion has been the *Wednesbury* unreasonableness test.[82] The court asks whether the administrative decision or conduct is "irrational" or "perverse", *i.e.* "so unreasonable that no reasonable authority could ever have come to it", or "which no sensible authority acting with due appreciation of its responsibilities would have decided to adopt".[83] In

---

[71] See, *mutatis mutandis, Klass v. Germany* (1978) 2 E.H.R.R. 214, para. 69. However see *Chahal v. United Kingdom*, November 15, 1996, R.J.D., 1996–II, No. 22; 23 E.H.R.R. 413: while the use of confidential material to justify detention may be unavoidable in national security cases, detention must still be subject to safeguards which both accommodate legitimate security concerns and yet accord the individual a substantial measure of procedural justice (paras 130–133). See the Special Immigration Appeals Commission Act 1997 passed in consequence of the *Chahal* judgment, and the Special Immigration Appeals Commission (Procedure) Rules 1998 (S.I. 1998 No. 1881). *cf. CCSU v. Minister for the Civil Service* [1985] A.C. 374, 402; *R. v. Home Secretary, ex parte Cheblak* [1991] 1 W.L.R. 890, 904; *R. v. Secretary of State for the Home Department, ex parte McQuillan* [1995] 4 All E.R. 400, 411–415, 423–426. The ECJ is less reluctant to intervene in such cases: see, *e.g.* Case C–83/94 *Leifer* [1995] E.C.R I–3231.
[72] As to domestic law, see *CCSU v. Minister for the Civil Service* [1985] A.C. 374, 398, 418; *Ex parte Molyneaux* [1986] 1 W.L.R. 331, 336.
[73] *James v. United Kingdom* (1986) 8 E.H.R.R. 123, para. 46.
[74] *R. v. Cambridge Health Authority, ex parte B* [1995] 2 All E.R. 129; *R. v. Criminal Injuries Compensation Board, ex parte P* [1995] 1 W.L.R. 895; *R. v. Chief Constable of Sussex ex parte International Trader's Ferry* [1999] 1 All E.R. 129.
[75] *National and Provincial Building Society & ors v. United Kingdom*, October 23, 1997, R.J.D., 1997–VII, No. 55; 25 E.H.R.R. 127; *R. v. Secretary of State for the Environment, ex parte Nottinghamshire CC* [1986] A.C. 240, 247, 250–251; *R. v. Secretary of State for the Environment, ex parte Hammersmith & Fulham LBC* [1991] 1 A.C. 521, 593, 601.
[76] *Abdulaziz, Cabales and Balkandali v. United Kingdom* (1987) 7 E.H.R.R. 471, para. 67.
[77] *W v. U.K.* (1988) 10 E.H.R.R. 29; *R. v. United Kingdom* (1988) 10 E.H.R.R. 74; *B v. United Kingdom* (1988) 10 E.H.R.R. 87; *O v. United Kingdom* (1988) 10 E.H.R.R. 82; *H v. United Kingdom* (1988) 10 E.H.R.R. 95.
[78] *United Communist Party of Turkey v. Turkey* (1998) 26 E.H.R.R. 121; *Sidiropoulos v. Greece* (1999) 27 E.H.R.R. 633. But *cf.*, for misplaced deference, *R. v. Radio Authority, ex parte Bull* [1997] 2 All E.R. 561, 573, criticised by Stevens & Feldman, [1997] P.L. 615.
[79] *Markt Intern and Beerman v. FRG* (1990) 12 E.H.R.R. 161. *cf. Hertel v. Switzerland* judgment of August 25, 1998.
[80] See above, para. 5–15.
[81] See generally Ellis (ed.), *The Principle of Proportionality in the Laws of Europe* (1999), esp. 85 (Craig), 107 (Hoffmann) and 117 (Feldman); De Smith, Woolf & Jowell, *Judicial Review of Administrative Action* (5th ed.), paras 13–070–13–086; de Burca in Andenas (ed.), *English Public Law and the Common Law of Europe* (1998) p. 53.
[82] *Associated Provincial Picture Houses Ltd v. Wednesbury Corporation* [1948] 1 K.B. 223, 228–230.
[83] *ibid.*, 228–230 (Lord Greene M.R.); *Secretary of State for Education v. Tameside MBC* [1977] A.C. 1014, 1064; *CCSU v. Minister for the Civil Service* [1985] A.C. 374, (Lord Diplock).

Ex parte Brind it was said that proportionality is a different and more stringent test than *Wednesbury* unreasonableness[84] and that this is of significance because the application of proportionality could lead to courts substituting their views on the issue for those of the person or body designated by statute or under the prerogative to decide it. So it was said that, under the principle of proportionality, an inquiry into the merits cannot be avoided and concern was expressed about judges conducting a balancing exercise on a matter which Parliament had remitted to a minister or an administrative body.[85] Those taking this view considered that the process of review was different in cases involving E.C. law, where, as we have seen, proportionality applies.[86] But the approach in *Ex parte Brind* been questioned on two separate grounds.

5–20 First, it is correctly pointed out that application of the principle of proportionality does not involve the court acting as an appellate rather than a reviewing body and that, even under the *Wednesbury* test, the standard of review varies according to subject-matter and circumstances. So, Laws J. has stated that in review based on proportionality " . . . the court is not concerned to agree or disagree with the decision; that would be to travel far beyond the boundaries of proper judicial authority, and usurp the primary decision-maker's function".[87] It is clear that even review on *Wednesbury* grounds goes beyond "irrationality" and "perversity". The process of *implying* purposes for statutory powers and determining which considerations are "relevant" and which "irrelevant" involves some balancing, as do the determination of whether an improper purpose is "dominant"[88] and the way the "relevant considerations" test operates in practice.[89]

---

[84] *R. v. Secretary of State for the Home Department, ex parte Brind* [1991] 1 A.C. 696, 762 (Lord Ackner); *R. v. Secretary of State for the Environment, ex parte NALGO* (1993) 5 Admin. L.R. 785, 800. *cf. R. v. Secretary of State for Transport, ex parte Pegasus Holdings (London) Ltd* [1988] 1 W.L.R. 990, 1001; *R. v. Secretary of State for Health, ex parte US Tobacco Inc.* [1992] 1 Q.B. 353, 366 (proportionality merely an aspect of the *Wednesbury* principle).

[85] *R. v. Secretary of State for the Home Department, ex parte Brind* [1991] 1 A.C. 696, 750, 762–3, 767 (Lord Roskill, Lord Ackner, Lord Lowry), *cf.* pp. 749, 751 (Lord Bridge and Lord Templeman). See also *R. v. Ministry of Defence, ex parte Smith* [1996] Q.B. 517, 541 (Simon Brown L.J.) and Lord Hoffmann's concern quoted above, para. 5–17. But this has been questioned, see Jowell & Lester in Jowell & Oliver (eds.), *New Directions in Judicial Review* (1989), p. 51; Laws [1993] P.L. 59, 71, 73–75.

[86] *R. v. Ministry of Agriculture, Fisheries and Food, ex parte Roberts* [1990] 1 C.M.L.R. 555; *R. v. International Stock Exchange, ex parte Else (1982) Ltd* [1983] Q.B. 534; *R. v. Secretary of State for the Home Department, ex parte Adams* [1995] All E.R. (E.C.) 177; *R. v. Ministry of Agriculture, Fisheries and Food, ex parte First City Trading* [1997] 1 C.M.L.R. 250; *R. v. Chief Constable of Sussex, ex parte International Trader's Ferry* [1999] 1 All E.R. 129. The last case raised both *Wednesbury* and E.C. justifications, and the facts could have given rise to a Convention point as well: see *Plattform Ärtzte für das Leben v. Austria* (1991) 13 E.H.R.R. 204.

[87] *R. v. Ministry of Agriculture, Fisheries and Food, ex parte First City Trading* [1997] 1 C.M.L.R. 250, 278–279, in the context of E.C. law, on which see further above, para. 5–15. That this is so in the Strasbourg context is shown by *R. v. Secretary of State for the Environment, ex parte NALGO* (1993) 5 Admin. L.R. 785, 801 (proportionality allows a "margin of appreciation", but a narrower one than *Wednesbury*), the application of the "margin of appreciation" and sensitivity to justiciability: see above, paras 5–14, 5–16—5–17.

[88] *Westminster Corp. v. L & NW Railway Co.* [1905] A.C. 426.

[89] *R. v. Barnet & Camden Rent Tribunal, ex parte Frey Investments Ltd* [1972] 2 Q.B. 342, 364–365, 368; *Pickwell v. Camden LBC* [1983] Q.B. 962, 999–1000 (quality or character of decision rather than methods by which it is reached should be examined); *R. v. Secretary of State for Social Services, ex parte Wellcome Foundation Ltd* [1987] 2 All E.R. 1024, 1032 (entitled to ignore factors which, if relevant, would not affect the decision because of the comparative weight of other relevant factors); *W. Glamorgan CC v. Rafferty* [1987] 1 W.L.R. 457, 477 (the court was "not precluded from finding a decision [*Wednesbury* unreasonable] merely because there are admissible factors on both sides of the question"; a "decision which required the weighing of factors according to the personal judgment of the councillors . . . does not permit complete freedom of choice or assessment because legal duty must be

As well as the "anxious scrutiny" in human rights cases, the effective scope of review is affected by considerations of justiciability.[90]

5–21   The second qualification to *Ex p. Brind*'s approach to the relationship between *Wednesbury* and proportionality is more problematic. It is that the two tests may lead to the same result in practice even allowing for a difference in onus,[91] and that the *Wednesbury* test could be reformulated as "whether the decision in question was one which a reasonable authority could reach".[92] Again, Laws J. has stated that the two "are different models–one looser, one tighter–of the same juridical concept, which is the imposition of compulsory standards on decision-makers so as to secure the repudiation of arbitrary power".[93] So also Sedley J. has favoured the integration of proportionality into the domestic standard of review.[94] These statements must, however, be understood in their context, and must not be taken as a projection of proportionality as an alternative formulation of the *Wednesbury* principle.[95] While the result may be the same and, at a theoretical level the concepts may be the same, there is a substantial difference of approach in practice. As Laws J. recognises, a court applying the proportionality principle "will test the solution arrived at, and pass it only if substantial factual considerations are put forward in its justification: considerations which are relevant, reasonable and proportionate to the aim in view".[96]

5–22   Proportionality requires the court to assess the fairness of the balance struck by the authority and the relative weight accorded to the competing considerations. The court is not limited to ensuring that the measure in issue was reasonable and adopted for proper purposes, or that only relevant considerations were taken into account. There is also the difference in onus,[97] the need for "substantial factual considerations" to be put forward, and for a more reasoned justification of an authority's policy choices.[98] These mean that, in practice and notwithstanding the developments where fundamental rights or E.C. law are involved, review on the ground of proportionality is likely in general to involve closer and more intensive scrutiny than review under the *Wednesbury* principle, even if the result is the same.

---

given proper weight"). See also *R. v. Devon CC, ex parte G* [1989] A.C. 573, 577 (Lord Donaldson M.R.).

[90] See above, paras 5–17—5–18. See further Craig, *Administrative Law*, (4th ed., 1999), pp. 536, 582–586, 598–600; Craig in Ellis (ed.), *The Principle of Proportionality in the Laws of Europe* (1999), pp. 96–99; Laws in Forsyth & Hare (eds.), *The Golden Metwand and the Crooked Cord* (1998), pp. 185–202.

[91] *R. v. Chief Constable of Sussex, ex parte International Trader's Ferry* [1999] 1 All E.R. 129, 145H–J (Lord Slynn).

[92] *ibid.*, 157d (Lord Cooke).

[93] *R. v. Ministry of Agriculture, Fisheries and Food, ex parte First City Trading* [1997] 1 C.M.L.R. 250, 279.

[94] *R. v. Secretary of State for the Home Department, ex parte McQuillan* [1995] 4 All E.R. 400, 428, but by raising the domestic standard. See also *R. v. MAFF, ex parte Hamble Fisheries* [1995] 4 All E.R. 714.

[95] This problem is identified by Feldman in Ellis (ed.), *The Principle of Proportionality in the Laws of Europe* (1999), p. 122. Others do not see it as a problem; see Hoffmann, *ibid.*, p. 109, treating irrationality as a higher level concept which includes lack of proportionality as one of its forms.

[96] *ibid.* Compare the formulation adopted by the Strasbourg Court, for example in *Buckley v. United Kingdom*: "The Court's task is to determine . . . whether the reasons relied on to justify the interference in question are relevant and sufficient under Article 8(2)." (1997) 23 E.H.R.R. 101, para. 77. Laws J. has described the process as building differential principles within the *Wednesbury* principle ([1993] P.L. 59, 71) and has stated that "proportionality *need not* be a separate category for it to have an independent life (in Forsyth & Hare (eds), *The Golden Metwand and the Crooked Cord* (1998), p. 201).

[97] See below, para. 5–39; above, para. 5–21, n. 96.

[98] See above, para. 5.21; below, para. 5–40.

J. Non-discrimination:

5–23 An interference with a Convention right which is otherwise lawful and necessary will be unacceptable if its effect is unjustifiably discriminatory.[99] Thus, Article 14 comes into play whenever it is necessary to justify a restriction on the Convention rights or whenever a benefit falling within the scope of a Convention right is afforded to some groups but not others. Under the Convention, discrimination is established where a distinction in treatment "has no reasonable and objective justification".[1] The effect will be that certain decisions, hitherto dealt with on conventional *Wednesbury* grounds, will be dealt with on the ground of improper discrimination.[2] It will also mean that where there is a policy or a regular practice which citizens can reasonably expect to continue, it must be applied in a non-discriminatory way. To that extent it will be possible to give substantive protection to a person who has a legitimate expectation, whether arising from an express promise by a public authority or from the existence of a policy or practice. It has been clear that in English law such legitimate expectations generate procedural protection, *i.e.* the right to a hearing or to be consulted before a decision concerning them is made.[3] However, it is not clear that in its present state of development, the substantive benefit of the policy or practice can be protected.[4]

The consideration of "reasonable and objective justification" for a distinction has much in common and may overlap with the consideration of whether a particular restriction is "necessary in a democratic society". In both cases, it must be shown that the measure—in the case of Article 14 the difference of treatment—pursues a legitimate aim and that there is a reasonable relationship of proportionality between the means employed and the aim sought to be realised.[5] But the questions are, in principle, distinct—for restrictions that are reasonable when applied uniformly may be unreasonable if applied in a different way to different groups of people. Moreover, some grounds of distinction, such as race, sex, nationality and legitimacy are naturally regarded as especially suspect, and the respondent will have to advance "very weighty reasons" to justify them.[6]

---

[99] See below, paras 5–39—5–40.

[1] *Belgian Linguistics Case* (1968) 1 E.H.R.R. 252, para. 10.

[2] See, *e.g. Wheeler v. Leicester CC* [1985] A.C. 1054, noted above, para. 3–37.

[3] *CCSU v. Minister for Civil Service* [1985] A.C. 375; *Attorney-General (Hong Kong) v. Ng Yuen Shiu* [1983] 2 A.C. 629.

[4] Favouring some substantive protection, see, *e.g. R. v. Secretary of State for the Home Department, ex parte Ruddock* [1987] 1 W.L.R. 1482; *R. v. Board of Inland Revenue, ex parte MFK* [1990] 1 All E.R. 91; *R. v. Ministery of Agriculture, Fisheries & Food, ex parte Hamble Fisheries* [1995] 2 All E.R. 714; *R. v. IRC Comms, ex parte Unilever* [1996] S.T.C. 681; *R. v. North and East Devon H.A., ex parte Coughlan*, *The Times*, July 20, 1999. But, *cf. R. v. Secretary of State for Transport, ex parte Richmond on Thames LBC* [1994] 1 W.L.R. 74, 92 and *R. v. Secretary of State for the Home Department, ex parte Hargreaves* [1997] 1 All E.R. 397 (CA) where such protection was described as "heresy". See further De Smith, Jowell & Woolf, *Judicial Review of Administrative Action* (5th ed.), 13–026–13–036; Forsyth [1988] C.L.J. 238; Craig (1992) 108 L.Q.R. at 87–98 and [1996] C.L.J. 289. For the position in E.C. law, see above, para. 5–09, n. 32.

[5] Where the Court has found a breach of a substantive Article of the Convention, it has usually considered it unnecessary to consider the case under Article 14 unless "a clear inequality of treatment in the enjoyment of the right in question is a fundamental aspect of the case": see *Chassagnou and others v. France*, Applications Nos 25088/94, 28331/95 and 28443/95, judgment of April 29, 1999, para. 89; *Dudgeon v. the United Kingdom* (1982) 4 E.H.R.R. 149, para. 67.

[6] *Burghartz v. Switzerland* (1994) 18 E.H.R.R. 101; *Schuler-Zgraggen v. Switzerland* (1994) 16 E.H.R.R. 405; *Schmidt v. Germany* (1994) 18 E.H.R.R. 513, para. 24; *Gaygusuz v. Austria*, September 16, 1996, R.J.D., 1996–IV, No. 14; 23 E.H.R.R. 364, para. 32; *Inze v. Austria*, 10 E.H.R.R. 394, para. 41.

4. THE NATURE AND INTENSITY OF JUDICIAL CONTROL: REVIEW OR APPEAL AND THE EFFECT OF ARTICLE 6 ON QUESTIONS OF FACT AND REASONS

5–24   The application of Article 6 to administrative decision-making, and the consequences for judicial review of administrative action, have caused particular difficulty in the Strasbourg case law. A public authority which determines disputes about civil rights can never fulfil some of the requirements of Article 6, such as independence of the executive. Considerations of economy and administrative necessity may prevent it in practice from fulfilling other requirements, such as public hearing. As we shall see, the response of the Strasbourg institutions has been to hold that such shortcomings do not violate Article 6 if the individual can bring his case before a court with "full jurisdiction". The particular question which has exercised the Commission and the Court is the extent to which judicial review of administrative action satisfies this requirement. Where private rights and interests are in issue, how far should public law proceedings be equated with the traditional role of a civil court in finding facts and applying the law and how far, by contrast, should the conventional approach of courts to judicial review of administrative action be accepted?

5–25   Outside the area of traditional civil trials, *i.e.* in relation to administrative proceedings, the discussion below identifies tensions and contradictions in the Strasbourg case law. We shall see that the approach of the Commission in its admissibility practice in relation to Article 6 has been narrower than that of the Strasbourg Court.[7] In the court, moreover, a minority of judges has consistently favoured a relatively narrow threshold to determine when Article 6(1) is applicable and requires access to a court of full jurisdiction.[8] In the late 1980s there were discussions concerning the adoption of an additional Protocol to deal explicitly with procedural guarantees over administrative proceedings that impact on civil rights, but these did not result in an agreed text. The dissenting judgments, the discussions about a possible Protocol, and the reticence of the Commission are explained by concern over the practicality and the appropriateness of requiring a uniform standard of control by national courts regardless of the origin of the dispute. So far, the court's case law has not adopted a flexible approach, similar to that developed under Article 5(4),[9] where the nature of what is in issue determines whether or not it is compatible with the Convention to limit the court's reviewing power to one of legality. We suggest, however, that the foundations for such an approach exist, and that it offers a way in which the case law can be rationalised in a manner which can be properly reconciled with the text of Article 6(1) itself as well as with the practical and sensible limits of the judicial function.

A. Effective access to judicial remedies: application to administrative action

5–26   The Convention requires that individuals should have effective access to judicial remedies, which is an important aspect of respect for the rule of law. Some

---

[7] See below, paras 5–32—5–38. By contrast the Commission has been less willing than the Court to regard judicial review as an effective remedy for Article 13 purposes: see below, paras 5–29, C13–11 *et seq.*
[8] See especially the dissents in *Benthem v. Netherlands* (1986) 8 E.H.R.R. 1, *Feldbrugge v. Netherlands* (1986) 8 E.H.R.R. 425 and *Deumeland v. Germany* (1986) 8 E.H.R.R. 448.
[9] On this, see below, paras C5–71 *et seq.*

provisions contain express entitlements to judicial protection in various circumstances.[10] Others import an implied requirement of effective (usually judicial) remedies as a necessary condition of the lawfulness and justifiability of an administrative interference with fundamental rights: interference may be acceptable only if it is attended by adequate and effective safeguards against abuse. Thus, for example, in relation to administrative powers of search and seizure given to French customs officers, the court found a violation of Article 8 because:

" . . . the customs authorities had very wide powers; in particular, they had exclusive competence to assess the expediency, number, length and scale of inspections. Above all, in the absence of any requirement of a judicial warrant the restrictions and conditions provided by law . . . appear too lax and full of loopholes for the interferences with the applicant's right to have been strictly proportionate to the legitimate aim pursued."[11]

What this and other decisions make clear is the importance which the Strasbourg institutions attach to the need for effective safeguards as a measure of the lawfulness and proportionality of an interference with a Convention right. This requirement applies to any interference, not just in the area of "civil rights and obligations". In one case, for example, the court found a violation of Article 8 for lack of safeguards, describing as "astonishing" the fact that an official, without supervision by an independent judge, had been given the task of identifying which of a lawyer's telephone calls were legally privileged and therefore exempt from interception.[12] It is important to note, therefore, that a need for effective judicial control may arise from the substantive provisions of the Convention as well as from its procedural guarantees. The issues to be discussed here arise in their most acute form in relation to the position under Article 6(1).

5–27   The issues arising under Article 6(1) in relation to "civil rights and obligations" are dealt with in the commentary on the Strasbourg case law.[13] At this stage it suffices to say that the concept of "civil" rights and obligations is an autonomous one, independent of the classification in English law. The very early case law appeared to exclude public law from the concept of "civil rights and obligations", but this narrow construction was rejected in *Ringeisen v. Austria*.[14] This case established that Article 6(1) can apply to proceedings that are of a public law character if they are directly decisive for civil rights and obligations, and Article 6(1) has since been found applicable to a wide range of disputes between administrative authorities and citizens. In *Editions Periscope*,[15] the court was concerned with a dispute originating from a denial of a fiscal benefit. It noted " . . .

---

[10] Issues arise especially under Article 5 (review of detention by a court), Article 6 (right to a court), and Article 13 (right to an effective remedy before a national authority—which need not be a court—when a Convention violation is claimed). Note, however, that "the requirements of . . . Article [13] are less strict than, and are here absorbed by, those of [Article 6]". *Sporrong and Lönnroth v. Sweden* (1983) 5 E.H.R.R. 35, para. 88.

[11] *Funke v. France* (1993) 16 E.H.R.R. 297, para. 57. See also in *McCann, Farrell and Savage v. United Kingdom* (1996) 21 E.H.R.R. 97, para. 161 (Article 2); *Aksoy v. Turkey* Decemsber 18, 1996, R.J.D., 1996–IV, No. 26; 23 E.H.R.R. 553, para. 84 (Articles 3 and 15). See further the cases cited below at para. C8–53.

[12] *Kopp v. Switzerland* (1999) 27 E.H.R.R. 91, para. 74. See further below, paras C8–38—C8–42.

[13] See below, C6–06 *et seq.*

[14] (1971) 1 E.H.R.R. 455, para. 94.

[15] (1992) 14 E.H.R.R. 597, para. 40.

that the subject-matter of the applicant's action was 'pecuniary' in nature and that the action was founded on an alleged infringement of rights which were likewise pecuniary rights. The right in question was therefore a 'civil right', notwithstanding the origin of the dispute and the fact that the administrative courts had jurisdiction". Other examples of areas in which the test is likely to be met are the fields of land use, planning or licensing, access to a profession, withdrawal of a licence to carry on an economic activity, and issues concerning social insurance and welfare benefits. Disciplinary proceedings which may result in a person losing his entitlement to practise a profession or carry on business have been held to relate to a civil right.[16] This includes proceedings leading to suspension as much as to striking off,[17] and an application for enrolment as a trainee[18] as well as to restoration to the professional roll.[19] Article 6 applies to an application for a licence to carry on any business activity.[20] But the subject-matter of the proceedings must be a *right* rather than a discretionary benefit or an *ex gratia* payment, so that a person who fulfils the eligibility criteria will have an enforceable claim.[21] The protection of Article 6 will apply only to proceedings which are directly decisive for civil rights and obligations; a tenuous or remote link is not enough.[22] Matters that have been held to fall outside the scope of Article 6(1) include the admission and expulsion of aliens,[23] disciplinary proceedings against members of professions which cannot lead to their suspension from practice,[24] investigative proceedings by companies inspectors,[25] aspects of employment in the public service[26] and detention on remand.[27]

B.   Access to a court of full jurisdiction: fact and law.

5–28   A difficult question arises where, as will often happen, the administrative procedure leading to the original determination of a "civil right" does not satisfy the Article 6 requirements of an "independent tribunal"[28] or a "fair and public

---

[16] *Le Compte, van Leuven & de Meyere v. Belgium* (1982) 4 E.H.R.R. 1; *Albert & Le Compte v. Belgium* (1983) 5 E.H.R.R. 533.

[17] *Everest v. U.K.* (1997) 23 E.H.R.R. CD 180.

[18] *de Moor v. Belgium* (1994) 18 E.H.R.R. 372 which concerned an application to enrol as a pupil barrister.

[19] *H v. Belgium* (1988) 10 E.H.R.R. 339.

[20] *Pudas v. Sweden* (1988) 10 E.H.R.R. 380 (taxi licence); *Tre Traktorer Aktiebolag v. Sweden* (1991) 13 E.H.R.R. 309 (licence to serve alcohol drinks).

[21] *Rolf Gustafson v. Sweden*, August 1, 1997, R.J.D., 1997–IV, No. 41; 25 E.H.R.R. 623, which concerned a claim for criminal damage compensation; and *Masson & van Zon v. Netherlands* (1996) 22 E.H.R.R. 491, which concerned the power of the court to make an award of compensation "for reasons of equity" in respect of pre-trial detention of a suspect who was subsequently acquitted, without the need to show that the detention was unlawful. The Court said that *"The grant to a public authority of a [large] measure of discretion indicates that no actual right is recognised by law"* (para. 51 of the judgment).

[22] *Le Compte, van Leuven & de Meyere v. Belgium* (1982) 4 E.H.R.R. 1; *Albert & Le Compte v. Belgium* (1983) 5 E.H.R.R. 533; *Balmer-Schafroth v. Switzerland* (1998) 25 E.H.R.R. 598.

[23] App. Nos 2991 and 2992/66 *Alam Khan & Singh v. U.K.* 10 Yb 478 and 8244/78; *Uppal & Others v. U.K.* (1980) 3 E.H.R.R. 391. But *cf.* App. No. 42225/98 *JED v. United Kingdom* (decision of February 2, 1999) (Article 6 applies but judicial review an effective remedy) and see the Advocate-General in Joint Cases C–65/95 and C–111/95 *R. v. Secretary of State for the Home Department, ex parte Shingara and Radiom* [1997] E.C.R. I–3343.

[24] App. Nos 8249/78 *v. Belgium* 20 D. & R. 40, 10059/82 *v. FRG* 43 D. & R. 5 and 11869/85 *v. Belgium* (1989) 11 E.H.R.R. 76.

[25] *Fayed v. U.K.* (1994) 18 E.H.R.R. 393, paras 39, 57–63.

[26] Recruitment, employment and retirement: see *Lombardo v. Italy* (1992) 18 E.H.R.R. 205; *Muti v. Italy* (1994) Series A No. 281–C; *Neigel v. France*, March 17, 1997, R.J.D., 1997–II, No. 32.

[27] *Neumeister v. Austria* (1968) 1 E.H.R.R. 91. See also App. No. 8000/77 *v. Switzerland* 13 D. & R. 82 and 7830/77 *v. Austria* 14 D. & R. 200.

[28] See below, paras C6–52 *et seq.* This can be shown where there is a tribunal presided over by a lawyer working in independent practice: see, *e.g. A.P.B. Ltd, A.P.P. & E.A.B v. United Kingdom* (1998) 25 E.H.R.R. C.D. 141, 149 (IMRO's membership and appeal tribunals).

hearing". Where a civil right is in issue, Article 6 requires that the individual have access to a court with "full jurisdiction" to determine the matter. In *Le Compte, Van Leuven and de Meyere v. Belgium*, the Strasbourg Court defined the concept of access to a court of full jurisdiction in the following terms:

> "Article 6(1) draws no distinction between questions of fact and questions of law. Both categories of question are equally crucial for the outcome of proceedings relating to 'civil rights and obligations'. Hence, the 'right to a court' and the right to a judicial determination of the dispute cover questions of fact just as much as questions of law."[29]

No issue of principle arises over access to a court of full jurisdiction in relation to traditional civil law suits before the courts (or criminal charges),[30] although compliance may be in issue in particular cases. In domestic law at present an administrative decision on the facts is generally reviewable only on *Wednesbury* grounds.[31] Where, however, Article 6(1) applies because administrative action has been decisive of civil rights, there may be a determination of civil rights and obligations. In such a case, does the Convention require a reviewing court to determine all questions of fact afresh, if necessary by receiving new evidence? If so, does this mean that the distinction between review and appeal is no longer significant in the context of distinction between review and appeal is no longer significant in the context of "civil" rights? Must the judicial review court act not in a supervisory but in an appellate role?

5–29   Later in this chapter we consider the approaches of the Court and the Commission to Article 6's applicability to administrative mattters.[32] At least in its earlier judgments, the court appeared to take the view that a fair hearing entailed a right to a tribunal with full jurisdiction to consider all questions of law and fact. By contrast, where Article 13 is concerned the court has been more willing than the Commission to regard judicial review as an effective remedy in cases involving administrative action,[33] and later judgments and decisions suggest that it may adopt a similarly flexible approach to the requirements of Article 6.[34] It is therefore

---

[29] (1981) 4 E.H.R.R. 1, para. 51 of the judgment.

[30] But in relation to questions of immunity from suit see the discussion of the Court's judgment of October 28, 1998 in *Osman v. United Kingdom* [1999] Fam. Law 86, in *Barrett v. London Borough of Enfield* [1999] 3 W.L.R. 79, 84–85 (Lord Browne-Wilkinson) and *Gibson v. Chief Constable of Strathclyde Police, The Times*, May 11, 1999 (Court of Session Outer House). Hoffmann (1999) 62 M.L.R. 1, 4–6 states that the decision in *Osman* fills him with apprehension.

[31] *e.g. Din v. Wandsworth LBC* [1983] 1 A.C. 657, 664; *R. v. Hillingdon LBC, ex parte Puhlhofer* [1986] A.C. 484, 518; *Bugdaycay v. Secretary of State for the Home Department* [1987] A.C. 514. On the position of a decision wholly unsupported by evidence, see below, para. 5–30, n. 39.

[32] See paras 5–32 and 5–33 *et seq.*

[33] *Vilvarajah v. United Kingdom* (1992) 14 E.H.R.R. 248, paras 123–124; *Soering v. U.K.* (1989) 11 E.H.R.R. 439, paras 116–124. *cf. Chahal v. United Kingdom*, November 15, 1996, R.J.D., 1996–II, No. 22; 23 E.H.R.R. 413; *Smith and Grady v. U.K.*, judgment of September 27, 1999 (judicial review insufficient).

[34] See, for example, App. No. 42225/98, *JED v. United Kingdom*, decision of February 2, 1999 (judicial review of refusal of asylum). Without deciding on the applicability of Article 6(1), the Court (Third Section) declared the case inadmissible as manifestly ill-founded on the ground that the applicant was able to seek judicial review of the Secretary of State's decision and that the High Court proceedings did not indicate any element of unfairness. For a recent Commission decision see App. No. 28530/95, *X v. United Kingdom* January 19, 1998: Secretary of State's decision that the was applicant not a fit and proper person to be chief executive of an insurance company–judicial review was considered adequate in the circumstances but the Commission limited itself to considering whether he had been given sufficient information about the grounds of the decision to enable him to challenge it effectively.

possible that, even where Article 6 applies, in many cases there will be no need for a fundamental change from present practice concerning factual matters in judicial review. But the sharp distinction between the approach to questions of law and that to questions of fact, and the general unwillingness to go behind the facts found or the inferences drawn by the decision-maker will require reconsideration where a case involves Convention rights.[35] Before considering the Strasbourg jurisprudence, the traditional approach of the domestic judicial review jurisdiction is summarised.

C. Review of facts in purely domestic judicial review proceedings.

5–30   In purely domestic judicial review proceedings, whereas the reviewing court will subject questions of law to full reconsideration, only rarely will it reopen questions of fact and conduct a full review of the merits.[36] This is because in practice all errors of law go to jurisdiction and deprive an administrative body of its jurisdiction,[37] but only exceptionally will the existence or the non-existence of a particular fact be held to go to the jurisdiction of the administrative body.[38] The effective scope of review over questions of fact is, however, widened in two ways. First, a finding of primary fact wholly unsupported by evidence, or an inference wholly unsupported by the primary facts, constitutes an error of law and will accordingly be reviewable.[39] But such a case will probably be rare, even in the context of the "anxious scrutiny" to which decisions concerning human rights are subjected in domestic law.[40] Secondly, on the "logical" or "analytical" view that is often taken, inferences from primary fact, particularly where they are of a technical nature, are likely to be held to be matters of law and accordingly subjected to full review.[41]

5–31   Even where a fact is "jurisdictional", the court may be inhibited in its investigation of it by the nature of judicial review proceedings, in particular since evidence in such proceedings is on affidavit, and conflicts are difficult to resolve without the benefit of cross-examination, which is rarely permitted. It has been said that the court should appraise the quality of the evidence, decide whether it justifies the conclusion reached, and if it is not satisfied with any part of the evidence remit the matter for reconsideration or itself receive further evidence. It should only quash the decision if the evidence is not such as the authority should have relied on or where the evidence received does not justify the decision reached.[42] A reviewing

---

[35] See below, paras 5–39 et seq.

[36] See further De Smith, Woolf & Jowell, *Judicial Review of Administrative Action* (5th ed.), paras 5–078–5–091; Wade & Forsyth, *Administrative Law* (7th ed.) pp. 302–306, 311–320.

[37] *Anisminic v. Foreign Compensation Commission* [1969] 2 A.C. 147; *Pearlman v. Harrow School* [1979] Q.B. 56; *R. v. Hull University Visitor, ex parte Page* [1993] A.C. 682; *R. v. Monopolies and Mergers Commission, ex parte South Yorkshire Transport Ltd* [1993] 1 W.L.R. 23.

[38] *Khawaja v. Secretary of State for the Home Department* [1984] A.C. 74.

[39] *e.g. Allinson v. General Council of Medical Education* [1894] 1 Q.B. 750, 760–763; *R. v. Governor of Brixton Prison, ex parte Armah* [1968] A.C. 192, 234; *Coleen v. Minister of Housing and Local Government* [1971] 1 W.L.R. 433; *Global Plant v. Secretary of State for Social Services* [1972] 1 Q.B. 139, 155. On what constitutes "evidence", see *Mahon v. Air New Zealand* [1984] A.C. 808, 821.

[40] For a case in which it did, see *Bugdaycay v. Secretary of State for the Home Department* [1987] A.C. 514, esp. 532–534. See also *R. v. Ministry of Defence, ex parte Smith* [1996] Q.B. 517, 531–533, 537H–538C, 541 (Simon Brown L.J.) 558 (Sir Thomas Bingham M.R.). See further below, para. 5–40.

[41] See, *e.g. Baldwin & Francis Ltd v. Patents Appeal Tribunal* [1959] A.C. 663; *Pearlman v. Harrow School* [1979] Q.B. 56; *ACT Ltd v. Customs & Excise Commissioners* [1981] 1 W.L.R. 49; Beatson (1984) 4 Ox. J.L.S. 22, 39 et seq. The alternative, "pragmatic" view is that within a zone of reasonable conclusions an inference will be a question of fact and degree but outside that zone it will be a question of law: *Edwards v. Bairstow* [1965] A.C. 14, 33.

[42] *Khawaja v. Secretary of State for the Home Department* [1984] A.C. 74. On disputed questions of fact, see also *R. v. Fulham, Hammersmith & Kensington Rent Tribunal, ex parte Zerek* [1951] 2 K.B. 1.

court will be more willing to set aside the inferences an administrative body has made from the primary facts than its findings of primary fact,[43] but even with regard to inferences it will take account of the expertise of the administrative body.[44] The very limited scope of review of factual issues has also affected the attitude of the courts to applications for discovery (now known as disclosure and inspection[45]) and cross-examination.[46]

D. "Full jurisdiction": the approach of the Strasbourg Commission.

5–32   In the Strasbourg jurisprudence, the reluctance to require a court or tribunal to determine all questions of fact and law (as opposed to questions of legality administrative action alone) stems from the Commission's opinion in its 1980 Report in *Kaplan v. United Kingdom*. The case concerned a complaint by a director of an insurance company, who had been the subject of a DTI inquiry. This had resulted in a determination that he was not a proper person to control the company and the imposition of restrictions on its ability to enter into or vary insurance contracts. The Commission noted that:

> "there is no question of the present applicant having been denied access to the existing court remedies in which he could seek judicial review of the Secretary of State's decisions. His complaint is that these remedies were inadequate in scope because the courts could not go fully into the merits of the Secretary of State's decision and substitute their decision for his if they disagreed with him. The question therefore arises whether he had a 'right to a court' with jurisdiction to determine the full merits of the matter."[47]

The Commission, unanimously, found that there had been no violation of Article 6(1). It observed that " . . . (a)n interpretation of Article 6(1) under which it was held to provide a right to a full appeal on the merits of every administrative decision affecting private rights would . . . lead to a result which is inconsistent with the existing, and long-standing, legal position of most of the Contracting States".[48] More recently, the Commission has declared inadmissible a complaint concerning the limits of judicial review of the IMRO Membership and Appeal Tribunals, which had declared that the applicant was not a fit and proper person to conduct investment business and terminated its membership of IMRO.[49] Noting that the scope of judicial review was no more restrictive than that approved by the Commission and the court in an earlier decision concerning a statutory appeal,[50]

---

[43] *Benemax v. Austin Motor Co.* [1955] A.C. 310.
[44] *Commission for Racial Equality v. Associated Newspapers* [1978] 1 W.L.R. 905, 909–910.
[45] CPR 31.
[46] See *O'Reilly v. Mackman* [1983] 2 A.C. 237, 282–283; *R. v. City of Westminster CC, ex parte Moozary-Oraky* (1994) 26 H.L.R. 213, 221. See generally, *R. v. IRC, ex parte National Federation of Self-Employed and Small Businesses* [1982] A.C. 617, 635, 654; *R. v. Secretary of State for the Home Department, ex parte Harrison* [1988] 3 All E.R. 86 (Div. Ct.), December 10, 1987 (CA); *R. v. Secretary of State for the Home Department, ex parte Fayed* [1998] 1 W.L.R. 763, 775. Discovery was allowed in *R. v. Inland Revenue Commissioners, ex parte J Rothschild Holdings plc* [1986] S.T.C. 410 [1987] S.T.C. 163 and *R. v. Secretary of State for the Home Department, ex parte Herbage (No. 2)* [1987] Q.B. 1077. See further the discussion and authorities cited in the Law Commission's Report *Judicial Review and Statutory Appeals* Law Com. No. 226 (1994) paras 7.4–7.12. On the effect of the Human Rights Act 1998, see below, para. 5–39.
[47] (1980) 4 E.H.R.R. 64, para. 158.
[48] *ibid.* para. 161.
[49] *APB Ltd & others v. United Kingdom* (1998) 25 E.H.R.R. C.D. 141, 150.
[50] *Bryan v. United Kingdom* (1996) 21 E.H.R.R. 342, considered below, para. 5–34.

the Commission stated that "the subject-matter of the decision of the Appeal Tribunal—fitness to engage in business as a member of one of the self-regulatory bodies envisaged under the Financial Services Act 1986—was governed by specialised rules which could reasonably justify some limits on judicial review of the establishment of facts by the tribunal of IMRO".[51] This decision goes some way to reconciling the Commission's approach with that of the court, which is considered next.

E.   "Full jurisdiction": the approach of the Strasbourg Court:

5–33   In 1981, the year after the Commission's Report in *Kaplan*'s case, the court gave judgment in *Le Compte, Van Leuven and de Meyere v. Belgium*.[52] In the *Le Compte* case, the applicants had had their licences to practise medicine suspended in proceedings conducted before the disciplinary organs of the Belgian Ordre des Médecins, which did not comply in full with Article 6(1). Although an appeal lay to the Cour de Cassation, which did comply with Article 6(1) in other respects, that court had no jurisdiction to rectify factual errors or to examine whether the sanction was proportionate to the fault. The court found that Article 6(1) had been violated due to the lack of access to a court of full jurisdiction. In its later decision, *Albert & Le Compte v. Belgium*, the court re-iterated that, where decision-making bodies do not comply with Article 6(1), their decisions must be " . . . subject to subsequent control by a judicial body that has full jurisdiction and does provide the guarantees of Article 6(1)".[53] In *Zumtobel v. Austria*,[54] the court rejected a complaint by a company affected by an expropriation order. The company had alleged that the Austrian Administrative Court had only reviewed the question of lawfulness and could not be considered equivalent to a full review. The respondent and the Commission submitted that the powers of the Administrative Court "are as wide as those required by Article 6(1)" and enabled enquiry "into almost all the shortcomings in the way in which the facts were presented".[55] The court unanimously found no violation of Article 6(1) noting that:

> "The Administrative Court, in fact considered [the applicant company's] submissions on their merits, point by point, without ever having to decline jurisdiction in replying to them or in ascertaining various facts . . .
> Regard being had to the respect which must be accorded to decisions taken by the administrative authorities on grounds of expediency and to the nature of the complaints made by the Zumtobel partnership, the review of the Administrative Court satisfied the requirements of Article 6(1)."[56]

5–34   In *Bryan v. United Kingdom* the court found that an appeal to the English High Court from the decision of a planning inspector did comply with the

---

[51] (1998) 25 E.H.R.R. C.D. 141, 150. See also App. No. 28530/95, *X v. United Kingdom*, January 19, 1998, in which the Commission was careful to confine its decision to the facts and not to make any general pronouncement on the adequacy of judicial review.
[52] (1980) 4 E.H.R.R. 1. *Kaplan's* case was not referred to the Court.
[53] (1983) 5 E.H.R.R. 533, para. 31. See also later judgments, including *W v. United Kingdom* (1987) 10 E.H.R.R. 29; *Belilos v. Switzerland* (1988) 10 E.H.R.R. 466 and *Obermeier v. Austria* (1991) 13 E.H.R.R. 290.
[54] (1994) 17 E.H.R.R. 116, see para. 32.
[55] *ibid.* para. 28.
[56] *ibid.* para. 32.

requirements of Article 6(1) despite the fact that the High Court's jurisdiction on appeal was limited in that it was on "points of law" only and the High Court could not substitute its own decision on the merits for that of the inspector. This was explained by the fact that:

" . . . apart from the classic grounds of unlawfulness under English law (going to such issues as fairness, procedural propriety, independence and impartiality), the inspector's decision could have been quashed by the High Court if it had been made by reference to irrelevant factors or without regard to relevant factors; or if the evidence relied on by the inspector was not capable of supporting a finding of fact; or if the decision was based on an inference from facts which was perverse or irrational in the sense that no inspector properly directing himself would have drawn such an inference."[57]

While the High Court could not substitute its own findings of fact for those of the inspector, it had the power to ensure that the findings of fact made by the inspector and the inferences drawn from them were neither perverse nor irrational. This case suggests that Article 6(1) does not always require a full appeal on the merits and that a supervisory jurisdiction by way of review may sometimes suffice. However, such a restricted right of appeal may satisfy the requirements of Article 6(1) only where, as in *Bryan*'s case, the court is dealing with a specialised area of law like town and country planning, in which the administrative procedure is relatively formal, or with an area with a high policy content.[58] In *Bryan*'s case the court stated that:

"Such an approach by an appeal tribunal on questions of fact can reasonably be expected in specialised areas of law as the one at issue, particularly where the facts have already been established in the course of a quasi-judicial procedure governed by many of the safeguards required by Article 6(1)."[59]

5–35 The importance of the nature of the administrative process and whether it is formal is also shown by the judgment of the court in *Terra Woningen v. Netherlands*. The case concerned in which the rent board reduced the rent of a flat in a block owned by the applicant following a finding by the provincial executive that the ground on which the block stood was polluted. On appeal, the District Court considered itself bound by the board's finding and did not investigate the facts of the matter. The Strasbourg Court held that the provincial executive was not a tribunal within the meaning of Article 6(1) and the District Court had deprived itself of jurisdiction to examine facts which were crucial to determination of the dispute. Therefore the applicant had had no access to a court with sufficient jurisdiction to decide the case before it.[60]

The state of the Strasbourg jurisprudence means that it is not possible to say with precision when less than complete determination of factual issues will suffice. But it

---

[57] (1996) 21 E.H.R.R. 342, para. 44. n. that in that case there was no dispute as to the primary facts nor any challenge to the factual inferences drawn by the inspector; *ibid.*, para. 47.
[58] *Zumtobel v. Austria* (1994) 17 E.H.R.R. 116, above. (expropriation). See also App. No. 20490/92 76A DR 90, 111 (1994) *Ikscon v. U.K.*. But *cf.* App. No. 42225/98 *JED v. United Kingdom* (decision of February 2, 1999) for indications of a more tolerant approach to the adequacy of judicial review. See also App. No. 28530/95, *X v. United Kingdom*, January 19, 1998.
[59] (1996) 21 E.H.R.R. 342, para. 47.
[60] December 17, 1996, R.J.D., 1996–VI, No. 25; 24 E.H.R.R. 456.

is possible to identify certain pointers in the existing Strasbourg case law which indicate the extent to which the Article 6 "independent and impartial tribunal" may accord to the primary fact-finding administrative body the deference that an appellate court would accord to a court of first instance.

5–36   In the first place, the degree of intervention required will depend upon the nature of the subject-matter: if it is a matter which is by its very nature one which requires a certain degree of secrecy, the requirement that the "tribunal" re-make findings of fact will necessarily be diminished.[61] Where the subject-matter is technical and specialised, such as planning,[62] or the regulation of competence or fitness to practise in financial or professional fields,[63] the "tribunal" will be able to pay a certain deference to a specialist body, the more so where its findings are the fruit of quasi-judicial procedures which are not themselves the subject of criticism.[64] Clearly the judicial review court will not want to replace the fact-finding exercise undertaken by administrative body, especially in cases concerning complex factual or technical questions which the court is not qualified to determine. Again, where the decision is based not simply on fact but on opinions as to administrative expediency or whether an environmental or health hazard exists, that may be an issue for the specialist body, with only limited review.[65]

5–37   Another relevant factor may be the nature of what is at stake in the proceedings. A degree of intervention is generally required, for example, where the individual is subject to a "criminal" penalty or in cases of interference with family life, rather than in cases of interference with commercial property.[66] This notion is similar to that of "anxious scrutiny" with which the judicial review court is already familiar. So, where the administrative act involves imposition of a penalty which may be classified as "criminal" for the purposes of the Convention, the court has reiterated that " . . . regard must be had to the complaints raised in that court by the applicant as well as the defining characteristics of a 'judicial body that has full jurisdiction'. These include the power to quash in all respects, on questions of fact

---

[61] *Klass v. Germany* (1978) 2 E.H.R.R. 214, para. 69. But compare the Court's approach in *Chahal v. United Kingdom*, November 15, 1996, R.J.D., 1996–II, No. 22; 23 E.H.R.R. 413, paras 130–131; *cf. R. v. Home Secretary, ex parte Cheblak* [1991] 1 W.L.R. 890, 904.

[62] *Bryan v. United Kingdom* (1996) 21 E.H.R.R. 342; *Fischer v. Austria* (1995) 20 E.H.R.R. 349.

[63] See the reasoning concerning the applicablity of Article 6 in *van Marle v. Netherlands* (1986) 8 E.H.R.R. 483, para. 36 (professional competence) and *H v. Belgium* (1988) 10 E.H.R.R. 339, para. 43 ("matters of fact and capable of judicial assessment"). See also the Commission's Report in *APB Ltd v. U.K.* (1998) 25 E.H.R.R. C.D. 141, 150, above, para. 5–32. *cf.* the important dissenting opinions of Judge Martens in *Fischer v. Austria* (1995) 20 E.H.R.R. 349, paras 6–8 and *Schmautzer v. Austria* (1995) 21 E.H.R.R. 511, below, n. 67.

[64] In *Bryan v. United Kingdom* (1996) 21 E.H.R.R. 342 the complaint about the planning inspector was that he was not independent of the executive and there was no dispute as to the primary facts nor any challenge to the factual inferences drawn by the inspector; *ibid.*, para. 47.

[65] *Zumtobel v. Austria* (1994) 17 E.H.R.R. 116, para. 32 (expropriation); *Fischer v. Austria* (1995) 20 E.H.R.R. 349, para. 34 (revocation of refuse tip operator's licence on environmental grounds).

[66] Compare *W v. United Kingdom* (1988) 10 E.H.R.R. 29, paras 82 and 49; *R. v. United Kingdom* (1988) 10 E.H.R.R. 74; *B v. United Kingdom* (1988) 10 E.H.R.R. 87; *O v. United Kingdom* (1988) 10 E.H.R.R. 82 and *H v. United Kingdom* (1988) 10 E.H.R.R. 95 (parents right of access to children in care) with *Agosi v. United Kingdom* (1987) 9 E.H.R.R. 1, paras 59–60 (confiscation). But *cf.*, in the context of Articles 3 and 13, the asylum cases, *Vilvarajah v. United Kingdom* (1992) 14 E.H.R.R. 248, paras 123–126; *Chahal v. United Kingdom*, November 15, 1996, R.J.D., 1996–II, No. 22; 23 E.H.R.R. 413, paras 148, 152–153; App. No. 42225/98 *JED v. United Kingdom* (decision of February 2, 1999).

and law, the decision of the body below."[67] Article 6 does not prevent the administrative imposition of penalties. But, at least where the Convention classifies a penalty as "criminal", an individual is entitled to challenge the penalty before an independent tribunal. Article 6 requires that the tribunal have power to entertain all the individual's complaints and to overturn the administrative decision, both on fact and law.[68]

5–38   The approach outlined in the previous two paragraphs should enable the "tribunal" to give due deference to the facts found by the administrative decision-maker in appropriate cases, in particular in matters which are not readily capable of judicial assessment. Findings of fact, and inferences drawn from them, will not be acceptable where they are the fruit of an unfair procedure or where they are supported by no evidence or no sufficient evidence. What is sufficient evidence will depend upon the seriousness of the right which is being interfered with, so that the more drastic the interference, the less readily the "tribunal" should accept the administrator's findings of fact. This approach is similar to that enunciated by Mr Nicolas Bratza in his important concurring opinion in the Commission's Report in *Bryan v. United Kingdom*,[69] in which he said:

> "It appears to me that the requirement that a court or tribunal should have 'full jurisdiction' cannot be mechanically applied with the result that, in all circumstances, and whatever the subject matter of the dispute, the court or tribunal must have full power to substitute its own findings of fact, and its own inferences from those facts, for that of the administrative body concerned. Whether the power of judicial review is sufficiently wide to satisfy the requirements of Article 6 must in my view depend on a number of considerations, including the subject matter of the dispute, the nature of the decision of the administrative authorities which is in question, the procedure, if any, which exists for review of the decision by a person or body acting independently of the authority concerned and the scope of that power of review."[70]

5.   EVIDENTIAL QUESTIONS

5–39   Even where Article 6 does not require a court to substitute its own findings of fact, the requirements that interference with a Convention right must be justified according to Convention principles (see above), and those of a fair trial are likely to mean that a wider range of evidence will have to be before the court. The

---

[67] *Schmautzer v. Austria* (1995) 21 E.H.R.R. 511, para. 36. In his separate opinion in that case, Judge Martens strongly criticises the inference that may be drawn from this statement, *i.e.* that in cases which are "administrative" under national law the safeguards afforded by a tribunal are lower where the case is "civil" for purposes of the Convention than where it is "criminal" for purposes of the Convention. He states: "I cannot see any justification for such differentiation, which does not find support in the wording or the purpose of Article 6 this differentiation is contrary to the Court's case-law.".
[68] See also the Opinion of the Commission, para. 51: " . . . whilst in civil matters a somewhat limited review of the decisions of administrative authorities may, in certain circumstances, satisfy the requirements of Article 6 of the Convention, criminal cases may require a different approach . . . [W]here a defendant desires a court to determine a criminal charge against him, there is no room for limitation on the scope of review required of the decisions of administrative authorities. Accordingly, the applicant in the present case, who wished to have determined by a court at least one question of fact, was entitled to, but did not have the benefit of, a court which could consider all the facts of the case.".
[69] (1996) 21 E.H.R.R. 342, 353.
[70] *ibid.*, p. 354.

greater significance of factual issues may also mean that a more open approach is to be taken to disclosure of documents, and perhaps cross-examination, in applications for judicial review.[71] Further, although Article 6 does not expressly refer to it, the court has developed a requirement to give reasons for decisions.[72] This follows also from the shift of the burden in relation to justification.

The burden of justifying an interference is placed fairly and squarely on the respondent public authority, which will be required to satisfy the court as to what the reasons were and that they were relevant and sufficient.[73] This approach is not entirely novel, since it already exists where a state authority seeks to justify interference with a right or freedom deriving from Community law.[74] But the consequence is that an authority asserting that the purpose of an interference is "legitimate" may have to put forward evidence in circumstances in which it is not necessary under traditional *Wednesbury* review. So much was recognised in *R. v. Ministry of Defence, ex parte Smith*[75] and confirmed by the Strasbourg Court in *Smith and Grady v. United Kingdom*.[75a] A court which is required to conduct its balancing exercise and to determine whether an interference is "necessary in a democratic society", "answers a pressing social need" and is "proportionate to the legitimate aim pursued", may well need evidence of social policy in order to carry out its task.

5–40   *Ex p. Smith* concerned the legality of a policy that homosexuality was incompatible with service in the armed forces. It was said that, had the Convention been enforceable at that time by domestic courts, evidence by the Government would have been required.[76] It would have been necessary for the Government to show that the policy answered a pressing social need and was proportionate to its aims of securing morale and unit effectiveness, and the protection of minors. At least one of the judges who decided the case considered that, had such evidence been necessary, it was unlikely that the policy could have been justified[77] and the Strasbourg Court has indeed since held that the government had failed to justify it. But evidence of this sort is not needed on the conventional *Wednesbury* approach: notwithstanding the anxious scrutiny used in human rights cases,[77a] the threshold of

---

[71] See above, para. 5–31 and note that in cases involving civil rights a public authority's failure to disclose documentation without good cause may constitute a denial of a fair hearing: *McGinley & Egan v. United Kingdom* (1999) 27 E.H.R.R. 1, para. 88. The more restrictive approach to disclosure under the Civil Procedure Rules (see CPR 31) is balanced by a duty to act reasonably in exchanging information and documents (CPR 1.1(2)(a)–(c)). See *R. v. Secretary of State for the Home Department, ex parte Zighem* [1996] Imm. AR 194 and other cases on Home Office Policy DP/2/93 (discussed in Hunt, *Using Human Rights Law in English Courts* (1996), pp. 233–242.) which suggest that even where Article 8 of the Convention is directly in play disclosure will not be widely necessary.

[72] *H v. Belgium* (1988) 10 E.H.R.R. 339; *Van de Hurk v. Netherlands* (1994) 18 E.H.R.R. 481.

[73] See *Buckley v. United Kingdom* (1997) 23 E.H.R.R. 101, para. 77. See further below, para. 5–43.

[74] *R. v. Chief Constable of Sussex, ex parte International Trader's Ferry* [1999] 1 All E.R. 129, 145 *per* Lord Slynn; *R. v. Ministry of Agriculture, Fisheries and Food, ex parte First City Trading* [1997] 1 C.M.L.R. 250, 279.

[75] [1996] Q.B. 517, 558 (Sir Thomas Bingham M.R.). See also *R. v. Secretary of State for the Home Department, ex parte Simms & O'Brien* [1999] 3 W.L.R. 328 (comments on cogency of evidence adduced on behalf of Home Secretary). See further *R. v. Secretary of State for the Home Department, ex parte Zighem* [1996] Imm. A.R. 194.

[75a] Judgment of September 27, 1999.

[76] [1996] Q.B. 517, 564E–F, 566B (Henry and Thorpe L.JJ.).

[77] [1996] Q.B. 517 at 541 (Simon Brown L.J.).

[77a] *Budaycay v. Secretary of State for the Home Department* [1987] A.C. 514; *R. v. Secretary of State for the Home Department ex parte Brind* [1991] 1 A.C. 517; *R. v. Ministry of Defence, ex parte Smith* [1996] Q.B. 517; *R. v. Lord Saville of Newdigate, ex parte A, The Times,* July 29, 1999, 149 N.L.J. 965, 1201.

irrationality which an applicant is required to surmount is a high one.[77b] Consequently, although the justification for the policy "may to many seem unconvincing", it was not "outrageous in its defiance of logic"[78] and the application for judicial review failed. In the same case, Henry L.J. recognised that in determining policy issues under the Convention the court might also be assisted by "Brandeis briefs",[79] a notion which received further encouragement from the Lord Chancellor during the course of the Government's defence of its narrow "victim" requirement for standing under the HRA.[80] Again the courts will be familiar with this wider approach to evidence in relation to Community law cases.[81] The inadequacy of the conventional *Wednesbury* approach adopted in *ex parte Smith* was demonstrated when the case reached Strasbourg. In *Smith & Grady v. United Kingdom*[81a] the Strasbourg Court held that, in the circumstances of that case, the threshold at which the domestic courts could find that the policy was *Wednesbury* unreasonable or irrational "was placed so high that it effectively excluded any consideration . . . of whether the interference with the applicants' rights answered a pressing social need or was proportionate to the national security and public order aims pursued"[81b] by the government. Accordingly, in such circumstances, reviewability on the ground of unreasonableness did not constitute an "effective remedy" as required by Article 13.

5–41 As under the pre-HRA judicial review jurisprudence, "the more substantial the interference with human rights, the more the court is likely to require by way of justification before it is satisfied" that an administrative decision has been justified.[82] But the evidential issues "should be approached with realism and good sense, and kept in proportion".[83] The Judicial Committee of the Privy Council,

---

[77b] In *R. v. Ministry of Defence, ex parte Smith* [1996] Q.B. 517, 538, *per* Simon Brown L.J. stated that the "threshold of unreasonableness" is not lowered in human rights cases but *cf R. v. Lord Saville of Newdigate, ex parte A, The Times*, July 29, 1999, 149 N.L.J. 965, 1201. The Court of Appeal pointedly refrained from agreeing with Simon Brown L.J. It stated that "when a fundamental right such as the right of life is engaged, the options available to the reasonable decision maker are curtailed" because "it is not open to the decision maker to risk interfering with fundamental rights in the absence of compelling justification" and the court will anxiously scrutinise "the strength" of the countervailing crcumstances and "the degree of the interference" with the human right involved.

[78] *ibid.*

[79] *ibid.*

[80] *Hansard*, H.L., November 24, 1997, col. 832. See further above, paras 4–37—4–40. For support of third party interventions see *R. v. Chief Constable of the North Wales Police, ex parte Thorpe* [1999] Q.B. 396, 426 (Lord Woolf M.R.).

[81] See, for example, *R. v. Secretary of State for Employment, ex parte Equal Opportunities Commission* [1995] A.C. 1 in which the respondent sought to justify differences of treatment by reference to a wide range of policy considerations.

[81a] Judgment of September 27, 1999.

[81b] Judgment dated September 27, 1999, paras 136–139. *Vilvarajah v. United Kingdom* (1992) 14 E.H.R.R. 248 and *Soering v. U.K.* (1989) 11 E.H.R.R. 439 were distinguished (para. 138) on the ground that the test applied by the domestic courts in those judicial review proceedings coincided with the Strasbourg Court's own approach under Article 3 of the ECHR. *Quaere* whether the broader approach of the Court of Appeal in *R. v. Lord Saville of Newdigate, ex parte A*, above, n. 77b, to *Wednesbury* reasonableness will be easier to justify under Article 13.

[82] *R. v. Ministry of Defence, ex parte Smith* [1996] Q.B. 517, 554 (Sir Thomas Bingham M.R. approving the applicants' submission as to the correct approach). *R. v. Lord Saville of Newdigate, ex parte A*, above n. 77b, see also *R. v. Chief Constable of Sussex, ex parte International Trader's Ferry* [1999] 1 All E.R. 129, 159 (Lord Cooke of Thorndon), company's needs "purely commercial". *cf.* in the context of Article 28 (formerly Article 30) of the E.C. Treaty to assess whether restrictions on intra-Community trade are justified the national court is said to require "as complete as possible a set of empirical data": Joined Cases C–306/88, C304/90, and C169/91 *Stoke-on-Trent CC & Norwich CC v. B & Q plc* [1992] E.C.R. I–6635, para. 35 [1993] A.C. 900, 945C.

[83] *A.G. of Hong Kong v. Lee Kwong-kut* [1993] A.C. 951, 976.

considering the evidence that would be required under the Hong Kong Bill of Rights to establish that an interference with individual rights was justified, stated that "in order to maintain the balance between the individual and society as a whole, rigid and inflexible standards should not be imposed on the legislature's attempts to resolve the difficult and intransigent problems with which society is faced when seeking to deal with serious crime".[84]

5–42   Courts should have little difficulty in developing a less restrictive approach to disclosure of documents and the giving of reasons. Even without a general obligation to give reasons when a decision is made, the respondent needs to explain the decision to the court,[85] and is further expected to approach the matter "with all the cards face upwards on the table".[86] These requirements are now reinforced by the provisions of the Civil Procedure Rules which provide that, even where pre-action Protocols do not exist for the matter, "the court will expect the parties, in accordance with the overriding objective and the matters referred to in CPR 1.1(2)(a), (b) and (c),[87] to act reasonably in exchanging information and documents relevant to the claim and generally in trying to avoid the necessity for the start of proceedings".[88] Applicants will be expected to write letters of claim and respondents to answer them giving reasons and disclosing relevant documents. Moreover, the Strasbourg Court has held that in cases involving civil rights a public authority's failure without good cause to disclose documents which would assist the applicant in establishing his case would be to deny him a fair hearing in violation of Article 6(1).[89] Although the Civil Procedure Rules refer to the principle of proportionality, both in the general conduct of proceedings and in relation to disclosure,[90] this principle must be interpreted subject to the Convention requirement of a fair hearing, which a desire to save resources does not excuse.[91]

5–43   As to reasons, the now well-established approach of the common law is that there is no general duty to give reasons.[92] In its recent decision in *Stefan v. General Medical Council* the Judicial Committee of the Privy Council, while declining to depart from from the common law rule, indicated that it was:

> " . . . of the possible re-appraisal of the whole position which the passing of the Human Rights Act 1998 may bring about. The provisions of Article 6(1) of the Convention on Human Rights, which are now about to become directly accessible in national courts, will require closer attention to be paid to the duty to give reasons, at least in relation to those cases where a person's civil rights and obligations are being determined."[93]

---

[84] *ibid.*

[85] *R. v. Civil Service Appeal Board, ex parte Cunningham* [1991] 4 All E.R. 310; *R. v. Secretary of State for the Home Department, ex parte Fayed* [1998] 1 W.L.R. 763. See also *R. v. Secretary of State for the Home Department, ex parte Zighem* [1996] Imm. A.R. 194 (need to identify reasons for decision).

[86] *R. v. Lancashire C.C., ex parte Huddleston* [1986] 2 All E.R. 941, 945, *per* Lord Donaldson M.R., pointing out that "the vast majority of the cards will start in the authority's hands".

[87] *i.e.* ensuring that the parties are on an equal footing, saving expense and dealing with the case in ways which are proportionate.

[88] Practice Direction—Protocols, B0–001, para. 4 (Civil Procedure, p. 800).

[89] *McGinley and Egan v. United Kingdom* (1999) 27 E.H.R.R. 1, para. 86.

[90] CPR 1.1(2)(c) and, in relation to inspection, CPR 31.3(2).

[91] *Airey v. Ireland* (1979) 2 E.H.R.R. 305. See further below, para. C6–74.

[92] *R. v. Secretary of State for the Home Department, ex parte Doody* [1994] 1 A.C. 531, 561, 564–566; *R. v. Higher Education Funding Council, ex parte Institute of Dental Surgery* [1994] 1 W.L.R. 242, 259, 262.

[93] [1999] 1 W.L.R. 1293, 1299 (Lord Clyde). See also *R. v. Secretary of State for the Home Department, ex parte Zighem* [1996] Imm. A.R. 194.

CHAPTER 6

Remedies

1. INTRODUCTION

6–01 The HRA will have a considerable impact on the remedial regime of domestic law. Its reach will go beyond the creation of a new free-standing right of action against public authorities for unlawful infringements of Convention rights.[1] It affects legal relationships not only between individuals and public authorities but also those between private parties. The interpretative obligation in section 3(1),[2] will require courts to scrutinise on human rights grounds those legislative provisions which clothe public authorities with apparent authority to interfere with Convention rights, or which are the basis of a prosecution, or which may be the foundation of private law rights asserted in relations between private parties.[3] In some cases, the combination of the interpretative obligation and the operation of the *ultra vires* doctrine will lead the court to declare invalid provisions of subordinate legislation on which a public authority relies as purporting to empower it, for example, to interfere with a person's liberty or property; and such disapplication may occur equally in proceedings between individuals which are founded on a provision of subordinate legislation whose validity is questioned.[4] The fact that a person may claim in *any* legal proceedings[5] that an act of a public authority unlawfully violates a Convention right means that acts which affect, or are the foundation of, the rights and obligations of private parties between themselves, may be questioned in proceedings between those parties. The indirect influence of the HRA, or the obligation on the court as a public authority,[6] may lead to the development of new causes of action.[7] Public authorities will face proceedings for, or be met with a defence claiming, unlawful breaches of Convention rights.

6–02 Save in proceedings against a public authority in which an unlawful act is alleged,[8] for the most part the court will be applying human rights principles within the framework of existing causes of action or public law rules: the remedies which the court applies will be familiar, and the principles well-established. The human rights context, and in particular the obligation–including positive obligations[9]—on courts under section 6, will no doubt affect the court's approach,[10] the nature of

---

[1] Section 6(1), see above, paras 4–01 *et seq.*, 4–45 *et seq.*
[2] Discussed above, paras 3–01 *et seq.*
[3] See the approach in *R. v. Secretary of State for the Home Department, ex parte Simms & O'Brien* [1999] 3 W.L.R. 328. See further above, paras 3–12, 3–34.
[4] See above, para. 4–47.
[5] s. 7(1)(b).
[6] See above, para. 4–45.
[7] See above, paras 4–53 *et seq.*
[8] s. 7(1)(a).
[9] See above, paras 4–49—4–52.
[10] See, *e.g.* Sir Thomas Bingham M.R. in *R. v. Ministry of Defence, ex parte Smith & ors* [1996] Q.B. 517. See further above, Chap. 5, especially paras 5–39—5–40.

the remedy, and the manner in which the court exercises its discretion, but the court will not be faced with a new remedy. So, for example, where the effect of the Act is to remove the statutory authority which would excuse what is otherwise a tort, the claim in tort will be made out and a remedy will be dispensed according to the applicable rules; the rights of individuals will be determined by reference to a conforming interpretation of a legislative provision. Again, in judicial review proceedings an *ultra vires* provision will be declared unlawful or quashed. We have canvassed these matters in previous chapters.

By contrast, the higher courts' power to make declarations of incompatibility, and Ministers' power to make remedial orders amending legislation in consequence either of such a declaration or of a decision of the Strasbourg Court, are entirely novel. So are certain aspects of the manner in which the Act requires remedies to be afforded.

Declarations of incompatibility have been considered in Chapter 3, dealing with the Act's effect on legislation. This chapter will consider judicial proceedings and remedies in respect of unlawful acts and the ministerial power to make remedial orders.

2.   A NEW STATUTORY RIGHT OF ACTION

6–03   As we have seen, the Act creates a new statutory right of action.[11] Provided that he or she is or would be a victim of the act,[12] a person may claim that a public authority has committed or proposes to commit an unlawful act under section 6(1), either by bringing proceedings against the authority under the Act or by relying on Convention right in any legal proceedings.[13] However, consistently with the Act's respect for parliamentary sovereignty, an authority does not act unlawfully where, as a result of one or more provisions of primary legislation, it could not have acted differently,[14] or if it is giving effect to or enforcing provisions of, or made under, irreconcilably incompatible primary legislation.[15]

The statutory right of action is free-standing and can thus be relied upon even where there is no pre-existing cause of action. Proceedings are to be brought in the "appropriate court or tribunal", which will be determined in accordance with rules[16] and a claim under the Act may be made by way of a private law claim or counterclaim, in judicial review proceedings or before an appropriate appellate body.[17] Proceedings claiming that a judicial act is unlawful may be brought only by exercising a right of appeal, on an application for judicial review,[18] or in such other forum as may be prescribed by rules.[19] However, this does not affect any rule of law

---

[11] Prior to its enactment, although the Convention could influence domestic proceedings, an action could not be directly founded on a breach of the Convention: *Malone v. Metropolitan Police Commissioner* [1979] Ch. 344, 353. See further above, para. 1–02.

[12] See above, para. 4–26.

[13] s. 7(1).

[14] s. 6(2)(a).

[15] s. 6(2)(b).

[16] s. 7(2). For proceedings in Scotland, rules will be made by the Secretary of State for Scotland; elsewhere, rules will be made by the Lord Chancellor or by the appropriate Secretary of State: s. 7(9).

[17] See cll. 55 and 50, 52, 54 of the Immigration and Asylum Bill 1999.

[18] In Scotland a petition.

[19] s. 9(1). s. 9(3), which places limits on the power to award of damages in respect of judicial acts, is considered below, para. 6–18. "Judicial act" includes a judicial act of a court, and includes an act done on the instructions, or on behalf, of a judge, including a member of a tribunal, a justice of the peace and a clerk or other officer entitled to exercise the jurisdiction of a court: s. 9(5).

which prevents a court from being subject to judicial review,[20] for example section 29(3) of the Supreme Court Act 1981 which excludes judicial review of a matter relating to a trial on indictment, and no new avenue of judicial review is created in such cases. Courts or tribunals will have to take account of an individual's right to an effective remedy under Article 13 of the Convention when considering whether to grant permission to appeal or permission to apply for judicial review.[21] This is considered further below at paragraphs 6–12 *et seq.*

6–04   A party relying on a Convention right is not prevented from relying on any other right or making any other claim available in national law.[22] In some cases, the interpretative obligation in section 3 or the *ultra vires* doctrine may operate to remove presumed statutory authority to interfere with Convention rights.[23] In practice, therefore, in most proceedings a claimant will rely on existing common law and statutory rights and on the Act pleaded in the alternative. For example, an individual complaining about arrest or detention will plead false imprisonment. If the defendant pleads a lawful authority, the court will be required to read and give effect to any governing statutory power, so far as it is possible to do so, to render the exercise of that power compatible with Article 5 of the Convention, which guarantees the right to liberty and security of the person. If the power of arrest can be construed in accordance with the Convention, then any action in excess of it will not be justified by lawful authority and will amount to the tort of false imprisonment.[24] The result will be the same if, for example, the power of arrest derives from subordinate legislation which is adjudged *ultra vires* on Convention grounds[25]; or if the power is exercisable upon the commission of an offence which was created by subordinate legislation which is itself *ultra vires*. Conversely, if the arrest is within the statutory power it will not be false imprisonment; and it will not be unlawful under section 6 because it will be protected by section 6(2). If the statutory power of arrest and detention is itself irreconcilably incompatible with Article 5, the court's only course will be to consider making a declaration of incompatibility. Where the law recognises an established tort, therefore, the Act may only have a subsidiary effect, serving mainly to limit the range of defences available to the defendant authority. Given the limits which the Act seeks to place on the remedies available for breaches of Convention rights,[26] a claimant will be well-advised to pursue his or tort tort remedies in the first instance. An allegation of breach of a Convention right will serve principally as a back stop, in particular where existing law does not afford a remedy.

6–05   The new statutory wrong is likely to be of additional significance in relation to breaches of the Convention by public authorities exercising non-statutory powers or discretions or enforcing non-statutory rules. Any such authority

---

[20] s. 9(2).
[21] An effective remedy must afforded only in respect of an "arguable" claim of violation of a Convention right: *Silver & others v. United Kingdom* (1983) 5 E.H.R.R. 347; *Boyle & Rice v. United Kingdom* (1988) 10 E.H.R.R. 425. The test of what is arguable may not be the same as the tests for permission to appeal or to apply: as to the case law relating to Article 13, see below, paras C13–01 *et seq.*
[22] s. 11.
[23] See *R. v. Secretary of State for the Home Department, ex parte Simms & O'Brien* [1999] 3 W.L.R. 328
[24] But see *Percy & another v. Hall* [1997] Q.B. 924, CA, which will have to be reconsidered in the light of the Human Rights Act.
[25] See above, para. 3–42.
[26] See below, paras 6–16 *et seq.*

will have a duty under section 6(1) to act in a manner which is compatible with Convention rights and, since its activities are not the subject of statute, it will not be able to avail itself of the section 6(2) defence. Consequently, in addition to any other liability which it may incur, the authority will be liable under section 6 for actions or proposed actions which are incompatible with Convention rights. If no pre-existing wrong has been committed, an individual can claim a breach of section 6 alone.

Courts will be acting unlawfully if they fail to exercise their powers and discretions in accordance with Convention rights, even where that exercise conflicts with existing precedent. In public law, section 6 creates a discrete head of illegality[27]: challenges to the exercise of statutory powers hitherto couched in the language of irrationality will henceforth challenge its legality[28]: the court will be asking, for example, not whether a decision is rational but whether a decision interfering with a Convention right pursued a legitimate aim and whether the action taken is proportionate to the aim to be achieved.

3. RELIANCE ON CONVENTION RIGHTS IN LEGAL PROCEEDINGS

6–06 A person who claims that a public authority has acted or proposes to act in a way which is unlawful under Article 6(1) may rely on the Convention right(s) concerned in any legal proceedings.[29] Where the proceedings were brought by or at the instigation of a public authority, the claim may be raised even if the unlawful act in question took place before the coming into force of the Act,[30] and a public authority instituting proceedings before the Act is brought into force is obliged to take account of the likely effect of the Convention on those proceedings, for example if it is likely that the substantive hearing or any appeal will be heard after the coming into force of the Act.[31] The reference to legal proceedings "includes" those brought by or at the instigation of a public authority and an appeal against the decision of a court or tribunal,[32] but unlike section 7(1)(a), the proceedings covered by this provision are not limited to those to which a public authority is a party. So an allegation that a public authority has committed an unlawful act may be raised (a) as a defence to proceedings brought by or at the instigation of a public authority; or (b) in any proceedings between private parties where the lawfulness of the act of a public authority is in issue.

A. Proceedings brought by a public authority

6–07 An individual may raise as a defence to proceedings brought by a public authority[33] a claim that an act or proposed act of that authority is or would be unlawful by virtue of section 6(1). For example, a person prosecuted for assaulting or impeding a police officer in the lawful execution of his or her duty may plead in

---

[27] See above, para. 4–01.
[28] See above, paras 3–33 et seq., 5–02, 5–39—5–40. To the same effect see Feldman [1998] E.H.R.L.R. 691.
[29] s. 7(1)(b).
[30] s. 22(4). Otherwise, s. 7(1) applies only to acts committed after the coming into force of s. 7.
[31] See R. v. Director of Public Prosecutions, ex parte Kebeline & ors [1999] 3 W.L.R. 175 (Divisional Court). The Court also suggested that the authority should take account of the likely outcome of any Strasbourg proceedings. The House of Lords allowed an appeal on October 28, 1999, see above, paras 5–09—5–13.
[32] s. 7(6).
[33] Such as those in Wandsworth LBC v. Winder [1985] A.C. 46; DPP v. Hutchinson [1990] 2 A.C. 783.

defence that the officer was committing a breach of a Convention right and was accordingly not acting in the lawful execution of his or her duty.[34] A criminal defendant may seek to exclude evidence which he or she argues was obtained unlawfully.[35] A person disciplined by his or her professional association for contravening a rule against advertising could claim in defence that the association has adopted an unlawful rule.[36]

B. Proceedings between individuals

6–08 It follows from the use of the expression "any legal proceedings" in section 7(1)(b)[37] that an individual can plead the unlawfulness of an act of a public authority in any proceedings in which it is relevant, even if the authority is not a party. Where an individual brings or defends proceedings founded on an act of a public authority, it appears, therefore, that the other party may plead that the act in question is unlawful.[38]

An individual may also rely, in his defence, on the obligation of the court, as a public authority, to comply with Convention rights. For example, if the court is considering making a search order (formerly an *Anton Piller* order),[39] or an order requiring disclosure of a source of information,[40] the defendant may plead in his defence that such an order would be a breach of a Convention right. It is immaterial in such a case that the claimant is not a public authority.

C. Appeals

6–09 If a court or tribunal makes an order which infringes a Convention right, a party may appeal on that ground.[41] Again, it does not matter that the opposing party is an individual or private body. In such a case, the claim is that the court itself has committed the unlawful act.

D. Period within which proceedings may be brought

6–10 Proceedings against a public authority by a victim of an unlawful act under section 7(1)(a) must be brought within one year beginning with the date on which the act complained of took place, or such longer period as the court or tribunal considers equitable having regard to all the circumstances.[42] However, this time limit is expressed to be "subject to any rule imposing a stricter time limit in relation to the procedure in question".[43] So, for example, where proceedings in respect of an unlawful act are brought by way of judicial review, application must

---

[34] See the facts in *Brazil v. Chief Constable of Surrey* [1983] 1 W.L.R. 1155 and *Piddington v. Bates* [1961] 1 W.L.R. 162. The offence is contained in Police Act 1996, s. 89(1).
[35] *R. v. Khan (Sultan)* [1990] 1 A.C. 109.
[36] See, *mutatis mutandis, Casado Coca v. Spain* (1994) 18 E.H.R.R. 1.
[37] See, *mutatis mutandis,* s. 6(3) and (5).
[38] *e.g.* that the grant of planning permission for an activity is unlawful: although at common law planning permission does not prevent the activity from constituting a nuisance, *Wheeler v. JJ Saunders Ltd* [1996] Ch. 19, it may affect the availability of injunctive relief, *Gillingham BC v. Medway (Chatham) Dock Ltd* [1993] Q.B. 343. Also, where a private person assists the police in apprehending another and is later sued for trespass, the other party may plead that the conduct of the police was unlawful: *Clerk & Lindsell on Torts* (17th ed.), paras 12–63.
[39] *Chappell v. United Kingdom* (1990) 12 E.H.R.R. 1.
[40] *Goodwin v. United Kingdom*, March 27, 1996, R.J.D., 1996–II, No. 7; 22 E.H.R.R. 123; *Camelot v. Centaur Communications* [1998] I.R.L.R. 80, CA.
[41] s. 9(1).
[42] s. 7(6).
[43] *ibid.*

be made "promptly and in any event within three months from the date when the grounds for the application first arose".[44] Proceedings by way of appeal must be brought within the time limits laid down for appealing.

4. REMEDIES FOR UNLAWFUL ACTS GENERALLY

6–11 Where a court or tribunal finds that an act or proposed act of a public authority is or would be unlawful under section 6(1), it may "grant such relief or remedy, or make such order, within its powers, as it considers just and appropriate".[45] A Minister with power to make rules in respect of any tribunal may by order add to the relief or remedies which a tribunal may grant, or to the grounds on which it may grant any of them, to the extent that he or she considers necessary to ensure that it can provide "an appropriate remedy".[46] In the next section, we consider the general approach to the question of what is an appropriate remedy.

A. The right to an effective remedy: the relevance of Article 13

6–12 The power to grant remedies is deliberately framed in the widest possible terms. Although the right to an effective remedy guaranteed by Article 13 is not among the articles to which section 1(1) of the Act gives effect, a court or tribunal considering any Convention question under the Act, including the question as to what remedy is "just and appropriate", must take account of all the relevant case law of the Strasbourg institutions, including that relating to Article 13.[47] The Government made this clear when resisting amendments intended either to include Article 13 in the list of Convention rights or to amend the Long Title to refer to provision of effective remedies for violations of Convention rights. In view of the significance of Article 13 and the fact that the effect of its omission from the statutory list is not clear on the face of the HRA, the Government's justification for omitting it and explanation of its effect is important. The Lord Chancellor stated:

"The Bill gives effect to Article 1 by securing to people in the United Kingdom the rights and freedoms in the Convention. It gives effect to Article 13 by establishing a scheme under which Convention rights can be raised before our domestic courts. To that end, remedies are provided in Clause 8 . . . We have set out in the Bill a scheme to provide remedies for violations of convention rights and we do not believe that it is necessary to add to it. We also believe that it is undesirable to provide for Articles 1 and 13 in the Bill in this way. The courts would be bound to ask themselves what was intended beyond the

---

[44] RSC, Ord. 53, r. 4 (1).

[45] s. 8(1). *"Court"* in s. 8 includes a tribunal: s. 8(6). The use of the word "appropriate" echoes the dictum of the European Court of Human Rights in its judgment in *Chahal v. United Kingdom*, November 15, 1996, R.J.D.; 1996–II, No. 22; 23 E.H.R.R. 413, at 472: "The effect of [Article 13] is thus to require the provision of a domestic remedy allowing the competent national authority both to deal with the substance of the relevant Convention complaint and to grant *appropriate relief* . . . "para. 145 (emphasis added).

[46] s. 7(11). This provision was included to make it clear that any constraints placed on a particular tribunal which prevent it from considering whether an order would be incompatible with an individual's Convention rights may be removed. (Those so restricting special adjudicators under s. 8 of the Asylum and Appeals Act 1993 will be removed by cl. 55 of the Immigration and Asylum Bill 1999). It is the clear intention of the Act that, even though tribunals are of limited jurisdiction, they should be able to give effect to Convention rights. See the explanation of the Minister of State, Mr O'Brien, *Hansard*, H.C., June 24, 1998, cols 1109–1110.

[47] The requirements of Article 13 are considered below, paras C13–01 *et seq.*

existing scheme of remedies set out in the Bill. It might lead them to fashion remedies other than the Clause 8 remedies, which we regard as sufficient and clear. We believe that Clause 8 provides effective remedies before our courts . . ."[48]

6–13 The Lord Chancellor was asked whether it was the Government's intention that the courts should not be entitled to have regard to Article 13 and the Strasbourg case law. He prefaced his reply by saying that "One always has in mind *Pepper v. Hart* when one is asked questions of that kind. I will reply as candidly as I can".

Referring to the obligation on courts and tribunals under section 2(1) to take the Strasbourg case law into account he continued:

"That means what it says. The court must take into account such material . . . My response . . . is that the courts may have regard to Article 13. In particular they may wish to do so when considering the very ample provisions of Clause 8(1) . . ."[49]

The position was summarised by Lord Lester of Herne Hill Q.C., in what may be described as a surrogate *Pepper v. Hart* statement:

"The . . . Lord Chancellor agrees that under the Bill the courts are fully entitled to have regard to Article 13, even if it is not directly incorporated. He also agrees that the courts are obliged to have regard to the Strasbourg case-law on Article 13 to the extent that it is relevant. The issue which remains is whether . . . it is sensible for Clause 1(1) to allow the judges to look at Articles 16, 17 and 18 in construing the substantive articles of the Convention, but not to look at Article 13.

I can think of several practical examples where in real cases it will help the courts to know that they can have regard to Article 13, even if it is not directly incorporated. Perhaps I may give two examples. First, the Turkish cases in which there is no proper post-mortem or police investigation into a suspicious murder. I am not suggesting that in practice such circumstances are likely to arise in this country, but in those cases the Strasbourg Court stated that Article 6, which is to be incorporated into U.K. law, is not the right Article. It stated that Article 13 is the right Article and it is the one to which domestic courts should have regard . . .

Perhaps I may take an example closer to home, which is the case of *Chahal*.[50] . . . Parliament had to enact special legislation on immigration appeals to give effect to the European Court's judgment in *Chahal*. The vice was a breach of Article 13. That breach arose because there was no proper judicial procedure where a suspected terrorist was facing deportation to a country where he would face torture or inhuman or degrading treatment or punishment. Therefore, we had to spend time enacting a new Bill.

If there were no clear inconsistency in the primary legislation and the courts could have regard to Article 13 when construing their remedial powers under

---

[48] *Hansard*, H.L., November 18, 1997, col. 475.
[49] *ibid.*, cols 476–477.
[50] *Chahal v. United Kingdom*, November 15, 1996, R.J.D., 1996–II, No. 22; 23 E.H.R.R. 413.

Clause 8 of the Bill that would greatly assist them in fashioning the effective remedy. There is nothing between . . . the Lord Chancellor and myself about the aim. We are concerned only about making the Bill clear on its face so that legal scholars, publishers, barristers, solicitors and, in the end, judges are not troubled by having to read this debate in order to arrive at the simple conclusion that it was the intention of Parliament that the courts would have regard to Article 13 of the Convention."[51]

6–14 During the House of Lords' Report Stage, further amendments were moved to make clear that the main purpose of the Act is to provide effective remedies for violations of Convention rights, and to include Article 13 in section 1(1). Resisting such amendments, the Lord Chancellor insisted that it would add nothing to the remedies already available within the structure of the Bill. He said:

"Our courts are rich in remedies and have every freedom under Clause 8 . . . The Bill has been constructed in a way that affords ample protection for individuals' rights under the convention. We have adopted an intentionally wide definition of public authority under Clause 6, and Clause 8(1), which I have already read, gives the courts ample scope for doing justice when unlawful acts are committed. I would say that these are measures of a government determined to deliver a strong form of incorporation, not a government fighting shy of enhancing our citizens' rights . . . Our objection is that the amendments add nothing to the Bill . . . [in answer to a question from Lord Ackner] . . . My Lords, I have not the least idea what the remedies the courts might develop outside Clause 8 could be if Article 13 was included. The noble and learned Lord has really made my point for me. *Clause 8(1) is of the widest amplitude.*"[52]

B. Summary

6–15 The position may be summarised as follows:

(a) where a court or tribunal finds that an actual or potential act of a public authority is an unlawful breach of a Convention right, it may grant such remedy as is just and appropriate, provided that the remedy in question is within its powers, and subject to any other limits in the Act.[53] Section 8(1) is not intended to confer a power to devise new remedies which are not within the powers of the court or tribunal in question;

(b) with those qualifications, the court or tribunal has the widest possible powers to adjudicate upon claims and grant effective remedies for a violation of a Convention right;

(c) the Act is intended to give effect to Article 13 of the Convention. Consequently, in exercising its powers, the court or tribunal is to take account of the right to an effective remedy guaranteed by that Article and to the case-law of the Strasbourg institutions relating to it.

---

[51] *Hansard*, H.L., November 18, 1997, cols 480–481.
[52] *Hansard*, H.L., January 19, 1998, col. 1266 (emphasis added).
[53] See the limitations on the power to award damages in ss. 8(2)–(4) and 9(3) and (4): below, paras 6–17—6–21.

However, there may still be cases, such as those referred to by Lord Lester of Herne Hill Q.C. in the passage quoted above, in which a court or tribunal is unable to grant an effective remedy. In such cases, it will be left to the Minister concerned to extend the competence and powers of the relevant tribunal to remedy the omission.[54]

5. DAMAGES

6–16 Despite the "wide amplitude" of section 8 to which the Lord Chancellor referred, the Government's desire to furnish protection by way of remedies was apparently tempered by a wish not to place an undue burden on the public purse, and the Act seeks to limit the circumstances in which damages may be awarded. The Act imposes limits on the courts or tribunals which, and the circumstances in which, an award of damages may be made in respect of an act of a public authority which is unlawful under section 6(1).[55] To the extent that this attempt at limitation has succeeded, however, courts will have to exercise their other remedial powers in such a way as to ensure that they provide remedies which are just and appropriate. This may entail the adaptation or extension of existing remedies to fulfil the statutory objective.

We shall first consider the limitations which the Act places on the power to award damages and then look at the other remedies which may be available.

A. Jurisdictional limitations

6–17 Damages may be awarded only by a court or tribunal which has power to award damages, or to order the payment of compensation, in civil proceedings.[56] The Act does not confer any new power on courts or tribunals to award damages for unlawful acts, although a Minister may, by order, make rules to add a power to award damages or compensation if he or she considers it necessary to ensure that a tribunal can provide an appropriate remedy.[57] Damages will be available in the High Court, in county courts, and in certain specialist tribunals such as employment tribunals.

There may be a question whether the power to award damages is intended to extend to the High Court on an application for judicial review. It has been held that such proceedings are not "civil proceedings" for the purpose of section 139 of the Mental Health Act 1983.[58] However, the use of the expression in section 8(2) is not intended to limit the power of the High Court to award compensation on an application for judicial review, in particular since such compensation may be awarded only where damages "could also have been awarded in an action begun by writ".[59] During the Committee Stage in the House of Lords the Lord Chancellor was asked[60] whether the judicial review court would be able to award damages for a public law tort of breaking the Convention, or whether the applicant would have to institute separate private law proceedings in an ordinary civil court. He ventured

---

[54] Under s. 7(11).
[55] "Damages" means damages for an unlawful act of a public authority: s. 8(6).
[56] s. 8(2). The Civil Liability (Contribution) Act 1978 and s. 3 of the Law Reform (Miscellaneous Provisions) Act 1940 apply to awards of damages against public authorities under the Act: s. 8(5).
[57] s. 7(11).
[58] *Re Waldron* [1986] Q.B. 824.
[59] RSC, Ord. 53, r. 7(1)(b) and s. 31(4)(b) of the Supreme Court Act 1981.
[60] By Lord Lester of Herne Hill QC: *Hansard*, H.L., November 24, 1997, col. 855.

the tentative response that an award of damages can be made in such circumstances if, in the terms of section 8(3), "the award is necessary to afford just satisfaction to the person in whose favour it is made".[61]

B.   Limits on the power to award damages for judicial acts

6–18   There are additional procedural[62] and substantive limitations on the remedies available in respect of judicial acts. Damages may not be awarded in respect of a judicial act done in good faith otherwise than to the extent required by Article 5(5) of the Convention, which provides that any person detained in breach of Article 5 shall have an enforceable right to compensation.[63] Any such award of damages is to be made against the Crown. No award may be made unless the appropriate person, if not a party, is joined.[64] The appropriate person is the Minister responsible for the court concerned, or a person or department nominated by him.[65]

In England and Wales, it is envisaged that the jurisdiction under section 9(3) and Article 5(5) will normally be exercised on appeal by the Court of Appeal, Criminal Division, or on appeal or by way of an application for judicial review by the Divisional Court. By contrast, in Scotland, the High Court on appeal has no power to award damages and an appellant would normally have to seek a remedy in the civil courts. To avoid such duplication of proceedings, section 9(1) provides that proceedings will be brought in such other forum as may be prescribed by rules.[66]

The purpose of the limitation on the power to award damages is to preserve the common law and statutory position by which the Crown is not liable in tort for judicial acts,[67] and that judges and magistrates acting within their jurisdiction, or outside their jurisdiction but in good faith, are immune from proceedings brought against them personally.[68] However, the enforceable right to compensation in Article 5(5) applies to all cases of arrest or detention in breach of the provisions of Article 5, including those resulting from a judicial act. In addition, the right is not conditional on fulfilment of the conditions in Article 41, formerly Article 50.[69] That

---

[61] *ibid.*, col. 856. The authority of the Lord Chancellor's reply to Lord Lester is perhaps diminished by his qualification that "I feel a moderate degree of confidence that the noble Lord could argue both sides of the question depending upon the client who instructed him."

[62] s. 9(1), which deals with limitations relating to the bringing of proceedings in respect of allegedly unlawful judicial acts, is considered above, para. 6–03.

[63] s. 9(3). This appears impliedly to overrule Justices of the Peace Act 1997, s. 52 which provides that damages for unlawful detention pursuant to an order of a magistrates' court can only be awarded if the claimant proves malice. But note the statutory right to compensation under the Criminal Justice Act 1988, s. 133. "Judicial act" includes a judicial act of a court, and includes an act done on the instructions, or on behalf, of a judge, including a member of a tribunal, a justice of the peace and a clerk or other officer entitled to exercise the jurisdiction of a court: s. 9(5). "Bad faith" in this context should be understood as meaning not simply a malicious desire to injure, but consciousness on the part of the judge that the power purportedly exercised is unlawful. See *Re McC (a Minor)* [1985] A.C. 528, 540. Article 5(5) is considered below, paras C5–78 *et seq.*

[64] s. 9(4).

[65] s. 9(5). In cases concerning judges and magistrates in England and Wales, the appropriate person will normally be the Lord Chancellor; in Scotland, it will normally be the Secretary of State for Scotland.

[66] s. 9(1)(c). See the Lord Chancellor's explanation of this provision at the Report Stage: *Hansard.* H.L., January 29, 1998, col. 389.

[67] Crown Proceedings Act 1947, s. 2(5).

[68] See the Lord Chancellor: *Hansard*, H.L., November 24, 1997, col. 857.

[69] Although an applicant must show some kind of pecuniary or non-pecuniary damage: *Wassink v. Netherlands*, September 27, 1990, Series A No. 185–A. Curiously, however, hitherto the Court has not made an award of compensation under Article 50 (now Article 41) in any case where it has found a violation of Article 5(5): see Harris, O'Boyle and Warbrick, *Law of the European Convention on Human Rights*, p. 160.

Article is addressed primarily to the international tribunal, whereas the primary obligation of the domestic court is to provide an enforceable right to compensation for arrest or detention in breach of the provisions of the Convention.

C. Limits on the circumstances in which damages may be awarded: the requirement of "just satisfaction"

6–19 No award of damages is to be made unless the court is satisfied that the award is necessary to afford "just satisfaction" to the person in whose favour it is made[70]; and in reaching its decision, the court must take account of all the circumstances of the case, including any other relief or remedy granted, or order made in relation to the act in question (by that or any other court), and the consequences of any decision (of that or any other court) in respect of the act.[71]

In determining whether to award damages and, if so, the amount of any award, the court must also take account of the principles applied by the ECHR in relation to an award of compensation under Article 41 of the Convention.[72] We have suggested[73] that the use of the term "just satisfaction" in the Act, a concept unfamiliar to domestic law, indicates that the concept itself has been incorporated into law, together with the case law elaborating the meaning of the expression. This does not sit entirely comfortably with the weaker direction to "take account" of the principles applied by the Strasbourg Court, which is the ultimate arbiter of the meaning of just satisfaction.[74]

The reference to Article 41 is a curiosity, since the Article is designed to empower the ECHR to afford just satisfaction only " . . . if the internal law . . . [of the respondent state] allows only partial reparation to be made . . ." for the consequences of the decision or measure which the court has found to be completely or partially in conflict with the state's obligations. The provision is therefore addressed to the supranational body which is considering a case which has completed its process through national law,[75] whereas the domestic court considering section 8(3) is part of the internal legal system which is the precursor of an application to Strasbourg. Although the Act's approach to damages is consistent with the legislative choice of not making the Convention rights part of domestic law, it creates other inconsistencies to the extent that remedies other than damages are fully available whereas damages are conceived of only as a subsidiary form of redress. Effectively, sections 8(3) and 8(4) place the domestic court or tribunal in a position similar to that of the Strasbourg Court.

6–20 The court or tribunal should have resort first to pre-existing domestic law, the right to rely on which is expressly reserved,[76] and, if necessary, to remedies

---

[70] Article 41 allows the award of just satisfaction to be made the "injured party". This term is "synonymous with the term 'victim' as used in Article [34]; [it denotes] the person directly affected by the act or omission in issue": *De Wilde, Ooms and Versyp v. Belgium (No. 2)* (1971) 1 E.H.R.R. 438, para. 23.

[71] s. 8(3).

[72] s. 8(4).

[73] See above, para. 2–02.

[74] There is also a technical point since the case law to date has arisen under Article 50 of the (pre-Protocol 11) Convention, which is in slightly different form. But the differences in wording are not material and the practice of the Court under Article 41 is no different from that adopted under Article 50. Despite the reference to Article 41, guidance may also be found in the jurisprudence that has grown up around Article 50.

[75] As Harris, O'Boyle & Warbrick explain, "the language of Article [41] thus reflects the general principle of international law that the state must first be given an opportunity to provide redress", *Law of the European Convention on Human Rights*, p. 683.

[76] s. 11.

under section 8 of the Act other than damages. If the aggregate of these remedies provides full reparation for the consequences of the violation, an award of damages under the Act will be unnecessary. Thus damages will already be available where a violation of a Convention right also founds an existing cause of action. A court having regard to all the circumstances of the case—the considerations to which the Act draws express attention are enumerated above—will only find it "necessary" to award additional damages under the Act where the available causes of action have not provided full reparation. Where breach of a Convention right does not amount to an existing wrong, a court with power to award damages in civil proceedings[77] will be able to make an award in respect of breach of the section 6(1) duty. But again it should do so only where the other available remedies or consequences do not afford just satisfaction.

Courts and tribunals are also likely to be largely frustrated in their search for the "principles" applied by the ECHR in determining the availability and amount of compensation. The Court has treated its power under Article 50 of the Convention as a broad discretionary exercise, to be considered in the circumstances of each case. Concern has been expressed about the consistency of, for example, the case law concerning the treatment of criminal fines as pecuniary damage and the method for valuing property. It has also been said that, while the Court makes moral judgments about the nature of different types of applicants, such as convicted criminals and terrorists, when evaluating their claims for just satisfaction, it generally fails to make express reference to these considerations or justify their use.[78] The Court's decisions contain regrettably little hard reasoning and in consequence it is difficult to distil any consistent statement of principle from its judgments.[79]

6–21   With these caveats in mind, it is, however, possible to offer the following broad summary of the approach adopted by the ECHR in exercising its power to afford just satisfaction, in particular in the form of an award of compensation:

(a) If the nature of the breach which the Court has found allows of *restitutio in integrum*, it is for the respondent state to effect it.[80] Applied at the domestic level, this means that for the national court the overriding purpose of the exercise of the power to afford just satisfaction is, where possible, to provide *restitutio in integrum*.[81]

(b) However, the power may be exercised even where it is not possible to "wipe out entirely the consequences of a violation . . .".[82] In such a case, Article 41 empowers the Court to afford the injured party "such satisfaction as appears to it to be appropriate".[83] The aim of an award should be, so far as possible, to put an end to the breach and to make reparation for its consequences in such a way as to restore as far as possible the situation existing before the breach.[84]

---

[77] s. 8(2), see above, para. 6–17.
[78] Mowbray [1997] P.L. 647, 658.
[79] See Harris, O'Boyle & Warbrick, *Law of the European Convention on Human Rights*, pp. 682–688; Mowbray [1997] P.L. 647.
[80] *Papamichalopoulos and others v. Greece* (1996) 21 E.H.R.R. 439, para. 34.
[81] *De Wilde, Ooms and Versyp v. Belgium (No. 2)*, (1971) 1 E.H.R.R. 438, para. 20.
[82] *ibid.*
[83] *ibid.*, para. 34.
[84] *Clooth v. Belgium*, judgment of March 5, 1998, para. 14.

(c) The Court will reject a claim where the applicant has not established a clear causal connection between the proven violation of the Convention and the damage claimed,[85] although in some cases, this may be presumed without specific proof.[86]

(d) Compensation may be awarded for both pecuniary and non-pecuniary damage. Pecuniary damage includes loss of earnings,[87] the value of expropriated property,[88] and the loss of an opportunity, for example to bring legal proceedings.[89] Non-pecuniary damage includes feelings of distress, anxiety and humiliation caused by the breach of the Convention which the Court has found.[90]

(e) The Court will take account of the applicant's conduct in deciding whether to award compensation.[91] This is a function of the Court's oft-repeated *dictum* that compensation is awarded "on an equitable basis", a phrase which it has never attempted to define, or reduce to a set of principles.

(f) In many cases, the Court considers that the finding of a violation will itself be sufficient just satisfaction and no award of compensation is made.[92]

The Court has used the "equitable basis" formulation to cloak the fact that, to all appearances, the figures which it arrives at are based neither on any detailed calculation nor on any discernible principle. The student of the Court's practice is left wondering whether the process by which the Court arrives at its judgments is anything more sophisticated than sticking a finger in the air or tossing a coin. While this criticism may be less than just where straightforward awards of pecuniary loss are concerned, the same cannot be said of its awards for non-pecuniary damage. One commentator concluded that "[t]he Court has not proved unduly generous in its approach to awarding compensation under any of the heads".[93]

6. NON-PECUNIARY REMEDIES

6–22 In the previous section we discussed the Strasbourg Court's approach to the award of just satisfaction in the context of the power to award damages. What

---

[85] See, for example, *Saunders v. United Kingdom*, December 17, 1996, R.J.D., 1996–II, No. 24; 23 E.H.R.R. 313.
[86] *Pine Valley Developments Ltd v. Ireland* (1993) 16 E.H.R.R. 379, 385, para. 17.
[87] *Young, James and Webster v. United Kingdom* (1981) 4 E.H.R.R. 38.
[88] *Papamichalopoulos and others v. Greece* (1996) 21 E.H.R.R. 439.
[89] *Weeks v. United Kingdom* (1988) 10 E.H.R.R. 293, para. 13 (loss of the opportunity for period review of continued lawfulness of discretionary life sentence); *Tinnelly & Sons Ltd & ors v. United Kingdom; McElduff & ors v. United Kingdom* (1999) 27 E.H.R.R. 249: awards of £15,000 and £10,000 for loss of the opportunity to have an adjudication on the merits of their complaints before the domestic courts following the issue of (public interest immunity) certificates under s. 42 of the Fair Employment (Northern Ireland) Act 1976. By contrast, in many cases, particularly those involving procedural breaches of fair trial guarantees, the Court has refused to award compensation on the basis that it is not prepared to speculate as to what the outcome would have been: *e.g. Saunders v. United Kingdom*, December 17, 1996, R.J.D., 1996–VI, No. 24; 23 E.H.R.R. 313, para. 86.
[90] See, among many, *Campbell and Cosans v. United Kingdom* (1982) 4 E.H.R.R. 293; *McMichael v. United Kingdom* (1995) 20 E.H.R.R. 205;.
[91] *McCann, Farrell and Savage v. United Kingdom* (1995) 21 E.H.R.R. 97, para. 219, the "Death on the Rock" case (the Court did not consider it appropriate to make an award of compensation since the applicants, three terrorist suspects, had been intending to plant a bomb in Gibraltar).
[92] *Saunders v. United Kingdom*, December 17, 1996, R.J.D., 1996–VI, No. 24; 23 E.H.R.R. 313; *Benham v. United Kingdom*, June 10, 1996, R.J.D. 1996–III, No. 11; 22 E.H.R.R. 293; *Niemietz v. Germany* (1993) 16 E.H.R.R. 97.
[93] Karen Reid, *A Practitioner's Guide to the European Convention on Human Rights*, p. 398, and pp. 399–425 for a useful tabulation of the Court's recent Article 41 case law.

does emerge clearly from the case law is the principle that once a violation has been found, it is the responsibility of the state, including the courts, to do everything possible to place the injured party in the position in which he would have been had the violation not occurred. The effect of section 8(3) is to direct the courts to seek to achieve the aim of full reparation primarily by non-pecuniary remedies, leaving damages as a subsidiary remedy where this cannot be done. In turn this may prompt courts, within their powers, to develop and adapt their remedial powers in more imaginative ways in order to achieve reparation in ways other than awarding damages. A legal system which has developed *Mareva* injunctions, *Anton Piller* orders and schemes for multi-party actions can adapt to the challenge which the requirement to provide "full reparation" poses. For example, in certain minor breaches of privacy by a public authority it may be sufficient to require an apology, say in a local newspaper, and where a public authority has wrongfully disseminated personal material, it may be sufficient to require it to recall documentation it has issued. Remedies other than damages may be particularly apposite where a court is faced with systemic issues, affecting a large group of people in a complex area of social policy. The inherent jurisdiction of the High Court offers the possibility of creative development of remedies. In practice any court with power to grant injunctions will have similar opportunities. A tribunal whose jurisdiction is limited by statute will find such development more difficult, but not impossible. For example, if an employment tribunal found a violation of a Convention right, it might adjourn to allow the parties to reach agreement on remedies. In doing so, it could indicate—after hearing argument—its view of what just satisfaction required. The tribunal could take account of a respondent's failure to accept its views when it decides what compensation to award.

7. NON-JUDICIAL "REMEDIES": REMEDIAL ORDERS

6–23   Because the Act is not intended to interfere with parliamentary sovereignty it does not empower courts to strike down primary legislation for incompatibility with the Convention. Where primary legislation is found to be incompatible with a Convention right[94] the normal course would be the introduction of primary legislation to amend or repeal the offending provision in order to remove any incompatibility. However, section 10 of the Act empowers Ministers in prescribed circumstances to take remedial action by order to amend legislation to remove an incompatibility with Convention rights or with obligations of the United Kingdom arising from the Convention. In the case of legislation by Order in Council,[95] the power is exercisable by Her Majesty in Council.[96] The power applies to the amendment of primary legislation[97] which is either itself incompatible or which prevents removal of an incompatibility in subordinate legislation. It also extends to subordinate legislation which has been declared incompatible,[98] and to cases in which a Minister wishes to use the emergency order procedure[99] to amend

---

[94] On the presumption of compatibility, see above, paras 3–01 *et seq.*, and on declarations of incompatibility, see above, paras 3–43 *et seq.*.
[95] Which is "primary legislation" for the purposes of the Act: s. 21(1).
[96] s. 10(5).
[97] Except a Measure of the Church Assembly or of the General Synod of the Church of England: s. 10(6)(b).
[98] *i.e.* where the primary legislation under which it is made prevents removal of the incompatibility: s. 4(4).
[99] Sched. 2, para. 2(b). See further below, para. 6–32.

subordinate legislation which has been quashed or declared invalid.[1] Being an "order . . . made under primary legislation . . . which . . . amends any primary legislation",[2] a remedial order is itself treated as primary legislation for the purpose of the Act. While it is subject to the interpretative obligation, it cannot be quashed or declared invalid like subordinate legislation, although it may be the subject of a declaration of incompatibility.

A. Conditions precedent to the exercise of the remedial power

6–24   As the remedial power enables a member of the executive to amend primary legislation by ministerial order,[3] the circumstances in which it may be exercised are subject to a number of conditions and limitations. Three conditions must exist before the ministerial power may be exercised:

(a) a declaration by a court under section 4 of the Act that a provision of legislation[4] is incompatible with a Convention right or, in certain cases, a decision of the ECHR ("judicial decision");

(b) necessity to amend legislation to remove the incompatibility or to enable it to be removed ("necessity"); and

(c) compelling reasons for proceeding by order ("compelling reasons").

(1) Judicial decision

6–25   Where a court makes a declaration of incompatibility,[5] a remedial order may be made if no appeal lies, or if all parties who may appeal[6] have stated in writing that they do not intend to appeal, or no party has appealed before expiry of the time for appealing, or any such appeal has been determined or abandoned.[7]
An order may also be made following a decision of the ECHR if the following conditions are fulfilled[8]:

(a) the decision is made after the coming into force of section 10[9];

(b) it is made in proceedings against the United Kingdom;

(c) it appears to a Minister of the Crown (or to Her Majesty in Council in relation to primary legislation consisting of an Order in Council) that, having regard to the finding of the Court, a provision of legislation is incompatible with an obligation of the United Kingdom arising from the Convention. Where decisions of the Strasbourg Court are concerned, the

---

[1] s. 10(4).
[2] s. 21(1).
[3] Known as a "Henry VIII" clause because one of the most striking pieces of delegation ever effected by Parliament was the Statute of Proclamations 1539 by which Henry VIII was given wide power to legislate by proclamation: see Wade & Forsyth, *Administrative Law* (7th ed.), pp. 860–862.
[4] This may be primary or subordinate legislation: see s. 10(3).
[5] See above, para. 3–43.
[6] A Minister of the Crown (or a person nominated by him) or a member of the Scottish Executive is entitled to be joined as a party to proceedings in which a court is considering whether to make a declaration of incompatibility: s. 5(2). A person who has been made a party to criminal proceedings (other than in Scotland) may, with leave, appeal to the House of Lords: s. 5(4).
[7] s. 10(1)(a).
[8] s. 10(1)(b).
[9] *i.e.* after October 2, 1999.

power is not limited to remedying incompatibility with the Convention rights referred to in section 1(1) but includes, for example, Article 13 or Article 34.[10]

(2) Necessity

6–26 The second condition is that, once a court has declared the incompatibility of a legislative provision, or once such incompatibility appears to the Minister following a decision of the Strasbourg Court, the Minister must consider it "necessary" to remove the incompatibility. This is implicit in the wording of section 10(2), which empowers him or her to make such amendments as he or she considers "necessary to remove the incompatibility". It is explicit in section 10(3), relating to incompatible subordinate legislation, which provides that the Minister must consider that it is "necessary to amend the primary legislation under which the subordinate legislation in question was made, in order to enable the incompatibility to be removed".

(3) Compelling reasons

6–27 Thirdly, the Minister (or Her Majesty in Council) must consider that there are "compelling reasons" for proceeding by way of remedial order rather than by ordinary legislation.[11] No definition is given of what reasons might be considered compelling. It is not self-evident that it is co-extensive with urgency, since the Act makes separate provision for urgent cases within the order-making procedure.[12] However, it is anticipated that the power will be used when the legislative time-table does not permit the early introduction of an amending Bill and the declaration indicates a breach of a serious and possibly widespread nature, for example relating to the liberty of the subject.[13] The courts will be slow to interfere with the Minister's discretion as to whether the case for making an order is compelling.

B. Ambit of the remedial power

6–28 The Minister (or Her Majesty in Council) may amend or repeal the relevant legislative provisions, or may apply them subject to modifications.[14] The power extends only to the making of such amendments to legislative provisions as are necessary to remove the incompatibility with a Convention right or with a Convention obligation of the United Kingdom.[15] An order may contain such incidental, supplemental, consequential or transitional provision as the maker considers appropriate,[16] which includes a power to amend, repeal or revoke primary or subordinate legislation other than that which contains the incompatible provision.[17]

6–29 The order may have retrospective effect,[18] save that no person is to be guilty of an offence solely as a result of such effect.[19] An order may make provision

---

[10] Formerly Article 25.

[11] s. 10(2) and (3). See Sched. 3 to the Competition Act 1997 ("exceptional and compelling reasons"); Local Government (Miscellaneous Provisions) Act 1976, s. 64 ("compelling reasons").

[12] Sched. 2, paras 2(b) and 4.

[13] for examples, see the Home Secretary, *Hansard*, H.C., June 24, 1998, cols 1137–1138.

[14] s. 10(6)(a).

[15] s. 10(2).

[16] Sched. 2, para. 1(1)(a).

[17] Sched. 2, para. 1(2)(a).

[18] Sched. 2, para. 1(1)(b), although on principle such effect should not pre-date the coming into force of the Act.

[19] Sched. 2, para. 1(3). Otherwise, there would be a risk of violation of Article 7(1) of the Convention, which prohibits the creation of retrospective criminal liability: see below, paras C7–01 *et seq.*

for the delegation of specific functions and may make different provision for different cases.[20] There has been some discussion as to how the remedial power might be used in relation to individual proceedings concerning a Convention right; for example whether it might be used to compensate an individual who has instigated proceedings leading to a declaration of incompatibility; or whether a court which has made a declaration of incompatibility might then adjourn or grant a stay of execution to see whether a retrospective amendment to the legislation in issue might provide the individual with a remedy leading to a different disposal of the case.[21] During the Committee Stage, Lord Ackner introduced a probing amendment, which would have had the effect of empowering the Minister, following a declaration of incompatibility, to grant relief to the individual in whose case the declaration was made or to any other person. The Lord Chancellor responded in the following terms:

"There are several difficulties in making remedies of this kind subject to a statutory provision in the manner proposed. First, the amendments could extend the scope of remedial orders wider than is desirable. The specific purpose of these orders is to put right incompatible legislation. It is for this purpose that we have concluded that the power to amend primary legislation by order is necessary. The amendments proposed would bolt on remedies for individuals of a wholly different character from remedies which are designed to put right incompatible legislation to make it compatible. Individual remedies do not naturally fit into that. The amendments would open up the prospect of legislative amendments being made by order under the Bill but having a much wider extension than the present drafting of the Bill permits.

As at present advised, we think that that would create too sweeping a provision. It would threaten the ability of the Minister to consider whether and to what extent a retrospective remedy was required by the facts of the case; and it would threaten the sovereignty of Parliament, since any order for its approval would be bound to contain such provisions. It is no answer to point to the words 'such amendments as may be appropriate and necessary'. *We believe that in practice those words would entail a presumption that a remedy would be necessary.*

We think it more appropriate for decisions on what remedy should be given to individuals affected by a particular act to be taken by the Government in light of the individual circumstances of every case—and they will vary infinitely. There are existing ways in which this could be achieved. For example, should it be necessary for a remedial order affecting legislation to take effect from a date earlier than that on which the order was made, this will be possible under the Bill; Clause 11(1)(b)[22] so provides. This will not of itself provide a direct remedy to individuals affected by the legislation which has been retrospectively amended; but, following the order, it may be open to them to seek such a remedy. In addition to these powers in the Bill, there are prerogative powers which can be exercised and other ex gratia actions that could be taken to grant remedies in appropriate circumstances."[23]

---

[20] Sched. 2, para. 1(c) and (d).
[21] This possibility is advanced by Wade in Cambridge Centre for Public Law, *Constitutional Reform in the United Kingdom: Practice and Principles* (1998), p. 67. The possibility was also canvassed by Lord Lester of Herne Hill Q.C.: *Hansard*, H.L., November 3, 1997, col. 1243.
[22] This is now in Sched. 2, para. 1(1)(b).
[23] *Hansard*, H.L., November 27, 1997, col. 1108 (emphasis added).

6–30   It appears, therefore, that a remedial order may be made so as to have a retrospective effect on the case in which the declaration of incompatibility was made. It has been suggested, therefore, that once a court has made a declaration, it should adjourn until the Minister has had an opportunity to consider the making of an order. The difficulty with this course, however, is that the power to make an order arises only after all rights of appeal have been exhausted, lost or abandoned. We have suggested, therefore, that questions of incompatibility should be dealt with as a preliminary issue so that the court is not *functus officio* once the declaration has been made and the remedial power exercised. Sir William Wade has suggested that what amounts to the determination of civil rights and obligations by ministerial order may itself amount to a violation of the right to a fair trial under Article 6.[24] While this argument has some force in the context of a remedial order with retrospective effect, it may be stated too broadly. There are a number of objections to it as a general proposition. First, the ministerial power applies to remedy incompatibility between domestic legislation and "Convention rights" but not all Convention rights are also "civil rights" to which Article 6 applies.[25] Secondly, a declaration of incompatibility does not alter the content of domestic law or bind the parties. Consequently, where an individual has lost, it will often be because the court has held that, Convention rights notwithstanding, domestic law does not recognise any right in the particular circumstances. Article 6 will not apply in such a case, since it "does not in itself guarantee any particular content for (civil) 'rights and obligations' in the substantive law of the Contracting States".[26] It follows from this that the Minister will not be "determining" a "dispute" relating to a civil right. The court will already have made the determination.[27]

6–31   Another question is whether the power to make remedial orders may be used, for example in discrimination cases, in a way which will reduce the level of protection of human rights. For example, in the case of *Abdulaziz & others v. United Kingdom*,[28] the ECHR found that the United Kingdom had discriminated against women in the enjoyment of their right to respect for family life, since the Immigration Rules entitled a man settled in the United Kingdom to be joined by his wife but did afford a corresponding right to a woman in relation to her husband. The Government's response to the judgment was to remove the discrimination by taking away the man's right. There is some support for the argument that the remedial power cannot be used in this way. First, the purpose of the Act is to increase rather than reduce protection of individual rights. Secondly, rejecting proposals that draft remedial orders should be capable of parliamentary amendment, the Lord Chancellor said that "the remedial order will have the sole purpose

---

[24] In Cambridge Centre for Public Law, *Constitutional Reform in the United Kingdom: Practice and Principles* (1998), p. 67.

[25] See further below, paras C6–10 *et, seq.*

[26] *James v. United Kingdom* (1986) 8 E.H.R.R. 123, para. 81 of the judgment; but compare the Strasbourg Court's approach in *Osman v. United Kingdom*, [1999] Fam. Law 86, where an "immunity" was held not to preclude the operation of Article 6; and see Lord Browne-Wilkinson in *Barrett v. Enfield LBC* [1999] 3 W.L.R. 79, 84–85.

[27] But in some cases the retrospective cancellation of an award or judgment may raise issues under Article 6 or Article 1 of the First Protocol: see, for example, *Stran Greek Refineries and Stratis Andreadis v. Greece* (1995) E.H.R.R. 319; *The National and Provincial Building Society, The Leeds Permanent Building Society and the Yorkshire Building Society v. United Kingdom*, October 23, 1997, R.J.D., 1997–VII, No. 55; 25 E.H.R.R. 127; and App. Nos. 28160/95 and 28382/95 *Preda and Dardari v. Italy*, decision of February 23, 1999. See further below, paras C6–38, P/11–10.

[28] (1985) 7 E.H.R.R. 471.

of improving human rights by removing a closely defined incompatibility."[29] Regrettably, however, this may not be a firm enough foundation to prevent the use of the power to reduce rather than enhance the protection of Convention rights in such cases.

C. Procedure for making a remedial order

6–32   The ordinary procedure for making a remedial order is as follows:

(a) the person proposing to make an order must lay before Parliament a document which contains a draft of the proposed order and the "required information",[30] *i.e.*

   (i) an explanation of the incompatibility sought to be removed by the order, including particulars of the relevant judicial decision, and

   (ii) a statement of the reasons for using the remedial order power (rather than introducing an amending Bill) and for making an order in those terms[31];

(b) a period of 60 days[32] must elapse from the date on which the document is laid. During this period, representations about the order may be made to the person making the order[33];

(c) no draft of the order may be laid before Parliament until after the end of the period. If any representations have been made, the draft must be accompanied by a statement containing a summary of the representations and details of any changes to the proposed order as a result of the representations[34];

(d) no order may be made unless, after the end of a further period of 60 days, the draft order has been approved by a resolution of each House of Parliament.[35]

The Act also provides for the following urgency procedure:

(a) an order may be made if it is declared that it appears to the person making it that, because of the urgency of the matter, it is necessary to make the order without the draft being approved[36];

(b) the person making the order must lay it before Parliament, together with the required information;

(c) a period of 60 days must elapse, beginning with the date on which the original order was made. During this period, representations about the order may be made to the person making it[37];

---

[29] *Hansard*, H.L., November 27, 1997, col. 1145.
[30] Sched. 2, para. 3(1)(a).
[31] Sched. 2, para. 5.
[32] Excluding any time during which Parliament is dissolved or prorogued or both Houses of Parliament are adjourned for more than four days: Sched. 2, para. 6.
[33] Sched. 2, para. 3(1)(b) and (2). Representations includes any relevant Parliamentary report or resolution: *ibid.*, para. 5.
[34] Sched. 2, para. 3(2).
[35] Sched. 2, para. 2(a).
[36] Sched. 2, para. 2(b).
[37] Sched. 2, para. 4(2).

    (d) if any representations have been made, then after the end of that period the person making the order must lay before Parliament a statement containing a summary of the representations and details of any changes to the original order which he or she considers it appropriate to make as a result of the representations.[38] In that event, the maker must make a further remedial order replacing the original order and lay it before Parliament[39];

    (e) the original or replacement order will cease to have effect if it has not been approved by a resolution of each House of Parliament by the end of the period of 120 days beginning on the day on which the original order was made. The maker may make a fresh remedial order.[40]

6–33   It would seem that a remedial order which amends primary legislation may not be quashed on Convention grounds: since it is an order made under primary legislation which amends primary legislation, a remedial order is itself regarded as "primary legislation" under section 21(1). A higher court could declare a provision of a remedial order to be incompatible with a Convention right.[41] Moreover, failure or refusal to make a remedial order is not open to challenge under the Act,[42] and accordingly the Act does not enable an individual to force the introduction of amendments to primary legislation.[43]

---

[38] Sched. 2, para. 4(2)(b).
[39] Sched. 2, para. 4(3).
[40] Sched. 2, para. 4(4). However, this does not affect anything done under either order.
[41] s. 4(1) and 4(2).
[42] s. 6(6)(b).
[43] See further, above, para. 4–23.

CHAPTER 7

Devolution

1. INTRODUCTION

7–01 When implemented, the HRA 1998 will apply throughout the United Kingdom.[1] A curious feature of the measure, however is that it has already been brought into force in a qualified manner in Scotland and Wales and that it may be brought into effect in Northern Ireland at some point before the date of formal implementation.[2] This unusual, indeed–from a constitutional perspective–rather peculiar situation, results from the speedy achievement by the Labour Government, elected on May 1, 1997, of another of its key manifesto commitments, on devolution.

In its election manifesto, the Party promised that "[a]s soon as possible after the election, we will enact legislation to allow the people of Scotland and Wales to vote in separate referendums on our proposals". As far as Scotland was concerned this was to involve the "creation of a parliament with law-making powers . . . including defined and limited financial powers to vary revenue". Wales was promised an assembly with new forms of "democratic control of the existing Welsh Office functions" and a range of "secondary legislative powers" with an assembly with the capacity "to reform and democratise the quango state".[3] These ambitious pledges were speedily redeemed with the publication in July 1997 of proposals for new measures relating to self-government for Scotland[4] and Wales[5]; and these initiatives were followed within a matter of months by referendums in which a majority of those voting in both jurisdictions expressed support for the Government's proposals. The resulting Bills emerged from the parliamentary process as the Scotland Act 1998 and the Government of Wales Act 1998. After the necessary elections, the formal commencement of devolution in each jurisdiction occurred on July 1, 1999.[6]

---

[1] See s. 22(6).

[2] This depends on the full implementation of the Northern Ireland Act 1998 which is in turn dependent on further progress being made in the current peace process in the Province.

[3] *New Labour, because Britain deserves better* (London, 1997), p. 33.

[4] Scotland's Parliament (Cm. 3658, The Scottish Office, The Stationery Office, Edinburgh, 1997).

[5] "A Voice for Wales. The Government's Proposals for a Welsh Assembly" (Cm. 3718. The Stationery Office, London, 1997). A good study of the Government's proposals at this early stage is A Tomkins (ed.), *Devolution and the British Constitution* (Key Haven Publications, London, 1998). Also very valuable is Cambridge Centre for Public Law, *Constitutional Reform in the United Kingdom: Practice and Principles* (Hart Publishing, Oxford, 1998), which contains five essays on devolution by, respectively, Professor V. Bogdanor, R Reed Q.C., Professor A Bradley, Professor Sir D Williams Q.C. and (on Northern Ireland) Professor Brigid Hadfield. An article which deals with the legislation in its final form from a legal perspective is P. Craig and M Walters, "The Courts, Devolution and Judicial Review" [1999] P.L. 274. For a less legal but valuably political perspective, see R Hazell and B O'Leary, "A Rolling Programme of Devolution: Slippery Slope or Safeguard of the Union?" in R Hazell (ed.), *Constitutional Futures. A History of the Next Ten Years* (Oxford, Oxford University Press, 1999), Ch. 3.

[6] The Northern Ireland timetable was equally if not more ambitious but it has been less successful in terms of achieving devolution than has been the case in Scotland and Wales.

7–02   Given the speed of these constitutional changes, it is hardly surprising that the exact nature of the relationship between them and the Government's equally far-reaching proposals on human rights should not have been crystal clear from the outset. Neither of the July 1997 consultation papers was specific on the relationship between their proposed devolutionary measures and the Human Rights Bill which was then also in its early planning stages. The Scottish White Paper raised the issue only to say that the "implications for devolution of incorporating the European Convention on Human Rights into domestic law will be dealt with as part of the process of legislating for incorporation", with the Government promising to set out its "proposals for this in a White Paper to be published later this year".[7] This duly arrived with the publication in October 1997 of 'Rights Brought Home: The Human Rights Bill'.[8]

In this document, it was made clear that "the Scottish Parliament [would] have no power to legislate in a way which [was] incompatible with the Convention; and similarly that the Scottish Executive [would] have no power to make subordinate legislation or to take executive action which [was] incompatible with the Convention".[9] It followed that it would "accordingly be possible to challenge such legislation and actions in the Scottish courts on the ground that the Scottish Parliament or Executive has incorrectly applied its powers. If the challenge is successful then the legislation or action would be held to be unlawful".[10] In terms of enforcement, the Government promised "a procedure for inferior courts to refer such issues to the superior Scottish courts" with those courts in turn being empowered "to refer the matter to the Judicial Committee of the Privy Council". If the issue were "decided by the superior Scottish courts, an appeal from their decision [would] be to the Judicial Committee".[11] On Wales, the Government promised in a similar vein that "the Welsh Assembly will not have power to make subordinate legislation or take executive action which is incompatible with the Convention. It will be possible to challenge such legislation and action in the courts, and for them to be quashed, on the ground that the Assembly has exceeded its powers".[12]

2. THE NEW DEVOLVED ARRANGEMENTS IN SCOTLAND AND WALES

7–03   The legislation for both Scotland and Wales has translated the broad themes set out in 'Rights Brought Home' into the necessary statutory language.As far as the new legislative powers in Scotland are concerned, "[a]n Act of the Scottish Parliament is not law so far as any provision of the Act is outside the legislative competence of the Parliament".[13] A provision is outside that competence if, *inter alia*, "it is incompatible with any of the Convention rights".[14] The term "Convention rights" is assigned "the same meaning as in the Human Rights Act

---

[7] See above n. 4, para. 4.20.
[8] Cm. 3782 (The Stationery Office, London, 1997) *cf.* Labour, *Bringing Rights Home: Labour's plans to incorporate the European Convention on Human Rights into U.K. law (A Consultation Paper, December 1996).*
[9] *ibid.*, para. 2.21.
[10] *ibid.*
[11] *ibid.*
[12] *ibid.*, para. 2.23.
[13] s. 29(1).
[14] s. 29(2)(d).

1998".[15] As a result of these provisions, the Convention has the potential to be a powerful ring-fence around Scotland's apparent autonomy, with the judges being required to act as vigilant gatekeepers.

It is interesting to note in this regard that the constraints on the Scottish Parliament potentially extend beyond the Convention to embrace other human rights instruments; under section 35(1)(a) "[i]f a Bill contains provisions which the Secretary of State has reasonable grounds to believe would be incompatible with any international obligations . . . he may make an order prohibiting the Presiding Officer from submitting the Bill for Royal Assent". In the context of the Scotland Act, "international obligations" means "any international obligations of the United Kingdom other than obligations to observe and implement Community law or the Convention rights".[16] It is probable that the identification of conflicting international obligations in respect of various apparently *intra vires* proposals of the Scottish Parliament will frequently be attempted by people who want to prevent the enactment of measures to which they are opposed. But it is clear that the Secretary of State's power to stifle the emergence of such measures is discretionary, and that its exercise is itself potentially susceptible to judicial review.

7–04   As indicated in the White Paper on the Principality, the Welsh Assembly has been given no equivalent legislative powers under the Government of Wales Act. As promised by the Government, however, the new authority has been given various powers (including the power to make certain delegated legislation) which had previously been exercised by the U.K. government.[17] However, the Act is clear that the "Assembly has no power: (a) to make, confirm or approve any subordinate legislation, or (b) to do any other act, so far as the subordinate legislation or act is incompatible with any of the Convention rights".[18] There are also constraints in respect of U.K. international obligations similar to those discussed above in respect of Scotland: "[i]f a Minister of the Crown considers that any action proposed to be taken by the Assembly would be incompatible with any international obligation, he may by order direct that the proposed action shall not be taken"[19] and if "a Minister of the Crown considers that any action capable of being taken by the Assembly is required for the purpose of giving effect to any international obligation, he may by order direct the Assembly to take the action".[20]

Turning now to the constraints on the powers of the new Executive established in Scotland, "[a] member of the Scottish Executive has no power to make any subordinate legislation, or to do any other act, so far as the legislation or act is incompatible with any of the Convention rights or with Community law".[21] This provision does not however apply to an act of the Lord Advocate "(a) in prosecuting any offence, or (b) in his capacity as head of the systems of criminal prosecution and investigation of deaths in Scotland, which, because of subsection (2) of section 6 of the Human Rights Act 1998, is not unlawful under subsection (1)

---

[15] s. 126(1), which means that it embraces "the rights and fundamental freedoms set out in (a) Articles 2 to 12 and 14 of the Convention, (b) Articles 1 to 3 of the First Protocol, and (c) Articles 1 and 2 of the Sixth Protocol, as read with Articles 16 to 18 of the Convention" (Human Rights Act 1998, s. 1(1)).
[16] s. 126(10).
[17] See, generally, Government of Wales Act 1998, Pt 3.
[18] s. 107(1).
[19] s. 108(1).
[20] s. 108(2). The provisions on delegated legislation–which are in similar terms–are at s. 108(3) and (4). See further s. 108(7). "International obligations" are defined in s. 108(6) in terms similar to those to be found in the Scotland Act.
[21] s. 57(2).

of that section".[22] Once again, an important limitation is being placed on the new Scottish Executive, one which is over and above the normal constraints of such a body to act within the *vires* of its parent statute. The full extent of the constraint on action that is involved here will only be fleshed out over time, when litigation has clarified the exact application of the Convention in this sphere.

7–05   Furthermore, as is also the case with the Parliament, the Secretary of State "may by order direct that [a] proposed action shall not be taken" if he or she "has reasonable grounds to believe that [such] action proposed to be taken by a member of the Scottish Executive would be incompatible with any international obligations".[23] The Secretary of State also enjoys the power, if he or she "has reasonable grounds to believe that any action capable of being taken by a member of the Scottish Executive is required for the purpose of giving effect to any such obligations", to "by order direct that the action shall be taken".[24] The term "action" in both s 58(1) and (2) "includes making, confirming or approving subordinate legislation and, in subsection (2), includes introducing a Bill in the Parliament".[25] In a similar vein, section 58(4) provides that "[i]f any subordinate legislation made or which could be revoked by a member of the Scottish Executive contains provisions . . . which the Secretary of State has reasonable grounds to believe to be incompatible with any international obligations . . . the Secretary of State may by order revoke the legislation".

7–06   All these orders under section 58 must be supported by reasons[26] and it is not hard to envisage a future in which some of the major battles between Whitehall and Edinburgh (and indeed possibly also Whitehall and Cardiff[27]) will be fought out over rival perceptions of what is required of the United Kingdom by international law. The ambit of the subject is of course far wider than human rights, but it includes many international treaties on the subject which cumulatively make up a far more detailed and wide ranging code of human rights protection than is to be found in the European Convention on Human Rights.[28] Thus while these will be largely political disputes, their battleground will be rival perceptions of the nature of international law. Difficult questions are also certain to arise if action in either devolved body is thought to be in violation of U.K. international obligations, but in respect of which the relevant Minister declines to intervene. In such a situation, it would be not difficult to envisage judicial review applications being initiated, probably most appropriately designed to force the Minister to act.

3.   ENFORCING THE DEVOLUTION LEGISLATION: THE ROLE OF THE COURTS

7–07   As mentioned above, both the Scottish and the Welsh measure have been brought into force before the HRA. This has required a special and unusual

---

[22] s. 57(3).
[23] s. 58(1).
[24] s. 58(2).
[25] s. 58(3).
[26] s. 58(5).
[27] Note the requirement in the Government of Wales Act, s. 108(5) that the Minister consult with the Assembly before making an order under s. 108(2), (3) or (7) (but not s. 108(1)).
[28] A good source book is F Ermacora, M Nowak and H Tretter (eds), *International Human Rights* (Law Books in Europe, Vienna, 1993).

provision in both the devolution measures,[29] under which the HRA is deemed to "have effect until the time when that Act is fully in force as it will have effect after that time".[30] It is unusual for a statute to be brought partially into force by another Act in this way. However, the restrictions placed upon those who can rely on the HRA also apply to the Scottish and Welsh measures. Under section 100 of the Scotland Act, the "Act does not enable a person: (a) to bring any proceedings in a court or tribunal on the ground that an act is incompatible with the Convention rights, or (b) to rely on any of the Convention rights in any such proceedings, unless he would be a victim for the purposes of Article 34 of the Convention (within the meaning of the Human Rights Act 1998) if proceedings in respect of the Act were brought in the European Court of Human Rights".[31] Furthermore the Scotland Act "does not enable a court or tribunal to award any damages in respect of an act which is incompatible with any of the Convention rights which it could not award if sections 8(3) and (4) of the Human Rights Act 1998 applied".[32]

As anticipated in the White Paper, the means by which matters relating to devolution and human rights will fall to be litigated is of no little complexity. The United Kingdom is unusual not only in incorporating three (and now after the Government of Wales Act, four) jurisdictions in one unitary state, but also in its absence of a written constitution and of a purpose-built constitutional court, and in its continuing denial that a separation needs to be made between the civil and the administrative spheres. The price paid for this continuing commitment to traditional constitutional arrangements will be a certain degree of opacity in the judicial system. Matters are likely to come to a head in the context of disputes between the devolved bodies on the one hand and litigants and other public authorities on the other as to the true extent of the power of the former bodies. It is probable that the Convention will be a frequent reference point in such disputes, and that the litigation thereby generated will need to be resolved by the judiciary in a context that is certain to be highly political on occasion.[33]

7–08   The schemes pertaining in Scotland and Wales are broadly similar. The starting point as far as Scotland is concerned is section 98, which provides that Schedule 6 (which makes provision in relation to devolution issues) shall have effect.[34] A "devolution issue" includes firstly "a question whether an Act of the Scottish Parliament or any provision of an Act of the Scottish Parliament is within the legislative competence of the Parliament",[35] and this clearly will include

---

[29] s. 129(2) of the Scotland Act; s. 153(2) of the Government of Wales Act.

[30] This is the wording in the Scottish measure. It may be that before the Human Rights Act is implemented in England, there will be the potential for interesting jurisdictional disputes where Scottish judges are asked to sanction conduct by a public authority in England acting under the instructions of a member of the Scottish executive which, were such action to take place in Scotland, would be vulnerable to review for compliance with the Convention. For an illustration of the procedural context in which such an issue could arise see *R. v. Manchester Stipendiary Magistrate, ex parte Granada Television Ltd* (1998) 148 N.L.J. 1603. The same issue could also conceivably arise in relation to Wales-England matters.

[31] An "act" here means (a) making any legislation or (b) any other act or failure to act, if it is the act or failure of a member of the Scottish Executive": s. 100(4). The restriction on standing does not apply to the Lord Advocate, the Advocate-General, the Attorney-General or the Attorney-General for Northern Ireland: s. 100(2). For the similar terms in the Government of Wales Act see s. 107(2), (3), (4) and (5).

[32] s. 100(3). Compare the Government of Wales Act, s. 107(4)(b).

[33] The tenure of Scottish judges was a matter of high controversy during the passage of the Scotland Act. See now s. 95 and for the background R Reed Q.C., "Devolution and the Judiciary" in Cambridge Centre for Public Law, above nn. 5, 21 and CMG Himsworth, "Securing the Tenure of Scottish Judges: a Somewhat Academic Exercise?" [1999] P.L. 14.

[34] See Government of Wales Act, s. 109 and Sched. 8 for the analogous procedures to those about to be outlined in respect of Scotland.

[35] Sched. 6, para. 1(a).

challenges to *vires* based on compatibility with the Convention. Secondly the term "devolution issue" also covers "a question whether a purported or proposed exercise of a function by a member of the Scottish Executive is, or would be, incompatible with any of the Convention rights . . .".[36] It embraces thirdly "a question whether a failure to act by a member of the Scottish Executive is incompatible with any of the Convention rights . . .".[37] A "devolution issue" as so defined can then come before the various courts of the United Kingdom in a number of ways, though in respect of a term in Scottish legislation which "could be read in such a way as to be outside competence"[38] (section 100(1)) the courts are enjoined to read such a provision "as narrowly as is required for it to be within competence, if such a reading is possible . . .".[39]

7–09   In Scotland itself, a devolution issue arising in non-criminal proceedings can be referred by a court (other than the House of Lords or any court consisting of three or more judges of the Court of Session) to the Inner House of the Court of Session.[40] A tribunal from which there is no appeal is obliged to make, and other tribunals may make, the same reference to the same court.[41] In criminal proceedings, "[a] court, other than any court consisting of two or more judges of the High Court of Justiciary, may refer any devolution issue which arises in criminal proceedings before it to the High Court of Justiciary".[42] Apart from this system of referrals within the ordinary court system, the Judicial Committee of the Privy Council may also become involved in resolving devolution issues, in three ways. First, there are powers of referral by the law officers. The Advocate General, the Lord Advocate or the Attorney General "may refer the question of whether a Bill or any provision of a Bill would be within the legislative competence of the Parliament to the Judicial Committee for decision".[43] The same public officials and the Attorney-General for Northern Ireland may also refer to the Privy Council "any devolution issue which is not the subject of proceedings"[44]). These officials may also "require any court or tribunal to refer to the judicial committee any devolution issue which has arisen in proceedings before it to which he is a party".[45]

7–10   Secondly, there is a system of referrals from Scottish courts to the Privy Council. Any "court consisting of three or more judges of the Court of Session may refer any devolution issue which arises in proceedings before it . . . to the Judicial Committee",[46] but cases which have already been referred to it by another court or tribunal under the procedure described above may not be referred on in this way. Any court "consisting of two or more judges of the High Court of Justiciary may refer any devolution issue which arises in proceedings before it . . . to the Judicial Committee",[47] except once again for those criminal cases which have already been

---

[36] Sched. 6, para. 1(d).
[37] Sched. 6, para. 1(e).
[38] s. 100(1).
[39] s. 100(2). See for possible difficulties between this clause and s. 3 of the Human Rights Act: AW Bradley, "Constitutional Reform, The Sovereignty of Parliament and Devolution" in Cambridge Centre for Public Law, above nn. 5, 33, p. 37.
[40] Sched. 6, para. 7.
[41] Sched. 6, para. 8.
[42] Sched. 6, para. 9.
[43] s. 33(1). There are time limits in respect of this process: see s. 33(2) and (3).
[44] Sched. 6, para. 34. On which see further Sched. 6, para. 35.
[45] Sched. 6, para. 33.
[46] Sched. 6, para. 10.
[47] Sched. 6, para. 11.

referred to it by a lower court. Thirdly, the Judicial Committee is to have a new appellate role in U.K. law. Issues will also find themselves in the Privy Council by way of appeal, in cases which were initially referred by a lower court or tribunal to either the Inner House of the Court of Session or the High Court of Justiciary.[48] An appeal will also exceptionally lie against a determination of a devolution issue by "a court of three or more judges of the Court of Session from which there is no appeal to the House of Lords", albeit only with leave of the court or special leave from the judicial committee itself.[49]

7–11   These are complicated provisions[50] but they do not exhaust the mechanisms set out in Schedule 6 for dealing with devolution issues, since the drafters have also had to take into consideration the possibility of matters of this nature arising in U.K. courts outside Scotland. Accordingly an analogous system of referrals and of appeals, also involving the Judicial Committee, from the courts in England, Wales and Northern Ireland is set out in the Act.[51] Additionally, "[a]ny devolution issue which arises in judicial proceedings in the House of Lords shall be referred to the Judicial Committee unless the House considers it more appropriate, having regard to all the circumstances, that it should determine the issue".[52]

The Government of Wales Act also defines a "devolution issue"[53] and provides similar duties in respect of notice of relevant proceedings wherever arising in the United Kingdom.[54] It also allows the Attorney-General to institute proceedings in relation to devolution issues in England and Wales,[55] the Advocate-General for Scotland to do so in Scotland[56] and the Attorney-General for Northern Ireland to do the same in his or her jurisdiction.[57] Separate provision similar to that in Scotland is made for litigation arising in the House of Lords[58] and for direct references to the Judicial Committee by the relevant law officers or the Assembly.[59] There are broadly analogous provisions dealing with litigation in Scotland and in Northern Ireland.[60] As far as litigation relating to "devolution issues" arising in England and Wales is concerned, the same system of referrals is adopted, from the magistrates' court to the High Court, or any other court (except the House of Lords) to the Court of Appeal, in civil proceedings.[61] A tribunal from which there is no appeal shall refer a devolution issue to the Court of Appeal and any other tribunal may make such a reference (Schedule 8, paragraph 8). Criminal matters of a summary nature may be referred to the High Court and proceedings on

---

[48] Sched. 6, paras 12 and 13.
[49] Sched. 6, para. 13.
[50] To which should be added the notice requirements where a devolution issue has emerged (Sched. 6, paras 5, 6, 16, 17, 26 and 27) which facilitate the involvement of law officers in cases raising devolution issues. Note also that the Attorney-General and the Attorney-General for Northern Ireland may each institute proceedings for the determination of a devolution issue: Sched. 6, para. 15(1) and 25(1) but that in each case such proceedings may be defended by the Lord Advocate: Sched. 6, paras 15(2) and 25(2).
[51] Sched. 6, paras 14–31.
[52] Sched. 6, para. 32.
[53] Sched. 8, para. 1.
[54] Sched. 8, paras 5, 14 and 24.
[55] Sched. 8, para. 4.
[56] Sched. 8, para. 13.
[57] Sched. 8, para. 23.
[58] Sched. 8, para. 29.
[59] Sched. 8, paras 30, 31. See Sched. 8, paras 32–34 for further general provisions in relation to the Judicial Committee. Similar provisions are to be found in the Scotland Act, s. 103.
[60] See Sched. 8, Pt III and Pt IV respectively.
[61] Sched. 8, paras 6 and 7.

indictment may be referred to the Court of Appeal.[62] The Court of Appeal "may refer any devolution issue which arises in proceedings before it [otherwise than on a reference under paragraphs 7, 8 or 9–see above] to the Judicial Committee"[63] and an appeal against a determination of a devolution issue by the High Court or the Court of Appeal on a reference under paragraphs 6, 7, 8 or 9 shall lie to the Judicial Committee, "but only (a) with leave of the court concerned, or (b) failing such leave, with special leave of the Judicial Committee".[64]

4. CONCLUSION

7-12   It is much too early to be clear about the likely impact of the HRA on the devolutionary arrangements that have been put in place for Scotland and Wales. The potential certainly exists for the Convention to play a lead role in circumscribing the power of all the bodies exercising newly devolved power, but this in turn very much depends on the substance of the exercise of power by these authorities.It is as yet also unclear which of the many judicial mechanisms for the resolution of devolution disputes described above will emerge as the main source of adjudication in this novel constitutional arena. It is tempting to anticipate the emergence of the Judicial Committee of the Privy Council as a respected court of last resort for these quasi-colonial disputes but nothing in the legislation makes such an outcome inevitable. Indeed it is also possible that this plethora of litigious devices will continue to jostle uneasily side by side into the indefinite future, though the forthcoming further reform of the House of Lords, to which the Government is committed, may provide an opportunity for a fundamental reappraisal of the United Kingdom's entire judicial arrangements.

A third area of possible change lies in the precedent set by Northern Ireland in relation to Part VII of its Devolution Act.[65] Though in other respects reflecting the same process in respect of the interrelationship between the HRA and devolution as we have already outlined in respect of both Scotland and Wales,[66] the Northern Ireland Act provides in Part VII for the establishment of a Northern Ireland Human Rights Commission[67] and for an Equality Commission for Northern Ireland.[68] Each authority is to enjoy dynamic new powers for the protection and assertion of the rights within its remit.[69] In particular the Northern Ireland Human Rights Commission is empowered to advise the Secretary of State and the Executive Committee of the Assembly of legislative and other measures which ought to be taken to protect human rights,[70] and to advise the Assembly on the compatibility of Bills with human rights. Such advice may be published.[71] It can also assist litigants in Northern Ireland in proceedings involving the law or practice relating to human rights or may bring such proceedings itself.[72] However, the legislation maintains the

---

[62] Sched. 8, para. 9.
[63] Sched. 8, para. 10.
[64] Sched. 8, para. 11.
[65] Northern Ireland Act 1998, ss. 68–78.
[66] See, in particular, ss. 6(2)(c), 24(1)(a), 71, 79 and Scheds 10, 98(1), 100(1) and Sched. 14, para. 1.
[67] s. 68.
[68] s. 73.
[69] They have been established before the devolution arrangement has been finally established, and their survival is not expected to be contingent on the successful achievement of devolution in the Province.
[70] And as to its own effectiveness: s. 69(2). "Human rights" includes, but is not limited to, Convention rights: s. 69(11)(b).
[71] s. 69(9). The Commission may also publish the outcome of research and investigations conducted under s. 69(8).
[72] ss. 69(5) and 70(1).

Government's approach to standing by providing that only a victim may rely on Convention rights.[73]

7–13 The Government of the Republic of Ireland has also recently announced its intention to introduce a Bill which would establish a Human Rights Commission within that jurisdiction.[74] In announcing the measure the Government referred not only to the Good Friday Agreement but also to the fact that regard had also been had "to relevant legislative developments in other jurisdictions, notably Canada, Australia and New Zealand".[75] It is probable that such initiatives so close to home will greatly increase pressure for the establishment of similar bodies in Great Britain.

---

[73] s. 71(1).
[74] See Human Rights Commission Bill, 1999 (No. 44 of 1999).
[75] Minister's press conference on publication of the Human Rights Commission Bill, July 8, 1999.

PART II

THE EUROPEAN CONVENTION ON HUMAN RIGHTS

Commentary on the case law

1. INTRODUCTION

C0–01   The first part of this book considered the effect of the Human Rights Act (HRA) 1998 and discussed questions which courts are likely to encounter when giving effect to the Convention through the common law and the Act. In the course of that discussion, reference was made to some of the Convention principles and case law by way of illustration. Part II concentrates on the Convention. This first section summarises the general principles which the Convention institutions have adopted in interpreting and applying the Convention. It is essential to have an appreciation of those principles in order to understand the Convention case law. The succeeding sections of Part II summarise the most important jurisprudence article by article. Because much of the case law is formulaic in style, we have quoted extensively from it.

We shall see that the overriding principle is that the Convention should be given a broad interpretation in accordance with its object and purpose, leading to a construction which will give life to the Convention rights in the world of today. Secondly, emphasis is placed on the importance of the rule of law and the unacceptability of arbitrary power. In consequence, the extent of public power and the constraints on it must be clear for all to see, and there must be adequate and effective safeguards against abuse. This in turn leads to the restrictive approach to the review of state interference, which must be justified by reference to a "pressing social need" and must be proportionate to the need. The Court has also developed the notion of the "margin of appreciation", mentioned elsewhere and dealt with briefly here.

2. THE CONVENTION PRINCIPLES

A. The purposive approach to interpretation

C0–02   From its earliest judgments, the Court has refused to construe the rights guaranteed by the Convention narrowly, regarding such an approach as insufficient to "realise the aim and achieve the object" of the Convention.[1] Instead it has stressed the importance of giving full weight to the object and purpose of the Convention.[2]

---

[1] See *Wemhoff v. Germany* (1968) 1 E.H.R.R. 55, para. 8; *Golder v. United Kingdom* (1975) 1 E.H.R.R. 524.
[2] *Brogan v. United Kingdom* (1989) 11 E.H.R.R. 117, para. 58; *Groppera Radio A.G. v. Switzerland* (1990) 12 E.H.R.R. 321, para. 61; *Van der Mussele v. Belgium* (1984) 6 E.H.R.R. 163, para. 49.

In doing so, it has relied upon the general principle that treaties should be interpreted "in good faith in accordance with the ordinary meaning to be given to the terms of the treaty in their context and in the light of its object and purpose".[3] Convention concepts must be interpreted in a spirit of "pluralism, tolerance and broadmindedness without which there is no 'democratic society'".[4] This overriding principle has led the Court to approach the interpretation of the Convention so as to make its safeguards "practical and effective",[5] and to treat the Convention as "a living instrument which must be interpreted in the light of present-day conditions".[6] These approaches and their consequences are considered in the following paragraphs.

(1) Convention rights should be practical and effective

C0–03   Insistence that the exercise of rights must be practical and effective has led the Court to go beyond the text of the Convention to establish the very essence of the rights which it seeks to guarantee. In consequence, it has read in guarantees which are not provided in the express terms of the text, but which are nonetheless necessary in order to give the rights real practical effect. For example, where Article 6(3)(c) guarantees a criminal defendant the right to defend himself through legal assistance, the Court has held that that state's obligation is not fulfilled merely by the nomination of a lawyer who refuses to act.[7] The effective right of defence is not thereby guaranteed. By the same token, the protection of the right to life under Article 2 has been held to require that public authorities carry out an effective official investigation into a death following the use of force by agents of the state.[8] The principle of effectiveness has also led to the identification of implied or inherent rights within the Convention, to the imposition of positive obligations on states to secure the enjoyment of certain rights and to the attribution of "autonomous" meanings to Convention concepts in order to prevent their curtailment by states.

(2) Inherent rights and positive obligations

C0–04   Probably the most important implied or inherent rights have been derived from Article 6, the guarantee of a right to a fair trial. Holding that the guarantee includes an inherent right of access to a court, the Court said:

"Were Article 6(1) to be understood as concerning exclusively the conduct of an action which had already been initiated before a court, a Contracting State could, without acting in breach of that text, do away with its courts, or take away their jurisdiction to determine certain classes of civil actions and entrust it to organs dependent on the Government. Such assumptions, indissociable

---

[3] Vienna Convention on the Law of Treaties, Art. 31. For an application of the Vienna Convention see *Golder v. United Kingdom* (1975) 1 E.H.R.R. 524, paras 29–36, where the Court considered that Art. 6 of the ECHR implied a right of access to a court.

[4] *Handyside v. United Kingdom* (1976) 1 E.H.H.R. 737, para. 49. See to similar effect Sedley L.J. in *Redmond-Bate v. Director of Public Prosecutions, The Times,* July 28, 1999 (DC).

[5] *Loizidou v. Turkey* (1995) 20 E.H.R.R. 99, para. 72. See also *Artico v. Italy* (1980) 3 E.H.R.R. 1, para. 33.

[6] *Matthews v. United Kingdom* (1999) 28 E.H.R.R. 361, para. 39.

[7] *Artico v. Italy* (1980) 3 E.H.R.R. 1, para. 33.

[8] *McCann, Farrell and Savage v. United Kingdom* (1996) 21 E.H.R.R. 97, para. 161. Similar obligations arisefrom a combination of Arts 3 and 13: *Aksoy v. Turkey,* December 18, 1996, R.J.D., 1996–IV, No. 26; 23 E.H.R.R. 553, para. 98; and from Art. 5: *Kurt v. Turkey* (1999) 27 E.H.R.R. 373, paras 123–124.

from a danger of arbitrary power, would have serious consequences which are repugnant to the aforementioned principles[9] and which the Court cannot overlook.

It would be inconceivable, in the opinion of the Court, that Article 6(1) should describe in detail the procedural guarantees afforded to parties in a pending lawsuit and should not first protect that which alone makes it in fact possible to benefit from such guarantees, that is, access to a court. The fair, public and expeditious characteristics of judicial proceedings are of no value at all if there are no judicial proceedings.[10]

In the case in question the Court found Article 6(1) violated by the Home Secretary's refusal to allow a prisoner to contact his solicitor with a view to issuing proceedings for libel against a prison officer. Although there was no legal impediment to issuing proceedings, a "hindrance in fact"[11] was sufficient to found a violation. The right of access to a court was also violated where an impecunious litigant was not granted legal aid in respect of complex judicial separation proceedings.[12] Although the applicant could have appeared in person, she could not have presented her own case effectively and the right to appear in person was therefore "theoretical and illusory".[13] Other fair trial rights inherent in the principle of effectiveness include the right of an accused person in detention to have access to counsel,[14] and the right to silence.[15]

C0–05 The notion of inherent rights arising out of effective realisation of the object of the Convention has also spawned the concept of positive obligations. Although in general terms the provisions of the Convention which protect substantive rights impose a negative obligation—to abstain from interference—positive obligations may be inherent in the rights themselves. Such obligations fall broadly into two classes. The first, developed by the Court in its earlier case law, still focuses on the relationship between the individual and the state. In effect it is an extension of the negative obligations which the Convention sets out expressly. In this kind of case, the state is obliged to rearrange its legal relations with, or provision to, the individual, but it is not directly concerned with the relations between individuals. In one of its earliest judgments, for example, the Court found such a positive obligation inherent in the notion of "respect" for family life in Article 8, obliging states to ensure that domestic law provided safeguards for the integration of illegitimate children into the family.[16] *Airey v. Ireland*, considered above, may also be classified as a positive obligation case: Article 6 obliged the state not only to refrain from placing obstacles in the way of access to a court but also imposed a positive obligation to provide legal assistance to ensure that access was effective.[17] In a series of cases, the Court has considered the extent to which Article 8 imposes a positive obligation on the state to recognise the new sexual identity of

---

[9] *i.e.* the universally recognised fundamental principles of law.
[10] *Golder v. United Kingdom* (1975) 1 E.H.R.R. 524, para. 35. See also *Osman v. United Kingdom* [1999] Fam. Law 86.
[11] 1 E.H.R.R. 524, para. 26.
[12] *Airey v. Ireland* (1979) 2 E.H.R.R. 305.
[13] *ibid.*, para. 24.
[14] *Campbell and Fell v. United Kingdom* (1984) E.H.R.R. 165, paras 97–99.
[15] *Saunders v. United Kingdom*, December 17, 1996, R.J.D., 1996–VI, No. 24; 23 E.H.R.R. 313, para. 68.
[16] *Marckx v. Belgium* (1979) 2 E.H.R.R. 330, para. 31.
[17] See above, n. 12.

a post-operative transsexual. In *B v. France*,[18] the Court found that the difficulties of social and professional integration and other inconveniences associated with the French system of registration of civil status gave rise to a detriment of sufficient seriousness that the positive obligation inherent in the notion of "respect" for private life had been violated. Applicants from the United Kingdom have been less successful, although the majorities against violation have been getting slimmer.[19] Other positive obligations include that of protecting individuals from polluting activities,[20] providing information about health hazards,[21] and taking into account the philosophical convictions of parents in the education field.[22] In certain circumstances, it appears, a state may be required to take positive steps to ensure that disabled people can enjoy the same leisure facilities as others, at least where there is a "direct and immediate link between the measures sought by an applicant and the latter's private and/or family life".[23]

C0–06   The case law of the Court has gone further, however, by holding that "effective" enjoyment of certain rights must be secured by protecting the individual not only from state interference but also from interference by other private parties. This kind of positive obligation affects third parties, requiring the state to impose obligations and penalties on other individuals in order to secure enjoyment of the right. An assault on a person's physical integrity must be punished by criminal sanctions,[24] and in general the state is under an obligation to protect a person's dignity[25] and religious sensibilities.[26] The full extent of positive obligations arising out of Article 11's guarantee of freedom of association is unclear, although it extends at least to ensuring that demonstrators can hold peaceful demonstrations without having to fear that they will be subjected to physical violence by their opponents. According to the Court, "[g]enuine, effective freedom of peaceful assembly cannot . . . be reduced to a mere duty on the part of the State not to interfere . . . Like Article 8, Article 11 sometimes requires positive measures to be taken . . .".[27] However, the Commission and the Court have disagreed on whether the state had to penalise trade union action taken with the aim of forcing an individual to join an employers' association.[28] We shall see that when establishing the extent of a positive obligation, the Court has regard to the factors which justify interference, for example, the protection of health or morals, or the rights and freedoms of others.[29]

(3)   Autonomous concepts

C0–07   Another facet of the "practical and effective" doctrine is the treatment of Convention terms as "autonomous concepts", independent of the legal systems

---

[18] (1993) 16 E.H.R.R. 1. See further below, para. C8–36.
[19] For the most recent judgment relating to the U.K. see *Sheffield and Horsham v. United Kingdom* (1997) 27 E.H.R.R. 163, para. 59 (no violation by 11 votes to 9, the Commission having found a violation by 15 votes to 1). See further below, para. C8–36.
[20] *Lopez-Ostra v. Spain* (1995) 20 E.H.R.R. 277. See further below, para. C8–70.
[21] *Guerra and others v. Italy*(1998) 26 E.H.R.R. 357 (information for residents living in the vicinity of a high risk factory); see also *McGinley & Egan v. United Kingdom* (1999) 27 E.H.R.R. 1 (information for individuals exposed to atmospheric tests of nuclear weapons).
[22] *Valsamis v. Greece*, December 18, 1996, R.J.D., 1996–VI, No. 27; 24 E.H.R.R. 294.
[23] *Botta v. Italy* (1998) 26 E.H.R.R. 241, para. 34.
[24] *X & Y v. Netherlands* (1985) 8 E.H.R.R. 235.
[25] *S.W. v. United Kingdom* (1996) 21 E.H.R.R. 363, para. 44.
[26] *Otto-Preminger Institute v. Austria* (1994) 19 E.H.R.R. 34; *Wingrove v. United Kingdom*, November 25, 1996, R.J.D., 1996–V, No. 23; 24 E.H.R.R. 1.
[27] *Plattform Ärtzte für das Leben v. Austria* (1991) 13 E.H.R.R. 204, para. 32.
[28] *Gustafsson v. Sweden*, April 25, 1996; R.J.D., 1996–II, No. 9; 22 E.H.R.R. 409.
[29] *Rees v. United Kingdom* (1987) 9 E.H.R.R. 56, para. 37. See also *B v. France* (1993) 16 E.H.R.R. 1, para. 44.

of the Contracting States. As with its approach to the inherent right of access to a court, the intention is to ensure that unilateral state action cannot undermine the efficacy of the Convention guarantee. The Court articulated this consideration most recently in its judgment in *Chassagnou v. France*, concerning the legal obligation imposed on landowners to belong to local hunt associations. The Government had argued that the associations were public law bodies, to which the right to freedom of association—and the negative right, not to associate—did not apply. For the Court, however:

> " . . . the question is not so much whether in French law [the associations] are private associations, public or para-public associations, or mixed associations, but whether they are associations for the purposes of Article 11 of the Convention.
>
> If Contracting States were able, at their discretion, by classifying an association as 'public' or 'para-administrative', to remove it from the scope of Article 11, that would give them such latitude that it might lead to results incompatible with the object and purpose of the Convention, which is to protect rights that are not theoretical or illusory but practical and effective . . .[30]
>
> The term 'association' therefore possesses an autonomous meaning; the classification in national law has only relative value and constitutes no more than a starting-point."[31]

The notion of "autonomy" has been of particular importance in determining what is a "civil right",[32] and a "criminal charge"[33] within the meaning of Article 6(1). As a result, the guarantees of Article 6 apply to proceedings which are not classed as criminal in U.K. law[34] and to disciplinary and public law proceedings, not commonly thought of as "civil".[35] Other autonomous concepts are the notion of when a person has been "charged" with an offence,[36] and what is a "penalty" within the meaning of Article 7.[37] In Article 1 of the First Protocol, the notion of possessions has an autonomous meaning which is not synonymous with ownership.[38]

(4)   *The Convention is to be interpreted as a "living instrument"*

C0–08   The Convention propounds the rights it guarantees in broad terms, to which it is possible to attach different scope at different times. As we have already

---

[30] See *Artico v. Italy* (1980) 3 E.H.R.R. 1, para. 33, and, more recently, *United Communist Party of Turkey and Others v. Turkey*, January 30, 1988, R.J.D., 1998–I, Nos 18–19; (1998) 26 E.H.R.R. 121, para. 33.
[31] App. Nos. 25088/94, 28331/95 and 28443/95, para. 100.
[32] *König v. Germany* (1978) 2 E.H.R.R. 170, para. 87–88; *Ringeisen v. Austria* (1971) 1 E.H.R.R. 455, para. 94; *Stran Greek Refineries and Stratis Andreadis v. Greece* (1995) E.H.R.R. 319, para. 39.
[33] *Engel and others v. The Netherlands* (1976) 1 E.H.R.R. 647, para. 81.
[34] *e.g.* prison and military discipline, failure to pay community charge. See further cases cited at para. C6–22.
[35] See para. 6–17 as to "civil proceedings". See also the approach of the ECHR to the existence of a "civil right" in *Osman v. United Kingdom* [1999] Fam. Law 86, and the reaction of Lord Browne-Wilkinson in *Barrett v. Enfield LBC* [1999] 3 W.L.R. 79, 84–85. See also *Gibson v. Chief Constable of Strathclyde Police*, *The Times*, May 11, 1999 (Court of Session Outer House); and Hoffmann (1999) 62 MLR 1.
[36] *Deweer v. Belgium* (1980) 2 E.H.R.R. 439; *Funke v. France* (1993) 16 E.H.R.R. 297.
[37] *Welch v. United Kingdom* (1995) 20 E.H.R.R. 247, see para. 28 (confiscation order under the Drug Trafficking Offences Act 1986, following conviction for offence committed before the Act came into force).
[38] *Matos e Silva LDA & ors v. Portugal*, September 16, 1996, R.J.D., 1996–IV, No. 14; 24 E.H.R.R. 573.

seen with the notion of inherent rights, the Strasbourg institutions are not wedded to the words of the Convention or the intentions of the drafters at the time, since such an approach would allow the Convention rights to ossify, rendering them incapable of reflecting contemporary values. The Court and the Commission have stated that the Convention is "a living instrument" which must be interpreted in the light of present-day conditions, an approach which is "firmly rooted" in its case law.[39] This "living instrument" approach is most evidently appropriate in matters of social policy or morality, for example in deciding whether corporal punishment of juveniles amounted to "degrading" punishment, or whether the right to respect for family life imposed positive obligations in respect of children born outside marriage.[40] The justifiability of restrictions on homosexual activity has been the subject of consider-able scrutiny in order to determine what interference may be regarded as "necessary in a democratic society" in the light of modern conditions and social developments.[41] The same kind of inquiry has been necessary to establish the scope of states' positive obligations to recognise the status of transsexuals.[42] The Court has looked in particular at developments in medical science, and in social attitudes, for example as evidenced by the adoption of international conventions[43] which might indicate a consensus among the parties to the Convention.[44] The Court has also taken account of political developments. For example the emergence of the E.U. and its citizenship had a considerable effect on the Strasbourg institutions' approach to the application of Article 16 to a German M.E.P. in a French Overseas Territory.[45] More recently, the Court considered that Article 3 of the First Protocol, which guarantees free elections to choose the "legislature", applied to elections to the European Parliament:

> "The mere fact that a body was not envisaged by the drafters of the Convention cannot prevent that body from falling within the scope of the Convention. To the extent that Contracting states organise common constitutional or parliamentary structures by international treaties, the Court must take these mutually agreed structural changes into account in interpreting the Convention and its Protocols."[46]

The "living instrument" approach is not limited to questions of justifiability and positive obligations, but has been applied to the Convention's enforcement provisions.[47]

(5) The purposive approach in U.K. law

C0–09 The courts of the United Kingdom will find nothing alien in the purposive approach to construction in general. Lord Clyde accepted in *Clarke v.*

---

[39] *Matthews v. United Kingdom*, (1999) 28 E.H.R.R. 361, para. 39.
[40] *Tyrer v. United Kingdom* (1978) 2 E.H.R.R. 1; *Marckx v. Belgium* (1979) 2 E.H.R.R. 330; *Inze v. Austria* (1988) 10 E.H.R.R. 394.
[41] *Dudgeon v. United Kingdom* (1981) 4 E.H.R.R. 149; *Sutherland v. United Kingdom* [1998] E.H.R.L.R. 117.
[42] *Sheffield & Horsham v. United Kingdom* (1999) 27 E.H.R.R. 163; *X, Y & Z v. United Kingdom*, April 22, 1997, R.J.D., 1997–II, No. 35; 24 E.H.R.R. 143.
[43] See, *e.g.*, *Marckx v. Belgium* (1979) 2 E.H.R.R. 330, para. 41 and *Inze v. Austria* (1988) 10 E.H.R.R. 394, para. 41 (illegitimacy); *Soering v. United Kingdom* (1989) 11 E.H.R.R. 439, para. 102 (death penalty).
[44] See for example *Sheffield & Horsham v. United Kingdom* (1997) 27 E.H.R.R. 163, para. 58.
[45] *Piermont v. France* (1995) 20 E.H.R.R. 301.
[46] *Matthews v. United Kingdom*, (1999) 28 E.H.R.R. 361, para. 39.
[47] *Loizidou v. Turkey* (1995) 20 E.H.R.R. 99, para. 71 (validity of territorial restrictions on Turkey's acceptance of the right of individual petition the competence of the Court—applicability to Turkish-occupied North Cyprus). The Court added that the object and purpose of the Convention as an instrument for the protection of human beings required an interpretation which made its safeguards practical and effective: *ibid.*, para. 72.

Kato that "it may be perfectly proper to adopt even a strained construction to enable the object and purpose of legislation to be fulfilled",[48] although there are limits to this approach.[49] Further, experience of interpretation of Commonwealth Bills of Rights shows that there already exists a tradition of giving a broad and generous approach to "constitutional instruments" suitable to give individuals the full measure of the fundamental rights and freedoms[50] and avoiding what has been called the "austerity of tabulated legalism".[51]

The "living instrument" approach to construction and application is similar to the common law presumption, noted above, that Parliament intends the court to apply–particularly to provisions expressing a dynamic concept–a construction which allows for changes since the legislation was initially framed.[52] This means that in its application on any date the language of the Act, though necessarily embedded in its own time, is nevertheless to be construed in accordance with the need to treat it as current law. Sir John Laws has described the approach as more akin to the incremental development of the common law,[53] and indeed it has already been articulated in the common law's approach to the rationality of restrictions on fundamental rights. Thus, in *R. v. Ministry of Defence, ex parte Smith*[54] the Master of the Rolls stated that the lawfulness of the discharge of homosexual servicemen was to be judged as at the date of their discharge, and indicated that "a belief which represented unquestioned orthodoxy in year X may become questionable by year Y and unsustainable by year Z".[55]

As with the "margin of appreciation",[56] the Strasbourg approach to the "living instrument" doctrine must be adapted for use at home. It may not be necessary to find a European consensus as to the scope of a particular right in order to determine whether, within the U.K., a positive obligation should be recognised or an interference should be considered necessary. The Strasbourg institutions accord state authorities a margin of appreciation, within which they will not interfere, in recognition that states themselves have the primary responsibility to achieve the balance between individual rights and the general interest. The Court shows the same deference by insisting that "present-day conditions" must be assessed by reference to European consensus. For the domestic court, however, the values and requirements of society within the U.K. will be more important, at least where they lead to a greater level of protection of Convention rights. U.K. law may well exceed the level of protection required by international consensus, although it cannot fall below it.

---

[48] [1998] 1 W.L.R. 1647, 1655 (HL).
[49] See further above, para. 3–39.
[50] *Minister of Home Affairs v. Fisher* [1980] A.C. 319, 328–329; *Thornhill v. A.G. Trinidad & Tobago* [1981] A.C. 61, 69; *Jobe v. AG Gambia* [1984] A.C. 689, 700; *Vasquez v. The Queen* [1994] 1 W.L.R. 1304, 1313; *Matadeen v. Pointu* [1999] A.C. 98, 108; *A.G. of Hong Kong v. Lee Kwong-kut* [1993] A.C. 951, 966; *Huntley v. A.G. for Jamaica* [1995] 2 A.C. 1, 12; *US v. Cretoni* [1989] 1 S.C.R. 1469, 1480.
[51] *Minister of Home Affairs v. Fisher* [1980] A.C. 319, 328, per Lord Wilberforce, dubbed by Paul Rishworth (*The Struggle for Simplicity in Law*, 1997, p. 321) "the celebrated Cardozo-via-Wilberforce aphorism".
[52] See above, para. 3–31. See also *R. v. Secretary of State for the Home Department, ex parte Adan and others*, *The Times*, July 28, 1999 (CA), in which the Court of Appeal held that the Convention and Protocol relating to the Status of Refugees had to be interpreted as a "living instrument" in order to ensure protection from persecution by non-state agents.
[53] [1998] P. L. 254, 264.
[54] [1996] Q.B. 517.
[55] [1996] Q.B. 517, 554. See also 563 (Henry L.J.).
[56] See further above, paras 2–05 and 5–16, and below, para. C0–17.

b. The rule of law and the requirement of lawfulness[57]

C0–10 The Convention uses the words "law" and "lawful" 39 times. The preamble refers to the "common heritage of . . . the rule of law" which the states parties share, and which the Court has described as "one of the fundamental principles of a democratic society, [which] is inherent in all the Articles of the Convention . . .".[58] The death penalty must be "provided by law"; arrest and detention must be "in accordance with a procedure prescribed by law", and "lawful"; tribunals must be "established by law"; no one may be punished for an act or omission which did not constitute an offence under national or international law when committed; interference with private and family life, home and correspondence must be "in accordance with the law"; limitations on religious freedom, freedom of expression and freedom of association, must be "prescribed by law"; deprivation of possessions must be "subject to the conditions provided for by law". Found principally where the Convention permits exceptions to or interference with Convention rights, lawfulness imports additional limitations on the state's power of interference. The requirement of lawfulness means first that a measure which interferes with a Convention right must have some basis in domestic law. If it does not, then it cannot be justified.[59] But compliance with domestic law is not enough by itself. The requirement of lawfulness is also a guarantee against arbitrariness, [60] and to be recognised as "law", a norm must be of a certain quality. It must be accessible, in the sense both that it is available to the citizen and that he or she is able to have an indication that is adequate, in the circumstances, of the legal rules applicable to a given case. A further important principle articulated by the Court is that:

" . . . a norm cannot be regarded as a 'law' unless it is formulated with sufficient precision to enable the citizen to regulate his conduct: he must be able—if need be with appropriate advice—to foresee, to a degree that is reasonable in the circumstances, the consequences which a given action may entail."[61]

A law which confers a discretion must indicate its scope. However, the law itself may leave some discretion to public authorities and if the circumstances so require, non-statutory guidance may set out the manner in which discretion is to be exercised.[62] "Law" covers not only statute but also unwritten law,[63] as long as it is sufficiently clear.

C0–11 There must also be adequate safeguards against abuse, so that the requirement of lawfulness was not fulfilled where a pre-emption procedure operated by the revenue authorities in cases of alleged sale at undervalue "operated

---

[57] See also 5–08 et seq.
[58] Iatridis v. Greece judgment of March 25, 1999, para. 62.
[59] ibid.
[60] James v. United Kingdom (1986) 8 E.H.R.R. 123, para. 67.
[61] Silver v. United Kingdom (1983) 5 E.H.R.R. 347, paras 87–88. See also Lüdi v. Switzerland (1993) 15 E.H.R.R. 173.
[62] ibid.
[63] Sunday Times v. United Kingdom (1979) 2 E.H.R.R. 245, para. 47. See also S.W. v. United Kingdom (1996) 21 E.H.R.R. 363, para. 36/34 (gradual clarification of criminal law by judicial decision is compatible with Art. 7 provided that the resultant development is consistent with the essence of the offence and could reasonably be foressen).

arbitrarily and selectively and was scarcely foreseeable, and it was not attended by basic procedural guarantees".[64] The need for safeguards has been an important feature of the Court's case law relating to "lawfulness", [65] and will go some way to compensate for the omission of Article 13, the right to an effective remedy, from the list of Convention rights in section 1(1) of the HRA. In many cases, lawfulness will require some form of judicial intervention, either authorising or supervising an interference, or providing a remedy after the event.[66]

As we have indicated elsewhere, in many cases the requirement that interference must be authorised by law effects no change to U.K. law, for it is an established constitutional principle that where a common law right is infringed, specific legal authority must be found.[67] Similarly, the requirement of protection against arbitrariness finds echoes in existing constitutional practice. It embodies Dicey's first conception of the rule of law as "the absolute supremacy or predominance of regular law as opposed to the influence of arbitrary power, [which] excludes the existence of arbitrariness",[68] a concept reflected in administrative law's strong presumption against "unfettered" discretion.[69] But we have suggested that a rigorous application of the principle of lawfulness will change the way in which the courts view some statutory or common law powers.[70]

C. Necessity, proportionality, fair balance and the margin of appreciation: the approach to justification and to positive obligations

C0–12   To be justified, interference with a Convention right must satisfy the requirement of lawfulness and it must pursue a legitimate aim, *i.e.* one of those set out in the provisions which permit exceptions. In addition, while some provisions stipulate expressly that interference must be "necessary in a democratic society", the requirements implicit in this phrase apply whenever the state seeks to justify an exception.

(1) The meaning of "necessary"

C0–13   The case law discloses a settled approach to consideration of exceptions. The Court restated the principles in a recent judgment:

> " . . . in assessing the necessity of a given measure a number of principles must be observed. The term 'necessary' does not have the flexibility of such expressions as 'useful' or 'desirable'. In addition, pluralism, tolerance and broadmindedness are hallmarks of a 'democratic society'. Although individual interests must on occasion be subordinated to those of a group, democracy does not simply mean that the views of a majority must always prevail: a

---

[64] *Hentrich v. France* (1994) 18 E.H.R.R. 440, para. 42.
[65] At times the Court has said that this requirement derives from the principle of proportionality rather than the requirement of lawfulness: see, *e.g.*, *Camenzind v. Switzerland*, (1999) 28 E.H.R.R. 458, para. 45.
[66] See, for example, *Kopp v. Switzerland* (1999) 27 E.H.R.R. 91. See also *Valenzuela Contreras v. Spain* (1999) 28 E.H.R.R. 483, para. 46, where the Court set out what it regards as the minimum safeguards against abuse of power in the area of interception of communications. See further, para. C8–41. See also, in relation to Art. 5, *Amuur v. France*, June 10, 1966, R.J.D., 1996–III, No. 10, para. 36; 22 E.H.R.R. 533, paras 50, 53.
[67] See above, para. 5–09. See also *Entick v. Carrington* (1765) 2 Wils. 275, and the cases on the common law presumptions, particularly the principle of legality, considered above, para. 3–12.
[68] *The Law of the Constitution* (10th ed., Macmillan, 1959), p. 202.
[69] *Padfield v. Minister of Agriculture, Fisheries and Food* [1968] A.C. 997.
[70] See further above, para. 5–09.

balance must be achieved which ensures the fair and proper treatment of minorities and avoids any abuse of a dominant position. Lastly, any restriction imposed on a Convention right must be proportionate to the legitimate aim pursued."[71]

It is for national authorities to make the initial assessment of the "necessity" for an interference, as regards both the choice of legislative framework and the particular measure of implementation. The margin of appreciation—the area of freedom of action—which the Court accords states varies according to, *inter alia*, the right in issue, its importance for the individual and the nature of the activities which are the subject of restriction.[72] For example, because of the importance of freedom of the press, exceptions to the right to freedom of expression must be narrowly interpreted and the necessity for any restrictions convincingly established.[73] Similarly, the importance of the right to the home must be taken into account when considering the scope of the state's margin of appreciation in relation to interference based on planning control.[74]

C0–14   The state bears the burden of showing necessity for an interference. It must show not only that the considerations relied upon are a relevant reason for the interference, *i.e.* that they are reasonably related to it, but also that those considerations constitute a sufficient reason.[75] This means that the actual interference in issue must be proportionate to the legitimate aim pursued. The adjective "necessary" implies the existence of a "pressing social need",[76] and proportionality must be assessed by the standards of a "democratic society", characterised by "pluralism, tolerance and broadmindedness".[77] The availability of less restrictive ways of achieving the aim in view will be an important consideration, to which evidence of practice in other countries will be relevant.[78] The availability of procedural safeguards is also relevant to determine whether the state has remained within its margin of appreciation in fixing the regulatory framework,[79] and legislation and practice governing interference must provide adequate and effective safeguards against abuse if the test of proportionality is to be satisfied.[80] For example, in considering the proportionality of a house search, the Court looked at the manner in which it was conducted, whether the applicant was present and represented, the number of personnel involved, the time taken, the physical extent

---

[71] *Chassagnou and others v. France*, App. Nos 25088/94, 28331/95 and 28443/95, judgment of April 29, 1999, para. 112. See also, *e.g. Young, James and Webster v. United Kingdom* (1981) 4 E.H.R.R. 38, para. 63.

[72] *Buckley v. United Kingdom* (1997) 23 E.H.R.R. 101, para. 74.

[73] *The Observer and The Guardian v. United Kingdom* (1992) 14 E.H.R.R. 153, para. 59.

[74] *Buckley, loc. cit.*, para. 76.

[75] See, *e.g. The Observer and the Guardian, loc. cit.*, paras 62 *et seq.*; *Buckley v. United Kingdom, loc. cit.*, para. 77.

[76] *Rekvényi v. Hungary*, App. No. 25390/94, judgment of May 20, 1999, para. 42 (Art. 10, restriction on freedom of expression for police); *Matter v. Slovakia*, App. No. 31534/96, judgment of July 5, 1999, para. 66 (Art. 8, forcible medical examination); *Chassagnou and others v. France*, App. Nos 25088/94, 28331/95 and 28443/95, judgment of April 29, 1999 (Art. 11, obligation to belong to a local hunt association).

[77] *Handyside v. United Kingdom* (1976) 1 E.H.R.R. 737, para. 49.

[78] *Informationsverein Lentia v. Austria* (1993) 17 E.H.R.R. 93, para. 40; *Hentrich v. France* (1994) 18 E.H.R.R. 440.

[79] *ibid.* See also *Air Canada v. United Kingdom* (1995) 20 E.H.R.R. 150, para. 44 (adequacy of the grounds for judicial review and the possibility of obtaining reasons for decision); *Gasus Dosier- und Födertechnik GmbH v. Netherlands* (1995) 20 E.H.R.R. 403.

[80] *Camenzind v. Switzerland* (1999) 28 E.H.R.R. 458, para. 45 (search and seizure).

of the search, and the information given to the applicant.[81] The more intrusive the measure, and the more important the right, the stricter the scrutiny which the Court has exercised.[82] The greater the element of policy involved in the choice of measures, the greater the latitude which Strasbourg will allow to the state. Thus, while the use of lethal force by agents of the state must be "strictly proportionate" to the aim of protecting people against unlawful violence,[83] the Court would not interfere in leasehold reform policy unless the measure in question was "manifestly without reasonable foundation".[84] The Court has been prepared to allow a state a broader margin of appreciation where it seeks to justify an interference on the ground that it is necessary in order to protect the Convention rights and freedoms of others. According to the Court, "(i)t is precisely this constant search for a balance between the fundamental rights of each individual which constitutes the foundation of a 'democratic society'". By contrast, " . . . only indisputable imperatives" can justify interference with enjoyment of a Convention right where a state seeks to protect rights and freedoms which are *not* set out in the Convention.[85]

(2) Application to inherent and implied rights

C0–15 The principles of necessity and proportionality apply not only to the express exceptions laid down by the Convention. They are also relevant to the delimitation of inherent or implied rights. Thus a limitation on the implied right of access to a court will not be compatible with Article 6(1) unless it pursues a legitimate aim and there is a reasonable relationship of proportionality between the means employed and the aim sought to be achieved.[86]

(3) Application to positive obligations

C0–16 Proportionality or fair balance also plays a role in the establishment of the scope of positive obligations. Although the Convention only expressly requires that these issues be addressed in relation to "interferences", the Court has held that "(i)n determining whether or not a positive obligation exists, regard must be had to the fair balance that has to be struck between the general interest of the community and the interests of the individuals . . . In striking this balance the aims mentioned in the second paragraph of Article 8 may be of a certain relevance . . .".[87] Finally, proportionality is relevant to the question whether a difference of treatment amounts to discrimination contrary to Article 14 of the Convention. That the same principles apply is clear from the following passage:

" . . . the principle of equality of treatment is violated if the distinction has no objective and reasonable justification. The existence of such a justification must be assessed in relation to the aim and effects of the measure under considera-

---

[81] *Camenzind v. Switzerland*, (1999) 28 E.H.R.R. 458, para. 46.
[82] See, *e.g. Johansen v. Norway*, August 7, 1996, R.J.D., 1996–III, No. 13; 23 E.H.R.R. 33, para. 64.
[83] *McCann, Farrell and Savage v. United Kingdom* (1996) 21 E.H.R.R. 97, para. 194.
[84] *James v. United Kingdom* (1986) 8 E.H.R.R. 123, para. 46.
[85] *Chassagnou and others v. France*, App. Nos 25088/94, 28331/95 and 28443/95, judgment of April 29, 1999, para. 113.
[86] *Ashingdane v. United Kingdom* (1985) 7 E.H.R.R. 528, para. 57. See also *Osman v. United Kingdom* [1999] Fam. Law 86, para. 151.
[87] *Rees v. United Kingdom* (1987) 9 E.H.R.R. 56, para. 37. See also *B v. France* (1993) 16 E.H.R.R. 1, para. 44.

tion, regard being had to the principles which normally prevail in democratic societies. A difference of treatment in the exercise of a right laid down in the Convention must not only pursue a legitimate aim; Article 14 is likewise violated when it is clearly established that there is no reasonable relationship of proportionality between the means employed and the aim sought to be realised."[88]

(4) Margin of appreciation

C0–17 We have dealt with the margin of appreciation at length elsewhere.[89] It is a degree of latitude or deference accorded to national authorities, including national courts, by the Strasbourg Court in recognition of the fact that they "are in principle in a better position than the international judge to give an opinion on the exact content of" restrictions on Convention rights.[90] National authorities, in particular the courts, may also have had the benefit of direct contact with the parties and witnesses and are in a better position to assess questions of justification. For those reasons, the Court is reluctant to substitute its own view for that of the domestic authorities.[91] However, the Strasbourg Court sets limits on the area of freedom of action, depending on context. The limits vary according to matters such as the importance of the right at stake, the particular purpose pursued by the state, and the degree to which practice varies among Convention States.

We have suggested above[91a] that, as an expression of subsidiarity, the margin of appreciation does not translate into the domestic context. On the contrary, the Strasbourg Court can take a back seat only because the national authorities—courts in particular—have engaged with the substance of issues of justification and proportionality. The need for such engagement is embedded in the very structure of the Convention which obliges states to secure the Convention rights and to provide effective remedies, which individuals must exhaust before applying to Strasbourg. This is not to say that the Convention obliges domestic courts to re-take every decision from scratch—to do so would manifestly exceed the proper limits of the judicial function—but the national court will have to adopt a more intensive review than traditional judicial review has required.

Courts will be familiar with the concept of variable intensity of scrutiny[92] depending on the seriousness of the right in issue. While not to be imported wholesale, the Strasbourg jurisprudence on the margin of appreciation will help courts establish which rights attract a higher level of scrutiny and the considerations which enable them to identify the hierarchy of Convention rights. Not surprisingly, those considerations will find echoes in domestic law. But this familiarity should not seduce courts into thinking that the judicial review court can simply carry on business as usual. For reasons which we have developed elsewhere,[93] the notions of proportionality are different from the traditional *Wednesbury* approach, and the margin of appreciation does not relieve the national court of its responsibility to scrutinise the substance of justification.

---

[88] *Belgian Linguistics case* (1968) 1 E.H.R.R. 252 at 284, para. 10.
[89] See paras 2–05 and 5–16.
[90] *Handyside v. United Kingdom* (1976) 1 E.H.R.R. 737, para. 49; *Brannigan & McBride v. United Kingdom* (1994) 17 E.H.R.R. 539.
[91] See, *e.g., Johansen v. Norway*, August 7, 1996. R.J.D., 1996–III, No. 13; 23 E.H.R.R. 33, para. 64.
[91a] See above, para. 2–05
[92] *Bugdaycay v. Secretary of State for the Home Department* [1987] A.C. 514; *R. v. Secretary of State for the Home Department, ex parte Brind* [1991] 1 A.C. 696, 748–749; *R. v. Ministry of Defence, ex parte Smith* [1996] Q.B. 517.
[93] See, in particular, paras 5–16, 5–17 and 5–19.

ARTICLE 1

OBLIGATION TO RESPECT HUMAN RIGHTS

C1–01   **The High Contracting Parties shall secure to everyone within their jurisdiction the rights and freedoms defined in Section I of this Convention.**

C1–02   This provision indicates that the Convention (and its Protocols) binds ratifying states in respect of interferences with rights defined in the Convention and Protocols and occurring with the jurisdiction of the state concerned.

C1–03   Within its sphere of application, the Convention rights are guaranteed to "everyone". The Convention may be invoked by nationals, non-nationals and stateless persons regardless of residence or domicile. Companies and other non-natural persons are also covered. It cannot, however, be invoked by one government authority against another of the same State.[1]

C1–04   States must "secure" the rights protected. The Court has stated that this means that the rights and freedoms must be "directly secured to anyone within the jurisdiction of the Contracting States".[2] Most ratifying states have incorporated the Convention into domestic law but there is no obligation to incorporate; ratifying states have discretion over how to secure the rights domestically.[3] The obligation to secure Convention rights applies whether or not the person is technically in the country concerned. In *D v. United Kingdom*[4] the U.K. Government argued that it was not responsible under the Convention because Mr D had never been granted leave to enter the United Kingdom, but had been on "temporary admission" for the duration of his prison sentence. The Commission dismissed this argument as:

> "an artificial and technical construction . . . which fails to take into account the fact that the applicant was present in the United Kingdom for over three years under the responsibility of the authorities who prosecuted and imposed a sentence of imprisonment on him."[5]

C1–05   The Convention makes further provision in Articles 13 and 14 as to how states must "secure" rights and freedoms.These respectively require an "effective remedy before a national authority" and that Convention rights and freedoms must be "secured without discrimination on any ground".[6]

C1–06   The applicability of the Convention may be extended by a ratifying state "to all or any of the territories for whose international relations it is responsible". The Commission explained the concept of jurisdiction as follows:

> ". . . [N]ationals of a State, including registered ships and aircraft are partly within its jurisdiction, wherever they may be, and . . . that authorised agents of

---

[1] See, *e.g.* the Commission's admissibility decision of September 15, 1998 in *Province of Bari, Sorrentino and Messeni Nemaga v. Italy* (Appl. No. 41877/98).
[2] *Ireland v. U.K.* (1978) 2 E.H.R.R. 25, para. 239.
[3] *Swedish Engine Drivers' Union v. Sweden* (1976) 1 E.H.R.R. 617 para. 50.
[4] May 2, 1997, R.J.D., 1997–III, No. 37; 24 E.H.R.R. 423.
[5] *ibid.*, para. 55.
[6] For commentary on these provisions see pp. 317, 322.

a State including diplomatic or consular agents and armed forces, not only remain under its jurisdiction when abroad but bring any other persons or property 'within the jurisdiction' of that State to the extent that they exercise authority over such persons or property. In so far as, by their acts or omissions, they affect such persons or property, the responsibility of the State is engaged."[7]

This admissibility decision was amongst those approved in *Drozd and Janousek v. France and Spain*,[8] where, unanimously, the Court stated:

"The term 'jurisdiction' is not limited to the national territory of the High Contracting Parties; their responsibility can be involved because of acts of their authorities producing effects outside their own territory."[9]

C1–07 A Contracting State may incur responsibility for removing an individual from its territory or refusing admission when sufficient evidence and circumstances exist that the action risks treatment contrary to Article 3 and/or fails to respect family life under Article 8.[10]

C1–08 On the other hand, care is taken to avoid extending the Convention to non-Contracting States indirectly through the responsibility of Contracting States for their actions within their jurisdiction. In *Bertrand Russell Peace Foundation v. United Kingdom*,[10a] the applicants complained of failure to take action in respect of the Soviet Union for alleged interferences with mail in breach of the Universal Postal Union Constitution. The Commission ruled that there was no right under the Convention to the diplomatic and other measures sought by the applicant; it declared the complaint incompatible with the Convention:

"Even though, as the applicant points out, Article 10 of the Convention guarantees the right to receive and impart information 'regardless of frontiers', this does not imply any right to intervention in respect of the acts of non-contracting state for which the Contracting State is in no way responsible. It merely implies that the Contracting State must, in the exercise of its jurisdiction, itself respect that right".[10b]

C1–09 Sometimes complex issues of jurisdiction can arise. In *Drozd and Janousek v. France and Spain*,[11] for example, both the Commission and Court were very divided on whether France bore responsibility under Article 5 of the Convention for imprisoning the applicant in France after he had been transferred, as was customary, to serve his sentence following a trial in Andorra which was alleged to have been unfair in some material respects. The Court's decision of no violation under Article 5 was by 12 votes to 11. Several other difficult jurisdictional issues have arisen and some have yet to be fully resolved, in particular, what

---

[7] App. No. 6780/74 and 6950/75 *Cyprus v. Turkey* (1976) 4 E.H.R.R. 482 at 586, para. 8 of the May 1925 admissibility decision.
[8] (1992) 14 E.H.R.R. 745.
[9] Para. 91 of the judgment.
[10] See below, paras C3–09—C3–11 and C8–55—C8–59.
[10a] App. No. 7597/76 14 D. & R. 117.
[10b] *ibid.*, p. 124.
[11] (1992) 14 E.H.R.R. 745.

responsibility the Contracting States have for acts done by E.C. institutions or pursuant to E.C. laws. In analysing questions of jurisdiction, principles of public international law play a significant role. In its judgment in *Matthews v. United Kingdom,* which concerned the rights of citizens of Gibraltar to vote in European Parliament elections, the Court held that:

> "The United Kingdom, together with all the other parties to the Maastricht Treaty, is responsible *ratione materiae* under Article 1 of the Convention and, in particular, under Article 3 of Protocol No. 1, for the consequences of that Treaty".[12]

C1–10   The obligations under the Convention and Protocols may be reduced by reservations made in accordance with Article 57 or subject to derogations complying with Article 15 and made by a state "in time of war or other public emergency threatening the life of the nation".[13]

---

[12] (1999) 28 E.H.R.R. 361, para. 33.
[13] See further the commentary on these provisions. The text of reservation and derogation now in force is set out below, p. 397.

Article 2
Right to life

C2–01

1 Everyone's right to life shall be protected by law. No one shall be deprived of his life intentionally save in the execution of a sentence of a court following his conviction of a crime for which this penalty is provided by law.

2 Deprivation of life shall not be regarded as inflicted in contravention of this article when it results from the use of force which is no more than absolutely necessary:

a in defence of any person from unlawful violence;

b in order to effect a lawful arrest or to prevent the escape of a person lawfully detained;

c in action lawfully taken for the purpose of quelling a riot or insurrection.

Article 1 of the Sixth Protocol
Abolition of the death penalty

C2–02 The death penalty shall be abolished. No one shall be condemned to such penalty or executed.

Article 2 of the Sixth Protocol
Death penalty in time of war

C2–03 A State may make provision in its law for the death penalty in respect of acts committed in time of war or of imminent threat of war; such penalty shall be applied only in the instances laid down in the law and in accordance with its provisions. The State shall communicate to the Secretary General of the Council of Europe the relevant provisions of that law.

C2–04 No derogation from Article 2 is permitted under Article 15 "except in respect of deaths resulting from lawful acts of war".[1] As the Court has repeatedly stated, Article 2: "ranks as one of the most fundamental provisions in the Convention and, together with Article 3 of the Convention, enshrines one of the basic values of the democratic societies that making up the Council of Europe".[2]

C2–05 Article 2 contains three distinct elements:

(a) The requirement in Article 2(1), first sentence that "everyone's right to life shall be protected by law";

---

[1] As to Article 15 see below, p. 364.
[2] *Cakici v. Turkey* judgment of July 8, 1999, para. 86, referring, *inter alia*, to its judgment in *McCann, Farrell and Savage v. United Kingdom* (1996) 21 E.H.R.R. 97, paras 146–147.

(b) Article 2(1), second sentence which covers intentional deprivation of life; and

(c) Article 2(2) which covers death resulting (but not intended) from the use of potentially lethal force.

Comments on each of these elements follow.

1. THE REQUIREMENT THAT "EVERYONE'S RIGHT TO LIFE SHALL BE PROTECTED BY LAW"

C2–06 According to the Court and Commission, this imposes a broader obligation on the state than that contained in the second sentence; it "enjoins the State not only to refrain from taking life 'intentionally' but, further, to take appropriate steps to safeguard it".[3] In *Association X v. United Kingdom*, the Association alleged that failings in the administration of the baby vaccination programmes had caused deaths and thus involved a breach of the first sentence of Article 2(1). The Commission, however, readily found that "the system of control and supervision established by the State is sufficient to comply with its obligation to protect life under Article 2".[4]

C2–07 The first sentence of Article 2 is concerned with alleged failures to take sufficient measures to protect life and, in common with the Convention practice on positive obligations, restraint is shown in reviewing the state's conduct. Thus the Commission rejected a number of complaints brought by relatives of murder victims who claimed that special protection should have been afforded to the deceased because he had been at risk.[5] The Commission's case law shows an appreciation of the difficulties of resource allocation which states face. A complaint will only be considered seriously if objective grounds exist on which the state can reasonably be criticised for having failed to act. Evidence that the state has fallen short of accepted European standards would be important, though not necessarily decisive.

C2–08 The Court has repeatedly confirmed this approach. For instance, in *Osman v. United Kingdom*,[6] which concerned the alleged failure by the police to protect the applicants and their family from the threat posed by a known individual, the Court stated that it was common ground that the state's obligation under Article 2:

"extends beyond its primary duty to secure the right to life by putting in place effective criminal law provisions to deter the commission of offences against the person backed up by law-enforcement machinery for the prevention, suppression and sanctioning of breaches of such provisions. It is thus accepted by those appearing before the Court that Article 2 of the Convention may also imply in certain well-defined circumstances a positive obligation on the authorities to take preventive operational measures to protect an individual whose life is at risk from the criminal acts of another individual."[7]

---

[3] Commission Opinion in App. No. 7154/75 *Association X v. United Kingdom* 14 D. & R. 31 at 32.
[4] *ibid.* at 35.
[5] *e.g.*, App. No. 9837/82 *M v. United Kingdom and Ireland* 47 D. & R. 27.
[6] [1999] Fam. L.R. 86.
[7] *ibid.*, para. 115.

The Court set out the scope of this positive obligation as follows:

> "For the Court, and bearing in mind the difficulties involved in policing modern societies, the unpredictability of human conduct and the operational choices which must be made in terms of priorities and resources, such an obligation must be interpreted in a way which does not impose an impossible or disproportionate burden on the authorities. Accordingly, not every claimed risk to life can entail for the authorities a Convention requirement to take operational measures to prevent that risk from materialising. Another relevant consideration is the need to ensure that the police exercise their powers to control and prevent crime in a manner which fully respects the due process and other guarantees which legitimately place restraints on the scope of their action to investigate crime and bring offenders to justice, including the guarantees contained in Articles 5 and 8 of the Convention.
>
> In the opinion of the Court where there is an allegation that the authorities have violated their positive obligation to protect the right to life in the context of their above-mentioned duty to prevent and suppress offences against the person, it must be established to its satisfaction that the authorities knew or ought to have known at the time of the existence of a real and immediate risk to the life of an identified individual or individuals from the criminal acts of a third party and that they failed to take measures within the scope of their powers which, judged reasonably, might have been expected to avoid that risk. The Court does not accept the Government's view that the failure to perceive the risk to life in the circumstances known at the time or to take preventive measures to avoid that risk must be tantamount to gross negligence or wilful disregard of the duty to protect life. Such a rigid standard must be considered to be incompatible with the requirements of Article 1 of the Convention and the obligations of Contracting States under that Article to secure the practical and effective protection of the rights and freedoms laid down therein, including Article 2.[8] For the Court, and having regard to the nature of the right protected by Article 2, a right fundamental in the scheme of the Convention, it is sufficient for an applicant to show that the authorities did not do all that could be reasonably expected of them to avoid a real and immediate risk to life of which they have or ought to have knowledge. This is a question which can only be answered in the light of all the circumstances of any particular case." [9]

Having examined the facts of that case, the Court found that there had been no violation of Article 2.

C2–09   However, the positive obligation to protect the right to life requires not only prevention of the use of force but also that "there should be some form of effective investigation when individuals have been killed as a result of the use of force."[10] In its judgment in *Kaya v. Turkey*,[11] the Court explained that:

> " . . . [T]he procedural protection for the right to life inherent in Article 2 of the Convention secures the accountability of agents of the State for their use of

---

[8] See, *mutatis mutandis, McCann and Others*, (1996) 21 E.H.R.R. 97, para. 146.
[9] Judgment of October 28, 1998, para. 106.
[10] See, *inter alia, Yasa v. Turkey*, (1999) 28 E.H.R.R. 408, para. 98; *Çakici v. Turkey* judgment of July 8, 1999, para. 86.
[11] (1999) 28 E.H.R.R. 1, see also *Güleç v. Turkey*, (1999) 28 E.H.R.R. 121, para. 78.

lethal force by subjecting their actions to some form of independent and public scrutiny capable of leading to a determination on whether the force used was or was not justified in a particular set of circumstances."[12]

2. INTENTIONAL DEPRIVATION OF LIFE

C2–10 Except for the death penalty, which is considered below, Article 2(1) unequivocally provides that "no one shall be deprived of his life intentionally". What is meant by "intentional deprivation of life" and how, if at all, does its prohibition affect the discretion of Contracting States in relation to medical and moral issues on when life begins and ends for the purposes of this provision? To date the Convention bodies have not had to rule on these potentially difficult issues. The current position is outlined in the next two paragraphs.

A. Abortion

C2–11 Complaints under Article 2 have been brought by applicants opposed to abortion but, as yet, the only admissible applications related to other provisions of the Convention. In *Paton v. United Kingdom*,[13] a father's complaint that his wife had a termination against his wishes was rejected. The Commission did not have to decide "whether Article 2 does not cover the foetus at all or whether it recognises a 'right to life' of the foetus with implied limitations". "If one assumes that this provision applies at the initial stage of the pregnancy", it found, abortion can be "covered by an implied limitation, protecting the life and health of the woman at that stage". Issues relating to abortion have also been raised under Articles 8 and 10 of the Convention.[14] In *Open Door Counselling v. Ireland*,[15] the Government argued that Article 2 of the Convention protected unborn life and that the injunction on information about abortion services in England should be assessed accordingly. The Court did not consider it necessary to rule on Article 2, concluding instead that Article 10 had been violated.[16]

B. Medical issues relating to the ending of life and euthanasia

C2–12 The Convention organs have not yet been called on to address the difficult medical and legal issues that can arise in relation to the definition of death and the granting or withholding of medical treatment in such cases. The Court is likely to show considerable restraint in assessing such issues and may well adopt an approach similar to its examination of the medical assessment of mental illness under Article 5(1)(e). In *Winterwerp v. Netherlands*,[17] the Court focussed on the adequacy of checks and safeguards but explicitly recognised the discretion of national authorities who have to assess the medical evidence and take the clinical decisions. By contrast, any formal legalisation of euthanasia would pose difficult and substantial questions if challenged under the Convention.

C. Death penalty

C2–13 Article 2(1) itself permits capital punishment provided the death sentence is prescribed by law for the crime in question and, clearly, provided the fair

---

[12] para. 87.
[13] App. No. 8416/78, 3 E.H.R.R. 408.
[14] See below, paras C8–33, C10–31.
[15] (1993) 15 E.H.R.R. 244.
[16] *ibid.* paras 65 and 66.
[17] (1979) 2 E.H.R.R. 387.

trial and legality requirements of Articles 6 and 7 of the Convention are satisfied. But two important qualifications should be noted. First, Protocol 6 amends Article 2 for ratifying states by requiring abolition of the death penalty other than when the law provides "for the death penalty in respect of acts committed in time of war or of imminent threat of war". Secondly, quite apart from Protocol No. 6, the obligations in Article 3 restrict capital punishment and the extradition of suspects who would face the risk of capital punishment in circumstances where this violates the prohibition on inhuman and degrading treatment or punishment.[18]

3. ARTICLE 2(2): DEATH RESULTING FROM THE USE OF POTENTIALLY LETHAL FORCE

C2–14   The use of lethal force received extensive consideration in *McCann, Farrell and Savage v. United Kingdom*,[19] the "Death on the Rock" case, which concerned the fatal shooting of three members of an IRA "active service unit" in Gibraltar. The Commission and the Court were largely in agreement about the principles to be applied, although there was extensive disagreement about the result in the case. The Commission found no violation by 11 votes to 6, whereas the Court found a violation by 10 votes to 9. The Court held that the sphere of protection afforded by Article 2 goes beyond the intentional deprivation of life. It observed that:

> " . . . the text of Article 2, read as a whole, demonstrates that paragraph 2 does not primarily define instances where it is permitted intentionally to kill an individual, but describes the situations where it is permitted to 'use force' which may result, as an unintended outcome, in the deprivation of life. The use of force, however, must be no more than 'absolutely necessary' for the achievement of one of the purposes set out in paragraphs (a), (b) or (c)."[20]

The provisions of Article 2 must be strictly construed.[21]

C2–15   To be acceptable, potentially lethal force must be "absolutely necessary".[22] In *Ogur v. Turkey*, the Court expressly stated that:

> " . . . the use of the term 'absolutely necessary' in Article 2(2) indicates that a stricter and more compelling test of necessity must be employed than that normally applicable when determining whether State action is 'necessary in a democratic society' under paragraph 2 of Articles 8 to 12 of the Convention. In particular, the force must be strictly proportionate to the achievement of the aims set out in sub-paragraphs 2(a), (b) and (c) of Article 2." [23]

The significance of any formal difference will depend on the manner in which it is applied in practice.

---

[18] *Soering v. United Kingdom* (1989) 11 E.H.R.R. 439. See below, para. C3–09.
[19] (1996) 21 E.H.R.R. 97.
[20] *ibid.*, para. 148.
[21] *ibid.*, para. 147.
[22] Although Article 2 of the Gibraltar Constitution propounded "reasonably necessary" as the standard of justification, the Court considered that the difference in the two standards was not sufficiently great to found a violation of Article 2(2) on that ground alone: *ibid.*, para. 155.
[23] App. No. 21594/93, judgment of May 20, 1999, para. 78.

C2–16   At issue in *McCann* was the adequacy of checks and safeguards required to ensure compliance with Article 2, including the adequacy of the Gibraltar inquest. The Court held that:

> "The obligation to protect the right to life under this provision, read in conjunction with the State's general duty under Article 1 of the Convention to 'secure to everyone within their jurisdiction the rights and freedoms defined in [the] Convention', requires by implication that there should be some form of effective official investigation when individuals have been killed as a result of the use of force by, *inter alios*, agents of the State."[24]

However, the Court was unanimous in rejecting the applicants' allegations as to the shortcomings of the inquest, holding that they did not substantially hamper the carrying out of a "thorough, impartial and careful examination" of the circumstances surrounding the killings.[25]

C2–17   The Commission and the Court agreed that Article 2 applies not only to the acts of the soldiers on the ground but also to the conduct and planning of the operation. For the majority of the Commission:

> "In these circumstances, the use of lethal force would be rendered disproportionate if the authorities failed, whether deliberately or through lack of proper care, to take steps which would have avoided the deprivation of life of the suspects without putting the lives of others at risk."[26]

The majority and the minority of the Court agreed that:

> " . . . in determining whether the force used was compatible with Article 2, the Court must carefully scrutinise . . . not only whether the force used by the soldiers was strictly proportionate to the aim of protecting persons against unlawful violence but also whether the anti-terrorist operation was planned and controlled by the authorities so as to minimise, to the greatest extent possible, recourse to lethal force."[27]

and they also agreed that:

> " . . . the use of force by agents of the State in pursuit of one of the aims delineated in Article 2(2) of the Convention may be justified under this provision where it is based on an honest belief which is perceived, for good reasons, to be valid at the time but which subsequently turns out to be mistaken. To hold otherwise would be to impose an unrealistic burden on the State and its law enforcement personnel in the execution of their duty, perhaps to the detriment of their lives and those of others."

They concluded, therefore that the actions of the soldiers did not in themselves, violate Article 2. By contrast there was strong division in the Court about the

---

[24] *ibid.*, para. 161.
[25] *ibid.*
[26] Commission report, *ibid.*, para. 235.
[27] Judgment, *ibid.*, para. 194.

responsibility of the state in the planning and control of the operation, the majority finding that the authorities had failed in their obligation to take proper care to minimise the risk to life.

C2–18   The extent of the authorities' duty of care in control and planning was also at issue in *Andronicou and Constantinou v. Cyprus*[28] which concerned a hostage rescue. The Court considered that its role was to evaluate:

" . . . whether in the circumstances the planning and control of the rescue operation including the decision to deploy the MMAD [police special forces] officers showed that the authorities had taken appropriate care to ensure that any risk to the lives of the couple had been minimised and that they were not negligent in their choice of action."[29]

[28] (1998) 25 E.H.R.R. 491.
[29] *ibid.*, para. 181.

ARTICLE 3

PROHIBITION OF TORTURE

C3–01 **No one shall be subjected to torture or to inhuman or degrading treatment or punishment.**

C3–02 Article 3 prohibits conduct which has serious physical or psychological effects on the individual concerned. In the case of torture and inhuman or degrading treatment or punishment, the physical or mental suffering must have reached a sufficient level of severity. In the case of degrading treatment or punishment, the key element is humiliation but the principle is the same: the humiliation must have reached a sufficient level of severity.[1] By way of example, in *Selçuk and Asker v. Turkey*,[2] the Court found that:

> "Mrs Selçuk and Mr Asker were aged respectively 54 and 60 at the time and had lived in the village of Islamköy all their lives. Their homes and most of their property were destroyed by the security forces, depriving the applicants of their livelihoods and forcing them to leave their village. It would appear that the exercise was premeditated and carried out contemptuously and without respect for the feelings of the applicants. They were taken unprepared; they had to stand by and watch the burning of their homes; inadequate precautions were taken to secure the safety of Mr and Mrs Asker; Mrs Selçuk's protests were ignored, and no assistance was provided to them afterwards.
>
> Bearing in mind in particular the manner in which the applicants' homes were destroyed[3] and their personal circumstances, it is clear that they must have been caused suffering of sufficient severity for the acts of the security forces to be categorised as inhuman treatment within the meaning of Article 3."[4]

The Court regards torture as deliberate inhuman treatment causing very serious and cruel suffering.[5]

C3–03 No derogation from Article 3 is permitted.[6] "The Convention prohibits in absolute terms torture and inhuman and degrading treatment or punishment irrespective of the victim's conduct."[7] Further, the Court has not countenanced any implied or inherent limitations to Article 3, and in *Tomasi v. France* it observed that "the requirements of the investigation and the undeniable difficulties inherent in the fight against crime, particularly with regard to terrorism, cannot result in limits being placed on the protection to be afforded in respect of the physical integrity of individuals."[8]

C3–04 We summarise the principal issues and cases considered under Article 3 below.

---

[1] *Ireland v. United Kingdom* 2 E.H.R.R. 25, paras 162–164 and *Tyrer v. United Kingdom* 2 E.H.R.R. 1, para. 30.
[2] 26 E.H.R.R. 477 (1998).
[3] *Akdivar and Others v. Turkey*, September 16, 1996, R.J.D., 1996–IV, No. 15; 23 E.H.R.R. 143, para. 91.
[4] Judgment of April 24, 1998, paras 77 to 78.
[5] *Aksoy v. Turkey*, December 18, 1996, R.J.D., 1996–IV, No. 26; 23 E.H.R.R. 553, para. 63.
[6] See Art. 15(2).
[7] *Ireland v. United Kingdom* 2 E.H.R.R. 25, para. 162.
[8] (1993) 15 E.H.R.R. 1, para. 115.

1. INTERROGATION TECHNIQUES

C3–05 In *Ireland v. United Kingdom*[9] the Commission and Court considered the five techniques previously used in Northern Ireland for interrogating detainees suspected of having information about terrorism. The Court held that they amounted to inhuman and degrading treatment but not torture as had been found by the Commission. The five techniques consisted of "interrogation in depth which involved the combined application of five particular techniques" *viz.* wall standing, hooding, subjection to noise, deprivation of sleep and deprivation of food and drink.[10] The Court concluded that these constituted inhuman treatment since, even if they did not cause actual bodily injury, they caused intense physical and mental suffering and led to acute psychiatric disturbances during interrogation. They were degrading since they were "such as to arouse in their victims feelings of fear, anguish and inferiority capable of humiliating and debasing them and possibly breaking their physical and moral resistance". In the Court's view, however, the techniques did not occasion suffering of the particular intensity and cruelty implied by the word torture.[11] In *Tomasi v. France* the Court found that the applicant had been subjected to inhuman and degrading treatment in breach of Article 3. Tomasi had been ill-treated "for a period of some 40 hours by some of the police officers responsible for his interrogation: he had been slapped, kicked, punched and given forearm blows, made to stand for long periods and without support, hands handcuffed behind the back; he had been spat upon, made to stand naked in front of an open window, deprived of food, threatened with a firearm and so on".[12]

C3–06 The facts constituting a violation must be proved beyond a reasonable doubt.[13] Where, however, injuries are sustained during detention in the custody of the state, the government is under an obligation to provide a plausible explanation of how the injuries were caused.[14] Where an individual has an arguable claim that he has been tortured by agents of the state, Article 13 of the Convention obliges states to carry out a thorough and effective investigation.[15] In the case of *Tekin v. Turkey*,[16] the Commission had found that, while in detention, Mr Tekin had been held in a cold and dark cell, blindfolded, and treated, in connection with his interrogation, in a way which left wounds and bruises on his body. The Court held:

> " . . . in respect of a person deprived of his liberty, recourse to physical force which has not been made strictly necessary by his own conduct diminishes human dignity and is in principle an infringement of the right set forth in Article 3.[17] It considers that the conditions in which the applicant was held, and the manner in which he must have been treated in order to leave wounds and bruises on his body, amounted to inhuman and degrading treatment within the meaning of that provision."[18]

---

[9] 2 E.H.R.R. 25.
[10] *ibid.*, paras 96–104, 106–107 and 165–168.
[11] *ibid.*, para. 167. As to interrogation techniques under the "Colonels' régime", see also the *Greek* case (1969) 12 Yearbook p. 186.
[12] (1993) 15 E.H.R.R. 1, para. 108.
[13] *Ireland v. United Kingdom* 2 E.H.R.R. 25, paras 160, 161.
[14] *Ribitsch v. Austria* (1996) 21 E.H.R.R. 573, para. 34.
[15] *Aksoy v. Turkey*, December 18, 1996, R.J.D., 1996–IV, No. 26; 23 E.H.R.R. 553, para. 98. See further below, para. C13–09.
[16] Judgment of June 9, 1999.
[17] see *Ribitsch v. Austria*, para. 38.
[18] para. 53.

2. CORPORAL PUNISHMENT

C3–07   Judicial corporal punishment was held to be degrading and contrary to Article 3 in *Tyrer v. United Kingdom*.[19] Corporal punishment in schools has also been considered under Articles 3 and 8 of the Convention and Article 2 of Protocol No. 1.[20] Since that decision the Court has considered two cases on corporal punishment in private schools. The first, *Y v. United Kingdom*,[21] resulted in a settlement under which the applicant received £8,000 in addition to his costs without any admission as to liability being made. In the second, *Costello-Roberts v. United Kingdom*,[22] a seven-year old boy was hit three times on his bottom by a teacher at a private boarding school. By a bare majority of 5 to 4, the Court found the matter insufficiently serious to come within Article 3. There was, however, a vigorous dissent and the Court specifically kept open the possibility of finding certain forms of ill-treatment in breach of Article 8. The Convention is a living instrument,[23] and accordingly the narrow decision in *Costello-Roberts* may fall to be reconsidered. The Court has recently decided the case of *A v. United Kingdom*,[24] in which a nine-year-old boy complained that his stepfather had beaten him on the legs with a garden cane with considerable force on a number of occasions. The beatings had been severe enough to leave a number of bruises which were visible several days later. The stepfather was prosecuted but acquitted of causing actual bodily harm. The Commission had concluded unanimously that the punishment caused physical injury, pain and humiliation which were serious enough to constitute degrading treatment or punishment contrary to Article 3. The Court agreed that treatment of such a kind reached the level of severity prohibited by Article 3. State responsibility was engaged by its failure to provide adequate protection to the child by means of the criminal law.

3. DISCRIMINATION

C3–08   In *East African Asians v. United Kingdom*,[25] the Commission found that the denial of entry to the United Kingdom violated Article 3 in the difficult circumstances experienced by the applicants who held British nationality and passports but did not have the "right of abode" in the United Kingdom. It observed:

> "A special importance should be attached to discrimination based on race; that publicly to single out a group of persons for differential treatment on the basis of race might in certain circumstances constitute a special form of affront to human dignity; and that differential treatment of a group of persons on the basis of race might therefore be capable of constituting degrading treatment when differential treatment on some other ground would raise no such question."[26]

---

[19] 2 E.H.R.R. 1.
[20] see further: *Campbell & Cosans v. United Kingdom* (1982) 4 E.H.R.R. 293; *Warwick v. United Kingdom*, App. No. 9471/81, 60 D. & R. 5.
[21] (1994) 17 E.H.R.R. 238.
[22] (1995) 19 E.H.R.R. 112.
[23] See above, para. C0–08.
[24] (1999) 27 E.H.R.R. 611.
[25] App. No. 4403/70 etc. (1973) 3 E.H.R.R. 76.
[26] *ibid.*, para. 207.

The Committee of Ministers, however, failed to reach a decision on the Commission's Report in this case by the required two-thirds majority. In *Abdulaziz, Cabales and Balkandali v. United Kingdom*, the Court did not accede to the discrimination argument, while leaving the position open for the future:

> "Most immigration policies–restricting as they do, free entry–differentiate on the basis of people's nationality and indirectly their race, ethnic origin and possibly their colour. Whilst a Contracting State could not implement 'policies of a purely racist nature', to give preferential treatment to its nationals or to persons from countries with which it had the closest links did not constitute 'racial discrimination'".[27]

The *East African Asians* case, of course, is to be distinguished: it concerned denial to nationals of entry into their State on grounds which differentiated on grounds of colour and racial origin. Restricting entry by nationals is plainly different from immigration controls over non-nationals. In contexts other than immigration controls, distinctions on grounds of race may well be sufficiently serious to be classified as degrading for the purposes of Article 3. The Court in *Abdulaziz* said that "the advancement of the equality of the sexes is today a major goal in the Member States of the Council of Europe".[28] On appropriate facts, a complaint could be brought under Article 3 relating to sufficiently serious and degrading treatment resulting from discrimination, particularly on grounds of race or sex. An allegation of degrading treatment was made by the transsexual applicant in *B v. France*.[29] It was rejected by the Commission[30] and not pursued before the Court, which nonetheless found a violation of Article 8. In general, where it is possible it will be wiser and easier to bring a case of discrimination under Article 8, either read alone or in conjunction with Article 14, than to do so under Article 3.

4. EXTRADITION

C3–09 In *Soering v. United Kingdom*, the Court unanimously ruled that it would be contrary to Article 3 for the applicant, a German national, to be extradited to face capital murder charges in the United States:

> "Having regard to the very long period of time spent on death row in such extreme conditions, with the ever present and mounting anguish of awaiting execution of the death penalty and to the personal circumstances of the applicant, especially his age and mental health at the time of the offence, the applicant's extradition to the United States would expose him to real risk of treatment going beyond the threshold set by Article 3."[31]

The Court, however, explicitly indicated that Article 3 had not yet operated so as to abrogate the permissibility of capital punishment under Article 2(1) of the Convention for States which have not ratified Protocol No. 6.[32]

---

[27] (1985) 7 E.H.R.R. 471, para. 84.
[28] *ibid.*, para. 78.
[29] (1993) 16 E.H.R.R. 1.
[30] paras 76 to 87 of the Report. See also *Smith and Grady v. United Kingdom*, judgment of September 27, 1999, para. 121 in which the Court held that it would not exclude the application of Article 3 to discrimination against homosexuals based on a predisposed bias on the part of a heterosexual majority.
[31] (1989) 11 E.H.R.R. 439, para. 111.
[32] See above, para. C2–14 in relation to Art. 2 and see earlier Commission admissibility decision in App. No. 10479/83 *Kirkwood v. United Kingdom* (1984) 6 E.H.R.R. 373.

5. ASYLUM AND EXPULSION

C3–10 The Court has confirmed well-established Commission case law to the effect that:

> "expulsion by a Contracting State of an asylum seeker may give rise to an issue under Article 3, and hence engage the responsibility of that State under the Convention, where substantial grounds have been shown for believing that the person concerned faced a real risk of being subjected to torture or to inhuman or degrading treatment or punishment in the country to which he was returned."[33]

Clear evidence of the "real risk" is required to bring a case under Article 3, although that risk may emanate not only from agents of the receiving State but also from other elements holding substantial power there if it is unlikely that any public authority could protect them from it.[34] By way of example, in its admissibility decision in *Ould Barar v. Sweden*,[35] the Court was faced with the threatened return to Mauritania of an applicant who had sought to escape slavery and who alleged that he would be without protection by the authorities against any punishment meted out to him by his father's master. The Court noted that there was evidence that the Mauritanian Government had not taken sufficient steps against slavery, the existence of which practice the Swedish Government acknowledged. It held that, in certain circumstances, the expulsion of a person to a country where there is officially recognised slavery might raise Article 3 issues. In this case, however, the Court found that, on the evidence, there was no indication that he would be subject to "harsh punishment of run-away slaves" in Mauritania. He had lived an independent life with his mother's family in the capital where he had studied and set up in business, he had not taken part in political activities, had not received any threats from the authorities, his clan or his father's master, and had not performed slave labour. The application was therefore declared inadmissible as manifestly ill-founded.

C3–11 Exceptionally, Article 3 may prevent expulsion where the source of the proscribed treatment in the receiving country stems from factors which cannot engage the responsibility of the public authorities of that country (*i.e.* threats from "non-state agents") or which, taken alone, do not in themselves infringe the standards of the Article. For example:

  (a) in *HLR v. France*,[36] the Court accepted that where the threat of torture, inhuman or degrading treatment emanates from persons other than the state, expulsion could still engage Article 3. In that case, the applicant had been convicted of drug-trafficking offences and had given information to the police that led to the arrest and conviction of other drug couriers; he complained that if removed to Colombia, he would be subjected to treatment contrary to Article 3. The Court held:

---

[33] *Vilvarajah v. United Kingdom* (1992) 14 E.H.R.R. 248, para. 103 following *Cruz Varas v. Sweden* (1992) 14 E.H.R.R. 1.
[34] *Ahmed v. Austria*, December 17, 1997, R.J.D, 1996–VI, No. 26; 24 E.H.R.R. 278, para. 44.
[35] App. No. 42367/98, Decision of January 19, 1999 (First Section).
[36] April 29, 1997, R.J.D., 1997–III, No. 36; 26 E.H.R.R. 29 (concerning threats by the Colombian drug mafia).

"Owing to the absolute character of the right guaranteed, the Court does not rule out the possibility that Article 3 of the Convention may also apply where the danger emanates from persons or groups of persons who are not public officials. However, it must be shown that the risk is real and that the authorities of the receiving State are not able to obviate the risk by providing appropriate protection" (para. 40).

Again, on the evidence in that case, no violation of Article 3 was found.

(b) in *D v. United Kingdom*,[37] the Court held that the removal to St Kitts of a terminally-ill AIDS sufferer would be a violation because of the acute physical and mental suffering to which he would be exposed by virtue of inadequate health care provision and the absence of the carers with whom he had formed a bond.

Once evidence of a real risk of such suffering is provided, however, there is no room to balance that risk against the undesirability of the individual's continued presence in the country.

"The prohibition provided by Article 3 against ill-treatment is equally absolute in expulsion cases. Thus, whenever substantial grounds have been shown for believing that an individual would face a real risk of being subjected to treatment contrary to Article 3 if removed to another State, the responsibility of the Contracting State to safeguard him or her against such treatment is engaged in the event of expulsion. In these circumstances, the activities of the individual in question, however, undesirable or dangerous, cannot be a material consideration. The protection afforded by Article 13 is thus wider than that provided by Articles 32 and 33 of the United Nations 1951 Convention on the Status of Refugees."[38]

When such cases were brought before the Commission, an urgent application was often introduced coupled with a request that the Commission request, under Rule 36 of Commission's Rules of Procedure, that the government suspend the person's removal pending a Commission investigation. Although Rule 36 requests were not to be binding on the state, if a state chose not to comply, "any subsequent breach of Article 3 found by the Convention organs would have to be seen as aggravated by the failure to comply with the indication".[39] The new Court has an equivalent power, under Rule 39 of the Rules of Court adopted on November 4, 1998, to "indicate to the parties any interim measures which it considers should be adopted in the interests of the parties or of the proper conduct of the proceedings before it."[40]

6. CONDITIONS OF DETENTION

C3–12 Detainees are entitled to be held in conditions which are not inhuman or degrading. Many detainees have alleged that their conditions of detention have

---

[37] May 2, 1997 R.J.D., 1997–III, No. 37; 24 E.H.R.R. 423. See also *Nasri v. France* (1996) 21 E.H.R.R. 458, considered in relation to Art. 8, below, para. C8–58.
[38] *Chahal v. United Kingdom*, November 15, 1996, R.J.D., 1996–II, No. 22; 23 E.H.R.R. 413, para. 80.
[39] *Cruz Varas v. Sweden* (1992) 14 E.H.R.R. 1, para. 103.
[40] The Rules of Court are reproduced in (1999) 27 E.H.R.R. 123.

violated Article 3. Complaints have been made about solitary confinement, overcrowding and insanitary conditions. Nearly all have failed, most at the admissibility stage. The Commission has shown great reluctance ever to classify undesirable detention conditions as inhuman or degrading. Breach of the European Prison Rules does not suffice to establish breach of Article 3. In practice, Article 3 liability has been virtually confined to deliberately inflicted ill-treatment: for example, even in *Hilton v. United Kingdom*,[41] where the majority of the Commission found that the applicant was detained in "extremely unsatisfactory conditions" it found that those conditions did not violate Article 3. The Commission noted that "there were, and still are, regrettable limitations on normal prisons, because of understaffing and overcrowding, which makes it difficult to give special attention to an individual prisoner's problems".[42]

C3–13   In *Raninen v. Finland*,[43] the Commission found that the handcuffing of a conscientious objector "as a security measure during his transportation" violated Article 3: the Ombudsman had found that the handcuffing—which had taken place in the prison yard in the full view of the applicant's supporters—was unlawful and unjustified, and the Commission considered it sufficiently humiliating to amount to a violation. The Court disagreed, considering that handcuffing did not normally give rise to issue under Article 3 when it was imposed in connection with lawful arrest or detention and did not entail the use of force or public exposure exceeding what was reasonably considered necessary in the circumstances. Although the applicant had felt humiliated appearing handcuffed in front of members of his support group, it had not adversely affected his mental state, nor was it aimed at debasing or humiliating him. In consequence it had not attained the minimum level of severity required for a violation of Article 3.

C3–14   Conditions of detention may amount to inhuman treatment where they are such as to cause the detainee ill-health, and in such cases, particular attention will be paid to the availability of medical treatment.[44] In addition, detention of persons of unsound mind in an unsatisfactory, or non-therapeutic, environment may amount to a violation of Article 5.[45] Removal from association does not normally amount to inhuman or degrading treatment, but it will depend on the conditions, duration, purpose and the effects on the person concerned.[46]

---

[41] (1981) 3 E.H.R.R. 104.
[42] para. 101.
[43] (1997) 26 E.H.R.R. 563.
[44] *Lukanov v. Bulgaria* (1995) 19 E.H.R.R. CD 65.
[45] *Aerts v. Belgium* 61/1997/845/1051, judgment of July 30, 1998.
[46] *Koskinen v. Finland* (1994) 18 E.H.R.R. CD 146.

ARTICLE 4

PROHIBITION OF SLAVERY AND FORCED LABOUR

C4–01

1 No one shall be held in slavery or servitude.

2 No one shall be required to perform forced or compulsory labour.

3 For the purpose of this article the term "forced or compulsory labour" shall not include:

    a any work required to be done in the ordinary course of detention imposed according to the provisions of Article 5 of this Convention or during conditional release from such detention;

    b any service of a military character or, in case of conscientious objectors in countries where they are recognised, service exacted instead of compulsory military service;

    c any service exacted in case of an emergency or calamity threatening the life or well-being of the community;

    d any work or service which forms part of normal civic obligations.

C4–02   Article 4 distinguishes between the prohibition of "slavery or servitude" on the one hand and that of "forced labour" on the other.

1. SLAVERY AND SERVITUDE

C4–03   Slavery and servitude are prohibited absolutely. No derogation is permitted under Article 15 nor can the circumstances listed in Article 4(3) ever be used to justify treatment which objectively falls within the scope of Article 4(1). In defining these terms reference is made to the Slavery Convention of 1926 and to the Supplementary Convention of 1956. The 1926 Convention refers to "status or condition of a person over whom any or all of the powers attaching to the right of ownership are exercised". Complaints have been made relating to Article 4(1) but no violation has ever been found. In *Van Droogenbroeck v. Belgium*, the Court had no difficulty confirming the Commission's opinion that the applicant had not been subjected to servitude when, as a criminal recidivist, a Court ordered that he be "placed at the Government's disposal":

> "The situation complained of did not violate Article 5(1). Accordingly, it could have been regarded as servitude only if it involved a 'particularly serious' form of 'denial of freedom', which was not so in the present case".[1]

It then proceeded to examine the case in relation to "forced labour" and found the work authorised under Article 4(3)(a) as "required to be done in the ordinary course of detention".

C4–04   Only in extreme circumstances, falling under the terms of, or closely analogous to, the 1926 or 1956 Conventions, will a situation be characterised as

---

[1] (1982) 4 E.H.R.R. 443, para. 58.

raising an issue under Article 4(1). Most cases likely to arise will relate to "forced or compulsory labour" and fall to be considered under Article 4 (2) and/or (3).

2. FORCED LABOUR

A. Definition of forced labour

C4–05 The first point to consider in relation to Article 4(2) or (3) is whether the conduct complained of can properly be characterised as "forced labour". In the leading case of *Van der Mussele v. Belgium*, the Court unanimously found no "forced labour" in the obligation on pupil advocates in Belgium to represent clients without payment if so directed by the Belgian Bar. Guidance was given on how "forced or compulsory labour" should be defined:

> "The first of these adjectives brings to mind the idea of physical or mental constraint . . . As regards the second adjective, it cannot refer just to any form of legal compulsion or obligation. For example work to be carried out in pursuance of a freely negotiated contract cannot be regarded as falling within the scope of Article 4 on the sole ground that one of the parties has undertaken with the other to do that work and will be subject to sanctions if he does not honour his promise . . . What there has to be is work 'exacted . . . under the menace of any penalty'; and also performed against the will of the person concerned, that is work for which he 'has not offered himself voluntarily'."[2]

The Court referred to Convention 29 of the International Labour Organisation in arriving at *this* interpretation of "forced or compulsory labour". The Court acknowledged that "the state of affairs complained of undoubtedly caused . . . some prejudice" but added that this had "not been shown to be excessive".[3] In the Commission's opinion, in addition to being performed against the individual's will, forced labour "must be either unjust or oppressive or the service itself must constitute an avoidable hardship".[4]

B. Discrimination and forced labour

C4–06 Even where work does not otherwise fall within the definition of "forced labour", it may still be possible to raise an issue under the Convention by reference to the prohibition of discrimination in Article 14. This possibility was examined (and rejected) in *Van Der Mussele v. Belgium*, as the Court put it:

> "The criteria which serve to delimit the concept of compulsory labour include the notion of what is in the normal course of affairs. Work or labour that is itself normal may be rendered abnormal if the choice of the groups or individuals bound to perform it is governed by discriminatory factors . . . "[5]

---

[2] (1984) 6 E.H.R.R. 163, para. 34.
[3] *ibid.*, para. 40.
[4] *Van Der Mussele v. Belgium*, para. 93 of the Commission's Report Series B (judgment of the Court at (1984) 6 E.H.R.R. 163); and see further App. No. 9322/81, 32 D. & R. 180 (complaint about the Dutch football transfer fee system was manifestly ill-founded, it did not involve forced labour) and App. No. 23866/94 *Reitmayr v. Austria* (1995) 20 E.H.R.R. CD 89 (complaint about the obligation of medical practitioner to conduct examinations without charge was manifestly ill-founded).
[5] (1984) 6 E.H.R.R. 163, para. 43.

As is explained in relation to Article 14, much turns on how much discretion Contracting States are allowed in determining which categories of situations are different.[6]

C4–07 In such case law as exists on Articles 4 and 14, the Court and Commission have allowed states a broad margin of appreciation. In *Van Der Mussele* the applicant failed to impress the Strasbourg institutions with comparisons made between the Bar and other professions, including the judicial and parajudicial professions. In its Report in *Grandrath v. Germany*,[7] the Commission rejected a complaint by a Jehovah's Witness "bible study conductor" that he had suffered discrimination by being required to undertake civilian service whilst Catholic and Protestant ordained ministers were exempt from both military and substitute service; ministers of other religions were likewise exempted provided their functions were equivalent to those of an ordained minister. Grandrath, who had a full-time job doing "ordinary work", was not found to satisfy this criterion. More recently the Commission rejected as manifestly ill-founded a complaint by a Dutch conscientious objector that he had to spend 18 months and 20 days doing substitute civilian service whereas the normal duration of military service was 14 months,[8] and in *Spöttl v. Austria*,[9] the Commission rejected a complaint that male conscientious objectors were required to carry out substitute civilian service while no corresponding obligation was placed on women, for whom there was no compulsory military service.

C4–08 The Court did, however, find a violation of Article 14 read with Article 4(3)(d) in *Schmidt v. Germany*.[10] Men, but not women, were required to serve as local firemen or pay a service levy in lieu. Since there were in fact already enough volunteer firefighters, both male and female, in practice the only obligation was to pay the levy. The Court found that sex discrimination could not be justified in relation to the imposition of this financial burden.

C4–09 It is therefore clearly possible to invoke Article 14 in appropriate cases in conjunction with either Article 4(2) or any of the heads of Article 4(3) and it remains important to check this issue in considering any possible complaint touching the subject-matter of Article 4.

C. Circumstances in which work may be required that otherwise would be qualified as "forced"

C4–10 Article 4(3) excludes four categories of work or service. The Commission has examined several complaints relating to Article 4(3) but no violations have yet been found. In considering any possible complaint under sub-paragraphs (a), (c) or (d), it would be important to consider whether the work or service required can be shown not to be "ordinary" (the term used in relation to work by detainees in sub-paragraph (a)) or "normal" (the term used in relation to civic obligations in sub-paragraph (d)). In turn this is very likely to require reference to accepted European standards. Only if the matters complained of can be demonstrated to

---

[6] See below, p. 33.
[7] App. No. 2299/64, 10 Yearbook 626.
[8] App. No. 11850/85, 51 D. & R. 180.
[9] App. No. 22956/93 (1996) 22 E.H.R.R. CD 88.
[10] (1994) 18 E.H.R.R. 513.

depart from such standards will there be any real prospect of a successful complaint under these sub-paragraphs.

C4–11   Article 4(3)(b) calls for some additional comments:

(a) There is no right to conscientious objection under the Convention. This is indicated in the terms of the sub-paragraph and the early case law of the Commission, which has been repeatedly re-affirmed.[11]

(b) A relevant Council of Europe recommendation exists on conscientious objection. It is evidence that European standards are evolving towards recognition of rights of conscientious objection.

(c) Sub-paragraph (b) covers regular soldiers, not just conscripts. This was established in the early admissibility decision in the *"Boy Soldiers"* case.[12] Doubt must exist whether the admissibility decision would be followed now in its acceptance of minors of 15 and 16 volunteering for military service and committing themselves to serve nine years after reaching the age of 18. Even with parental consent, the practice looks highly questionable in the light of subsequent Court judgments which have emphasised the importance of showing clear consent to any waiving of rights and to developments on the rights of the child, especially the International Convention of 1989.[13] However this may be, no question mark exists over the Commission's position that volunteer military service is included in the scope of sub-paragraph (b), since neither its terms nor policy considerations suggest any other interpretation.

C4–12   Article 4(3) excludes certain compulsory work from the prohibition under Article 4(2). This includes work undertaken by prisoners. [14] Military service is expressly permitted and alternative civilian service is not required under the text of the Convention.

---

[11] *Grandrath v. Germany* App. No. 2299/64,10 Yearbook 626, and see, *e.g.*, App. No. 10600/83 *Johansen v. Norway* 44 D. & R. 155.
[12] App. No. 3435–3438/67 *W, X, Y & Z v. United Kingdom* 11 Yearbook 562.
[13] (1989) 28 *International Legal Materials* 1448, on which see Van Bueren, *The International Convention on the Rights of the Child* (1995).
[14] *Van Droogenbroeck v. Belgium* (1982) 4 E.H.R.R. 443 (paras 57–60).

ARTICLE 5

RIGHT TO LIBERTY AND SECURITY

C5–01

1 Everyone has the right to liberty and security of person. No one shall be deprived of his liberty save in the following cases and in accordance with a procedure prescribed by law:

a the lawful detention of a person after conviction by a competent court;

b the lawful arrest or detention of a person for non-compliance with the lawful order of a court or in order to secure the fulfilment of any obligation prescribed by law;

c the lawful arrest or detention of a person effected for the purpose of bringing him before the competent legal authority on reasonable suspicion of having committed an offence or when it is reasonably considered necessary to prevent his committing an offence or fleeing after having done so;

d the detention of a minor by lawful order for the purpose of educational supervision or his lawful detention for the purpose of bringing him before the competent legal authority;

e the lawful detention of persons for the prevention of the spreading of infectious diseases, of persons of unsound mind, alcoholics or drug addicts or vagrants;

f the lawful arrest or detention of a person to prevent his effecting an unauthorised entry into the country or of a person against whom action is being taken with a view to deportation or extradition.

2 Everyone who is arrested shall be informed promptly, in a language which he understands, of the reasons for his arrest and of any charge against him.

3 Everyone arrested or detained in accordance with the provisions of paragraph 1.c of this article shall be brought promptly before a judge or other officer authorised by law to exercise judicial power and shall be entitled to trial within a reasonable time or to release pending trial. Release may be conditioned by guarantees to appear for trial.

4 Everyone who is deprived of his liberty by arrest or detention shall be entitled to take proceedings by which the lawfulness of his detention shall be decided speedily by a court and his release ordered if the detention is not lawful.

5 Everyone who has been the victim of arrest or detention in contravention of the provisions of this article shall have an enforceable right to compensation.

C5–02   Article 5 of the Convention is a fundamental provision which safeguards the individual from unlawful arrest; there has been very extensive case law on the provision.

C5–03   The Court has repeatedly described the overall approach to Article 5 thus:

" . . . the list of exceptions to the right to liberty secured in Article 5(1) is an exhaustive one and only a narrow interpretation of those exceptions is consistent with the aim and purpose of that provision, namely to ensure that no one is arbitrarily deprived of his or her liberty."[1]

As a consequence, where an individual continues to be detained after his detention ceases to be justified under one sub-paragraph of Article 5(1) and before it becomes justified under another, such detention will amount to a breach of Article 5(1). In *Quinn v. France*, the applicant had been in detention on remand until, at 9 a.m. on August 4, 1989, his release "forthwith" was ordered in his absence. He was not, however, notified of this decision or released "forthwith" but continued to be detained for another 11 hours, by which time extradition proceedings had been initiated and a legal basis found to re-arrest the applicant at the prison. In respect of those 11 hours, the Court, unanimously, found a violation of Article 5(1).[2]

C5–04   In its judgment in *Kurt v. Turkey*, the Court further stated:

" . . . the authors of the Convention reinforced the individual's protection against arbitrary deprivation of his or her liberty by guaranteeing a corpus of substantive rights which are intended to minimise the risk of arbitrariness by allowing the act of deprivation of liberty to be amenable to independent judicial scrutiny and by securing the accountability of the authorities for that act. The requirements of Article 5(3) and (4) with their emphasis on promptitude and judicial control assume particular importance in this context. Prompt judicial intervention may lead to the detection and prevention of life-threatening measures or serious ill-treatment which violate the fundamental guarantees contained in Articles 2 and 3 of the Convention. What is at stake is both the protection of the physical liberty of individuals as well as their personal security in a context which, in the absence of safeguards, could result in a subversion of the rule of law and place detainees beyond the reach of the most rudimentary forms of legal protection.

The Court emphasises in this respect that the unacknowledged detention of an individual is a complete negation of these guarantees and a most grave violation of Article 5. Having assumed control over that individual it is incumbent on the authorities to account for his or her whereabouts. For this reason, Article 5 must be seen as requiring authorities to take effective measures to safeguard against the risk of disappearance and to conduct a prompt effective investigation into an arguable claim that a person has been taken into custody and has not been seen since."[3]

In that case the Court found a "particularly grave violation of the right to liberty" because, the applicant's son having been held by soldiers, his detention was not logged and there was no official trace of his whereabouts or fate.

C5–05   The existing case law concerning Article 5 mainly concerns questions of legality of detention of an individual by the state party to the Convention. In its

---

[1] *Quinn v. France* (1996) 21 E.H.R.R. 529, para. 42. See also *Van der Leer v. Netherlands* (1990) 12 E.H.R.R. 567 and *Loukanov v. Bulgaria* (1997) 24 E.H.R.R. 121.
[2] *cf. Johnson v. United Kingdom*, October 24, 1997, R.J.D., 1997–VII, No. 55; 27 E.H.R.R. 296.
[3] (1999) 27 E.H.R.R. 373, paras 123–124.

admissibility decision in *M.A.R. v. United Kingdom*,[4] however, the Commission declared admissible a complaint that the removal of the applicant to Iran, where he would run a very real risk of detention and trial in flagrant breach of the rights guaranteed, *inter alia*, by Articles 5 and 6, would amount to a violation of those provisions attributable to the United Kingdom. The applicant's argument relied strongly on an application by analogy of the Strasbourg jurisprudence in relation to Article 3.[5] No opinion on the merits of this complaint was ever adopted by the Commission, as the case was settled: the deportation order against the applicant was revoked and he was granted indefinite leave to remain and the right to apply for a Home Office travel document.[6]

C5–06 The scope of Article 5 and the case law which has arisen under it are shown in the following paragraphs by examining the following issues:

(a) definition of detention;

(b) circumstances in which detention is permitted under Article 5;

(c) procedural guarantees Article 5 requires detainees to receive; and

(d) right to compensation for those who have suffered detention in contravention of Article 5.

C5–07 Article 5 may be subject to derogations made in accordance with Article 15 of the Convention.[7] Certain of the guarantees of Article 5, however, may in practice be close to non-derogable. The right to *habeas corpus* was held to be specially protected by the Inter-American Court of Human Rights.[8] Article 27 of the American Convention differs from Article 15 of the European Convention in providing explicitly that no derogation shall be made to "the judicial guarantees essential for the protection of [non-derogable] rights". How far a similar requirement is implicit in the European Convention was been raised in the case of *Brannigan and McBride v. United Kingdom*.[9] The Court rejected submissions of lack of effective safeguards, it "was satisfied that such safeguards do in fact exist and provide an important measure of protection against arbitrary behaviour and incommunicado detention".[10] The Court took account of "the existence of basic safeguards against abuse" in finding that the respondent had not exceeded its margin of appreciation.[11]

1. DEFINITION OF "DETENTION"

C5–08 The guarantees in Article 5 apply only to restrictions on liberty amounting to detention. Lesser restrictions on freedom of movement, not involving actual detention, fall outside its scope but may raise issues under other Convention

---

[4] App. No. 28038/95, (1997) 23 E.H.R.R. CD 120.
[5] See above, paras C3–09—C3–11 and, in particular, the Court's dictum in *Ahmed v. Austria*, December 17, 1997, R.J.D., 1996–VI, No. 26; 24 E.H.R.R. 278, para. 44.
[6] Report of the Commission dated September 19, 1997.
[7] See *Lawless v. Ireland* (1961) 1 E.H.R.R. 15 and *Ireland v. United Kingdom* (1978) 2 E.H.R.R. 25.
[8] See *Habeas Corpus in Emergency Situations* (1988) 11 E.H.R.R. 33.
[9] (1994) 17 E.H.R.R. 539.
[10] para. 62.
[11] para. 66.

provisions notably Article 2 of Protocol No. 4. Three points should be noted in relation to Article 2 of Protocol No. 4. First, it does not require state parties to provide the extensive procedural guarantees of Article 5. Secondly, some state parties, including the United Kingdom, have not ratified Protocol No. 4 and so are not bound by its provisions. Thirdly, there is relatively little case law relating to Article 2 of Protocol No. 4. In considerable measure, however, this may be understood in view of the important and extensive protection of rights of freedom of movement under E.C. law, often extending to non-nationals of E.C. Member States.

C5–09   The Convention case law provides guidance on the degree of restraint required for restrictions to amount to "detention" and so to attract the guarantees of Article 5. Detention in prisons, mental hospitals or other places of detention clearly qualifies as did "strict arrest" imposed on soldiers for disciplinary offences in *Engel v. Netherlands*.[12] In *Guzzardi v. Italy*[13] the Court held that an order for compulsory residence of a suspected Mafia member on a small island subject to strict police supervision was a deprivation of liberty. By contrast, no "detention" occurred during his period of restriction on a larger island subject to a less strict regime.[14]

C5–10   In *Guzzardi*'s case, the Court observed that:

"the difference between deprivation of and restriction upon liberty is nonetheless merely one of degree or intensity, and not one of nature or substance".[15]

Detention did not occur when a 10–year old girl was questioned about some thefts for some two hours at a police station but without at any point being arrested, locked up or formally detained.[16] Even very short periods of detention, however, come within Article 5, for example, when a compulsory blood test was performed following a court order.[17]

C5–11   When faced with the issue of asylum seekers held in an "international zone" at Paris-Orly airport, the Court accepted that this amounted to "detention" within the meaning of Article 5. The French Government had argued, and the Commission had accepted, that this did not amount to "detention" and therefore Article 5 did not apply because "the applicants could at any time have removed themselves from the sphere of application of the measure in issue".[18]

C5–12   In calculating the period of detention the Court, in its judgment in *Kemmache v. France (No. 3)*,[19] indicated that detention, for the purposes of Article 5, will be taken to have ended at the time of the applicant's actual release and not

---

[12] (1976) 1 E.H.R.R. 647.
[13] (1981) 3 E.H.R.R. 333.
[14] See further *Ciulla v. Italy* (1989) 13 E.H.R.R. 346; *Raimondo v. Italy* (1994) 18 E.H.R.R. 237; as well as the Commission in App. No. 16360/90 *F v. Switzerland*, Decision of March 2, 1994, unpublished (confinement to a small part of Switzerland) and App. No. 26249/95 *Dick v. United Kingdom* (1996) 21 E.H.R.R. CD 107 (Saisie issued by Jersey courts preventing departure from island).
[15] para. 93 of the judgment.
[16] App. No. 8819/79, 24 D. & R. 158.
[17] App. No. 8278/78 18 D. & R. 154.
[18] *Amuur v. France*, June 10, 1996, R.J.D., 1996–III, No. 10, para. 36; 22 E.H.R.R. 533, para. 46.
[19] (1995) 19 E.H.R.R. 349, para. 34.

the date on which the relevant court or authority ordered his release subject to payment of a security.

C5–13   Detention presupposes constraint: it does not cover cases where the individual consents to the restriction, for example, voluntary mental patients. Consent, however, must be clearly established in such cases for the guarantees of Article 5 to be inapplicable. In *De Wilde, Ooms and Versyp v. Belgium* (*the "Vagrancy Case"*),[20] consent to a detention order for vagrancy was not found merely because the individuals concerned had "reported voluntarily to the police" as a result of homelessness and distressed circumstances. The Court found the confinement to have been compulsory. By contrast, in *Nielsen v. Denmark*,[21] a narrow majority of the Court found that no deprivation of liberty had occurred when a 12–year–old boy's mother consented to his confinement in a psychiatric hospital against his wish and that of his father. In finding that no detention had occurred, the court took account of, (a) the fact his mother had sole legal guardianship of the child, (b) the conditions in the ward, and (c) the child's opportunities for leaving it. Although it is a recent decision, there must be doubt how far, if at all, *Nielsen's* case will be followed in future. In considering any similar issue today, account should be taken of the Convention on the Rights of the Child 1989.

2.   CIRCUMSTANCES IN WHICH DETENTION IS PERMITTED UNDER ARTICLE 5

A.   Detention is only permitted under Article 5(1) if it comes within one of the grounds listed in Article 5(1)(a) to (f)

C5–14   Before outlining the scope of each of these grounds, an explanation is necessary of the general requirements, common to all the grounds in Article 5(1), that any deprivation of liberty must be "lawful" and effected "in accordance with a procedure prescribed by law". As the Court expressed it in *Herczegfalvy v. Austria* "if detention is to be lawful . . . it must essentially comply with national law and the substantive and procedural rules thereof".[22]

C5–15   These general requirements mean that any detention must be lawful under domestic law, imposed for a proper purpose and effected in a procedurally regular manner. These are specific instances of the general requirement in the Convention that the rule of law must be properly observed. If this does not occur, the Convention will be violated. These requirements protect against extreme human rights violations such as the disappearance of prisoners. The Commission, in its second *Cyprus v. Turkey* Report, stated that:

"[a]ny deprivation of liberty must be subject to control . . . any unaccounted disappearance of a detained person must be considered as a particularly serious violation of [Article 5(1)], which can be considered as a guarantee against such disappearances".[23]

---

[20] (1971) 1 E.H.R.R. 373, para. 65.
[21] (1989) 11 E.H.R.R. 175.
[22] (1993) 15 E.H.R.R. 432, para. 63.
[23] (1993) 15 E.H.R.R. 509, para. 119.

These principles also require states to act with careful respect for legal process when keeping anyone in detention.

C5–16 The Court, in its judgment in *Kemmache v. France (No. 3)* made clear that:

> "Although it is not normally the Court's task to review the observance of domestic law by the national authorities, it is otherwise in relation to matters where, as here, the Convention refers directly back to that law; for, in such matters, disregard of the domestic law entails a breach of the Convention, with the consequence that the Court can and should exercise a certain power of review."[24]

This does not, however, extend to the assessment of whether detention is "lawful" within the context of Article 5(1)(c), where the Court, in principle, will not assess itself the facts which have led the national court to adopt one decision rather than another. The Court will merely examine whether the decisions disclose an abuse of authority, bad faith or arbitrariness.[25]

C5–17 The cases of *Bozano v. France*[26] and *Bouamar v. Belgium*[27] well illustrate the Convention approach. Article 5(1)(f) was the Convention provision potentially relevant in *Bozano*; it permits detention "of a person against whom action is being taken with a view to deportation or extradition". Bozano had been arrested in France for extradition to Italy where he had been convicted in his absence and sentenced to life imprisonment. The French courts, however, denied extradition on the ground that it would be contrary to French public policy. Nevertheless, Bozano was arrested at night, detained by police, served with a deportation order and forthwith deported to Switzerland, from where he was later returned to Italy. The deportation order and the manner of its execution were subsequently declared wholly irregular and illegal by the French courts. The European Court therefore found that the arrest and detention had not been "lawful":

> "depriving Mr Bozano of his liberty in this way amounted in fact to a disguised extradition designed to circumvent the negative ruling [of the French Court] and not to 'detention' necessary in the ordinary course of 'action . . . taken with a view to deportation'."[28]

C5–18 Article 5(1)(d) was the Convention provision potentially relevant in *Bouamar*; it permits "the lawful detention of a minor by lawful order for the purpose of educational supervision". The Court rejected the Government's reliance on Article 5(1)(d) in respect of Bouamar who had been detained for a total of 119 days out of a period of 291 days and again thereafter; the Court stated:

> "the nine placement orders, taken together, were not compatible with sub-paragraph (d). Their fruitless repetition had the effect of making them less and

---

[24] (1995) 19 E.H.R.R. 349, para. 37.
[25] *ibid.*, para. 45.
[26] (1987) 9 E.H.R.R. 297.
[27] (1989) 11 E.H.R.R. 1.
[28] *ibid.*, para. 60.

less 'lawful' under sub-paragraph (d), especially as Crown Counsel never instituted criminal proceedings in respect of the alleged offenses against him."[29]

C5–19   Together *Bozano* and *Bouamar* show how the Convention requires that any arrest or detention must be effected in good faith for a legitimate purpose and conducted in a regular procedural manner. The Convention bodies have competence to check whether domestic standards have been respected.[30] In the absence of a finding by the national court that the detention was irregular in some way, the Strasbourg bodies will only intervene where a clear cut case of irregularity at the domestic level can be shown. It is not the function of the Strasbourg institutions to review the decisions of national authorities under the Convention, those authorities enjoy "a certain discretion" and it is not the Convention's role or function to duplicate it.

B.   Article 5(1)(a)—detention after conviction

C5–20   Article 5(1)(a) provides that the state may detain an individual after his or her conviction by a competent court. The Court has explained, in *Weeks v. United Kingdom* that:

> "the word 'after' in sub-paragraph (a) does not simply mean that the detention must follow the 'conviction' in point of time: in addition, the detention must result from, 'follow and depend upon' or occur 'by virtue of" the "conviction'. In short, there must be a sufficient causal connection between the conviction and the deprivation of liberty at issue."[31]

C5–21   In *Weeks v. United Kingdom*, the original conviction and sentence to life imprisonment were held not to justify recall several years after the applicant had been released on licence. It should be noted, however, that Weeks had been sentenced to life imprisonment, not because of the gravity of his offence but because, at the time of sentence, he was judged dangerous because of instability and personality disorder, grounds "by their very nature susceptible of change with the passage of time".

C5–22   When a sentence of imprisonment is imposed under Article 5(1)(a) after conviction, the judicial supervision of the lawfulness of detention required by Article 5(4) is incorporated in the decision of the trial court.[32] Subsequent judicial supervision, however, is still required where continued imprisonment is insufficiently linked to the original sentence as in the *Weeks* case.[33] In *Thynne, Wilson and Gunnell v. United Kingdom*,[34] the Court held that separate Article 5(4) proceedings were required when it was clear that "the punitive period" of the life sentences had expired, notwithstanding that the applicants had been convicted of "offences of the utmost gravity meriting lengthy terms of imprisonment". In *Thynne, Wilson and*

---

[29] (1987) 9 E.H.R.R. 297, para. 53.
[30] *Bozano v. France* (1987) 9 E.H.R.R. 297, para. 58.
[31] (1988) 10 E.H.R.R. 293, para. 42.
[32] *De Wilde, Ooms and Versyp v. Belgium (The Vagrancy case)* (1971) 1 E.H.R.R. 373, para. 76.
[33] See above, para. C5–12: see also *Van Droogenbroeck v. Belgium* (1982) 4 E.H.R.R. 443 and *E v. Norway* (1994) 17 E.H.R.R. 666.
[34] (1991) 13 E.H.R.R. 666.

Gunnell v. United Kingdom, the Court accepted that there is an important difference between mandatory and discretionary life sentences with regard to Article 5(4), namely that discretionary life sentences were imposed not by reason of the inherent gravity of the offence but because of the presence factors which were susceptible to change with the passage of time, such as mental instability and dangerousness. A discretionary life sentence was therefore considered to have a protective purpose.[35] In *Hussain (and Singh) v. United Kingdom*, the Court held that detention "during Her Majesty's pleasure" (HMP) after the tariff period has expired is more comparable to a discretionary life sentence,"[36] and that in consequence the applicant was entitled to continued protection under Article 5(4). In *T & V. v. United Kingdom*, which concerned the HMP detention of two young boys convicted of murder, the Commission considered that Article 5(4) entitled the applicants to a periodic judicial review of their detention after a very short period. Since HMP detention is justified only by considerations of risk to the public, only a short tariff is permissible: children aged eleven might be expected to develop physically, intellectually and emotionally over the following years, so that the considerations of risk may change. The Commission considered that there was a violation since the applicants had been detained for five years without review and with no prospect of an early review.[37]

C5–23   In *Wynne v. United Kingdom*, the Court unanimously rejected the applicant's complaint on the basis that the applicant's detention was based both on a (revoked) mandatory life sentence and a subsequent discretionary life sentence. The Court rejected the applicant's attempt submission that it should re-visit its earlier ruling on the distinction between mandatory and discretionary life sentences.[38]

C5–24   Article 5(1)(a) justifies detention even if an appeal has been lodged against the original conviction and sentence.[39] Article 5(1)(a) does not require a "lawful" conviction, it only speaks of a "lawful" detention. Thus a successful appeal against a conviction does not retroactively affect the lawfulness of the detention which followed that conviction. Even if the domestic court, in convicting the applicant, committed errors in applying domestic law the detention may nevertheless be "lawful".[40] However, in relation to the latter, any finding of lawfulness will depend upon the circumstances of the individual case in light of the objective of Article 5 to protect the individual from arbitrariness.[41]

C5–25   The term "competent court" means a competent judicial body that offers adequate procedural guarantees and operates independently of the executive and the parties to a given case: see the *Vagrancy* case[42] and *Engel*.[43]

---

[35] *ibid.*, paras 73 and 74.
[36] February 21, 1996, R.J.D., 1996–I, No. 4; 22 E.H.R.R. 1, para. 54.
[37] App. No. 24724/94, Report of the Commission dated December 4, 1998.
[38] (1995) 19 E.H.R.R. 333.
[39] *Wemhoff v. Federal Republic of Germany* (1976) 1 E.H.R.R. 55 and see *Van Droogenbroeck v. Belgium* (1982) 4 E.H.R.R. 443.
[40] See Commission Decisions in *Krzycki v. Germany* (1978) 13 D. & R. 57 and in App. Nos. 19233 and 19234/91 *Tsirlis and Kouloumpas v. Greece*, July 1, 1997, R.J.D., 1997–IV, No. 4; 21 E.H.R.R. CD 30.
[41] *Tsirlis and Kouloumpas v. Greece* (1998) 25 E.H.R.R. 198 (detention following conviction had no basis in domestic law and was therefore arbitrary); and see also Commission Opinion in App. No. 6694/74 (1977) 8 D. & R. 73.
[42] (1971) 1 E.H.R.R. 373.
[43] (1976) 1 E.H.R.R. 647, para. 68.

C. Article 5(1)(b)–non-compliance with the lawful order of a court or in order to secure the fulfilment of any obligation prescribed by law

C5–26   Article 5(1)(b) Care has been taken to construe Article 5(1)(b), potentially a very open-ended provision, so that it can only be relied on in limited circumstances when to do so does not effectively circumvent requirements for detention under other paragraphs of Article 5(1). Thus Article 5(1)(b) was held not to justify the internment of a suspected member of the IRA[44] nor the detention of Dutch soldiers for breach of military discipline.[45] The Court has interpreted the phrase "secure the fulfilment of any obligation prescribed by law" as concerning "only cases where the law permits the detention of a person to compel him to fulfil a specific and concrete obligation which he has until then failed to satisfy". It rejected a wide interpretation justifying "administrative internment meant to compel a citizen to discharge, in relation to any point whatsoever, his general duty of obedience to the law".[46] Subsequently, the Commission took account of the problem of terrorism in Northern Ireland and held that Article 5(1)(b) could justify detention for questioning under the Prevention of Terrorism Order. It was made clear, however, that the circumstances were exceptional and that normally only a person's refusal or neglect to comply with a specific legal obligation can justify detention to secure its fulfilment. Further, the nature of the obligation whose fulfilment is sought must be compatible with the Convention and could not consist "in substance merely of an obligation to submit to detention".[47] This latter point has been stressed by the Court in two other judgments: it stated that Article 5(1)(b) "denotes an obligation of a specific nature already incumbent on the person concerned".[48]

C5–27   In *Benham v. United Kingdom* the Court held that the applicant's imprisonment for non-payment of community charge could be justified under Article 5(1)(b), as its purpose was to "secure the fulfilment of B's obligation to pay the community charge owed by him".[49] The applicant in that case had complained that his detention was not "lawful" under domestic law, or arbitrary. The Commission, in its opinion, held that the original decision had not been "lawful" as the magistrates had failed to conduct an adequate inquiry into whether the applicant's failure to pay was due to culpable neglect. The Court, however, held that, although the Divisional Court had quashed the magistrates' order, it had not been established "with any degree of certainty" that the order for detention was unlawful under national law. Article 5(1)(b) had therefore not been violated. *Perks v. United Kingdom*,[50] a complaint concerning the imprisonment of the applicant, who was in receipt of invalidity benefit, for failing to pay his community charge, provides a contrast. The Commission declared this application admissible despite express reliance by the respondent government on the Court's decision in *Benham*.

C5–28   It should be noted that Protocol No. 4, Article 1 (which does not feature among the Convention rights to which the HRA gives effect) prohibits state

---

[44] *Lawless v. Ireland* (1961) 1 E.H.R.R. 13.
[45] *Engel v. Netherlands* 1 E.H.R.R. 647.
[46] *ibid.*, para. 69.
[47] App. Nos 8022, 25 & 27/77 McVeigh, O'Neill & Evans v. United Kingdom (1983) 5 E.H.R.R. 71.
[48] *Cuilla v. Italy* (1991) 13 E.H.R.R. 346, para. 36 and see *Guzzardi v. Italy* (1980) 3 E.H.R.R. 333, para. 101.
[49] June 10, 1996, R.J.D., 1996–III, No. 10; 22 E.H.R.R. 293, para. 39.
[50] Application 25277/94 (1997) 24 E.H.R.R. CD 35.

parties from depriving persons of liberty "merely because of inability to fulfil a contractual debt".

D. Article 5(1)(c)—suspected criminals

C5–29   Article 5(1)(c) permits the arrest of suspected criminals (a) for the purpose of bringing them to trial, (b) to prevent the commission of a criminal offence, and (c) to prevent a person fleeing after a criminal offence has been committed. The provision "sets out three alternative circumstances in which detention may be effected for the purpose of bringing a person before a competent authority".[51] It is sufficient if the detention is justified by any one of the three circumstances. Persons detained pursuant to Article 5(1)(c) are entitled to the guarantees of Article 5(3) in addition to all other procedural guarantees under the Convention.

C5–30   The first of the circumstances specified in Article 5(1)(c) "requires that the purpose of the arrest or detention should be to bring the person concerned before the competent legal authority".[52] But the fact that a person is neither charged nor brought before a court does not necessarily mean that the purpose of his detention is not in accordance with Article 5(1)(c):

"The existence of such a purpose must be considered independently of its achievement and Article 5(1)(c) does not presuppose that the police should have obtained sufficient evidence to bring charges, either at the point of arrest or while the applicants were in custody."[53]

(1)   Reasonable grounds

C5–31   Detention under Article 5(1)(c) must be based on reasonable grounds. In assessing whether reasonable grounds exist, the fact that domestic legislation does not impose a requirement of "reasonable suspicion" is relevant but not decisive; the Court will seek to assess whether on the facts of the individual case the objective standard of "reasonable suspicion" was met.[54] In *Fox, Campbell and Hartley v. United Kingdom*, the Court stated:

"The 'reasonableness' of the suspicion on which an arrest must be based forms an essential part of the safeguard against arbitrary arrest and detention . . . Having a 'reasonable suspicion' presupposes the existence of facts or information which would satisfy an objective observer that the person concerned may have committed the offence."[55]

However, the " . . . facts which raise the suspicion need not be of the same level as those necessary to justify a conviction or even the bringing of a charge".[56]

C5–32   In *Fox, Campbell and Hartley*, the Court also stated that what may be regarded as reasonable will depend on all the circumstances and took account of

---

[51] *De Jong, Baljet and Van den Brink v. Netherlands* (1986) 8 E.H.R.R. 20, para. 43.
[52] *Brogan v. United Kingdom* (1989) 11 E.H.R.R. 117, para. 52.
[53] *ibid.*, para. 53.
[54] *Murray v. United Kingdom* (1995) 19 E.H.R.R. 193, para. 50.
[55] (1991) 13 E.H.R.R. 157, para. 32; see also *K.-F. v. Germany*, November 27, 1997, R.J.D., 1997–VI, No. 54; 26 E.H.R.R. 390, para. 57.
[56] *Murray v. United Kingdom* (1995) 19 E.H.R.R. 193, para. 55 and *K.-F. v. Germany*, November 27, 1997, R.J.D., 1997–VI, No. 54; 26 E.H.R.R. 390, para. 57.

the difficulties inherent in investigating terrorist crime. Nevertheless, the "essence of the safeguard" had to be respected and in that case it found that *bona fide* suspicions against the applicants did not suffice to meet the standard of Article 5(1)(c). The Government had not provided the "material on which the suspicion against the applicants was based" and its explanations were therefore found not to meet the minimum standard.

C5–33   In *Murray v. United Kingdom* the Court reiterated that in the circum-stances of terrorist offences it was "prepared to attach some credence to the respondent Government's declaration concerning the existence of reliable but confidential information grounding the suspicion against Mrs Murray".[57] This declaration together with the fact that, unlike in *Fox, Campbell and Hartley*'s case, the underlying facts and the applicant's allegations had been reviewed by the national courts (up to the House of Lords) in civil proceedings for false imprison-ment, led the Court to conclude that there "did exist sufficient facts or information which could form a plausible and objective basis for a suspicion".[58] The national courts, having heard the witnesses and assessed their credibility, had concluded that the applicant had genuinely been suspected of having been involved in a criminal offence.

C5–34   In *Murray v. United Kingdom* the Court further indicated that "the length of the deprivation of liberty at risk may also be material to the level of suspicion required."[59] In that case, the legislation in question permitted detention for a maximum of four hours compared to the 44 hours, 44 hours and five minutes and 30 hours 15 minutes at issue in *Fox, Campbell and Hartley*.

E.   Article 5(1)(d)—detention of minors

C5–35   Article 5(1)(d) has given rise to little case law. The leading decision is *Bouamar v. Belgium*,[60] where the Court found a violation in the applicant's repeated detention in a remand prison. "The juvenile courts ordered this detention nine times and then released him on or before the expiry of the statutory limit of fifteen days".[61] This shuttling to and fro between prison and family was found not to have been for the purpose of "educational supervision". The Court, however, observed:

> "The confinement of a juvenile in a remand prison does not necessarily contravene Article 5(1)(d), even if it is not in itself such as to provide for the person's 'educational supervision'. As is apparent from the words 'for the purpose of' ('pour'), the detention referred to in the text is a means of ensuring that the person concerned is placed under 'educational supervision', but, the placement does not necessarily have to be an immediate one. Just as Article 5(1) recognises–in sub-paragraphs (c) and (a)–the distinction between pre-trial detention and detention after conviction, so sub-paragraph (d) does not preclude an interim custody measure being used as a preliminary to a regime of supervised education, without in itself involving any supervised

---

[57] (1995) 19 E.H.R.R. 193, para. 59.
[58] *ibid.*, para. 63.
[59] *ibid.*, para. 56.
[60] (1989) 11 E.H.R.R. 1.
[61] *ibid.*, para. 51.

education. In such circumstances, however, the imprisonment must be speedily followed by actual application of such a regime in a setting (open or closed) designed and with sufficient resources for the purpose."[62]

C5–36   The guarantees of Article 5(4) apply to detention under this provision and the Court has held that "it is essential not only that the individual concerned should have the opportunity to be heard in person but that he should also have the effective assistance of his lawyer".[63]

F. Article 5(1)(e)–infectious diseases, persons of unsound mind, alcoholics, drug addicts and vagrants

C5–37   Article 5(1)(e) covers the detention of a number of categories of persons, especially for medical reasons and in order to prevent the spreading of infectious diseases. The language of this head of Article 5(1) is decidedly dated today. Case law has interpreted the phrases "vagrants" and "persons of unsound mind". The *Vagrancy* judgment accepted that the definition in the then Belgian law was compatible with the Convention: "vagrants are persons who have no fixed abode, no means of subsistence and no regular trade or profession".[64] In *Winterwerp v. Netherlands*, the Court said that the term "persons of unsound mind":

> "is not one that can be given a definitive interpretation . . . it is a term whose meaning is constantly evolving as research in psychiatry progresses, an increasing flexibility in treatment is developing and society's attitudes to mental illness change, in particular so that a greater understanding of the problems of mental patients is becoming more widespread.
> In any event, Article 5(1)(c) obviously cannot be taken as permitting the detention of a person simply because his views or behaviour deviate from the norms prevailing in a particular society."[65]

C5–38   The national authorities are given considerable discretion over the assessment of medical evidence but the Court has stressed the importance of good procedures avoiding the risk of arbitrary decisions:

> "Except in emergency cases, the individual concerned should not be deprived of his liberty unless he has been reliably shown to be of "unsound mind". The very nature of what has to be established . . . calls for objective medical expertise. Further, the mental disorder must be of a kind or degree warranting compulsory confinement. What is more, the validity of continued confinement depends upon the persistence of such a disorder".[66]

C5–39   In relation to the last of these criteria, the persistence of the disorder, the Court rejected the applicant's submission in *Johnson v. United Kingdom* that once there is a finding by an expert authority that the disorder has ceased the applicant "should as a consequence have been immediately and unconditionally released from detention":

---

[62] *ibid.*, para. 50.
[63] *ibid.*, para. 60.
[64] (1971) 1 E.H.R.R. 373, para. 68.
[65] (1979) 2 E.H.R.R. 387, para. 37.
[66] *Winterwerp v. Netherlands* (1979) 2 E.H.R.R. 387, para. 39.

"Such a rigid approach to the interpretation of that condition would place an unacceptable degree of constraint on the responsible authority's exercise of judgment to determine in particular cases and on the basis of all the relevant circumstances whether the interests of the patient and the community into which he is to be released would in fact be best served by this course of action."[67]

In that case, the Court accepted that the Mental Health Review Tribunal was justified in not releasing the applicant immediately but ordering a phased conditional discharge. However, the imposition of a hostel residence requirement and deferring release until arrangements had been made meant that the applicant's release was deferred indefinitely; the Court held that this violated Article 5(1), *inter alia*, because neither the Tribunal nor the authorities possessed the power to ensure that this condition could be implemented in a reasonable time.

C5–40   When a trial court deals with a person convicted of a criminal offence by ordering detention in a mental hospital, for the purposes of the Convention, initially at least, the detention may be justified under both Article 5(1)(a) and (e).[68] However, in order for detention to be lawful under Article 5(1)(e) it must:

"be effected in a hospital, clinic or other appropriate institution authorised for that purpose. However, subject to the foregoing, Article 5(1)(e) is not in principle concerned with suitable treatment or conditions."[69]

C5–41   In *Aerts v. Belgium*, the applicant was held in provisional detention in the psychiatric wing of a prison for some seven months until a place became available in the Social Protection Centre designated as place of detention. According to the information before the Court, the former was not regarded as an appropriate institution for persons of unsound mind by the Belgian Government, as there was no regular medical attention nor a therapeutic environment. Furthermore, the Mental Health Board, on application by the applicant, had found that the situation was in fact harmful to Mr Aerts. In light of these factors, the Court found a violation of Article 5(1), as "the proper relationship between the aim of the detention and the conditions in which it took place was therefore deficient".[70]

C5–42   Procedural guarantees, particularly Article 5(4), have taken prominence in the cases relating to mental patients brought under the Convention. In *Winterwerp*, the Court said of Article 5(4):

"It is essential that the person concerned should have access to a court and some opportunity to be heard either in person or, where necessary, through some form of representation, failing which he will not have been afforded the fundamental guarantees of procedure applied in matters of deprivation of liberty. Mental illness may entail restricting or modifying the manner of the exercise of such a right, but it cannot justify impairing the very essence of the

---

[67] October 24, 1997, R.J.D., 1997–VII, No. 55; 27 E.H.R.R. 296, para. 61.
[68] *X v. United Kingdom* (1981) 4 E.H.R.R. 188, para. 39.
[69] *Ashingdane v. United Kingdom* (1985) 7 E.H.R.R. 528, para. 44: see also *Aerts v. Belgium* judgment of July 30, 1998, para. 46. See further above, para. C3–14.
[70] *Aerts v. Belgium*, judgment of July 30, 1998, para. 49.

right. Indeed, special procedural safeguards may prove to be called for in order to protect the interests of persons who, on account of their mental disabilities, are not fully capable of acting for themselves."[71]

C5–43 While Article 5(4) is confined to challenges to the lawfulness of detention, and does not extend to complaints about treatment or nature of hospital in which the patient is detained,[72] there must be a "proper relationship between the aim of the detention and the conditions in which it [takes] place". It appears that Article 5(4) will require proceedings which are capable of bearing on that question[73] whether that relationship is deficient.

G. Article 5(1)(f)—unauthorised immigration, deportation or extradition

C5–44 The scope of the guarantee in Article 5(1)(f) is restricted to protecting against unlawful detention under the provision. It does not, however, provide any substantive guidance about the circumstances when entry into a country is "unauthorised" and/or when deportation or extradition is possible. Other provisions of the Convention place certain limits on states' action in these matters.[74] The restricted and usually formalistic character of Article 5(1)(f) is well illustrated by the Commission's Report in *Zamir v. United Kingdom*, which was accepted by the Committee of Ministers. The Commission stated:

"The use of the words 'person against whom action is being taken with a view to deportation' in Article 5(1)(f) indicates that the Commission should examine whether the person is being detained in accordance with national law with the intention of being deported . . . However, a legal situation may occur, where . . . national law makes the lawfulness of the detention dependent on the lawfulness of the deportation. While Article 5(1)(e), requires that the substantive conditions justifying detention are met—i.e. the existence of a mental disorder warranting compulsory confinement . . .—Article 5(1)(f) does not require the Commission to provide its own interpretation on questions of national law concerning the legality of the detention or deportation. The scope of the Commission's review is limited to examining whether there is a legal basis for the detention and whether the decision of the courts on the question of lawfulness could be described as arbitrary in the light of the facts of the case".[75]

C5–45 The Court confirmed this approach in its judgment in *Chahal v. United Kingdom*, where it stated:

"Article 5(1)(f) does not demand that the detention of a person against whom action is being taken with a view to deportation be reasonably considered necessary, for example to prevent his committing an offence or fleeing; in this respect Article 5(1)(f) provides a different level of protection from Article 5(1)(c).

---

[71] *Winterwerp v. Netherlands* (1979) 2 E.H.R.R. 387, para. 60. See further *X v. United Kingdom* (1981) 4 E.H.R.R. 188 and *Ashingdane v. United Kingdom* (1985) 7 E.H.R.R. 528.
[72] *Ashingdane* (1985) 7 E.H.R.R. 528, para. 52.
[73] *Aerts v. Belgium*, judgment of July 30, 1998, paras 49 and 55.
[74] See, in particular, commentary on Arts 3, 8 and 14.
[75] App. No. 9174/80 (1986) 8 E.H.R.R. 108, para. 87.

Indeed, all that is required under this provision is that 'action is being taken with a view to deportation'. It is therefore immaterial, for the purposes of Article 5(1)(f), whether the underlying decision to expel can be justified under national or Convention law."[76]

C5–46   Although the Court will not examine the legality of the underlying extradition proceedings, in *Quinn v. France* it stated that:

"It is clear from the wording of both the French and the English version of Article 5(1)(f) that deprivation of liberty under this sub-paragraph will be justified only for so long as extradition proceedings are being conducted. It follows that if such proceedings are not being prosecuted with due diligence, the detention will cease to be justified under Article 5(1)(f)."[77]

In its judgment in *Quinn*, the Court unanimously found a violation of Article 5(1)(f) on the basis that the extradition proceedings had lasted almost two years. By contrast, in its judgment in *Chahal* the Court (contrary to the conclusions of the Commission) held that deportation proceedings lasting more than 3 and a half years were not excessive and therefore there was no violation of Article 5(1).

C5–47   In assessing the "lawfulness" of the detention under domestic law the Court will, however, assess the "quality" of the legal rules applicable to the persons concerned:

"Quality in this sense implies that where a national law authorises deprivation of liberty–especially in respect of a foreign asylum seeker–it must be sufficiently accessible and precise, in order to avoid all risk of arbitrariness. These characteristics are of fundamental importance with regard to asylum seekers at airports, particularly in view of the need to reconcile the protection of fundamental rights with the requirements of States' immigration policies."[78]

In this decision, *Amuur v. France*,[79] the Court concluded that neither the Decree nor the Circular invoked to provide a domestic law basis for the detention "constituted a 'law' of sufficient 'quality' within the meaning of the Court's case law; there must be adequate legal protection in domestic law against arbitrary interferences by public authorities with the rights safeguarded by the Convention".[80] Neither document provided such safeguards: neither of them allowed the ordinary courts to review the conditions of detention nor to impose a limit on the length of such detention nor did they provide for legal, humanitarian and social assistance or at least procedures for access to such assistance.

C5–48   Procedural guarantees, especially Article 5(4), apply in conjunction with Article 5(1)(f). The limited scope of Article 5(1)(f) is reflected, however, in the limited scrutiny called for by national courts under Article 5(4):

"[D]etention is justified under Article 5(1)(f) where a person is detained in accordance with national law with the intention of deporting him. Accordingly

---

[76] November 15, 1996, R.J.D., 1996–II, No. 22; 23 E.H.R.R. 413, para. 112.
[77] (1996) 21 E.H.R.R. 529, para. 48.
[78] *Amuur v. France*, June 10, 1996, R.J.D., 1996–III, No. 10, para. 36; 22 E.H.R.R. 533, para. 50.
[79] June 10, 1996, R.J.D., 1996–III, No. 10, para. 36; 22 E.H.R.R. 533, para. 50.
[80] *ibid.*, para. 53.

Article 5(4) is satisfied if the courts are empowered to examine the lawfulness under domestic law of the applicant's detention and whether he is being detained with a view to deportation or removal. It is not a requirement of this provision . . . that judicial control of detention under Article 5(1)(f) extend to a complete review on all questions of fact of the exercise of the power to detain."[80a]

3. PROCEDURAL GUARANTEES REQUIRED BY ARTICLE 5

A. Article 5(2)—right to be informed of reasons for arrest

C5–49 Article 5(2) requires that anyone arrested or detained should be "informed promptly, in a language which he understands, of the reasons for his arrest and of any charge against him". This information must be given to all who are detained, not just criminal suspects; thus, for example, it also applies to mental patients.[81] Information must be sufficient to enable the person to know why he is detained especially to enable legal proceedings challenging the lawfulness of the detention if this is considered appropriate. The mere recital of the legal basis for the arrest, on its own, is insufficient.[82] As was said in *Murray v. United Kingdom,* it may, however, be sufficient for the purposes of Article 5(2) if the alleged offence for which she was detained "must have been apparent" to the detainee in the course of her questioning.[83] As Mrs Murray was interviewed only 1 hour and 20 minutes after her initial arrest, the Court found that the requirement of "promptness" imposed by Article 5(2) was satisfied.

C5–50 The information required to be given varies depending on why the person is detained. For example, where the reason was that detention was a form of security check to establish whether the detainees were involved in terrorism, it was held sufficient to supply this information; details about any specific suspicions against them were not required.[84] By contrast, when the reason for arrest is suspicion of a criminal offence, there is an entitlement to:

"be informed sufficiently about the facts and the evidence which are proposed to be the foundation of a decision to detain him. In particular, he should be asked whether he admits or denies the alleged offence".[85]

C5–51 Once charges are brought there is the additional entitlement under Article 6(3)(a) to be "informed in sufficient detail of the nature and cause of the accusation against him". Note both Articles 5(2) and 6(3)(a) require information to be given "promptly" and in a language understood by the detained person.

B. Article 5(3)—prompt production before a judge, trial within a reasonable time and bail

C5–52 Article 5(3) provides additional procedural guarantees for persons detained pursuant to Article 5(1)(c). The provision has three elements:

[80a] *Zamir v. United Kingdom* (1986) 8 E.H.R.R. 108, para. 100.

[81] *Van Der Leer v. Netherlands* (1990) 12 E.H.R.R. 567, paras 28 and 29.

[82] *Fox, Campbell and Hartley v. United Kingdom* (1991) 13 E.H.R.R. 157; *Murray v. United Kingdom* (1995) 19 E.H.R.R. 193.

[83] *Murray v. United Kingdom* (1995) 19 E.H.R.R. 193, para. 77.

[84] App. Nos 8022, 25 & 27/77 *McVeigh, O'Neill and Evans v. United Kingdom* (1983) 5 E.H.R.R. 71, para. 210.

[85] App No. 8098/77 *X v. Germany* 16 D. & R. 111.

(a) to be "brought promptly";

(b) "before a judge or other officer authorised by law to exercise judicial power";

(c) "entitled to trial within a reasonable time or to release pending trial".

Each of these elements is examined in turn in the paragraphs which follow.

C5–53 The overall compliance with the requirements of Article 5(3) of the denial of bail for certain offences introduced by section 25 of the Criminal Justice and Public Order Act 1994 was raised before the Commission in *BH v. United Kingdom*.[86] By a decision of December 1, 1997, the Commission declared this complaint admissible.

(1) The requirement of "promptness"

C5–54 In *Brogan v. United Kingdom* the Court stated that this requirement needs to be construed in the light of the object and purpose of Article 5 which is "the protection of the individual against arbitrary interferences by the State with his right to liberty".[87] Although "the issue of promptness must be assessed in each case according to its special features",[88] the Court has clearly stated that:

> "the significance to be attached to those features can never be taken to the point of impairing the very essence of the right guaranteed by Article 5(3), that is the point of effectively negativing the State's obligation to ensure a prompt release or a prompt appearance before a judicial authority . . .
> The scope for flexibility in interpreting and applying the notion of "promptness" is very limited."[89]

C5–55 In *Brogan*, the Court found that the promptness requirement had been infringed by delays of four days and six hours and longer in bringing detainees before a court:

> "The undoubted fact that the arrest and detention of the applicants were inspired by the legitimate aim of protecting the community as a whole from terrorism is not on its own sufficient to ensure compliance with the specific requirements of Article 5(3)."[90]

C5–56 In *Brannigan and McBride v. United Kingdom*,[91] however, the Court upheld the United Kingdom's Article 15 derogation from its obligations under Article 5. In the context of that derogation, individuals suspected of terrorist offences could be detained for up to seven days without judicial control. By contrast, the Court in *Aksoy v. Turkey*,[92] relying on its judgment in *Brogan*'s case, confirmed that a period of 14 or more days of being detained without being

---

[86] App. No. 30307/96 (1998) 25 E.H.R.R. CD 136.
[87] (1989) 11 E.H.R.R. 117, para. 58.
[88] *De Jong, Baljet & Van den Brink v. Netherlands* (1986) 8 E.H.R.R. 20, para. 52.
[89] *Brogan v. United Kingdom* (1989) 11 E.H.R.R. 117, paras 59 and 62.
[90] *ibid.*, para. 62. See further *Koster v. Netherlands* (1992) 14 E.H.R.R. 396.
[91] (1994) 17 E.H.R.R. 539.
[92] December 18, 1996, R.J.D., 1996–IV, No. 26; 23 E.H.R.R. 553.

brought before a judge or other judicial officer did not satisfy the requirement of promptness. This was despite the fact that the applicant's detention was also covered by a derogation under Article 15. In this last case, however, the Court held that (incommunicado) detention without judicial control for such a long period "was not strictly required by the exigencies of the situation"[93] and found a violation of Article 5(3).

C5–57 In *Rigopoulos v. Spain*[94] the authorities inspected a ship on the open Atlantic in connection with an investigation into international drug trafficking. As a result of the search a large quantity of cocaine was discovered on board. Due to resistance by crew members, delaying the ship's escort to the nearest Spanish port, the ship's captain was brought before a Spanish court after some 16 days had elapsed. The Court held that, in principle, a period of 16 days cannot be considered to be compatible with the requirement of promptness; only exceptional circumstances could justify such a long period of time. In this case, the inspection was carried out more than 5,500km from the Spanish coast and it took 16 days to reach the nearest Spanish port. It was technically impossible for the Spanish authorities to bring the applicant before the investigating judge within a shorter period of time. For this reason the application under Article 5(3) was held to be inadmissible as manifestly ill-founded.

(2) "Before a judge or other officer authorised by law to exercise judicial power"

C5–58 The Court gave important guidance on the interpretation of this requirement in *Schiesser v. Switzerland*:

> "In providing that an arrested person shall be brought promptly before a 'judge' or 'other officer', Article 5(3) leaves the contracting States a choice between two categories of authorities . . .
> The 'officer' is not identical with the 'judge' but must nevertheless have some of the latter's attributes, that is to say, he must satisfy certain conditions each of which constitutes a guarantee for the person arrested.
> The first of such conditions is independence of the executive and of the parties. This does not mean that the 'officer' may not be to some extent subordinate to other judges or officers provided that they enjoy similar independence.
> In addition, under Article 5(3), there is both a procedural and a substantive requirement. The procedural requirement places the 'officer' under the obligation of himself hearing the individual brought before him; the substantive requirement imposes on him the obligations of reviewing the circumstances militating for or against detention, of deciding, by reference to legal criteria, whether there are reasons to justify detention and of ordering release if there are no such reasons."[95]

C5–59 No violation was found in *Schiesser* although the district attorney was subordinate to the public prosecutor and exercised investigative functions in

---

[93] *ibid.*, para. 86.
[94] App. No. 37388/97.
[95] (1979) 2 E.H.R.R. 417, paras 27 and 31.

criminal cases. In reaching its conclusion, the Court emphasised that the district attorney "intervened exclusively as an investigating authority" and "did not exercise concurrent investigating and prosecuting functions".[96] By contrast, a violation was found in Dutch military cases, in which the "officer" could "be called on to perform the function of prosecuting authority" and so was not "independent of the parties".[97] To comply with Article 5(3), the "officer" must have power to order release; recommendations are not sufficient.[98]

(3) "Entitled to trial within a reasonable time or to release pending trial"

C5–60 In its early case law, the Court indicated that:

> "this provision cannot be understood as giving the judicial authorities a choice between either bringing the accused to trial within a reasonable time or granting him provisional release even subject to guarantees. The reasonableness of the time spent by an accused person in detention . . . must be assessed in relation to the very fact of his detention. Until conviction, he must be presumed innocent and the purpose of the provision . . . is essentially to require his provisional release once his continuing detention ceases to be reasonable".[99]

C5–61 But early case law accepted long periods of detention on remand as reasonable in complex cases. So, for example, in *Wemhoff v. Germany*,[1] Wemhoff was detained for some three years and five months before the conclusion of his trial at first instance, yet the Court found no violation. Judge Zekia dissented vigorously pointing out that:

> "In a country where the common law system is followed, the time taken in bringing the person before a trial court and having him tried is relatively much shorter than the time needed for such a trial under the continental system."[2]

C5–62 Understandably the Court and Commission did not adopt a radical interpretation in the earlier cases. Nevertheless, over the years, the approach has become gradually stricter as measures have been introduced to combat delays in criminal proceedings in various Council of Europe countries and standards have evolved. It is important to note that each case must be individually assessed to determine whether the requirements of Article 5(3) have been met; a delay acceptable in one case may not be in another. The current approach for assessing the issues under the Convention was summarised as follows by the Court:

> "It falls in the first place to the national judicial authorities to ensure that, in a given case, the pre-trial detention of an accused person does not exceed a reasonable time. To this end, they must examine all the facts arguing for or against the existence of a genuine requirement of public interest justifying, with due regard to the principle of the presumption of innocence, a departure

---

[96] *ibid.*, para. 34.
[97] *De Jong, Baljet & Van den Brink v. Netherlands* (1986) 8 E.H.R.R. 20, para. 49.
[98] *De Jong*, paras 47 and 48 and see *Ireland v. United Kingdom* (1978) 2 E.H.R.R. 25, para. 199.
[99] *Neumeister v. Austria* (1968) 1 E.H.R.R. 91, para. 4.
[1] 1 E.H.R.R. 55.
[2] para. 8 of his dissenting judgment, p. 87.

from the rule of respect for individual liberty and set them out in their decisions on the applications for release. It is essentially on the basis of the reasons given in these decisions and of the true facts mentioned by the applicant in his appeals, that [the Convention organs are] called upon to decide whether there has been a violation of Article 5(3) of the Convention. · The persistence of reasonable suspicion that the person has committed an offence is a condition *sine qua non* for the validity of the continued detention, but, after a certain lapse of time, it no longer suffices: the Court must then establish whether the other grounds cited by the judicial authorities continue to justify the deprivation of liberty. Where such grounds are 'relevant' and 'sufficient', the Court must also ascertain whether the national authorities displayed 'special diligence' in the conduct of the proceedings."[3]

C5–63   In accordance with Article 6(1), all criminal proceedings must be brought to trial within a "reasonable time", irrespective of whether the accused is detained.[4] But the fact of detention on remand requires "special diligence" in handling the case.[5] What is "reasonable" for Article 6(1) purposes may not be "reasonable" in relation to detention on remand and Article 5(3).

C5–64   In assessing whether a prolonged period of detention remains "reasonable" the mere complexity of the case itself will not be sufficient. Furthermore, in weighing the public interest to maintain public order it will have to be established that "it is based on facts capable of showing that the accused's release would actually prejudice public order. In addition, detention will continue to be legitimate only if public order remains actually threatened".[6] The gravity of the crime with which he or she is charged in itself is insufficient in that it is irreconcilable with the presumption of innocence.[7]

C5–65   However, in the context of a major Spanish investigation into drug trafficking, described as the largest of its kind ever to take place in Europe, a period of detention pending trial of some three years and 2 months has been held to be "reasonable". The Court refused to entertain the argument that the applicant's minor charges should never have been transferred to the national investigation (the transfer accounting for one year, eight months and 24 days of the delay), as that decision could not be held to have been unreasonable.[8]

C5–66   In *Scott v. Spain*[9] the Court held that a period of detention of some four years and 16 days in connection with an allegation of rape, the trial of which was of no great complexity, was not a "reasonable time". The Court expressly rejected an argument by the Spanish Government that the authorities' difficulties with the implementation of international letters rogatory (such as translation of documents, transmission by diplomatic channels, repeated summons of the complainant) could justify the delay in bringing this case to trial.

---

[3] *Letellier v. France* (1992) 14 E.H.R.R. 83, para. 35; see also *Yağci and Sargin v. Turkey* (1995) 20 E.H.R.R. 505.
[4] See further below, p. 249.
[5] *Tomasi v. France* (1992) 15 E.H.R.R. 1; *Herczegfalvy v. Austria* (1992) 15 E.H.R.R. 437 and *Abdoella v. Netherlands* (1995) 20 E.H.R.R. 585.
[6] *Tomasi v. France* (1992) 15 E.H.R.R. 1, para. 91.
[7] Commission Opinion in App. No. 17831/91 *Morganti v. France* (1996) 21 E.H.R.R. 34, para. 62.
[8] *Van der Tang v. Spain* (1996) 22 E.H.R.R. 363.
[9] December 18, 1996, R.J.D., 1996–VI, No. 27; 24 E.H.R.R. 391.

(4) "Release may be conditioned by guarantees to appear for trial"

C5–67   In *Neumeister*, the Court emphasised that the amount of bail must be set so as to secure "the presence of the accused at the hearing":

> "Its amount must therefore be assessed principally by reference to him, his assets and his relationship with the persons who are to provide the security, in other words, to the degree of confidence that is possible that the loss of the security or of action against the guarantors in case of his non-appearance at trial will act as a sufficient deterrent to dispel any wish on his part to abscond."[10]

C5–68   However, failure by the national courts even to consider other ways of ensuring that the accused appears for trial, such as the provision of a recognisance, on an application for release, may invalidate any finding that there is a risk of absconding and thereby undermine the sufficiency of the grounds given for continued detention.[11]

C.   Article 5(4)—review of lawfulness of detention

C5–69   Unlike Article 5(3), which only applies to persons detained under Article 5(1)(c), the guarantees of Article 5(4) apply to all detainees:-

> "the purpose of Article 5(4) is to assure to persons who are arrested or detained the right to a judicial supervision of the lawfulness of the measure to which they are thereby subjected."[12]

C5–70   The supervision of lawfulness must occur "speedily" and before a court providing "the fundamental guarantees of procedure applied in matters of deprivation of liberty."[13] In that sense, Article 5(4) provides a *lex specialis* in relation to the more general requirements for an effective remedy as set out in Article 13.[14]

C5–71   Although Article 5(4) applies to all cases of deprivation of liberty, what it requires can vary considerably as explained in the commentary on the various heads of Article 5(1) above. It will be recalled that for those convicted after criminal trials, the requirements of Article 5(4) will have been fully satisfied in the trial itself; it is only when detention ceases to be sufficiently linked to the trial sentence that further review to comply with Article 5(4) will be required.[15] Important differences between what has to be established for detention to be lawful under the various heads of Article 5(1) are mirrored in the review and procedural guarantees called for under Article 5(4).[16] Detention of a person who is considered to be of "unsound mind" under Article 5(1)(e) calls for periodic review with a hearing and representation so that the medical need for continued detention can be reviewed and the lawfulness checked; control of the legality of detention equivalent to "judicial review" is

---

[10] *Neumeister v. Austria* (1968) 1 E.H.R.R. 91, para. 14.
[11] Commission Opinion in App. No. 17831/91 *Morganti v. France* (1996) 21 E.H.R.R. 34, paras No. 65–66.
[12] *Vagrancy* case (1971) 1 E.H.R.R. 373, para. 76.
[13] *ibid.*
[14] See *Chahal v. United Kingdom*, November 15, 1996, R.J.D., 1996–II, No. 22; 23 E.H.R.R. 413. As to Art. 13, see p. 317.
[15] See above, para. C5–22.
[16] See *Chahal v. United Kingdom*, November 15, 1996, R.J.D., 1996–II, No. 22; 23 E.H.R.R. 413, para. 127.

insufficient, as was held in relation to habeas corpus.[17] In the different context of Article 5(1)(f), however, "judicial review" has been held sufficient to check the lawfulness of a person's detention as an illegal entrant with a view to deportation.[18]

C5–72   In *Chahal v. United Kingdom*, the Court was again faced with the adequacy of judicial review in the context of an Article 5(4) review of detention under Article 5(1)(f). In that case, however, the judicial review proceedings had been conducted in the context of national security. The Court reiterated that:

> " . . . it is clear that Article 5(4) does not guarantee a right to judicial review of such breadth as to empower the court, on all aspects of the case including questions of pure expediency, to substitute its own discretion for that of the decision-making authority. The review should, however, be wide enough to bear on those conditions which are essential for the 'lawful' detention of a person according to Article 5(1)."[19]

In light of the fact that the domestic courts were not in a position to review whether the decisions to detain the applicant and to keep him detained were justified on national security grounds; and before the advisory panel (the "three wise men" procedure) set up to consider such cases, the applicant had no right to legal representation, the applicant would only receive an outline of the reasons on which the intention to deport him was based, the panel had no power of decision and its advice to the Secretary of State was neither binding nor published; the Court concluded that neither judicial review or habeas corpus nor the advisory panel satisfied the requirements of Article 5(4). The Court further noted that:

> "This shortcoming is all the more significant given that Mr Chahal has undoubtedly been deprived of his liberty for a length of time which is bound to give rise to serious concern."[20]

C5–73   Just as there are differences in what must be reviewed to verify the lawfulness of different classes of detention, there are differences in the procedural guarantees required. In all cases, proceedings must be before a "court" which implies certain "fundamental features, of which the most important is independence of the executive and of the parties to the case".[21] There must also be the "guarantees of judicial procedure" but the "forms of the procedure" can vary.[22] This point was illustrated in *Sanchez-Reisse v. Switzerland*,[23] in which the Court indicated that the possibility of submitting written comments would have been an appropriate procedure in proceedings to challenge the lawfulness of detention in an extradition case under Article 5(1)(f). Unlike cases under Article 5(1)(c) or (e), the Court did not consider that, under Article 5(1)(f), the fundamental guarantees of

---

[17] *X v. United Kingdom* (1981) 4 E.H.R.R. 188, paras 134–137.
[18] *Zamir v. United Kingdom* (1986) 8 E.H.R.R. 108 and see above, para. I–5.028.
[19] November 15, 1996, R.J.D., 1996–II, No. 22; 23 E.H.R.R. 413, para. 127.
[20] *ibid.*, para. 132; see also above, para. C5–45. As a consequence of this finding, the Respondent Government set up a Special Immigration Appeals Commission Act 1997 in order to hear national security deportation appeals: see the Special Immigration Appeals Commission and the Special Immigration Appeals Commission (Procedure) Rules 1998 (S.I. 1998 No. 1881).
[21] *Vagrancy* case (1971) 1 E.H.R.R. 373, para. 78.
[22] *ibid.*
[23] (1987) 9 E.H.R.R. 71.

procedure required proceedings in which the detainee could be heard either in person or through some form of representation; for supervision of Article 5(1)(f) detention, a written procedure respecting the principles of adversarial procedure could suffice.[24] In that case a violation was found because no such opportunity had been given and the initial written request to be released did not suffice as it did not allow the detainee to respond to and to criticise a later report from the authorities which was before the Court. The Court will, however, always seek to ensure that equality of arms between the detainee and the prosecutor is maintained. Where that would require the right of the detainee to appear at the same time as the prosecutor but no such right is available, the Court will find a violation of Article 5(4).[25]

C5–74   In the context of review of imprisonment under Article 5(1)(a) "during her Majesty's pleasure", the Court found that the Parole Board did not comply with the requirements of Article 5(4) because:

(a) the Parole Board cannot order the release of a prisoner;

(b) there are no adversarial proceedings before the Board;

(c) in the view of the Court, both factors prevent the Parole Board from being regarded as a court or court-like body for the purposes of Article 5(4).

> "The Court recalls in this context that, in matters of such crucial importance as the deprivation of liberty and where questions arise which involve, for example, an assessment of the applicant's character or mental state, it has held that it may be essential to the fairness of the proceedings that the applicant be present at an oral hearing.
> The Court is of the view that, in a situation such as that of the applicant, where a substantial term of imprisonment may be at stake and where characteristics pertaining to his personality and level of maturity are of importance in deciding on his dangerousness, Article 5(4) requires an oral hearing in the context of an adversarial procedure involving legal representation and the possibility of calling and questioning witnesses."[26]

C5–75   The caution in respect of guarantees for detainees under Article 5(1)(f) may well reflect concern not to impose unreasonable procedures on Contracting States in relation to controls on illegal immigration and an awareness of the potential volume of cases involved. It is well-established, however, that, in controlling the entry and removal of persons from their territory, states must have regard to and respect the requirements of the Convention, particularly Articles 3, 8 and 14.[27] Cases may likewise exist, it is suggested, where lawfulness of detention under Article 5(1)(f) calls for a more detailed review and procedures than those indicated so far in the case law. To exclude this would risk adopting an over-mechanical approach to the Convention's application, whereas the Court has indicated that "regard must be had to the particular nature of the circumstances" in determining whether proceedings provide adequate guarantees for the purposes of Article 5(4).[28]

---

[24] *ibid.*, para. 51.
[25] *Kampanis v. Greece* (1996) 21 E.H.R.R. 43.
[26] *Hussain v. United Kingdom*, February 21, 1996, R.J.D., 1996–I, No. 4; 22 E.H.R.R. 1, paras 59 and 60. See, *mutatis mutandis*, *Kremzow v. Austria* (1994) 17 E.H.R.R. 322, para. 67.
[27] See commentary on these provisions at paras C3–09 *et seq.*, (Article 3), C8–55 *et seq.*, (Article 8) and C14–02 (Article 14).
[28] *Vagrancy* case (1971) 1 E.H.R.R. 373, para. 78.

C5–76 Article 5(4) proceedings must be determined "speedily":

"In the Court's view, this concept cannot be defined in the abstract; the matter must–as with the "reasonable time" stipulation in Article 5(3) and Article 6(1) . . .–be determined in the light of the circumstances of each case."[29]

C5–77 In *Sanchez-Reisse*, delays of 31 and 46 days in determining requests to be released were found not to have been "speedy". Violations have been established in several other cases, including *De Jong, Baljet and Van den Brink v. Netherlands*[30] and *Bezicheri v. Italy*.[31] In *Bezicheri*'s case, the Court rejected the Government's argument that account should be taken of the "excessive workload" of the investigating judge.[32] In *Letellier v. France*[33] the Court, while expressing "certain doubts", reversed the Commission's opinion and found no violation when requests for release had been dealt with in periods from 8 to 20 days.

D. Article 5(5)–compensation for detention in contravention of Article 5

C5–78 The effect of this provision is to require an enforceable claim for compensation before the national courts whenever a breach of the other paragraphs of Article 5 has occurred.[34] This is distinct from and without prejudice to the power of the ECHR to award "just satisfaction" under Article 41 of the Convention.[35] It should be noted, however, Article 5(5) does not come into play merely because detention is overturned by domestic courts, for example, when an appeal against criminal conviction and a sentence of imprisonment succeeds. In such a case, normally no breach of Article 5 guarantees will have occurred.[36]

---

[29] *Sanchez-Reisse v. Switzerland* (1987) 9 E.H.R.R. 71, para. 55.
[30] (1986) 8 E.H.R.R. 20.
[31] (1990) 12 E.H.R.R. 210.
[32] *ibid.*, para. 25.
[33] (1992) 14 E.H.R.R. 83, paras 54–57.
[34] See, for example, *Brogan v. United Kingdom* (1989) 11 E.H.R.R. 117, para. 67 and *Tsirlis and Kouloumpas v. Greece* (1998) 25 E.H.R.R. 198, para. 66.
[35] See *Neumeister v. Austria* (1968) 1 E.H.R.R. 91, para. 30 and *Brogan*, para. 67.
[36] Protocol No. 7, Art. 3, to which the HRA does not give effect, creates a right to compensation subject to certain conditions when "a newly discovered fact shows conclusively that there has been a miscarriage of justice".

Article 6

Right to a fair trial

C6–01

1 In the determination of his civil rights and obligations or of any criminal charge against him, everyone is entitled to a fair and public hearing within a reasonable time by an independent and impartial tribunal established by law. Judgment shall be pronounced publicly but the press and public may be excluded from all or part of the trial in the interests of morals, public order or national security in a democratic society, where the interests of juveniles or the protection of the private life of the parties so require, or to the extent strictly necessary in the opinion of the court in special circumstances where publicity would prejudice the interests of justice.

2 Everyone charged with a criminal offence shall be presumed innocent until proved guilty according to law.

3 Everyone charged with a criminal offence has the following minimum rights:

   a. to be informed promptly, in a language which he understands and in detail, of the nature and cause of the accusation against him;
   b. to have adequate time and facilities for the preparation of his defence;
   c. to defend himself in person or through legal assistance of his own choosing or, if he has not sufficient means to pay for legal assistance, to be given it free when the interests of justice so require;
   d. to examine or have examined witnesses against him and to obtain the attendance and examination of witnesses on his behalf under the same conditions as witnesses against him;
   e. to have the free assistance of an interpreter if he cannot understand or speak the language used in court.

1. Introduction

C6–02   Article 6 is the Convention's single most frequently invoked provision, whose importance has been stressed on many occasions. For example, in *Delcourt v. Belgium* the Court stated that:

"In a democratic society within the meaning of the Convention, the right to a fair administration of justice holds such a prominent place that a restrictive interpretation of Article 6(1) would not correspond to the aim and the purpose of that provision."[1]

C6–03   The provision overlaps with Article 5, which also guarantees access to judge,[2] and the principles of lawfulness and proportionality may also require

---

[1] 1 E.H.R.R. 355, para. 26.
[2] For example, issues about the lawfulness of detention, and entitlement to damages for unlawful detention, fall within both Arts 5(4) and 5(5) and may constitute civil rights within Art. 6(1): see, for example, *Aerts v. Belgium* judgment of July 30, 1998, para. 59.

judicial safeguards.[3] There may also be an overlap with Article 13, which guarantees the right to an effective remedy, but there are significant differences. Article 13 applies to claims that Convention rights have been violated rather than to disputes about civil rights and obligations or criminal charges. Moreover, Article 13 guarantees a remedy before a "national authority", which need not be a "tribunal". Although certain guarantees of procedure and independence are implicit in Article 13, its requirements are not as stringent as those of Article 6. Consequently, where a court finds a violation of Article 6, it is unnecessary to consider Article 13 "because the requirements of the latter Article are less strict than, and are . . . absorbed by, those of the former".[4] States may derogate from the requirements of Article 6 when "strictly required by the exigencies of the situation" in accordance with Article 15 of the Convention,[5] but even when derogations are made, there must be "basic safeguards against abuse".[6]

C6–04 The Court has analysed Article 6 as containing three distinct elements: access to a court, a set of guarantees concerning the organisation and the composition of the court and a set of guarantees concerning the conduct of proceedings.[7] The commentary below considers the case law on the following topics:

1. Proceedings to which Article 6 applies
2. The right of access to a court
3. The requirement that a court should have "full jurisdiction" over the dispute
4. Organisation and composition of the court
5. Conduct of the proceedings
6. Additional guarantees for persons charged with criminal offences

C6–05 While Article 6(1) applies to both criminal and civil proceedings, Articles 6(2) and (3) apply directly only to people who have been "charged with a criminal offence". Article 6(2) guarantees the presumption of innocence, Article 6(3) prescribes minimum rights of defence. It is important, however, to remember that the rights in Article 6(2) and 6(3) are additional to the basic guarantees of a fair trial in Article 6(1), to which reference should be made where an issue is not explicitly covered under Articles 6(2) or (3). In civil cases it can be worthwhile considering Articles 6(2) and (3) by analogy, since they are regarded as elements of the right to a fair hearing in Article 6(1). In consequence, the principles they embody are often used as a yardstick to measure the fairness of non-criminal proceedings.[8]

2. PROCEEDINGS TO WHICH ARTICLE 6 APPLIES

A. Civil rights and obligations and criminal charges autonomous concepts

C6–06 The guarantees of Article 6(1) apply to "the determination of . . . civil rights and obligation and of any criminal charge". Article 6(1) must be respected in

---

[3] See further above, para. C0–14.
[4] *Sporrong and Lönnroth v. Sweden* (1983) 5 E.H.R.R. 35, para. 88.
[5] *Ireland v. United Kingdom* (1978) 2 E.H.R.R. 25, para. 235. As to Art. 15, see further below, paras C15–01 *et seq.*
[6] *Brannigan & McBride v. United Kingdom* (1994) 17 E.H.R.R. 539, para. 66.
[7] *Golder v. United Kingdom* 1 E.H.R.R. 524, para. 36.
[8] *Albert and Le Compte v. Belgium* (1983) 5 E.H.R.R. 533, para. 30.

any case where domestic law classifies a person's rights as "civil" or as a "criminal charge", so that where a state decides that the Article 6(1) guarantees should apply, the Strasbourg institutions will not question that exercise of discretion. The position is otherwise where national law seeks to exclude the operation of Article 6 as the Court has made clear:

> "The converse choice, for its part, is subject to stricter rules. If the Contracting States were able at their discretion to classify an offence as disciplinary instead of criminal, or to prosecute the author of a mixed offence on the disciplinary rather than the criminal plane, the operation of the fundamental clauses of Article 6 and 7 would be subordinated to their sovereign will. A latitude extending thus far might lead to results incompatible with the purpose and object of the Convention. The Court has jurisdiction, under Article 6, even without reference to Articles 17 and 18 to satisfy itself that the disciplinary does not improperly encroach upon the criminal.
> In short the 'autonomy' of the concept of 'criminal' operates, as it were, one way only."[9]

C6–07 This important statement of principle equally to the definition of "civil rights". As with the notion of a "criminal charge", the concept of "civil rights and obligations" is autonomous, and "cannot be interpreted solely by reference to the domestic law of the respondent State",[10] but by reference to the substantive content and effects of the right.[11] In *Stran Greek Refineries and Stratis Andreadis v. Greece* the Court made clear that:

> "Article 6(1) applies irrespective of the status of the parties, of the nature of the legislation which governs the manner in which the dispute is to be determined and of the character of the authority which has jurisdiction in the matter; it is enough that the outcome of the proceedings should be decisive for private rights and obligations."[12]

C6–08 As will be seen below, the case law shows tensions and contradictions when applied outside the area of traditional civil trials. In particular it is not clear to what extent the traditional approach of courts towards judicial review of administrative action should be accepted and how far administrative law courts have to make their own findings of fact and decisions on the merits.[13] These are important questions yet to be fully resolved in the Convention's case law. But these unresolved issues should not be taken as clouding the clear application of the guarantees to traditional civil and criminal proceedings. When reading the case law, it is therefore important to take account of the context in which Article 6(1) has been applied.

---

[9] *Engel v. Netherlands* 1 E.H.R.R. 647, para. 81.
[10] *König v. Germany* 2 E.H.R.R. 170, para. 88; *Ringeisen v. Austria* 1 E.H.R.R. 455, para. 94.
[11] *König v. Germany* 2 E.H.R.R. 170, para. 89.
[12] (1995) E.H.R.R. 319, para. 39 ("the right to recover the sums awarded [to the applicants] by the arbitration court" was a civil right). See also *Editions Periscope v. France* (1992) 14 E.H.R.R. 597, where a dispute concerning denial of a fiscal benefit was held to concern a "civil right" notwithstanding the origin of the dispute and the fact that it fell within the jurisdiction of the administrative courts. For the Court, it was" . . . 'pecuniary' in nature and . . . the action was founded on an alleged infringement of rights which were likewise pecuniary rights".
[13] For an example of the Court conducting a careful balancing exercise between the public law elements of a dispute and its private law elements in order to determine whether the dispute was covered by Art. 6(1), see *Schouten and Meldrum v. Netherlands* (1995) 19 E.H.R.R. 432.

C6–09   The paragraphs below consider in turn the applicability of Article 6(1) to the determination of "civil rights and obligations" and "criminal charges". In each instance, the commentary concentrates on the boundaries of the Convention's applicability.

(1)   Civil Rights and Obligations

C6–10   Article 6(1) applies to proceedings which involve a determination of "civil rights and obligations". In the earliest case law, this concept was thought to reflect the civil law distinction between private and public law, with Article 6(1) covering only the former. In *Ringeisen v. Austria* the Court understandably rejected this narrow construction, holding that 6(1) "covers all proceedings the result of which is decisive for civil rights and obligations".[14] It is the substance of the rights in issue which is decisive, not the formal designation of the proceedings. Article 6(1) can thus apply to proceedings that are of a public law character if they are decisive for civil rights and obligations.

C6–11   (a)   **Existence of a "contestation" (dispute) concerning a (civil) right.** Article 6(1) applies to any genuine dispute over the existence, scope or manner of exercise of civil rights or obligations which can be said, at least on arguable grounds, to be recognised under domestic law.[15] There must be a dispute—this requirement comes from the word *"contestation"* in the French text—and it must concern a right rather than, for example, a discretionary benefit. The dispute must be "genuine and serious", although "a claim submitted to a tribunal for determination must be presumed to be genuine and serious unless there are indications to the contrary".[16] *i.e.* unless there is a clear indication that it is frivolous, vexatious or otherwise lacking in foundation. A tenuous connection with, or remote consequences for, a right do not suffice to bring Article 6(1) into play: civil rights and obligations must be the object—or one of the objects—of the dispute.[17]

C6–12   The concept of a dispute must not be construed too technically, and "should be given a substantive rather than a formal meaning".[18] The same approach appears to apply to the question of whether the dispute concerns a right which can be said, at least on arguable grounds, to be recognised under domestic law. But the subject matter of the proceedings must be a *right* rather than a discretionary benefit or an *ex gratia* payment, so a right is involved where that a person who fulfils the eligibility criteria for a benefit will have an enforceable claim.[19] By contrast "[t]he grant to a public authority of a [large] measure of discretion indicates that no actual right is recognised by law".[20] Matters dependent upon expert judgment, for example, questions of fitness to practise a profession which involve an evaluation of

---

[14] 1 E.H.R.R. 455, para. 94.

[15] *Le Compte Van Leuven and De Meyere v. Belgium* (1981) 4 E.H.R.R. 1, paras 45 and 49; *Benthem v. Netherlands* (1986) 8 E.H.R.R. 1, para. 32; *James v. United Kingdom* (1986) 8 E.H.R.R. 123, para. 81.

[16] *Rolf Gustafson v. Sweden*, August 1, 1997, R.J.D., 1997–IV, No. 41; 25 E.H.R.R. 623, para. 39. The Court found that the applicant's application under a criminal injuries compensation scheme gave rise to a genuine and serious dispute about his fulfilment of the eligibility criteria and entitlement to payments.

[17] *Le Compte, Van Leuven and De Meyere v. Belgium* (1981) 4 E.H.R.R. 1, para. 47.

[18] *Le Compte, Van Leuven and De Meyere v. Belgium* (1981) 4 E.H.R.R. 1, para. 45.

[19] *Rolf Gustafson v. Sweden*, August 1, 1997, R.J.D., 1997–IV, No. 41; 25 E.H.R.R. 623.

[20] *Masson & Van Zon v. Netherlands* (1996) 22 E.H.R.R. 491, para. 5. The case concerned the power of the court to make an award of compensation "for reasons of equity" in respect of pre-trial detention of a suspect who was subsequently acquitted, without the need to show that the detention was unlawful.

knowledge and experience by a professional registration body, are largely within the discretion of the primary decision-making body. But questions of fact susceptible to judicial assessment may form the subject-matter of a civil right. Thus in *Van Marle & others v. Netherlands*,[21] a disagreement as to the correctness of an assessment of professional competence was held to fall outside Article 6(1), but the Court indicated that an Article 6(1) dispute could have arisen if the domestic proceedings had centred on procedural irregularities or the arbitrary or *ultra vires* character of the original decision.

C6–13   Although Article 6(1) applies to all proceedings "the result of which is decisive for private rights and obligations",[22] its guarantees are available only to those whose civil rights and obligations are directly affected and which constitute the subject-matter of the dispute.

"A tenuous connection or indirect consequences or repercussions do not suffice for Article 6(1)."[23]

On that basis both the Court and the Commission concluded that:

"Neither Article 6 nor Article 13 imply that under the national law of the Contracting State shareholders in a limited company should have the right to bring an action seeking an injunction or damages in respect of an act or omission that is prejudicial to 'their' company."[24]

However, in its more recent judgment in *Pafitis and others v. Greece*,[25] the Court accepted that bank shareholders proceedings challenging increases in capital, *inter alia* on the ground that they had not been ordered by a duly constituted general meeting of shareholders, constituted a dispute over the shareholders civil rights and obligations since:

" . . . they could arguably claim under Greek and European Community legislation the right to vote on the increase in the bank's capital and thus participate in decisions concerning the value of their shares."[26]

The difference between the two cases is that in the first the shareholders were seeking to assert a right belonging to the company whereas in the second the right was that of the shareholders themselves.

C6–14   In planning and environmental matters, an objector must apparently show a specific and imminent effect on him or her to be able to rely on Article 6. In *Balmer-Schafroth v. Switzerland* the Court found that Article 6(1) was not applicable to proceedings concerning the extension of an operating licence for a

---

[21] (1986) 8 E.H.R.R. 483.
[22] *Ringeisen v. Austria* (1971) 1 E.H.R.R. 455, para. 94.
[23] *Agrotexim et al. v. Greece* (1996) 21 E.H.R.R. 250, Commission Report. See further para. 1/1.017. See also *Le Compte, Van Leuven and de Meyere v. Belgium* (1982) 4 E.H.R.R. 1; *Albert and Le Compte v. Belgium* (1983) 5 E.H.R.R. 533; *Balmer-Schafroth v. Switzerland*, August 26, 1997, R.J.D., 1997–IV, No. 43, para. 32; 25 E.H.R.R. 598.
[24] Judgment at para. 73.
[25] (1999) 27 E.H.R.R. 566.
[26] *ibid.*, para. 87.

nuclear power station, where objectors to the extension complained of a failure to
provide access to a "tribunal". For the Court the connection between the decision
and the right invoked by the applicants was too tenuous and remote:

> " . . . they did not . . . establish a direct link between the operating conditions
> of the power station which were contested by them and their right to
> protection of their physical integrity, as they failed to show that the operation
> of Mühlberg power station exposed them personally to a danger that was not
> only serious but also specific and, above all, imminent."[27]

C6–15   (b)   **No guarantee of any particular content for civil rights.**   Subject to
what has been said about the autonomous nature of the concept of "civil rights",
and except where a Convention right is itself a civil right,[28] the Convention does
not require any particular substantive content for civil rights. In consequence
Article 6 is not violated where no right recognised in domestic law is involved. For
example, in *James v. United Kingdom* landlords had no means of challenging the
tenant's right to enfranchise and acquire title once the criteria laid down in the
Leasehold Reform Act were satisfied. The Court found that there had been no
violation of the right of access, since Article 6 "does not in itself guarantee any
particular content for (civil) 'rights and obligations' in the substantive law of the
Contracting States".[29] This *dictum* has been followed repeatedly by the Commission,[30] although some of its decisions are open to doubt. In particular the absence
of a right in domestic law cannot be conclusive where the "civil right" which an
individual seeks to enforce is a substantive Convention right. The state is required
to secure that right by law, and the right to a court cannot be excluded by failure to
accord the substantive right adequate recognition in domestic law. In such
instances, there is a powerful argument of principle that Article 6(1) should apply,
not least so as to promote effective domestic judicial protection for fundamental
rights. The contrary construction undermines the autonomous interpretation of
civil rights. The judgment in *James* can easily be reconciled with this principle since
in *James* there was no civil right in play either by virtue of domestic law or by
operation of the autonomous notion of "civil rights" under the Convention. In
summary, where a Convention right is also a "civil right" within the autonomous
Article 6 meaning, the right should receive both substantive protection in domestic

---

[27] August 26, 1997, R.J.D., 1997–IV, No. 43; 25 E.H.R.R. 598, para. 40. See also *LM & R. v.
Switzerland* 22 E.H.R.R. CD 130 (holding in transit of nuclear waste at a railway station near the
applicants' homes); see also *Zander v. Sweden* (1994) 18 E.H.R.R. 175 (right of landowner to challenge
authorisation to dump waste on adjacent tip, with risk to drinking water—Article 6); *Greenpeace
Schweiz & others v. Switzerland* (1997) 23 E.H.R.R. CD 116 (complaint of lack of access to court for
neighbours to challenge award of licences to run a nuclear power station affected neighbours' health and
related to their use of property either as proprietor or tenant and therefore a civil right under Article 6).
See also para. C8–70 and see below, para. C6–17(h).
[28] For example the right to liberty, see *Aerts v. Belgium* judgment of July 30, 1998.
[29] (1986) 8 E.H.R.R. 123, para. 81.
[30] See, for example *Kaplan v. United Kingdom*, Commission's Report, (1980) 4 E.H.R.R. 64, para. 134;
App. Nos 8282/78 Church of Scientology v. Sweden 21 D. & R. 109; *Application 9803/82 v. United
Kingdom* (1983) 5 E.H.R.R. 465, *Application 7443/76 v. United Kingdom* 8 D. & R. 216; *10096/82
Pinder v. United Kingdom* (1985) 7 E.H.R.R. 464; *10475/83 Dyer v. United Kingdom* (1985) 7 E.H.R.R.
460; *9310/81 Baggs v. United Kingdom* (1987) 9 E.H.R.R. 235.

law and procedural protection under Article 6. Convention rights which are not also "civil rights" benefit only from the remedial guarantees of Article 13.[31]

C6–16   In other cases, the Convention organs have interpreted the concept of "a right which can be said, at least on arguable grounds, to be recognised under domestic law" in the broadest possible manner. In *W v. United Kingdom*, for example, the Court considered that despite the adoption of a parental rights resolution natural parents could at least arguably claim a "right" of access to their children who had been taken into care. Although parental access became a matter within the local authority's discretion, domestic law recognised the desirability of continued access and the parental rights resolution did not extinguish all the rights and responsibilities of the natural parent. According to the Court, extinction of all parental rights of access would scarcely be compatible with the fundamental notions of family life and the family ties which Article 8 was designed to protect.[32] A similar approach has been taken in a consistent line of Court judgments, and this is to be preferred, both on grounds of principle and authority, to contrary indications in some Commission admissibility decisions.[33]

C6–17   (c)   **Examples of disputes which concern civil rights and obligations.** Article 6(1) has been found applicable in a wide range of disputes relating to:

(a) refusal of administrative authorities to approve contracts concluded between private parties or to authorise the retention of property bought at a compulsory sale;[34]

(b) access to (or disqualification from practice in) one of the liberal professions;[35]

(c) withdrawal of a licence to engage in an economic activity;[36]

(d) expropriation or land consolidation proceedings;[37]

---

[31] However, see the judgment in *Osman v. United Kingdom* judgment of October 28, 1998 [1999] Fam. Law 86, considered below, where the Court found that Art. 6 applied to guarantee access to a court despite the existence of a common law "immunity" from tort liability for the police in relation to the prevention and detection of crime. See the comment of Lord Browne-Wilkinson in *Barrett v. London Borough of Enfield* [1999] 3 W.L.R. 79, 84–85 and see *Gibson v. Chief Constable of Strathclyde Police, The Times*, May 11, 1999 (Court of Session Outer House). Hoffmann (1999) 62 M.L.R. 1, 4–6 states that the decision in *Osman* fills him with apprehension.

[32] (1988) 10 E.H.R.R. 29. But *cf. McMichael v. United Kingdom* (1995) 20 E.H.R.R. 205 (care proceedings before a sheriff court in Scotland not a "determination" of the civil rights of the father of an illegitimate child who did not take the necessary steps in order to "obtain legal recognition of his status as a father").

[33] See *Pudas v. Sweden* (1988) 10 E.H.R.R. 380; *Boden v. Sweden* (1988) 10 E.H.R.R. 367; *H v. Belgium* (1988) 10 E.H.R.R. 339; *Tre Traktorer Aktiebolag v. Sweden* (1991) 13 E.H.R.R. 309; *Allan Jacobsson v. Sweden* (1990) 12 E.H.R.R. 56; *Skarby v. Sweden* (1991) 13 E.H.R.R. 90; *Mats Jacobsson v. Sweden* (1991) 13 E.H.R.R. 79.

[34] *Ringeisen v. Austria, Sramek v. Austria* (1989) 7 E.H.R.R. 351; *Håkansson and Sturesson v. Sweden* (1993) 13 E.H.R.R. 1.

[35] *König v. Germany* (1978) 2 E.H.R.R. 170; *Le Compte, Van Leuven and De Meyere v. Belgium* (1981) 4 E.H.R.R. 1; *Albert and Le Compte v. Belgium* (1983) 5 E.H.R.R. 533; *H v. Belgium* (1987) 10 E.H.R.R. 339; *Kraska v. Swizterland* (1993) 18 E.H.R.R. 188; *Diennet v. France* (1996) 21 E.H.R.R. 554; *Philis v. Greece (No. 2)*, February 27, 1997, R.J.D., 1992–IV, No. 40; 25 E.H.R.R. 417.

[36] *Benthem v. Netherlands* (1986) 8 E.H.R.R. 1; *Pudas v. Sweden* 40 D. & R. 234; *Tre Traktörer Aktiebolag v. Sweden* (1989) 13 E.H.R.R. 309.

[37] *Sporrong and Lönnroth v. Sweden* (1983) 5 E.H.R.R. 35; *Lithgow v. United Kingdom* (1988) 6 E.H.R.R. 329; *Erkner and Hofauer v. Austria* (1987) 9 E.H.R.R. 464; *Ettl v. Austria* (1988) 10 E.H.R.R. 255; *Poiss v. Austria* (1988) 10 E.H.R.R. 231; *Boden v. Sweden* (1988) 10 E.H.R.R. 367.

(e) disputes about entitlement to benefits under,[38] or contributions to,[39] social insurance and welfare assistance schemes.

(f) access to children in care and related wardship and adoption proceedings;[40]

(g) actions for damages against the state or a public body,[41] which includes actions for compensation for detention following a conviction which is later quashed on appeal;[42]

(h) refusal or grant of a permission to exploit or build on privately owned land.[43] In *Ortenberg v. Austria* the Court held that a landowner's public law appeal against the grant of planning permission for adjoining land constituted a "civil right or obligation" because:

" ... she wished to avoid any infringement of her pecuniary rights, because she considered that the works on the land adjoining her property would jeopardise her enjoyment of it and would reduce its market value"[44];

(i) loss of civil capacity upon confinement in a psychiatric hospital;[45]

(j) the right to liberty (as protected by Article 5);[46]

(k) a party's right to recover sums awarded by an arbitration court;[47]

(l) the right to compensation for expropriation arising out of an agreement between two states, where the agreement provided for compensation to be paid from one state to the other with the apportionment of that compensation left to the national authorities;[48]

(m) defamation proceedings, both as plaintiff[49] and as defendant;[50]

(n) patent applications;[51]

---

[38] *Feldbrugge v. Netherlands* (1986) 8 E.H.R.R. 425; *Deumeland v. Germany* (1986) 8 E.H.R.R. 448; *Giancarlo Lombardo v. Italy* November 26, 1992, Series A No. 249–B; *Francesco Lombardo v. Italy* (1996) 21 E.H.R.R. 188; *Schuler-Zgraggen v. Swizterland* (1993) 16 E.H.R.R. 405; *Salesi v. Italy* (1998) 26 E.H.R.R. 187.

[39] *Schouten and Meldrum v. Netherlands* (1995) 19 E.H.R.R. 432 ("the private law features are of greater significance than those of public law", para. 60.)

[40] *W v. United Kingdom* (1988) 10 E.H.R.R. 29; *R. v. United Kingdom* (1988) 10 E.H.R.R. 74; *B v. United Kingdom* (1988) 10 E.H.R.R. 87; *O v. United Kingdom* (1988) 10 E.H.R.R. 82 and *H v. United Kingdom* (1988) 10 E.H.R.R. 95.

[41] *H v. France* (1990) 12 E.H.R.R. 74; *Neves and Silva v. Portugal* (1991) 13 E.H.R.R. 535; *Baraona v. Portugal* (1991) 13 E.H.R.R. 329; *X v. France* (1992) 14 E.H.R.R. 483; *Editions Periscope v. France* (1992) 14 E.H.R.R. 597.

[42] *Georgiadis v. Greece*, May 29, 1997, R.J.D., 1997–III, No. 38; 24 E.H.R.R. 606; *Werner and Szücs v. Austria* (1998) 26 E.H.R.R. 310.

[43] *Fredin v. Sweden* (1991) 13 E.H.R.R. 784, *Allan Jacobsson v. Sweden* (1990) 12 E.H.R.R. 56, *Skarby v. Sweden* (1991) 13 E.H.R.R. 90, *Mats Jacobsson v. Sweden* (1991) 13 E.H.R.R. 79 and *Oerlemans v. Netherlands* (1993) 15 E.H.R.R. 561.

[44] (1995) 19 E.H.R.R. 524, para. 28.

[45] *Winterwerp v. Netherlands* (1979) 2 E.H.R.R. 387.

[46] *Aerts v. Belgium* judgment of July 30, 1998.

[47] *Stran Greek Refineries and Stratis Andreadis v. Greece* (1995) E.H.R.R. 319.

[48] *Beaumartin v. France* (1995) 19 E.H.R.R. 501. Despite the origin of the right, and the fact that the administrative courts had jurisdiction, the right was "unquestionably a pecuniary right and consequently a civil one", para. 28.

[49] *Helmers v. Sweden* (1993) 15 E.H.R.R. 285.

[50] *Tolstoy Miloslavsky v. United Kingdom* (1995) 20 E.H.R.R. 442.

[51] *British American Tobacco Company Ltd v. Netherlands* (1996) 21 E.H.R.R. 409 (the Commission held, and the parties agreed, that the decision to refuse a patent constituted "the determination of civil rights and obligations").

(o) disputes over the allocation of EC milk quotas;[52]

(p) a claim for compensation as a victim of crime under a criminal injuries compensation scheme;[53]

(q) claims of discrimination on grounds of religious belief or political opinion.[54]

C6–18   (d) Examples of disputes which do not concern civil rights and obligations.   The previous case law indicates that the following matters do not involve a determination of civil rights and obligations and are therefore excluded from the scope of application of Article 6(1):

(a) disputes concerning the recruitment, employment, retirement or dismissal of civil servants as well as assessment and promotion of military officers.[55] In *Maillard v. France* the Court expressly stated that:

"The mere fact that the consequences were also partly pecuniary does not suffice to make the proceedings in issue 'civil' ones."[56]

However, a dispute about the entitlement of a retired public servant to an enhanced pension was held to fall within Article 6(1) because:

" . . . what is concerned here is essentially an obligation on the State to pay a pension to a public servant in accordance with the legislation in force. In performing this obligation the State is not using discretionary powers and may be compared, in this respect, with an employer who is a party to a contract of employment governed by private law."[57]

The distinction in the case law is not readily accessible.

(b) Taxation.[58] But in the context of restitution proceedings (for the recovery of allegedly overpaid tax) the Court held that Article 6 applied because these proceedings "were decisive for the determination of private law rights to quantifiable sums of money";[59]

(c) the admission and expulsion of aliens, including the grant of asylum;[60]

---

[52] *Van De Hurk v. Netherlands* (1994) 18 E.H.R.R. 481.

[53] *Rolf Gustafson v. Sweden*, August 1, 1997, R.J.D., 1997–IV, No. 41; 25 E.H.R.R. 623.

[54] *Tinnelly & Sons Ltd and Others and McElduff and Others v. United Kingdom* (1999) 27 E.H.R.R. 249 (claim under the Fair Employment (Northern Ireland) Act 1976).

[55] *Francesco Lombardo v. Italy* (1996) 21 E.H.R.R. 188, para. 17 and *App. Nos 8496/79 v. U.K.* 21 D. & R. 168 and *Application 8686/79 v. Italy* 21 D. & R. 208; *Huber v. France* (1998) 26 E.H.R.R. 457; *Maillard v. France* (1999) 27 E.H.R.R. 232.

[56] (1999) 27 E.H.R.R. 232, para. 37.

[57] *Francesco Lombardo v. Italy* (1996) 21 E.H.R.R. 188, para. 17. See also *Süßmann v. Germany*, September 16, 1996, R.J.D., 1996–IV, No. 15; 25 E.H.R.R. 64.

[58] *App. Nos 2145/64 v. Belgium* 18 Coll 1 and *Application 8903/80 v. Austria* 21 D. & R. 246.

[59] *The National and Provincial Building Society, The Leeds Permanent Building Society and the Yorkshire Building Society v. United Kingdom*, October 23, 1997; R.J.D., 1997–VII, No. 55; 25 E.H.R.R. 127, para. 97. This conclusion was not affected by the fact that the proceedings had their background in tax legislation. Judicial review proceedings brought to challenge the regulations which retrospectively sought to legalise the tax imposed were also held to have been covered by Art. 6 because "these were closely interrelated with the . . . restitution proceedings." (*Ibid.*).

[60] *App. Nos 2991 and 2992/66 Alam, Kahn and Singh v. United Kingdom.* 10 Yb 478 and 8244/78 *Uppal and Others v. United Kingdom* (1980) 3 E.H.R.R. 391. See more recently the Court's admissibility decision in *J.E.D. v. United Kingdom*, App. No. 42225/98, decision of February 2, 1999, where the Court found it unnecessary to examine whether Article 6 entitled the applicant to a court procedure to challenge the rejection of his asylum request, holding that in any event the judicial review proceedings which he had been able to bring were adequate for the purpose. See also *Maaoui v. France* App. No. 39652/98; decision of January 12, 1999, where the Court has communicated to the respondent government a complaint under Article 6(1) about proceedings challenging the refusal to regularise the applicant's immigration position and to issue him with a residence permit.

(d) disciplinary proceedings against members of the liberal professions which cannot lead to their suspension from practice;[61]

(e) detention on remand;[62]

(f) investigations under the Companies Act by DTI inspectors. They are "essentially investigative", leading only to publication of a report, and do not "determine" the subject's right to a good reputation;[63]

(g) hearings concerning allegations that a candidate had exceeded his permitted election expenditure, leading to an order for repayment of the excess, disqualification from standing for election for one year and forfeiture of the seat.[64]

C6–19   While it is safe to assume that Article 6 *will* apply to the cases of the kind set out in paragraph C6–18, more caution is required before assuming that the cases in paragraph C6–18 exclude Article 6 as a matter of principle. In every case, the applicability of Article 6 will depend very much on the facts.

(2)   Criminal Charges

C6–20   The second category of proceedings to which Article 6(1) applies is those which involve the determination of a criminal charge. The state is free to bring Article 6(1) into play by classifying a matter as criminal, but it cannot exclude it simply by classifying an offence as disciplinary, regulatory or civil. The concept of a criminal charge under the Convention has autonomous meaning, which is not bound by the way in which domestic law characterises an act.[65]

C6–21   The applicability of Article 6(1) is determined by reference to three criteria originally adopted in the *Engel* case: the first is the classification of the offence under national law. However, this is only the starting point. The second criterion is the very nature of the offence (*i.e.* whether it is in essence criminal) and the scope of the allegedly violated rule. The classification adopted in other states parties to the Convention is of relevance here. The third criterion is the nature and severity of the possible penalty.[66]

C6–22   Using these criteria the Court has so far considered that the following types of proceedings involve a determination of a criminal charge:

(a) military disciplinary proceedings where the penalties may include deprivation of liberty, with the exception of penalties which by their nature, duration or manner of execution cannot be appreciably detrimental;[67]

(b) prisoners' disciplinary proceedings where the accused risks incurring substantial loss of remission;[68]

---

[61] *App. Nos 8249/78 v. Belgium* 20 D. & R. 40, *10059/82 v. Germany* 43 D. & R. 5 and *11869/85 v. Belgium* (1989) 11 E.H.R.R. 76.

[62] (1968) *Neumeister v. Austria* 1 E.H.R.R. 91. See further *App. No. 8000/77 v. Swizterland* 13 D. & R. 82 and *7830/77 v. Austria* 14 D. & R. 200.

[63] *Fayed v. United Kingdom* (1994) 18 E.H.R.R. 393.

[64] *Pierre-Bloch v. France*, October 21, 1997, R.J.D., 1997–VI, No. 53; 26 E.H.R.R. 202 ("proceedings do not become 'civil' merely because they also raise an economic issue"; para. 51).

[65] *Engel and others v. Netherlands* (1976) 1 E.H.R.R. 647, para. 81 (see above). On the additional protection in criminal cases see below, paras C6–81 *et seq.*

[66] *ibid.*, para. 50.

[67] *Engel v. Netherlands* (1976) 1 E.H.R.R. 647.

[68] *Campbell and Fell v. United Kingdom* (1985) 7 E.H.R.R. 165.

(c) committal to prison for failure to pay Community Charge;[69]

(d) proceedings for regulatory offences which could be committed by any member of the population and which are punishable either by a fine or by deprivation of liberty, for example road traffic offences.[70] In countries where road traffic cases are classified as regulatory, for example, they nonetheless involve a criminal charge, *inter alia*, because default in payment of a fine may be enforced by an order for committal to prison;

(e) proceedings for offences classified as disciplinary under domestic law which potentially affect the entire population and attract a punitive sanction, for example breach of the confidentiality of the judicial investigation by one of the parties and breach of parliamentary privilege by an ordinary citizen;[71]

(f) "regulatory" fines in competition and fiscal cases.[72] In *Bendenoun v. France*,[73] the Court held that administrative "tax surcharges" were criminal in character taking account of the deterrent and punitive character, and the substantial amounts, of the surcharges.

C6–23   No criminal charges, however, were found to be involved in military or prisoners' disciplinary proceedings involving short periods of deprivation of liberty, loss of remission of up to 180 days, cellular confinement, and fines; nor in the proceedings of civil servants and professional associations leading to dismissal from the civil service, loss of earnings, or reprimand.[74] Furthermore, the Court held that a charge of exceeding the maximum election expenditure allowance was not a criminal charge, although the finding would have led to an order for repayment of the excess, forfeiture of the seat and temporary disqualification from standing.[75]

C6–24   Article 6 also implies an "autonomous approach" to the question of when a procedure which might lead to a determination of a criminal charge has been instituted. From what point in time do Article 6 guarantees first apply? Can an individual be considered an "accused" person within the meaning of Article 6, despite the fact that no charges have been formally preferred in accordance with national law? In several cases an individual has been found to be "accused" when facing an administrative investigation for the purpose of gathering evidence for impending criminal proceedings.[76]

C6–25   It has been held that no determination of a criminal charge occurred in detention on remand proceedings, administrative proceedings leading to the

---

[69] *Benham v. United Kingdom*, June 10, 1996, R.J.D., 1996–III, No. 10; 22 E.H.R.R. 293.
[70] *Oztürk v. Germany* (1984) 6 E.H.R.R. 409; *Umlauft v. Austria* (1996) 22 E.H.R.R. 76 (administrative "sentence order" for refusal to submit to a breath test); *Schmautzer v. Austria* (1996) 21 E.H.R.R. 511 (administrative "sentence order" for failing to wear a safety-belt).
[71] *Weber v. Switzerland* (1990) 12 E.H.R.R. 508 and *Demicoli v. Malta* (1992) 14 E.H.R.R. 47.
[72] *Société Stenuit v. France* (1992) 14 E.H.R.R. 509 (administrative proceedings leading to fine for breach of competition rules).
[73] (1994) 18 E.H.R.R. 54, para. 47.
[74] *Eggs v. Switzerland*, Commission's Report, 15 D. & R. 35 and *App. Nos 8249/78 v. Belgium* 20 D. & R. 40; *10059/82 v. Germany* 43 D. & R. 5; *11869/85 v. Belgium* (1989) 11 E.H.R.R. 76; *8778/79 v. Switzerland* 20 D. & R. 240; *6224/73 Kiss v. United Kingdom* 7 D. & R. 55; *10365/83 v. Germany* 39 D. & R. 237, *8317/78 Mcfeely v. United Kingdom* 3 E.H.R.R. 161; *9208/80 Carvalho v. Portugal* 26 D. & R. 262 and *8496/79 v. United Kingdom* 21 D. & R. 168.
[75] *Pierre-Bloch v. France*, October 21, 1997, R.J.D., 1997–VI, No. 53; 26 E.H.R.R. 202.
[76] *Deweer v. Belgium* (1980) 2 E.H.R.R. 439; *Funke v. France* (1993) 16 E.H.R.R. 297. *cf. Saunders v. United Kingdom*, December 17, 1996, R.J.D., 1996–VI, No. 24; 23 E.H.R.R. 313.

removal of an illegal entrant and proceedings for the forfeiture of illegally imported goods which belong to a third party.[77] Again, however, a warning must be given against mechanistic application of previous decisions.

3.   RIGHT OF ACCESS TO A COURT

(A)   Access to legal advice and proceedings

(1)   right of access generally

C6–26   When civil rights and obligations are in issue, the Convention guarantees "the right to institute proceedings before courts"[78] and similarly there is a right to defend a civil right before a court. This "right to a court" is an inherent element of the notion of a fair trial embodied in Article 6(1),[79] which the Court explained in the following terms:

> "It would be inconceivable . . . that Article 6(1) should describe in detail the procedural guarantees afforded to parties in a pending lawsuit and should not first protect that which alone makes it in fact possible to benefit from such guarantees, that is access to a court. The fair, public and expeditious characteristics of judicial proceedings are of no value at all if there are no judicial proceedings."[80]

C6–27   Violation of the right of access has been found where the Home Secretary prevented a prisoner from consulting a solicitor;[81] where a litigant lacking the means to employ a lawyer is not granted legal aid in respect of complex proceedings;[82] where a statutory body is subrogated to its members' rights and has the sole capacity to institute proceedings for recovery of their fees;[83] where uncertainty in the law deprives an individual of a clear, practical and effective opportunity to challenge administrative acts which interfere with his rights;[84] where an individual or body is denied legal capacity.[85]

(2)   Right of access applies to all stages of legal proceedings

C6–28   The right of access to court relates not only to the "trial" proper but also to the enforcement of a judgment given by any court. Execution proceedings arising from a party's failure to give effect to a judgment "must . . . be regarded as

---

[77] *Neumeister v. Austria* (1979–80) 1 E.H.R.R. 91, *AGOSI v. United Kingdom* (1987) 9 E.H.R.R. 1, App. No. 9174/80 *Zamir v. United Kingdom* 29 D. & R. 153; *Air Canada v. United Kingdom* (1995) 20 E.H.R.R. 150.
[78] *ibid.*
[79] *Golder v. United Kingdom* (1975) 1 E.H.R.R. 524, para. 36.
[80] *ibid.* (Home Secretary's refusal of permission for a prisoner to contact a solicitor with a view to instituting proceedings). See also *Silver v. United Kingdom* (1983) 5 E.H.R.R. 347; *Campbell and Fell v. United Kingdom* (1985) 7 E.H.R.R. 165.
[81] *Golder v. United Kingdom* (1975) 1 E.H.R.R. 524.
[82] *Airey v. Ireland* 2 E.H.R.R. 305.
[83] *Philis v. Greece* (1991) 13 E.H.R.R. 741.
[84] *De la Pradelle v. France*, December 16, 1992, Series A, No. 253–B (uncertainty as to the calculation of the time limits for bringing appeals).
[85] *Holy Monasteries v. Greece* (1995) 20 E.H.R.R. 1; *Canea Catholic Church v. Greece* (1999) 27 E.H.R.R. 521.

an integral part of the 'trial' for the purposes of Article 6(1)",[86] as must proceedings relating to costs following judgment.[87]

C6–29   There is, however, no implied right of access to an appeal. The only explicit provision for appeals is in Article 2 of Protocol No. 7, which guarantees such a right in respect of criminal proceedings.[88] But where appeal procedures do exist under domestic law Article 6(1), read in conjunction with the anti-discrimination provisions of Article 14, guarantees equality of access to the appellate stages. As the Court put it in the second *Belgian Linguistic* case:

> "Article 6 of the Convention does not compel States to institute a system of appeal courts. A State which does set up such courts consequently goes beyond its obligations under Article 6. However, it would violate that Article read in conjunction with Article 14, were it to debar certain persons from these remedies without a legitimate reason while making them available to others in respect of the same class of actions".[89]

C6–30   In spite of the general rule, Article 6 may require access to an appeal where the court of first instance has ruled that it has no jurisdiction to consider the substance of the dispute, for in such a case the dispute has not been determined. That appears to be the rationale in *Aerts v. Belgium*, where the applicant was refused legal aid to appeal to the Cour de Cassation against the lower court's refusal to review the lawfulness of his continued detention in the psychiatric wing of a prison. The lower court had decided that the decision to transfer the applicant was an administrative act not subject to judicial review. The Strasbourg Court found that the refusal of legal aid, coupled with the requirement of representation by counsel before the Cour de Cassation, violated the very essence of the right of access.[90]

(3)   Limitations on the right of access

C6–31   The right of access to a court is not absolute and it may be impliedly limited.[91] The Court's approach to this question is a familiar one as the following passage illustrates:

> "The right of access . . . may be subject to limitations: . . . Nonetheless, the limitations applied must not restrict or reduce the access left to the individual in such a way or to such an extent that the very essence of the right is impaired. Furthermore, a limitation will not be compatible with Article 6(1) if it does not pursue a legitimate aim and if there is not a reasonable relationship

---

[86] *Hornsby v. Greece*, March 19, 1997, R.J.D., 1997–II, No. 33; 24 E.H.R.R. 250, para. 40. The Court went on to state that these "principles are of even greater importance in the context of administrative proceedings concerning a dispute whose outcome is decisive for a litigant's civil right.".
[87] *Robins v. United Kingdom*, September 23, 1997, R.J.D., 1997–V, No. 49; 26 E.H.R.R. 527.
[88] The substantive guarantees in the Seventh Protocol are not among the Convention rights to which the HRA gives effect.
[89] 1 E.H.R.R. 252, 283, para. 8.
[90] *Aerts v. Belgium* 61/1997/845/1051, judgment of July 30, 1998. Compare the Court's approach to the similar case of *Ashingdane v. United Kingdom* (1985) 7 E.H.R.R. 528. See further below, paras C6–39—C6–40.
[91] *Golder v. United Kingdom* (1975) 1 E.H.R.R. 524; although the fact that a person is in prison is not a ground for restricting his access to the court.

of proportionality between the means employed and the aim sought to be achieved".[92]

The legitimacy of limitations on access to justice are tested by these criteria. The following paragraphs examine some of those restrictions which the Convention institutions have considered.

C6–32   (a) **Security for costs.** Whether an order for security for costs is an acceptable restriction on access to a court will depend on the purpose of the order and its proportionality. Thus the dismissal of, *inter alia*, a civil-party application in criminal proceedings[93] following the applicant's failure to pay FF80,000 in security for costs was found to be disproportionate, where the applicant's legal aid application had been rejected and he had been assessed as having no assets.[94] Although an order for security pursued the legitimate aim of ensuring payment by the applicant of a civil fine in the event of the application failing, in the circumstances it impaired the very essence of the right of access. By contrast an order for payment of security for the costs of an appeal in libel proceedings in the sum of nearly £125,000 has been considered acceptable. The order had the legitimate aim of protecting the opposing party from irrecoverable costs and the Court of Appeal had taken account of the merits of the appeal in reaching its decision. Security for costs therefore protected the rights of others and the interests of justice, and did not impair the essence of the right.[95]

C6–33   (b) **Limitation periods.** Limitation periods are a common feature in the legal systems of the state parties to the Convention and the Court has normally regarded them as within the state's margin of appreciation so long as they are not so short as to impair the very essence of the right of access. The Commission and Court considered the issue in depth in relation to the limitation period for claims of intentional personal injury brought by victims of childhood sexual abuse. The Commission found no justification for the difference of treatment between this group and victims of negligence, for whom there was a discretion to extend time. For the Court, however, the limitation did not impair the very essence of the right, it pursued a legitimate aim and was proportionate. The Court noted in particular that the practice of European states showed no uniformity, and the matter therefore fell within the state's discretion.[96]

C6–34   (c) **Public interest immunity certificates.** Public interest immunity certificates may constitute a denial of access to the courts. By virtue of certain

---

[92] (1985) 7 E.H.R.R. 528, para. 57. See further *Fayed v. United Kingdom* (1994) 18 E.H.R.R. 393, *Tolstoy Miloslavsky v. United Kingdom* (1995) 20 E.H.R.R. 442; *Lithgow v. United Kingdom* (1986) 8 E.H.R.R. 329, paras 193 to 197; *App. Nos 3374/67 v. Austria* 29 Coll 29; *7729/76 Agee v. United Kingdom* 7 D. & R. 164; *7443/76 v. United Kingdom* 8 D. & R. 216; *10096/82 Pinder v. United Kingdom* (1985) 7 E.H.R.R. 464; *10475/83 Dyer v. United Kingdom* (1985) 7 E.H.R.R. 460; and *Société Levage Prestations v. France* (1997) 24 E.H.R.R. 351; *Waite and Kennedy v. Germany* judgment of February 18, 1999 and *Beer and Regan v. Germany* judgment of February 18, 1999, in all of which cases, no violation was found; *Osman v. United Kingdom* [1999] Fam. Law 86 in which a violation was found.
[93] *i.e.* joinder of the victim in criminal proceedings for the purpose of claiming compensation.
[94] *Aït-Mouhoub v. France* judgment of October 28, 1998.
[95] *Tolstoy Miloslavsky v. United Kingdom* (1995) 20 E.H.R.R. 442, para. 62.
[96] *Stubbings v. United Kingdom*, October 22, 1993, R.J.D., 1996–IV, No. 18; 23 E.H.R.R. 213. See further, Reid, *A Practitioner's Guide to the European Convention of Human Rights* (Sweet and Maxwell, 1998), p. 65.

statutory provisions, a certificate by the Secretary of State that an act was done, or that documents should not be disclosed, on grounds of national security, is conclusive of the matters which it certifies.[97] Such a certificate has been held to constitute a violation of the right to a determination by a court because it removes the certified issue from the primary fact finding body. This was held to be so in particular where the High Court, on an application for judicial review, considered that it was unable to go behind the certificate to verify the truth of the matters.[98] According to the Court, even having regard to the fair balance between national security interests and the right of access to court:

"The right guaranteed to an applicant under Article 6(1) of the Convention to submit a dispute to a court or tribunal in order to have a determination on questions both of fact and law cannot be displaced by the *ipse dixit* of the executive."[99]

C6–35 **(d) Immunities and disabilities.** The immunity from jurisdiction enjoyed by many international organisations pursues a legitimate object in that it:

" . . . is an essential means of ensuring the proper functioning of such organisations free from unilateral interference by individual governments."[1]

Whether the immunity is proportionate to the aim pursued depends on whether the intending litigant has available to him or her reasonable alternative means of effectively protecting his or her rights under the Convention.[2] Thus the grant of jurisdictional immunity did not amount to a breach of the right of access to court under Article 6(1) where employees of an international organisation could bring their complaints to its Appeals Board, and workers on secondment could sue the firms which had seconded them in the German courts.[3]

C6–36 Statutory limitations on liability and access may be justified. For example, the Court considered legitimate a requirement[4] that a patient obtain leave before bringing proceedings against the authorities in respect of alleged failure to comply with the Mental Health Act and a limit on liability to acts done in "bad faith or without reasonable care "[5] The restrictions pursued the legitimate aim of reducing the risk of unfair harassment of those responsible for the care of mental patients. The requirement of bad faith or negligence did not impair the very essence of the right, and it was a proportionate response.

C6–37 By contrast, the Court found that a breach of the right of access arose from the "immunity" which English common law[6] accords to the police from

---

[97] *e.g.* s. 42 of the Fair Employment (Northern Ireland) Act 1976.
[98] *Tinnelly & Sons and others and McElduff and others v. United Kingdom* (1999) 27 E.H.R.R. 249. See also Case 222/84 *Johnston v. Chief Constable of the Royal Ulster Constabulary* [1986] E.C.R. 1651, [1986] 3 C.M.L.R. 240.
[99] *ibid.*, para. 77.
[1] *Waite and Kennedy v. Germany* judgment of February 18, 1999, para. 63; see also *Beer and Regan v. Germany* judgment of February 18, 1999.
[2] *Waite and Kennedy*, para. 68.
[3] *Waite and Kennedy* and *Beer and Regan*.
[4] In s. 141 of the Mental Health Act 1959.
[5] *Ashingdane v. United Kingdom* (1985) 7 E.H.R.R. 528.
[6] *Hill v. Chief Constable of West Yorkshire* [1989] A.C. 53.

actions in negligence in relation to acts or omissions in the investigation and suppression of crime. Although it accepted that the immunity pursued a legitimate aim, namely the maintenance of the effectiveness of the police service, and the prevention of crime and disorder, the Court considered that the grant of absolute immunity was disproportionate. In its judgment in *Osman v. United Kingdom*, the Court reasoned that:

> " . . . the application of the rule in this manner without further enquiry into the existence of competing public interest considerations only serves to confer a blanket immunity on the police for their acts and omissions during the investigation and suppression of crime and amounts to an unjustifiable restriction on an applicant's right to have a determination on the merits of his or her case against the police in deserving cases."[7]

The circumstances of the case were striking, in that the police had failed to protect a boy and his father from an attack (fatal in the father's case) by a teacher who had become obsessed with the boy. The subsequent action in negligence was struck out on the basis that it was not fair, just or reasonable to hold the police liable in such cases. The Strasbourg Court considered that the applicants were " . . . entitled to have the police account for their actions and omissions in adversarial proceedings".[8] Lord Browne-Wilkinson has expressed serious reservations about the Court's reasoning.[9] In particular, he suggests that the consequence of deciding that imposing liability would not be "fair, just and reasonable" is that no "right" exists under domestic law. He also questioned the Court's analysis that the rule in *Hill v. Chief Constable of West Yorkshire* allows a court to assess in each case whether or not it is fair, just and reasonable to apply the exclusionary rule. However, in *Osman* there clearly existed a relationship of proximity to the police, and the harm caused was foreseeable. The Strasbourg Court appears to have been influenced by the facts of case, and the consequence of the rule in *Hill's* case that a failure by the police to act had not been the subject of a judicial investigation at the instance of the family.

C6–38   **(e) Retrospective legislative removal of civil rights.** Legislative intervention to influence the outcome of pending judicial proceedings is viewed with considerable suspicion. Although it may be justified:

> "Respect for the rule of law and the notion of fair trial require that the reasons adduced to justify such measures be treated with the greatest possible degree of circumspection."[10]

Reasons justifying such intervention will therefore be subject to "close scrutiny".[11] In an earlier judgment, the Court had gone further and suggested that the principle

---

[7] *Osman v. United Kingdom* [1999] Fam. L.R. 86, para. 151.
[8] *ibid.*, para. 153.
[9] See Lord Browne-Wilkinson in *Barrett v. Enfield LBC* [1999] 3 W.L.R. 79, 84–85. See also *Gibson v. Chief Constable of Strathclyde Police, The Times,* May 11, 1999 (Court of Session Outer House); and Hoffmann (1999) 62 M.L.R. 1.
[10] In *The National and Provincial Building Society, The Leeds Permanent Building Society and the Yorkshire Building Society v. United Kingdom,* October 23, 1997; R.J.D., 1997–VII, No. 55; 25 E.H.R.R. 127, para. 112.
[11] *ibid.*, para. 107.

of the rule of law and the notion of a fair trial "preclude any interference by the legislature with the administration of justice designed to influence the judicial determination of the dispute".[12] Subsequently, however, it appears to have back-tracked, deciding that Article 6(1) "cannot be interpreted to prevent any interference by public authorities with pending legal proceedings to which they are a party".[13] Thus, while the cancellation of an enforceable judgment, the fruit of nine years litigation against the State, violated Article 6, no violation arose from retrospective legislation to prevent building societies from securing an unexpected tax windfall by frustrating the original intention of Parliament when enacting tax legislation.[14]

B. Legal aid in civil proceedings

C6–39   While Article 6(3)(c) provides that in criminal proceedings, a person without adequate means is to be given free legal assistance when the interests of justice so require,[15] there is no express provision for legal aid in civil proceedings. The Court has made it clear that legal aid is not required for every dispute relating to a "civil right". The assistance of a lawyer will be required, when it:

" . . . proves indispensable for an effective access to a court either because legal representation is rendered compulsory, as is done by the domestic law of certain Contracting States for various types of litigation, or by reason of the complexity of the procedure or of the case."[16]

Free legal aid does not have to be available for every case in which a person cannot afford legal assistance. The circumstances of each case will determine whether it is too complex to expect a litigant to appear in person.

C6–40   Where legal representation is required and the applicant does not have sufficient funds to pay for it, denial of legal aid on the basis of a merits assessment by the legal aid authorities can amount to a breach of the right of access to court. It is for the court, and not the legal aid authorities, to determine the merits.[17]

C. The right of access in criminal proceedings

C6–41   The right of access to a court applies equally in criminal matters. Certain qualifications need to be noted:

(a) The accused is not guaranteed an absolute right to have the charges against him or her determined by a finding of guilty or not guilty. The prosecution

---

[12] *Stran Greek Refineries and Stratis Andreadis v. Greece* (1995) 19 E.H.R.R. 319, para. 49.

[13] *The National Provincial Building Society, loc. cit.*

[14] See also the Commission's Report in *Pressos Compania Naviera S.A. & ors v. Belgium* (1996) 21 E.H.R.R. 301. The case concerned retrospective legislation depriving shipowners of their claims for compensation for damage from collisions allegedly arising from the negligence of Belgian pilots. The Court dealt with the case under Article 1 of the First Protocol and decided that it was unnecessary to deal with Article 6.

[15] See below, paras C6–92 *et seq.*

[16] *Airey v. Ireland* (1979) 2 E.H.R.R. 305, para. 26, and see App. No. 10871/84 *Winer v. United Kingdom* (1986) 48 D. & R. 154.

[17] "By refusing the application on the ground that the appeal did not at that time appear to be well-founded, the Legal Aid Board impaired the very essence of [the applicant's] right to a tribunal.": *Aerts v. Belgium*, 61/1997/845/1051, judgment of July 30, 1998, para. 60. The case concerned an appeal to the Court of Cassation. *Sed quaere* where the lack of merit is such that there is no "genuine and serious" dispute about a right.

may, for example, decide to discontinue the case and the court may terminate the proceedings without a ruling.[18] But Article 6(2) will be violated if such closure of the proceedings involves an implication of guilt.[19]

(b) The right of access may be waived, for example, by plea bargaining. A waiver given under duress or constraint, however, will not be upheld.[20]

(c) The right of access to a court in relation to a criminal charge is that of the accused, not that of the victim:

"The right of access to the courts afforded by Article 6(1) does not include a right to have criminal proceedings instituted against a third party."[21]

However, the victim of a crime may have a civil right in respect of which he or she enjoys a right of access to a court. Further, the Convention may impose positive obligations requiring access to a criminal court. For example, Article 8 requires that serious sexual abuse be punished by effective deterrence and criminal law provisions;[22] and it may be necessary to allow private prosecutions at the instance of someone offended by a serious blasphemous libel.[23]

D. Waiver of the right of access to a Court

C6–42   The right of access to a court can be waived in both civil and criminal cases. In criminal cases, as noted above, the right of access to a court may be waived, for example by engaging in plea-bargaining. But the Court will not uphold a waiver tainted with constraint.[24] In civil cases, the most common forms of waivers are arbitration agreements and settlements.

(1) Arbitration agreements

C6–43   The case law establishes a distinction between "voluntary and compulsory arbitration":

"Normally Article 6 poses no problem where arbitration is entered into voluntarily.[25] If on the other hand, arbitration is compulsory in the sense of being required by law . . . the parties have no option but to refer their dispute to an Arbitration Board, and the Board must offer the guarantees set forth in Art. 6(1) . . . "[26]

(2) Settlement of a claim

C6–44   Settlement of a claim may amount to a waiver of the right of access to a court under Article 6(1).[27] Settlement must be voluntary, and any purported waiver

---

[18] Deweer v. Belgium (1980) 2 E.H.R.R. 439, para. 49.
[19] See para. C6–82 as to the presumption of innocence.
[20] Deweer v. Belgium, para. 50. See further below, para. C6–42.
[21] App. No. 7116/75 7 D. & R. 91 and App. No. 9777/82 34 D. & R. 158.
[22] X & Y v. Netherlands (1985) 8 E.H.R.R. 235.
[23] App. No. 8710/79 Gay News and Lemon v. United Kingdom (1983) 5 E.H.R.R. 123, para. 12: Commission decision on admissibility.
[24] Deweer v. Belgium (1979–1980) 2 E.H.R.R. 439, para. 50.
[25] cf. App. No. 1197/61, 5 Yb 88.
[26] App. Nos 8858 & 8859/79 Bramelid & Malmstrom v. Sweden (1986) 8 E.H.R.R. 116, paras 30 and 32 of the Commission's Report.
[27] Settlement may also deprive an applicant of his or her status as a victim under Art. 34/25 of the Convention: see, e.g. App. Nos 5577–5583/72 Donelly v. United Kingdom 4 D. & R. 4 at 78 and see paras 4–25 et seq.

of a Convention right must be established in an unequivocal manner. In order to be effective for Convention purposes, a waiver of procedural rights requires minimum guarantees commensurate to its importance. In other words, the law should prescribe the procedure for waiver and it should be attended by guarantees, for example legal representation.[28]

E. The right of access to a court is not infringed by preliminary administrative proceedings that do not comply with Article 6(1)

C6–45 The initial stages of disciplinary or administrative proceedings which involve the determination of civil rights and obligations or criminal charges are frequently conducted by bodies which do not fully comply with the requirements of Article 6(1). This non-compliance does not violate Article 6, provided that there is an appeal to a judicial body which has full jurisdiction and does provide the guarantees of Article 6(1).[29] The requirement of "full jurisdiction" is considered in the next section.

4. ACCESS TO A COURT WITH "FULL" JURISDICTION[30]

C6–46 In *Le Compte, Van Leuven and De Meyer v. Belgium*, the Court defined the concept of access to a court of full jurisdiction in the following terms:

" . . . Article 6(1) draws no distinction between questions of fact and questions of law. Both categories of question are equally crucial for the outcome of proceedings relating to 'civil rights and obligations'. Hence, the 'right to a court' and the right to a judicial determination of the dispute cover questions of fact just as much as questions of law."[31]

C6–47 Full jurisdiction means that the tribunal which determines an individual's civil rights and obligations must be competent to entertain and rule upon all relevant questions of law and fact which a party wishes to raise.[32] In professional disciplinary matters, for example, this may extend to determining whether the penalty imposed was proportionate to the misconduct.[33] The requirement is not satisfied where a court considers itself bound by findings of fact made by another body on material issues, thereby depriving itself of jurisdiction to determine facts which are crucial to the dispute.[34] Nor is it satisfied, for example, where a court is required to seek, and is bound to accept, the interpretation of an international treaty from the executive.[35]

C6–48 As we have indicated earlier,[36] no issue of principle arises over access to a court of full jurisdiction in relation to traditional civil law suits before the courts

---

[28] *Pfeifer and Plankl v. Austria* (1992) 14 E.H.R.R. 692, para. 37. See further *Oberschlick v. Austria* (1995) 19 E.H.R.R. 389, para. 51.
[29] *Le Compte, Van Leuven and De Meyer v. Belgium* (1981) 4 E.H.R.R. 1, para. 51; *Albert and Le Compte v. Belgium* (1983) 5 E.H.R.R. 533, para. 29; *British American Tobacco Company Ltd v. Netherlands* (1996) 21 E.H.R.R. 409, para. 78; *Ortenberg v. Austria* (1995) 19 E.H.R.R. 524, para. 31; *Fischer v. Austria* (1995) 20 E.H.R.R. 349, para. 28.
[30] See also paras 5–28 *et seq.*
[31] (1981) 4 E.H.R.R. 1, para. 51.
[32] See, *e.g.*, *Zumtobel v. Austria* (1994) 17 E.H.R.R. 116.
[33] *Diennet v. France* (1996) 21 E.H.R.R. 554.
[34] *Terra Woningen v. Netherlands*, December 17, 1996, R.J.D., 1996–VI, No. 25; 24 E.H.R.R. 456.
[35] *Beaumartin v. France* (1995) 19 E.H.R.R. 485.
[36] See para. 5–28.

(or criminal charges), although compliance may be in issue in particular cases. The full jurisdiction requirement has given rise to problems, however, where Article 6(1) applies because an administrative decision-maker takes action which is decisive of civil rights and obligations. Typically in such a case, the administrative body has full jurisdiction but does not satisfy the requirements of independence, while the reviewing court is independent and impartial but traditional grounds of judicial review may fall short of full jurisdiction. The Strasbourg institutions have had to grapple with the question of whether Article 6 requires the judicial review court to act not in a supervisory but in an appellate role, re-opening all questions of fact, law and discretion. This problem has arisen because Article 6 has been a victim of its own success. As the scope of the notion of a civil right has expanded to encompass areas of administrative decision-making beyond the traditional boundaries of private law, so there has been a need to adapt the requirements of the "full jurisdiction" doctrine to accommodate the reality of public administration. The Commission summarised its approach to this question in its unanimous 1980 Report in *Kaplan v. United Kingdom*,[37] where it said that "[a]n interpretation of Article 6(1) under which it was held to provide a right to a full appeal on the merits of every administrative decision affecting private rights would . . . lead to a result which is inconsistent with the existing, and long-standing, legal position of most of the Contracting States". As we have explained earlier,[38] there are indications in the case law that the Court also accepts a more pragmatic application of the full jurisdiction requirement. In *Bryan v. United Kingdom*, for example, the Court explicitly recognised that the limited scope for appeal from an administrative decision is "not infrequently the case in relation to administrative law appeals in the Council of Europe Member States".[39]

C6–49 The application of the full jurisdiction requirement to administrative decision-making is discussed in Chapter 5 of Part I, above, and in particular at paragraphs C5–24—C5–25 and C5–28—C5–38. From that discussion, it is possible to identify the following considerations which are relevant in order to decide the extent to which a reviewing court should intervene in the merits of an administrative decision.

  (a) **The nature of what is at stake in the proceedings:** where the individual is subject to a "criminal" penalty, the defining characteristics of "full jurisdiction" include the power "to quash in all respects, on questions of law and fact, the decision of the body below".[40] Similarly, where the administrative decision interferes with an important right, for example family life, a greater degree of judicial intervention is required than, for example, in cases of interference with commercial property.[41]

---

[37] (1980) 4 E.H.R.R. 64, para. 158, discussed above, para. I–5.4.9.
[38] See above, paras 5–33 *et seq.*
[39] (1996) 21 E.H.R.R. 342, para. 44 (appeal to the High Court against the decision of a planning inspector).
[40] *Umlauft v. Austria* (1996) 22 E.H.R.R. 76, para. 39; *Schmautzer v. Austria, Umlauft v. Austria* and *Pfarrmeier v. Austria* (1996) 22 E.H.R.R. 175 and *Mauer v. Austria*, February 18, 1997, R.J.D., 1997–I, No. 28; 25 E.H.R.R. 91.
[41] Compare *W v. United Kingdom* (1988) 10 E.H.R.R. 29, paras 82 and 49; *R. v. United Kingdom* (1988) 10 E.H.R.R. 74; *B v. United Kingdom* (1988) 10 E.H.R.R. 87; *O v. United Kingdom* (1988) 10 E.H.R.R. 82 and *H v. United Kingdom* (1988) 10 E.H.R.R. 95 (parents right of access to children in care) with *AGOSI v. United Kingdom* (1987) 9 E.H.R.R. 1, paras 59–60 (confiscation). But *cf.* in the context of Articles 3 and 13, the asylum cases, *Vilvarajah v. United Kingdom* (1992) 14 E.H.R.R. 248, paras 123–126; *Chahal v. United Kingdom*, November 15, 1996, R.J.D. 1996–II, No. 22; 23 E.H.R.R. 413, paras 148, 152–153; App. No. 42225/98 *J.E.D. v. United Kingdom* (decision of February 2, 1999).

(b) **The nature of the subject-matter of the proceedings:** The requirement that the tribunal re-make findings of fact is likely to be diminished where:

    (i) the matter is by its very nature one which requires a certain degree of secrecy;[42]

    (ii) the subject-matter is technical and specialised, such as planning,[43] or the regulation of competence or fitness to practise in financial or professional fields;[44]

    (iii) the court is dealing with an area with a high policy content;[45]

    (iv) the decision is based not simply on fact but on opinions as to administrative policy or expediency, or whether an environmental or health hazard exists; in such cases the issue may be one for the specialist body, with only a limited review by the court;[46]

(c) **The fairness of the decision-making process leading to the administrative decision:** In general, findings of fact, and inferences drawn from them, will not be acceptable where they are the fruit of an unfair procedure or where they are supported by no evidence or no sufficient evidence. What is sufficient evidence will depend upon the seriousness of the right which is being interfered with, so that the more drastic the interference, the less readily the Article 6 "tribunal" should accept the administrator's findings of fact.[47] Contrast the situation where the administrative findings are the fruit of relatively formal (quasi-judicial) procedures which are not themselves the subject of criticism.[48]

(d) **The nature of the submissions which the applicant actually wishes to advance:** The question of a court's jurisdiction will not be considered as an abstract issue. No issue will therefore arise if, in the circumstances of the particular case, the Article 6 "tribunal" reviewing the decision of the administrative body can in fact consider the applicant's submissions on their merits. Where a tribunal has in fact dealt with the applicant's submissions, point by point, without declining jurisdiction in addressing them or in ascertaining various facts, the Strasbourg Court has found no breach of Article 6.[49]

---

[42] *Klass v. Germany* 2 E.H.R.R. 214, para. 69. *cf. Chahal v. United Kingdom*, November 15, 1996, R.J.D. 1996–II, No. 22; 23 E.H.R.R. 413, paras 130–131. See also *R. v. Home Secretary, ex parte Cheblak* [1991] 1 W.L.R. 890, 904.

[43] *Bryan v. United Kingdom* (1996) 21 E.H.R.R. 342; *Fischer v. Austria* (1995) 20 E.H.R.R. 349.

[44] See by analogy the reasoning concerning the applicability of Article. 6 in *Van Marle v. Netherlands* (1986) 8 E.H.R.R. 483, para. 36 (professional competence) and *H v. Belgium* (1988) 10 E.H.R.R. 339, para. 43 ("matters of fact and capable of judicial assessment"). See also the Commission's Report in *APB Ltd v. U.K.* (1998) 25 E.H.R.R. CD 141, 150, above, para. 5–32. *cf.* the important dissenting opinions of Judge Martens in *Fischer v. Austria* (1995) 20 E.H.R.R. 349, paras 6–8 and *Schmautzer v. Austria* (1995) 21 E.H.R.R. 511.

[45] *Zumtobel v. Austria* (1994) 17 E.H.R.R. 116, above (expropriation). See also App. No. 20490/92 *IKSCON v. United Kingdom* 76A DR 90, 111 (1994).

[46] *Zumtobel v. Austria* (1994) 17 E.H.R.R. 116, para. 32 (expropriation); *Fischer v. Austria* (1995) 20 E.H.R.R. 349, para. 34 (revocation of refuse tip operator's licence on environmental grounds).

[47] *Bryan v. United Kingdom* (1996) 21 E.H.R.R. 342, 353–354 (see Mr Nicolas Bratza's important concurring opinion in the Commission's Report).

[48] In *Bryan* the complaint about the planning inspector was that he was not independent of the executive and there was no dispute as to the primary facts nor any challenge to the factual inferences drawn by the inspector; *ibid.*, para. 47. See also cases cited below, n. 49.

[49] *Bryan v. United Kingdom* (1996) 21 E.H.R.R. 342, paras 44, 47; *Zumtobel v. Austria* (1994) 17 E.H.R.R. 116, paras 28, 32. See also *Ortenberg v. Austria* (1995) 19 E.H.R.R. 524, para. 31 *and Fischer v. Austria* (1995) 20 E.H.R.R. 349, para. 28 *cf. Terra Woningen v. Netherlands*, December 17, 1996, R.J.D., 1996–VI, No. 25; 24 E.H.R.R. 456.

5. THE ORGANISATION AND COMPOSITION OF THE COURT

C6-50   Certain consequences—in particular as to power and jurisdiction—flow from the requirement that the deciding body should be a "tribunal" as they do from the requirement of a "court" in Article 5. Both terms imply impartiality and independence, and procedural guarantees, many of which are also specified in Article 6(1).[50] A tribunal within the meaning of the Convention is an independent body whose function is to determine matters within its competence on the basis of rules of law, following proceedings conducted in a prescribed manner.[51] The term does not refer exclusively to "courts of the classic kind", "integrated within the standard judicial machinery of the country". It includes a variety of bodies which satisfy these requirements, including "administrative authorities" and "jurisdictional organs of professional associations".[52] The fact that a body performs several functions other than its judicial function does not prevent it from being a tribunal.[53]

C6-51   As the Court stated in its judgment in *Van De Hurk v. Netherlands*:

" . . . the power to give a binding decision which may not be altered by a non-judicial authority to the detriment of an individual party is inherent in the very notion of a 'tribunal', as is confirmed by the word 'determination' ('*qui décidera*').[54] This power can also be seen as a component of the 'independence' required by Article 6(1)."[55]

In that case, Article 6 was violated because domestic law empowered the Government to decide that judgments of the relevant tribunal should not be implemented.

A. An "independent" tribunal

C6-52   Article 6(1) requires the tribunal be independent of both the executive and the parties to the case. Several factors should be taken into account in determining whether a tribunal is independent for the purposes of Article 6(1). Regard must be had to:

" . . . the manner of appointment of its members and the duration of the terms of their office, the existence of guarantees against outside pressures and the question whether the body presents an appearance of independence."[56]

Applying this test, the Court has held that planning inspectors do not possess the requisite appearance of independence. Although required to decide a case in a quasi-judicial, independent, impartial and fair manner, an inspector is appointed by the Secretary of State who " . . . can revoke his appointment at any time".[57]

C6-53   In practice, however, the Convention organs have been reluctant to conclude that a court coming under their supervision lacks independence. Such a

---

[50] *Le Compte, Van Leuven and De Meyere* (1983) 5 E.H.R.R. 183, para. 55.

[51] *Sramek v. Austria* (1985) 7 E.H.R.R. 351, para. 36.

[52] *De Cubber v. Belgium,* (1991) 13 E.H.R.R. 422, para. 32.

[53] *H v. Belgium* (1988) 10 E.H.R.R. 339, para. 50.

[54] Compare *Benthem v. The Netherlands* (1986) 8 E.H.R.R. 1, para. 40; *H v. Belgium* (1988) 10 E.H.R.R. 339, para. 50; and *Belilos v. Swizterland* (1988) 10 E.H.R.R. 466, para. 64.

[55] (1994) 18 E.H.R.R. 481, para. 45.

[56] *Campbell and Fell v. United Kingdom* (1985) 7 E.H.R.R. 165, para. 78.

[57] *Bryan v. United Kingdom* (1996) 21 E.H.R.R. 342, para. 38.

finding would cast doubt on the Contracting State's adherence to the rule of law and the common political traditions which underlie co-operation within the Council of Europe.[58] One of the rare findings of violation of the "independence" requirement concerned the role of the "convening officer" in the U.K. courts-martial system, prior to the changes introduced by the Armed Forces Act 1996. The convening officer had wide-ranging responsibilities and powers in relation to the bringing and withdrawal of charges, constituting, convening and dissolving the court-martial, dealing with questions of evidence and witnesses and giving effect to the court's decision by confirming it. He also had the power to vary the sentence imposed as he saw fit. For the Court the position of the convening officer cast serious doubt on the court's independence and impartiality.[59]

C6–54   The Commission has also found that the Royal Court in Guernsey lacks the required independence because its President is Bailiff of Guernsey, who also presides over the island's legislature and is head of its administration.[60] Perhaps with the Lord Chancellor's position in mind, Mr Nicolas Bratza limited his finding of violation to proceedings where the executive was a party. In his view, "different considerations would . . . apply where the Bailiff sat in cases involving a dispute between private parties, in which there was no lack of the requisite appearance of independence". However, that appears to be more a question of the appearance of impartiality rather than of independence.

B.   An impartial tribunal

C6–55   The requirement of impartiality, on the other hand, has given rise to more litigation. As the Court observed in *Piersack v. Belgium*,[61] "impartiality normally denotes absence of prejudice or bias". Compliance is assessed by a twofold test, distinguishing between a "subjective" and an "objective approach". The subjective approach involves "endeavouring to ascertain the personal conviction of a given judge" while the objective approach involves "determining whether he offered guarantees sufficient to exclude any legitimate doubt in this respect".[62]

C6–56   Personal impartiality is to be presumed until there is proof to the contrary,[63] and a finding of violation will not be made lightly. The structural or objective impartiality of the tribunal, on the other hand, is more readily open to challenge on the basis of the maxim that justice must not only be done, but it must be seen to be done.

C6–57   Although the case-law does not provide a cut and dried answer as to when justice is not seen to be done, the Convention organs have closely scrutinised cases where:

---

[58] See *Ringeisen v. Austria* (1979–80) 1 E.H.R.R. 455; *Engel v. Netherlands* (1979–80) 1 E.H.R.R. 647; *Le Compte, Van Leuve and De Meyere v. Belgium* (1983) 5 E.H.R.R. 183; *Lithgow v. United Kingdom* (1986) 8 E.H.R.R. 329; *Ettl v. Austria* (1988) 10 E.H.R.R. 255; *H v. Belgium* (1988) 10 E.H.R.R. 339.
[59] *Findlay v. United Kingdom*, February 25, 1997, R.J.D., 1997–I, No. 30; 24 E.H.R.R. 221. It also found a violation of the "impartiality" requirement.
[60] App. No. 28488/95 *McGonnell v. United Kingdom* (Commission's Report dated October 20, 1998).
[61] para. 30.
[62] *Piersack v. Belgium*, (1983) 5 E.H.R.R. 169, para. 30.
[63] *Le Compte, Van Leuven and De Meyere v. Belgium* (1983) 5 E.H.R.R. 183, para. 58; *Debled v. Belgium* (1995) 19 E.H.R.R. 506, para. 37.

(a) The judge has been previously involved in the case.[64] However previous involvement is not an automatic bar. Whether misgivings about a judge's impartiality should be treated as justified depends on the circumstances of each particular case; and the mere fact that the trial judge has also dealt with the case at the pre-trial stage does not in itself justify fears about his impartiality.[65] The Court found the applicant's misgivings objectively were justified where the same judge sat both at first instance and presided over the appeal tribunal sitting with two lay judges.[66]

(b) The tribunal or some of its members have close links with the administration,[67] or to one of the defendants.[68]

(c) Members of the tribunal have been appointed by organisations whose interests are in conflict with those of a litigant.[69]

(f) The complainants and victims of the offence participate in the proceedings leading to conviction and sentence.[70]

(g) The distinction between the functions of the prosecution and the trial court, or between the court and the state as party to the proceedings, become blurred.[71]

(h) Members of the tribunal have previously advised in relation to the drafting of the legislation at issue in the case before them.[72]

While the general rule is that appearances are very important for the administration of justice, the standpoint of the parties is not in itself decisive. The misgivings of the

---

[64] *Piersack v. Belgium* (1983) 5 E.H.R.R. 169, *De Cubber v. Belgium* (1991) 13 E.H.R.R. 422, *Ben Yaacoub v. Belgium* (1991) 13 E.H.R.R. 418; *Hauschildt v. Denmark* (1990) 12 E.H.R.R. 266; *Ringeisen v. Austria* (1979–80) 1 E.H.R.R. 455; *Saint-Marie v. France* 16 E.H.R.R. 116; *Fey v. Austria* 16 E.H.R.R. 387, *Padovani v. Italy* February 26, 1993, Series A/257B, *Nortier v. Netherlands* (1994) 17 E.H.R.R. 273; *Bulut v. Austria*, February 22, 1996, R.J.D., 1996–II, No. 3; 24 E.H.R.R. 84.
[65] *Bulut v. Austria*, February 22, 1996, R.J.D., 1996–II, No. 3; 24 E.H.R.R. 84, para. 33.
[66] *De Haan v. Netherlands*, August 26, 1997, R.J.D., 1997–IV, No. 44; 26 E.H.R.R. 417.
[67] *Sramek v. Austria* (1985) 7 E.H.R.R. 351, *Ettl v. Austria* (1988) 10 E.H.R.R. 255, *Benthem v. Netherlands* (1986) 8 E.H.R.R. 1, *Belilos v. Swizterland* (1988) 10 E.H.R.R. 466, *Stallinger and Kuso v. Austria* (1998) 26 E.H.R.R. 81.
[68] *Higgins and others v. France* judgment of February 19, 1998.
[69] *Langborger v. Sweden* (1989) 12 E.H.R.R. 416. *Gautrin and others v. France* (1999) 28 E.H.R.R. 196.
[70] *Demicoli v. Malta* (1991) 14 E.H.R.R. 47 (conviction and fine of an editor for publishing an Article critical of members of House of Representatives, who took part in the House's proceedings thereon).
[71] See *Delcourt v. Belgium, Borgers v. Belgium* 15 E.H.R.R. 92 and *Thorgeisen v. Iceland* in relation to criminal trials and *Lobo Machado v. Portugal*, February 20, 1996, R.J.D., 1996–I, No. 3; 23 E.H.R.R. 79 in relation to civil proceedings. In *Lobo Machado's* case the Court found a violation of Article 6(1) on the basis of the role played by the Deputy Attorney-General (representing the State) in the context of civil proceedings before the Supreme Court in accordance to the rules of procedure: he gave an opinion to the Court that the appeal should be dismissed, the applicant was unable to obtain a copy of the opinion and reply to it and he was present during the private sittings of the Supreme Court. In *Reinhard and Slimane-Kaid v. France* (1999) 28 E.H.R.R. 59, the reporting judge had submitted the whole of his report and the draft judgment to the Advocate-General (including that part of the report relating to the deliberations of the Court) and not to the applicants. The Advocate-General, who is not a member of the Court but who advises the judges on the solution in each case, likewise did not communicate his submissions to the applicants. The Court found a violation of the right to a fair trial under Article 6(1).
[72] *Procola v. Luxembourg* (1996) 22 E.H.R.R. 193. This case concerned the independence of the Luxembourg Conseil d'Etat, which, like the House of Lords, both deliberates on draft legislation and has a Judicial Committee. Four of the five members of the Conseil d'Etat hearing a case concerning the legality of the retrospective application of a regulation had previously been involved in advising on the legislation at issue, and in particular had drafted the bill which gave it retrospective effect.

individuals before the courts must in addition be "capable of being held to be objectively justified".[73]

C.   Juries and impartiality and independence

C6–58   The requirements of impartiality and independence of tribunals apply to jurors just as they do to professional or lay judges,[74] and those presiding over trial by jury must ensure the impartiality of its members. Thus the Convention was violated where a court refused to take formal notice of a juror's written statement that she had overheard another juror say that he was racist. In consequence the defendant, who was North African, was prevented from seeking to remedy the possible defect. For the Court:

> "Article 6(1) of the Convention imposes an obligation on every national court to check whether, as constituted, it is 'an impartial tribunal' within the meaning of that provision where, as in the instant case, this is disputed on a ground that does not immediately appear to be manifestly devoid of merit."[75]

C6–59   In another case there was no violation of the independence and impartiality requirements even though one member of the jury had been employed by one of the two key prosecution witnesses. On the facts, the juror had only been a junior employee within the witness's firm and had not worked on the project which formed the background to the prosecution, and he had been given notice of redundancy three days before the start of the trial. Further, the Court was of the view that the system provided adequate safeguards. The juror was only one of 15 randomly selected jurors, all of whom had been directed to assess the credibility of the witnesses dispassionately, and had sworn an oath to do so.[76]

C6–60   The requirement of impartiality and the requirement of a fair trial generally, will require that particular care be given to pre-trial publicity where a jury is involved. The Commission has recognised that:

> "in certain cases, and in particular in cases where laymen participate as jurors in the proceedings, th[e] guarantee (of impartiality) may be seriously impaired by a virulent press campaign against the accused, which so influences public opinion and thereby the jurors that a hearing can no longer be a fair hearing within the meaning of Article 6 of the Convention."[77]

This matter is considered further in the commentary relating to the right to freedom of expression.[78]

---

[73] *Kraska v. Swizterland* (1993) 18 E.H.R.R. 188, para. 32.
[74] *Holm v. Sweden* (1994) 18 E.H.R.R. 79; *Remli v. France*, April 23, R.J.D., 1996–II, No. 8; 22 E.H.R.R. 253; *Gregory v. United Kingdom*, February 25, 1997, R.J.D., 1997–I, No. 31; 25 E.H.R.R. 577.
[75] *Remli v. France*, April 23, 1996, R.J.D., 1996–II, No. 8; 22 E.H.R.R. 253, para. 48. Compare *Gregory v. United Kingdom*, February 25, 1997, R.J.D., 1997–I, No. 31; 25 E.H.R.R. 577, where the discharge of one of juror and a firmly worded direction to the remaining members was held to be sufficient to deal with an allegation that the jury was "showing racial overtones".
[76] *Pullar v. United Kingdom*, June 10, 1996, R.J.D., 1996–III, No. 11; 22 E.H.R.R. 391.
[77] *App. No. 1476/62 v. Austria* 11 Coll. 31.
[78] See below, paras C10–14—C10–15.

D. A tribunal established by law

C6–61 The requirement that the tribunal be established by law aims primarily at ensuring a measure of parliamentary control over the organisation of the courts.[79] By interpreting, however, the words "established by law" as "in accordance with national law" the Convention organs have reserved for themselves competence to review the legality under domestic law of almost every aspect of the operation of an Article 6(1) tribunal.[80] However, this competence will be exercised with great caution.

6. CONDUCT OF THE PROCEEDINGS

A. The right to a fair hearing generally

C6–62 "[T]he Convention does not define the notion of fair trial".[81] However, the Convention organs regard the right to a fair hearing as the general principle which underlies all the guarantees of Article 6.[82] Thus, the specific guarantees which the provision sets out expressly are not exhaustive. As the Commission observed *Nielsen v. Denmark*:

> "a trial may not conform to the general standard of a fair trial, even if the minimum rights guaranteed by paragraph 3—and also the rights set forth in paragraph 2—have been respected . . ."[83]

This passage suggests that the more complex question of the overall fairness of the proceedings should be addressed only when no violation of the specific guarantees of Article 6 can be established. In fact, the reverse tendency appears to prevail in more recent case law.[84] The Court will not engage in a detailed examination of the Article 6(3) guarantees if it can safely conclude that overall the accused has had a fair or unfair hearing.[85]

C6–63 In many cases the specific guarantees in Article 6 will not be applicable and an applicant's complaints will have to be examined under the general fair hearing rule. In such cases:

> " . . . the question whether the trial conforms to the standard laid down by paragraph 1 [will be] decided on the basis of a consideration of the trial as a whole, and not on the basis of an isolated consideration of one particular incident. Admittedly one particular incident or one particular aspect . . . may have been so prominent or may have been of such importance as to be decisive for the general evaluation of the trial as a whole. Nevertheless, even in this contingency, it is on the basis of an evaluation of the trial in its entirety that the answer must be given to the question whether there has been a fair trial."[86]

---

[79] *Zand v. Austria*, Commission's Opinion, 15 D. & R. 70.
[80] See *Oberschlick v. Austria* (1991) 19 E.H.R.R. 389; *Pfeifer and Plank v. Austria* (1992) 14 E.H.R.R. 692.
[81] *Nielsen v. Denmark* (1989) 11 E.H.R.R. 175, Commission's Opinion, para. 52.
[82] *Golder v. United Kingdom*, (1979–80) 1 E.H.R.R. 524, para. 36.
[83] Commission's Opinion, para. 52.
[84] See below.
[85] See *Barberà, Messegué and Jabardo v. Spain* (1988) 11 E.H.R.R. 360.
[86] *Nielsen v. Denmark* (1988) 11 E.H.R.R. 175, para. 52.

C6–64 This method of examination allows for the rejection of complaints about secondary procedural flaws which have caused no prejudice, or about lack of procedural protection which has been cured by a higher court.[87] Conversely it also allows account to be taken of the cumulative impact of a series of apparently minor procedural shortcomings.[88]

C6–65 The Convention organs have, moreover, relied on the general right to a fair hearing to articulate several more concrete rights:

(a) The right to adversarial proceedings.[89] The parties are entitled to be heard on all important issues. This right was violated where the applicant was unable to obtain, or comment on, an opinion from the Attorney-General's department submitting to the Supreme Court that his appeal be dismissed.[90]

(b) The right to equality of arms, which affords a party a reasonable opportunity of presenting his or her case to the court under conditions which do not place him at a substantial disadvantage *visà-vis* his or her opponents.[91]

(c) The right to be present at certain court hearings.[92] This right includes hearings before an appellate court, but only where those hearings involve questions of fact bearing on the assessment of the applicant's guilt or innocence or the severity of any sentence imposed.

(d) The right to know the grounds on which a court decision is based.[93] In *Van De Hurk v. Netherlands* the Court held that:

"Article 6(1) obliges courts to give reasons for their decisions, but cannot be understood as requiring a detailed answer to every argument. Nor is the European Court called upon to examine whether arguments are adequately met."[94]

The extent of the obligation to state reasons may also vary according to the nature of the decision and the circumstances of each case.[95]

(e) The right (for a person accused of a criminal offence) to remain silent and not to incriminate himself.[96]

---

[87] See *App. No. 9000/80 v. Switzerland* 28 D. & R. 133 and *Schuler-Zgraggen v. Switzerland* (1993) 16 E.H.R.R. 405.
[88] *Barberà, Messegué and Jabardo v. Spain* (1989) 11 E.H.R.R. 560.
[89] *Feldbrugge v. Netherlands* (1986) 8 E.H.R.R. 425; *Kamasinski v. Austria* (1991) 13 E.H.R.R. 36; *Kraska v. Switzerland* (1994) 18 E.H.R.R. 188 and *Ruiz-Mateos v. Spain* (1993) 16 E.H.R.R. 505.
[90] *Lobo Machado v. Portugal*, February 20, 1996, R.J.D., 1996–I, No. 3; 23 E.H.R.R. 79. See also *Vermeulen v. Belgium*, February 20, 1996, R.J.D., 1996–I, No. 3 and *Van Orshoven v. Belgium*, June 25, 1997, R.J.D., 1997–III, No. 39; 26 E.H.R.R. 55.
[91] App. No. 10938/84 *Kaufman v. Belgium* (1986) 50 D. & R. 98, 115. See also *Delcourt v. Belgium* (1970) 1 E.H.R.R. 355; *Neumeister v. Austria* (1979–80) 1 E.H.R.R. 91; *Borgers v. Belgium* (1993) 15 E.H.R.R. 92. The content of this principle is considered below, para. C6–67.
[92] *Colozza v. Italy* (1985) 7 E.H.R.R. 516; *Monnell and Morris v. United Kingdom* (1988) 10 E.H.R.R. 205; *Ekbatani v. Sweden* (1991) 13 E.H.R.R. 504; *Brozicek v. Italy* (1990) 12 E.H.R.R. 371; *FCB v. Italy* (1991) 14 E.H.R.R. 909; *Kamasinski v. Austria* (1991) 13 E.H.R.R. 36; *Kremzow v. Austria* (1994) 17 E.H.R.R. 322.
[93] *Hadjianastassiou v. Greece* (1993) 16 E.H.R.R. 219.
[94] (1994) 18 E.H.R.R. 481, para. 61.
[95] *Ruiz Torija v. Spain* (1995) 19 E.H.R.R. 553; *Hiro Balani v. Spain* (1995) 19 E.H.R.R. 566. See also *Georgiadis v. Greece*, May 29, 1997, R.J.D., 1997–III, No. 38; 24 E.H.R.R. 606 (failure to give sufficiently detailed reasons).
[96] *Funke v. France* (1992) 16 E.H.R.R. 297; *Murray v. United Kingdom*, February 8, 1996, R.J.D., 1996–I, No. 1; 22 E.H.R.R. 29. *Saunders v. United Kingdom*, December 17, 1996, R.J.D., 1996–VI, No. 24, 23 E.H.R.R. 313. See further, below, paras C6–68 *et seq.*

(f) Access to information necessary to bring the case effectively. In *McGinley and Egan v. United Kingdom*, where the applicants claimed that they had been exposed to dangerous levels of radiation while serving in the armed forces, the Court stated that:

" . . . if it were the case that the respondent State had, without good cause, prevented the applicants from gaining access to, or falsely denied the existence of, documents in its possession which would have assisted them in establishing [their claim] . . . this would have been to deny them a fair hearing in violation of Article 6(1)."[97]

C6–66   Finally "although it is not the function (of the Court) to deal with errors of fact or law allegedly committed by a national court" and "although . . . Article 6 . . . does not lay down any rules on the admissibility of evidence as such", it is the Court's task "to ascertain whether the proceedings in their entirety, including the way in which evidence was taken, were fair".[98] The Court is increasingly asserting supervisory powers in this field.[99] For example, it has adopted a strict approach to the use of undercover agents or *agents provocateurs*, which:

" . . . must be restricted and safeguards put in place even in cases concerning the fight against drug-trafficking. While the rise in organised crime undoubtedly requires that appropriate measures be taken, the right to a fair administration of justice nevertheless holds such a prominent place that it cannot be sacrificed for the sake of expediency. The general requirements of fairness embodied in Article 6 apply to proceedings concerning all types of criminal offences, from the most straight forward to the most complex. The public interest cannot justify the use of evidence obtained as a result of police incitement."[1]

B.   The principle of equality of arms

C6–67   The principle of equality of arms means that a person must be afforded a reasonable opportunity of presenting his case to the court under conditions which do not place him at a substantial disadvantage *vis-à-vis* his opponent.[2] Each party must be able to make known any evidence it requires for its claim to succeed, and each must have knowledge of, and be able to comment effectively on, all the evidence adduced or observations filed with a view to influencing the court's decision. Article 6(1) will be violated where these requirements are not met, irrespective of whether the applicant can show any "quantifiable unfairness flowing from a procedural inequality".[3] The following examples illustrate the content and operation of this principle:

---

[97] (1999) 27 E.H.R.R. 1, para. 86.
[98] *Schenk v. Switzerland* (1988) 13 E.H.R.R. 242, paras 45–46, and *Edwards v. United Kingdom* (1993) 15 E.H.R.R. 417, para. 34. See further Reid, *A Practitioner's Guide to the European Convention of Human Rights* (Sweet and Maxwell, 1998) p. 84.
[99] See *Unterpertinger v. Austria* (1991) 13 E.H.R.R. 175; *Barberà, Messegué and Jabardo v. Spain*; *Vidal v. Belgium* April 22, 1992, Series A, No. 235–B; *Schuler-Zgraggen v. Swizterland* [1994] 1 F.C.R. 453; (1993) 16 E.H.R.R. 405 (on which see the comments below, para. C14–10.
[1] *Teixeira de Castro v. Portugal* (1999) 28 E.H.R.R. 101, para. 36.
[2] App. No. 10938/84 *Kaufman v. Belgium* (1986) 50 D. & R. 98, 115. See also *Delcourt v. Belgium* (1970) 1 E.H.R.R. 355; *Neumeister v. Austria* (1979–80) 1 E.H.R.R. 91; *Borgers v. Belgium* (1993) 15 E.H.R.R. 92.
[3] *ibid.*, para. 49.

(a) Failure to furnish documents to a party: proceedings on appeal from a custody and access hearing were not fair because documents lodged with the court, in particular reports previously before the children's hearing, were not made available to an appellant parent. This was said to reveal "a basic inequality [which] placed the parent at a substantial disadvantage both in respect of bringing an appeal and in the subsequent presentation of any appeal".[4]

(b) Failure to give reasons or serve pleadings on a party: the principle of equality of arms was violated where the Attorney-General submitted observations to the Supreme Court, merely opposing the appeal without giving any reasons, and without serving them on the defence.[5] By contrast, there was no infringement of the principle of equality of arms where a court whose decision was under appeal transmitted its observations to the appeal court but to *neither* of the parties.[6]

(c) Court appointed experts: where evidence is produced on the order of the court rather than on behalf of a party there may also be a breach if a party is not able to comment effectively on it. There was such a breach in *Mantovanelli v. France*,[7] where the court had ordered an expert to provide the answer to a question it had posed. The question posed was identical to the issue the court had to determine and was therefore highly likely to be determinative, even though the court was not, strictly speaking, bound by the expert's opinion. The applicants were not permitted to be associated with the production of the report, which was based on interviews with a number of individuals and referred to correspondence which they had not seen. They were "not able to comment effectively on the main piece of evidence".[8]

(d) Refusal to admit evidence: in *De Haes and Gijsels v. Belgium* the Court found a violation of the principle of equality of arms in defamation proceedings brought by a number of judges and Advocates General against two journalists who had criticised their handling of a case. The applicants were not allowed to produce the opinions of three professors which had prompted the writing of their articles. They wished to do this to counter the statement made by the judges and Advocates-General that the criticism was not supported by the facts of the case. The Court concluded: that "[c]oming as it did from the judges and Advocate-General who had handled the case, that statement had such credibility that it could hardly be seriously challenged in the courts if the defendants could not adduce at least some relevant documentary or witness evidence to that end".[9]

C. The right to remain silent and the privilege against self-incrimination

C6–68 Article 6 does not expressly mention the right to silence and the privilege against self-incrimination. Drawing on generally recognised international

---

[4] *McMichael v. United Kingdom* (1995) 20 E.H.R.R. 205, para. 82.

[5] *Bulut v. Austria*, February 22, 1996, R.J.D., 1996–II, No. 3; 24 E.H.R.R. 84.

[6] *Niederöst-Huber v. Switzerland*, February 18, 1997, R.J.D., 1997–I, No. 29; 25 E.H.R.R. 709. Failure to notify the parties that the first instance court had made observations, to copy the observations to them and to give them an opportunity to comment on them, violated the general right to a fair trial/adversarial proceedings.

[7] March 18, 1997, R.J.D., 1997–II, No. 32; 24 E.H.R.R. 370.

[8] *ibid.*, para. 36.

[9] February 24, 1997, R.J.D., 1997–I, No. 30; 25 E.H.R.R. 1, para. 54.

standards, however, the Court has implied them as rights which "lie at the heart of the notion of fair procedure under Article 6".[10] They apply to all types of crime, no matter how complex, and departures from principle are not justified by appeal to the public interest, for example in the effective prosecution of serious or complex fraud.[11] The privilege against self-incrimination is closely linked with the presumption of innocence in Article 6(2), in that it presupposes that the prosecution should prove its case without resort to evidence obtained by coercion or oppression in defiance of the accused's will.[12] Despite the link with Article 6(2), however, the Court's practice has been to approach the matter from the standpoint of overall fairness in Article 6(1), violation of which makes it unnecessary to consider Article 6(2) separately.[13]

C6–69 The essence of the right is that the accused should be protected from improper compulsion by the authorities, thereby contributing to the avoidance of miscarriages of justice and securing the aim of Article 6.[14] Where it applies, the rule against compulsion extends not only to the answering of questions but also to the imposition of a requirement, on pain of criminal sanctions, to produce documentation which would furnish evidence of offences which the authorities believe the individual has committed.[15] However, it does not extend to the use in criminal proceedings of material obtained through the use of other compulsory powers " . . . but which has an existence independent of the will of the suspect such as, *inter alia*, documents acquired pursuant to a warrant, breath, blood and urine samples and bodily tissue for the purpose of DNA testing".[16]

C6–70 It appears from the Court's judgment in *Saunders v. United Kingdom* that the right to silence does not necessarily operate to prevent the compulsory *obtaining* (as opposed to the use) of evidence by inspectors carrying out an investigation under section 432(2) of the Companies Act 1985.[17] The Court considers that financial regulation would be unduly hampered by the application of the guarantees of Article 6(1) to such an investigation, which it regards as preparatory in nature.[18] The limits of the Court's approach are not readily apparent, however, and it is suggested that the right to silence should apply at least where an investigation is primarily intended to gather information for a criminal prosecution.

C6–71 In any event, where information is obtained by compulsion, Article 6 will prevent its use in subsequent criminal proceedings.[19] The rule against compul-

---

[10] *Murray v. United Kingdom*, February 8, 1996, R.J.D., 1996–I, No. 1; 22 E.H.R.R. 29, para. 45; *Saunders v. United Kingdom*, December 17, 1996, R.J.D; 1996–VI, No. 24; 23 E.H.R.R. 313, para. 68.
[11] *Saunders v. United Kingdom*, para. 74.
[12] *Saunders v. United Kingdom*, loc. cit.
[13] See *Funke v. France* (1993) 16 E.H.R.R. 297, para. 45.
[14] *Murray v. United Kingdom*, February 8, 1996, R.J.D., 1996–I, No. 1; 22 E.H.R.R. 29, para. 45.
[15] *Funke v. France* (1993) 16 E.H.R.R. 297. In *Saunders*, the Court did not deal specifically with the use in criminal proceedings of documents obtained compulsorily pursuant to s. 434.
[16] *Saunders*, para. 69.
[17] *Saunders*, para. 67.
[18] *Fayed v. United Kingdom* (1994) 18 E.H.R.R. 393, paras 61 and 62. This conclusion does not sit easily with the Court's insistence elsewhere on the autonomous nature of the concept of a person charged with a criminal offence and the date of institution of proceedings. And compare the Court's approach in its earlier judgment in *Funke v. France* (1993) 16 E.H.R.R. 297, where it considered that the special features of customs law could not justify departure from the Article 6 guarantees (para. 44).
[19] *Saunders*, para. 67.

sion is not limited to statements making admissions or other statements which are directly incriminating. Statements of fact relating to apparently neutral matters could subsequently be used to cast doubt on a defendant's credibility. For the Court, " . . . what is of the very essence in this context is the use to which evidence obtained under compulsion is made in the course of the criminal trial".[20] Answers to apparently innocuous questions could be equally damaging if deployed in a manner which would tend to incriminate a defendant.

C6–72 In *Murray v. United Kingdom* the Court said that the right to silence is not absolute, so that in some circumstances a court might legitimately draw inferences from the silence of the accused. Whether the drawing of an inference infringes Article 6 is to be determined:

> "in the light of all the circumstances of the case, having particular regard to the situations where inferences may be drawn, the weight attached to them by the national courts in their assessment of the evidence and the degree of compulsion inherent in the situation."[21]

While it would be incompatible with Article 6 to base a conviction solely on the accused's refusal to give evidence,[22] there may be circumstances in which the drawing of inferences from silence is acceptable. The Court has had regard to the safeguards available to the accused, to the weight of the evidence against him, *i.e.* whether it calls for an explanation, and to the constitution of the court hearing the matter (the judge alone or judge and jury).[23]

D. Hearing within a reasonable time

C6–73 There are no general time-limits by which to assess compliance with the right to a hearing within a "reasonable time", which must be judged according to the circumstances of each case. In criminal cases the Convention organs will have regard to the *complexity* of the case and the *conduct* of the applicant and the competent authorities.[24] In civil cases they take account, in addition, of the *behaviour of the other parties* to the case and *what is at stake* in the litigation for the applicant.[25] Although in civil cases the conduct of the litigation is in the hands of the parties, this does not absolve the authorities from ensuring the trial of the actions as expeditiously as required by Article 6.[26] The Convention organs usually concentrate on the *conduct of authorities* to examine whether they have been responsible for delays which were neither the result of the complexity of the case nor caused by the applicant himself—or in civil proceedings by the opposing party.[27] Having looked at individual periods of delay, the Court also makes a global assessment of the overall length of proceedings.[28]

---

[20] *Saunders*, para. 71.
[21] *Murray v. United Kingdom*, February 8, 1996, R.J.D., 1996–I, No. 1; 22 E.H.R.R. 29, para. 47. Compare *Saunders*, para. 69, where the Court said that it did not need to decide whether the right not to incriminate oneself is absolute or whether infringements may be justified in particular circumstances.
[22] *ibid.*
[23] *ibid.*, paras 50 and 51. But even where the drawing of an inference from silence may be legitimate, the risk of such an inference being drawn will be an additional reason for requiring that the suspect should have access to legal advice at the earliest stage: *ibid.*, paras 66–68.
[24] See *Eckle v. Germany* (1983) 5 E.H.R.R. 1, para. 80.
[25] See *Buchholz v. Germany* (1981) 3 E.H.R.R. 597, para. 49.
[26] *ibid.*, para. 50.
[27] *Feldbrugge v. Netherlands. cf. Pretto v. Italy.*
[28] *Santilli v. Italy* (1992) 14 E.H.R.R. 421; *Pugliese v. Italy (No. 1)* (1992) 14 E.H.R.R. 413. See also *Robins v. United Kingdom*, September 23, 1997, R.J.D., 1997–V, No. 49; 26 E.H.R.R. 527, where the Court found Art. 6 violated by costs proceedings lasting four years following judgment in a neighbour dispute between legally aided parties.

C6–74 Save in exceptional circumstances, structural deficiencies, including those arising from shortage of resources, will not be accepted as a defence, since:

> "the Convention places a duty on Contracting States to organise their legal systems so as to allow their courts to comply with Article 6(1), including ensuring trial within a reasonable time."[29]

Although in its earlier judgments the Court appeared ready to tolerate quite lengthy proceedings,[30] the Convention standard has recently become much more stringent.[31] Any significant periods of stagnation in the proceedings will almost certainly attract a finding of violation.[32] In *Philis v. Greece (No. 2)*[33] the Court reiterated this proposition, holding that a period of inactivity of some three years between the date of the applicant's appeal and the date on which his conviction was quashed was excessive. There are, however, certain delays which will be tolerated in the interests of the proper administration of justice, for example the decision not to proceed with a case in order to await the outcome of related proceedings.[34]

C6–75 The authorities are under a positive obligation to exercise exceptional diligence in the conduct of certain cases, where time is of the essence because of what is at stake.[35] This class of case will include those relating to access to, and the adoption of, children taken into public care,[36] social security cases,[37] and cases concerning civil status and capacity.[38] In a number of cases, the Court has paid particular regard to the position of those bringing proceedings for compensation following infection with the AIDS virus through contaminated blood.[39] The consideration of what is at stake for the individuals in those proceedings has been of crucial importance in view of the disease from which they were suffering, and has been an important factor in assessing the reasonableness of the length of proceedings. For example, in one case involving a haemophiliac infected through blood transfusion, the Court found a reasonable time had been exceeded where the domestic court took one year and 10 months to determine the amount of compensation to be paid following friendly settlement of the applicant's previous application under the Convention.[40]

---

[29] *Buchholz v. Germany* (1981) 3 E.H.R.R. 597, para. 51. See also *Zimmermann and Steiner v. Switzerland* (1984) 6 E.H.R.R. 17; *Guincho v. Portugal* (1994) 17 E.H.R.R. 223; *Baggetta v. Italy* (1988) 10 E.H.R.R. 325; *Martins Moreira v. Portugal* (1991) 13 E.H.R.R. 517, a series of cases concerning backlogs.

[30] See, *e.g. Neumeister v. Austria* (1979–80) 1 E.H.R.R. 91.

[31] See, *e.g. Maj v. Italy* (1992) 14 E.H.R.R. 405; *Santilli v. Italy* (1992) 14 E.H.R.R. 421; *Bunkate v. Netherlands*, 26.5.1990.

[32] See *Zimmermann and Steiner v. Switzerland* (1984) 6 E.H.R.R. 17; *Bunkate v. Netherlands* (1995) 19 E.H.R.R. 477; *Massa v. Italy* (1994) 18 E.H.R.R. 266, (1993) 19 E.H.R.R. 477; *Scuderi v. Italy* (1993) 19 E.H.R.R. 187; *Ruiz-Mateos v. Spain*, (1993) 16 E.H.R.R. 505.

[33] February 27, 1997, R.J.D., 1997–IV, No. 40; 25 E.H.R.R. 417. See also *Süßmann v. Germany*, September 16, 1996, R.J.D., 1996–IV, No. 15; 25 E.H.R.R. 64.

[34] *Boddaert v. Belgium* (1993) 16 E.H.R.R. 242.

[35] *A and others v. Denmark*, February 8, 1996, R.J.D., 1996–I, No. 2; 22 E.H.R.R. 458.

[36] *H v. United Kingdom* (1988) 10 E.H.R.R. 95.

[37] *Schuler-Zgraggen v. Switzerland* (1993) E.H.R.R. 405.

[38] *Bock v. Germany* (1990) 12 E.H.R.R. 247.

[39] *X v. France* (1992) 14 E.H.R.R. 483; *Vallée v. France* (1994) 18 E.H.R.R. 549; *Karakaya v. France*, August 26, 1994, Series A, No. 289–B and *A and others v. Denmark*, February 8, 1996, R.J.D; 1996–I, No. 2; 22 E.H.R.R. 458.

[40] *Pailot v. France*, 93/1997/877/1089, judgment of April 22, 1998. The Court rejected an argument that, by virtue of the settlement, the applicant had waived his right to make a further application to the Commission and the Court.

C6–76 A recurrent theme in criminal cases is how to determine the beginning and end of the period to be taken into consideration when calculating the length of proceedings. In accordance with the Convention organs' constant case law, the right to a hearing within a reasonable time accrues to every person who is "charged" within the meaning of Article 6(1).[41] The notion of a "charge" has been defined as:

> "the official notification given to an individual by the competent authority of an allegation that he has committed a 'criminal offence', a definition that also corresponds to the test whether the 'situation of the [suspect] has been substantially affected".[42]

The period to be taken into consideration does not end until the person ceases to be "affected" by the charge, normally after final acquittal, or following final conviction and setting of sentence.[43] In this respect Article 6(1) offers a different kind of guarantee from Article 5(3), which, as noted above, in paragraph II-5.XX, applies to defendants remanded in custody only from the moment of the initial arrest until the first instance determination of the charges or their release.

E. Public hearing and public pronouncement of the judgment

(1) Hearings

C6–77 The Court has repeatedly affirmed the importance of the right to a public hearing. "The public character of the proceedings . . . protects litigants against the administration of justice in secret with no public scrutiny; it is also one of the means whereby confidence in the courts, superior and inferior, can be maintained. By rendering the administration of justice visible, publicity contributes to the aim of Article 6(1), namely a fair trial, the guarantee of which is one of the fundamental principles of any democratic society, within the meaning of the Convention".[44] Unless there are exceptional circumstances that could justify dispensing with an oral hearing, the right to a "public hearing" also includes an entitlement to an "oral hearing".[45]

---

[41] See *Wemhoff v. Germany* (1968) 1 E.H.R.R. 55, para. 19 and *Neumeister v. Austria* (1979–80) 1 E.H.R.R. 91, para. 18.

[42] *Eckle v. Germany* (1983) 5 E.H.R.R. 1, para. 73.

[43] *ibid.* There is some uncertainty in the case law as to whether proceedings before constitutional courts, whether in criminal or civil proceedings, should be included in the relevant period: *Buchholz v. Germany* (1981) 3 E.H.R.R. 597 (German Federal Constitutional Court did not rule upon the right in dispute between the applicant and his employers, para. 48); compare *Deumeland v. Germany* (1986) 8 E.H.R.R. 448 (German Federal Constitutional Court to be taken into account because although it did not rule on the merits—it dealt with procedural complaints made by the applicant—its decision was "capable of affecting the outcome of the claim", para. 77); and, to similar effect, *Poiss v. Austria* (1988) 10 E.H.R.R. 231, para. 52. A question may arise about the applicability of Article 6 to proceedings, rare though they may be, where the only relief sought is a declaration of incompatibility. Arguably, even if the right in issue is civil or criminal, the court considering the matter does not "determine" the right, because the making of a declaration "is not binding on the parties to the proceedings in which it is made": HRA, s. 4(6)(b). As to declarations on incompatibility, see further above, paras 3–43—3–51.

[44] *Axen v. Germany* (1984) 6 E.H.R.R. 195, para. 25. See also *Sutter v. Switzerland* (1984) 6 E.H.R.R. 272; *Schuler-Zgraggen v. Switzerland* (1994) 16 E.H.R.R. 405; *Diennet v. France* (1996) 21 E.H.R.R. 554.

[45] *Fredin v. Sweden (No. 2)*, (1991) 13 E.H.R.R. 784; *Fischer v. Austria* (1995) 20 E.H.R.R. 349 and *Stallinger and Kuso v. Austria*, April 23, 1994, R.J.D., 1997–II, No. 35; 26 E.H.R.R. 81. Indeed the notion of a public hearing without the consideration of oral evidence or argument is surreal.

C6-78 The right to publicity for all judicial hearings is, however, subject to certain specified exceptions. The court hearing the matter may rule that there be no publicity "in the interests of morals, public order or national security in a democratic society, where the interests of juveniles or the protection of the private life of the parties so require, or to the extent strictly necessary in the opinion of the court in special circumstances where publicity would prejudice the interests of justice". However, a private hearing must be "strictly required by the circumstances", in general there should be no automatic rule excluding the public,[46] and the tribunal should consider whether the whole of the proceedings need be conducted in private or whether they might adjourn into chambers only if it became necessary.[47]

C6-79 The case law allows for some exceptions to this general rule. In *Campbell and Fell v. United Kingdom*[48] the Court considered that a state could provide that all disciplinary proceedings in prisons should be held in camera on the basis of considerations of public order and security. There was no need for the tribunal to balance the conflicting interests in each particular case. The Court has also upheld practices of routinely holding certain types of proceedings in private, on the basis of the express or tacit consent of the parties concerned.[49] Although, such waiver should be unequivocal, the Court has not applied very strict criteria to determine what constitutes unequivocal waiver. Thus, where an applicant knew that in practice a particular tribunal held its hearings in private, the Court found that failure to request a public hearing could reasonably be considered to amount to an unequivocal waiver.[50] And indeed, the Court has approved a system, in the social security field, whereby hearings are generally held in private save on application by a party or of the judge's own motion. The applicant's failure to request a public hearing was held to be an unequivocal waiver.[51] Finally, the Court has found on occasion that by their nature certain proceedings on appeal do not require an oral hearing, or indeed public pronouncement of judgment. For the most part, the Court has considered that Article 6 will be satisfied by an oral hearing at first instance and the special features of appeal proceedings will normally justify the absence of a hearing on appeal. This is particularly so where the appeal court determines only questions of law. However, the question in each case will be whether, as a matter of fair trial, the appeal court can properly determine the issue before it without an oral hearing.[52]

---

[46] But see exceptions below.

[47] *Diennet v. France* (1996) 21 E.H.R.R. 554, para. 34. As to arbitration in the county court, see App. No. 33745/96, *Scarth v. United Kingdom* judgment of July 22, 1999.

[48] (1984) E.H.R.R. 165.

[49] *Le Compte, Van Leuven and De Meyere v. Belgium* (1982) 4 E.H.R.R. 1, para. 59; *Håkansson and Sturesson v. Sweden* (1991) 13 E.H.R.R. 1. But *cf. Adler v. Swizterland* No. 9486/81, (1985) 46 D. & R. 36 for the limits of this jurisprudence.

[50] *Zumtobel v. Austria* (1994) 17 E.H.R.R. 116; and see more recently *Rolf Gustafson v. Sweden*, August 1, 1997, R.J.D., 1997–IV, No. 41; 25 E.H.R.R. 623.

[51] *Schuler-Zgraggen v. Switzerland* (1993) 16 E.H.R.R. 405.

[52] *Axen v. Germany* (1984) 6 E.H.R.R. 195 (Federal Court of Justice: determined questions of law only, lower court held public hearing and the object of Article 6 satisfied by proceedings as a whole; *Sutter v. Swizterland* (1984) 6 E.H.R.R. 272 (Court of Cassation: reviewed only issues of law, and public hearing would not have provided any further guarantees of Article 6 rights not already guaranteed by public hearing before first instance court; judgment could be consulted or a copy obtained by anyone with any interest, and was subsequently published); *Schuler-Zgraggen v. Switzerland* (1993) 16 E.H.R.R. 405 (social security proceedings—applicant could apply for hearing: dispute raised no issue of public interest warranting hearing, it was highly technical and better dealt with in writing; national authorities could

(2) Judgments

C6–80 Although there are exceptions to the public hearing requirement, under Article 6(1) all judgments are to be made public.[53] In spite of the wording of Article 6(1), however, public pronouncement is not always required. Other methods of publicity, for instance depositing the judgment in a registry accessible to the public, may be justified in certain types of proceedings.[54]

7. ADDITIONAL PROTECTION IN CRIMINAL PROCEEDINGS

A. The presumption of innocence: Article 6(2)

C6–81 The Court stated in *Barberà, Messegué and Jabardo v. Spain* that Article 6(2):

> " . . . embodies the principle of the presumption of innocence. It requires, *inter alia*, that when carrying out their duties, the members of a court should not start with the preconceived idea that the accused has committed the offence charged; the burden of proof is on the prosecution, and any doubt should benefit the accused. It also follows that it is for the prosecution to inform the accused of the case that will be made against him, so that he may prepare and present his defence accordingly, and to adduce evidence sufficient to convict him."[55]

The presumption of innocence may be infringed not only by a judge or court but also by other public authorities. For example, unqualified public statements by, for example, the police or prosecutors which refer to a person as the perpetrator of an offence both encourage the public to believe in his guilt and prejudge a proper judicial assessment of the facts.[56]

C6–82 One consequence of the presumption of innocence is that a court may not make a decision reflecting an opinion that the accused was guilty:

> " . . . without the accused's having previously been proved guilty according to law and, notably, without his having had the opportunity of exercising his rights of defence . . . "[57]

---

have regard to demands of efficiency, and systematic holding of hearings could ultimately prevent compliance with 'reasonable time' requirement); But *cf. Ekbatani v. Sweden* (1991) 13 E.H.R.R. 504 (Court of Appeal determined both facts and law and made a full assessment of applicant's guilt or innocence; could not fairly and properly determine that question without a direct assessment of the applicant's evidence given in person) and *Helmers v. Sweden* (1993) 15 E.H.R.R. 285 (defamation proceedings–Court of Appeal came to different conclusion of law from that which had formed basis on which first instance court had made findings of fact. Court of Appeal could not make proper assessment of case without hearing parties evidence).

[53] *Campbell and Fell v. United Kingdom* (1985) 7 E.H.R.R. 165, para. 90.

[54] *Pretto v. Italy* (1984) 6 E.H.R.R. 182 (Court of Cassation—confined to reviewing questions of law and could not itself determine the suit; deposit of judgment in court registry and making it generally available sufficient); *Sutter v. Switzerland* (1984) 6 E.H.R.R. 272 (Court of Cassation: reviewed only issues of law; judgment could be consulted or a copy obtained by anyone with any interest, and was subsequently published); *Axen v. Germany* (1984) 6 E.H.R.R. 195 (action for negligence—appeal rejected without hearing or pronouncement or subsequent report; simply confirmed judgment below—object of Article 6 satisfied by the proceedings as a whole). But compare *Werner and Szücs v. Austria* (1998) 26 E.H.R.R. 310 (claims for compensation for detention—decisions of the regional court—first instance—not pronounced publicly, leave to inspect court file given only at the court's discretion and full texts of judgments not available to everyone).

[55] (1989) 11 E.H.R.R. 360, para. 77.

[56] *Allenet de Ribemont v. France* (1995) 20 E.H.R.R. 557, para. 41.

[57] *Minelli v. Switzerland* (1983) 5 E.H.R.R. 554, para. 37.

Typically, such decisions occur where defendants who have been acquitted, or against whom charges have been dropped, apply for costs or compensation. The Court's attitude appears to be less strict where such a decision is made after the proceedings have been terminated without any final decision on the substance, for example following dismissal of time-barred proceedings.[58] A stricter standard of compliance appears to operate where the judicial decision reflecting the accused's guilt is accompanied by a surrogate penalty[59] or where the decision is made despite the accused's final acquittal on the merits.[60] In such cases:

> "The voicing of suspicions regarding an accused's innocence is conceivable as long as the conclusion of criminal proceedings has not resulted in a decision on the merits of the accusation. However, it is no longer admissible to rely on such suspicions once an acquittal has become final."[61]

The Convention does not, however, guarantee to a person whose conviction is quashed on appeal "a right either to reimbursement of costs incurred in the course of criminal proceedings against him, however necessary the costs might have been, or to compensation for lawful restrictions on his liberty".[62]

C6–83 While presumptions of fact and law are not as such contrary to Article 6(2), an issue could arise in respect of over-broad presumptions.[63] Further, the automatic attribution of responsibility to the heirs of an alleged offender, irrespective of guilt, is contrary to the presumption of innocence. Thus Article 6(2) was violated where fines were imposed on a widow and children in respect of tax evasion by their late husband and father. While acknowledging that it was normal for tax *debts* to be paid out of the estate, the Court held:

> "It is a fundamental rule of criminal law that criminal liability does not survive the person who has committed the criminal act . . . In the Court's opinion, such a rule is also required by the presumption of innocence enshrined in Article 6(2) of the Convention. Inheritance of the guilt of the dead is not compatible with the standards of criminal justice in a society governed by the rule of law."[64]

B. The right to be informed promptly, in a language the accused understands, in detail of the charges: Article 6(3)(a)

C6–84 Article 6(3)(a) requires that the accused be informed of the acts with which he or she is charged and of their legal classification.[65] However, the relevant

---

[58] *Lutz v. Germany* (1988) 10 E.H.R.R. 182; *Englert v. Germany* (1991) 13 E.H.R.R. 392; *Nolkenbockhoff v. Germany* (1991) 13 E.H.R.R. 360; *Leutscher v. Netherlands*, March 26, 1996, R.J.D., 1996–II, No. 6; 24 E.H.R.R. 181.
[59] *Minelli v. Switzerland* (1983) 5 E.H.R.R. 554, para. 37.
[60] *Sekanina v. Austria* (1994) 17 E.H.R.R. 221.
[61] *Sekanina v. Austria* (1994) 17 E.H.R.R. 221, para. 30 (rejection of application for compensation on the ground that although the evidence was not strong enough to convict, the applicant had not dispelled the suspicion of guilt).
[62] *Masson and Van Zon v. Netherlands* (1996) 22 E.H.R.R. 491.
[63] *Salabiaku v. France* (1991) 13 E.H.R.R. 379 (unlawful importation or failure to declare goods presumed from fact of their possession: court in fact identified an element of intent, and did not apply impugned provision in a way which conflicted with presumption of innocence); *Hoang v. France* (1993) 16 E.H.R.R. 53. cf. *R. v. D.P.P., ex parte Kebeline* [1999] 3 W.L.R. 175 (DC) and H.L. judgment of October 28, 1999.
[64] *AP, MP and TP v. Switzerland* (1998) 26 E.H.R.R. 541, para. 48. See also Exodus 20, 5.
[65] App. No. 524/59 *Ofner v. Austria*.

information need not be given in writing,[66] as the Court appears to adopt a substantive rather than formalistic approach to this provision. Thus, a summary notification of the charges at the outset of the investigation can satisfy the requirements of Article 6(3)(a) where the national authorities had failed to communicate the official act of indictment to the accused.[67]

C6–85   By contrast, in *Kamasinski v. Austria* the Court stressed the importance of a duly served indictment in ensuring compliance with Article 6(3)(a):

> "An indictment plays a crucial role in the criminal process, in that it is from the moment of its service that the defendant is formally put on notice of the factual and legal basis of the charge against him. A defendant not conversant with the Court's language may in fact be put at a disadvantage if he is not also provided with a written translation of the indictment in a language he understands."[68]

Kamasinski, however, had neither requested a written translation of the indictment, nor complained to the court that he did not understand it. At his request, the indictment had been served upon his defence counsel, who had been appointed by the national court because he was fluent in English. As a result, the absence of a written translation of the indictment did not breach Article 6(3)(a). A violation was, found, however in *Brozicek*, where the summary notification of the charges in Italian was communicated by mail to the accused, who was neither of Italian origin, nor residing in Italy, and who had informed the authorities in an unequivocal manner of his lack of knowledge of Italian.

C6–86   The principles laid down in *Kamasinski* were applied in *Pélissier and Sassi v. France*,[69] where the applicants had been charged with criminal bankruptcy but were later convicted of "aiding and abetting" criminal bankruptcy. The Court endorsed the Commission's finding that the information provided in the indictment needs to be detailed. The applicants had at no time been made aware that the courts might return an alternative verdict of "aiding and abetting" criminal bankruptcy, an offence that required proof of additional elements not required for the charge of criminal bankruptcy. The Court found that there had been a violation of Article 6(3)(a). It appears, however, that the Court of Appeal, which had returned the alternative verdict, would have avoided the breach[70] if it had adjourned the hearing for argument to be addressed on the re-characterisation of the facts or had invited the applicants to provide written submissions on the issue.

C.   The right to adequate time and facilities for the preparation of the accused's defence: Article 6(3)(b)

C6–87   There is no significant case law interpreting the right to adequate time for the preparation of one's defence under Article 6(3)(b) and again compliance will be assessed in the light of the circumstances of each case.[71]

---

[66] *Kamasinski v. Austria* (1991) 13 E.H.R.R. 36.

[67] *Brozicek v. Italy* (1990) 12 E.H.R.R. 371 (judicial notification contained a list of alleged offences, with place and date, referred to legal provisions and named the victim).

[68] (1991) 13 E.H.R.R. 36, para. 80. See further Reid, *op, cit.*

[69] Judgment of March 25, 1999.

[70] Both of Article 6(3)(a) and of Article 6(1), which the Court also found violated.

[71] See *App. Nos 441/58 v. Germany* 2 Yb 391, 5523/72 *Huber v. Austria* 46 Coll 99 and 7628/76 *v. Belgium* 9 D. & R. 172.

C6–88 Article 6(3)(b) guarantees for the accused the opportunity to organise his or her defence in an appropriate way and without restriction as to the possibility to put all relevant defence arguments before the trial court, and thus to influence the outcome of the proceedings. For example, in *Brandstetter v. Austria*[72] the Court considered that the "rights of the defence" concept under Article 6(3)(c) would be overstrained if the accused could not be prosecuted where, in his defence, he had intentionally aroused false suspicions against a witness.

C6–89 The requirements of Article 6(3)(b), as with Article 6 generally, extend to the preparation of an appeal. Thus Article 6 was violated where the accused had not been informed of the reasons for his conviction, until well after the time-limit for lodging an appeal, nor was he told the time-limit for appealing, so that his appeal was rejected as out of time.[73] According to the Court on the facts:

" . . . States must ensure that everyone charged with a criminal offence benefits from the safeguards provided by Article 6(3). Putting the onus on convicted appellants to find out when an allotted period of time starts to run or expires is not compatible with the 'diligence' which the Contracting States must exercise to ensure that the rights guaranteed by Article 6 are enjoyed in an effective manner."[74]

(1) Access to case file and disclosure

C6–90 Some more specific rules have been developed in respect of access to the case file and disclosure. The Court in *Edwards v. United Kingdom* considered that:

" . . . it is a requirement of fairness . . . that the prosecution authorities disclose to the defence all material evidence for and against the accused."[75]

Moreover, in *Jespers v. Belgium*,[76] the Commission, took the view that:

"the 'facilities' which everyone charged with a criminal offence should enjoy include the opportunity of acquainting himself, for the purposes of preparing his defence, with the results of investigations carried out throughout the proceedings. Furthermore, the Commission has always recognised that although a right of access to the prosecution file is not expressly guaranteed by the Convention, such a right can be inferred from Article 6(3)(b) . . . it is clear that the facilities which must be granted to the accused are restricted to those which assist or may assist him in the preparation of his defence . . . In short, Article 6(3)(b) recognises the right of the accused to have at his disposal, for the purposes of exonerating himself or obtaining a reduction in his sentence, all relevant elements that have been or could be collected by the competent authorities."[77]

---

[72] See further *Melin v. France* (1994) 17 E.H.R.R. 1.

[73] *Hadjianastassiou v. Greece* (1993) 16 E.H.R.R. 219.

[74] The position may be different where the individual is himself a lawyer well versed in the practice of the court in question: *Melin v. France* (1994) 17 E.H.R.R. 1.

[75] (1993) 15 E.H.R.R. 417, para. 36. As to denial of disclosure on the ground of public interest immunity see the Commission's Report dated October 20, 1998 in App. No. 28901/95, *Rowe and Davis v. United Kingdom*.

[76] 27 D. & R. 61.

[77] *ibid.*, paras 56–58 of the opinion.

C6–91   In assessing compliance with Article 6(3)(b) the Convention organs take into consideration the facilities made available to defence counsel as well as those made available to the accused.[78]

D.   The right of the accused to defend himself in person or through legal assistance and the right to legal aid: Article 6(3)(c)

C6–92   The option of defending oneself in person or being represented is that of the accused, not the state. A person who chooses to be represented and cannot afford a lawyer is entitled to free legal assistance where the interests of justice so require.[79]

C6–93   The right of the accused to legal assistance applies at all stages of the criminal proceedings against the accused, so that an individual is entitled to access to counsel during the preliminary investigation into an offence by the police.[80] Although the Convention does not expressly guarantee it, the right of an accused in detention to have access to counsel is inherent in Article 6(3)(c).[81] It includes the "right [of the accused] to communicate with his advocate out of the hearing of a third person".[82] Note that, although the Court has expressly recognised the possibility for restrictions, Article 6(3)(c) provides a firmer basis for defending a detained person's right of access to counsel in connection with criminal proceedings than Article 6(3)(b).[83]

C6–94   The following rules emerge from the Court's judgment in *Pakelli v. Germany*[83a] when read in combination with previous case law:

(a)   states cannot force an accused to defend him or herself, or to use officially appointed counsel, where he can procure legal assistance for him or herself (see further *Goddi v. Italy*[83b]);

(b)   the possibility of defending oneself in person is not an acceptable substitute for the right to be given free legal assistance when the interests of justice so require;

(c)   although states are entitled to make defence by a lawyer mandatory and thus deprive the accused of the option of defending him or herself, they cannot prevent him or her from attending the hearing and addressing the court where such a right is guaranteed under Article 6(1); an accused who does not have sufficient means to pay for legal assistance is automatically entitled to free legal aid on such an occasion "when the interests of justice so require".[84]

---

[78] See *Kamasinski v. Austria* (1991) 13 E.H.R.R. 36, para. 88 and *Kremzow v. Austria* (1994) 17 E.H.R.R. 322.
[79] *Pakelli v. Germany* (1984) 6 E.H.R.R. 1, para. 31.
[80] *Imbrioscia v. Swizterland* (1994) 17 E.H.R.R. 441; *Murray v. United Kingdom*, February 8, 1996, R.J.D., 1996–I, No. 1; 22 E.H.R.R. 29. The individual does not have to show that the absence of a lawyer has caused actual prejudice, in the sense that he would have acted differently had he been able to consult a lawyer.
[81] *Campbell and Fell v. United Kingdom* (1985) 7 E.H.R.R. 165, paras 97–99.
[82] *S v. Switzerland* (1992) 14 E.H.R.R. 670, para. 48.
[83] See above, para. C6–88.
[83a] (1984) 6 E.H.R.R. 1
[83b] *Goddi v. Italy*, (1984) 6 E.H.R.R. 457.
[84] See further *Airey v. Ireland* 2 E.H.R.R. 305. Note, however, that these rules apply in respect of criminal cases only.

(d) the fact that the accused chooses not to appear in person cannot justify depriving him or her of right to be defended by counsel at the original trial or in any appeal by way of re-hearing, even if the accused has been properly summoned. As the Court put it in *Poitrimol v. France*:

"Although not absolute, the right of everyone charged with a criminal offence to be effectively defended by a lawyer, assigned officially if need be, is one of the fundamental features of a fair trial. A person charged with a criminal offence does not lose the benefit of this right merely on account of not being present at the trial."[85]

C6–95 The right of the accused to a lawyer of his or her own choice may be subject to certain limitations. States are entitled to limit the number of counsel and to make their appearance subject to regulations, and defence counsel may be excluded if they transgress principles of professional ethics.[86]

C6–96 The most interesting issues in the case law have arisen in connection with the right to free legal assistance. The Court has failed so far to develop any way by which to judge the sufficiency of the accused's means. Much will depend on the circumstances of each case and the *prima facie* good faith of the accused's claim.[87] Whether the interests of justice require legal assistance is, on the other hand, a question which the Convention organs have approached on a more systematic basis. In assessing the question, the Court will consider the case as a whole, including the way it developed after the initial refusal of legal aid.[88] The seriousness of the charges and the penalty threatened, the complexity of the legal and factual issues involved and the personal circumstances of the accused are the main considerations that the Convention organs take into account when addressing the issue.[89] The interests of justice will normally call for representation where liberty may be at stake.[90]

C6–97 A person seeking free legal assistance is not in principle entitled to choose counsel. The state may reasonably seek the reimbursement of legal aid costs if a convicted person acquires sufficient means after the conclusion of the proceedings.[91]

(1) Effectiveness of assistance

C6–98 The Convention organs will examine whether the legal assistance provided by the officially appointed counsel was real and effective. As the Court observed in *Artico v. Italy*

[85] (1994) 18 E.H.R.R. 130. See also *Campbell and Fell v. United Kingdom* (1984) 7 E.H.R.R. 165, para. 99, and, *mutatis mutandis*, *Goddi v. Italy* (1984) 6 E.H.R.R. 457, para. 30 and *F.C.B. v. Italy* (1991) 14 E.H.R.R. 909, para. 33. See further *Pelladoah v. Netherlands* (1995) 19 E.H.R.R. 81 (where the accused had been deported prior to his appeal hearing).
[86] See App. Nos 722/60 *v. Germany* 9 Coll 1; *5217/71 and 5376/72 v. Germany* 42 Coll 139 and 7572/76, 7586/76 and 7587/76 *Ensslin, Baader and Raspe v. Germany* 14 D. & R. 64.
[87] *Pakelli v. Germany* (1984) 6 E.H.R.R. 1, para. 34.
[88] *Granger v. United Kingdom* (1990) 12 E.H.R.R. 469.
[89] See *Pakelli v. Germany* (1984) 6 E.H.R.R. 1; *Monnell and Morris v. United Kingdom* (1988) 10 E.H.R.R. 205; *Granger v. United Kingdom* (1990) 12 E.H.R.R. 469; *Quaranta v. Switzerland*, May 25, 1991, Series A, No. 25; *Hoang v. France* (1993) 16 E.H.R.R. 53; *Maxwell v. United Kingdom* (1995) 19 E.H.R.R. 97 and *Boner v. United Kingdom* (1995) 19 E.H.R.R. 246.
[90] *Benham v. United Kingdom*, June 10, 1996, R.J.D., 1996–III, No. 10; 22 E.H.R.R. 293, para. 61 (applicant faced up to three months imprisonment. Only legal aid available was two hours advice on Green Form or ABWOR, under which the magistrates could have appointed a solicitor to represent him; violation as he was not entitled, as of right, to be represented).
[91] *Croissant v. Germany* (1993) 16 E.H.R.R. 135.

" . . . the Convention is intended to guarantee not rights that are theoretical or illusory but rights that are practical and effective . . . [M]ere nomination does not ensure effective assistance since the lawyer appointed for legal aid purposes may die, fall seriously ill, be prevented for a protracted period from acting or shirk his duties. If they are notified of the situation, the authorities must either replace him or cause him to fulfil his obligations."[92]

Note, however, that "a State cannot be held responsible for every shortcoming on the part of a lawyer appointed for legal aid purposes".[93] In *Kamasinski*[94] the Court held that Article 6(3)(c) required the competent national authorities to intervene only if the failure by legal aid counsel to provide effective representation is manifest or brought to their attention in some other way.

E. The right of the accused to examine witnesses against him and obtain the attendance and examination of witnesses on his behalf: Article 6(3)(d)

C6–99   Article 6(3)(d) contains two distinct rules, the first concerning the right to examine prosecution witnesses and the second concerning the admission of witnesses for the defence.

C6–100   Recent case law relating to the first rule tends to favour a more general principle deriving from Article 6(1). The testimony of a witness whom the accused has had no opportunity to question at any stage of the proceedings cannot form the exclusive or principal basis of a conviction. A number of findings of violation on this ground involve anonymous witnesses, close relatives availing themselves of the right not to testify at court, high ranking officers of state subject to special rules for the taking of evidence, or witnesses who simply could not be located by the police.[95] Recently the Court appears less inclined to reach a finding of violation on this last ground, at least in cases which do not involve anonymous witnesses.[96]

C6–101   However, the Court has made clear that the right to examine prosecution witnesses has to be balanced against the interests of the witnesses:

"It is true that Article 6 does not explicitly require the interests of witnesses in general, and those of victims called upon to testify in particular, to be taken into consideration. However, their life, liberty and security of person may be at stake, as may interests coming generally within the ambit of Article 8 of the Convention. Such interests of witnesses and victims are in principle protected by other, substantive provisions of the Convention, which imply that Contracting States should organise their criminal procedure in such a way that those interests are not unjustifiably imperilled."[97]

---

[92] (1980) 3 E.H.R.R. 1, para. 33 of the judgment.
[93] *Artico v. Italy* 3 E.H.R.R. 1, para. 36.
[94] (1991) 13 E.H.R.R. 36.
[95] See *Kostovski v. Netherlands* (1990) 12 E.H.R.R. 434; *Windisch v. Austria* (1991) 13 E.H.R.R. 281; *Delta v. France* (1992) 16 E.H.R.R. 574; *Unterpertinger v. Austria* (1991) 13 E.H.R.R. 175; *Barberà, Messegué and Jabardo v. Spain* (1989) 11 E.H.R.R. 360; *Bricmont v. Belgium* (1990) 12 E.H.R.R. 217; *Ludi v. Switzerland* (1993) 15 E.H.R.R. 173 and *Teixeira de Castro v. Portugal* (1999) 28 E.H.R.R. 101.
[96] See *Artner v. Austria*, August 28, 1992, Series A, No. 242–A; *Cardot v. France* (1991) 13 E.H.R.R. 853 and *Asch v. Austria* (1993) 15 E.H.R.R. 597. The general rule stated above remains good law (see *Saidi v. France* (1994) 17 E.H.R.R. 251).
[97] *Doorson v. Netherlands*, March 26, 1996, R.J.D., 1996–II, No. 6; 22 E.H.R.R. 330, para. 70 (conviction based on evidence of anonymous witnesses: no violation in the circumstances).

C6–102   In each case the trial court must carefully assess the concerns of the witnesses in order to determine their seriousness. Members of the police force are in a different position from civilian witnesses, in particular victims, and should be granted anonymity only in exceptional circumstances. Where anonymity is granted, the consequent handicaps under which the defence labours should be counterbalanced by the procedures which are followed, and restrictions on the rights of defence should be the minimum consistent with the interests of the witnesses. Thus the Court found a violation of Article 6 where anonymous police officers were interviewed by the investigating judge in a separate room from that of the accused and their counsel, the only communication being by sound link. The defence was not only unaware of the witnesses identity, but was also prevented from observing their demeanour under direct questioning, and thus from testing their reliability.[98]

C6–103   The second rule, as to the admission of defence evidence, has not been interpreted in a particularly broad manner by the Convention organs. Article 6(3)(d) has been expressly held not to require the attendance and examination of *every* witness on the accused's behalf. As the Court observed in *Engel and others v. Netherlands*:

> "Its essential aim, as indicated by the words 'under the same conditions', is a full equality of arms in the matter. With this proviso, it leaves it to the competent national authorities to decide upon the relevance of proposed evidence in so far as is compatible with the concept of a fair trial which dominates the whole of Article 6."[99]

C6–104   A defendant has the right to examine his own expert witness in the same circumstances as the expert witness for the prosecution, or an expert witness whom the accused has objectively justified reasons to identify with the prosecution. This is based on the principle of equality of arms, and derives from Article 6(3)(d), taken together with Article 6(1).[1]

C6–105   "The concept of 'equality of arms' does not, however, exhaust the content of paragraph 3(d) of Article 6 . . . ". There will be extreme cases where the domestic courts' failure to hear defence witnesses is so arbitrary that a violation of Article 6(3)(d) will be found, notwithstanding the domestic courts' margin of appreciation.[2]

F.   The right to free assistance of an interpreter: Article 6(3)(e)

C6–106   Most of the issues arising under Article 6(3)(e) were conclusively dealt with in the important case of *Luedicke, Belkacem and Koç v. Germany*.[3] The Court held that "the right protected by Article 6(3)(e) entails, for anyone who cannot speak or understand the language used in court, the right to receive the free assistance of an interpreter, without subsequently having claimed back from him payment of the costs thereby incurred".[4] According to the Court in the same case,

---

[98] For the principles in this paragraph see *Van Mechelen and others v. Netherlands*, April 23, 1997, R.J.D., 1997–III, No. 36; 25 E.H.R.R. 647.

[99] (1976) 1 E.H.R.R. 647, para. 91.

[1] See *Bönisch v. Austria* (1987) 9 E.H.R.R. 191 *cf. Brandstetter v. Austria* (1993) 15 E.H.R.R. 370.

[2] *Vidal v. Belgium*, April 22, 1992, Series A, No. 235.

[3] (1979) 2 E.H.R.R. 149.

[4] *ibid.*, para. 46.

Article 6(3)(e) guarantees "the right [of the accused] to the free assistance of an interpreter for the translation or interpretation of all those documents or statements in the proceedings instituted against him which it is necessary for him to understand in order to have the benefit of a fair trial".[5]

C6–107 The protection of Article 6(3)(e) also extends to the pre-trial phase. "The right . . . to the free assistance of an interpreter applies not only to oral statements made at the trial hearing but also to the documentary material and the pre-trial proceedings . . . However, paragraph 3(e) does not go so far as to require a written translation of all items of written evidence or official documents in the procedure. The interpretative assistance provided should be such as to enable the defendant to understand the case against him, notably by being able to put before the court his version of the events".[6]

C6–108 Article 6(3)(e) further requires the state to ensure that this right is effectively guaranteed in practice. Thus the obligation on the authorities may extend beyond mere appointment of an interpreter and require a degree of control over the quality of the interpretation provided.[7]

---

[5] *ibid.*, para. 48.
[6] *Kamasinski v. Austria* (1991) 13 E.H.R.R. 36, para. 74.
[7] *ibid.*

ARTICLE 7

NO PUNISHMENT WITHOUT LAW

C7–01

1 No one shall be held guilty of any criminal offence on account of any act or omission which did not constitute a criminal offence under national or international law at the time when it was committed. Nor shall a heavier penalty be imposed than the one that was applicable at the time the criminal offence was committed.

2 This article shall not prejudice the trial and punishment of any person for any act or omission which, at the time when it was committed, was criminal according to the general principles of law recognised by civilised nations.

C7–02   The first point to note is that that no derogation from this right is possible in time of war or other public emergency. The Court has been called upon to decide only very few cases under Article 7, and consequently there is little case law decided under this provision. In the important case of *Kokkinakis v. Greece*, the Court set out the general principle that:

> "Article 7(1) of the Convention is not confined to prohibiting the retrospective application of the criminal law to the accused's disadvantage. It also embodies, more generally, the principle that only the law can define a crime and prescribe a penalty (*nullum crimen, nulla poena sine lege*) and the principle that the criminal law must not be extensively construed to the accused's detriment, for instance by analogy; it follows from this that an offence must be clearly defined in law. This condition is satisfied where the individual can know from the wording of the relevant provision and, if need be, with the assistance of the courts' interpretation of it, what acts and omissions will make him liable".[1]

The Court has made clear that the guarantee that the act constituted an offence "under national or international law" applies to both written and unwritten law "and implies qualitative requirements, notably those of accessibility and foreseeability".[2] Thus in *Kokkinakis*, the Court approached the issue under Article 7 in the same way as it had the issue of foreseeability, under Article 9(2), of the limitation on the right to freedom of religion introduced by national law provisions which criminalised proselytism. It is clear, therefore, that the requirements that flow from the general principle of lawfulness in the restriction clauses (paragraphs 2 of Articles 8–11) are the same as the specific prohibition contained in Article 7.[3]

C7–03   Particular problems may arise in common law countries in respect of the law-making function of the courts. The issue arose in *Gay News Ltd and Lemon v. United Kingdom*, where the Commission observed:

> " . . . in the area of the criminal law it is excluded, by virtue of Article 7 of the Convention, that any acts not previously punishable should be held by the

---

[1] (1994) 17 E.H.R.R. 397, para. 52.
[2] *SW v. United Kingdom* (1996) 21 E.H.R.R. 363, para. 35.
[3] For the requirements that flow from the principle of lawfulness see paras C0–10—C0–11.

courts to entail criminal liability, or that existing offences should be extended to cover facts which previously clearly did not constitute a criminal offence. This implies that constituent elements of an offence such as, *e.g.* the particular form of culpability required for its completion may not be essentially changed, at least not to the detriment of the accused, by the case law of the courts. On the other hand it is not objectionable that the existing elements of the offence are clarified and adapted to new circumstances which can reasonably be brought under the original concept of the offence".[4]

In *SW v. United Kingdom*, the Court had to consider this issue in relation to the disappearance of a husband's common law immunity from prosecution for the rape of his wife. The Court observed that:

" . . . Article 7 of the Convention cannot be read as outlawing the gradual clarification of the rules of criminal liability through judicial interpretation from case to case, provided that the resultant development is consistent with the essence of the offence and could be reasonably foreseen."[5]

The Court went on to find that the decisions confirming discontinuance of the immunity did no more than continue a perceptible line of case law development and that recognition of the absence of the immunity had become a reasonably foreseeable development. The Court also implied that the State's positive obligation to protect the wife from interference with her Convention rights might require removal of the immunity.[6]

C7–04 The concept of a "penalty" in the second sentence of Article 7(1) applies not only to the sentence of the court, but may extend to ancillary orders. In *Welch v. United Kingdom*, the Court made clear that the concept has an autonomous meaning leaving the Court free to go behind formal classifications and assess the substance of the measure. In applying the concept, the Court observed:

"The wording of Article 7(1), second sentence, indicates that the starting point in any assessment of the existence of a penalty is whether the measure in question is imposed following conviction for a 'criminal offence'. Other factors that may be taken into account as relevant in this connection are the nature and purpose of the measure in question; its characterisation under national law; the procedures involved in the making and implementation of the measure; and its severity."[7]

That case concerned the making of a confiscation order under the Drug Trafficking Offences Act 1986, following conviction for a criminal offence committed before the Act came into force. The Court found a violation, as it did in *Jamil v. France*[8] where an increased term of imprisonment in default of payment of fine was ordered pursuant to a law passed after the offence was committed.

C7–05 In its admissibility decision in *Adamson v. United Kingdom*,[9] the Court considered the question of whether compulsory registration of sex offenders with

---

[4] (1983) 5 E.H.R.R. 123, para. 9. On retrospectivity, see further Reid, *op. cit.*
[5] (1996) 21 E.H.R.R. 363, para. 36.
[6] *ibid.*, para. 44.
[7] (1995) 20 E.H.R.R. 247, para. 28.
[8] (1996) 21 E.H.R.R. 65.
[9] App. No. 42293/98, Decision of the ECHR (Third Section) of January 26, 1999 (unreported).

the police under the Sex Offenders Act 1997 amounted to a "penalty" within the terms of Article 7. The Court concluded that it did not constitute a "penalty" and therefore Article 7 did not apply. This finding was based, *inter alia*, on the fact that:

(a) the Act's requirements "do not go beyond an obligation to furnish information to the authorities", which in itself cannot be regarded as severe;

(b) "the purpose of the measures in question is to contribute towards a lower rate of reoffending in sex offenders, since a person's knowledge that he is registered with the police may dissuade him from committing further offences and since, with the help of the register, the police may be enabled to trace reoffenders faster"; and

(c) unlike in *Welch*, independent criminal proceedings would have to be brought against a defaulter, "in which the degree of culpability in defaulting would be taken into account in sentencing".

C7–05 The provision does not apply to the retrospective application of new rules of evidence.[10]

C7–06 Note that Article 7 is one of the provisions in the Convention which empower the Convention organs to supervise, in certain circumstances, the correct application of national law by the national courts:

" . . . under Article 7 the application of a provision of municipal penal law to an act not covered by the provision in question directly results in a conflict with the Convention, so that the Commission can and must take cognisance of allegations of such false interpretation of municipal law".[11]

However, the Commission "exercises in this respect a purely supervisory function and must carry out its task with caution".[12]

C7–08 The exception to the general rule embodied in Article 7(2) was designed to allow the application of national and international war crimes legislation, enacted during and after World War II, to acts committed during the war.[13] The phrase in Article 7(2) "general principles of law recognised by civilised nations" has been directly taken from Article 38 of the Statute of the International Court of Justice. Due to this reference to "civilised nations" the law and practice of states other than those Party to the European Convention will be taken into account in determining whether a retroactive law should constitute an exception to Article 7(1).

---

[10] *Quinn v. United Kingdom* (1997) 23 E.H.R.R. CD 41.
[11] App. No. 1852/63 *X v. Austria* 8 Yb 190.
[12] *ibid.*
[13] App. No. 1038/61 *X v. Belgium* 4 Yb 324.

ARTICLE 8

THE RIGHT TO RESPECT FOR PRIVATE AND FAMILY LIFE

C8–01

> 1 Everyone has the right to respect for his private and family life, his home and his correspondence.
>
> 2 There shall be no interference by a public authority with the exercise of this right except such as is in accordance with the law and is necessary in a democratic society in the interests of national security, public safety or the economic well-being of the country, for the prevention of disorder or crime, for the protection of health or morals, or for the protection of the rights and freedoms of others.

C8–02   The extensive case law on this provision has addressed a wide range of overlapping and interrelated issues. This chapter will undertake initially a brief examination of the meaning of the main concepts in Article 8 and then consider the Convention organs' response to some of the more important categories of complaints that have arisen in this connection.

1. "RESPECT" FOR THE RIGHTS UNDER ARTICLE 8(1)

C8–03   Article 8 adopts a structure which features frequently in the Convention. The first paragraph sets out the rights—respect for private life, family life, home and correspondence—in broad terms. The second paragraph specifies the circumstances in which a public authority may justifiably interfere with them. From this it is clear that Article 8 imposes a negative duty on states not to interfere with the four rights in Article 8(1) unless such interference can be justified under Article 8(2). The Strasbourg institutions have analysed Article 8 issues by asking the following questions: (1) does the subject-matter fall within the scope of Article 8? (2) if so, has there been an interference by a public authority? (3) if so, was it "in accordance with the law"? (4) if so, did it pursue a legitimate aim, *i.e.* one of those set out in Article 8(2)? (5) if so, was it "necessary", *i.e.* did the interference correspond to a "pressing social need" and was it proportionate to that need?

C8–04   The Court has also interpreted the words "right to respect" in Article 8(1) as requiring the state to take positive steps, in some cases, to secure or protect the enjoyment of the rights in Article 8(1). As the Court observed in the important case of *Marckx v. Belgium*:

> "the object of the Article [8] is 'essentially' that of protecting the individual against arbitrary interference by the public authorities. Nevertheless, it does not merely compel the State to abstain from such interference: in addition to this primarily negative undertaking, there may be positive obligations inherent in an effective 'respect' for family life".[1]

The same approach applies to respect for private life, home and correspondence. The case law is still developing, but the Court has said that a positive obligation

---

[1] (1979) 2 E.H.R.R. 330, para. 31.

will exist where there is a "direct and immediate link between the measures sought by an applicant and the latter's private and/or family life".[2]

C8–05   The states parties' positive obligations may, furthermore, involve the adoption of measures designed to secure respect for the protected rights even in the sphere of the relations of individuals between themselves.[3] So far, in the field covered by Article 8 the Court has applied this concept of positive obligations to require states to establish a legal regime which will allow an unmarried mother, her child and the other members of her family to lead a normal family life[4]; to ensure effective access to a domestic court in order to petition for judicial separation[5]; to enable the guardians of a mentally defective girl to lodge a complaint with a view to instituting criminal proceedings against a man who had sexually assaulted her[6]; to establish a fair system whereby the question of access to the personal history files of a child in public care will be determined[7]; to take measures towards reunification of a parent with his or her child, even where the child had been placed in care with other relatives pursuant to a private arrangement[8]; to protect residents from exposure to noxious fumes from a waste treatment plant[9]; to furnish local residents with information about the effect of toxic emissions from a factory near their homes[10]; and to establish an effective and accessible procedure by which those who have been involved in hazardous activities on the state's behalf can obtain all relevant and appropriate information on the possible consequences for their health.[11] In addition, the Commission has found that Article 8 obliges a state to provide a remedy against persistent harassment of a person in his or her home[12]; and it has been suggested that there may be a positive obligation to provide an actionable remedy in respect of publication of private information.[13] It has also stated that "where the State has an obligation to provide medical care, an excessive delay of the public health service in providing a medical service to which the patient is entitled and the fact that such delay has, or is likely to have, a serious impact on the patient's health could raise an issue under Article 8(1) of the Convention".[14]

C8–06   If state action or inaction can be characterised as failure to comply with the positive obligation to "respect" the rights under Article 8(1) then a state will be found in breach of Article 8(1). Although this kind of "interference" cannot be justified by reference to Article 8(2), there are limits on this positive obligation.

---

[2] *Botta v. Italy* (1998) 26 E.H.R.R. 241, para. 34.
[3] *X and Y v. Netherlands* (1986) 8 E.H.R.R. 235; *Hoffmann v. Austria* (1994) 17 E.H.R.R. 293.
[4] *Marckx v. Belgium* (1979) 2 E.H.R.R. 330, para. 31.
[5] *Airey v. Ireland* (1979) 2 E.H.R.R. 305.
[6] *X and Y v. Netherlands*; see also *Stubbings v. United Kingdom*; October 22, 1996, R.J.D., 1996–IV, No. 18; 23 E.H.R.R. 213.
[7] *Gaskin v. United Kingdom* (1990) 12 E.H.R.R. 36.
[8] *Hokkanen v. Finland* (1995) 19 E.H.R.R. 139.
[9] *Lopez-Ostra v. Spain* (1995) 20 E.H.R.R. 277.
[10] *Guerra v. Italy* (1998) 26 E.H.R.R. 357.
[11] *McGinley & Egan v. United Kingdom* (1999) 27 E.H.R.R. 1.
[12] *Whiteside v. U.K.* (1994) 18 E.H.R.R. CD 126.
[13] *Spencer and Spencer v. United Kingdom* (1998) 25 E.H.R.R. CD 105. *cf. Winer v. United Kingdom* 10871/84 48 D. & R. 154.
[14] *Passannante v. Italy* (1998) 26 E.H.R.R. CD 153 (five months' wait to see hospital specialist; no. proof of serious impact on physical or psychological conditions); *cf. Scialacqua v. Italy* (1998) 26 E.H.R.R. CD 164 (no obligation under Article 2 to pay for medicines which are not listed as officially recognised).

These were discussed, in general terms, in the case of *Abdulaziz, Cabales and Balkandali v. United Kingdom*. The Court observed:

" . . . the notion of 'respect' is not clear-cut: having regard to the diversity of the practices followed and the situations obtaining in the Contracting States, the notion's requirements will vary considerably from case to case. Accordingly, this is an area in which the Contracting Parties enjoy a wide margin of appreciation in determining the steps to be taken to ensure compliance with the Convention with due regard to the needs and resources of the community and of individuals".[15]

Moreover, as observed by the Court in *Rees v. United Kingdom*:

"[i]n determining whether or not a positive obligation exists, regard must be had to the fair balance that has to be struck between the general interest of the community and the interests of the individuals . . . In striking this balance the aims mentioned in the second paragraph of Article 8 may be of a certain relevance, although this provision refers in terms only to 'interferences' with the right protected by the first paragraph–in other words is concerned with the negative obligations flowing therefrom."[16]

C8–07 The Court has afforded Contracting States a particularly generous margin of appreciation it appears in areas of the law where, for example, the right to respect for family life makes demands on immigration policy,[17] issues which raise "complex scientific, legal, moral and social issues, in respect of which there is no generally shared approach among the Contracting States",[18] and where the law appears to be in a transitional stage, as, for example, in the regulation of transsexualism.[19]

2. "INTERFERENCE" WITH THE GUARANTEED RIGHTS

C8–08 The notion of "interference" with a guaranteed right under the Convention refers not only to legal impediments (*i.e.* instances where an individual's rights are removed or restricted under the applicable rules of national law), but also to hindrances in fact, even temporary in character, of the effective exercise of a right.[20] It should also be noted that the Court and Commission have not always insisted that the legislation should have been enforced against an applicant before finding that there has been an interference with his Convention rights. As the Court observed in *Klass v. Germany*:

"a law may by itself violate the rights of an individual if the individual is directly affected by the law in the absence of any specific measure of implementation."[21]

---

[15] (1985) 7 E.H.R.R. 471, para. 67.
[16] (1987) 9 E.H.R.R. 56, para. 37. See also *B v. France* (1993) 16 E.H.R.R. 1, para. 44.
[17] *Abdulaziz, Cabales and Balkandali v. United Kingdom* (1987) 7 E.H.R.R. 471.
[18] *X, Y & Z v. United Kingdom*, April 22, 1997, R.J.D., 1997–II, No. 35; 24 E.H.R.R. 143, para. 52.
[19] *Rees v. United Kingdom*; see also *Sheffield & Horsham v. United Kingdom* (1999) 27 E.H.R.R. 163.
[20] *Golder v. United Kingdom* (1975) 1 E.H.R.R. 524, para. 26.
[21] (1983) 2 E.H.R.R. 214, para. 33.

C8–09   In relation to rights protected by Article 8 the Court has concluded on a number of occasions that individuals could claim to be so affected by secret surveillance measures the existence of which remained unknown to the persons being controlled,[22] the criminalisation of homosexual behaviour between consenting adults in private,[23] and family and inheritance laws which discriminate against children born outside marriage in their relationship with their mother and her family.[24] The Convention organs will not find an "interference" with a Convention right, however, if the individual remains largely responsible for the situation complained of.[25]

C8–10   A number of other issues arising in connection with the interpretation of the term "interference" are closely connected with the question of the actual content of the different rights protected under Article 8 and will be examined, as a result, below.

3.   "PRIVATE LIFE"

C8–11   The Court has declined to offer an exhaustive definition of the notion of "private life". It is closely linked with issues of personal autonomy and development, so that it goes further than simply a right to privacy. In its judgment in *Botta v. Italy*, which concerned the rights of disabled people to access to leisure facilities (in this case sea bathing), the Court said that "private life . . . includes a person's physical and psychological integrity; the guarantee afforded by Article 8 is primarily intended to ensure the development, without outside interference, of the personality of each individual in his relations with other human beings".[26]

C8–12   The Court has used this broad approach to give private life an extensive meaning. In *Niemietz v. Germany* it considered that:

" . . . it would be too restrictive to limit the notion to an 'inner circle' in which the individual may live his own personal life as he chooses and to exclude therefrom entirely the outside world not encompassed within that circle. Respect for private life must also comprise to a certain degree the right to establish and develop relationships with other human beings".[27]

In consequence, the notion of private life does not exclude activities of a professional or business nature: "it is, after all, in the course of their working lives that the majority of people have a significant, if not the greatest, opportunity of developing relationships with the outside world".[28]

---

[22] *Klass v. Germany* and *Malone v. United Kingdom* (1985) 7 E.H.R.R. 14. A complainant will need to show that there is a reasonable likelihood that he may be subject to such measures: *Halford v. United Kingdom*, June 25, 1997, R.J.D., 1997–III, No. 39; 24 E.H.R.R. 523; *Esbester v. United Kingdom* (1994) 18 E.H.R.R. CD 72.
[23] *Dudgeon v. United Kingdom* (1981) 4 E.H.R.R. 149; *Norris v. Ireland* (1988) 13 E.H.R.R. 186 and *Modinos v. Cyprus* (1993) 16 E.H.R.R. 485, *Sutherland v. United Kingdom* [1998] E.H.R.L.R 117.
[24] *Marckx v. Belgium* (1979) 2 E.H.R.R. 330.
[25] See further App. No. 8317/78 *Mcfeeley v. U.K.* 3 E.H.R.R. 161.
[26] (1998) 26 E.H.R.R. 241, para. 32.
[27] (1993) 16 E.H.R.R. 97, para. 29.
[28] *ibid.*, *cf. Reiss v. Austria* (1995) 20 E.H.R.R. CD 90: conviction for showing homosexual pornographic video in a private club. Although the club was private it was a business activity which could be separated from the applicant's private life.

There are, however, limits to the interpretation of the right to respect for private life. The Commission gave an indication of its understanding of where the boundaries of the concept might lie in its report in the case of *Brüggeman and Scheuten v. Germany*:

" . . . there are limits to the personal sphere. While a large proportion of the law existing in a given State has some immediate or remote effect on the individual's possibility of developing his personality by doing what he wants to do, not all of these can be considered to constitute an interference with private life in the sense of Article 8 . . . In fact, . . . , the claim to respect for private life is automatically reduced to the extent that the individual himself brings his private life into contact with public life or into close connection with other protected interests".[29]

For similar reasons, the Court has made clear that while sexual orientation and activity concern an intimate aspect of private life, not every sexual activity carried out in private falls within the scope of Article 8. The Court questioned whether private life was involved in a case involving sado-masochistic practices involving a large number of people, the use of specially equipped premises and the making of video-recordings of their activities for circulation among the group.[30]

C8–13   It is unclear to what extent a person can maintain a right to "private space" when he or she is in a public place. It appears that the taking of photographs of an individual participating in a public demonstration will not as such be an interference with private life,[31] although the retention and use of such photographs may raise separate issues.[32] It is therefore likely that a person will retain certain privacy rights in public whenever there is a reasonable expectation that he or she will not be overheard or watched.[33] However, not every such intrusion is a violation of privacy. The Commission's approach has been to examine first whether there has been an intrusion into a person's private sphere, for example his home, next whether the data in question relate to public or private matters and thirdly whether they are liable to be brought to public attention or are intended for limited use only.[34] In a recent Report, the Commission expressed itself as follows:

" . . . the fact that an activity of an individual occurs in a public place or is not intended to be kept secret does not necessarily make such an activity a matter outside the notion of private life in Article 8 para. 1 . . . Whether such an activity falls within the concept of private life or not must be judged on the basis of the nature of the activity itself. Thus, while Article 8 para. 1 of the

---

[29] (1981) 3 E.H.R.R. 244, para. 56 of the Report; and for further discussion see *Botta v. Italy* (1998) 26 E.H.R.R. 241, in particular the concurring opinion of Mrs Liddy and others, p. 250.

[30] *Laskey, Jaggard & Brown v. United Kingdom*, February 19, 1997, R.J.D., 1997–I, No. 29; 24 E.H.R.R. 39.

[31] See the Commission's Report in *Friedl v. Austria* (1995) 21 E.H.R.R. 83, paras 48 and 51. The case was referred to the Court, but a friendly settlement was reached.

[32] *Leander v. Sweden* (1987) 9 E.H.R.R. 433.

[33] See *Halford v. United Kingdom*, June 25, 1997, R.J.D., 1997–III, No. 39; 24 E.H.R.R. 523, para. 45, where the Court held that the applicant had a reasonable expectation of privacy in respect of calls on her office telephone.

[34] *Herbecq v. Belgium* 32200/96 & 32201/96, admissibility decision dated January 14, 1998. The case concerned the use of CCTV cameras in public places, without the making of video recordings. The Commission found that there had been no interference with Article 8 rights.

Convention might not protect public appearances of well-known figures which are intended to attract attention, the right to respect for private life would be interfered with if State agents were to follow the personal activities which an individual conducts in the open, record them and/or keep all relevant information."[35]

C8–14 The Court, moreover, in *Costello-Roberts v. United Kingdom* found that "not every act or measure which may be said to affect adversely the physical or moral integrity of a person necessarily gives rise to such an interference".[36] However, forcible medical examination and the removal of a person's legal capacity raise issues of private life.[37]

4. "Family life"

C8–15 The case law relating to the concept of family life in Article 8 involves three main groups of questions. First, which relationships amount to family life? Secondly, does a real family life exist? Thirdly, when it does, what interests or activities come within its scope?

A. Which relationships amount to family life?

C8–16 In answering the first question the Court held in *Abdulaziz, Cabales and Balkandali v. United Kingdom* that:

". . . [w]hatever else the word 'family' may mean, it must at any rate include the relationship that arises from a lawful and genuine marriage".[38]

In *Berrehab v. Netherlands* the Court added that:

"a child born of such a union is *ipso jure* part of the relationship; hence, from the moment of the child's birth and by the very fact of it, there exists between him and his parents a bond amounting to 'family life' even if the parents are not then living together".[39]

C8–17 Moreover, in the most important case of *Marckx v. Belgium*, the Court held that "Article 8 makes no distinction between the 'legitimate' and the 'illegitimate' family".[40] The following relationships have been held, as a result, to amount to "family life": an unmarried mother and her child, although under domestic law maternal affiliation could be established only by a formal act of recognition[41]; a child and its natural father even if at the time of the child's birth the parents were no longer living together or their relationship had ended[42]; a

---

[35] App. No. 28802/95 *Tsavachidis v. Greece* Report of the Commission dated October 28, 1997, para. 47. A friendly settlement was reached.
[36] (1995) 19 E.H.R.R. 112, para. 36; see further *Lüdi v. Switzerland* (1993) 15 E.H.R.R. 173, para. 40; *Raninen v. Finland* (1997) 26 E.H.R.R. 563.
[37] App. No. 31534/96 *Matter v. Slovakia* July 5, 1999.
[38] (1985) 7 E.H.R.R. 471, para. 62.
[39] (1989) 11 E.H.R.R. 322, para. 21. See also *Gül v. Switzerland*, February 19, 1996, R.J.D., 1996–I, No. 3; 22 E.H.R.R. 93, para. 32.
[40] (1979) 2 E.H.R.R. 330, para. 31.
[41] *Marckx v. Belgium* (1979) 2 E.H.R.R. 330.
[42] *Keegan v. Ireland* (1994) 18 E.H.R.R. 342.

couple who had gone through a ceremony of marriage, believed themselves to be married and genuinely wished to cohabit and lead a normal life, regardless of the actual validity of their wedding[43]; and the relationship between two people who had lived together for some 15 years without being married, and between each of them and their child.[44] Although as a rule co-habitation is required to create "family" ties outside marriage, exceptionally other factors, such as having children, will suffice to demonstrate that the relationship has sufficient constancy to constitute *de facto* family life.[45] In *X, Y & Z v. United Kingdom*,[46] the plenary Court considered the relationship of a post-operative male transsexual who lived as a male partner in a long term stable relationship with a natural born woman, and with her child. They jointly applied for the woman to have the child by AID. The man had been involved throughout the process and had acted as the child's father in every respect since the birth. The full Court held unanimously that Article 8 applied to the *de facto* family ties between the three of them. Finally, the Court held in *Marckx*'s case that family life includes "at least the ties between near relatives, for instance those between grandparents and grandchildren, since such relatives may play a considerable part in family life".[47] Recently, the Commission held that this included the relationship between a child whose father had died and his uncle who lived in close proximity and stayed frequently at weekends.[48] The Commission has held that Article 8 was not engaged where a woman with children claimed that to deport her and them would interfere with her family life with her parents and sisters. In the Commission's opinion, she and her children formed an independent family unit and therefore her relationship with her extended family was not family life within Article 8.[49] The existence of family life is an issue of fact in each case.

B. Does a real family life exist?

C8–18   The mere existence of family ties will not automatically bring the parties under the protection of Article 8. The Convention organs will usually enquire into the existence of continuing real ties.[50] This, however, "does not mean that all intended family life falls entirely outside its [Article 8's] ambit". The existence of a lawful and genuine marriage "must be considered sufficient to attract such respect as may be due under Article 8", even if a family life with the legitimate expectation of its enjoyment in a particular country has not yet been fully established.[51] Moreover, "(t)he Court . . . does not see cohabitation as a *sine qua non* of family life between parent and minor children".[52]

---

[43] *Abdulaziz, Cabales and Balkandali v. United Kingdom* (1987) 7 E.H.R.R. 471.
[44] *Johnston v. Ireland* (1987) 9 E.H.R.R. 203.
[45] *Kroon v. Netherlands* (1995) 19 E.H.R.R. 263. However, co-habitation and the strength of any other ties will be relevant when judging the justification for any interference: see *Söderbäck v. Sweden* October 28, 1998, para. 31 (113/1997/897/1109); *cf. Johansen v. Norway*, August 7, 1996, R.J.D., 1996–III, No. 13; 23 E.H.R.R. 33.
[46] *X, Y & Z v. United Kingdom*, April 22, 1997, R.J.D., 1997–II, No. 35; 24 E.H.R.R. 143. *cf. G v. Netherlands* (1993) 16 E.H.R.R. CD 38 (donation of sperm for artificial insemination does not of itself give donor a right to respect for the family life with the child. Applicant's contacts with the child insufficient to conclude that a close personal tie developed).
[47] *Loc. cit.*, para. 45 of the judgment.
[48] *Boyle v. United Kingdom* (1995) 19 E.H.R.R. 179, Commission Report—friendly settlement reached.
[49] *A & family v. Sweden* (1994) 18 E.H.R.R. CD 209.
[50] See *Marckx v. Belgium* (1979) 2 E.H.R.R. 330, *Berrehab v. Netherlands* (1989) 11 E.H.R.R. 322.
[51] *Abdulaziz, Cabales and Balkandali v. United Kingdom*, (1985) 7 E.H.R.R. 471, para. 62. As to what respect is due, see below, para. C8–55 relating to immigration.
[52] *Berrehab v. Netherlands*, para. 21; *Keegan v. Ireland* (1994) 18 E.H.R.R. 342.

C. What interests or activities come within the scope of family life?

C8–19 As regards, on the other hand, the interests and activities coming within the scope of family life, the Court stated in *Abdulaziz, Cabales and Balkandali* that "the expression 'family life', in the case of a couple, normally comprises cohabitation".[53] Furthermore in *Marckx* the Court held that family life does not include only social, moral or cultural relations but that it also includes interests of a material kind, for example intestate succession.[54] In *X, Y & Z v. United Kingdom*[55] the Court took into account, in addition, transmission of tenancies by operation of law, transmission of citizenship and immigration status when deciding whether the failure to allow X to register as Z's father struck a fair balance between the general interest and those of the applicants.

5. "HOME"

C8–20 There has been little case law specifically dealing with the right to respect for the home. The notion of home does not extend to an intended home, or a past home. According to the Court " . . . it would strain the meaning of the notion 'home' in Article 8 to include property on which it is planned to build a house for residential purposes. Nor can that term be interpreted to cover an area of a State where one has grown up and where the family has its roots but where one no longer lives".[56] It may extend to a professional person's office,[57] although a state's entitlement to interfere under the second paragraph of Article 8 "might well be more far-reaching where professional or business activities or premises were involved than would otherwise be the case".[58] By contrast, however, the concept does not apply to places which are freely accessible to the public and which are used as premises for activities which do not involve matters relating to the private sphere.[59] Whether a place constitutes a person's home is a question of fact and does not depend on the establishment of a proprietary interest. Accordingly, an applicant was able to complain about the burning of her "home" and forced evacuation from a village where she had lived for significant periods every year when she visited the village, and with which she had a strong family connection.[60] It is unnecessary to establish ownership if a person is an occupier,[61] nor is the concept of "home" limited to a residence which is lawfully established.[62] Long periods of absence from one's place of residence may, however, affect the degree of protection afforded under Article 8.[63]

C8–21 In addition to flagrant cases of interference where the constitutional right to respect for home is suspended to allow for night arrests,[64] or where

---

[53] para. 62.
[54] para. 52.
[55] April 22, 1997, R.J.D., 1997–II, No. 35; 24 E.H.R.R. 143, paras 48 and 49.
[56] *Loizidou v. Turkey* (1997) 23 E.H.R.R. 513, para. 66.
[57] *Niemietz v. Germany* (1993) 16 E.H.R.R. 97, para. 30. The Court placed particular reliance on the use of the word *"domicile"* in the French text as having broader connotation than *"home"*.
[58] *ibid.*, para. 31. For a similar approach to limitations on commercial speech see *Markt Intern and Beerman v. Germany* (1990) 12 E.H.R.R. 161 and *Hertel v. Switzerland* judgment of August 25, 1998.
[59] *Pentidis & ors v. Greece*, June 9, 1997, R.J.D., 1997–III, No. 39; 24 E.H.R.R. CD 1.
[60] *Mentes v. Turkey* (1998) 26 E.H.R.R. 595.
[61] See *Mentes v. Turkey*; *Khatun & 180 others v. United Kingdom* (1998) 26 E.H.R.R. CD 212, *cf. Hunter v. Canary Wharf Limited* [1997] 2 All E.R. 426.
[62] *Buckley v. United Kingdom* (1997) 23 E.H.R.R. 101, para. 54.
[63] *Gillow v. United Kingdom* (1989) 11 E.H.R.R. 335. See further para. C8–65 and *Cyprus v. Turkey (2nd case)* (1993) 15 E.H.R.R. 509, Commission's Opinion, para. 135.
[64] *Greek* case 12 Yearbook, Commission's Opinion, para. 345.

individuals are evicted from their homes or refused authorisation to return,[65] the Convention organs will examine under Article 8 cases where the interference with one's right to respect for his or her home has a more qualitative character. In *Lopez-Ostra v. Spain* the Court held, for example, that, "severe environmental pollution may affect individuals' well-being and prevent them from enjoying their homes in such a way as to affect their private and family life adversely, without, however, seriously endangering their health".[66]

6. "CORRESPONDENCE"

C8–22   Article 8 protects telephone conversations as well as written correspondence: see *Klass v. Germany*.[67] There have been no decisions yet on other forms of communication, such as e-mail. However, there is little doubt that the notion of correspondence will embrace them.

In the following paragraphs we consider the principal issues which have arisen for determination within the scope of Article 8.

7. PARENTS AND CHILDREN

A. Divorce or separation

C8–23   Many applications have been brought by parents who have lost custody of or have been denied access to their children. In a divorce or separation neither parent can claim a right to the custody of the child under Article 8 of the Convention.[68] Although an order awarding custody to one parent rather than another will constitute an interference with the non-custodial parent's right to family life, it will be normally considered necessary for the protection of the rights of the child.[69] The Convention organs will question a national court's custody decision only in the most extreme circumstances.

C8–24   However, loss of custody in divorce proceedings does not bring "family life" within the meaning of Article 8 to an end:

> "(T)he right to respect for family life within the meaning of Article 8 of the Convention includes the right of a divorced parent, who is deprived of custody following the break-up of marriage, to have access to or contact with his child, and . . . the state may not interfere with the exercise of that right otherwise than in accordance with the conditions set out in paragraph 2 of that Article . . . the natural link between a parent and a child is of fundamental importance

---

[65] *Cyprus v. Turkey (1st case)* (1976) 4 E.H.R.R. 482, Commission's Opinion, paras 208–209 and *Cyprus v. Turkey (2nd case)* (1993) 15 E.H.R.R. 509, Commission's Opinion, para. 135. As to denial of access because of foreign occupation of the land, see *Loizidou v. Turkey* (1997) 23 E.H.R.R. 513.

[66] (1995) 20 E.H.R.R. 277, para. 51. See also *Guerra & others v. Italy* (1998) 26 E.H.R.R. 357 (toxic emissions from a factory); *Powell & Rayner v. United Kingdom* (1990) 12 E.H.R.R. 355, in particular paras 40 and 41; *Rayner v. United Kingdom* 47 D. & R. 22; *Powell v. United Kingdom* (1987), 9 E.H.R.R. 241 (noise nuisance).

[67] (1978) 2 E.H.R.R. 214, para. 41.

[68] App. No. 172/56 *X v. Sweden* 1 Yb 211.

[69] *cf.*, *Hoffmann v. Austria* (1994) 17 E.H.R.R. 293, and see further para. C14–22 in relation to Article 14.

and . . . , where the actual 'family life' in the sense of 'living together' has
come to an end, continued contact between them is desirable and shall in
principle remain possible. Respect for family life within the meaning of Article
8 thus implies that this contact should not be denied unless there are strong
reasons, set out in paragraph 2 of that provision, which justify such an
interference".[70]

The same principle applies to the making of a care order in public law proceedings.

B. Public care and adoption generally

C8–25   The taking of children into public care raises similar issues, and
represents most of the case law relating to the relations between parent and child.
The Court considers that it is " . . . an interference of a very serious order to split
up a family. Such a step must be supported by sufficiently sound and weighty
considerations in the interests of the child; . . . it is not enough that the child would
be better off if placed in care".[71] In assessing the justification of a decision to take a
child into care, a refusal to terminate a care order, and any decisions made while a
child is in care, consideration of what is in the best interest of the child is "of
crucial importance".[72] In the same judgment the Court said that:

> " . . . a fair balance has to be struck between the interests of the child in
> remaining in public care and those of the parent in being reunited with the
> child. In carrying out this balancing exercise, the Court will attach particular
> importance to the interests of the child, which, depending on their nature and
> seriousness, may override those of the parent. In particular . . . the parent
> cannot be entitled under Article 8 of the Convention to have such measures
> taken as would harm the child's health and development."[73]

The Commission has said that where there is a serious conflict between the interests
of the parent and the child, which can be resolved only by a disadvantage to one of
them, it is legitimate under Article 8 to let the interests of the child prevail[74]; and
that the interests of the child are "of paramount importance".[75]

C8–26   Naturally, " . . . the family relationship is not terminated by reason of
the fact that the child is taken into public care".[76] Since "(t)he mutual enjoyment by
parent and child of each other's company constitutes a fundamental aspect of
family life", the natural parents retain a right of access which can be restricted only
in accordance with the second paragraph of Article 8. Where the adoption of a
child who has been taken into public care is not envisaged, the care decision should
be regarded as a temporary measure, to be discontinued as soon as circumstances
permit, and any measures of implementation should be consistent with the ultimate
aim of reuniting the family.[77]

---

[70] *Hendriks v. Netherlands* (1983) 5 E.H.R.R. 223, Commission's Opinion, paras 94–95.
[71] See *Olsson v. Sweden (No. 1)* (1989) 11 E.H.R.R. 259, para. 72.
[72] *Johansen v. Norway*, August 7, 1996, R.J.D., 1996–III, No. 13; 23 E.H.R.R. 33, para. 64.
[73] *ibid.*, para. 78.
[74] *Thorbergsson v. Iceland* (1994) 18 E.H.R.R. CD 205.
[75] *Asplund v. Sweden* (1994) 18 E.H.R.R. CD 111.
[76] *W v. United Kingdom* (1988) 10 E.H.R.R. 29, para. 59.
[77] *Johansen v. Norway*, August 7, 1996, R.J.D., 1996–III, No. 13; 23 E.H.R.R. 33, para. 78.

"The ties between members of the family and the prospects of their successful reunification will perforce be weakened if impediments are placed in the way of their having easy and regular access to each other".[78]

The state has an obligation to take measures with a view to parents being reunited with their children. However, parents have no absolute right in this respect. This is because public authorities must also respect the interests and Article 8 rights of the children, and because reunion may need some preparation, for example if the children have been fostered for some time. Where contacts with natural parents would harm the child's interests and rights, a fair balance must be struck. "What will be decisive is whether the national authorities have made such efforts to arrange the necessary preparations for reunion as can reasonably be demanded under the special circumstances of each case".[79]

C8–27   The Court has allowed states a margin of appreciation in relation to this area, " . . . if only because it has to base itself on the case file, whereas the domestic authorities had the benefit of direct contact with all those involved".[80] In its judgment in *Johansen v. Norway*, the Court explained this margin of appreciation by reference to two factors: first, that perceptions about the appropriateness of intervention by public authorities in the care of children varied from one Contracting State to another; and secondly that national authorities had the benefit of direct contact with all those concerned, often at the very stage when care measures are being envisaged or immediately after their implementation. For those reasons, the Court would not substitute its own view for that of the domestic authorities.[81] Clearly, this justification will not apply to the U.K. courts' consideration of care proceedings.[82] The Strasbourg approach to scrutiny of such decisions will nonetheless be significant.

C8–28   The degree to which the Commission and Court have scrutinised decisions in this area has depended upon the seriousness of the interests at stake. First, the nature of the interference is taken into account. Although the Strasbourg institutions have allowed national authorities a relatively wide margin of appreciation the justification for taking a child into public care, they have adopted a stricter level of scrutiny when considering further limitations such as restrictions on parental rights and access[83]: "Such further limitations entail the danger that the family relations between the parents and a young child are effectively curtailed".[84] In *Johansen v. Norway*, the Court had to deal with deprivation of parental rights and access in the context of permanent placement in a foster home with a view to adoption. The Court described such measures as particularly far-reaching in that they totally deprived the mother of her family life and were inconsistent with the aim of reuniting them. "Such measures should only be applied in exceptional circumstances and could only be justified if they were motivated by an overriding requirement pertaining to the child's best interests".[85] Secondly, the Commission

---

[78] See *Olsson v. Sweden (No. 1)* (1988) 11 E.H.R.R. 259, para. 81.
[79] *Olsson v. Sweden (No. 2)* (1994) 17 E.H.R.R. 134, para. 90. For a similar approach where a private care arrangement was made, see *Hokkanen v. Finland* (1995) 19 E.H.R.R. 139, para. 58.
[80] *Olsson v. Sweden (No. 2)* (1994) 17 E.H.R.R. 134, para. 90.
[81] *Johansen v. Norway*, August 7, 1996, R.J.D., 1996–III, No. 13; 23 E.H.R.R. 33, para. 64.
[82] As to the role of the margin of appreciation under the HRA, see above, paras 2–05 and 5–16.
[83] *Johansen v. Norway*, August 7, 1996, R.J.D., 1996–III, No. 13; 23 E.H.R.R. 33.
[84] *ibid.*, para. 64.
[85] *ibid.*, para. 78.

and Court have taken account of the nature of the relationship between parent and child. Thus is *Söderbäck v. Sweden*,[86] although the measure in issue was the same, the Court considered that the strict approach adopted in *Johansen* was inappropriate in a case where the applicant's links with the child were weaker. The case did not:

" . . . concern the severance of links between a mother and a child taken into public care but, rather, of links between a natural father and a child who had been in the care of her mother since she was born. Nor does it concern a parent who had had custody of the child or who in any other capacity had assumed the care of the child."[87]

C8–29 The Court has so far recorded findings of violation of Article 8 in cases where children of the same family were placed in separate homes and far away from the natural parents[88]; where severe restrictions were placed on meetings between the natural parent and the child as well as on communication by correspondence and telephone[89]; where, despite the lifting of the care order, the natural parent was prohibited from removing the child from the foster home and lacked enforceable access rights[90]; where a child was secretly placed for adoption without the natural father's knowledge or consent[91]; and where a mother was deprived of parental rights and access to her daughter when the "overriding requirement" of the child's best interests did not require such extreme measures.[92] In less extreme cases, however, the margin of appreciation which the Court has allowed to national authorities in this field has tipped the scales against a finding of violation.[93]

C8–30 Whatever the scope of the national margin of appreciation, however, the Convention organs' review has insisted on the existence of adequate procedural guarantees for the natural parents, who must "[be] involved in the decision-making process, seen as a whole, to a degree sufficient to provide them with sufficient protection of their interests".[94] This guarantee extends not only to the original public care decision[95] but also to any subsequent decisions on a wide range of issues from the regulation of access to the children to their eventual adoption.[96] The Court has also insisted that Article 8 requires the authorities to act with exceptional diligence in ensuring progress of care proceedings and associated matters because of the nature of the interests at stake for the parent and the serious and irreversible consequences which the taking into care may have for his or her family life.[97]

C8–31 The Commission has declared admissible two applications complaining about social services departments' care decisions and their immunity from suit

---

[86] Judgment of October 28, 1998 (113/1997/897/1109).
[87] *ibid.*, para. 31.
[88] *Olsson v. Sweden (No. 1)* (1989) 11 E.H.R.R. 259.
[89] *Andersson v. Sweden* (1992) 14 E.H.R.R. 615.
[90] *Eriksson v. Sweden* (1990) 12 E.H.R.R. 183.
[91] *Keegan v. Ireland* (1994) 18 E.H.R.R. 342.
[92] *Johansen v. Norway*, August 7, 1996 R.J.D., 1996–III, No. 13; 23 E.H.R.R. 33.
[93] *Reime v. Sweden* (1993) 16 E.H.R.R. 155; *Olsson v. Sweden (No. 2)* (1992) 17 E.H.R.R. 134; *Soderbäck v. Sweden* October 28, 1998 (113/1997/897/1109).
[94] *W v. United Kingdom* (1988) 10 E.H.R.R. 29, para. 64.
[95] *McMichael v. United Kingdom* (1995) 20 E.H.R.R. 205 (Scotland—failure to disclose social work reports when making decisions about custody and access).
[96] See, *e.g., Johansen v. Norway*, August 7, 1996, R.J.D., 1996–III, No. 13; 23 E.H.R.R. 33, para. 66.
[97] *Paulsen-Medalen & Svensson v. Sweden* (1998) 26 E.H.R.R. 260, para. 39 (delay in access proceedings).

following the House of Lords' decision in *X v. Bedfordshire County Council*.[98] One case complains about the authorities' failure to protect the applicants from inhuman and degrading treatment where they knew of serious neglect and abuse which the applicants suffered at home.[99] The other case deals with the allegedly "careless" removal of a child into care.[1]

C. Children born outside marriage

C8–32   In a number of other cases the Court has had to deal with the respect for the "family life" of parents and children born outside marriage. Although the Convention does not require states to establish for unmarried couples a status analogous to that of married couples,[2] any significant difference between the treatment of illegitimate and legitimate children under national law will lead to a finding of violation of Article 8 on its own or in combination with Article 14.[3] In the current state of the law, Article 8 does not impose a positive obligation to register a post-operative male transsexual as the father of his partner's child.[4]

Finally, in the case of *Rasmussen v. Denmark*[5] the existence of a statutory time limit for the institution of proceedings by the presumed father of a child with a view to contesting his paternity, and the difference in treatment with the mother for whom no statutory limit existed, was not found to amount to discrimination under Article 14 read together with Article 8.

8.   ABORTION

C8–33   The Commission has held that "Article 8(1) cannot be interpreted as meaning that pregnancy and its termination are, as a principle, solely a matter of the private life of the mother".[6] As a result, "not every regulation of the termination of unwanted pregnancies constitutes an interference with the right to respect for the private life of the mother".[7] Moreover, "the potential father's right to respect for his private and family life can(not) be interpreted so widely as to embrace . . . a right to be consulted, or a right to make applications (before a court), about an abortion which his wife intends to have performed on her".[8]

9.   SEX AND SEXUALITY

C8–34   The Court has expressly recognised that a person's private life entitled to respect under Article 8 includes his sexual life[9] although, as noted above, not every sexual activity carried out in private falls within the scope of Article 8.[10]

---

[98] [1995] 3 All E.R. 353.
[99] App. No. 29392/95 *KL v. United Kingdom* (1998) 26 E.H.R.R. CD 113.
[1] App. No. 28945/95 *TP & KM v. United Kingdom* (1998) 26 E.H.R.R. CD 84.
[2] *Johnston v. Ireland* (1987) 9 E.H.R.R. 203, para. 68.
[3] *Johnston v. Ireland, Marckx v. Belgium* 2 E.H.R.R. 330 and *Vermeire v. Belgium* (1993) 15 E.H.R.R. 488; *Keegan v. Ireland* (1994) 18 E.H.R.R. 342.
[4] *X, Y & Z v. United Kingdom*; April 22, 1997, R.J.D., 1997–II, No. 35; 24 E.H.R.R. 143.
[5] (1985) 7 E.H.R.R. 371.
[6] *Brüggeman and Scheuten v. Germany* (1981) 3 E.H.R.R. 244, para. 61.
[7] *ibid.*
[8] App. No. 8416/78 *Paton v. United Kingdom* (1980) 3 E.H.R.R. 408.
[9] *Dudgeon v. United Kingdom* 4 E.H.R.R. 149, para. 41 and *Norris v. Ireland* (1988) 13 E.H.R.R. 186, para. 38.
[10] *Laskey, Jaggard & Brown v. United Kingdom*, February 19, 1997; R.J.D., 1997–I, No. 29; 24 E.H.R.R. 39. See above, para. C8–12.

Criminal laws which prohibit homosexual acts, committed in private and between consenting adults, cannot be justified under Article 8(2).[11] [11a]

C8–35   However, in the cases referred to above the Court had to deal with extreme situations. "There can be no denial that some degree of regulation of male homosexual conduct, as indeed of other forms of sexual conduct, by means of the criminal law can be justified as 'necessary in a democratic society' . . . to provide for sufficient safeguards against exploitation and corruption of others, particularly those who are specially vulnerable because they are young, weak in body or mind, inexperienced or in a state of special physical, official or economic dependence".[12] In certain cases the right to respect for private life under the Convention requires the criminalisation of certain forms of sexual exploitation.[13] However, the Commission has found that the difference in the "age of consent" between male homosexuals and heterosexuals is no longer justified.[14]

C8–36   The Commission and Court have also dealt under Article 8 with a number of applications by transsexuals who have undergone sex-change operations and who complain that lack of official recognition of these changes causes them embarrassment.[15] Although the Court considered in the cases of *Rees*[16] and *Cossey*[17] that the United Kingdom was under no positive obligation to alter official birth records to accommodate changes in sex, the lack of recognition of a person's new sexual identity on a wider scale in France led to a finding of violation (13 votes to 5) in *B v. France*.[18] In that case the Court took into account the applicant's manifest determination to abandon the external marks of her original sex. Refusal to allow the applicant to change her forename to a female one of her choice was a relevant factor. Because of the regime regarding documents showing the discrepancy between legal and assumed gender, she was unable to hide her situation from, for example, a potential employer or an employer's administrative staff. This led to difficulties in social and professional integration. These inconveniences gave rise to a detriment of sufficient seriousness to override the state's margin of appreciation.[19] In July 1998 the Grand Chamber of the Court upheld its judgments in *Rees* and *Cossey* by a majority of 11 votes to 9, the majority holding that there had been no significant developments in either the law or in medical science, since *Cossey*.[20]

C8–37   The Court has also held that Article 8 does not include an obligation to allow a male transsexual (X) to be registered as the father of the child (Z) of his

---

[11] *Dudgeon*, paras 60–61, *Norris*, paras 46–47 and *Modinos v. Cyprus* (1993) 16 E.H.R.R. 485, para. 25.
[11a] See also *Lustig-Prean and Beckett v. United Kingdom, Smith and Grady v. United Kingdom*, judgments of September 27, 1999 (policy of excluding homosexuals from the armed forces an unjustified interference).
[12] *Dudgeon v. United Kingdom* 4 E.H.R.R. 149, para. 49.
[13] *X and Y v. Netherlands* (1986) 8 E.H.R.R. 235.
[14] *Sutherland v. United Kingdom* [1998] E.H.R.L.R 117.
[15] See *Van Oosterwijk v. Belgium* (1980) 3 E.H.R.R. 557, *Rees v. United Kingdom* (1987) 9 E.H.R.R. 56; *Cossey v. United Kingdom* (1991) 13 E.H.R.R. 622 and *B v. France* (1993) 16 E.H.R.R. 1. As to the margin of appreciation which the Court has left to the state, see above, para. C8–06 relating to the notion of "respect".
[16] (1987) 9 E.H.R.R. 56.
[17] (1991) 13 E.H.R.R. 622.
[18] (1993) 16 E.H.R.R. 1. See also para. C12–05 as to Article 12.
[19] *cf. Sheffield & Horsham v. United Kingdom* (1997) 27 E.H.R.R. 163, para. 59.
[20] *Sheffield & Horsham v. United Kingdom* (1997) 27 E.H.R.R. 163. The Commission had found a violation of Article 8 by 15 votes to 1.

female partner (Y). In the view of the majority (14 votes to 6), the inconveniences to which the applicants referred were either theoretical or they were capable of remedy, for example by obtaining a residence order.[21] For the majority, " . . . given that transsexuality raises complex scientific, legal, moral and social issues, in respect of which there is no generally shared approach among the Contracting States, the Court is of the opinion that Article 8 cannot, in this context, be taken to imply an obligation for the respondent state formally to recognise as the father of a child a person who is not the biological father".[22]

10. SECRET SURVEILLANCE OF POSTAL AND TELEPHONE COMMUNICATIONS

C8–38 Interception of communications constitutes an interference with the right to respect for both private life and correspondence. Since the latter term is not qualified by the word "private",[23] it covers both private and professional communications.[24] Article 8 applies not only to the placing of taps on telephones but also to the planting of listening devices in the home,[25] and in general the Court has been particularly aware of the need for legal protection to keep up with the development of increasingly sophisticated technology.[26]

C8–39 The general position of the Court on the issue is that "(p)owers of secret surveillance of citizens, characterising as they do the police state, are tolerable under the Convention only in so far as strictly necessary for safeguarding the democratic institutions".[27] The Court has, moreover, stressed the danger which laws authorising secret surveillance of postal and telephone communications pose of undermining or destroying democracy on the ground of defending it. As a result, before accepting that such measures could be justified under Article 8(2):

"(t)he Court must be satisfied that . . . there exist adequate and effective guarantees against abuse. The assessment has only a relative character: it depends on all the circumstances of the case, such as the nature, scope and duration of the possible measures, the grounds required for ordering such measures, the authorities competent to permit, carry out and supervise such measures, and the kind of remedy provided by national law".[28]

C8–40 The requirement of lawfulness has played a particularly important part in the Court's case law on this topic, the Court indicating that since interception is a particularly serious form of interference with private life and correspondence, it

---

[21] X, Y & Z v. United Kingdom, April 22, 1997, R.J.D., 1997–II, No. 35; 24 E.H.R.R. 143. The Commission found a violation by 13 votes to 6: see para. 71.
[22] ibid., para. 52.
[23] See, for example, Niemietz v. Germany (1993) 16 E.H.R.R. 97, para. 32.
[24] Halford v. United Kingdom, June 25, 1997, R.J.D., 1997–III, No. 39; 24 E.H.R.R. 523, para. 44. However, in that case the Court did consider whether the circumstances gave rise to an expectation of privacy.
[25] See, for example, App. No. 27237/95 Govell v. United Kingdom, Report adopted on January 14, 1998 (placing of covert listening devices not justified by Article 8(2) because not regulated by law. The case has gone to the Committee of Ministers). See generally Colvin, Under surveillance: Covert policing and human rights standards (JUSTICE, London, 1998).
[26] Kopp v. Switzerland (1999) 27 E.H.R.R. 91, para. 72.
[27] Klass v. Germany 2 E.H.R.R. 214, para. 42.
[28] ibid., para. 50.

must be based on a "law" that is "particularly precise".[29] To have a sense of the Court's approach in this area, it is instructive to compare the *Klass* case[30] where adequate and effective guarantees were found to exist, with *Malone v. United Kingdom*,[31] *Huvig v. France*,[32] *Kruslin v. France*,[33] *Kopp v. Switzerland*[34] and *Valenzuela Contreras v. Spain*[35] where the Court considered that the domestic laws of the four States which authorised the interception of postal and telephone communications did not introduce "foreseeable" restrictions to the right of respect for private life and correspondence. In *Malone* the Court reasoned as follows:

> "Undoubtedly, . . . , the requirements of the Convention, notably in regard to foreseeability, cannot be exactly the same in the special context of interception of communications for the purposes of police investigations as they are when the object of the relevant law is to place restrictions on the conduct of individuals. In particular, the requirement of foreseeability cannot mean that an individual should be enabled to foresee when the authorities are likely to intercept his communications so that he can adapt his conduct accordingly. Nevertheless, the law must be sufficiently clear in its terms to give citizens an adequate indication as to the circumstances in which and the conditions on which public authorities are empowered to resort to this secret and potentially dangerous interference with the right to respect for private life and correspondence . . . Since the implementation in practice of measures of secret surveillance of communications is not open to scrutiny by the individuals concerned or the public at large, it would be contrary to the rule of law for the legal discretion granted to the executive to be expressed in terms of an unfettered power. Consequently, the law must indicate the scope of any such discretion conferred on the competent authorities and the manner of its exercise with sufficient clarity, . . . , to give the individual adequate protection against arbitrary interference".[36]

C8–41   The Court has applied these requirements rigorously. Thus, legislation which appeared to preclude the interception of conversations covered by legal professional privilege but did not clearly state how, under what conditions and by whom, a distinction was to be drawn between matters specifically connected with a lawyer's work under instructions and those relating to activity other than that of counsel, did not meet them.[37] In particular, the Court found it " . . . to say the least, astonishing" that the task of identifying legally privileged calls from other activity should have been assigned to an official in the Post Office legal department, who is a member of the executive, without supervision by an independent judge.[38]

---

[29] *Kopp v. Switzerland* (1999) 27 E.H.R.R. 91, para. 72.
[30] 2 E.H.R.R. 214.
[31] (1985) 7 E.H.R.R. 14.
[32] (1990) 12 E.H.R.R. 528.
[33] (1990) 12 E.H.R.R. 547.
[34] (1999) 27 E.H.R.R. 91.
[35] (1999) 28 E.H.R.R. 483.
[36] *Malone v. United Kingdom* (1985) 7 E.H.R.R. 14, paras 67–68 of the judgment. *cf. Silver v. United Kingdom* (1983) 5 E.H.R.R. 347 where the Court ruled that a law which confers a discretion must indicate the scope of that discretion, although the detailed procedures and conditions to be observed do not necessarily have to be incorporated in rules of substantive law. See further *Lüdi v. Switzerland* (1993) 15 E.H.R.R. 173.
[37] *Kopp v. Switzerland* (1999) 27 E.H.R.R. 91.
[38] *ibid.*, para. 74.

The Court regards the following as the minimum safeguards that should be set out in the statute in order to avoid abuses of power:

" . . . a definition of the categories of people liable to have their telephones tapped by judicial order, the nature of the offences which may give rise to such an order, a limit on the duration of telephone tapping, the procedure for drawing up the summary reports containing intercepted conversations, the precautions to be taken in order to communicate the recordings intact and in their entirety for possible inspection by the judge and by the defence and the circumstances in which recordings may or must be erased or the tapes destroyed, in particular where an accused has been discharged by an investigating judge or acquitted by a court".[39]

C8–42   Guarantees prescribing the extent of the authorities' discretion and the manner of its exercise must be set out in detail in domestic law so that it has binding force which circumscribes the discretion in the application of such measures.[40] Further, it appears that standing to complain must be afforded to not only the person whose line is tapped but also to any third party whose conversation is intercepted in consequence. Otherwise a very large number of people would be deprived of the protection of the law, namely all those who had conversations on a telephone line other than their own and any protective machinery would be rendered largely devoid of substance.[41]

11.   PERSONAL INFORMATION IN PUBLIC AUTHORITIES' FILES

C8–43   The storage and use of information concerning a person's private life in the files of a public authority or in a secret police register amount to an interference with the right to respect for private life.[42]

C8–44   Any such interference will have to be justified under the second paragraph of Article 8, although the Court starts from the assumption that:

"(t)here can be no doubt as to the necessity, for the purpose of protecting national security, for the Contracting Parties to have laws granting the national authorities power, firstly, to collect and store in registers not accessible to the public information on persons and, secondly, to use this information when assessing the suitability of candidates for employment in posts of importance for national security".[43]

C8–45   The principles relating to covert interception of postal and telephone communications–in particular the consequences flowing from the requirement of

---

[39] *Valenzuela Contreras v. Spain*, (1999) 28 E.H.R.R. 493, para. 46.
[40] *ibid.*
[41] *Lambert v. France*, judgment of August 24, 1998, para. 38.
[42] *Leander v. Sweden* (1987) 9 E.H.R.R. 433 and *Hewitt and Harman v. United Kingdom* (1992) 14 E.H.R.R. 657. See further *Gaskin v. United Kingdom* (1990) 12 E.H.R.R. 36 where Article 8 imposed on the State a positive obligation to disclose to an individual information related to his history while in public care as a child; and *Guerra & ors v. Italy* (1998) 26 E.H.R.R. 357, where the Court found a positive obligation to disclose to residents information about the risk of serious environmental pollution from a "high risk" factory in the locality. See also *Adamson v. United Kingdom* 42293/98, Court decision on admissibility, January 26, 1999 (requirement on sex offender to register with police justified under Article 8(2)).
[43] *Leander v. Sweden*, para. 59.

lawfulness—apply with equal force in this area. But while the Convention requires adequate safeguards against abuse,[44] the Commission and Court have afforded national authorities a wide margin of appreciation in the area[45]; and due account must be taken of the special nature of terrorist crime, the threat it poses to democratic society and the exigencies of dealing with it.[46]

C8–46   As with secret surveillance of telephone and postal communications, an individual cannot be certain as to the existence of secret files concerning his person. In *Klass* the Court considered that:

" . . . an individual may, under certain conditions, claim to be the victim of a violation occasioned by the mere existence of secret measures or of legislation permitting secret measures, without having to allege that such measures were in fact applied to him".[47]

The Commission, however, in *Hewitt and Harman v. United Kingdom* did not consider that the:

" . . . case law can be interpreted so broadly as to encompass every person . . . who fears that the security service may have compiled information about him . . . [yet] an applicant cannot reasonably be expected to prove that information concerning his private life has been compiled and retained. It is sufficient, in the area of secret measures, that the existence of practices permitting secret surveillance be established and that there is a reasonable likelihood that the security service has compiled and retained information concerning private life."[48]

It is not necessary, therefore, that the information should have been used to the person's detriment, or indeed used in any way, since requiring that a person should have suffered identifiable damage would render the Convention guarantees in Article 8 of the Convention theoretical and illusory, whereas they are intended to be practical and effective.[49]

C8–47   Article 8 is also engaged where a public authority disseminates personal information which it holds, whether that information was obtained covertly or not. The Court found an interference where a clinic disclosed a patient's medical notes to another public authority verifying her claim to industrial injury benefit. Disclosure was held to be proportionate to the legitimate aim of protecting the economic well-being of the country and there were adequate safeguards.[50] In general, though, the Court's approach is that:

[44] The criteria in the Security Service Act 1989 are sufficiently well defined to satisfy the test of foreseeability and are therefore in accordance with the law; and in the absence of evidence or indication that the system is not functioning as required by domestic law, the framework of safeguards achieves a compromise between the requirements of defending democratic society and the rights of the individual which is compatible with the provisions of the Convention: *Esbester v. United Kingdom* (1994) 18 E.H.R.R. CD 72.
[45] See further *McVeigh, O'Neill and Evans v. United Kingdom* (1983) 5 E.H.R.R. 71, Commission's Opinion, paras 228–231.
[46] *Murray v. United Kingdom* (1995) 19 E.H.R.R. 193, para. 47.
[47] 2 E.H.R.R. 214, para. 34 of the judgment.
[48] (1992) 14 E.H.R.R. 657, para. 32 of the Report. See also *Esbester v. United Kingdom* (1994) 18 E.H.R.R. CD 72.
[49] *HA v. Switzerland*, Report of the Commission dated May 20, 1998: 27798/95, para. 55.
[50] *MS v. Sweden* (1999) 28 E.H.R.R. 313. See also *Andersson v. Sweden* (1998) 25 E.H.R.R. 722.

" . . . the protection of personal data, not least medical data, is of fundamental importance to a person's enjoyment of his or her right to respect for private and family life . . . Respecting the confidentiality of health data . . . Is crucial not only to respect the sense of privacy of a patient but also to preserve his or her confidence in the medical profession and in the health services in general."[51]

Disclosure must be justified by "an overriding requirement in the public interest"; and where highly intimate and sensitive information is concerned, any state measures compelling communication or disclosure of such information without the consent of the patient call for the most careful, as do the safeguards designed to secure an effective protection.[52]

C8–48 It is also possible to derive from Article 8 a right of access to information held by public authorities where it is sufficiently closely linked with private and family life, for example where the information relates directly to an aspect of a person's upbringing,[53] or health,[54] or to enable him or her to assess the risk from severe environmental pollution which may affect his or her well-being and prevent him from enjoyment of the home in such a way as to affect private and family life adversely.[55]

12. MEDIA INTRUSION AND PERSONAL DIGNITY

C8–49 Article 8 may also impose a positive obligation on the state to protect individuals against interference with the right to respect for their private life by other individuals or non-state bodies. The Court has not yet pronounced on the matter directly, but the Commission has given an indication of its approach in recent decisions. In *Spencer v. United Kingdom* it stated that it:

" . . . would not exclude that the absence of an actionable remedy in relation to the publications of which the applicants complain could show a lack of respect for their private lives. It has regard in this respect to the duties and responsibilities that are carried with the right to freedom of expression guaranteed by Article 10 of the Convention and to Contracting States' obligation to provide a measure of protection to the right of privacy of an individual affected by others' exercise of their freedom of expression".[56]

C8–50 In that case the applicants complained about the taking and subsequent publication of a photograph of Lady Spencer in the garden of a clinic for the treatment of eating disorders. The photograph was accompanied by an article containing information about the Spencers' marital affairs. The Commission declared the applications inadmissible on the ground that the applicants should have pursued an action for breach of confidence.[57] The Commission's approach was

---

[51] *Z v. Finland*, February 25, 1997, R.J.D., 1997–I, No. 31; 25 E.H.R.R. 371, para. 95.
[52] *ibid.*, para. 96.
[53] *Gaskin v. United Kingdom* (1990) 12 E.H.R.R. 36 (official information concerning childhood in care).
[54] *McGinley & Egan v. United Kingdom* (1999) 27 E.H.R.R. 1.
[55] *Guerra and others v. Italy* (1998) 26 E.H.R.R. 357.
[56] *Spencer v. United Kingdom* [1998] 25 E.H.R.R. CD 105 at 112.
[57] *cf.* App. No. 10871/84 *Winer v. United Kingdom* 48 D. & R. 154, where the Commission had considered the law relating to breach of confidence to be too uncertain to require the applicant to use it. The Commission had also concluded that in view of the remedies which were available, notably defamation, the absence of an actionable right to privacy under English law did not show a lack of respect for the applicant's private life and his home.

more explicit in *Whiteside v. United Kingdom*, in which the applicant complained of the State's failure to remedy the serious and persistent harassment of her and her family by her former partner. Holding that the harassment was of a level which could constitute an interference with her right to respect for her private life and enjoyment of her home, the Commission found that the State's responsibility was engaged and that it was under a positive obligation to secure her rights by providing adequate protection against deliberate persecution of this type.[58]

C8-51 Respect for private life in this area may thus require protection of personal information from disclosure and additionally may require protection of a person's reputation,[59] including his professional reputation.[60] The Court has recognised the tension between such privacy rights and freedom of expression, particularly freedom of the press, and has sought to achieve a balance between the two in determining the scope of the positive obligation under Article 8. This matter is considered further in the discussion of Article 10.[61] When the public acts of a public figure are at issue, there is no need to read Article 10 in the light of Article 8.[62] Publication of information obtained in breach of a duty of confidence may be justified if it contributes to a public debate on a matter of general interest; and the Court has held that there must be an overriding requirement in the public interest to justify a restriction on disclosure by the press[63]; and it is likely to be a rare case in which the protection of reputation outweighs "the vital public interest in ensuring an informed public debate over a matter of local and national as well as international interest".[64] In general, therefore, it appears that section 12(4) of the HRA reflects the approach of the Strasbourg institutions in directing that a court should have "particular regard to the importance of the Convention right to freedom of expression".[64a]

13. SEARCHES OF PREMISES AND SEIZURE OF PROPERTY

C8-52 Searches and seizure of property constitute interference with a person's right to respect for either home, or private life or correspondence or the three taken together.[65] Protection extends beyond a person's residence to their professional premises,[66] and applies to search by private individuals carried out with court sanction such as an *Anton Piller* order.[67]

---

[58] (1994) 18 E.H.R.R. CD 126 at 128. The Commission held that the applicant had failed to exhaust domestic remedies because she had not appealed against the refusal of an injunction based on harassment, trespass and nuisance. See also App. No. 19173/91, decision of January 8, 1993 (allegations of surveillance by applicant's insurance company; Commission acknowledges positive obligation but finds no evidence of the alleged interference). *cf.* App. No. 21120/93 *Bausson v. France*, decision of December 1, 1993 (allegations of clandestine recording of conversations by applicant's co-accused; Commission held State responsibility not engaged).
[59] See, for example, App. No. 10871/84 *Winer v. United Kingdom* D. & R. 154. See also *Stewart-Brady v. United Kingdom* (1997) 24 E.H.R.R. CD 38 (inability to bring libel proceedings).
[60] *T.E.E. v. United Kingdom* (1996) 21 E.H.R.R. CD 108 (suspension of applicant by LAUTRO). See also *Young v. Ireland* (1996) 21 E.H.R.R. CD 91: parliamentary immunity from libel.
[61] See below, p. 296.
[62] *Lingens v. Austria* (1986) 8 E.H.R.R. 407, para. 38. For a similar approach see *Fayed v. United Kingdom* (1998) 18 E.H.R.R. 393, para. 75.
[63] *Fressoz and Roire v. France*, App. No. 29183/95 judgment of January 21, 1999, para. 51.
[64] *Bladet Tromsø and Stensaas v. Norway*, App. No. 21980/93, judgment of May 20, 1999.
[64a] See above, para. 4–65.
[65] *Funke v. France* (1993) 16 E.H.R.R. 297; *Mialhe v. France* (1993) 16 E.H.R.R. 332; *Niemetz v. Germany* (1993) 16 E.H.R.R. 97 and *Chappell v. United Kingdom* (1990) 12 E.H.R.R. 1.
[66] *Niemietz v. Germany* (1993) 16 E.H.R.R. 97, para. 30.
[67] *Chappell v. United Kingdom* (1990) 12 E.H.R.R. 1. Now a 'search order' C.P.R. 25.1(h).

C8–53   In order for search and seizure to be permitted under the second paragraph of Article 8, the reasons adduced to justify such measures must be relevant and sufficient. In addition, the governing legislation and practice must afford adequate and effective safeguards against abuse if the test of proportionality is to be satisfied.[68] The Court has exercised particular judicial vigilance where the authorities are empowered under national law to order and effect searches without a judicial warrant. Very strict limits on such powers are called for in such cases in order to protect individuals from arbitrary interference by the authorities with the rights guaranteed under Article 8.[69] For example in *Camenzind v. Switzerland*, the Court considered that a search of residential premises for physical evidence of use of an unauthorised cordless telephone, pursued the legitimate aim of the prevention of disorder or crime. In concluding that Swiss law furnished adequate safeguards, the Court noted the following: the Swiss Act limited the number of senior officials who could issue a search warrant, the number of trained officers could carry it out, the premises which could be searched and the grounds on which search could be authorised. It specified the procedure for the conduct of the search and for the monitoring and recording of it. The occupier had to be told the reason for the search and invited to attend, and suspects were entitled to representation. There was also a procedure for applying to quash the warrant and for obtaining compensation in appropriate cases.[70] A similar conclusion was reached by the Court in its admissibility decision in *Banco de Finanzas e Inversiones SA v. Spain*.[71] In that case the applicant bank had complained not only about the execution of the search warrant but also about the fact that a detailed account of the search was broadcast on radio and television on that same day. Having concluded that the search itself did not violate Article 8, the Court went on to hold that the fact that the press had divulged information about the search could not by itself amount to a breach of the right to respect for the home.[72]

C8–54   As with other interference, the Court will examine whether the entry or search is a proportionate measure at all in the circumstances[73]; and the manner in which the search was conducted, for example whether the applicant was present and represented, the number of personnel who carried out the search, the time taken and the physical extent of the search, and the information given to the individual.[74]

14.   IMMIGRATION

C8–55   As a matter of well-established international law and subject to its treaty obligations, a state has the right to control the entry, residence and expulsion of non-nationals from its territory.[75] However, "measures taken in the field of immigration may affect the right to respect for family life under Article 8",[76] for

---

[68] *Camenzind v. Switzerland* (1999) 28 E.H.R.R. 458, para. 45.
[69] *ibid.*
[70] *ibid.*, para. 46.
[71] App. No. 36876/97 Decision of April 27, 1999 (Fourth Section), unpublished.
[72] *"Le seul motif que la presse ait divulguée des informations relatives à la perquisition ne saurait constituer en soi une atteinte au droit invoqué"* (para. 2).
[73] *McLeod v. United Kingdom* (1999) 27 E.H.R.R. 493 (police entry to premises in support of search held disproportionate—owner of the property absent, so no apprehension of breach of the peace).
[74] *Camenzind v. Switzerland*, para. 46.
[75] See, among other cases, *Moustaquim v. Belgium* (1991) 13 E.H.R.R., para. 43.
[76] *Abdulaziz, Cabales and Balkandali v. United Kingdom* (1985) 7 E.H.R.R. 471, para. 60. See also the discussion of immigration, above, para. C3–10.

example if a person is excluded from a country where members of his family are living. Two questions must be answered when deciding whether an exercise of immigration control violates Article 8. First, whether there exists "family life" worthy of protection within the meaning of Article 8.[77] Secondly, if so, whether that interference is justified. The case law of the Commission and the Court has developed a set of criteria to deal with these issues.

A. The existence of family life

C8–56   Not all family ties, however genuine, will be taken into account when considering an immigration issue under Article 8. The Commission has held that a mother and her children were to be regarded as an independent family unit for this purpose, so that the fact that their deportation separated them from their extended family raised no issue under Article 8.[78] The links between adult relatives are not usually protected in this context, and the relationship between a parent and an adult child will not be covered unless there is a situation of dependence.[79] However, a person may still enjoy family life with his child even though they do not live together.[80] The existence of family life is to be assessed at the time when the decision is made, so that no account will be taken of the establishment of family life between the making of a deportation order and its intended execution.[81]

B. Justification

C8–57   Once an interference has been found, it must be justified under the second paragraph of Article 8. The Convention organs appear to be asserting increasingly effective supervisory powers in this field, and the "economic well-being of the country" is unlikely to justify such an interference on its own.[82] In other cases, where "public safety" and the "prevention of crime" are invoked to justify the deportation of an immigrant with criminal convictions, the seriousness of the crime will be balanced against the personal circumstances of the individual and his or her real links with the country of nationality, or the country where he or she grew up or lived for a substantial part of his or her life.[83] The Commission summarised the approach to justification in its decision on admissibility in *PP & others v. United Kingdom*:

> " . . . Article 8 does not impose a general obligation to respect the choice of residence of a married couple or to accept the non-national spouse for settlement in that country.[84] . . . The Commission considers that this also

---

[77] See above, para. C8–15.
[78] *A & family v. Sweden* (1994) 18 E.H.R.R. CD 209.
[79] *Advic v. United Kingdom* (1995) 20 E.H.R.R. CD 125.
[80] *Boughanemi v. France*, April 24, 1996. R.J.D., 1996–II, No. 8; 22 E.H.R.R. 228.
[81] *Bouchelkia v. France*, January 29, 1997, R.J.D., 1997–I, No. 28; 25 E.H.R.R. 686. Compare the Court's approach under Article 3, which is to assess the risk of inhuman or degrading treatment at the time of its own consideration of the case: *D v. United Kingdom*, May 2, 1997, R.J.D., 1997–III, No. 37; 24 E.H.R.R. 423, para. 50.
[82] *Berrehab v. Netherlands*, (1989) 11 E.H.R.R. 322, para. 29.
[83] *Beldjoudi v. France* (1992) 14 E.H.R.R. 801; *Moustaquim v. Belgium* (1991) 13 E.H.R.R. 802; *Bouchelkia v. France*, January 29, 1997, R.J.D., 1997–I, No. 28; 25 E.H.R.R. 686; *Boughanemi v. France*, April 24, 1996, R.J.D., 1996–II, No. 8; 22 E.H.R.R. 228.
[84] See also the Court to similar effect in *Abdulaziz, Cabales and Balkandali v. United Kingdom*, para. 68: "The duty imposed by Article 8 cannot be considered as extending to a general obligation . . . to respect the choice by married couples of the country of their matrimonial residence and to accept the non-national spouses for settlement in that country".

applies to situations where members of a family, other than spouses, are non-nationals. Whether removal or exclusion of a family member from a Contracting State is incompatible with Article 8 will depend on a number of factors: the extent to which family life is effectively ruptured, whether there are insurmountable obstacles in the way of the family living in the country of origin of one or more of them, whether there are factors of immigration control (*e.g.* history of breaches of immigration law) or considerations of public order (*e.g.* serious or persistent offences) weighing in favour of exclusion.[85]

C8–58   As with spouses, the deportation of second-generation immigrants has been found to raise an issue under Article 8.[86] The same holds true for the expulsion of an immigrant from the country where his child lived with the immigrant's former wife.[87] In order to succeed, it must not be feasible for the family unit to be established elsewhere, or there must exist special reasons why this could not be expected of them.[88] Much will depend on the facts of each case. The Commission found that deportation following conviction for wounding was disproportionate in the case of a Moroccan in his twenties who had lived and been educated in the United Kingdom since the age of seven, and all of whose close relatives lived there. The applicant had no real ties with Morocco or acquaintance with its culture or language, and all his family and social ties were in the United Kingdom.[89] Even where the individual has committed a serious crime, deportation may be disproportionate in exceptional circumstances. Both the Commission and the Court found a violation in the case of an Algerian national who had lived virtually his whole life in France with his parents and eight siblings, some of whom had become French nationals. He was deaf and dumb from birth, had had little education, was illiterate and did not know a recognised sign language. He understood no Arabic. A deportation order was made following a number of petty offences and his participation in a gang rape. The Court took account of the "accumulation of special circumstances, notably his situation as a deaf and dumb person, capable of achieving psychological and social equilibrium only within his family, the majority of whose members are French nationals with no close ties with Algeria".[90]

C8–59   Article 14 provides an additional basis for European supervision in the field. Although immigration control necessarily distinguishes between a country's own nationals and others, immigration rules which discriminate on the basis of sex could be found to violate Article 14 in conjunction with Article 8 even in cases where the right to respect for family life is not in itself interfered with.[91]

15.   PRISONERS

C8–60   The most common ground for complaints by prisoners in the case law is restrictions on correspondence and visits. Some measure of control over prisoners'

---

[85] (1996) 21 E.H.R.R. CD 81, 84.
[86] *Beldjoudi v. France* (1992) 14 E.H.R.R. 801 and *Moustaquim v. Belgium* (1991) 13 E.H.R.R. 802.
[87] *Berrehab v. Netherlands* (1989) 11 E.H.R.R. 322.
[88] *Abdulaziz, Cabales and Balkandali v. United Kingdom* (1985) 7 E.H.R.R. 471 paras 59–69.
[89] *Lamguindaz v. United Kingdom* (1994) 17 E.H.R.R. 213.
[90] *Nasri v. France* (1996) 21 E.H.R.R. 458, para. 46.
[91] *Abdulaziz, Cabales and Balkandali v. United Kingdom* and *East African Asians v. United Kingdom* (1973) 3 E.H.R.R. 76. See further, in relation to Article 14, below, para. C14–02. As to Article 3 see above, para. 3–08.

correspondence is called for and is not of itself incompatible with the Convention.[92] However, prisoners' right to respect for their correspondence is not subject to implied limitations,[93] and any restrictions have to be justified under Article 8(2), although regard must be had to the ordinary and reasonable requirements of imprisonment when considering whether a restriction is necessary in a democratic society.[94]

C8–61   The approach to prison visits is broadly similar, and the Court has said that:

"When assessing the obligations imposed on the Contracting States by Article 8 in relation to prison visits, regard must be had to the ordinary and reasonable requirements of imprisonment and to the resultant degree of discretion which the national authorities must be allowed in regulating a prisoner's contact with his family".[95]

C8–62   However, a prisoner's contact with his counsel enjoys a privileged status under the Convention. In *Campbell v. United Kingdom* the Court referred to previous jurisprudence, in accordance with which the accused is guaranteed the right to communicate with his advocate out of the hearing of a third person, and considered that:

"similar considerations apply to a prisoner's correspondence with a lawyer concerning contemplated or pending proceedings where the need for confidentiality is equally pressing, particularly where such correspondence relates, . . . , to claims and complaints against the prison authorities. That such correspondence be susceptible to routine scrutiny, particularly by individuals or authorities which may have a direct interest in the subject matter contained therein is not in keeping with the principles of confidentiality and professional privilege attaching to relations between a lawyer and his client . . . Admittedly, . . . , the borderline between mail concerning contemplated litigation and that of general nature is especially difficult to draw and correspondence with a lawyer may concern matters which have little or nothing to do with litigation. Nevertheless the Court sees no reason to distinguish between the different categories of correspondence with lawyers which, whatever their purpose, concern matters of private and confidential character. In principle such letters are privileged under Article 8. This means that the prison authorities may open a letter from a lawyer to a prisoner when they have reasonable cause to believe that it contains an illicit enclosure which the normal means of detection have failed to disclose. The letter should, however, only be opened and should not be read. Suitable guarantees preventing the reading of the letter should be provided, *e.g.* opening the letter in the presence of the prisoner. The reading of a prisoner's mail to and from a lawyer, on the other hand, should only be permitted in exceptional circumstances when the authorities have reasonable cause to believe that the privilege is being abused in that the contents of the letter endanger prison security or the safety of others or are otherwise of a

---

[92] *Silver v. United Kingdom* (1983) 5 E.H.R.R. 347, para. 98.
[93] *Golder v. United Kingdom*, 1 E.H.R.R. 524, para. 44.
[94] *ibid.*, para. 45.
[95] *Boyle and Rice v. United Kingdom* (1988) 10 E.H.R.R. 425, para. 74.

criminal nature. What may be regarded as "reasonable cause" will depend on all the circumstances but it presupposes the existence of facts or information which would satisfy the objective observer that the privileged channel of communication was being abused."[96]

C8–63　The Commission has held that Article 8 does not require conjugal visits even if the husband and wife are detained in the same prison.[97]

C8–64　Finally, the Convention organs have decided two cases with important implications for incommunicado detention. In *McVeigh, O'Neill and Evans v. United Kingdom*,[98] people suspected of terrorist activities were prevented from contacting their wives to inform them of their detention. The applicants' detention, and the denial of contact with their wives, had lasted only for a relatively short time. However, the Commission considered that at a time when a person is arrested his or her ability to communicate rapidly with his or her family may be of great importance. The unexpected disappearance of a family member even for a short period of time may provoke great anxiety. The Commission accepted that in certain circumstances the existence of the risk that accomplices might be alerted and escape, destroy or remove evidence or commit offences may justify refusing for a time to allow an arrested person to contact the outside world. However, the Government had not claimed any specific reasons why, in the particular case, the applicants' wives could not be notified of their whereabouts. As a result Article 8 had been violated.

C8–65　The case must be read together with *Schonenberger and Durmaz v. Switzerland*[99] where the Court considered that stopping a letter sent by counsel to a detainee could not be justified under the second paragraph of Article 8, even though counsel had used this device to inform the detainee of his right of silence and to advise him to exercise it. It is significant that the Court did not attach any importance to the fact that counsel had been instructed by the detainee's wife rather than by the detainee himself.

16. HOUSING LAWS

C8–66　In cases concerning the right to respect for a person's home, Article 8 may have an impact on housing laws, but such case law as there is has tended to relate to Article 1 of Protocol No. 1.[1] Subjecting the occupation of privately owned residential property to a system of licences does not amount *per se* to a violation of the Convention; the question is whether special circumstances exist.[2] In one recent case, a retired civil servant complained that since he had his tenancy from the Government, he did not qualify for security of tenure as a "statutory tenant". The complaint was not made under Article 8 alone, but the Court held that questions of

---

[96] (1992) E.H.R.R. 137, paras 47–48. see further *McCallum v. United Kingdom* (1990) 13 E.H.R.R. 596 and *Herczegfalvy v. Austria* (1993) 15 E.H.R.R. 437.
[97] App. No. 8166/78 *X and Y v. Switzerland* 13 D. & R. 241 and further App. No. 9054/80 30 D. & R. 113.
[98] (1983) 5 E.H.R.R. 71, Commission's Report.
[99] (1989) 11 E.H.R.R. 202.
[1] See below, p. 332.
[2] *Gillow v. United Kingdom* (1989) 11 E.H.R.R. 335.

security of tenure come within its scope. In that case the applicant was found to be in a relevantly similar position to private tenants and since no reasonable justification had been advanced, the Court found a violation of Article 14 of the Convention in conjunction with Article 8.[3]

17. GYPSIES

C8–67 If gypsies have established a home in a caravan, the refusal of planning permission, and planning or other enforcement action, which prevents them from continuing to live there can amount to an interference with their right to respect for their home.[4] But Article 8 cannot be construed as conferring a right to take up residence on land belonging to others nor as imposing a positive obligation to ensure that there are vacancies on official sites, at least for those who wish to return to the traditional way of life of a gypsy after a number of years.[5]

C8–68 The Commission has accepted that living in a caravan may be an integral and deeply-felt part of a gypsy's traditional life-style, to which the guarantees of respect for private and family life and home may apply.[6] The Court found it unnecessary to rule on this point in its only judgment relating to gypsies, although it has said that the importance of the right to an applicant's home must be taken into account when determining the scope of the state's margin of appreciation. This is to be balanced against the enforcement of planning control, which pursues the aims of public safety, the economic well-being of the country and the protection of health[7]; and "Article 8 does not necessarily go so far as to allow individuals' preferences as to their place of residence to override the general interest".[8] The Court exercised very light supervision in *Buckley*, merely satisfying itself that procedural safeguards were available and the applicant's interests were taken into account.[9]

C8–69 In March 1998, the Commission declared admissible a further group of cases relating to planning enforcement action against gypsies. These cases are now pending before the Court.[10]

18. ENVIRONMENTAL POLLUTION

C8–70 The Court has accepted that "severe environmental pollution may affect individuals' well-being and prevent them from enjoying their homes in such a way as to affect their private and family life adversely, without, however, seriously endangering their health".[11] Whether the obligation which Article 8 creates is

---

[3] *Larkos v. Cyprus*, App. No. 29515/95, judgment of February 18, 1999.
[4] *Buckley v. United Kingdom* (1997) 23 E.H.R.R. 101, para. 60; see also, for example, *Beard v. United Kingdom* (1998) 25 E.H.R.R. CD 28.
[5] *Burton v. United Kingdom* (1996) 22 E.H.R.R. CD 134.
[6] *Buckley v. United Kingdom* (1997) 23 E.H.R.R. 101, para. 64 of the Commission's Report.
[7] *ibid.*, para. 63 of the judgment.
[8] *ibid.*, para. 81 of the judgment.
[9] *ibid.*, paras 81–84 of the judgment.
[10] *Beard v. United Kingdom* (1998) 25 E.H.R.R. CD 28; *Chapman v. United Kingdom* 25 E.H.R.R. CD 64; *Coster v. United Kingdom* 25 E.H.R.R. CD 24; *Smith v. United Kingdom* 25 E.H.R.R. CD 52.
[11] *Lopez-Ostra v. Spain* (1995) 20 E.H.R.R. 277, para. 51. See also *Rayner v. United Kingdom* 47 D. & R. 22; *Powell and Rayner v. United Kingdom* (1990) 12 E.H.R.R. 355 (noise nuisance).

positive or negative in these circumstances, public authorities have to strike a balance between the rights of the individual and whatever general interest may be served by the polluting activities.

C8–71   In some cases, the state may be obliged to protect people from polluting activities whether caused by public authorities or by private bodies.[12] In others, Article 8 creates a positive obligation to make available essential information that would enable individuals to assess the risks they and their families might run as a result of particular activities in their locality.[13] The right to respect for private and family life may also afford procedural guarantees in this area, so that those potentially affected by polluting activities have an opportunity to object to their authorisation.[14]

19.   SCHOOL DISCIPLINE

C8–72   The majority of complaints about school discipline have concerned the use of corporal punishment and in the main they have been considered under Article 3.[15] However, "[t]he Court does not exclude the possibility that there might be circumstances in which Article 8 could be regarded as affording in relation to disciplinary measures a protection that goes beyond that given by Article 3".[16] Not every act or measure which may be said to have an adverse effect on the physical or moral integrity of a person necessarily gives rise to an interference with that person's private life and as a result not every disciplinary measure will be found to constitute such an interference.[17] Further support for this conclusion may be derived from the Court's recognition in *Costello-Roberts v. United Kingdom* that " . . . the sending of a child to school necessarily involves some degree of interference with his or her private life", which, by implication, cannot give rise to an issue under Article 8.[18]

---

[12] *Lopez-Ostra v. Spain* (1995) 20 E.H.R.R. 277; *Khatun & 180 others v. United Kingdom* (1998) 26 E.H.R.R. CD 212 (serious dust contamination caused by construction of Limehouse Link Road—legitimate aim of urban regeneration; fair balance achieved).

[13] *Guerra and others v. Italy* (1998) 26 E.H.R.R. 357 (information for residents living in the vicinity of a high risk factory); see also *McGinley & Egan v. United Kingdom* (1999) 27 E.H.R.R. 1 (information for individuals exposed to atmospheric tests of nuclear weapons).

[14] *LM & R. v. Switzerland* 22 E.H.R.R. CD 130 (holding in transit of nuclear waste at a railway station near the applicants' homes); see also *Zander v. Sweden* (1994) 18 E.H.R.R. 175 (right of landowner to challenge authorisation to dump waste on adjacent tip, with risk to drinking water—Article 6); *Greenpeace Schweiz & others v. Switzerland* (1997) 23 E.H.R.R. CD 116 (complaint of lack of access to court for neighbours to challenge award of licences to run a nuclear power station affected neighbours' health and related to their use of property either as proprietor or tenant and therefore a civil right under Article 6).

[15] See above, para. C3–07.

[16] *Costello-Roberts v. United Kingdom* (1995) 19 E.H.R.R. 112, para. 36.

[17] *ibid.*

[18] *ibid.*

ARTICLE 9

FREEDOM OF THOUGHT, CONSCIENCE AND RELIGION

C9–01

1 Everyone has the right to freedom of thought, conscience and religion; this right includes freedom to change his religion or belief and freedom, either alone or in community with others and in public or private, to manifest his religion or belief, in worship, teaching, practice and observance.

2 Freedom to manifest one's religion or beliefs shall be subject only to such limitations as are prescribed by law and are necessary in a democratic society in the interests of public safety, for the protection of public order, health or morals, or for the protection of the rights and freedoms of others.

C9–02 The Court's general understanding of Article 9 is broadly set forth in *Kokkinakis v. Greece*:

"As enshrined in Article 9, freedom of thought, conscience and religion is one of the foundations of a 'democratic society' within the meaning of the Convention. It is, in its religious dimension, one of the most vital elements that go to make up the identity of believers and their conception of life, but it is also a precious asset for atheists, agnostics, sceptics and the unconcerned. The pluralism indissociable from a democratic society, which has been dearly won over the centuries, depends on it."[1]

C9–03

"The fundamental nature of the rights guaranteed in Article 9(1) is also reflected in the wording of the paragraph providing for limitations on them. Unlike the second paragraphs of Articles 8, 10 and 11, which cover all the rights mentioned in the first paragraphs of those Articles, that of Article 9 refers only to 'freedom to manifest one's religion or belief'. In so doing, it recognises that in democratic societies, in which several religions coexist within one and the same population, it may be necessary to place restrictions on this freedom in order to reconcile the interests of the various groups and ensure that everybody's beliefs are respected."[2]

C9–04 Of the Articles containing a restriction clause, Article 9 is the only one that does not permit the state to invoke "national security" to justify restricting the exercise of the protected right. But in *Kalaç v. Turkey*,[3] considered below, the Court considered that a person who chose to pursue a military career accepted a disciplinary system that by its nature implied the possibility of limitations on rights and freedoms, including freedom of religion.

C9–05 The Convention organs have not specifically addressed the issue of what the attributes of a "religion or a belief" are for the purposes of Article 9. In *Kokkinakis* the Court relied on the status of Jehovah's Witnesses as a "known

---

[1] (1994) 17 E.H.R.R. 397, para. 31.
[2] *ibid.*, para. 33.
[3] July 1, 1997, R.J.D., 1997–IV, No. 41; 27 E.H.R.R. 552.

religion" under domestic law. In *Arrowsmith v. United Kingdom* the Commission limited itself to observing that "pacifism as a philosophy . . . . falls within the ambit of the right to freedom of thought and conscience. The attitude of pacifism may therefore be seen as a belief (*'conviction'*) protected by Article 9(1)."[4]

C9–06   The Convention organs have had, on the other hand, the opportunity to deal in a number of decisions with the issue of what constitutes a manifestation of religion or beliefs within the meaning of Article 9. In *Kokkinakis* the Court observed:

"While religious freedom is primarily a matter of individual conscience, it also implies, *inter alia*, freedom to manifest [one's] religion".

Bearing witness in words and deeds is bound up with the existence of religious convictions.

C9–07   According to Article 9, freedom to manifest one's religion is not only exercisable in community with others, "in public" and within the circle of those whose faith one shares, but can also be asserted "alone" and "in private". Furthermore, in principle it includes the right to try to convince one's neighbour, for example through "teaching", without which "freedom to change [one's] religion or belief, enshrined in Article 9, would be likely to remain a dead letter."[5]

C9–08   However, in *Kalaç v. Turkey*,[6] the Court considered that Article 9 does not protect every act motivated or inspired by a religion or belief; and in *Arrowsmith v. United Kingdom* the Commission explained that:

"It is true that public declarations proclaiming generally the idea of pacifism and urging the acceptance of a commitment to non-violence may be considered as a normal and recognised manifestation of pacifist belief. However, when the actions of individuals do not actually express the belief concerned they cannot be considered to be as such protected by Article 9(1), even when they are motivated or influenced by it."[7]

C9–09   Moreover, in *X v. United Kingdom*[8] the Commission observed that:

"Article 9 primarily protects the sphere of personal beliefs and religious creeds, *i.e.* the area which is sometimes called the *forum internum*. In addition, it protects acts which are intimately linked to these attitudes, such as acts of worship or devotion which are aspects of the practice of a religion or a belief in a generally recognised form. However, in protecting this personal sphere, Article 9 of the Convention does not always guarantee the rights to behave in the public sphere in a way which is dictated by such a belief, for instance by refusing to pay certain taxes because part of the revenue so raised may be applied for military expenditure".

---

[4] (1980) 3 E.H.R.R. 218, para. 69.
[5] *Kokkinakis v. Greece* (1994) 17 E.H.R.R. 397, para. 31. On the relationship between the freedom to manifest one's religion alone and the freedom to manifest it in community with others see further App. No. 8160/78 *Ahmad v. United Kingdom* 4 E.H.R.R. 126.
[6] July 1, 1997, R.J.D., 1997–IV, No. 41; 27 E.H.R.R. 552.
[7] (1980) 3 E.H.R.R. 218, para. 71 of the Report.
[8] App. No. 10295/82, (1984) 6 E.H.R.R. 558.

C9–10   It should be noted that the Court has also held that "in exercising his freedom to manifest his religion, an individual may need to take his specific situation into account".[9] In *Kalaç v. Turkey* the Court found no interference under Article 9(1) in a case where a judge advocate in the air force with the rank of group captain, who was the high command's director of legal affairs, had been compulsorily retired on the ground that "his conduct and attitude revealed that he had adopted unlawful fundamentalist opinions". In the Court's view:

> "In choosing to pursue a military career Mr Kalaç was accepting of his own accord a system of military discipline that by its very nature implied the possibility of placing on certain of the rights and freedoms of members of the armed forces limitations incapable of being imposed upon civilians . . . States may adopt for their armies disciplinary regulations forbidding this or that type of conduct, in particular an attitude inimical to an established order reflecting the requirements of military service."[10]

In that case, the applicant's compulsory retirement was based not on his opinions and beliefs but on his conduct and attitude which breached military discipline and infringed the principle of secularism.

C9–11   The Commission has also rejected a number of complaints on the basis of the applicants' special contractual obligations or the fact that they are in detention.[11]

C9–12   Conscientious objectors cannot derive the right to alternative military service from the Convention. The Commission has stated that in interpreting Article 9:

> " . . . [it] has also taken into consideration the terms of Article 4(3)(b) of the Convention which states that forced or compulsory labour shall not include 'any service of a military character or, in case of conscientious objectors in countries where they are recognized, service exacted instead of compulsory military service'. This provision clearly shows that, by including the words 'in countries where they are recognized' in Article 4(3)(b), a choice is left to the High Contracting Parties to the Convention whether or not to recognize conscientious objectors and, if so recognized, to provide some substitute service for them."[12]

If, however, exemption from military service may be granted on, for example, grounds of religious belief, it must be accorded without unjustified discrimination.[13]

C9–13   Article 9 of the Convention may also impose a positive duty on the state to protect believers from provocative portrayals of objects of religious veneration,

---

[9] *Kalaç v. Turkey*, July 1, 1997, R.J.D., 1997–IV, No. 41; 27 E.H.R.R. 552.
[10] *ibid.*, para. 28.
[11] See App. No. 5422/72 *X v. United Kingdom* 1 D. & R. 41; App. No. 7374/76 *X v. Denmark* 5 D. & R. 157 and App. No. 8160/78 *Ahmad v. United Kingdom* 4 E.H.R.R. 126.
[12] *App. No. 5591/72 v. Austria* 43 Coll 161.
[13] See the Commission's Opinion in *Tsirlis v. Greece*, July 1, 1997, R.J.D., 1997–IV, No. 4; 21 E.H.R.R. CD 30 (the Court decided the case on the basis of Article 5 and found it unnecessary to deal with Article 9.

since such portrayals may be regarded as a malicious violation of the spirit of tolerance which must be a feature of democratic society.[14]

C9–14 A state is entitled to regulate alleged religious activity in order to verify, for the purpose of protecting public order, whether a movement or association carries on, ostensibly in pursuit of religious aims, activities which are harmful to the population. However, considerable weight is to be attached to the proportionality of any restriction imposed, and "strict scrutiny" must be applied. In particular:

> "The right to freedom of religion as guaranteed under the Convention excludes any discretion on the part of the State to determine whether religious beliefs or the means used to express such beliefs are legitimate."[15]

C9–15 It should also be noted that, unless it is exercising "governmental powers", a church or religious association constitutes a "non-governmental organisation" which can claim to be a "victim" within the meaning of Article 34 of the Convention.[16] In *Christian Association of Jehovah's Witnesses v. Bulgaria*[17] the Commission confirmed that, even without legal personality, a religious association could make a claim under Article 34 as a "group of individuals". This also means that decisions by church authorities relating to the internal organisation of the church do not constitute interference by the state.[18]

C9–16 Finally, there is considerable overlap between the protection afforded by Article 9 and a number of other provisions in the Convention, including Article 10 which guarantees the right to freedom of expression and to freedom to hold opinions. With the notable exception of *Kokkinakis v. Greece*[19] where the Court was confronted with a conviction for proselytism, an issue going to the heart of religious freedom, most cases have been so far examined under one of the other Convention provisions applicable in the situation.[20]

---

[14] *Otto-Preminger Institute v. Austria* (1994) 19 E.H.R.R. 34; see also the Commission's decision in *Dubowska & Skup v. Poland* (1997) 23 E.H.R.R. CD 204.
[15] *Manoussakis v. Greece*, September 26, 1996, R.J.D., 1996–IV, No. 17; 23 E.H.R.R. 387, para. 47.
[16] *Holy Monasteries v. Greece* (1995) 20 E.H.R.R. 1; see also *Christian Association of Jehovah's Witnesses v. Bulgaria* (1997) 24 E.H.R.R. CD 52.
[17] (1997) 24 E.H.R.R. CD 52.
[18] See *Hautanemi et al v. Sweden* (1996) 22 E.H.R.R. CD 155, which concerned a prohibition by the Church Assembly of the Church of Sweden on the use of Finnish liturgy.
[19] (1993) 17 E.H.R.R. 397.
[20] See *Darby v. Sweden* (1991) 13 E.H.R.R. 774; *Hoffmann v. Austria* (1994) 17 E.H.R.R. 293; *Johnston v. Ireland* (1987) 9 E.H.R.R. 203 and *Young, James and Webster v. United Kingdom* (1981) 4 E.H.R.R. 38.

ARTICLE 10

FREEDOM OF EXPRESSION

C10–01

1 Everyone has the right to freedom of expression. This right shall include freedom to hold opinions and to receive and impart information and ideas without interference by public authority and regardless of frontiers. This article shall not prevent States from requiring the licensing of broadcasting, television or cinema enterprises.

2 The exercise of these freedoms, since it carries with it duties and responsibilities, may be subject to such formalities, conditions, restrictions or penalties as are prescribed by law and are necessary in a democratic society, in the interests of national security, territorial integrity or public safety, for the prevention of disorder or crime, for the protection of health or morals, for the protection of the reputation or rights of others, for preventing the disclosure of information received in confidence, or for maintaining the authority and impartiality of the judiciary.

C10–02   Article 10(1) guarantees the right to freedom of expression. An interference with this right entails a violation of Article 10 if it does not fall within one of the exceptions provided for in paragraph 2.

C10–03   In the important case of *Handyside v. United Kingdom* the Court observed that freedom of expression constitutes one of the essential foundations of a democratic society and one of the basic conditions for its progress and for each individual's self-fulfilment:

> "Subject to Article 10(2), it is applicable not only to 'information' or 'ideas' that are favourably received or regarded as inoffensive or as a matter of indifference, but also to those that offend, shock or disturb the State or any sector of the population. Such are the demands of that pluralism, tolerance and broadmindedness without which there is no 'democratic society'."[1-2]

However:

> "whoever exercises his freedom of expression undertakes 'duties and responsibilities' the scope of which depends on his situation and the technical means he uses. The Court cannot overlook such a person's 'duties' and 'responsibilities' when it enquires . . . whether "restrictions" . . . were . . . 'necessary' in a 'democratic society'."[3]

These "duties and responsibilities", for example, mean that the protection provided by Article 10 to journalists is subject to the proviso that "they are acting in good faith in order to provide accurate and reliable information in accordance with the ethics of journalism".[4]

[1-2] (1976) 1 E.H.R.R. 737, para. 49.
[3] *ibid.*, para. 49.
[4] See *Bladet Tromsø and Stensaas v. Norway*, judgment of May 20, 1999, para. 65, discussed below, para. C10–13. See also *Fressoz and Roire v. France*, judgment of January 21, 1999, para. 54. See further below, para. C10–13.

C10–04 Moreover, "Article 10 protects not only the substance of the ideas and information expressed, but also the form in which they are conveyed".[5]

C10–05 The commentary below outlines the scope of Article 10 and the case law which has arisen by examining the following issues:

1. Freedom of speech and the political process

2. Freedom of speech and criticism of civil servants

3. Freedom of speech and other matters of public concern

4. Freedom of speech and the judicial process

5. Freedom of speech and prior restraints

6. Commercial free speech

7. Licensing of broadcasting facilities

8. Civil Service employment

9. Artistic expression

10. Obscene material

11. Blasphemous material

12. Racist speech

13. Access to information

14. Abortion information

15. Demonstrations

16. Libel awards

17. Protection of journalistic sources

1. FREEDOM OF SPEECH AND THE POLITICAL PROCESS

C10–06 In the important case of *Castells v. Spain*, which concerned the conviction and disqualification of an M.P. for insulting the Government, the Court considered that:

> " . . . while freedom of expression is important for everybody, it is especially so for an elected representative of the people. He represents his electorate, draws attention to their preoccupations and defends their interests. Accordingly, interferences with the freedom of expression of an opposition M.P., . . ., call for the closest scrutiny on the part of the Court."[6]

In finding a violation the Court relied heavily on the fact that the M.P. in question had not been allowed to establish the veracity of his allegations. In an earlier

---

[5] *Oberschlick v. Austria* (1995) 19 E.H.R.R. 389.
[6] (1992) 14 E.H.R.R. 445, para. 42.

equally important case, *Lingens v. Austria*. the Court pronounced on the importance of a free press for the political process in a democratic society:

> "Freedom of the press ... affords the public one of the best means of
> discovering and forming an opinion of the ideas and attitudes of political
> leaders. More generally, freedom of political debate is at the very core of the
> concept of a democratic society which prevails throughout the Convention.
> The limits of acceptable criticism are accordingly wider as regards a politician
> as such than as regards a private individual."[7]

The case concerned the conviction of a journalist for defaming the Austrian
Chancellor. The Court found a violation of Article 10 relying on the fact that the
accused was convicted for good-faith value judgments based on undisputed facts.
National law required the accused to prove the truth of his statements to escape
conviction. According to the Court, however, "[t]he existence of facts can be
demonstrated, whereas the truth of value judgments is not susceptible of proof".[8]
The measure employed against the applicant was disproportionate to the legitimate
aim pursued, to protect the reputation of others, and the limitation of his freedom
of expression not necessary in a democratic society.[9]

C10–07   The Commission and the Court have recognised the legitimacy in
principle of restrictions on electoral expenditure aimed at keeping candidates on an
equal footing. However, they have held to be disproportionate a restriction on the
distribution, by an independent third party, of leaflets informing the electorate of
candidates' views on single issues (abortion and human embryo experimentation).
In the Commission's opinion, "individual freedom of expression, as a key ingredient of a democratic society, must be considered inextricably linked with a free
election system and cannot be excluded without convincing justification".[10] The
Court has emphasised that:

> "Free elections and freedom of expression, particularly freedom of political
> debate, together form the bedrock of any democratic system. The two rights
> are interrelated and operate to reinforce each other: as the Court has observed
> in the past, freedom of expression is one of the 'conditions' necessary to
> 'ensure the free expression of the opinion of the people in the choice of the
> legislature'. For this reason it is particularly important in the period preceding
> an election that opinions and information of all kinds are permitted to
> circulate freely."[11]

Certain restrictions on freedom of speech may nonetheless be justified during
elections in the interest of guaranteeing equality between candidates.

C10–08   Special problems arise in relation to the fight against terrorism, and a
ban on the broadcast of the voices, but not the words, of Sinn Fein members was

---

[7] (1986) 8 E.H.R.R. 407, para. 42.
[8] para. 46.
[9] See further *Oberschlick v. Austria* (1995) 19 E.H.R.R. 389 and *Schwabe v. Austria*, August 28, 1992, Series A, No. 242–B.
[10] *Bowman v. United Kingdom* (1998) 26 E.H.R.R. 1, para. 46 of the Commission's Opinion.
[11] *Bowman v. United Kingdom* (1998) 26 E.H.R.R. 1, para. 42 of the judgment.

justified for the prevention of disorder and not disproportionate to the aim in view.[12] In *Ceylan v. Turkey*,[13] the Court was again faced with the balance to be struck between political speech and the concerns arising in the context of prevention of terrorism. In that case, the applicant, the president of the petroleum workers' union, had been convicted of incitement to hatred and hostility by making distinctions based upon ethnic or regional origin or social class for writing an article, the style of which was "virulent and the criticism of the Turkish authorities' actions in the relevant part acerbic, as demonstrated by the use of the words 'State Terrorism' and 'genocide'."[14] The applicant was sentenced to one year and eight months' imprisonment and a fine of TRL100,000. The Court found that the conviction amounted to a disproportionate interference with his right to free speech, relying in particular on the following three factors:

a) the applicant was writing as a "player on the Turkish political scene";

b) the article, despite its virulence, did not encourage the use of violence or armed resistance or insurrection; and

c) the penalty imposed upon the applicant was very severe.

2. FREEDOM OF SPEECH AND CRITICISM OF CIVIL SERVANTS

C10–09   In *Janowski v. Poland*,[15] a case in which the applicant had been convicted of insulting municipal guards by using words such as "oafs" and "dumb", the Commission had concluded that civil servants acting in an official capacity are subject to the same "wider limits of acceptable criticism" as politicians. However, the Court did not agree:

> "Admittedly those limits may in some circumstances be wider with regard to civil servants exercising their powers than in relation to private individuals. However, it cannot be said that civil servants knowingly lay themselves open to close scrutiny of their every word and deed to the extent to which politicians do and should therefore be treated on an equal footing with the latter when it comes to the criticism of their actions.
> What is more, civil servants must enjoy public confidence in conditions free of undue perturbation if they are to be successful in performing their tasks and it may therefore prove necessary to protect them from offensive and abusive verbal attacks when on duty".[16]

Since the case in question did not concern press comment or other open discussion on matters of public concern, there was no need to weigh the protection of public officials against press freedom. It must be open to doubt whether this judgment would be followed in the United Kingdom, in particular when one reads the persuasive dissenting judgment of Sir Nicolas Bratza, who found himself quite unable to accept the government's justification. In his view, the prosecution,

---

[12] *Brind v. United Kingdom* (1994) 18 E.H.R.R. CD 76.
[13] Judgment of July 8, 1999.
[14] para. 33.
[15] Judgment of January 21, 1999.
[16] *ibid.*, para. 33. *cf. Oberschlick v. Austria (No. 2)*, (1997) 25 E.H.R.R. 357, para. 29.

conviction and fining of the applicant was neither a response to a pressing social need, nor proportionate to any legitimate aim served.

3. FREEDOM OF SPEECH AND OTHER MATTERS OF PUBLIC CONCERN

C10–11 The importance of a free press is not, however, limited to the discussion of political issues. The Court has expressly said that "there is no warrant in its case-law for distinguishing between political discussion and discussion of other matters of public concern".[17] So, for example, a conviction of a journalist, who had reported in strong terms allegations of police brutality, for defamation of unspecified members of the police force was regarded in *Thorgeirson v. Iceland* as capable of discouraging open discussion of matters of public concern. A violation of Article 10 was found. One of the reported incidents was uncontested, the report aimed at instigating a public inquiry into the allegations and, most importantly, the Court considered it unreasonable to require a journalist who was reporting what was being said by others to establish the truth of his statements.

C10–12 In *Hertel v. Switzerland*[18], the Court held that the extent of the States' wide margin of appreciation which applied in the commercial sphere (see below, paragraph C10–18) had to be reduced "when what is at stake is not a given individual's purely 'commercial' statements, but his participation in a debate affecting the general interest, for example, over public health".[19] The case concerned an injunction, breach of which was punishable by the criminal law, restraining the applicant from repeating statements, based on his research, to the effect that food cooked in a microwave might be damaging to health in certain specified ways. Finding that the injunction was a disproportionate interference, the Court stated that:

> "The effect of the injunction was thus partly to censor the applicant's work and substantially to reduce his ability to put forward in public views which have their place in a public debate whose existence cannot be denied. It matters little that his opinion is a minority one and may appear to be devoid of merit since, in a sphere in which it is unlikely that any certainty exists, it would be particularly unreasonable to restrict freedom of expression only to generally accepted ideas."[20]

C10–13 We have noted that those exercising freedom of expression undertake "duties and responsibilities". For journalists, this means that the protection of Article 10 is available only if "they are acting in good faith in order to provide accurate and reliable information in accordance with the ethics of journalism."[21] In a recent case the Court referred to what it described as the media's "ordinary obligation to verify factual statements that [are] defamatory of private

---

[17] *Thorgeirson v. Iceland* (1992) 14 E.H.R.R. 843, para. 64.

[18] (1999) 28 E.H.R.R. 534.

[19] para. 47 of the judgment.

[20] para. 50 of the judgment.

[21] *Bladet Tromsø and Stensaas v. Norway*, judgment of May 20, 1999, para. 65, with reference to *Goodwin*, para. 39 and *Fressoz and Roire*, judgment of January 21, 1999, para. 54.

individuals".[22] However, " . . . the press should normally be entitled, when contributing to public debate on matters of legitimate concern, to rely on the contents of official reports without having to undertake independent research. Otherwise, the vital public-watchdog role of the press may be undermined".[23] In *Bladet Tromsø and Stensaas*,[24] a newspaper had reported "factual statements" based upon a government-appointed inspector's report into seal hunting. The newspaper, which had not verified this report by independent research, was found guilty of defamation against a group of seal hunters. The Court concluded that the convictions for defamation were disproportionate to the legitimate aim of protecting the seal hunters' reputations:

> "Having regard to the various factors limiting the likely harm to the individual seal hunters' reputation and to the situation as it presented itself to Bladet Tromsø at the relevant time, the Court considers that the paper could reasonably rely on the official Lindberg report, without being required to carry out its own research into the accuracy of the facts reported. It sees no reason to doubt that the newspaper acted in good faith in this respect."[25]

Of particular importance for the Court was the "vital public interest in ensuring an informed public debate over a matter of local and national as well as international interest".[26] It is noteworthy, however, that the Court did not adopt wholesale the Commission's *dictum* that:

> " . . . freedom of the press would be extremely limited if it were considered to apply only to information which could be proved to be true. The working conditions of journalists would be extremely limited if they were limited to publishing such information."[27]

4.   FREEDOM OF SPEECH AND THE JUDICIAL PROCESS

C10–14   The importance attached to the role of the press in a democratic society is further demonstrated by the position taken by the Court in cases concerning freedom of speech and the judicial process. As a matter of fact, it was in a case raising such issues, *Sunday Times v. United Kingdom*, that the foundations for the development of the jurisprudence mentioned above were laid. The case concerned a court injunction prohibiting publication of an article by the Sunday Times, on the grounds that it would constitute contempt of court. The Court held that:

> "[t]here is general recognition of the fact that the courts cannot operate in a vacuum . . . whilst the mass media must not overstep the bounds imposed on

---

[22] *ibid.*, para. 66. The reference to private individuals: the Court has said that the limits of permissible criticism or other statements are narrower in relation to a private citizen than in relation to politicians or governments: *Incal v. Turkey*, judgment of June 9, 1998, para. 54.

[23] App. No. 21980/93, *Bladet Tromsø and Stensaas v. Norway*, judgment of May 20, 1999, para. 68. See, *mutatis mutandis, Goodwin*, para. 39.

[24] App. No. 21980/93, *Bladet Tromsø and Stensaas v. Norway*, judgment of May 20, 1999.

[25] *ibid.*, para. 72.

[26] *ibid.*, para. 73.

[27] Commission's Report dated July 9, 1998, para. 80, referring also to *Incal v. Turkey*, judgment of June 9, 1998, para. 54.

them in the interests of the proper administration of justice, it is incumbent on them to impart information and ideas concerning matters that come before the courts just as in other areas of public interest. Not only do the media have the task of imparting such information and ideas: the public also has a right to receive them."[28]

The Court concluded on a violation of Article 10 relying on the breadth and unqualified nature of the injunction, the moderate nature of the prohibited article, the fact that it concerned civil proceedings which lay dormant over a number of years and the large degree of public interest surrounding the subject-matter of the article. In the light of all the above the interference was not "necessary in a democratic society".[29]

C10–15   However, in cases of direct criticism of judges the Court is more likely to consider press restrictions justified under the second paragraph of Article 10 for the protection of the authority and impartiality of the judiciary,[30] and although lawyers have rights too, they are subject to a particular duty of discretion and responsibility when it comes to public criticism of the judicial authorities.[31]

5.   FREEDOM OF SPEECH AND PRIOR RESTRAINTS

C10–16   The issue of prior restraints was dealt with in *The Observer and The Guardian v. United Kingdom* and *Sunday Times (No. 2).*[32] The Court held that the protection afforded to the press by Article 10 does not prohibit the imposition of prior restraints on publication. Yet:

" . . . the dangers inherent in prior restraint are such that they call for the most careful scrutiny on the part of the Court. This is especially so as far as the press is concerned, for news is a perishable commodity and to delay its publication, even for a short period, may well deprive it of all its value and interest."[33]

C10–17   Injunctions intended to prevent the disclosure of information that ought to be kept secret were considered justified under the second paragraph of Article 10. Injunctions the purpose of which had become confined to the promotion of the efficiency and reputation of the security service were not. It cannot be regarded as "necessary" to seek to prevent disclosure of information which is already in the public domain as was held in *Vereniging Weekblad Bluf! v. Netherlands*[34]

6.   COMMERCIAL FREE SPEECH

C10–18   The Court has indicated that information of a commercial nature is protected by Article 10.[35] However, the Court has, in effect, accepted that:

---

[28] (1979) 2 E.H.R.R. 245, para. 65.
[29] See further *Worm v. Austria*, August 29, 1997, R.J.D. 1997–V, No. 45; 25 E.H.R.R. 454.
[30] See *Barfod v. Denmark* (1989) 13 E.H.R.R. 493. See further *De Haes & Gijsels v. Belgium*, February 24, 1997, R.J.D., 1997–I, No. 30; 25 E.H.R.R. 1; *Worm v. Austria*, August 29, 1997, R.J.D., 1997–V, No. 45; 25 E.H.R.R. 454.
[31] *Schöpfer v. Switzerland* judgment of May 20, 1998 [1998] E.H.R.L.R. 646.
[32] (1992) 14 E.H.R.R. 153; (1992) 14 E.H.R.R. 229.
[33] *The Observer and The Guardian v. United Kingdom* (1992) 14 E.H.R.R. 153, para. 60.
[34] (1995) 20 E.H.R.R. 189, para. 44.
[35] *Markt Intern and Beermann v. Germany* (1990) 12 E.H.R.R. 161; see further App. No. 7805/77 *X and Church of Scientology v. Sweden*, 22 Yb 244.

" . . . in the field of competition, States enjoyed a wide discretion in order to take account of the specific situation in the national market . . . statements made 'for purposes of competition' fell outside the basic nucleus protected by the freedom of expression and received a lower level of protection than other 'ideas' or 'information'"[36]

The same wider margin of appreciation will apply to professional advertising, in particular where there is no uniformity of practice among the states parties to the Convention. "The Court's task is therefore confined to ascertaining whether the measures taken at a national level are justifiable in principle and proportionate."[37]

C10–19 Note, however, that the Convention organs are unlikely to characterise as commercial speech a contribution to the public debate which has a secondary advertising effect as was held in *Barthold v. Germany*,[38] or which may have an incidental effect on competition.[39]

7. LICENSING OF BROADCASTING FACILITIES

C10–20 The Court has held that both the means of transmission and the means of reception of information are covered by Article 10(1).[40] Moreover:

" . . . both broadcasting of programmes over the air and cable retransmission of such programmes are covered by the right enshrined in the first two sentences of Article 10(1), without there being any need to draw distinctions according to the content of the programmes."[41]

C10–21 Although Article 10(1) contains an express provision allowing states to regulate, through a licensing system, all broadcasting, television, or cinema enterprises, states must still justify their licensing requirements or practices by reference to Article 10(2), to which the third sentence of Article 10(1) is subject:

"[T]he purpose of the third sentence of Article 10(1) of the Convention is to make it clear that States are permitted to control by a licensing system the way in which broadcasting is organised in their territories, particularly in its technical aspects. It does not, however, provide that licensing measures should not otherwise be subject to the requirements of paragraph 2, for that would lead to a result contrary to the object and purpose of Article 10 taken as a whole."[42]

The Court registered a finding of violation when a private company was refused permission to receive, by means of a private dish aerial, uncoded TV programmes intended for the general public from a Soviet telecommunications satellite, without

[36] *Markt Intern and Beermann v. Germany* (1990) 12 E.H.R.R. 161, para. 32.
[37] *Casado Coca v. Spain* (1994) 18 E.H.R.R. 1.
[38] (1985) 7 E.H.R.R. 383.
[39] *Hertel v. Switzerland* (1999) 28 E.H.R.R. 534.
[40] *Autronic AG v. Switzerland* (1990) 12 E.H.R.R. 485.
[41] *Groppera Radio AG v. Switzerland* (1990) 12 E.H.R.R. 321, para. 55..
[42] *ibid.*, para. 61.

the permission of the broadcasting state.[43] The Court has held a refusal of a broadcasting licence, pursuant to a state broadcasting monopoly, to be an unjustified interference, since it did not correspond to any pressing social need deriving from technical justifications. "Supervision [by the convention institutions] must be strict because of the importance–frequently stressed by the Court–of the rights in question".[44]

C10–22 No violation was found, on the other hand, when a Swiss company was prohibited from transmitting by cable programmes broadcast from a station situated on Italian soil which did not comply with the conventions and agreements concluded under international radio and telecommunications law.[45]

8. CIVIL SERVICE EMPLOYMENT

C10–23 The Court has found that where a public authority takes account of an individual's opinions and attitudes merely in order to satisfy itself as to whether the individual possesses one of the necessary qualifications for a civil service post there can be no interference with the right guaranteed under Article 10(1).[46] Moreover, the state may restrict the Article 10 rights of its employees to the extent that this is required for fulfilment of the employees' functions.[47] In assessing whether the restrictions are justified under Article 10(2) the Court takes account of the specific "duties" and "responsibilities" incumbent on civil servants. However, as the Commission held in its opinion in the case of *Ahmed v. United Kingdom*,[48] the need for restrictions on freedom of expression of public officials must be convincingly justified, and they must be limited to what is necessary. The Court held in the same case[49] that restrictions on the political activities of certain categories of local government officers were justified in the interests of preserving their political neutrality in order to safeguard effective local democracy. However, the Court has also held that it will be more difficult to justify the dismissal of a civil servant who has been in post for some time without his activities or convictions having any discernible effect on the performance of his functions.[50]

C10–24 In *Rekvényi v. Hungary*,[51] the Court was faced with a newly introduced provision in the Hungarian constitution which prohibited members of the armed forces and the police from joining any political party and from engaging in any political activity. It stated:

"In the present case the obligation imposed on certain categories of public officials including police officers to refrain from political activities is intended

---

[43] *Autronic AG v. Switzerland* (1990) 12 E.H.R.R. 485.
[44] *Informationsverein Lentia v. Austria* (1993) 17 E.H.R.R. 93. See also *Radio ABC v. Austria*, (1998) 25 E.H.R.R. 185.
[45] *Groppera Radio AG v. Switzerland* (1990) 13 E.H.R.R. 321.
[46] *Glasenapp v. Germany* (1987) 9 E.H.R.R. 25 and *Kosiek v. Germany* (1987) 9 E.H.R.R. 328.
[47] See *Engel v. Netherlands* (1976) 1 E.H.R.R. 647, paras 94–101.
[48] 22954/93, adopted on May 29, 1997.
[49] Judgment of September 2, 1998.
[50] See *Vogt v. Germany* (1996) 21 E.H.R.R. 205. See also *VDSO v. Austria* (1990) 20 E.H.R.R. 56.
[51] Judgment of May 20, 1999.

to depoliticise the services concerned and thereby to contribute to the consolidation and maintenance of pluralistic democracy in the country. The Court notes that Hungary is not alone, in that a number of Contracting States restrict certain political activities on the part of their police. Police officers are invested with coercive powers to regulate the conduct of citizens, in some countries being authorised to carry arms in the discharge of their duties. Ultimately the police force is at the service of the State. Members of the public are therefore entitled to expect that in their dealings with the police they are confronted with politically-neutral officers who are detached from the political fray, to paraphrase the language of the recent judgment in the case of *Ahmed and Others v. the United Kingdom.*[52] In the Court's view, the desire to ensure that the crucial role of the police in society is not compromised through the corrosion of the political neutrality of its officers is one that is compatible with democratic principles.

This objective takes on a special historical significance in Hungary because of that country's experience of a totalitarian regime which relied to a great extent on its police's direct commitment to the ruling party.[53]
. . .

In view of the particular history of some Contracting States, the national authorities of these States may, so as to ensure the consolidation and maintenance of democracy, consider it necessary to have constitutional safeguards to achieve this aim by restricting the freedom of police officers to engage in political activities and, in particular, political debate."[54]

9. ARTISTIC EXPRESSION

C10–25 The term "expression" has been interpreted to include artistic expression as it "affords the opportunity to take part in the public exchange of cultural, political and social information and ideas of all kinds".[55] However:

"(a)rtists and those who promote their work are certainly not immune from the possibility of limitations as provided for in paragraph 2 of Article 10. Whoever exercises his freedom of expression undertakes, in accordance with the express terms of that paragraph, 'duties and responsibilities'."[56]

10. OBSCENE MATERIAL

C10–26 It would appear that Article 10 cannot be successfully invoked in the majority of circumstances to question measures designed to protect morals from "obscene material". According to the Court, the states parties still enjoy a wide margin of appreciation in this regard. This is because:

" . . . it is not possible to find in the domestic law of the various Contracting Parties a uniform European conception of morals. The view taken by their

---

[52] para. 53.
[53] See, *mutatis mutandis*, *Vogt v. Germany* (1996) 21 E.H.R.R. 205, para. 51.
[54] *Rekvényi v. Hungary*, paras 41 and 46.
[55] *Müller v. Switzerland* (1991) 13 E.H.R.R. 212, para. 27.
[56] *ibid.*, para. 34.

respective laws of the requirements of morals varies from time to time and from place to place, especially in our era which is characterised by a rapid and far-reaching evolution of opinions on the subject."[57]

C10–27   In the *Handyside* case,[58] which was decided in 1976, the Court failed to find a violation of Article 10 in respect of the destruction of a book and the conviction of the author of the book, which was addressed to children and adolescents aged from 12 to 18, and which contained sentences or paragraphs on sex that young people could have interpreted as an encouragement to indulge in precocious activities harmful for them or even to commit certain criminal offences. Although, as the Court itself accepted, conceptions of sexual morality have changed in recent years, Article 10 was unsuccessfully invoked in the *Müller* case,[59] decided in 1988, against the confiscation of paintings with emphasis on sexuality in some of its crudest forms, displayed in an exhibition which was unrestrictedly open to–and sought to attract–the public at large and the conviction of the painter and the organisers of the exhibition.

11.   BLASPHEMOUS MATERIAL

C10–28   Restrictions on freedom of expression may also be legitimately imposed on provocative or gratuitously offensive portrayals of objects of religious veneration. Such portrayals may be regarded as "a malicious violation of the spirit of tolerance which must be a feature of a democratic society" and may engage the state's responsibility to ensure respect for freedom of religion under Article 9 of the Convention. Seizure and forfeiture of the offending material may be justified in order to prevent others feeling that their religious beliefs are under unwarranted attack in an offensive manner.[60]

12.   RACIST SPEECH

C10–29   The publication or broadcast of statements or material inciting racial hatred, xenophobia and anti-Semitism or which is insulting to particular racial groups does not enjoy the protection of Article 10. However, the reporting of such statements should not be restricted in a democratic society unless, objectively viewed, it has as its purpose the propagation of racist views and ideas.[61] Journalists should be allowed a degree of latitude in reporting:

> " . . . the methods of objective and balanced reporting may vary considerably, depending among other things on the media in question. It is not for this Court, nor for the national courts for that matter, to substitute their own views

---

[57] *Handyside v. United Kingdom* (1976) 1 E.H.R.R. 737, para. 48.
[58] *ibid.*
[59] *Müller v. Switzerland* (1991) 13 E.H.R.R. 212.
[60] *Otto-Preminger Institute v. Austria* (1994) 19 E.H.R.R. 34. See also *Wingrove v. United Kingdom*, November 25, 1996, R.J.D., 1996–V, No. 23; 24 E.H.R.R. 1, where prior restraint by way of refusal of a classification certificate for a video on blasphemy grounds was held justified.
[61] *Jersild v. Denmark* (1994) 19 E.H.R.R. 1.

for those of the press as to what technique of reporting should be adopted by journalists."[62]

13. ACCESS TO INFORMATION

C10–30 In *Leander v. Sweden*[63] the Court held that " . . . the right to receive information basically prohibits a government from restricting a person from receiving information that others wish or may be willing to impart to him. Article 10 does not . . . confer on the individual a right of access to a register containing information on his personal position, nor does it embody any obligation on the government to impart such information to the individual".[64] Although the finding was expressly limited to the circumstances, it does reflect the general orientation of the Court on the issue. *Gaskin v. United Kingdom*[65] is an example in which the Court held that a right of access to official information concerning a person's childhood in care might be derived from Article 8, but not from Article 10; access to reports may be required in the context of legal proceedings, for example social work reports in proceedings relating to children as in the case of *McMichael v. United Kingdom*[65a] and *Guerra & ors v. Italy*[66], in which the Court held that Article 10 was inapplicable but that Article 8 imposed a positive obligation on the respondent state to furnish to people living close to a fertiliser factory information about emissions which would have enabled them to assess the risks of continuing to live near the factory.

14. ABORTION INFORMATION

C10–31 In the case of *Open Door and Dublin Well Woman v. Ireland* the Court examined the compatibility with the Convention of Supreme Court injunctions which imposed a perpetual restraint on the provision of information to pregnant women concerning abortion facilities abroad. The Court considered that:

" . . . the injunction limited the freedom to receive and impart information with respect to services which are lawful in other Convention countries and may be crucial to a woman's health and well-being. Limitations on information concerning activities which, notwithstanding their moral implications, have been and continue to be tolerated by national authorities, call for careful scrutiny by the Convention institutions as to their conformity with the tenets of a democratic society."[67]

The Court found that the absolute nature of the injunctions was disproportionate to the legitimate aim of the protection of morals and Article 10 had, as a result, been violated.[68]

---

[62] *loc. cit.*, para. 31.
[63] (1987) 9 E.H.R.R. 433.
[64] para. 74 of the judgment.
[65] (1990) 12 E.H.R.R. 36.
[65a] (1995) 20 E.H.R.R. 205.
[66] (1998) 26 E.H.R.R. 278.
[67] (1993) 15 E.H.R.R. 244, para. 72.
[68] See further commentary on the margin of appreciation, above, paras 2–05, 5–16 and C0–17.

15. DEMONSTRATIONS

C10–32 The prohibition of or interference with a demonstration by public authorities could raise an issue under Article 10. The Convention organs will, however, exercise only a very limited power of review of on-the-spot decisions by police officers to prevent breaches of the peace.[69] However, a fair balance must be struck between the prevention of disorder and freedom of expression, in particular where the speech in question is a contribution to democratic debate which does not call for violence or disorder.[70] In its judgment in *Steel & ors v. United Kingdom*,[71] the Court accepted that non-peaceful demonstrations which consisted of "physically impeding activities of which the applicants disapproved" amounted to "expressions of opinion" protected by Article 10. The applicants' resulting detention amounted to an interference, and as detention of the third to fifth applicants was not "lawful" within the terms of Article 5 (because the protest had been peaceful) it was not "prescribed by law" as required by Article 10(2). However, as the detention of the first and second applicants was "lawful" and therefore "prescribed by law", the Court went on to consider whether the detention pursued a legitimate aim and was "necessary in a democratic society", both of which it answered in the affirmative.

16. LIBEL AWARDS

C10–33 Awards of damages for libel amount to an interference with freedom of expression. Judicial control of awards, both at trial and on appeal, must be such as to offer adequate and effective safeguards against disproportionately large awards.[72]

17. PROTECTION OF JOURNALISTIC SOURCES

C10–34 The Court has held that limitations on the confidentiality of journalistic sources call for the most careful scrutiny:

> ". . . Protection of journalistic sources is one of the basic conditions for press freedom, as is reflected in the laws and the professional codes of conduct in a number of contracting states . . . Without such protection, sources may be deterred from informing the public on matters of public interest . . . Having regard to the importance of the protection of journalistic sources for press freedom in a democratic society and the potentially chilling effect an order of source disclosure has on the exercise of that freedom, such a measure cannot be compatible with Article 10 of the Convention unless it is justified by an overriding requirement in the public interest."[73]

---

[69] See *Chorherr v. Austria* (1993) 17 E.H.R.R. 358.
[70] *Piermont v. France* (1995) 20 E.H.R.R. 301.
[71] Judgment of September 23, 1998.
[72] *Tolstoy Miloslavsky v. United Kingdom* (1995) 20 E.H.R.R. 442.
[73] *Goodwin v. United Kingdom*, March 27, 1996, R.J.D., 1996–II, No. 7; 221 E.H.R.R. 123, para. 39.

ARTICLE 11

FREEDOM OF ASSEMBLY AND ASSOCIATION

C11–01

1 Everyone has the right to freedom of peaceful assembly and to freedom of association with others, including the right to form and to join trade unions for the protection of his interests.

2 No restrictions shall be placed on the exercise of these rights other than such as are prescribed by law and are necessary in a democratic society in the interests of national security or public safety, for the prevention of disorder or crime, for the protection of health or morals or for the protection of the rights and freedoms of others. This article shall not prevent the imposition of lawful restrictions on the exercise of these rights by members of the armed forces, of the police or of the administration of the State.

C11–02   Article 11 is yet another Convention provision which allows in its second paragraph for certain limitations of the rights guaranteed in the first. One particular feature, however, is the inclusion in Article 11(2) of a restriction not found elsewhere in the Convention to the effect that "(t)his article shall not prevent the imposition of lawful restrictions on the exercise of these rights by members of the armed forces, of the police or of the administration of the State". In the important case of *Groppera Radio v. Switzerland* the Court held that the restrictions referred to in this clause "are not covered by the restrictions in the first sentence of paragraph 2, except for that of lawfulness".[1] Article 11(2) therefore allows additional limitations over and above those contained in paragraphs (2) of Articles 8, 9 and 10. The clause has received little interpretation. In *Vogt v. Germany*, the Commission considered that a secondary school teacher was not a member of the administration of the State. The Court agreed with the Commission that the term should be interpreted narrowly, in the light of the post held by the official concerned; but it considered that it was unnecessary to decide the question in that case, concluding that her dismissal was in any event disproportionate.[2]

1.   THE RIGHT OF PEACEFUL ASSEMBLY

C11–03   The right of peaceful assembly is considered to be one of the foundations of a democratic society.[3] It covers both private meetings and meetings in public thoroughfares, static meetings as well as public processions.[4]

C11–04   In interpreting Article 11 the Convention organs have often examined whether the assembly in question was "peaceful" in order to determine whether an interference with the right has occurred. By contrast, even non-peaceful protest may constitute an expression of opinion falling within the scope of Article 10.[5]

---

[1] (1990) 12 E.H.R.R. 321, para. 61.
[2] (1996) 21 E.H.R.R. 205, paras 66 and 67.
[3] App. No. 8191/78 *Rassemblement Jurassien and Unité Jurassienne v. Switzerland* 17 D. & R. 93.
[4] See App. No. 8191/78 *Rassemblement Jurassien and Unité Jurassienne v. Switzerland* and App. No. 8440/78 *Christians Against Racism and Fascism v. United Kingdom* 21 D. & R. 138.
[5] *Steel & Others v. United Kingdom*, judgment of September 23, 1998, para. 92.

C11–05 Subjecting public meetings to an authorisation procedure would not normally encroach upon the essence of the right. In the *Christians Against Racism and Fascism* case the Commission observed that:

"Such a procedure is in keeping with the requirements of Article 11(1), if only in order that the authorities may be in a position to ensure the peaceful nature of a meeting, and accordingly does not as such constitute interference with the exercise of the right."[6]

However, " . . . to subject indoor meetings to the discretion of the police, . . . , without any clear prescription in law as to how this discretion is to be exercised and without further control, is to create a police state, which is the antithesis of a 'democratic society'."[7]

The right of peaceful assembly is:

" . . . a freedom capable of being exercised not only by the individual participants of such demonstration, but also by those organising it, including a corporate body such as the applicant association".[8]

The emphasis in the case law is, however, on individual responsibility. Thus, in the *Christians Against Racism and Fascism* case the Commission considered that a demonstration was within the ambit of Article 11 even though it might evoke violent opposition from opponents and extremists. Moreover, the Court has held that:

" . . . the freedom to take part in a peaceful assembly–in this instance a demonstration that has not been prohibited is of such an importance that it cannot be restricted in any way, even for an avocat, so long as the person concerned does not himself commit any reprehensible act on such an occasion".[9]

C11–06 In the important case of *Plattform 'Ärtze für das Leben' v. Austria* the Court found that a state may be required to take positive measures to safeguard freedom of association as guaranteed by Article 11. As the Court observed,

"[a] demonstration may annoy or give offence to persons . . . The participants must, however, be able to hold the demonstration without having to fear that they will be subjected to physical violence by their opponents; such a fear would be liable to deter associations or other groups supporting common ideas or interests from openly expressing their opinions on highly controversial issues affecting the community. In a democracy the right to counter-demonstrate cannot extend to inhibiting the exercise of the right to demonstrate. . . . Genuine, effective freedom of peaceful assembly cannot, therefore, be reduced to a mere duty on the part of the State not to interfere . . . Like Article 8, Article 11 sometimes requires positive measures to be taken . . ."[10]

---

[6] 21 D. & R. 138.
[7] *Greek* case 12 Yb, Commission's Opinion, para. 394.
[8] *Christians Against Racism and Fascism v. United Kingdom* 21 D. & R. 138.
[9] *Ezelin v. France* (1992) 14 E.H.R.R. 362, para. 53.
[10] (1991) 13 E.H.R.R. 204, para. 32.

However, the Convention does not require national authorities to provide an absolute guarantee that lawful demonstrations proceed peacefully.[11]

2. The right to freedom of association

C11–07 The right to freedom of association is a wider right. It is not simply a right to form and join trade unions.[12] and it is not therefore necessary that the association in question should be capable of being characterised as a trade union or an employers' association. So, religious organisations are within the scope of the right[13] as are political parties.[14] In *United Communist Party of Turkey and others v. Turkey* the Court stated that " . . . political parties are a form of association essential to the proper functioning of democracy. In view of the importance of democracy in the Convention system, there can be no doubt that political parties come within the scope of Article 11."[15] The Court has also held that the protection of personal opinions, enshrined in Article 10, is one of the objectives of freedom of association, and that consequently dismissal of a teacher following her refusal to dissociate herself from the Communist Party interfered with her rights under Article 11 in addition to the interference with her Article 10 rights.[16] In recent judgments, the Court has emphasised the fundamental importance of the right to freedom of association in a properly functioning democracy, with the result that exceptions must be narrowly construed and the state has only a limited margin of appreciation.[17]

C11–08 The Court has recently set out the scope of Article 11 in the following wide terms:

"That citizens should be able to form a legal entity in order to act collectively in a field of mutual interest is one of the most important aspects of the right to freedom of association, without which that right would be deprived of any meaning."[18]

It appears, therefore, that any group of individuals forming an association can in principle come within the scope of Article 11. The *Sidiropoulos*[19] case concerned what was, ostensibly at any rate, the formation of a Macedonian cultural and social association. However, in *Le Compte, Van Leuven and De Meyere v. Belgium*[20] the Court held that a professional organisation, established by the state, which performs public law functions is not to be considered as an "association" for the purposes of Article 11. But the fact that a professional association established under private law also performs some public law regulatory functions does not preclude it

---

[11] See *Plattform Ärtze für das Leben v. Austria* (1991) 13 E.H.R.R. 204, para. 34.
[12] See *Sigurjonsson v. Iceland* (1993) 16 E.H.R.R. 462.
[13] See *Christian Association of Jehovah's Witnesses v. Bulgaria* (1997) 24 E.H.R.R. CD 52, in which the Commission declared admissible a complaint under Article 11 in respect of failure to register the applicant association and interference with its activities.
[14] *United Communist Party of Turkey and others v. Turkey* R.J.D., 1998–I, Nos 18–19 (1998) 26 E.H.R.R. 121.
[15] (1998) 26 E.H.R.R. 121, para. 24.
[16] *Vogt v. Germany* (1996) 21 E.H.R.R. 205, paras 64 and 65.
[17] *United Communist Party of Turkey and others v. Turkey,* January 30, 1998, R.J.D., 1998–I, Nos 18–19; 26 E.H.R.R. 121; *Sidiropoulos v. Greece* (1999) 27 E.H.R.R. 633.
[18] *Sidiropoulos and others v. Greece* (1999) 27 E.H.R.R. 633, para. 40.
[19] *Sidiropoulos and others v. Greece* (1999) 27 E.H.R.R. 633.
[20] (1982) 4 E.H.R.R. 1, para. 64.

from being an "association" for the purposes of Article 11 if its predominant function is to promote interests of, and solidarity among, its members.[21]

C11–09   A particularly difficult issue arising in this area has been whether Article 11 guarantees not only freedom of association in the positive sense, but also a "negative right" not to be compelled to join an association or a union. Having avoided addressing the issue squarely in *Young, James and Webster v. United Kingdom*,[22] the Court in *Sigurjonsson v. Iceland* considered that the question could be answered positively:

> "Article 11 must be viewed as encompassing a negative right of association. It is not for the Court to determine . . . whether this right is to be considered on an equal footing with the positive right."[23]

A law which made membership of an automobile association a prerequisite for the acquisition of a taxi driver's licence violated Article 11.[24] In *Chassagnou and others v. France*[25] the Court held that a French law requiring landowners to be members of local hunters' associations, where the applicant landowners were opposed to hunting on ethical grounds, violated Article 11:

> "To compel a person by law to join an association such that it is fundamentally contrary to his own convictions to be a member of it, and to oblige him, on account of his membership of that association, to transfer his rights over the land he owns so that the association in question can attain objectives of which he disapproves, goes beyond what is necessary to ensure a fair balance is struck between conflicting interests and cannot be considered proportionate to the aim pursued."[26]

C11–10   The state may be obliged to protect this negative freedom even in relations between private parties. A form of compulsion to make a person join a union which strikes at the very substance of the negative right is an interference with the negative freedom and:

> "It follows that national authorities may, in certain circumstances, be obliged to intervene in the relationships between private individuals by taking reasonable and appropriate measures to secure the effective enjoyment of the negative right to freedom of association".[27]

C11–11   By contrast, the Court found no violation of Article 11 where a union took industrial action against an employer with the object of forcing him *either* to join an employers' association with whom the union had concluded a collective agreement *or* to conclude his own substitution agreement with the union. Disagreeing with the Commission, the Court held that:

> "Article 11 of the Convention does not as such guarantee the right not to enter into a collective agreement. The positive obligation incumbent on the State

---

[21] *Sigurjonsson v. Iceland* (1993) 16 E.H.R.R. 462.
[22] (1982) 4 E.H.R.R. 38.
[23] Para. 35.
[24] *Sigurjonsson v. Iceland.*
[25] Apps Nos 25088/94, 28331/95, 28443/95, judgment of April 29, 1999.
[26] *ibid.*, para. 117.
[27] *Gustafsson v. Sweden*, April 25, 1996; R.J.D., 1996–II, No. 9; 22 E.H.R.R. 409, para. 45.

under Article 11, including the aspect of protection of personal opinion, may well extend to treatment connected with the operation of a collective bargaining system, but only where such treatment impinges on freedom of association. Compulsion which, as here, does not significantly affect the enjoyment of that freedom, even if it causes economic damage, cannot give rise to any positive obligation under Article 11."[28]

3. THE RIGHTS OF TRADE UNIONS

C11–12 The right to form and join trade unions for the protection of one's interests has not been interpreted in a particularly broad manner in the Convention case law. In the most important case of *National Union of Belgian Police v. Belgium* the Court considered that:

" . . . while Article 11(1) presents trade union freedom as one form or a special aspect of freedom of association, the Article does not guarantee any particular treatment of trade unions, or their members, by the State . . ."[29]

Although the Court was at pains to affirm in the same case that the words "for the protection of his interests" were not redundant, their real impact on the case law appears minimal:

"These words, clearly denoting purpose, show that the Convention safeguards freedom to protect the occupational interests of trade union members by trade union action, the conduct and development of which the Contracting States must both permit and make possible . . . it follows that the members of a trade union have a right, in order to protect their interests, that the trade union should be heard. Article 11(1) certainly leaves each State a free choice of means to be used towards this end."[30]

As a result, failure to grant a trade union the right to be consulted or to conclude a collective agreement does not amount to a violation of Article 11.[31] Pursuing the same line of argument the Court considered in *Schmidt and Dahlstrom v. Sweden*[32] that Article 11 does not include an absolute right to strike.

The right to form trade unions guaranteed in Article 11 appears, finally, to guarantee some rights for trade union members *vis-à-vis* the trade union itself. Thus, in *Cheall v. U.K.*,[33] the Commission observed that:

" . . . the right to form trade unions involves, for example, the right of trade unions to draw up their own rules, to administer their own affairs and to establish and join trade union federations."

Although a state will not, in general, be responsible for essentially private disputes which arise between a trade union and its members, there are circumstances where the state should protect an individual member from abuse by his union.[34]

---

[28] *Gustafsson v. Sweden*, para. 53.
[29] (1975) 1 E.H.R.R. 578, para. 38.
[30] *National Union of Belgian Police v. Belgium*, para. 39.
[31] *National Union of Belgian Police v. Belgium* and *Swedish Engine Drivers Union v. Sweden* (1976) 1 E.H.R.R. 617.
[32] (1976) 1 E.H.R.R. 632, para. 36.
[33] App. No. 10550/83 (1985) 42 D. & R. 178.
[34] See also *Sibson v. United Kingdom* (1994) 17 E.H.R.R. 193, where an employee who resigned from his union was dismissed after union pressure and his refusal to work at another depot.

C11–13   The exercise of the rights in Article 11 may involve the holding and propagation of specific opinions, thus closely linking these rights with those guaranteed by Articles 9 and 10. Both the Court and Commission, accordingly, have either treated the rights guaranteed in Articles 9 and 10 as elements of Article 11 or held Article 11 to be a *lex specialis vis-à-vis* the other provisions.[35] In *Steel & others v. United Kingdom*,[36] by contrast, which concerned arrests for participating in demonstrations, the Court considered the complaints under Article 10 and held that no separate issue arose under Article 11.

---

[35] See *Young, James and Webster v. United Kingdom* (1983) 5 E.H.R.R. 201, *Ezelin v. France* (1992) 14 E.H.R.R. 362 and *Vogt v. Germany* (1996) 21 E.H.R.R. 205.
[36] Judgment of September 23, 1998.

ARTICLE 12

RIGHT TO MARRY

C12–01 Men and women of marriageable age have the right to marry and to found a family, according to the national laws governing the exercise of this right.

C12–02 The right to marry and found a family is subject to the domestic laws of the States Party to the Convention. In its Report in *Hamer v. United Kingdom* the Commission stated:

> "Such laws may thus lay down formal rules concerning matters such as notice, publicity and the formalities whereby marriage is solemnised. They may also lay down rules of substance based on generally recognised considerations of the public interest. Examples are rules concerning capacity, consent, prohibited degrees of consanguinity or the prevention of bigamy. However, in the Commission's opinion national law may not otherwise deprive a person or category of persons of full legal capacity. Nor may it substantially interfere with their exercise of the right."[1]

C12–03 The Commission's Report in *Hamer* was accepted by the Committee of Ministers, which found that the provision was infringed by denying prisoners the facilities to contract marriage. The Court found a breach of the provision in a prohibition on re-marriage for three years imposed on an applicant after his third divorce.[2]

C12–04 By contrast, the case law establishes the following restrictions or formalities are compatible with the requirements of Article 12:

(a) a constitutional prohibition on divorce and thus on re-marriage after a first marriage has irretrievably broken down[3];

(b) a denial of facilities for conjugal visits for prisoners, and thus for procreation: earlier admissibility decisions were referred to and confirmed in *Hamer*[4] and subsequently re-affirmed in *Khan v. United Kingdom*[5];

(c) prohibitions on marriage practices of minority religions and/or cultures (*e.g.*, lower age of consent or polygamy)[6];

(d) a requirement that the parties to a marriage must be of biologically opposite sexes and thus an effective bar on transsexuals (or homosexuals) engaging in matrimony with people of the "same" sex.[7]

C12–05 Both in relation to prisoners and transsexuals, however, emphasis has been placed on the Convention being a living instrument. It remains therefore

---

[1] (1979) 4 E.H.R.R. 139, para. 62 of the Report.
[2] *F v. Switzerland* (1988) 10 E.H.R.R. 411.
[3] *Johnston v. Ireland* (1987) 9 E.H.R.R. 203.
[4] *ibid.*, para. 58 of the Report.
[5] App. No. 11579/85, 48 D. & R. 253.
[6] App. No. 11579/85.
[7] *Rees v. United Kingdom* (1986) 9 E.H.R.R. 56 and *Cossey v. United Kingdom* (1991) 13 E.H.R.R. 622; *Sheffield & Horsham v. United Kingdom* (1998) 27 E.H.R.R. 163.

possible that acceptable standards will evolve and that some of the limitations previously found compatible with Article 12 will cease to be acceptable. In *Sheffield & Horsham v. United Kingdom*, the Court concluded that there was no violation (of Article 8) by a majority of 11 votes to 9 (the Commission having concluded in favour of a violation of that provision by 15 votes to 1).[8] The Court in its judgment went out of its way to reiterate the need to keep the legal position of transsexuals under review.[9] It should be emphasised that the findings of no violation in this area are based substantially on the Court's deference to the state's margin of appreciation. It is therefore open to the courts of the United Kingdom to reach a different conclusion as to the balance between the general interest of the community and the interests of the individual.

[8] (1998) 27 E.H.R.R. 163.
[9] See also the strong dissenting opinions and the concurring opinion of Sir John Freeland.

ARTICLE 13
RIGHT TO AN EFFECTIVE REMEDY

C13–01 Everyone whose rights and freedoms as set forth in this Convention are violated shall have an effective remedy before a national authority notwithstanding that the violation has been committed by persons acting in an official capacity.

C13–02 Although, controversially, Article 13 is not among the "Convention rights" listed in section 1(1)(a) of the Act, the Lord Chancellor has said[1] that domestic courts must take account of the Strasbourg case law relating to Article 13 when deciding how to exercise their remedial powers under section 8 of the Act. Indeed, he told the House of Lords that incorporation of Article 13 was unnecessary since section 8 was intended to meet the United Kingdom's obligations under Article 13. The scope of the right to an effective remedy therefore remains of prime importance, in particular for a court seeking to determining what relief, remedy or order is "just and appropriate" for the purposes of that section. Its requirements are less demanding than those under Article 6, so that it will not usually apply to cases involving "civil rights or obligations".[2] Sometimes, the need for procedural safeguards will be implied into the substantive right, leaving no scope for further application to Article 13. However, after a Cinderella existence, the provision has now found a place of its own in the Convention system of protection. It is not self-evident that this place is wholly filled by the section 8 of the Act. Whether it is will depend on the willingness of courts to adapt our law to accord with the Article 13 case law.

C13–03 Like Articles 14, 17 and 18, Article 13 is said to have "no independent existence" in the sense that it relates only to "rights and freedoms set forth in the Convention". Until 1978, hardly any case law existed on Article 13. Although frequently pleaded, the provision was virtually never considered: where the Commission found that a violation of the substantive provision invoked had occurred, it took the view that it was unnecessary to consider Article 13; where it found no violation of a substantive provision, it considered that Article 13 did not apply. The only significant exception was the finding of a breach of Article 13 in the inter-state case against Greece.[3]

C13–04 Despite this background, the Court carved out a discrete role for Article 13 in its important 1978 judgment in *Klass v. Germany*. In that case it gave the following interpretation to the provision:

> "Article 13 requires that where an individual considers himself to have been prejudiced by a measure allegedly in breach of the Convention, he should have a remedy before a national authority in order both to have his claim decided and, if appropriate, to obtain redress. Thus Article 13 must be interpreted as guaranteeing an "effective remedy before a national authority" to everyone who *claims* that his rights and freedoms under the Convention have been violated."[4]

---

[1] *Hansard*, H.L., November 18, 1997, col. 476–477.
[2] As to the relationship with Article 6, see above, para. C6–03.
[3] 12 Yb, p. 174.
[4] (1978) 2 E.H.R.R. 214, para. 64.

On the facts before it the Court found no violation: German law and practice provided some remedies against unnecessary secret surveillance and "an 'effective remedy' under Article 13 [had to] mean a remedy that is as effective as can be having regard to the restricted scope for recourse inherent in any system of secret surveillance".[5] However, what the case did establish was that Article 13 guarantees a right to bring a claim that a substantive Convention right has been violated, a right which exists even if it is eventually shown that there has been no violation of the substantive right; and if the claim is made out, the national authority concerned must provide an effective remedy. What that means in practice will vary according to the nature of the breach.

C13–05   Since the decision in *Klass*, however, Article 13 has had something of a chequered history. In the 15 or so years after the *Klass* case, the Convention institutions found very few violations of the Article, the subsequent case law being most noticeable for the limitations and glosses which were put on broad pronouncement in *Klass*. These may be summarised as follows:

(a) Article 13 is inapplicable when the alleged violation relates to the state of domestic law:

"Article 13 does not go so far as to guarantee a remedy allowing a Contracting State's laws as such to be challenged before a national authority on the ground of being contrary to the Convention or to equivalent domestic legal norms."[6]

In *Costello-Roberts v. United Kingdom*,[7] which concerned corporal punishment in an independent school, the Court overturned the Commission's finding of a violation of Article 13. The applicant could have brought county court proceedings for assault. Although a defence of "reasonable and moderate chastisement" was available, the concept of "reasonableness" permitted the courts to apply contemporary standards regarding the physical punishment of children and consequently the possibility of a remedy existed. However, if it turned out that the county court did consider itself able to give such an interpretation, and therefore did not provide such a remedy, that would be due not to the unavailability of a means of redress but to the state of domestic law, which Article 13 did not allow the applicant to challenge.[8]

(b) In respect of other alleged violations of the Convention, for Article 13 to apply, "the grievance must be an arguable one in terms of the Convention".[9]

(c) The Commission has usually regarded a claim as "arguable in terms of the Convention" only if it has succeeded in passing the admissibility threshold.[10] In *Powell and Rayner*, the Court explicitly rejected a distinction made by the majority of the Commission:

---

[5] *ibid.*, para. 69.
[6] *James v. United Kingdom* (1986) 8 E.H.R.R. 123, para. 85. See also *Holy Monasteries v. Greece* (1995) 20 E.H.R.R. 1.
[7] (1995) 19 E.H.R.R. 112.
[8] *ibid.*, para. 40.
[9] *Boyle and Rice v. United Kingdom* (1988) 10 E.H.R.R. 425, para. 52.
[10] *Boyle and Rice*, para. 54, and see further *Plattform "Ärtzte für das Leben" v. Austria* (1991) 13 E.H.R.R. 204 and *Powell and Rayner v. United Kingdom* (1990) 12 E.H.R.R. 355.

". . . between the notions of 'manifestly ill-founded' and lack of 'arguability'. It was 'implicit in the Commission's established case law that the term "manifestly ill-founded" extends further than the literal meaning of the word "manifest" would suggest at first reading.' Thus some serious claims might give rise to a *prima facie* issue but after 'full examination' at the admissibility stage, ultimately be rejected as manifestly ill-founded".[11]

Thus in Strasbourg, a substantive claim which the Commission had declared inadmissible could not give rise to any issue under Article 13. By contrast, Article 13 will be in issue in any case which has been declared admissible, *i.e.* which raises serious issues under the Convention which warrant further examination. For example, the Court held an Article 8 claim "arguable" where it had found that a search amounted to an interference with the applicant's home, which therefore required justification under Article 8(2), even though it found no violation of Article 8.[12]

(d) The Convention organs sometimes decide that it is unnecessary to examine Article 13 if violation of another provision is established.[13]

(e) In any event, Article 13 is inapplicable where other provisions of the Convention prescribe more specific guarantees in respect of remedies. In particular, Article 13 requirements are "less strict than and . . . entirely absorbed by" those of Article 6(1).[14]

(f) When applicable, Article 13 leaves the Contracting State discretion over how to implement the "effective remedy" requirement. The remedy need not be judicial. Furthermore, "although no single remedy may itself entirely satisfy the requirements of Article 13, the aggregate of remedies under domestic law may do so", *e.g.*, ministerial control subject to judicial review on grounds of lawfulness.[15]

C13–06 The notion of effectiveness requires that the alleged victim should be able to use the remedy in practice rather than just in theory. Considerations of this nature have led the Commission and the Court to insist upon the obligation of the authorities to carry out thorough investigation, at least where allegations of serious violation are concerned. In addition, while the national authority need not be a court, it must be independent, must have access to all relevant information and must be empowered to make a binding decision. In appropriate cases, the applicant may need legal representation and he or she should also have access to the relevant materials. In *Chahal v. United Kingdom*, the applicant had no legal representation before the panel which considered his case, and he was given only an outline of the grounds for deportation. The panel could only give the Secretary of State advice (which was not disclosed to the applicant) and could not make a binding decision. For these reasons, the Court considered that it did not provide an effective remedy.[16] Recently, in the case of *Govell v. United Kingdom*,[17] the Commission

---

[11] *ibid.*, para. 32.
[12] *Camenzind v. Switzerland* (1999) 28 E.H.R.R. 458; but compare the opinion of the majority of the Commission in *Friedl v. Austria* (1996) 21 E.H.R.R. 83.
[13] see, *e.g. Young, James and Webster v. United Kingdom* (1981) 4 E.H.R.R. 38, para. 67.
[14] *Airey v. Ireland* (1979) 2 E.H.R.R. 305, para. 35.
[15] *Silver and others v. United Kingdom* (1983) 5 E.H.R.R. 347, para. 113 *et seq.*
[16] November 15, 1996, R.J.D., 1996–II, No. 22; 23 E.H.R.R. 413, paras 153–154.
[17] App. No. 27237/95, Report dated January 14, 1998.

concluded, unanimously, that Article 13 was violated by the absence of an effective remedy in respect of a complaint of unlawful surveillance and bugging of his home: a Chief Constable has no obligation to refer complaints to the Police Complaints Authority (PCA) other than those relating to death or serious injury; it is unclear to what extent the PCA oversees the decision-making process undertaken by the Chief Constable; in any event, complaints are normally investigated by an officer from the same force; members of the PCA are appointed by the Home Secretary and must have regard to his guidance in the exercise of their powers. In the Commission's opinion, therefore, "the system of investigation of complaints does not meet the requisite standards of independence needed to constitute sufficient protection against abuse of authority and thus provide an effective remedy within the meaning of Article 13.[18] The case has not been referred to the Court. In some cases, effectiveness will require a preventive remedy, for example where the effects of a violation will be irreversible, but this will not invariably be the case. For example, in *M.S. v. Sweden* the applicant complained unsuccessfully about disclosure of her medical records to the Social Insurance Office (SIO) following a claim she had made for industrial injury benefit. Swedish law afforded no prior remedy, in particular because the applicant was not made aware of the intended disclosure in advance. The Court held that given the limited nature of the disclosure, to another public authority, and the fact that the SIO was obliged to maintain the confidentiality of the information, the various *ex post facto* remedies—criminal proceedings or a civil claim for damages—satisfied the requirements of Article 13.[19] In *Iatridis v. Greece*,[20] the Court found that Greek law did provide a remedy, *i.e.* an application to court to have the eviction order quashed; the applicant had successfully used the remedy and obtained a court order to that effect. But since the Minister of Finance refused to comply with the judgment of the domestic court, the Court found that the remedy was not "effective" and that there had been a breach of Article 13.

C13–07 More recently, the Convention institutions have used Article 13 to develop three aspects of the right to an effective remedy: (a) the right to locus or access; (b) the right to an effective investigation; and (c) the right to independent scrutiny. Each will be examined briefly.

1. Locus and access

C13–08 Article 13 has been found to be violated by the complete absence of a remedy, regardless of whether a violation of the substantive right has been found. Thus in *Valsamis v. Greece*, the Court found that although a one-day suspension of a child for failing (on religious grounds) to take part in a parade did not violate Article 2 of the First Protocol, or Articles 3 or 9, the absence of any avenue of recourse—whether a claim for damages or an administrative action—constituted a violation of Article 13.[21] Article 13 has also been found to be violated where the applicant could not seek relief at a national level in respect of interception of her office telephone, because of the absence of legal regulation of interception of calls on an internal communications system.[22]

---

[18] *ibid.*, para. 70. The case has not been referred to the Court.
[19] (1999) 28 E.H.R.R. 313.
[20] Judgment of March 25, 1999.
[21] December 18, 1996, R.J.D., 1996–VI, No. 27; 24 E.H.R.R. 294.
[22] *Halford v. United Kingdom*, June 25, 1997, R.J.D., 1997–III, No. 39; 24 E.H.R.R. 523; see also *Camenzind v. Switzerland*, above, n. 12, where the applicant, whose home had been searched, was denied locus before the domestic courts because the measure in question had ceased and he therefore had no present interest entitling him to bring proceedings.

2. EFFECTIVE INVESTIGATION

C13–09 The development this aspect of Article 13 has been fuelled largely by the activities of the Turkish security forces, particularly in relation to Kurds: the Convention institutions have found proven allegations of torture, rape, other forms of ill-treatment, house burning and unlawful arrest. It is inherent in allegations of this nature that the applicant will have been isolated, frightened and in no state to identify the perpetrators, let alone to pin-point dates or places. Yet violations of this kind are the most serious which can arise under the Convention. Clearly, they will call for imposition of criminal sanctions.[23] The victim must also be entitled to claim damages. But the effectiveness of such remedies is dependent upon the availability of information, which it will be beyond the victim's ability to secure. In such cases, Article 13 imposes an obligation on the state to carry out an effective investigation. In *Aksoy v. Turkey*, which concerned the detention of a member of the Kurdish Workers' Party, the Court found violations of Articles 3 and 5(3). In respect of Article 13 the Court said:

> "The scope of the obligation under Article 13 varies depending on the nature of the applicant's complaint under the Convention. Nevertheless, the remedy required by Article 13 must be 'effective' in practice as well as in law, in particular in the sense that its exercise must not be unjustifiably hindered by the acts or omissions of the authorities of the respondent State."[24]
> "Given the fundamental importance of the prohibition of torture and the especially vulnerable position of torture victims, Article 13 imposes, without prejudice to any other remedy available under the domestic system, an obligation on States to carry out a thorough and effective investigation of incidents of torture."[25]

C13–10 Accordingly, in addition to a remedy of compensation, at least in cases where there is an arguable claim of murder, torture or ill-treatment in custody, there must be a thorough investigation capable of leading to identification and punishment of those responsible and effective access to the investigation by the victim. Such an investigation requires the appropriate authorities to take the initiative in seeking out the evidence, verifying information given by suspects and promptly instructing appropriate experts.[26] Although the Act does not incorporate Article 13, it is likely that the courts will take account of these strictures when scrutinising the activities of the prosecuting authorities.

3. INDEPENDENT SCRUTINY

C13–11 Again in the context of substantive complaints under Article 3, the Convention institutions have developed the notion of the effectiveness of the remedy in relation to the degree of scrutiny that national authorities must exercise. In *Chahal v. United Kingdom*, which concerned the proposed deportation of a Sikh

---

[23] See, *mutatis mutandis*, *X & Y v. Netherlands* (1985) 8 E.H.R.R. 235.
[24] December 18, 1996, R.J.D., 1996–IV, No. 26; 23 E.H.R.R. 553, para. 95.
[25] *ibid.*, para. 98.
[26] *Aydin v. Turkey*, September 25, 1997, R.J.D., 1997–VI, No. 50; 25 E.H.R.R. 251; see also *Mentes v. Turkey* (1998) 26 E.H.R.R. 595.

the Court held that the national authorities must be able to assess the strength of his claim that he would be subjected to inhuman treatment if returned to India:

> "In such cases, given the irreversible nature of the harm that might occur if the risk of ill-treatment materialised and the importance the Court attaches to Article 3, the notion of an effective remedy under Article 13 requires independent scrutiny of the claim that there exist substantial grounds for fearing a real risk of treatment contrary to Article 3. This scrutiny must be carried out without regard to what the person may have done to warrant expulsion or to any perceived risk to the national security of the expelling State."[27]

C13–12   In *Chahal* the Court found the scope of judicial review to be restricted because the case involved national security. The Court distinguished its dictum in *Klass v. Germany* to the effect that a remedy must be "as effective as can be" where national security is involved. For the Court, that was an appropriate test in cases involving Articles 8 and 10, but not for the examination of a complaint that deportation would expose the applicant to a real risk of treatment in breach of Article 3. In such cases, considerations of national security are immaterial, and since the judicial review court had simply investigated whether the Home Secretary had balanced that risk against the considerations of national security, it had failed to provide an effective remedy as required by Article 13. By contrast, the Court held that judicial review did furnish an effective remedy in *D v. United Kingdom*.[28] The case concerned the proposed deportation of a terminal AIDS patient to St. Kitts, where only limited treatment and support were available. The Court held that his deportation in the circumstances would amount to inhuman treatment. As to Article 13, the Court considered that since Court of Appeal had applied "the most anxious scrutiny" in assessing the rationality of the Secretary of State's decision, it had in effect considered the substance of D's complaint; and absent considerations of national security, it had been able to conduct an independent scrutiny of the facts. However, it is doubtful whether the Strasbourg Court was right in this case. In practice, before the entry into force of the Human Rights Act 1998, the judicial review court could not quash an otherwise rational decision on the sole ground that it was a violation of a Convention right.

Recently, in *Smith & Grady v. U.K.*,[28a] the Strasbourg Court held that where a blanket policy barring homosexuals from serving in the armed forces could be reviewed only for *Wednesbury* unreasonableness or irrationality, this did not constitute an "effective remedy" as required by Article 13. The domestic courts had placed the threshold of irrationality "so high that it effectively excluded any consideration by the domestic courts of the question whether the interference with the applicants' rights answered a pressing social need or was proportionate to the national security and public order aims pursued".

---

[27] November 15, 1996, R.J.D., 1996–II, No. 22; 23 E.H.R.R. 413, para. 151.

[28] May 2, 1997, R.J.D., 1997–III, No. 37; 24 E.H.R.R. 423. See also *Vilvarajah v. United Kingdom* (1992) 14 E.H.R.R. 248, paras 123–124 and *Soering v. United Kingdom* (1989) 11 E.H.R.R. 439, paras 116–124.

[28a] Judgment of September 27, 1999, paras 136–139. See further, above, para. 5–40. *Vilvarajah v. United Kingdom* (1992) 14 E.H.R.R. 248 and *Soering v. United Kingdom* (1989) 11 E.H.R.R. 439 were distinguished (para. 138) on the ground that the test applied by the domestic courts in those judicial review proceedings coincided with the Strasbourg Court's own approach under Article 3 of the E.C.H.R.

C13–13 Notwithstanding the restrictive application given to it, Article 13 remains a much pleaded provision of the Convention. No doubt sometimes this reflects a failure fully to understand quite how restrictive the case law has become but there are certainly other explanations. Even in what appear to be the most serious and well-founded applications, at the stage of submitting, there can be questions over how the facts will emerge after the government's response, assuming the Court communicates the case, and still further uncertainty over how the Court will assess matters when deciding on admissibility. Coupled with the possibility of further development in the case law, these unpredictable elements go some way to explain the frequency with which Article 13 is pleaded, notwithstanding how rarely a violation is found.

ARTICLE 14

PROHIBITION OF DISCRIMINATION

C14–01　The enjoyment of the rights and freedoms set forth in this Convention shall be secured without discrimination on any ground such as sex, race, colour, language, religion, political or other opinion, national or social origin, association with a national minority, property, birth or other status.

C14–02　Unlike Article 26 of the International Covenant on Civil and Political Rights, Article 14 does not provide a free-standing prohibition of discrimination in general. It prohibits discrimination only in relation to enjoyment of the rights and freedoms guaranteed by the Convention:

> " . . . this guarantee has no independent existence in the sense that under the terms of Article 14 it relates solely to 'rights and freedoms set forth in the Convention'."[1]

This does not exclude the possibility that discrimination which is not related to the enjoyment of a Convention right might nonetheless violate other provisions of the Convention. Thus in its report on the *East African Asians* case, the Commission expressed the opinion that:

> "A special importance should be attached to discrimination based on race; that publicly to single out a group of persons for differential treatment on the basis of race might in certain circumstances constitute a special form of affront to human dignity; and that differential treatment of a group of persons on the basis of race might therefore be capable of constituting degrading treatment when differential treatment on some other ground would raise no such question."[2]

The *East African Asians* case was not referred to the Court, which has not ruled on this issue. The Committee of Ministers failed to achieve the requisite two-thirds majority either to adopt or reject the Commission's opinion, and consequently took no further action.[3] In *Abdulaziz, Cabales & Balkandali v. United Kingdom*, the Court rejected an invitation to hold that the refusal to allow women settled in the United Kingdom to be joined by their husbands, being racially motivated, amounted to degrading treatment contrary to Article 3. However, the judgment is silent as to whether racial discrimination might amount to degrading treatment in severe cases.[3a]

C14–03　Despite its terms, however, the applicability of Article 14 is not limited to cases in which there is an accompanying violation of another provision in the Convention, and:

> " . . . a measure which in itself is in conformity with the requirements of the Article enshrining the right or freedom in question may however infringe this

---

[1] *Belgian Linguistic* case (1968) 1 E.H.R.R. 252 at 283, para. 9.
[2] (1973) 3 E.H.R.R. 76, para. 207.
[3] *ibid.* at pp. 102–103.
[3a] (1985) 7 E.H.R.R. 471. See also *Smith and Grady v. United Kingdom*, judgment of September 27, 1999 (severe discrimination against homosexual minority might violate Article 3).

Article when read in conjunction with Article 14 for the reason that it is of a discriminatory nature."[4]

Or, as the Court more succinctly put it:

"The notion of discrimination within the meaning of Article 14 includes in general cases where a person or group is treated, without proper justification, less favourably than another, even though the more favourable treatment is not called for by the Convention".[5]

C14–04 The Convention's approach to discrimination has significant differences from the treatment of discrimination under domestic statutes, which will be considered in more detail below. The first is that Article 14 applies to discrimination on any ground. The list given in Article 14 is illustrative only, and is not exhaustive. One consequence of the wide reach of Article 14 is that all discrimination, on whatever ground, is capable of being justified. Even in the absence of any express exceptions, a state can seek to justify direct racial or gender discrimination by reference to the legitimacy of the aim pursued. However, the Strasbourg institutions have recognised that differential treatment on some grounds is more suspect than on others, and the margin of appreciation which is left to the state should be correspondingly restricted. In consequence, the state will carry a greater burden of justification in relation to those grounds. Thus the Court has said that "very weighty reasons" will be needed to justify differences of treatment based solely on gender;[6] or on nationality.[7] Differences on the ground of race or illegitimacy will be approached in a similar manner. The extent of the burden of justification will depend on the importance which a democratic society attaches to the ground on which the state has differentiated between two groups; and that importance may well change over time.

C14–05 Secondly, the concept of discrimination under the Convention does not appear to admit to the possibility of indirect discrimination unless it is a covert form of intentional discrimination. In *Abdulaziz*, the Court was invited to find that there had been racial discrimination in that the immigration rules in question had the effect of preventing the entry into the United Kingdom of substantially more men from the New Commonwealth and Pakistan than from elsewhere. The Court confined itself to noting that the rules were generally applicable and were motivated by economic rather than racial considerations. As to the discriminatory result of the rules the Court said that:

" . . . it is an effect which derives not from the content of the 1980 Rules but from the fact that, among those wishing to immigrate, some ethnic groups outnumbered others."[8]

The Court's approach to this case may have been coloured by its particular context, which involved allegations of racial discrimination arising *de facto* from rules on

---

[4] *Belgian Linguistic* case (1968) 1 E.H.R.R. 252 at 283, para. 9.
[5] *Abdulaziz, Cabales and Balkandali v. United Kingdom*. See also, for example, decision of the Commission in *A.P. v. Austria* (20458/92) (1995) 20 E.H.R.R. CD 63, 66.
[6] *Burghartz v. Switzerland* (1994) 18 E.H.R.R. 101; *Schmidt v. Germany* (1994) 18 E.H.R.R. 513, para. 24.
[7] *Gaygusuz v. Austria*, September 16, 1996, R.J.D., 1996–IV, No. 14; 23 E.H.R.R. 364, para. 32 of the judgment.
[8] (1985) 7 E.H.R.R. 471, para. 85.

immigration. The Court accepted the view of the majority of the Commission that "most immigration policies differentiated on the basis of people's nationality, and indirectly their race, ethnic origin and possibly their colour . . . to give preferential treatment . . . to persons from countries with which [a state] had the closest links did not constitute 'racial discrimination'."[9] Immigration being a very sensitive area where states traditionally assert the right to exercise the greatest possible discretion, the Court may well have adopted a more cautious approach than it would have done in other contexts. There is every reason in principle why the notion of discrimination should extend to measures and practices which, whether intentional or not, have a disproportionate and unjustifiable adverse impact on particular groups.

C14–06   Clearly, however, Article 14 does not forbid every difference of treatment in the exercise of the rights and freedoms guaranteed in the Convention:

> "The competent national authorities are frequently confronted with situations and problems which, on account of differences inherent therein, call for different legal solutions; moreover, certain legal inequalities tend only to correct factual inequalities".[10]

C14–07   The Court propounded the test for assessing compliance with the requirements of Article 14 in the *Belgian Linguistic* case decided in 1968, and continues to rely on broadly the same formulation. The principles are set out in the following passage of the judgment:

> " . . . the principle of equality of treatment is violated if the distinction has no objective and reasonable justification. The existence of such a justification must be assessed in relation to the aim and effects of the measure under consideration, regard being had to the principles which normally prevail in democratic societies. A difference of treatment in the exercise of a right laid down in the Convention must not only pursue a legitimate aim; Article 14 is likewise violated when it is clearly established that there is no reasonable relationship of proportionality between the means employed and the aim sought to be realised."[11]

C14–08   When examining a complaint under Article 14 the Convention organs will ask themselves the following four questions:

(a) Do the facts of the case fall within the ambit of one or more of the other substantive provisions of the Convention?

(b) Was there a difference of treatment?

(c) Were the objects of such differential treatment placed in analogous situations?

(d) Did the difference of treatment have an objective and reasonable justification, *i.e.* does it pursue a legitimate aim and does the differential treatment

---

[9] *ibid.*, para. 84.
[10] *Belgian Linguistic* Case (No. 2) (1968) 1 E.H.R.R. 252 at 284, para. 10.
[11] 1 E.H.R.R. 252 at 284, para. 10.

bear a reasonable relationship of proportionality to the aim sought to be achieved?[12]

Each of the stages in the Convention organs' process of reviewing compliance with Article 14 will be examined in the following paragraphs.

(1) Do the facts of the case fall within the ambit of one or more of the other substantive provisions of the Convention?

C14–09 Article 14 does not apply to cases where the facts of the case have no relationship whatsoever with the Convention. In *Engel v. Netherlands*, for example, the Court disposed of certain of the applicants' complaints relating to military discipline by observing that "since certain of the said penalties and measures did not involve any deprivation of liberty, the discrimination alleged in their connection does not give rise to any problem with regard to Article 14, in that it did not affect the enjoyment of the right set forth in Article 5(1)".[13]

C14–10 It would appear, however, that even the most tenuous link with another provision in the Convention will suffice for Article 14 to enter into play. Thus, although the right to receive welfare benefits falls largely outside the scope of the substantive provisions of the Convention, the Court was prepared to characterise emergency assistance payments to the unemployed as a "pecuniary right" and as such within the ambit of Article 1 of the First Protocol, which a person is entitled to enjoy without discrimination.[14] In so doing, the Court went further than the Commission, which had considered it necessary to rely on the fact that the benefits were available only to those who had made contributions, and therefore came within the obligation to pay "taxes or other contributions" to which Article 1 of the First Protocol refers. Again, despite its oft-repeated affirmation that Article 6 entitles it to pronounce only on the procedural fairness of a domestic case, as against its substantive merits, in *Schuler-Zgraggen v. Switzerland* the Court found a violation of Article 14 in conjunction with Article 6 relying on its competence to review the fairness of the taking of evidence under the second provision:

> "[The national court] adopted in its entirety the . . . assumption that women gave up work when they gave birth to a child. It did not attempt to probe the validity of that assumption itself by weighing arguments to the contrary. [The assumption] . . . constitutes the sole basis for the reasoning, thus being decisive, and introduces a difference of treatment based on the ground of sex only."[15]

C14–11 In addition, the prohibition of discrimination in Article 14 quite often serves to expand certain concepts in the Convention. In *Van der Mussele v. Belgium*, for example, the Court considered that "[t]he criteria which serve to delimit the concept of compulsory labour include the notion of what is in the normal course of affairs.[16] Work or labour that it is in itself normal may in fact be

---

[12] See, *mutatis mutandis*, *Rasmussen v. Denmark* (1985) 7 E.H.R.R. 371.
[13] (1976) 1 E.H.R.R. 647, para. 71.
[14] *Gaygusuz v. Austria*, September 16, 1996, R.J.D., 1996–IV, No. 14; 23 E.H.R.R. 364.
[15] (1993) 16 E.H.R.R. 405, para. 67.
[16] The Court was referring to Article 4(3)(d) of the Convention, which excluded from the term "forced or compulsory labour" "any work or service which forms part of normal civic obligations".

rendered abnormal if the choice of the groups or individuals bound to perform it is governed by discriminatory factors . . . "[17]

(2) Was there a difference of treatment?

C14–12 Any difference of treatment in connection with the enjoyment of a right guaranteed under the Convention will raise an issue under Article 14. As the Court articulated in the *Belgian Linguistic* case, Article 14 forms an integral part of each of the articles laying down rights and freedoms:

> "No distinctions should be made in this respect according to the nature of these rights and freedoms and of their correlative obligations, and for instance as to whether the respect due to the right concerned implies positive action or mere abstention."[18]

C14–13 So far as negative rights and obligations are concerned—*i.e.* where the Convention imposes a duty to refrain from interference—an interference which might otherwise be justified under the provision guaranteeing the substantive right will nonetheless violate Article 14 if it is applied in an unjustifiably discriminatory manner. For example, in *Sutherland v. United Kingdom*, while the Commission accepted that the setting of a minimum age for sexual acts could be justified under Article 8(2), it found to be unjustified the setting of different ages for homosexual and heterosexual acts.[19]

C14–14 In addition, Article 14 requires the extension to all persons and groups in comparable situations of positive measures which might not even be required under another provision in the Convention but which fall within its scope of application. Thus, although no provision of the Convention requires the making of emergency assistance payments to the unemployed, if made, such payments must be made without discrimination.[20]

C14–15 In this light it is highly unlikely that a serious application will be rejected on the basis that there was no difference in treatment to be complained of. Some controversy could, however, arise as to the relevance of the characteristics which a person or group allege to have formed the basis for different treatment. Article 14 prohibits discrimination "on any ground such as sex, race, colour, language, religion, political or other opinion, national or social origin, association with a national minority, property, birth or other status". The list of prohibited grounds is illustrative and not exhaustive.[21] However, in *Kjeldsen, Busk, Madsen and Pedersen v. Denmark*, where the applicants had complained that national law allowed parents to have their children exempted from religious instruction classes held in state schools, whilst it offered no similar possibility for integrated sex education, the Court found it difficult to discern the personal characteristic ("status") by which the applicants were distinguishable from any other group of parents.[22]

---

[17] (1984) 6 E.H.R.R. 163, para. 43.
[18] (1968) 1 E.H.R.R. 252 at 283, para. 8.
[19] [1998] E.H.R.L.R. 117.
[20] *Gaygusuz v. Austria*, September 16, 1996, R.J.D., 1996–IV, No. 14; 23 E.H.R.R. 364.
[21] *Engel v. Netherlands* (1976) 1 E.H.R.R. 647, para. 72.
[22] (1976) 1 E.H.R.R. 711.

C14–16 But more recently, the Convention organs appear to have taken a less strict approach to this aspect of discrimination. Indeed, in *Sutherland v. United Kingdom*, the Commission considered that it was

> "not required to determine whether a difference based on sexual orientation is a matter which is properly to be considered a difference on the grounds of 'sex' or of 'other status'. In either event, it is a difference in respect of which the Commission is entitled to seek justification."[23]

C14–17 A look at some of the grounds of differentiation which states have been called on to justify will serve to indicate the potential versatility of Article 14. Thus in recent years alone, in addition to religion, nationality and sex, the Convention institutions have entertained cases of differential treatment on the ground of lack of wealth[24]; a difference of treatment between victims of intentional trespass to the person and victims of negligently inflicted injury[25]; distinctions based on marital status[26]; different treatment of owners of non-residential as opposed to residential buildings in relation to suspension of orders for the eviction of tenants[27]; differential treatment of dog owners by reference to the breed of dog in question[28]; people injured at work not entitled to bring proceedings for personal injury by comparison with those suffering injury outside the workplace[29]; distinction in favour of those who had already brought legal proceedings for restitutionary remedies, in relation to exemption from the retrospective validation of invalid regulations[30]; a difference in treatment between small landowners (who were obliged to transfer their hunting rights to a local hunt association) and large landowners (who were not).[31]

(3) Were the comparators placed in analogous situations?

C14–18 A large number of complaints are rejected on the basis of lack of analogy in the situations invoked. In *Sunday Times v. United Kingdom*, for example, the Court dismissed a complaint brought under Article 10 in conjunction with Article 14 considering that " . . . the press and parliamentarians cannot be considered to be 'placed in comparable situations' since their respective 'duties and responsibilities' are essentially different".[32] On occasion, the Court's conclusion that comparators are not in an analogous situation has been influenced by its

---

[23] [1998] E.H.R.L.R. 117 (Report dated July 1, 1997), para. 51.
[24] *S & M v. United Kingdom* (1993) 18 E.H.R.R. CD 172 (the McDonalds two; absence of legal aid to defend libel proceedings).
[25] *Stubbings v. United Kingdom*, October 22, 1996, R.J.D., 1996–IV, No. 18; 23 E.H.R.R. 213. The Commission found this to be based on personal status, whereas the Court held that the two groups were not in analogous situations.
[26] *McMichael v. United Kingdom* (1995) 20 E.H.R.R. 205 (unmarried father of a child not entitled to custody or to participate in care proceedings).
[27] *Spadea & Scalabrino v. Italy* (1995) 21 E.H.R.R. 482; *Scollo v. Italy* (1996) 22 E.H.R.R. 514.
[28] *Bullock v. United Kingdom* (1996) 21 E.H.R.R. CD 85 (measures in respect of pit bull terriers).
[29] *Handwerker v. Germany* (1996) 22 E.H.R.R. CD 125.
[30] *The National and Provincial Building Society & ors v. United Kingdom*, October 23, 1997, R.J.D., 1997–VII, No. 55; 25 E.H.R.R. 127.
[31] App. Nos 25088/94, 28331/95 and 28443/95 *Chassagnou and others v. France* judgment of April 29, 1999.
[32] (1979) 2 E.H.R.R. 245, para. 72. See further *Van der Mussele v. Belgium*, (1984) 6 E.H.R.R. 163, para. 46; *Lithgow v. United Kingdom* (1986) 8 E.H.R.R. 329, para. 189; *Johnston v. Ireland* (1987) 9 E.H.R.R. 203, para. 60; *Moustaquim v. Belgium* (1991) 13 E.H.R.R. 802, para. 49; and *Observer and Guardian v. United Kingdom* (1992) 14 E.H.R.R. 153, para. 73.

conclusion that differential treatment is justified, *i.e.* the fact that their situations are not analogous justifies the drawing of a distinction between them: see for example *Stubbings v. United Kingdom*,[33] in which the Court held both that the victims of intentional torts and negligence were not in analogous situations and that, in any event, the distinction between them was justified. By contrast, the Commission had found unanimously that there was an unjustified distinction, based on personal status, between people in analogous situations.[34]

C14–19   However, quite often the Court will bypass the issue, arguing that the question of comparability is just one facet of the more general question whether the difference of treatment is justified.[35] In *Van Raalte v. Netherlands*,[36] for instance, the Government argued that unmarried childless men and women over 45 were not in comparable positions because women (who were not required to make child benefit contributions) were less likely to have children than men (who were not exempt). The Court said that it was precisely this difference which was at the heart of the question whether the difference could be justified. In fact, the character of the scheme was that obligation to contribute did not depend on potential entitlement, and in consequence the exemption ran counter to the underlying character of scheme.

(4) Does the difference of treatment have an objective and reasonable justification?

C14–20   Justification is another issue over which the Strasbourg institutions have been prepared to afford national authorities a margin of appreciation:

> " . . . the Contracting States enjoy a certain 'margin of appreciation' in assessing whether and to what extent differences in otherwise similar situations justify a different treatment in law. The scope of the margin of appreciation will vary according to the circumstances, the subject matter and its background; in this respect, one of the relevant factors may be the existence or non-existence of common ground between the laws of the Contracting States."[37]

C14–21   There are, however, certain differences of treatment which, independently of any national margin of appreciation, will not be easily tolerated in Strasbourg, discrimination based on gender or nationality or race, or against children born outside marriage being the most obvious cases:

> "(T)he advancement of the equality of the sexes is today a major goal in the member States of the Council of Europe. This means that very weighty reasons would have to be advanced before a difference of treatment on the ground of sex could be regarded as compatible with the Convention."[38]

---

[33] October 22, 1996, R.J.D., 1996–IV, No. 18; 23 E.H.R.R. 213.
[34] See also *The National and Provincial Building Society & ors v. United Kingdom*, October 23, 1997, R.J.D., 1997–VII, No. 55; 25 E.H.R.R. 127.
[35] *Rasmussen v. Denmark* (1985) 7 E.H.R.R. 371, para. 37.
[36] February 21, 1997, R.J.D., 1997–I, No. 39; 24 E.H.R.R. 503.
[37] *Rasmussen v. Denmark*, para. 40.
[38] *Abdulaziz, Cabales and Balkandali v. United Kingdom* (1985) 7 E.H.R.R. 471, para. 78; see also *Schuler-Zgraggen v. Switzerland* (1993) 16 E.H.R.R. 405.

"The question of equality of children born in and children born out of wedlock as regards their civil rights is today given importance in the member states of the Council of Europe . . . Very weighty reasons would accordingly have to be advanced before a difference of treatment on the ground of birth out of wedlock could be regarded as compatible with the Convention."[39]

C14–22   Although it has not made any similarly broad pronouncement on the issue, in recent cases the Court appears to have taken a firm line regarding discrimination in the field of freedom of religion. Thus in *Hoffmann v. Austria*,[40] the Court found a violation of Article 8 in conjunction with Article 14 where a national court decided a case concerning the custody of children on the basis of the parent's difference of religion alone. In *Darby v. Sweden*,[41] the Court found a violation of Article 1 of the First Protocol in conjunction with Article 14 where a non-permanent resident of Sweden was liable to pay a special tax benefiting a church to which he did not belong while permanent residents in comparable situations were not. It is notable, however, that the Court has been reluctant to rely on Article 9 of the Convention which guarantees religious freedom, instead showing a preference for other more neutral provisions. A recent example is *Canea Catholic Church v. Greece*,[42] which concerned the inability of the Catholic Church to take proceedings to protect its property, whereas the Greek Orthodox Church and Jewish Community could bring such proceedings. The Commission had considered the case under Articles 9 and 14 whereas the Court preferred to approach it as an issue under Articles 6 and 14.

C14–23   The existence of a national margin of appreciation is not *carte blanche*, however, and the Convention institutions have nonetheless been prepared to hold that certain justifications are not acceptable. Although the fact that the difference of treatment has been the subject of parliamentary debate and approval[43] carries some weight, it is by no means decisive; and in the recent case of *Sutherland v. United Kingdom*, the Commission rightly affirmed that of more importance than the fact of parliamentary approval is the validity of the reasons advanced to justify the difference of treatment in issue.[44] In that case, for example, the majority of the Commission was prepared to over-rule its previous case law in the light of changes in medical opinion and in the legislation of the majority of other members of the Council of Europe. It was also prepared to hold that society's claimed entitlement to indicate disapproval of homosexual conduct and preference for a homosexual lifestyle "could not in any event justify inequality of treatment under criminal law".[45]

C14–24   Where a complaint under Article 14 (always in conjunction with another Article) runs concurrently with a separate complaint under a substantive provision, the Court will initially concentrate on the latter:

"If the Court does not find a separate breach of one of those Articles that has been invoked both on its own and together with Article 14, it must also

---

[39] *Inze v. Austria* (1988) 10 E.H.R.R. 394, para. 41; see further *Marckx v. Belgium* (1979) 2 E.H.R.R. 330 and *Vermeire v. Belgium* (1993) 15 E.H.R.R. 488.
[40] (1994) 17 E.H.R.R. 293.
[41] (1991) 13 E.H.R.R. 774.
[42] (1999) 27 E.H.R.R. 521.
[43] As in *Abdulaziz Cabales and Balkandali v. United Kingdom* (1985) 7 E.H.R.R. 471, for example.
[44] [1998] E.H.R.L.R. 117, para. 62 of the Report.
[45] *ibid.*, para. 65.

examine the case under the latter Article. On the other hand, such an examination is not generally required when the Court finds a violation of the former Article taken alone. The position is otherwise if a clear inequality of treatment in the enjoyment of the right in question is a fundamental aspect of the case."[46]

However, where discrimination is the very essence of the matter of complaint, the matter may be considered primarily under Article 14, as in *Sutherland v. United Kingdom*.

C14–25   As in other aspects of its remedial jurisdiction, the Court has not always appeared consistent in its approach to the remedies to be provided following a finding of discrimination. Thus in *Van Raalte v. Netherlands*,[47] the Court found unanimously that there was no justification for requiring unmarried childless men over the age of 45 to pay contributions under the General Child Benefits Act while at the same time exempting comparable women. However, the Court dismissed the applicant's claim for compensation, holding that its judgment did not entitle him to retrospective exemption from the contributions. By contrast, in *Schmidt v. Germany*,[48] where the Court found Article 14 violated by the obligation, placed on men alone, to pay a levy in lieu of joining the fire service, the Court ordered the Government to reimburse the levy. Further, where the violation found is one of discrimination alone, there appears to be nothing to prevent a state from responding by "levelling down" to the standard afforded to the less favoured group, so long as in doing so it does not violate the substantive right taken by itself.

---

[46] *Airey v. Ireland* (1979) 2 E.H.R.R. 305, para. 30. See also App. Nos 25088/94, 28331/95 and 28443/95, *Chassagnou and others v. France* judgment of April 29, 1999, para. 89.
[47] February 21, 1997, R.J.D., 1997–I, No. 39; 24 E.H.R.R. 503.
[48] (1994) 18 E.H.R.R. 513.

ARTICLE 1 PROTOCOL 1:
PROTECTION OF PROPERTY

P1/1–01   Every natural or legal person is entitled to the peaceful enjoyment of his possessions. No one shall be deprived of his possessions except in the public interest and subject to the conditions provided for by law and by the general principles of international law.

The preceding provisions shall not, however, in any way impair the right of a State to enforce such laws as it deems necessary to control the use of property in accordance with the general interest or to secure the payment of taxes or other contributions or penalties.

P1/1–02   In one of its earliest decisions on Article 1 of the First Protocol, *Marckx v. Belgium*,[1] the Court confirmed that this provision guarantees in substance the right of property. Its aim is to protect a person's existing possessions, and it does not guarantee a right to acquire possessions.[2] Although the Court's ruling in *Marckx* was made in respect of the right to acquire possessions on intestacy or through voluntary dispositions, its scope appears to be more general.[3] The Protocol has not been interpreted as creating any right to social security payments, nor can it be said that it was the intention of its drafters that it should do so.[4]

P1/1–03   Despite many differences of both style and substance, Article 1 of the First Protocol is in essence similar to all of the Convention provisions which contain a limitation clause. While it guarantees the right of every person to "the peaceful enjoyment of his possessions", it also affords states the possibility of interfering with the right under certain circumstances.

P1/1–04   The wording of Article 1 of the First Protocol envisages two particular forms of state interference, "deprivation of possessions" and "control of the use of property" and subjects both to certain conditions: deprivation must be lawful, must serve the public interest, and must comply with the general principles of international law; controls of use must likewise be lawful, the state must deem them necessary and they must serve the general interest or another specifically enumerated purpose. In addition to the express limitations in the wording, the Court has built into its case law an important additional condition: any interference must strike a fair balance between the individual and the public interest, the principle of proportionality by another name.[5]

P1/1–05   Although Article 1 of Protocol No. 1 refers specifically only to deprivation and control of use, the generality of the first sentence makes clear that its application extends to all forms of state interference with the right to peaceful

---

[1] (1979) 2 E.H.R.R. 330, para. 63.

[2] *ibid.*, para. 50.

[3] See further *App. No. 8410/78 v. Germany* 18 D. & R. 216 and *App. 10438/83 Batelaan & Huiges v. Netherlands* 41 D. & R. 170).

[4] See *App. 4130/69 v. Netherlands* 14 Yb 224, *App. 6776/74 v. Sweden* 2 D. & R. 123 and *App. 10482/83 v. Germany* (1984) 6 E.H.R.R. 587. But see two recent discrimination decisions *Gaygusuz v. Austria*, September 16, 1996, R.J.D., 1996–IV, No. 14; 23 E.H.R.R. 364, where the Court held that emergency assistance payments to the unemployed were a "pecuniary right" which accordingly came within the scope of Article 1 of the First Protocol, and therefore Article 14 applied; *van Raalte v. Netherlands*, February 21, 1997, R.J.D., 1997–I, No. 39; 24 E.H.R.R. 503, concerning sex discrimination in respect of the obligation to pay contributions under the General Child Benefits Act. The Court held that since the case concerned the State's right to secure the payment of taxes and contributions, it came within the ambit of Article 1 of Protocol 1. See para. P1/1–14 below.

[5] As to the principle of proportionality, see above paras C0–12 *et seq.*

enjoyment of one's possessions. Moreover, although the first sentence does not contain any express exceptions, the case law of the Court recognises that some interferences may nevertheless be justified so long as they meet the criteria of lawfulness, legitimate aim and fair balance. In short, the same considerations apply whichever form of interference is in issue, although the considerations which are relevant to the question of proportionality may vary according to the nature of the interference under scrutiny.

P1/1–06 The Court has summarised its general approach to Article 1 of the First Protocol in the following passages:

> "That Article comprises three distinct rules. The first rule, which is of a general nature, enounces the principle of peaceful enjoyment of property; it is set out in the first sentence of the first paragraph. The second rule covers deprivation of possessions and subjects it to certain conditions; it appears in the second sentence of the same paragraph. The third rule recognises that the States are entitled, amongst other things, to control the use of property in accordance with the general interest, by enforcing such laws as they deem necessary for the purpose; it is contained in the second paragraph."[6]
>
> "The three rules are not, however, 'distinct' in the sense of being unconnected. The second and third rules are concerned with particular instances of interference with the right to peaceful enjoyment of property and should therefore be construed in the light of the general principle enunciated in the first rule."[7]

P1/1–07 Before enquiring whether the first general rule has been complied with, it must be decided whether the last two rules are applicable[8]; *i.e.* the Convention institutions have determined first whether there has been a deprivation or a control of use of property. If there has not, they consider, as a separate issue, whether there has been any other form of interference with the enjoyment of a person's possessions. The fact, however, that a measure of interference does not fall within the ambit either of the second sentence of the first paragraph (deprivation) or of the second paragraph (control of use) does not mean that it automatically violates the rule contained in the first sentence of the first paragraph[9]: lawful, legitimate and proportionate exceptions may still be permitted.

P1/1–08 The commentary below examines the following issues:

1. what constitutes a "possession" for the purposes of Article 1 of the First Protocol;

2. what are the principal component elements of the right to property;

3. whose property rights are guaranteed under Article 1 of the First Protocol;

4. what constitutes a deprivation of property under Article 1 of the First Protocol and when is such a deprivation justified under the Protocol;

---

[6] *Sporrong & Lönnroth v. Sweden* (1983) 5 E.H.R.R. 35, para. 61.
[7] *James v. United Kingdom* (1986) 8 E.H.R.R. 123, para. 37.
[8] *Sporrong & Lönnroth v. Sweden*, para. 61.
[9] *ibid.*, para. 69.

5. what constitutes a control of the use of property under Article 1 of the First Protocol and which controls are justified under the Protocol;

6. what other measures constitute interference with the right to peaceful enjoyment of one's possessions, and in what circumstances may they be justified?

1. WHAT CONSTITUTES A "POSSESSION" FOR THE PURPOSES OF ARTICLE 1 OF THE FIRST PROTOCOL?

P1/1–09 The majority of the complaints examined by the European Commission and Court in this connection have concerned rights of ownership over real or movable property.[10] There can be no doubt that these rights constitute "possessions" for the purposes of Article 1 of the First Protocol. However, the Court has made it clear that the notion of possessions has an autonomous meaning which is not synonymous with ownership,[11] and that certain other rights and interests constituting assets can also be regarded as property rights and thus possessions, whether they are rights of ownership or, for example, security rights *in rem*.[12] Thus the Strasbourg institutions have been prepared to entertain applications even where the ownership of the asset in question was in dispute,[13] in particular where the ground for disputing ownership is the very act of deprivation of which complaint is made.[14] However the extent of the concept of "possessions" has proved to be a contentious issue in certain areas.

A. Legal claims

P1/1–10 In a number of early decisions,[15] the Commission considered that a claim might constitute a "possession". However, in *Van der Mussele v. Belgium*[16] the Court held Article 1 to be inapplicable to the case of a pupil advocate who had been compelled to represent, without payment, a client in need of legal aid: no debt had ever arisen in favour of the applicant, as no assessment of fees could have been made due to the client's lack of means. In *Stran Greek Refineries & Stratis Andreadis v. Greece*,[17] which concerned a law cancelling an arbitration award in the applicants' favour, the Court reiterated that in order to determine whether the applicants had a "possession" it had to ascertain whether the award had given rise to a debt in their favour that was sufficiently established to be enforceable.[18] Since the arbitration award in the applicants' favour was final and binding and did not require any further enforcement measure, it clearly recognised the state's liability

---

[10] Or rights of a similar nature such as hunting rights *Chassagnou and Others v. France* judgment of April 29, 1999; or fishing rights *Huber, Staufer, Sportanglerbund Vöcklabruck & Eckhardt v. Austria* (1996) 22 E.H.R.R. CD 91.

[11] *Matos e Silva LDA & ors v. Portugal*, September 16, 1996, R.J.D., 1996–IV, No. 14; 24 E.H.R.R. 573.

[12] *Gasus Dosier- under Fördertechnik GmbH v. Netherlands* (1995) 20 E.H.R.R. 403 (property right of a vendor under a retention of title clause).

[13] *Iatridis v. Greece*, judgment March 25, 1999.

[14] *Panikian v. Bulgaria* (1997) 24 E.H.R.R. CD 63.

[15] App. Nos 7742/76 v. Germany 14 D. & R. 146, 7775/77 *De Napoles Pacheco v. Belgium* 15 D. & R. 143 and 10438/83 *Batelaan and Huiges v. Netherlands* 41 D. & R. 170. See also App. No. 12947/87 *Association of General Practitioners v. Denmark* 62 D. & R. 226.

[16] (1984) 6 E.H.R.R. 163.

[17] (1995) 19 E.H.R.R. 293.

[18] *ibid.*, para. 59.

and was therefore to be regarded as a possession.[19] However, in *Pressos Compania Naviera S.A. & ors v. Belgium*, which also concerned retrospective cancellation of claims, the Court held that a claim in tort was to be regarded as an asset and therefore a "possession" even though it was not final and binding: the asset appears to have been a legitimate expectation that the claimant's claim will be determined in accordance with the general law of tort.[20] The opportunity to clarify these authorities arose in *National and Provincial Building Society & ors v. United Kingdom*,[21] which concerned legislation retrospectively validating tax provisions, thereby extinguishing the applicants' restitution proceedings. Although the Court ultimately determined the case without deciding the question, it expressed considerable doubt as to whether the applicants' claims in that case constituted possessions: at the time when they instituted proceedings the applicants did not have an enforceable final judgment in their favour,[22] the law on restitution was not favourable to them at the time and it was questionable whether they had a "legitimate expectation" that the Government would not seek to cancel the benefit which they sought.[23] Accordingly, their proceedings could not be said to be sufficiently established or based on any legitimate expectation.[24] The decision appears to have been influenced by the Court's view that the claim which the applicants were seeking to enforce was in essence a windfall, arising out of a technical error in legislation changing the basis of assessment for the taxation of interest paid to building society investors. It seems, however, that in order to amount to a possession, a claim must either relate to an acknowledged or enforceable debt (as in the *Stran* case) or it must amount to a "legitimate" expectation that the claim will be dealt with in accordance with the general law (as in the *Pressos* case). It is the element of legitimacy which appears to have been present in the case of *Pressos* but, in the Court's view, absent in that of the *National and Provincial Building Society case*.

B. Licences

P1/1–11 Whether a licence to conduct an economic activity amounts to a "possession" depends, *inter alia*, on whether it gives rise to a reasonable and legitimate expectation of the lasting nature of the licence, and hence as to the possibility of continuing to draw benefits from the exercise of the licensed activity. No such expectation exists where the conditions attached to the licence are not or no longer fulfilled. Accordingly, no property right is affected where a provisional licence is withdrawn because the applicant has failed to show that he fulfils the conditions on which it was granted[25]; or where it is withdrawn in accordance with the provisions of the law which were in force when the licence was granted.[26]

P1/1–12 However, the economic interests connected with the running of a business are "possessions" and the withdrawal of a licence which is one of the

---

[19] *ibid.*, para. 61.

[20] (1996) 21 E.H.R.R. 301. The case concerned retrospective legislation depriving ship-owners of their claims for compensation for damage from collisions allegedly arising from the negligence of Belgian pilots. Unhelpfully the Court did not refer to or distinguish *Stran Greek Refineries*.

[21] October 23, 1997, R.J.D., 1997–VII, No. 55; 25 E.H.R.R. 127.

[22] *ibid.*, para. 67.

[23] *ibid.*, para. 68.

[24] *ibid.*, para. 69.

[25] *JS & ors v. Netherlands* (1995) 20 E.H.R.R. CD 42. See also the Commission's decision in App. No. 10426/83 *Pudas v. Sweden* (1984) 20 D & R 234 (licence granted under specific conditions by a public authority to run a road transport service found not to be a "possession"); *Gudmunsson v. Iceland* (1996) 21 E.H.R.R. CD 89 (withdrawal of taxi licence).

[26] *Gudmunsson v. Iceland, loc. cit.*

principal conditions for the carrying on of such a business has been considered to constitute an interference with such "possessions".[27] In *Van Marle and others v. Netherlands*, the Court held that the goodwill of an accountancy practice constituted an asset, which would be diminished by the refusal to register the applicants as certified accountants. Goodwill had in many respects the nature of a private right and it was therefore a possession within the meaning of the first sentence of Article 1.[28]

C. Company shares

P1/1–13 Company shares were also found by the Commission to be "possessions" giving rise to a property right in *Bramelid and Malmstrom v. Sweden*.[29]

D. Pensions and social security

P1/1–14 The making of contributions to a pension fund may, in certain circumstances, create a property right in a portion of the fund, which may be affected by the manner in which the fund is distributed.[30] In its report in *Müller v. Austria*,[31] however, the Commission drew a distinction between social security systems and private insurance companies. In the case of the former, the Commission considered that, even if it is assumed that Article 1 of the First Protocol guarantees those who have paid contributions to a social insurance system the right to derive benefit from the system, it cannot be interpreted as entitling that person to a pension of a particular amount. Only a substantial reduction of the amount of the pension could be regarded as affecting the very substance of the right. In its judgment in *Gaygusuz v. Austria*,[32] the Court appears to have confirmed that the right to receive contributory welfare is a "pecuniary right", to which Article 1 of Protocol 1 is applicable, although the particular case was decided primarily under Article 14. In its admissibility decision in *Bellet and others v. France*[33] the Court again confirmed that contributions made under a compulsory retirement scheme could in certain cases create a right of property in part of the fund. However, for such a right to accrue the applicant has to satisfy the conditions laid down by domestic law. *Bellet* concerned French civil servants seconded to Monaco, who had contributed to pension funds in both countries but were only entitled to receive one pension. The French statute clearly provided that civil servants on secondment overseas could not participate in a retirement scheme for the post for which they had been seconded or in such capacity acquire any rights to a pension, irrespective of the positions they had held during their career. The fact that the French authorities had for a number of years tolerated retired civil servants receiving both

---

[27] *Tre Traktörer Aktiebolag v. Sweden* (1991) 13 E.H.R.R. 309, para. 53 (licence to serve alcoholic beverages in a restaurant); *Fredin v. Sweden* (1991) 13 E.H.R.R. 784, para. 39 (licence to exploit gravel). *Zacher v. Germany* (1996) 22 E.H.R.R. CD 136 (milk quota).

[28] (1986) 8 E.H.R.R. 491, para. 41. See, however, App. No. 10438/83 *Batelaan and Huiges v. Netherlands* 41 D. & R. 170. See also *Iatridis v. Greece* judgment of 25 March 1999, para. 54, where the Court considered that the clientele associated with a business constituted in itself an asset, which is in principle protected from interference under Article 1 of the First Protocol.

[29] App. Nos 8588/79 and 8589/79 (1983) 5 E.H.R.R. 249.

[30] App. No. 4130/69 v. *Netherlands* 14 Yb 224; *Mann v. Germany* (1996) E.H.R.R. CD 157.

[31] Comm. Report 1.10.75, 43 D 7 R, p. 25, 19 Yb 994, paras 29–32 See also *Szumilas v. Poland* (1998) 26 E.H.R.R. CD 181.

[32] (1997) 23 E.H.R.R. 364. The case concerned discriminatory rules governing the availability of emergency social assistance, which took the form of an advance payment of a contributory pension. See further para. C14–10 above.

[33] App. Nos 40832/98, 40833/98 and 40906/98, Decision of April 20, 1998 (Third Section).

pensions, contrary to the requirements of statute, was insufficient to create a property right under Article 1 of Protocol No. 1.

E. Leases/licenses

P1/1–15 In *JLS v. Spain*,[34] upon his transfer to the provisional reserve, the applicant was required to return accommodation he had been allocated for use as a member of the armed forces. The property had been let to him, on the basis of an "administrative document for the allocation of special accommodation" for a rent well below the market rate. Though the applicant did not suggest that the arrangement could be compared to a private law lease, the Court stated that:

> "... a right to live in a given property without being the owner does not constitute 'property' within the meaning of Article 1.[35] Furthermore, allowing 'users' who, like the applicant, were not even tenants to stay indefinitely in accommodation belonging to the State would hinder the authorities in the exercise of their duty to administer the State's property in accordance with the provisions of the Constitution and the law."[36]

The Court was, however, careful to draw a distinction between the applicant in this case, who merely had the use of the property, and a tenant, who had signed a tenancy agreement and was subject to protection against eviction, as a matter of national law. The latter was the position in *Larkos v. Cyprus*,[37] where the Court found a violation of Article 8 in conjunction with Article 14 in relation to the eviction of a government tenant. In light of this finding, the Court, expressly, did not deal with the complaint (and applicability of) under Article 1 of the First Protocol.

2. WHAT ARE THE PRINCIPAL COMPONENTS OF THE RIGHT TO PROPERTY?

P1/1–16 In *Marckx v. Belgium*,[38] the Court considered that the right to dispose of one's property constitutes a traditional and fundamental aspect of the right to property. In *Sporrong and Lönnroth v. Sweden*,[39] the Court referred to the right to use, sell, devise, donate or mortgage property. The right to enjoy and use one's property as one pleases must be also seen as the second main component of this right,[40] as indeed is the right to refrain from, and prevent the carrying out of, any particular activity on one's land.[41] Even if a measure leaves intact a person's right to deal with his possessions as a matter of law, it may nonetheless constitute an interference if it greatly reduces his ability to do so in practice.[42]

---

[34] App. No. 41917/98, Decision of April 27, 1999 (Fourth Section).
[35] See App. No. 19217/91, *Durini v. Italy* 76 D & R 76.
[36] Translation adapted from Court press release.
[37] Judgment of February 18, 1999.
[38] *Gudmunsson v. Iceland, loc. cit.* para. 63; *App. Nos 7624/76 v. Austria* 19 D. & R. 100; *9776/82 v. United Kingdom* 34 D. & R. 153 and *10094/82 v. Austria* 38 D. & R. 84.
[39] (1983) 5 E.H.R.R. 35, para. 62.
[40] See, *mutatis mutandis, Sporrong & Lönnroth v. Sweden* (1983) 5 E.H.R.R. 35, para. 60 and *Mellacher v. Austria* (1990) 12 E.H.R.R. 391, para. 44.
[41] *Chassagnou and Others v. France* judgment of April 29, 1999 (right of land owners to refrain from, and prevent, hunting on their land).
[42] *ibid.*

3. WHOSE PROPERTY RIGHTS ARE GUARANTEED UNDER ARTICLE 1 OF THE FIRST PROTOCOL?

P1/1–17 Article 1 of the First Protocol guarantees the right of every natural or legal person to the peaceful enjoyment of his possessions. Although legal persons appear to derive protection from a number of other Convention provisions, this is the only Article which expressly envisages their protection. However, under Article 34[43] of the Convention only non-governmental organisations may submit individual applications, and in the result, the Protocol cannot be invoked by one branch of the state against another.[44] Particularly acute problems may arise in connection with the status of public corporations as victims. In *Holy Monasteries v. Greece*[45] the Government contested the claim of the applicant monasteries to be non-governmental organisations, claiming that they were public law bodies. The Court examined the activities in which the monasteries engaged in order to assess their claim and found that they were essentially ecclesiastical and spiritual, also social and cultural, but in any event "not such as to enable them to classed with government organisations established for public administration purposes". Their classification as public law entities was not conclusive, their only power consisted of making rules concerning the organisation and furtherance of spiritual life and the internal administration of each monastery; and they were under supervision of the local archbishop, not of the State.[46] As a result the monasteries could claim to be non-governmental organisations and victims of an interference with their property rights.[47]

P1/1–18 Shareholders can claim to be victims of interferences with the property rights of the company only in very limited circumstances.[48] The Commission has so far accepted cases where the individuals concerned held substantial majority shareholdings in the company, carried on their own business through the medium of the company and had a direct interest in the subject-matter of the complaint. In *Agrotexim Hellas SA and others v. Greece*,[49] the Commission, in accepting the applicant shareholders' claim to be victims of an interference with the company's property, had stressed the fact that the company was essentially under effective state control pursuant to a ministerial direction that the company be liquidated: as a result, in the Commission's view it could not reasonably be expected to lodge an application against the Greek State. The Court agreed that the right of a shareholder to complain about interference with the company's property rights cannot depend solely on whether he is a majority shareholder. However, it would be too wide a ground of *locus standi* to say that any infringement of company's property right which results in a fall in the value of its shares automatically entails infringement of a shareholder's right. In the Court's view, piercing of the corporate

---

[43] Formerly Article 25. The HRA maintains this position by stipulating that proceedings in respect of acts made unlawful by section 6 of the Act may only be brought by a person who is or would be a victim of that act: section 7(1).

[44] *Sixteen Austrian Communes and some of their Councillors v. Austria* 17 Yb 338 and App. No. 9267/81 *Moreaux and others v. Belgium* (1984) 6 E.H.R.R. 467.

[45] (1995) 20 E.H.R.R. 1.

[46] *ibid.*, para. 49.

[47] See also *Hautanemi et al. v. Sweden* (1996) 22 E.H.R.R. CD 155.

[48] *1706/62 v. Austria* 21 Coll 26, 7598/76 *Kaplan v. United Kingdom* (1980) 4 E.H.R.R. 64, paras 129–131 and 9266/81 *Yarrow Plc and three shareholders v. United Kingdom* (1983) 5 E.H.R.R. 498.

[49] (1996) 21 E.H.R.R. 250.

veil or disregarding the company's legal personality can be justified only in exceptional circumstances, in particular where it is clearly established that it is impossible for the company to apply under the Convention through its corporate organs or through its liquidators. Declining to entertain the *Agrotexim* case, the Court considered that the liquidators could have applied to Strasbourg as a matter of law, and were free to do so as a matter of fact.

4. WHAT CONSTITUTES A DEPRIVATION OF PROPERTY UNDER ARTICLE 1 OF THE FIRST PROTOCOL, AND WHEN IS SUCH A DEPRIVATION JUSTIFIED UNDER THE PROTOCOL?

P1/1–19   As already observed, when an interference with an applicant's property right is established, the first issue which the Court and the Commission will address is whether the interference amounts to a deprivation.

P1/1–20   The deprivation rule will normally apply where a formal and permanent deprivation has occurred, unless deprivation is ancillary to control of use or taxation, in which case the matter will be considered under the second paragraph of the Article.[50] But other measures have been considered as equivalent to deprivation in substance. For example in *Holy Monasteries v. Greece*,[51] the Court had to consider a law which created a presumption of State ownership. The effect of the law was to shift the burden of proof to the person claiming ownership, who could assert such ownership only if it derived from a duly registered title deed, from a statutory provision or from a final court decision against the State. The Court held that this deprived the applicants of the possibility of proving ownership through other means of acquisition such as adverse possession or a final court decision against an individual. The rule was not merely procedural but a substantive provision which effectively transferred full ownership, use and possession of the property. Retrospective legislation exempting the State from claims for compensation in respect of negligent acts for which it could have been liable has also been regarded as a deprivation.[52]

A.   Formal expropriation not required

P1/1–21   No formal act of expropriation is necessary for the deprivation rule to apply. Since the Convention is intended to safeguard rights which are practical and effective, the Court looks behind appearances and investigates the realities of each case. Absent a formal legal deprivation of title, a measure which amounts to *de facto* expropriation will nonetheless fall under the deprivation rule.[53]

P1/1–22   No *de facto* expropriation was found to have taken place in *Sporrong and Lönnroth v. Sweden*,[54] where the Government had issued expropriation

---

[50] See below, para. P1/1–27. But see *Hentrich v. France* (1994) 18 E.H.R.R. 440, where the exercise of a right of pre-emption in favour of the Commissioner of Revenue was treated as a deprivation even though it related to the levying and collection of taxes.

[51] (1995) 20 E.H.R.R. 1.

[52] *Pressos Compania Naviera S.A. & ors v. Belgium* (1996) 21 E.H.R.R. 301. Compare *Stran Greek Refineries & Stratis Andreadis v. Greece* (1995) 19 E.H.R.R. 293, where the cancellation of an arbitration award in favour of the applicants was regarded not as deprivation but as an interference falling within the first rule.

[53] *Sporrong and Lönnroth v. Sweden* (1982) 5 E.H.R.R. 35, para. 63.

[54] *ibid.*

permits—and issued prohibitions on construction—which remained in force for between 12 and 23 years without actually taking possession or ownership of the property; although the applicants' right of property had lost some of its substance, it did not disappear. Rent control legislation did not amount to a *de facto* expropriation either in *Mellacher v. Austria*[55]; there was no transfer of the applicants' property nor were they deprived of their right to use, let or sell it. *De facto* expropriation had, however, occurred in *Papamichalopoulos v. Greece*,[56] where under a law enacted in 1967 by the military government of the time, the Navy Fund took over possession of, but not title to, the applicants' land, the latter being unable either to make use of their property or to sell, bequeath, mortgage or make a gift of it. In the Court's view, "the loss of all ability to dispose of the land in issue, taken together with the failure of the attempts made so far to remedy the situation complained of, entailed sufficiently serious consequences for the applicants *de facto* to have been expropriated in a manner incompatible with their right to the peaceful enjoyment of their possessions".[57] The Commission and the Court also found that there was a *de facto* expropriation where a Commissioner of Revenue exercised a right of pre-emption where he considered that the applicant had bought a piece of land at under-value: exercise of the right of pre-emption had the effect of transferring ownership to the State.[58]

B. Temporary deprivation distinguished

P1/1–23 When it first considered the question of what constitutes a deprivation of property, in *Handyside v. United Kingdom*,[59] the Court clarified that a temporary deprivation of possessions does not infringe the second rule of Article 1, which protects against deprivations of ownership.[60] Accordingly, a deprivation of possessions must be first distinguished from measures of temporary interference in order to establish which rule in Article 1 applies. The following have not been considered to be deprivations: a provisional seizure of obscene publications[61]; the seizure of an aircraft subject to payment of money pursuant to a policy of preventing carriers bringing in, *inter alia*, prohibited drugs[62]; the provisional seizure and confiscation of the property of a defendant in criminal proceedings by way of preventive[63] or interim[64] measure; the provisional transfer of land under a consolidation plan[65]; and the operation of the procedures preliminary to expropriation, since they are not irreversible, they do not amount to expropriation.[66]

C. Withdrawal of a licence distinguished

P1/1–24 Deprivations of property must be also distinguished from other measures of a more permanent character, which do not however affect ownership

---

[55] (1990) 12 E.H.R.R. 391, para. 44.
[56] (1993) 16 E.H.R.R. 440, para. 43.
[57] *ibid.*, para. 45.
[58] *Hentrich v. France* (1994) 18 E.H.R.R. 440.
[59] (1976) 1 E.H.H.R. 737.
[60] *ibid.*, para. 62.
[61] *Handyside v. United Kingdom, loc. cit.*
[62] *Air Canada v. United Kingdom* (1995) 20 E.H.R.R. 150.
[63] *Raimondo v. Italy* (1994) 18 E.H.R.R. 237.
[64] *Venditelli v. Italy* (1995) 19 E.H.R.R. 465.
[65] *Erkner and Hofauer v. Austria* (1987) 9 E.H.R.R. 464, para. 74 and *Wiesinger v. Austria* (1993) 16 E.H.R.R. 258, para. 72.
[66] *Matos e Silva LDA & others v. Portugal*; September 16, 1996, R.J.D., 1996–IV, No. 14; 24 E.H.R.R. 573, para. 85. Compare *Papamichalopoulos v. Greece, loc. cit.*

rights. Withdrawals of licences to serve alcoholic drinks or to exploit gravel were not found to constitute deprivations of possessions in *Tre Traktorer Aktiebolag v. Sweden,*[67] and *Fredin v. Sweden.*[68] The findings reflect the non-proprietary character of the licence itself; the right interfered with in both cases was a more general one based on the economic interests connected with the running of a restaurant business in the first case and the exploitation of a gravel pit in the second.

D. Laws governing private law property relations distinguished

P1/1–25 A third category of measures which are distinguished from deprivations of property are laws governing private law relations between individuals which oblige one individual to surrender property to another. In *Bramelid and Malmstrom v. Sweden,*[69] for example, the Commission examined, under Article 1 of the First Protocol, Swedish legislation allowing for the compulsory purchase of a minority shareholding in a company by the majority shareholder. The Commission considered that the legislation in issue was in fact the expression and the application of a general policy with regard to the regulation of commercial companies and that, in enacting legislation of this type, the legislature was pursuing the general aim of reaching a system of regulation favourable to those interests which it regards as most worthy of protection. In this light, it concluded that it could not examine the applicants' complaints under the second rule of Article 1: the general aim of the legislation—the regulation of commercial companies—had nothing to do with the notion of the public interest as commonly understood in the field of expropriation.

P1/1–26 For the Commission this latter feature—in effect the difference between regulation and redistribution—was the distinguishing characteristic in *James v. United Kingdom.*[70] The Leasehold Reform Act, which afforded tenants of houses let on long leases the right to acquire the freehold or an extended lease on certain terms and conditions, went beyond the regulation of existing landlord/tenant relationships; it was a measure of social reform, to which the deprivation rule applied. Although the point was not contested before it, the Court concluded, without providing any explanation, that the applicants were deprived of their possessions.[71] In the light of this attitude of restraint on the part of the Court, it is probably safe to consider that the deprivation rule does not apply when "legislation governing private law relations between individuals . . . includes rules which determine the effects of these legal relations with respect to property and, in some cases, compel a person to surrender a possession to another": the division of inherited property and matrimonial estates, and the seizure of and sale of property in execution proceedings are examples of such rules expressly mentioned by the Commission.[72]

E. Deprivation as ancillary to control of use or taxation considered under the second paragraph of Article 1

P1/1–27 Deprivation of property will not be examined under the second rule of Article 1 where it forms a constituent element of a procedure for the control of the

---

[67] (1991) 13 E.H.R.R. 309.
[68] (1991) 13 E.H.R.R. 784, paras 42–47.
[69] (1986) 8 E.H.R.R. 116.
[70] (1986) 8 E.H.R.R. 123.
[71] (1986) 8 E.H.R.R. 123, para. 38.
[72] (1984) 6 E.H.R.R. 475, para. 100. See, however, *App. No. 11417/85 v. Sweden* (1986) 8 E.H.R.R. 106.

use of the property in question, i.e. a means of enforcing this control; or where the deprivation forms part of a system of taxation. In such cases, it will be examined under the second paragraph of Article 1 and not as a deprivation. In *AGOSI v. United Kingdom*,[73] for example, the Court considered under the third rule of Article 1 (on the control of the use of property) the forfeiture of gold coins illegally imported in the United Kingdom; and in *Handyside v. United Kingdom*,[74] the Court examined under the same rule the forfeiture and destruction of obscene publications, reasoning that "these measures were authorised by the second paragraph of Article 1 of Protocol No. 1, interpreted in the light of the principle of law, common to the contracting parties, whereunder items whose use has been lawfully adjudged illicit and dangerous to the general interest are forfeited with a view to destruction".[75] In *Gasus Dosier- und Fördertechnik GmbH v. Netherlands*,[76] the applicants complained of seizure by the tax authorities of goods which they owned under a retention of title clause, in order to meet the purchasers' tax debts. The Court considered the case under the second paragraph of Article 1 of the First Protocol on the basis that in essence the case concerned right of states to enact laws for the purpose of securing the payment of taxes.

F. Justifying deprivation

P1/1–28 Once a deprivation of property is found to have occurred, it is necessary to examine whether it was lawful, whether it was in the public interest, whether a reasonable or fair balance was struck between the public interest and individual rights and whether the general principles of international law were respected.

(1) Lawfulness

P1/1–29 The Court has ruled that the term "law" in Article 1 of the First Protocol, as in other provisions of the Convention, does not merely refer back to domestic law,[77] but relates also to the quality of law, requiring it to be compatible with the rule of law.[78] The Court has affirmed its competence to satisfy itself that the law is not arbitrary,[79] which entails that it should sufficiently satisfy the requirements of precision and foreseeability implied by the concept of law within the meaning of the Convention. In appropriate cases, the Court will also require that a proposed deprivation should be attended by procedural guarantees. Thus in a case concerning pre-emption by the tax authorities based on an allegation of sale at undervalue, the Court held that the decision could not be legitimate in the absence of adversarial proceedings that comply with the principle of equality of arms, enabling argument to be presented on the issue of the underestimation of the price and, consequently, on the Revenue's position.[80]

---

[73] (1987) 9 E.H.R.R. 1.
[74] (1976) 1 E.H.R.R. 737.
[75] *ibid.*, para. 63.
[76] (1995) 20 E.H.R.R. 403.
[77] Indeed the Court's power to review actual compliance with domestic law is very limited: see *Tre Traktörer Aktiebolag v. Sweden* (1991) 13 E.H.R.R. 309, para. 58; see further *Fredin v. Sweden* (1991) 13 E.H.R.R. 784, para. 50, and *Håkånsson and Sturesson v. Sweden* (1991) 13 E.H.R.R. 1, para. 47.
[78] *James v. United Kingdom* (1986) 8 E.H.R.R. 123, para. 67.
[79] *ibid.*
[80] *Hentrich v. France* (1994) 18 E.H.R.R. 440.

(2) Public interest

P1/1–30 The Strasbourg Court has allowed national authorities a wide margin of appreciation as regards the requirement that deprivation should be in the public interest[81]:

> "Because of their direct knowledge of their society and its needs, the national authorities are in principle better placed than the international judge to appreciate what is "in the public interest". Under the system of protection established by the Convention, it is thus for the national authorities to make the initial assessment both of the existence of a problem of public concern warranting measures of deprivation of property and of the remedial action to be taken. Here, as in other fields to which the safeguards of the Convention extend, the national authorities accordingly enjoy a certain margin of appreciation.
>
> Furthermore, the notion of 'public interest' is necessarily extensive. In particular, . . . , the decision to enact laws expropriating property will commonly involve consideration of political, economic and social issues on which opinions within a democratic society may reasonably differ. *The Court, finding it natural that the margin of appreciation available to the legislature in implementing social and economic policies should be a wide one, will respect the legislature's judgment as to what is 'in the public interest' unless that judgment be manifestly without reasonable foundation.* In other words, although the Court cannot substitute its own assessment for that of the national authorities, it is bound to review the contested measures under Article 1 of Protocol No. 1 and, in so doing, to make an inquiry into the facts with reference to which the national authorities acted."[82]

P1/1–31 Exercising this "rational basis" form of review, the Court so far accepted the following measures as being in the public interest: the promotion of the rationalisation in agriculture in a case concerning the compulsory resale after two years of an agricultural estate bought at a compulsory auction[83]; the prevention of illegal sales of land, encroachments on it or its abandonment or uncontrolled development in a case concerning the creation of a presumption of state ownership[84]; the need to protect the state's financial interests, to re-establish legal certainty in the field of tort and to bring legislation into line with that of neighbouring countries in the case of legislation exempting the state and other organisers of pilot services from their liability for negligent acts[85]; and the object of securing greater social justice in the sphere of ownership of peoples' homes in a case concerning leasehold reform.[86] In reaching the last conclusion the Court considered that a deprivation of property effected for no reason other than to confer a private benefit on a private party cannot be in the public interest.[87] However, the requirement that deprivation must be in the public interest does not

---

[81] As to the applicability of the margin of appreciation in the application of the HRA, see above para. 2–05.

[82] *James v. United Kingdom*, para. 46, emphasis added.

[83] *Håkansson and Sturesson v. Sweden* (1991) 13 E.H.R.R. 1, para. 44.

[84] *Holy Monasteries v. Greece* (1995) 20 E.H.R.R. 1.

[85] *Pressos Compania Naviera S.A. & ors v. Belgium* (1996) 21 E.H.R.R. 301.

[86] *James v. United Kingdom*, para. 47.

[87] *ibid.*, para. 40.

mean that the transferred property should be put into use for the general public or that of the community generally, or even a substantial proportion of it:

> "The taking of property in pursuance of a policy calculated to enhance social justice within the community can properly be described as being 'in the public interest'. In particular, the fairness of a system of law governing the contractual or property rights of private parties is a matter of public concern and therefore legislative measures intended to bring about such fairness are capable of being 'in the public interest', even if they involve the compulsory transfer of property from one individual to another."[88]

(3) Fair balance

P1/1–32 Pursuit of a legitimate goal does not in itself render a deprivation of property justifiable under the second rule of Article 1 of the First Protocol. "There must also be a reasonable relationship of proportionality between the means employed and the aim sought to be realised". A fair balance must be struck between the demands of the general interest of the community and the requirements of the protection of the individual's fundamental rights. The requisite balance will not be found if the person concerned has had to bear an individual and excessive burden.[89] The test which the Court has applied in this connection by the Court is not one of strict necessity. The Court will examine "whether the means chosen could be regarded as reasonable and suited to achieving the legitimate aim being pursued, having regard to the need to strike a "fair balance".[90] A number of factors have been taken into account in order to determine whether this balance has been struck. These are considered in the following paragraphs.

P1/1–33 The fact that alternative solutions are available does not in itself render a measure unjustified, since it is not for the Court to say whether the measure in question represented the best solution for dealing with the problem. However, it constitutes one fact, along with others, which is relevant to the question whether a fair balance has been struck.[91] Thus in *Hentrich v. France*,[92] the Court found a violation in respect of a right of pre-emption, the application of which was unsystematic and unforeseeable: in doing so it relied on the fact that the State had other suitable methods at its disposal for discouraging tax evasion, and it considered that the systematic use of legal proceedings to recover unpaid tax and, if necessary, the imposition of tax fines, "should be an adequate weapon".[93] The Court's attitude in that case was also influenced by the fact that the impugned system seemed to have no equivalent in any other state party to the Convention.

P1/1–34 Another element in the assessment of proportionality is the degree of protection from arbitrariness which is available to the subject of the deprivation. The fact that a deprivation measure is not applied systematically, and that its application is not foreseeable, will be relevant in this connection, as will the fact

---

[88] *ibid.*, para. 41.
[89] *ibid.*, para. 50.
[90] *ibid.*, para. 51.
[91] *ibid.* For a recent re-affirmation of this approach, see the Commission's decision in *Panikian v. Bulgaria* (1997) 24 E.H.R.R. CD 63.
[92] (1994) 18 E.H.R.R. 440.
[93] *ibid.*, para. 47.

that the decision whether to apply the measure to any particular transaction is taken solely for the purpose of deterring others from avoiding taxes.[94] The availability of procedural guarantees is important, and the fair balance may be upset if the individual has no possibility of effectively challenging the measure in issue[95]; for example, the Court found a violation in a case where the applicants' land was expropriated for the building of the road and a presumption that they would benefit from the proposed development prevented them from proving their alleged damage and asserting their right to full compensation before the domestic courts.[96]

P1/1–35   The availability of compensation is a key element in the Court's examination:

" . . . compensation terms are material to the assessment whether the contested legislation respects a fair balance between the various interests at stake and, notably, whether it does not impose a disproportionate burden on the applicants . . . [T]he taking of property without payment of an amount reasonably related to its value would normally constitute a disproportionate interference which could not be considered justifiable under Article 1. Article 1 does not, however, guarantee a right to full compensation in all circumstances. Legitimate objectives of 'public interest', such as pursued in measures of economic reform or measures designed to achieve greater social justice, may call for less than reimbursement of full market value".[97]

P1/1–36   States enjoy a wide margin of appreciation[98] in the choice of compensation terms and conditions, subject of course to European supervision.[99] In exercising its power of review the Court takes into account all the aspects of the case, but has often cast its findings in an unhelpfully *ad hoc* manner. In *James v. United Kingdom*, for example, the Court considered it justifiable that a landlord should be paid compensation in respect of the site but not of the buildings on the site, as the objective of the leasehold reform legislation was to prevent a perceived unjust enrichment accruing to him on reversion of the property. In *Lithgow v. United Kingdom* the Court upheld, taking into account a variety of considerations, the reasonableness of a valuation method which had in many cases resulted in wide divergences between the value of the companies on a vesting day and the compensation actually paid.

P1/1–37   However, the Court has put some limits on the wide margin of appreciation which states enjoy in the choice and method of calculation of compensation terms. Thus, although full compensation is not required,[1] "the taking of property without payment of an amount reasonably related to its value will normally constitute a disproportionate interference and total lack of compensation

---

[94] *ibid.*, para. 48.
[95] *ibid.*, para. 49.
[96] *Papachelas v. Greece*, judgment of March 25, 1999.
[97] *James v. United Kingdom* (1986) 8 E.H.R.R. 123, para. 54.
[98] As to the applicability of the margin of appreciation in the application of the HRA, see above, para. 2–05.
[99] *James v. United Kingdom*, para. 54, and *Lithgow v. United Kingdom* (1986) 8 E.H.R.R. 329, para. 122.
[1] For a recent case in which the Court accepted a method of calculation which was less than market value see *Papachelas v. Greece* Judgment of March 25, 1999.

can be considered justifiable under Article 1 only in exceptional circumstances".[2] In *Papamichalopoulos v. Greece*,[3] the Court found a violation as the Greek state, despite repeated attempts, had been unable to secure adequate compensation for the applicants whose property had been improperly taken away by the Navy Fund during the military dictatorship. In *Papachelas v. Greece*,[4] the fair balance was upset since the applicants were unable to argue that the road works for which their land had been taken had been of no benefit—or of less benefit—to them or had caused them varying degrees of loss.[5]

P1/1–38 Further, certain principles of a more general nature emerge from the case law on compensation. First, the standard of compensation required in a nationalisation case may be different from that required in regard to other takings of property, provided of course that a fair balance is struck between the individual and public interest.[6] Second, when examining whether a fair balance has been struck, the Court will not lose sight of the fact that there are certain cases which call for the adoption of uniform formulae for the assessment of compensation, for example the nationalisation of an entire industry and land expropriation implementing a programme of social and economic reform. Such schemes are not always capable of doing entire justice in the diverse circumstances of the very large number of different individuals concerned and this is something which the Court appears prepared to tolerate.[7] However, this principle appears to be inapplicable outside the fields of nationalisation and social reform, and in a recent judgment, the Court criticised a system for the assessment of the loss and damage caused to property owners adjoining a major road development: application of a presumption that the road was of economic benefit without the owners being able to present contrary argument was "too inflexible and takes no account of the diversity of situations, ignoring as it does the differences due in particular to the nature of the works and the layout of the site".[8]

(4) Respect for international law

P1/1–39 The fourth and final requirement of the second rule in Article 1 is that the general principles of public international law should be respected; and it applies only to the limited category of deprivations affecting the property of non-nationals. The general principles of international law were specifically developed for the benefit of non-nationals and provided for compensation for the expropriation of their property. In *James v. United Kingdom* the Court rejected the suggestion that Article 1 rendered them applicable to nationals as well:

> "[T]hose principles are incorporated into that Article, but only as regards those acts to which they are normally applicable, that is to say acts of a State in

---

[2] *Holy Monasteries v. Greece* (1995) 20 E.H.R.R. 1, para. 70.
[3] (1996) 21 E.H.R.R. 439.
[4] Judgment of March 25, 1999.
[5] See also *Guillemin v. France*, February 21, 1997, R.J.D., 1997–I, No. 29; 25 E.H.R.R. 435, which concerned an unlawful expropriation. Since the applicant's land had been sold on, compensation was the only available course to provide reparation for unlawful deprivation. The Court held that "Compensation for the loss sustained can only constitute adequate reparation where it also takes into account the damage arising from the length of the deprivation. It must moreover be paid within a reasonable time" (para. 54).
[6] *Lithgow v. United Kingdom* (1986) 8 E.H.R.R. 329, para. 121.
[7] *Lithgow v. United Kingdom*, para. 121 and *James v. United Kingdom* (1986) 8 E.H.R.R. 123, para. 68.
[8] *Papachelas v. Greece* judgment of March 25, 1999, para. 53.

relation to non-nationals. . . . [T]he words of a treaty should be understood to have their ordinary meaning, and to interpret the phrase in question as extending the general principles of international law beyond their normal sphere of applicability is less consistent with the ordinary meaning of the terms used, notwithstanding their context".[9]

There are several reasons for the incorporation of these principles in Article 1:

"Firstly, it enables non-nationals to resort directly to the machinery of the Convention to enforce their rights on the basis of the relevant principles of international law, whereas otherwise they would have to seek recourse to diplomatic channels or to other available means of dispute settlement to do so. Secondly, the reference ensures that the position of non-nationals is safe-guarded, in that it excludes any possible argument that the entry into force of Protocol No. 1 has led to a diminution of their rights".[10]

Moreover, there are a number of grounds for drawing a distinction between nationals and non-nationals in this field.

"[N]on-nationals are more vulnerable to domestic legislation: unlike nationals, they will have generally played no part in the election or designation of its authors nor have been consulted on its adoption. Secondly, although a taking of property must always be effected in the public interest, different considera-tions may apply to nationals and non-nationals and there may well be legitimate reason for requiring nationals to bear a greater burden in the public interest than non-nationals".[11]

5. WHAT CONSTITUTES A CONTROL OF THE USE OF PROPERTY UNDER ARTICLE 1 OF THE FIRST PROTOCOL AND WHICH CONTROLS ARE JUSTIFIED UNDER THE PROTOCOL?

A. Controls of use

P1/1–40   If an interference with the peaceful enjoyment of one's possessions does not amount to a deprivation, it must next be determined whether it constitutes a control of the use of property. Regrettably, the Court and the Commission have not formulated any general rules in accordance with which to address the issue. They have so far accepted the following as constituting controls on the use of property: the provisional seizure of the matrix and of copies of a book under the Obscene Publications Act 1959[12]; rent control[13]; suspension of eviction from residential property[14]; a prohibition on construction[15]; a zoning designation, but

---

[9] *James v. United Kingdom*, para. 61 of the judgment.
[10] *ibid.*, para. 62.
[11] *ibid.*, para. 63.
[12] *Handyside v. United Kingdom* (1979–80) 1 E.H.R.R. 737, para. 62.
[13] *Mellacher v. Austria* (1990) 12 E.H.R.R. 391, para. 44.
[14] *Spadea and Scalabrino v. Italy* (1996) 21 E.H.R.R. 482; *Scollo v. Italy* (1996) 22 E.H.R.R. 514.
[15] *Sporrong and Lönnroth v. Sweden*, para. 64 and *Allan Jacobsson v. Sweden* (1990) 12 E.H.R.R. 56, para. 54. But compare *Katte Klitsche de la Grange v. Italy* (1995) 19 E.H.R.R. 368: see below, para. P1/1–53.

not the decision refusing a building permit on the ground that it was contrary to the zoning[16]; the annulment of an outline planning permission[17]; the provisional seizure and confiscation of the property of a defendant in criminal proceedings by way of preventive[18] or interim[19] measure; the withdrawal of a licence to serve alcohol[20] or to exploit gravel[21]; retroactive tax measures to prevent tax-payers from obtaining an unintended windfall[22]; and the compulsory transfer of the hunting rights over land.[23] Refusal of a licence to carry on professional activities has also been regarded as a control of use which falls to be examined under the second paragraph of Article 1. Thus in *Van Marle v. Netherlands*, the refusal to register the applicants as certified accountants radically affected the professional activities which they had previously undertaken over a substantial period of time before the certification system was introduced and the scope of these activities was reduced. Their income fell, as did the value of their clientele and, more generally, their business. Consequently, the Court considered that they had been the subject of measures controlling the use of the possessions.[24]

P1/1–41   The Convention organs have also considered under the rule contained in the second paragraph of Article 1 (the third rule) forfeitures of property, the aim of which is to enforce controls on the use of this property, such as the seizure of items imported in contravention of a prohibition on importation[25]; and the seizure of an aircraft subject to payment of money pursuant to a policy of preventing carriers bringing in, *inter alia*, prohibited drugs.[26]

P1/1–42   An expropriation permit, however, which constituted an initial step in a procedure leading to a deprivation of possessions, was not considered to be a control on the use of property.[27] The same conclusion was reached in respect of a provisional transfer of property under a consolidation plan[28]; and in respect of a land-use plan imposing a development ban.[29]

B.   Justifying control of use

P1/1–43   In accordance with the third rule, a control on the use of property will be justified under the Protocol if it is lawful; if it has a legitimate aim, *i.e.* either if it is in accordance with the general interest or if it aims at securing the payment of taxes or other contributions or penalties; and if it is deemed necessary by the State.

---

[16] *Schertler v. Austria* (1996) E.H.R.R. CD 212.
[17] *Pine Valley Developments v. Ireland* (1992) 14 E.H.R.R. 319, para. 56.
[18] *Raimondo v. Italy* (1994) 18 E.H.R.R. 237.
[19] *Venditelli v. Italy* (1995) 19 E.H.R.R. 465.
[20] *Tre Traktörer Aktiebolag v. Sweden*, (1991) 13 E.H.R.R. 309, para. 55.
[21] *Fredin v. Sweden*, (1991) 13 E.H.R.R. 784, para. 47.
[22] *The National and Provincial Building Society & ors v. United Kingdom*, October 23, 1997, R.J.D., 1997–VII, No. 55; 25 E.H.R.R. 127.
[23] *Chassagnou and Others v. France* judgment of April 29, 1999.
[24] (1986) 8 E.H.R.R. 483 paras 42 and 43 of the judgment.
[25] *AGOSI v. United Kingdom* (1987) 9 E.H.R.R. 1, para. 51.
[26] *Air Canada v. United Kingdom* (1995) 20 E.H.R.R. 150.
[27] *Sporrong and Lönnroth v. Sweden*, para. 65. See also *Matos e Silva LDA and others v. Portugal* (1997) 24 E.H.R.R. 573.
[28] *Erkner and Hofauer v. Austria* (1987) 9 E.H.R.R. 464, para. 74; *Poiss v. Austria* (1988) 10 E.H.R.R. 231, para. 64 and *Wiesinger v. Austria* (1993) 16 E.H.R.R. 258, para. 72.
[29] *Katte Klitsche de la Grange v. Italy* (1995) 19 E.H.R.R. 368.

(1) Lawfulness

P1/1–44 The Court has exercised only a limited review of the legality of measures of control on the use of property, similar to that exercised in accordance with the second (deprivation) rule of Article 1.[30]

(2) Legitimate aim

P1/1–45 The Court has accepted the following as legitimate aims in the general interest under the second paragraph of Article 1: the protection of morals[31]; the structuring of a profession that is important to the entire economic sector[32]; reducing excessive and unjustified disparities between rents for equivalent flats and combating property speculation so that accommodation would be more easily made available at reasonable prices to less affluent members of the population, while at the same time providing incentives for the improvement of sub-standard properties[33]; protecting tenants from homelessness during a serious housing shortage[34]; facilitating town planning[35]; the protection of the environment[36]; avoiding unregulated hunting[37]; controlling the use of alcohol[38]; the preservation of evidence and prevention of aggravation of a suspected offence[39]; and combating international drug-trafficking.[40] In *Marckx v. Belgium*, the Court considered that the general interest may in certain cases induce a legislature to control the use of property in the area of dispositions *inter vivos* or by will,[41] and in *AGOSI v. United Kingdom*,[42] the Court found that a prohibition on the importation of Krugerrands was in the public interest, without providing any further explanation in either of the two cases.[43]

P1/1–46 The Court initially appeared inclined to exercise only limited review over the state's choice of measures of control. In *Handyside v. United Kingdom*, for example, it considered that the second paragraph of Article 1 "sets the Contracting States up as sole judges of the 'necessity' for an interference", with the Court restricting itself "to supervising the lawfulness and the purpose of the restriction in question".[44] However, its more recent decisions have not adopted this hands-off approach, and its attitude to measures falling within the second paragraph of

---

[30] *Fredin v. Sweden* (1991) 13 E.H.R.R. 784, para. 50, *Tre Traktörer Aktiebolag v. Sweden* (1991) 13 E.H.R.R. 309, para. 58 and *Allan Jacobsson v. Sweden* (1990) 12 E.H.R.R. 56, para. 57. A similar approach is adopted in relation to the requirement of lawfulness in the first (general) rule: *Iatridis v. Greece* judgment of March 25, 1999, para. 58. See further below, para. P1/1–58.

[31] *Handyside v. United Kingdom*, para. 62.

[32] *Van Marle v. Netherlands* (1986) 8 E.H.R.R. 483, para. 43.

[33] *Mellacher v. Austria* 12 E.H.R.R. 391, para. 47.

[34] *Spadea & Scalabrino v. Italy* (1995) 21 E.H.R.R. 482.

[35] *Allan Jacobsson v. Austria* 12 E.H.R.R. 56, para. 57.

[36] *Pine Valley Developments v. Ireland* 14 E.H.R.R. 319, para. 57; *Fredin v. Sweden* 13 E.H.R.R. 784, para. 48; *Matos e Silva LDA & ors v. Portugal*, September 16, 1996, R.J.D., 1996–IV, No. 14; 24 E.H.R.R. 573.

[37] *Chassagnou and Others v. France* judgment of April 29, 1999.

[38] *Tre Traktörer Aktiebolag v. Sweden* 13 E.H.R.R. 309, para. 57.

[39] *Venditelli v. Italy* (1995) 19 E.H.R.R. 465.

[40] *Air Canada v. United Kingdom* (1995) 20 E.H.R.R. 150.

[41] (1979) 2 E.H.R.R. 330, para. 64.

[42] (1987) 9 E.H.R.R. 1, para. 52.

[43] For cases concerning the payment of contributions see App. Nos 7995/77 *National Federation of Self-Employed v. United Kingdom* 15 D. & R. 198 and 15434/89 *Antoniades v. United Kingdom* 64 D. & R. 232.

[44] See para. 62 of the judgment; see also *Marckx v. Belgium* (1979–80) 2 E.H.R.R. 330, para. 64.

Article 1 is the same as it is in respect of the other rules in the Article. Thus in *AGOSI v. United Kingdom*, the Court expressly affirmed its power to review proportionality[45]; and in its more recent formulations the Court has no longer found it necessary to distinguish between the different parts of Article 1. In The *National and Provincial Building Society & ors v. United Kingdom*, the Court said that:

> "According to the Court's well-established case law, an interference, including one resulting from a measure to secure the payment of taxes, must strike a 'fair balance' between the demands of the general interest of the community and the requirements of the protection of the individual's rights. The concern to achieve this balance is reflected in the structure of Article 1 as a whole, including the second paragraph: there must therefore be a reasonable relationship of proportionality between the means employed and the aims pursued."[46]

In the same passage, however, the Court recognised that, in particular in framing and implementing policies in the area of taxation, the state enjoys a wide margin of appreciation "and the Court will respect the legislature's assessment in such matters unless it is devoid of reasonable foundation".[47] Again, the test employed is not that of strict necessity, as the Court appears to imply in *Mellacher v. Austria*:

> "The possible existence of alternative solutions does not in itself render the contested legislation unjustified. Provided that the legislature remains within the bounds of its margin of appreciation, it is not for the Court to say whether the legislation represented the best solution for dealing with the problem or whether the legislative discretion should have been exercised in another way".[48]

P1/1–47 In the light of the states' margin of appreciation, the Court has so far accepted as justified a wide variety of measures of control: the abolition of the right of unqualified accountants to practise as members of the newly regulated profession of "accountants" by a law which, however, enabled them to gain entry to the new profession on prescribed conditions[49]; lengthy building prohibitions under legislation which recognised the possibility of exemptions and provided for a regular examination of their necessity[50]; the withdrawal of a licence to serve alcoholic drinks following discovery of serious discrepancies in book-keeping[51]; the withdrawal of a licence to exploit gravel which could have been foreseen by the applicants at the time of making their investment[52]; the annulment of an outline planning permission with no compensation in a case where the applicants were aware of the zoning plan and of the opposition of the local authority to any departure from it[53]; the seizure and confiscation of real and movable property reasonably suspected of being the proceeds of organised crime, for the purpose of

---

[45] (1987) 9 E.H.R.R. 1, para. 52.
[46] (1998) 25 E.H.R.R. 127, para. 80.
[47] *ibid*. See also *Gasus Dosier- und Fördertechnik GmbH v. Netherlands* (1995) 20 E.H.R.R. 403, para. 60.
[48] See para. 53 of the judgment.
[49] *Van Marle v. Netherlands* (1986) 8 E.H.R.R. 483.
[50] *Allan Jacobsson v. Sweden* (1990) 12 E.H.R.R. 56.
[51] *Tre Traktörer Aktiebolag v. Sweden* (1991) 13 E.H.R.R. 309.
[52] *Fredin v. Sweden* (1991) 13 E.H.R.R. 784.
[53] *Pine Valley Developments v. Ireland* (1992) 14 E.H.R.R. 319.

ensuring that the Mafia could derive no benefit from them and that they would be available for permanent confiscation if necessary[54]; the seizure and retention of an aircraft against payment of a sum of £50,000 as a measure to secure an improvement in the carrier's security procedures in pursuance of a policy to prevent the importation of prohibited drugs[55]; the power of the tax authorities to maximise tax yields by recovering property in the possession of a tax debtor which is nominally owned by a third party under a retention of title clause[56]; suspension of evictions in order to prevent disorder and social tension which might be caused by the simultaneous eviction of a considerable number of tenants whose leases were expiring at or around the same time[57]; retrospective validation of tax regulations, extinguishing restitution claims, for the "obvious and compelling public interest to ensure that private entities do not enjoy the benefit of a windfall in a changeover to a new tax payment regime and do not deny the Exchequer revenue simply on account of defects in the tax enabling legislation . . . ".[58]

P1/1–48 Two cases in particular show the breadth of the state's freedom of action. In *Mellacher v. Austria* the Court accepted rent control legislation which resulted, in the particular cases, in rent reductions which were "striking in their amount". For the Court:

> "[I]n remedial social legislation and in particular in the field of rent control . . . it must be open for the legislature to take measures affecting the further execution of previously concluded contracts in order to attain the aim of the policy adopted."[59]

Moreover, "legislation instituting a system of rent control and aiming, *inter alia*, at establishing a standard of rent for equivalent apartments at an appropriate level must, perforce, be general in nature". It was therefore justifiable not to make the reductions of rent dependent on the specific situation of each tenant.[60] In this light and in the light of various safeguards provided for in the legislation, the Court decided that the interference was proportionate."[61]

P1/1–49 In *AGOSI v. United Kingdom*[61a], the Court considered it justifiable that the UK authorities had ordered the forfeiture of illegally imported goods which, however, belonged to someone other than the person from whose possession they

---

[54] *Raimondo v. Italy* (1994) 18 E.H.R.R. 237. However, once measures had been annulled, the fact that the measures remained on the public register amounted to an interference which was neither provided for by law nor necessary in the general interest: *ibid.*, para. 36. See also *Venditelli v. Italy* (1995) 19 E.H.R.R. 465.

[55] *Air Canada v. United Kingdom* (1995) 20 E.H.R.R. 150.

[56] *Gasus Dosier- und Fördertechnik GmbH v. Netherlands* (1995) 20 E.H.R.R. 403. The Court considered that the state might legitimately differentiate between retention of title and other forms of ownership since the "retaining" owner is not interested so much in retaining link of ownership with the goods as receiving the purchase price.

[57] *Spadea & Scalabrino v. Italy* (1996) 21 E.H.R.R. 482. The Court also took account of the fact that Italian law provided exemptions from the postponement provisions for landlords who urgently needed to recover their property or who were owed arreas of rent.

[58] *The National and Provincial Building Society & ors v. United Kingdom*, October 23, 1997, R.J.D., 1997-VII, No. 55; 25 E.H.R.R. 127, para. 81.

[59] (1990) 12 E.H.R.R. 391, para. 51.

[60] *ibid.*, para. 53.

[61] see also App. No. 15434/89 *Antoniades v. United Kingdom* 64 D. & R. 232.

[61a] (1987) 9 E.H.R.R. 1.

were forfeit. Although the Court considered that the authorities should have taken into account the behaviour of the owner of the property, including the degree of fault or care he had displayed, that was only one element of the entirety of circumstances. As the procedures available under domestic law had afforded the applicant company a reasonable opportunity of putting its case to the responsible authorities, the Court did not find that the forfeiture of the goods amounted to a disproportionate interference with the applicant company's possessions. The availability of effective judicial review now appears to be an important feature in deciding proportionality in other cases decided under the second paragraph of Article 1.[62]

6. WHAT OTHER MEASURES CONSTITUTE INTERFERENCE WITH THE RIGHT TO PEACEFUL ENJOYMENT OF ONE'S POSSESSIONS, AND IN WHAT CIRCUMSTANCES MAY THEY BE JUSTIFIED?

A. Interference with the right to peaceful enjoyment

P1/1–50   As we have already noted, deprivation of property and the control of its use are only particular instances of interference with the right to peaceful enjoyment of one's possessions. The Court and Commission have recognised, however, that Article 1 protects from forms of interference which fall within neither rule. The Convention institutions have examined first whether the measure in question falls within one of the specific rules and, if not, whether it nonetheless constitutes an interference with the applicant's property. The following paragraphs give examples of measures falling within the general rule.

(1)   Action prior to expropriation

P1/1–51   In *Sporrong and Lönnroth v. Sweden*, the Court considered that an expropriation permit, which recognised before the event that any expropriation would be lawful and authorised a local authority to expropriate when it found it expedient to do so, amounted to an interference with the applicants' right of property. Not only did the permit reduce significantly the possibility of exercising the owners' right to use and dispose of their property, but it also rendered the applicants' right of property precarious and defeasible.[63] Although such measures may leave intact the landowner's legal right to deal with and use the land, they greatly reduce their ability to do so in practice; and the advance recognition of the lawfulness of any future expropriation affects the very substance of ownership.[64]

(2)   Compulsory transfer of hunting rights

P1/1–52   "The compulsory transfer of the hunting rights over their land to [a municipal hunter's association] prevents them from making use of the right to

---

[62] See *Air Canada v. United Kingdom* (1995) 20 E.H.R.R. 150, para. 44, where the Court considered the adequacy of the grounds for judicial review and the possibility of obtaining reasons for the Commissioner's decision; see also *Gasus Dosier- und Fördertechnik GmbH v. Netherlands* (1995) 20 E.H.R.R. 403.

[63] (1983) 5 E.H.R.R. 35, para. 60. See, to similar effect, *Matos e Silva LDA & ors v. Portugal*; September 16, 1996, R.J.D., 1996–IV, No. 14; 24 E.H.R.R. 573.

[64] *Matos e Silva LDA & ors v. Portugal*, para. 79.

hunt, which is directly linked to the right of property, as they see fit. In the present case the applicants do not wish to hunt on their land and object to the fact that others may come onto their land to hunt. However, although opposed to hunting on ethical grounds, they are obliged to tolerate the presence of armed men and gun dogs on their land every year. This restriction on the free exercise of the right of use undoubtedly constitutes an interference with the applicants' enjoyment of their rights as the owners of property."[65]

(3) Land-use plans

P1/1–53 The adoption of a land use plan, like a structure plan, which imposes a development ban on land, has been held to interfere with a person's enjoyment of his possessions, while not amounting to a deprivation or control of use.[66]

(4) Land consolidation plans

P1/1–54 The provisional transfer of land under a land consolidation plan has also been considered an interference. The transfer could be made irrevocable only on the entry into force of a consolidation plan; nor was the provisional transfer designed to restrict or control the use of the land.[67]

(5) Regulation of private legal relations

P1/1–55 State rules as to the effects on property or legal relations between individuals will amount to an interference with the peaceful enjoyment of their possessions only if they create an imbalance between the parties which would arbitrarily and unjustly deprive one party of his or her goods for the benefit of another. An Act which in certain circumstances required minority shareholders to sell their shares at a price to be fixed by arbitration, while recognising their right to insist on their being purchased on the same conditions if they so wished, was held not to establish an excessive imbalance to the point of violating their right to peaceful enjoyment of possessions.[68]

(6) Other examples

P1/1–56 In *Van der Mussele v. Belgium* the Court considered that no interference with possessions had occurred in the case of non-reimbursement of the expenses of a pupil advocate who had been required to represent without payment a client in need of legal aid:

> "In many cases, a duty prescribed by law involves a certain outlay for the person bound to perform it. To regard the imposition of such a duty as constituting in itself an interference with possessions for the purposes of Article 1 of Protocol No. 1 would be giving the Article a far-reaching interpretation going beyond its object and purpose".[69]

P1/1–57 Legislation rendering an arbitration award against the state invalid and unenforceable, which made it impossible for the beneficiaries of the award to

---

[65] *Chassagnou v. France*, judgment of April 29, 1999, para. 74,
[66] *Katte Klitsche de la Grange v. Italy* (1995) 19 E.H.R.R. 368.
[67] *Erkner and Hofauer v. Austria* (1987) 9 E.H.R.R. 464, para. 74; *Poiss v. Austria* (1988) 10 E.H.R.R. 231, para. 62; *Wiesinger v. Austria* (1993) 16 E.H.R.R. 258.
[68] App. Nos 8588/79 and 8589/79 *Bramelid and Malmstrom v. Sweden* (1983) 5 E.H.R.R. 249.
[69] (1984) 6 E.H.R.R. 163, para. 49.

enforce it, was held to constitute an interference.[70] The proprietor of a cinema who was unlawfully evicted from a cinema and subsequently kept out of possession by the authorities' subsequent refusal give effect to the judicial decision quashing the eviction, was held to be the victim of an interference falling within the first sentence of Article 1; because he held only a lease of the business premises, this interference was held to be neither expropriation nor control of use.[71]

B. Justification

P1/1–58 When testing an interference against the first rule the Court applies the same tests as for the other rules. In the first instance, it will consider whether the interference is lawful. In *Iatridis v. Greece*,[72] where the authorities had failed to give effect to a judgment declaring the applicant's eviction unlawful, the Court considered it unnecessary to ascertain whether a fair balance had been struck since the interference was "manifestly in breach of Greek law".[73] The Court said that:

> " . . . the rule of law, one of the fundamental principles of a democratic society, is inherent in all the Articles of the Convention . . . and entails a duty on the part of the State or other public authority to comply with judicial orders or decisions against it . . . It follows that the issue of whether a fair balance has been struck between the demands of the general interest of the community and the requirements of the protection of the individual's funda-mental rights . . . becomes relevant only once it has been established that the interference in question satisfied the requirement of lawfulness and was not arbitrary."[74]

Once lawfulness is established, the legitimate aim and fair balance tests are applied.[75] Indeed, the Court first propounded the test in *Sporrong and Lönnroth v. Sweden*, a case concerning the first rule under Article 1.[76] As already seen, the test was subsequently extended in all other areas of Article 1. In *Sporrong and Lönnroth v. Sweden* the Court found that the prolonged extension of the expropriation permits and prohibition on construction upset this balance and imposed an excessive burden on the applicants which could have been rendered legitimate only if Swedish law had allowed the applicants to seek a reduction of the time-limits for expropriation or to claim compensation. Since no such remedies existed or were available to them, this amounted to a violation of Article 1 of the First Protocol. A similar conclusion was reached in two cases concerning the provisional transfer of land under a consolidation plan.[77] The relevant legislation provided no means, before the entry into force of a consolidation plan, by which affected landowners could alter their position or be compensated for damage they might have sustained in the time up to the final award of the statutory compensation in land. As a result the Court considered that the necessary balance between protection of the right to property and the requirements of the public interest was lacking.[78] Even though the

---

[70] *Stran Greek Refineries & Stratis Andreadis v. Greece* (1995) 19 E.H.R.R. 293. Compare *Pressos Compania Naviera S.A. & ors v. Belgium* (1996) 21 E.H.R.R. 301.
[71] *Iatridis v. Greece* judgment of March 25, 1999, para. 55.
[72] Judgment of March 25, 1999.
[73] *ibid.*, para. 62.
[74] *ibid.*, para. 58.
[75] See above, paras P1/1–28—P1/1–38 and P1/1–43—P1/1–49.
[76] See (1983) 5 E.H.R.R. 35, para. 69.
[77] *Erkner and Hofauer v. Austria* (1987) 9 E.H.R.R. 464 and *Poiss v. Austria* (1998) 10 E.H.R.R. 231.
[78] *cf. Wiesinger v. Austria* where the Court reached a different conclusion.

measures in issue pursue a legitimate public interest such as town and country planning for the purpose of protecting the environment, what the Court examines is the degree to which the measures in issue have hindered the ordinary enjoyment of the right to property, the length of time for which those measures have continued and, in appropriate cases, the effective availability of compensation within a reasonable time.[79] In *Chassagnou v. France*[80] the Court, again, found that there was no option available to the applicants to absolve them from the statutory obligation to transfer the hunting rights over their land. The Court, therefore, concluded that:

" . . . notwithstanding the legitimate aims of the Loi Verdeille when it was adopted, the Court considers that the result of the compulsory-transfer system which it lays down has been to place the applicants in a situation which upsets the fair balance to be struck between protection of the right of property and the requirements of the general interest. Compelling small landowners to transfer hunting rights over their land so that others can make use of them in a way which is totally incompatible with their beliefs imposes a disproportionate burden which is not justified under the second paragraph of Article 1 of Protocol No. 1."[81]

---

[79] See, for example, *Matos e Silva LDA & others v. Portugal* (1997) 24 E.H.R.R. 573.
[80] Judgment of April 29, 1999.
[81] *ibid.*, para. 85.

Article 2 Protocol 1
Right to Education

P1/2–01 No person shall be denied the right to education. In the exercise of any functions which it assumes in relation to education and to teaching, the State shall respect the right of parents to ensure such education and teaching in conformity with their own religious and philosophical convictions.

P1/2–02 Article 2 of the First Protocol is unusual in its formulation. Although it does refer to "rights", it is cast in distinctly negative terms: "no person shall be denied". Despite this negative formulation, "[t]here is . . . no doubt that Article 2 does enshrine a right".[1] However, the negative formulation of the provision is not without consequence. As the Court considered in the *Belgian Linguistic Case*,

> "[t]he negative formulation indicates that the Contracting Parties do not recognize such a right to education as would require them to establish at their own expense, or to subsidise, education of any particular type or at any particular level".[2]

The Court was quick to attribute this rather restrictive interpretation to certain realities which existed at the time of the adoption of the Protocol.

> "[A]ll member States of the Council of Europe possessed at the time of the opening of the Protocol to their signature, and still do possess, a general and official educational system. There neither was, nor is now, therefore, any question of requiring each State to establish such a system . . . ".[3]

The judgment of the Court allows, however, room for a more extensive interpretation in the unlikely event that a state party decides to dismantle its official educational system.

P1/2–03 Presently, however, Article 2 of the First Protocol guarantees "to persons subject to the jurisdiction of the Contracting Parties the right, in principle, to avail themselves of the means of instruction existing at a given time".[4]

P1/2–04 The right of access to educational institutions existing at a given time is only a part of the right guaranteed under Article 2. Another aspect of this right was discussed by the Court in the *Belgian Linguistic Case*:

> "For the right to education to be effective, it is further necessary that, *inter alia*, the individual who is the beneficiary should have the possibility of drawing profit from the education received, that is to say, the right to obtain, in conformity with the rules in force in each State, and in one form or another, official recognition of the studies which he has completed".[5]

---

[1] *Belgian Linguistic Case* (1968) 1 E.H.R.R. 252, s. 1.B of the judgment, para. 3.
[2] *ibid.*
[3] *ibid.*
[4] *Belgian Linguistic Case, ibid.* For a case where this right was violated see *Campbell and Cosans v. United Kingdom* (1982) 4 E.H.R.R. 293, para. 41.
[5] Section 1.B of the judgment, para. 4.

P1/2–05 However, the most important aspect of the right is guaranteed in the second sentence of Article 2 of the First Protocol which enjoins states "in the exercise of any functions which [they] assum[e] in relation to education and to teaching" to "respect the right of parents to ensure such education and teaching in conformity with their own religious and philosophical convictions".

P1/2–06 It would appear that Article 2 guarantees the right to establish private schools:

"Whilst they indisputably demonstrate . . . the importance attached by many members of the Consultative Assembly and a number of governments to freedom of teaching, that is to say, freedom to establish private schools, the 'travaux préparatoires' do not for all that reveal the intention to go no further than a guarantee of that freedom".[6]

P1/2–07 However, the scope of the second sentence of Article 2 is much broader:

"The second sentence of Article 2 aims in short at safeguarding the possibility of pluralism in education which possibility is essential for the preservation of the 'democratic society' as perceived by the Convention".[7]

P1/2–08 Pluralism means respect for the parents' religious and philosophical convictions, and the Court has devoted considerable attention in interpreting the latter concept. As it said in *Campbell and Cosans v. United Kingdom*:

"In its ordinary meaning the word 'convictions', taken on its own, is not synonymous with the words 'opinions' and 'ideas', such as are utilised in Article 10 of the Convention, which guarantees freedom of expression; it is more akin to the term 'beliefs' . . . appearing in Article 9—which guarantees freedom of thought, conscience and religion—and denotes views that attain a certain level of cogency, seriousness, cohesion and importance.
As regards the adjective 'philosophical', it is not capable of exhaustive definition and little assistance as to its precise significance is to be gleaned from the *travaux préparatoires*. The Commission pointed out that the word 'philosophy' bears numerous meanings: it is used to allude to a fully-fledged system of thought, or rather loosely, to views on more or less trivial matters. The Court agrees with the Commission that neither of these two extremes can be adopted for the purposes of interpreting Article 2: the former would too narrowly restrict the scope of a right that is guaranteed to all parents and the latter might result in the inclusion of matters of insufficient weight or substance".[8]

P1/2–09 Article 2, however, refers only to "such convictions as are worthy of respect in a 'democratic society' and are not incompatible with human dignity. In addition they must not conflict with the fundamental right of the child to education, the whole of Article 2 being dominated by its first sentence".[9]

---

[6] *Kjeldsen, Busk Madsen and Pedersen v. Denmark* (1976) 1 E.H.R.R. 711, para. 50.
[7] *ibid.*
[8] (1982) 4 E.H.R.R. 293, para. 36. see also *Valsamis v. Greece*, December 18, 1996, R.J.D., 1996–VI, No. 27; 24 E.H.R.R. 294, para. 25 and *Efstratiou v. Greece*, judgment of December 18, 1996.
[9] *ibid.*

P1/2–10 In determining whether membership of the Jehovah's Witnesses amounts to "religious or philosophical convictions" protected by Article 2, the Court in *Valsamis v. Greece* reiterated what it had said in *Kjeldsen, Busk Madsen and Pedersen v. Denmark,* namely that "the two sentences of Article 2 [of Protocol No. 1] must be read not only in the light of each other but also, in particular, of Articles 8, 9 and 10 of the Convention".[10] The Court went on to look at its Article 9 jurisprudence on Jehovah's Witnesses[11] in order to conclude that they are entitled to rely on the right to respect for their religious convictions within the meaning of Article 2.

P1/2–11 The Court has so far accepted as "philosophical convictions" for the purposes of Article 2 parents' views on sex education[12] and corporal punishment.[13] In connection with the latter the Court observed the following:

"The applicants' views relate to a weighty and substantial aspect of human life and behaviour, namely the integrity of the person, the propriety or otherwise of the infliction of corporal punishment and the exclusion of the distress which the risk of such punishment entails. They are views which satisfy each of the various criteria listed above; it is this that distinguishes them from opinions that might be held on other methods of discipline or on discipline in general".[14]

P1/2–12 The Commission, on the other hand, has so far skilfully avoided the issue of whether parents' various opinions constitute "philosophical beliefs" by insisting that Article 2 does not guarantee an absolute right to have children educated in accordance with the philosophical convictions of the parents but a right to respect for these convictions.[15] This interpretation is to a large degree borne out by the approach of the Court in *Kjeldsen, Busk Madsen and Pedersen v. Denmark.*[16] In *Valsamis v. Greece,* the Court said that "respect" means more than "acknowledge" or "take into account". "In addition to a primarily negative undertaking, it implies some positive obligations on the part of the State",[17] with a balance to be struck which ensures proper treatment of minorities and avoids any abuse of a dominant position.

P1/2–13 However, the terms of Article 2 impose certain limits on the interpretation of the term "philosophical convictions". Parents' linguistic preferences, for example, do not have to be respected. "[T]he object of the second sentence of Article 2 was in no way to secure respect by the State of a right for parents to have education conducted in a language other than that of the country in question".[18]

P1/2–14 What is the extent of the obligations that the second sentence of Article 2 entails for states parties? In accordance with the letter of the provision,

---

[10] December 18, 1996, R.J.D., 1996–VI, No. 27; 24 E.H.R.R. 294, para. 25.
[11] *Kokkinakis v. Greece* (1994) 17 E.H.R.R. 397.
[12] *Kjeldsen, Busk Madsen and Pedersen v. Denmark,* 1 E.H.R.R. 711.
[13] *Campbell and Cosans v. United Kingdom* (1982) 4 E.H.R.R. 293.
[14] *Campbell and Cosans v. United Kingdom,* para. 36.
[15] *App. Nos 7527/76 v. United Kingdom* 11 D. & R. 147, *8811/79 v. Sweden* 29 D. & R. 104, *9461/81 v. United Kingdom* 31 D. & R. 210 and *10233/83 v. United Kingdom* 37 D. & R. 105.
[16] para. 53.
[17] *Valsamis v. Greece,* December 18, 1996, R.J.D., 1996–VI, No. 27; 24 E.H.R.R. 294, para. 27, referring to its *Campbell and Cosans* judgment, para. 37.
[18] *Belgian Linguistic Case,* section 1B of the judgment, para. 6.

states must respect the rights it guarantees for parents "in the exercise of any functions which [they] assum[e] in relation to education and to teaching". We shall see that the effects of this qualification are in fact minimal. Thus, in *Kjeldsen, Busk Madsen and Pedersen v. Denmark* the Court considered that:

> "[t]he second sentence of Article 2 is binding upon the Contracting States in the exercise of each and every function that they undertake in education and teaching . . ."[19]

P1/2–15 Building on these findings the Court observed in *Campbell and Cosans v. United Kingdom*, that:

> "the education of children is the whole process whereby, in any society, adults endeavour to transmit their beliefs, culture and other values to the young, whereas teaching or instruction refers in particular to the transmission of knowledge and to intellectual development."[20]

P1/2–16 It appears to the Court somewhat artificial to attempt to separate matters relating to internal administration as if all such matters fall outside the scope of Article 2. The use of corporal punishment may, in a sense, be said to belong to the internal administration of a school, but at the same time it is, when used, an integral part of the process whereby a school seeks to achieve the object for which it was established, including the development and moulding of the character and mental powers of its pupils.[21] Moreover, as the Court pointed out in *Kjeldsen, Busk Madsen and Pedersen*, the second sentence of Article 2 is binding upon the Contracting States in the exercise of "each and every function that they undertake in education and teaching, so that the fact that a given function may be considered to be ancillary is of no moment in this context".[22]

P1/2–17 The state is bound by the obligations in the second sentence of Article 2 even when the education in question is provided in private schools. Thus although the case of *Costello-Roberts v. United Kingdom* concerned corporal punishment in a private school, the Court pointed out that the obligation to secure the right to education rests with the state, that the right is guaranteed equally to pupils in state and independent schools, and that the state cannot absolve itself from responsibility by delegating its functions.[23] Although the Court accepted that an application could be brought against the state in this connection and although it held expressly that corporal punishment in private schools could amount to a violation of Article 3 or 8, it still is still open to question whether Article 2 of the First Protocol would be violated, if the parents had the option of sending their children to a state school where no corporal punishment was administered.

P1/2–18 The final but most fundamental issue to be addressed in this connection is what measures the state should take to ensure compliance with the second

---

[19] Para. 50.
[20] (1982) 4 E.H.R.R. 293, para. 33 of the judgment.
[21] *Campbell and Cosans*, para. 33; *Valsamis v. Greece*, December 18, 1996, R.J.D., 1996–VI, No. 27; 24 E.H.R.R. 294, para. 29.
[22] Para. 33 of the judgment. To similar effect see *Valsamis v. Greece*, December 18, 1996, R.J.D., 1996–VI, No. 27; 24 E.H.R.R. 294, paras 27 and 28.
[23] (1995) 19 E.H.R.R. 112, para. 27.

sentence of Article 2. The issue was addressed extensively in *Kjeldsen, Busk Madsen and Pedersen v. Denmark*. Article 2 does not imply solely the right for parents to have their children exempted from classes offering religious instruction of a denominational character:

"it enjoins States to respect parents' convictions, be they religious or philosophical, throughout the entire State education programme".[24]

However:

"the setting and planning of the curriculum fall in principle within the competence of the Contracting States. This mainly involves questions of expediency on which it is not for the Court to rule and whose solution may legitimately vary according to the country and the era. In particular the second sentence of Article 2 of the Protocol does not prevent States from imparting through teaching or education information or knowledge of a directly or indirectly religious or philosophical kind. It does not even permit parents to object to the integration of such teaching or education in the school curriculum, for otherwise all institutionalised teaching would run the risk of proving impracticable. In fact, it seems very difficult for many subjects taught at school not to have, to a greater or lesser extent, some philosophical complexion or implications. The same is true of religious affinities if one remembers the existence of religions forming a very dogmatic and moral entity which has or may have answers to every question of a philosophical, cosmological or moral nature.
The second sentence of Article 2 implies on the other hand that the State, in fulfilling the functions assumed by it in regard to education and teaching, must take care that information or knowledge included in the curriculum is conveyed in an objective, critical and pluralistic manner. The State is forbidden to pursue an aim of indoctrination that might be considered as not respecting parents' religious and philosophical convictions. That is the limit that must not be exceeded".[25]

P1/2–19   In examining whether this delicate balance is observed the Court will concentrate on state teaching. However, although the aim of pluralism must be realised above all through this medium, the granting of assistance to private schools must be also taken into account.[26] In this light, and although the Court has never expressly said so, it could be argued that subsidising private education may be mandatory under the Convention, if the religious and philosophical conviction of a category of parents are not respected within the state system of education.[27]

---

[24] see para. 51.
[25] *ibid.*, para. 53.
[26] *Kjeldsen, Busk Madsen and Pedersen v. Denmark*, para. 50.
[27] See *App. No. 7782/77 v. United Kingdom*. For a series of cases concerning the education of handicapped children, see *App. Nos 10233/83 v. United Kingdom*.

Article 3 Protocol 1
Right to free elections

P1/3–01 The High Contracting Parties undertake to hold free elections at reasonable intervals by secret ballot, under conditions which will ensure the free expression of the opinion of the people in the choice of the legislature.

P1/3–02 Article 3 of the First Protocol is a key provision for the human rights system established under the European Convention. "Since it enshrines a characteristic principle of democracy, Article 3 of Protocol No. 1 is accordingly of prime importance in the Convention system".[1]

P1/3–03 Article 3 is not cast in the usual "rights" terms. However, as observed by the Court in the first judgment it gave under the provision:

" . . . the inter-State colouring of the wording of Article 3 does not reflect any difference of substance from the other substantive clauses in the Convention and Protocols. The reason for it would seem to lie rather in the desire to give greater solemnity to the commitment undertaken and in the fact that the primary obligation in the field concerned is not one of abstention or non-interference as with the majority of the civil and political rights, but one of adoption by the State of positive measures to 'hold' democratic elections".[2]

The provision guarantees, accordingly, subjective rights of participation, the right to vote and the right to stand for election to the legislature.[3]

P1/3–04 These rights, however, are not absolute:

"Since Article 3 recognises them without setting them forth in express terms, let alone defining them, there is room for implied limitations. In their internal legal orders the Contracting States make the rights to vote and stand for election subject to conditions which are not in principle precluded under Article 3. They have a wide margin of appreciation in this sphere, but it is for the Court to determine in the last resort whether the requirements of Protocol No. 1 have been complied with; it has to satisfy itself that the conditions do not curtail the rights in question to such an extent as to impair their very essence and deprive them of their effectiveness; that they are imposed in pursuit of a legitimate aim; and that the means employed are not disproportionate. In particular, such conditions must not thwart 'the free expression of the opinion of the people in the choice of the legislature'."[4]

P1/3–05 The Commission has so far pronounced that restrictions on the right to vote may be imposed, in certain circumstances, on convicted persons serving their sentence[5] and people residing abroad.[6] It has also accepted the imposition of a minimum age requirement for those wishing to stand for election.[7]

---

[1] *Mathieu-Mohin and Clerfayt v. Belgium* (1988) 10 E.H.R.R. 1, para. 47.
[2] *ibid.*, para. 50.
[3] *ibid.*, para. 51.
[4] *ibid.*, para. 52; see also *Gitonas v. Greece*, July 1, 1997, R.J.D., 1997–IV, No. 42; 26 E.H.R.R. 691, para. 39.
[5] *App. Nos 2728/66 v. Germany* 10 Yb 336 and *9914/82 v. Netherlands* 33 D. & R. 242.
[6] *App. Nos 7566/76 v. United Kingdom* 9 D. & R. 121, *7730/76 v. United Kingdom* 15 D. & R. 137 and *8612/79 Alliance Des Belges De La Communaute Europeenne v. Belgium* 15 D. & R. 259.
[7] *App. No. 6745/76 v. Belgium* 18 Yb 236. For a rather unusual limitation on the right to stand for election see *App. No. 10316/83 v. United Kingdom*, 37 D. & R. 129.

P1/3–06 Article 3 of the First Protocol guarantees the right to vote and the right to stand for election to the "legislature", or at least one of its chambers if it has two or more.[8] In its ordinary meaning, the word "legislature" does not necessarily mean only the national parliament; it has to be interpreted in the light of the constitutional structure of each state.[9] The apparent intention of the Court is to allow for a wide range of constitutional arrangements.[10] These arrangements must, however, respect the characteristic principle of democracy enshrined in Article 3 of the First Protocol. It must be assumed that the assignment of extensive law-making powers to non-elective bodies could put this principle in jeopardy.

P1/3–07 Until very recently, the Commission and Court had left open the issue whether the European Parliament can be considered as a "legislature" for the purposes of Article 3.[11] Thus in *Ahmed and others v. United Kingdom*, the Court, in finding no violation of Article 3, did so "without taking a stand on whether local authority elections or elections to the European Parliament are covered by Article 3 of Protocol No. 1".[12] Finally, in *Matthews v. United Kingdom*, the Court had to tackle the issue of elections to the European Parliament under Article 3 head on. The Commission had held that to include the European Parliament would extend the scope of Article 3 beyond what was intended and beyond the object and purpose of Article 3. The Court disagreed:

> "The mere fact that a body was not envisaged by the drafters of the Convention cannot prevent that body from falling within the scope of the Convention. To the extent that Contracting States organise common constitutional or parliamentary structures by international treaties, the Court must take these mutually agreed structural changes into account in interpreting the Convention and its Protocols."[13]

P1/3–08 Referring to, *inter alia*, the precedence of EC law over (conflicting) domestic law, the Court concluded that to exclude the European Parliament from the protection of Article 3 "would risk undermining one of the fundamental tools by which 'effective political democracy' can be maintained."[14]

P1/3–09 In relation to the question of whether the European Parliament is a "legislature" the Court held:

> " . . . whatever its limitations, the European Parliament, which derives democratic legitimation from the direct elections by universal suffrage, must be seen as that part of the European Community structure which best reflects concerns as to 'effective political democracy'."[15]

P1/3–10 As regards the method of appointment of the "legislature", Article 3 provides for free elections at reasonable intervals, by secret ballot and under

---

[8] *Mathieu-Mohin and Clerfayt v. Belgium* (1998) 10 E.H.R.R. 1, para. 53; see also App. No. 15344/89 *Habsburg-Lothringen v. Austria* 64 D. & R. 210 where the Commission held that Article 3 does not apply in connection with the appointment of the head of state.

[9] *Mathieu-Mohin and Clerfayt v. Belgium*, para. 53.

[10] See further *App. Nos 5155/71 v. United Kingdom* 6 D. & R. 13, *8873/80 v. United Kingdom* 28 D. & R. 99 and *9926/82 v. Netherlands* 32 D. & R. 274.

[11] See, *inter alia*, App. No. 8364/78 *Lindsay v. United Kingdom* 15 D. & R. 247 and *Téte v. France* (1987) 54 D. & R. 52.

[12] Judgment of September 2, 1998, para. 76. See further the discussion under Article 10.

[13] (1999) 28 E.H.R.R. 361, para. 39.

[14] *ibid.*, para. 43.

[15] *ibid.*, para. 52. See also, in relation to Article 16, *Piermont v. France* (1995) 20 E.H.R.R. 301.

conditions which will ensure the free expression of the opinion of the people. "Subject to that, it does not create any 'obligation to introduce a specific system' such as proportional representation or majority voting with one or two ballots".[16] As a matter of fact states are accorded, in this connection, a wide margin of appreciation for the following reasons:

> "Electoral systems seek to fulfil objectives which are sometimes scarcely compatible with each other; on the one hand, to reflect fairly faithfully the opinions of the people, and on the other, to channel currents of thought so as to promote the emergence of a sufficiently clear and coherent political will. In these circumstances the phrase 'under conditions which will ensure the free expression of the opinion of the people in the choice of legislature' implies essentially . . . the principle of equality of treatment of all citizens in the exercise of their right to vote and their right to stand for election.
> It does not follow, however, that all votes must necessarily have equal weight as regards the outcome of the election or that all candidates must have equal chances of victory. Thus no electoral system can eliminate 'wasted votes'."[17]

P1/3–11 The general position of the Court on this issue is the following:

> "For the purposes of Article 3 of Protocol No. 1, any electoral system must be assessed in the light of the political evolution of the country concerned; features that would be unacceptable in the context of one system may accordingly be justified in the context of another, at least so long as the chosen system provides for conditions which will ensure the 'free expression of the opinion of the people in the choice of the legislature'."[18]

P1/3–12 These general considerations are reflected in the outcome both of *Mathieu-Mohin and Clerfayt v. Belgium* and of a series of cases examined by the Commission.[19]

P1/3–13 More recently, the Court, on a number of occasions, had to address the issue of the disqualification of civil/public servants from standing for election. In *Gitonas v. Greece*, the Court held that:

> " . . . the States enjoy considerable latitude to establish in their constitutional order rules governing the status of parliamentarians, including criteria for disqualification. Though originating from a common concern—ensuring the independence of members of parliament, but also the electorate's freedom of choice—the criteria vary according to the historical and political factors peculiar to each State. The number of situations provided for in the constitutions and legislation on elections in many member States of the Council of Europe shows the diversity of possible choice on this subject. None of these criteria should, however, be considered more valid than any other provided that it guarantees the expression of the will of the people through free, fair and regular elections."[20]

---

[16] *Mathieu-Mohin and Clerfayt v. Belgium*, para. 54.
[17] *ibid.*
[18] *ibid.*
[19] *App. Nos 7140/75 v. United Kingdom* 7 D. & R. 95; 8364/78 *Lindsay v. United Kingdom* 15 D. & R. 247 and 8765/78 *Liberal Party v. United Kingdom* 21 D. & R. 211.
[20] *Gitonas v. Greece* (1998) 26 E.H.R.R. 691, para. 39.

P1/3–14 In *Gitonas* the Court found no violation of Article 3. Under the Greek Constitution, holders of public office (including salaried public servants and members of staff of public-law entities and public undertakings) are excluded from standing for election in any constituency where they have performed their duties for more than three months in the last three years. In effect this meant that an individual had to resign his position 33 months or more before an election in order to be entitled to stand.

P1/3–15 In *Ahmed et al. v. United Kingdom*,[21] the Court was faced with a challenge to the restrictions on the involvement of senior local government officers in political activities imposed by the Local Government and Housing Act 1989 and the Local Government Officers (Political Restrictions) Regulations 1990. Reiterating its previous jurisprudence, the Court, unanimously, concluded that there had been no violation of Article 3.

P1/3–16 Dealing with the issue under Article 10, the Commission and the Court have recognised the legitimacy in principle of restrictions on electoral expenditure aimed at keeping candidates on an equal footing. However, in *Bowman v. United Kingdom* they held to be disproportionate a restriction on the distribution, by an independent third party, of leaflets informing the electorate of candidates' views on single issues (abortion and human embryo experimentation). In the Commission's opinion, "individual freedom of expression, as a key ingredient of a democratic society, must be considered inextricably linked with a free election system and cannot be excluded without convincing justification".[22] The Court emphasised that:

> "Free elections and freedom of expression, particularly freedom of political debate, together form the bedrock of any democratic system. The two rights are interrelated and operate to reinforce each other: as the Court has observed in the past, freedom of expression is one of the 'conditions' necessary to 'ensure the free expression of the opinion of the people in the choice of the legislature'. For this reason it is particularly important in the period preceding an election that opinions and information of all kinds are permitted to circulate freely."

Certain restrictions on freedom of speech may nonetheless be justified during elections in the interest of guaranteeing equality between candidates.

P1/3–17 No attempt has been made in the Convention organs' case law to link the guarantee of Article 3 of the First Protocol with the requirement of "lawfulness" which appears in a series of Convention articles allowing for limitations of the rights they guarantee, in the sense that the "laws" providing for such limitations must have been adopted or approved by a "legislature" elected in accordance with Article 3.

---

[21] Judgment of September 2, 1998.
[22] *Bouman v. United Kingdom* (1998) 26 E.H.R.R. 1, para. 46 of the Commission's Report.

Article 15

Derogation in time of emergency

C15–01

1 In time of war or other public emergency threatening the life of the nation any High Contracting Party may take measures derogating from its obligations under this Convention to the extent strictly required by the exigencies of the situation, provided that such measures are not inconsistent with its other obligations under international law.

2 No derogation from Article 2, except in respect of deaths resulting from lawful acts of war, or from Articles 3, 4 (paragraph 1) and 7 shall be made under this provision.

3 Any High Contracting Party availing itself of this right of derogation shall keep the Secretary General of the Council of Europe fully informed of the measures which it has taken and the reasons therefor. It shall also inform the Secretary General of the Council of Europe when such measures have ceased to operate and the provisions of the Convention are again being fully executed.

C15–02 Article 15 permits a state party to derogate, in times of national emergency, from observance of most of the rights enshrined in the Convention, although the second paragraph lists certain Convention rights from which no derogation is permissible. The provision contains both substantive and procedural requirements which a state must fulfil before it can legitimately invoke Article 15 as a basis for derogation.

C15–03 Although Article 15 is not mentioned in section 1(1) of the Act, section 1(2) provides that the Convention rights are to have effect subject to any designated derogation, to which sections 14 and 15 refer. The fact that the Act provides that the Convention rights are to have effect subject to any designated derogation entitles domestic courts to review the legitimacy of any claimed derogation. The courts will therefore be able to investigate whether the state of affairs giving rise to the derogation fulfils the criteria of Article 15. As with other areas of review, the Strasbourg margin of appreciation does not apply in the same way to exclude or limit the domestic court's power of review. So much is clear from the reference in *Ireland v. United Kingdom* to the national "authorities'" (including the national courts') direct and continuous contact with the pressing needs of the moment.[1]

C15–04 While there has been relatively little case law concerning Article 15, the cases have examined at some length both the substantive and procedural requirements of a valid derogation.

1. Substantive requirements

C15–05 For a derogation to be valid Article 15 requires, first, that a public emergency exist in a country, secondly, that any measures taken to deal with it are strictly required by the exigencies of the situation, thirdly, that any such measures

---

[1] 2 E.H.R.R. 25, para. 207.

are not inconsistent with the state's other obligations under international law and, fourthly, that they do not involve a derogation from the rights qualified as non-derogable in Article 15(2) or other equivalent provisions.

A. Existence of a public emergency threatening the life of the nation

C15–06 The case law indicates with sufficient clarity the conditions which must exist within a country before a state can invoke Article 15 to justify derogation from the Convention rights. In its judgment in the important case of *Lawless v. Ireland*, the Court declared that a public emergency threatening the life of the nation is an "exceptional situation of crisis or emergency which affects the whole population and constitutes a threat to the organised life of the community of which the State is composed".[2]

C15–07 In the *Greek* Case, the Commission identified four separate requirements in the definition given by the Court in *Lawless*:

(a) the public emergency must be actual or imminent;

(b) its effects must involve the whole nation;

(c) the continuance of the organised life of the community must be threatened; and

(d) the crisis or danger must be exceptional, in that the normal measures or restrictions permitted by the Convention for the maintenance of public safety, health and order, are plainly inadequate.[3]

Requirement (b) may be in need of some refinement, in the light of the judgment of the Court in *Ireland v. United Kingdom*, where the derogation applied only to Northern Ireland and *Sakik and Others v. Turkey*,[4] where the Court rejected the Government's submission that it should be able to rely on a derogation outside the particular part of its territory in respect of which it was made. The submission was made on the basis that the facts of the case constituted only the prolongation of a terrorist campaign being conducted from inside the area where the state of emergency had been proclaimed, in south-east Turkey, and in fact the terrorist threat was not confined to any particular part of Turkish territory. The Court preferred to take a strict view of the construction of derogations, refusing to extend them beyond their express terms.

C15–08 In determining whether the "public emergency" requirement is met in a given case the Convention institutions have afforded states a considerable margin of appreciation:

"It falls in the first place to each Contracting State, with its responsibility for 'the life of [its] nation', to determine whether that life is threatened by a 'public emergency' . . . By reason of their direct and continuous contact with the pressing needs of the moment, the national authorities are in principle in a better position than the international judge to decide . . . on the presence of

---

[2] (1961) 1 E.H.R.R. 15, para. 28.
[3] 12 Yb 1, para. 153.
[4] November 26, 1997, R.J.D., 1997–III, No. 58; 26 E.H.R.R. 662.

such an emergency . . . In this matter, Article 15(1) leaves those authorities a wide margin of appreciation".[5]

C15–09   Naturally, the domestic margin of appreciation is not unlimited. The Court makes its own assessment in the light of all the material before it[6]; and it gives "appropriate weight to such relevant factors as the nature of the rights affected by the derogation, the circumstances leading to, and the duration of, the emergency situation".[7]

C15–10   However, in the vast majority of the circumstances the Convention organs have not questioned a democratic government's opinion as to the actual existence of a public emergency. Thus, having engaged in a detailed review of the question in *Lawless v. Ireland*, in *Ireland v. United Kingdom* the Court deferred to the agreement of the parties as the existence of an emergency in Northern Ireland.[8] In doing so, the Court appears to have disregarded the requirement that the emergency must be one threatening the life of the whole nation.[9] Moreover, in *Brannigan and McBride v. United Kingdom* the Court accepted at face value the respondent Government's assertion that a public emergency requiring a derogation from Article 5(3) existed in Northern Ireland and elsewhere in the United Kingdom, presumably since 1974 when the contested legislation was effectively introduced, despite the withdrawal in 1984 of an earlier Article 15 derogation by the United Kingdom. The Court appeared to attach great importance to the fact that the respondent Government genuinely believed at the time of the withdrawal of the earlier derogation that section 12(1)(s) of the Prevention of Terrorism Act, which suspended the normal requirement to bring the accused before a court not later than 48 hours after his arrest, complied with Article 5(3); when this legislation was subsequently found in *Brogan and others v. United Kingdom*[10] to be in violation of the Convention, the Government considered that its only option was to re-introduce its Article 15 derogation in order to ensure the survival of section 12(1)(s) which it believed to be "strictly required by the exigencies of the situation".

C15–11   It was only in the *Greek* case that a Convention organ reached a different conclusion than the respondent Government as to the existence of an emergency situation under Article 15. The Commission's more assertive stance must be attributed to the particular circumstances of the case. This was the only case where a Convention organ was confronted with an attempt by an non-democratically elected government to introduce emergency measures in order to consolidate its rule.

B. The measures taken are strictly required by the exigencies of the situation

C15–12   The Convention institutions have equally afforded states a comparatively broad margin of appreciation when addressing the issue whether the

---

[5] *Ireland v. United Kingdom* 2 E.H.R.R. 25, para. 207.
[6] *Brannigan and McBride v. United Kingdom* (1994) 17 E.H.R.R. 539.
[7] *ibid.*, para. 43.
[8] See para. 205.
[9] *cf. Lawless v. Ireland, supra.*
[10] (1988) 11 E.H.R.R. 117.

measures taken are strictly required by the exigencies of the situation.[11] The Convention organs equally exercise a certain measure of European supervision.[12]

C15–13   It is important to note that the Court, when examining whether the measures taken are strictly required, will not substitute its own assessment of what measures would have been desirable. As it observed in *Ireland v. United Kingdom*:

> "[t]he Court must do no more than review the lawfulness, under the Convention, of the measures adopted by that Government . . . For this purpose the Court must arrive at its decision in the light, not of a purely retrospective examination of the efficacy of those measures, but of the conditions and circumstances reigning when they were originally taken and subsequently applied".[13]

C15–14   The emphasis appears to be on allowing the state a certain flexibility to operate in difficult and unpredictable circumstances, if necessary through the progressive establishment of sufficient safeguards which will ensure the proportionality of the measures taken under Article 15. As observed by the Court in *Ireland v. United Kingdom*:

> "[w]hen a State is struggling against a public emergency threatening the life of the nation, it would be rendered defenceless if it were required to accomplish everything at once, to furnish from the outset each of its chosen means of action with each of the safeguards reconcilable with the priority requirements for the proper functioning of the authorities and for restoring peace within the community. The interpretation of Article 15 must leave a place for progressive adaptations".[14]

C15–15   In the light of these observations, the Court has considered justifiable far-reaching measures, such as arrests for the sole purpose of obtaining information about the activities of others, stressing, however, the very exceptional character of the situation.[15] It has also accepted lengthy periods of administrative detention in the course of which the right to have access to a court with power to review the reasonableness of the suspicion, in accordance with Article 5(4), was suspended, but in respect of which the respondent Government had gradually built alternative administrative guarantees.

C15–16   The scope of the review of the Convention organs is not identical in every case. In exercising this supervision, they:

> " . . . give appropriate weight to such relevant factors as the nature of the rights affected by the derogation, the circumstances leading to, and the duration of, the emergency situation".[16]

---

[11] *Ireland v. United Kingdom* (1978) 2 E.H.R.R. 25, para. 207.
[12] *ibid.*
[13] 2 E.H.R.R. 25, para. 214.
[14] See para. 220 of the judgment. See further, para. 54.
[15] *Ireland v. United Kingdom*, para. 212.
[16] *Brannigan and McBride v. United Kingdom* (1994) 17 E.H.R.R. 539, para. 54.

C15–17 Thus, in the *Greek* case the Commission, addressing a purely theoretical question, considered that, even if an emergency had existed, the measures introduced by the Government would not have been strictly required under Article 15. The circumstances leading to their introduction, *i.e.* imposition of martial law by a military government in violation of the Constitution, must have coloured the Commission's findings. Moreover, in *Brannigan and McBride v. United Kingdom,* the Court's emphasis on alternative safeguards was much more pronounced than in the earlier *Ireland v. United Kingdom* case. In this case Court appeared to base its finding of non-violation on the availability of habeas corpus proceedings, in accordance with Article 5(4). The unavailability, however, of a similar safeguard in *Ireland v. United Kingdom* did not lead to a finding of violation. The more stringent standard of review in *Brannigan and McBride* is explicable partly by the fact that the only purpose of the United Kingdom's notice of derogation was to preserve anti-terrorist legislation already found in violation of Article 5(3), which had been introduced in respect of a lasting emergency situation. However, the Court has adopted the *Brannigan* test in its judgment in *Aksoy v. Turkey*,[17] requiring that measures derogating from the right to liberty should nonetheless be accompanied by sufficient safeguards against abuse. Thus in *Aksoy*, the Court held that it was "not persuaded that the exigencies of the situation necessitated the holding of the applicant on suspicion of involvement in terrorist offences for 14 days or more in incommunicado detention without access to a judge or judicial officer".[18]

C. Compliance with other obligations under international law

C15–18 This requirement has not played an important part in the case law of either the Court or Commission. In the cases of *Lawless* and *Ireland v. United Kingdom* the Court found no evidence that this requirement had been infringed. In *Brannigan and McBride v. United Kingdom* the Court addressed the issue whether the emergency relied on by the respondent Government had been "officially proclaimed", in accordance with Article 4 of the United Nations International Covenant on Civil and Political Rights 1966, which the United Kingdom had ratified. A statement in the House of Commons was considered to have satisfied the requirement.[19]

D. Non-derogable rights

C15–19 Article 15(2) lists certain provisions in the Convention from which no derogation is permissible:

- *Article 2* which guarantees the right to life; note, however, that there is a limited derogation to allow for deaths resulting from lawful acts of war; note, moreover, that Article 2 itself permits "action lawfully taken for the purpose of quelling a riot or insurrection" and the death penalty following conviction and sentence. While the Sixth Protocol, to which the Act gives effect, abolishes the death penalty, Article 2 preserves it "in respect of acts committed in time of war or of imminent threat of war". Notably, however, it does not extend to cases of "other public emergency" to which Article 15 applies.

---

[17] December 18, 1996, R.J.D., 1996–IV, No. 26; 23 E.H.R.R. 553.
[18] *ibid.*, para. 84.
[19] See paras 72–73 of the judgment.

- *Article 3* which prohibits torture or inhuman or degrading treatment or punishment.

- *Article 4(1)*, which guarantees the right to freedom from slavery or servitude; although states are permitted to derogate from the prohibition of forced or compulsory labour, guaranteed under Article 4(2).

- *Article 7* which guarantees the right not to subjected to the retroactive application of criminal laws and penalties.

C15–20   Article 4(3) of Protocol No. 7 has added one more non-derogable right to the list, the right to freedom from double jeopardy as defined in the first and second paragraphs of this provision.

2. PROCEDURAL REQUIREMENTS UNDER ARTICLE 15

C15–21   Although Article 15 of the Convention does not require expressly, as the Covenant does, that the emergency situation be "officially proclaimed", the Commission has held that some formal and public act of derogation is necessary, unless the state is prevented from doing so.[20] A notice of derogation must be addressed to the Secretary-General of the Council of Europe in accordance with Article 15(3), "without delay".[21] The purpose of the notice is to inform the Secretary-General of the measures taken and the reasons therefor. It does not appear that the Convention organs are particularly demanding as regards the extent of the reasoning required.[22] Moreover, it has been held that the Convention contains no obligation for a state to promulgate in its territory the notice of derogation addressed to the Secretary-General.

C15–22   The Convention organs have on several occasions left open the question of the consequences of a failure of the state to notify the Secretary-General of a public emergency in accordance with Article 15(3).[23] In *Aksoy v. Turkey*, the Court asserted that it was competent to examine of its own motion whether a notice of derogation complied with the formal requirements of Article 15(3), " . . . and in particular whether [it] contained sufficient information about the measure in question . . . to satisfy the requirements of Article 15(3)".[24] From this use of language, and on a reasonable construction of *Brogan and others v. United Kingdom* and *Brannigan and McBride v. United Kingdom* it would appear that failure to notify properly would preclude a state party from relying on the existence of an emergency situation to escape a finding of violation in litigation before the Convention organs.[25]

C15–23   In the *Brogan* case the Court had to examine whether section 12(1)(s) of the Prevention of Terrorism Act violated Article 5(3). The Court considered that

---

[20] *Cyprus v. Turkey (No. 1)* (1976) 4 E.H.R.R. 482, para. 527; see further *Brannigan and Mcbride v. United Kingdom* (1994) 17 E.H.R.R. 539.
[21] *Lawless v. Ireland (No. 3)* 1 E.H.R.R. 15, para. 47.
[22] *ibid.*
[23] See *Lawless v. Ireland*, Commission's Opinion, Ser. B, para. 80 and *Cyprus v. Turkey (No. 1)*, (1976) 4 E.H.R.R. 482, para. 526.
[24] (1997) 23 E.H.R.R. 533, paras 85 and 86.
[25] See also *Cyprus v. Turkey (No. 1)* where the respondent state's failure to issue a formal and public act of derogation internally was held to have such an effect.

there was "no call in the present proceedings to consider whether any derogations from the United Kingdom's obligations under the Covenant might be permissible under Article 15" in view of an earlier withdrawal of a notice of derogation which had relied on an emergency in Northern Ireland.[26] (Note,however, that the notice of derogation did not concern the legislation in question.) It then went on to find a violation of Article 5(3). The United Kingdom did not repeal the offending legislation, considering it a necessary instrument in its fight against terrorism. Instead, it submitted to the Secretary-General a new notice of derogation. The derogation was challenged in *Brannigan and McBride*. Although there was no evidence that the situation in Northern Ireland had deteriorated to a significant degree in the intervening period, the Court considered that a public emergency did exist and that the derogation from Article 5(3) was strictly required. The implications for *Brogan* are clear: the Court was prevented in that case from taking into consideration an emergency situation which did exist, due to the absence of a duly notified derogation act under Article 15(3).

C15–24 The importance of the notice of derogation under Article 15(3) is paramount. As it has been stressed by the Commission in a statement it submitted to the Court in the *Lawless* case:

" . . . the obligations to inform the Secretary-General of a measure derogating from the Convention is an essential link in the machinery provided in the Convention for the ensuring the observance of the engagements of the High Contracting Parties in the Convention. Without such information, the other parties to the Convention will not know their position under Article 24 of the Convention. Without such information the Commission itself will be unaware of facts which for the time being may radically affect the extent of its own jurisdiction to entertain applications either from States or from individuals with respect to the acts of the State in question . . . it is impossible to foresee all the possible circumstances in which a government may fail to comply with the requirements of paragraph 3; a government might, for example, deliberately withhold information from the Secretary-General in order not to attract attention to controversial measures".[27]

---

[26] *Brogan and others v. United Kingdom* (1988) 11 E.H.R.R. 117, para. 48.
[27] See Series B, pp. 335–336.

ARTICLE 16

RESTRICTIONS ON POLITICAL ACTIVITY OF ALIENS

C16–01   Nothing in Articles 10, 11 and 14 shall be regarded as preventing the High Contracting Parties from imposing restrictions on the political activity of aliens.

C16–02   The fact that Article 16 has been considered by the Court only once during the lifetime of the Convention system gives some indication of the limited importance of this provision.

C16–03   By its very terms, Article 16 purports to limit only Articles 10, 11 and 14, and it applies to only "political activities". To the extent that aliens may enjoy the right to participate in political activities under any other provision of the Convention, states must justify any restriction by reference to the ordinary limitation clauses in those other provisions.

C16–04   Secondly, the provision does not define political activities; does it include or exclude trade union activities? It is submitted that the provision should be construed strictly and that the reference to Article 11 should be limited to rights of freedom of assembly and association only to the extent that they impinge directly on politics narrowly defined.

C16–05   Thirdly, it is submitted that the provision does not exclude Article 14 altogether: Article 16 means simply that the prohibition, in Article 14, of discrimination *on the ground of nationality* does not prevent restrictions on the political activities of aliens. However, it does not legitimise discrimination on other grounds, for example race, religion or colour, which may have the practical effect of restricting the political activities of aliens. Despite the word "nothing" in Article 16, this narrower construction may be more appropriate for a limitation clause. Additionally, Article 18 remains applicable and may itself prohibit excessive restrictions. It must also be open to question to what extent Article 16 allows discrimination between different classes of aliens. Such discrimination would, it is submitted, still have to be objectively justified.

C16–06   The only guidance—and that is of limited application—is to be found in *Piermont v. France*[1] which concerned a German M.E.P. who visited French Polynesia in February 1986 and took part in pro-independence and anti-nuclear demonstrations. The authorities made an order expelling Polynesia and excluding her from New Caledonia with the aim of prevention of disorder, and territorial integrity. The French Government raised Article 16. The majority of the Commission (who found a violation of Article 10 by eight votes to six) apparently regarded Article 16 as something of an anachronism, which accepted at a time when the general unlimited restriction of the political activities of aliens was considered to be legitimate.[2] However, applying the "living instrument" doctrine,[3] in particular given the evolution of Community law and the role of the European Parliament,

---

[1] (1995) 20 E.H.R.R. 301.
[2] *ibid.*, para. 58 of the Report.
[3] See above, para. C0–08.

the majority concluded that that since the applicant was acting as an M.E.P. she could not be regarded as an "alien" within the meaning of Article 16.[4]

C16–07   The Court was also divided on the import of Article 16, finding a violation by five votes to four. The majority held that it could not:

" . . . accept the [applicant's] argument based on European citizenship, since the Community treaties did not at the time recognise any such citizenship. Nevertheless it considers that Mrs Piermont's possession of nationality of a Member State of the European Union and, in addition, her status as a member of the European Parliament do not allow Article 16 of the Convention to be raised against her, especially as the people of the OTs take part in European Parliament elections."[5]

C16–08   Reasoning for this conclusion is rather thin on the ground. The most reasoned basis in principle is to be found in the minority opinions of Mr Danelius and others in the Commission and Judge Ryssdal and others in the Court. They seek to ascribe some place to Article 16 while not allowing states an unfettered discretion:

"Account must be taken of the increased internationalisation of politics in modern circumstances, and, so far as the present case in particular is concerned, of the interest which nowadays an MEP may legitimately have in the affairs of a Community territory. In the light of these developments, limits may have to be admitted to the restrictions on the political activity of aliens permissible under Article 16. With this in mind, and having regard to the approach adopted by the Court in its *Groppera Radio AG and Others* judgment to the interpretation of the third sentence of paragraph 1 of Article 10, we would accept that the object and purpose of Article 16 should, like that sentence, be examined in the context of paragraph 2 of Article 10. In particular, when the proportionality of the interference with Mrs Piermont's freedom of expression is under consideration, account should be taken of the principle embodied in Article 16."[6]

In the light of Article 16, the minority did not regard the interference as disproportionate.

C16–09   *Piermont* related to events which took place before Community law recognised the concept of citizenship of the European Union, and it seems likely that this development will make a significant difference to the approach to Article 16 in the European Union context.[7] However, in view of the strong prohibition of discrimination on grounds of nationality under EC law, in particular EC Treaty Article 12, it is likely that any disputes will be first considered in the framework of EC law including the various association agreements before the Convention becomes relevant. In these circumstances the dearth of Article 16 cases may continue.

---

[4] (1995) 20 E.H.R.R. 301, para. 69.
[5] *ibid.*, para. 64 of the judgment.
[6] *ibid.*, para. 5 of the joint partly dissenting judgment, at p. 346.
[7] See *Matthews v. United Kingdom* (1999) 28 E.H.R.R. 361.

ARTICLE 17

PROHIBITION OF ABUSE OF RIGHTS

C17–01   Nothing in this Convention may be interpreted as implying for any State, group or person any right to engage in any activity or perform any act aimed at the destruction of any of the rights and freedoms set forth herein or at their limitation to a greater extent than is provided for in the Convention.

C17–02   Article 17 is another provision which has to date received little direct consideration at the level of the Court, although it has been referred to directly or by implication. Unlike other Convention provisions, it is addressed to the activities of both the individual and the state. However, the injunction addressed to the state appears to be circular *i.e.* that nothing in the Convention empowers the state to limit Convention rights to a greater extent than provided for in the Convention—and seems to add little if anything to the principles of necessity and proportionality which form such an important part in the reasoning of the Convention institutions.

C17–03   The Commission has summed up the effect on individuals and non-governmental organisations in the following passage:

> "The general purpose of Article 17 is to prevent totalitarian groups from exploiting in their own interests the principles enunciated by the Convention. To achieve that purpose, it is not necessary to take away every one of the rights and freedoms guaranteed from persons found to be engaged in activities aimed at the destruction of any of the rights and freedoms. Article 17 covers essentially those rights which, if invoked, will facilitate the attempt to derive therefrom a right to engage personally in activities aimed at the destruction of any of the rights and freedoms set forth in the Convention."[1]

Glimmerveen and Hagenbeek were members of a Dutch political party which advocated repatriation of "undesired aliens" and "so-called guest workers". They had been convicted for distributing leaflets found to contain incitement to racial discrimination; they had also been barred from standing in a municipal election; they alleged breaches of Article 10 and Protocol No. 1, Article 3. The Commission dismissed the complaints as incompatible with the Convention, holding that by reason of Article 17 the applicants could not rely on those provisions. The Commission followed this decision in 1988 in rejecting the complaint of a journalist who had been sentenced to three years and four months imprisonment for breach of the German Penal Code through Neo-Nazi propaganda and agitation.[2] The Court endorsed the Commission's *Glimmerveen* decision in its judgment in *Jersild v. Denmark* when it confirmed that racist remarks which were "more than insulting to members of the targeted groups did not enjoy the protection of Article 10".[3] In its most recent decision, the Commission appears to have approached Article 17 as providing an additional justification for interference with the applicant's Convention rights rather than imposing an absolute bar to his or her

---

[1] App. Nos 8348 & 8406/78 *Glimmerveen & Hagenbeek v. Netherlands* (1979) 4 E.H.R.R. 260 at 267, para. 16 of the admissibility decision.
[2] App. No. 12194/86 *Kuhnen v. Germany* 56 D. & R. 205.
[3] (1994) 19 E.H.R.R. 1, para. 35 of the judgment.

complaint. So in *Ochsenberger v. Austria*,[4] where the applicant had been convicted for National Socialist activities, and for writing, editing, publishing and distributing articles inciting readers to racial hatred, anti-Semitism and xenophobia, the Commission referred to Article 17 and found that the applicant was seeking to use Article 10 as a means of destroying rights protected by the Convention, but held that the convictions were justified under Article 10(2).

C17–04   In practice, Article 17 has been largely concerned with applications brought in respect of measures restricting the dissemination of racist propaganda, an area in which states have been allowed considerable discretion. Indeed, in *Jersild v. Denmark*, the Court emphasised that it was "particularly conscious of the vital importance of combating racial discrimination in all its forms and manifestations" (paragraph 30 of the judgment) and of the need to interpret the Convention "to the extent possible" so as to be reconcilable with the objects of the UN Convention on the Elimination of All Forms of Racial Discrimination.[5] On the other hand the rights of those whose views are unpopular must be protected and Article 17's potential field of application must be carefully defined. The following paragraphs outline three important limitations on the applicability of Article 17.

C17–05   **Freedom of expression applies to ideas that shock or disturb and is especially important in the political sphere and for opposition politicians.** The Court has repeatedly emphasised the importance to be attached to the right to freedom of expression, in particular where politicians and journalists are concerned. See, for example *Castells v. Spain*.[6] Accordingly the expression of unpopular, shocking or offensive opinions has to be tolerated. It is only where that expression threatens to undermine or destroy the rights of others that Article 17 has any place. But even where freedom of expression may violate the rights of others, the Convention institutions have preferred to rely on Article 10(2) rather than Article 17, since this enables them more easily to assess questions of proportionality. See, for example, *Otto-Preminger Institute v. Austria*,[7] where seizure of a film offending religious sensibilities was held to be a proportionate interference with freedom of expression.

C17–06   **Article 17 does not operate so as to deprive members of "totalitarian groups" of all their rights under the Convention; it only applies to rights and freedoms which are being actively used to interfere with the rights of others under the Convention.** This point is mentioned in the passage from the Commission's report in *Glimmerveen*, quoted above. It was established in the very first case decided by the Court.[8] Article 17 did not operate so as to deprive Lawless, a suspected IRA member, of his rights under Article 5 and 6 of the Convention; the Government had to justify its actions by derogation under Article 15. Article 17 is likely to be applied only to Article 10 and 11 of the Convention and to Article 3 of Protocol No. 1. While its application to certain other provisions cannot be excluded (*e.g.*, public manifestations of belief under Article 9), Article 17 is manifestly inapplicable to some Convention provisions, for example Article 3.

---

[4] (1994) 18 E.H.R.R. CD 170.
[5] (1994) 19 E.H.R.R. 1 para. 30. See above, para. C10–29.
[6] (1992) 14 E.H.R.R. 445. See above, para. C10–06.
[7] (1994) 19 E.H.R.R. 34. See above, para. C10–28.
[8] *Lawless v. Ireland* (No. 3) 1 E.H.R.R. 15, paras 4–7.

C17–07   **Proportionality and Article 17.**   Even when it is applicable, Article 17 justifies only limitations of rights and freedoms which are necessary to prevent acts aimed at the destruction of Convention rights and freedoms. Its application is subject to a test of proportionality. This point is well-illustrated in the Commission's report in *De Becker v. Belgium*.[9] De Becker had collaborated during the war by acting as the editor of the newspaper *Le Soir*; he was originally sentenced to death, then reprieved but subjected to a life-long ban on publishing. The Commission took the view that Article 17 could not justify this measure and found a breach of Article 10:

> "Article 17 is of a somewhat limited scope; it applies only to persons who threaten the democratic system of the Contracting States and then only to an extent strictly proportionate to the seriousness and duration of such a threat, as is confirmed by Article 18. Accordingly Article 17 cannot be used to deprive an individual of his rights and freedoms permanently merely because at some given moment he displayed totalitarian convictions."[10]

As there was no evidence that De Becker sought freedom to publish in order to propagate pro-Nazi views, the Commission considered Article 17 inapplicable and found a violation of Article 10. Belgium reformed its law while the case was pending before the Court and the case was therefore struck out before judgment on the merits.[11] Accordingly, the Commission's analysis remains authoritative.

---

[9] (1961) Series B, No. 4.
[10] *ibid.*, paragraph 279 of the Commission's Report.
[11] See 1 E.H.R.R. 43.

ARTICLE 18

LIMITATION ON USE OF RESTRICTIONS ON RIGHTS

C18–01   The restrictions permitted under this Convention to the said rights and freedoms shall not be applied for any purpose other than those for which they have been prescribed.

C18–02   Like Article 14, this provision has no independent existence, in the sense that there can be no breach of Article 18 by itself: it can be violated only in conjunction with another provision of the Convention, and indeed only one which expressly authorises a state to impose restrictions on Convention rights. The provision has been of virtually no practical effect, in view of the overwhelming evidential difficulties which applicants have faced in convincing the Convention institutions that a state has interfered with Convention rights other than for reasons authorised by the Convention.

C18–03   The Strasbourg institutions have concentrated primarily on whether the state has justified the pleaded interference by reference to one of the authorised restrictions. In doing so, they have sometimes referred to Article 18 as supporting the proposition that the concept of "lawfulness" (or likewise "in prescribed by/in accordance with the law") presuppose conformity with the purposes of the permitted restrictions.[1] But where the Commission or Court has found a violation of a substantive provision, it has considered it unnecessary to consider Article 18 as well.[2] However, this exercise in judicial economy may be misplaced in cases where the applicant seeks to aggravate the seriousness of the violation by showing that the state has been acting in bad faith.[3]

Where an interference has been found to be justified, it remains open to the applicant—in theory at least—to argue that the justification advanced by the state is in fact not the real justification for the interference. In practice, no applicant has ever succeeded in convincing the Convention institutions of such an argument, even in the most serious of cases. For example, in *Akdivar v. Turkey*[4] and *Mentes v. Turkey*,[5] the Commission found the allegations of abuse of power unsubstantiated, and the Court confined itself to adopting the Commission's finding.[6]

---

[1] See, for example, *Ashingdane v. United Kingdom* (1985) 7 E.H.R.R. 528, para. 44.
[2] See, for example *United Communist Party of Turkey and others v. Turkey* (1998) 26 E.H.R.R. 121; *Lukanov v. Bulgaria* (1997) 24 E.H.R.R. 121; *Sporrong & Lönnroth v. Sweden* (1983) 5 E.H,R.R. 35.
[3] Where a practice in breach of the Convention is found, the violation is to be considered as much more serious: *Ireland v. United Kingdom*, Report of the Commission dated January 25, 1976, part II.A.3(c).
[4] (1997) 23 E.H.R.R. 143.
[5] (1998) 26 E.H.R.R. 595.
[6] See also *Engel and others v. Netherlands* 1 E.H.R.R. 647; *Handyside v. United Kingdom* 1 E.H.R.R. 737.

PART III

Appendices

APPENDIX I

Human Rights Act 1998

1998 CHAPTER 42

ARRANGEMENT OF SECTIONS

Introduction

12. Freedom of expression.

13. Freedom of thought, conscience and religion.

Derogations and reservations

14. Derogations.

15. Reservations.

16. Period for which designated derogations have effect.

17. Periodic review of designated reservations.

Judges of the European Court of Human Rights

18. Appointment to European Court of Human Rights

Parliamentary procedure

19. Statements of compatibility.

Supplemental

20. Orders etc. under this Act.

21. Interpretation, etc.

22. Short title, commencement, application and extent.

SCHEDULES
    Schedule 1 – The Articles.
        Part I – The Convention.
        Part II – The First Protocol.
        Part III – The Sixth Protocol.
    Schedule 2 – Remedial Orders.
    Schedule 3 – Derogation and Reservation.
        Part I – Derogation.
        Part II – Reservation.
    Schedule 4 – Judicial Pensions.

An Act to give further effect to rights and freedoms guaranteed under the European Convention on Human Rights; to make provision with respect to holders of certain judicial offices who become judges of the European Court of Human Rights; and for connected purposes.

[9th November 1998]

BE IT ENACTED by the Queen's most Excellent Majesty, by and with the advice and consent of the Lords Spiritual and Temporal, and Commons, in this present Parliament assembled, and by the authority of the same, as follows:-

Introduction

The Convention Rights.
   1.–(1)
In this Act "the Convention rights" means the rights and fundamental freedoms set out in-

    (a) Articles 2 to 12 and 14 of the Convention,

    (b) Articles 1 to 3 of the First Protocol, and

    (c) Articles 1 and 2 of the Sixth Protocol,

as read with Articles 16 to 18 of the Convention.

(2) Those Articles are to have effect for the purposes of this Act subject to any designated derogation or reservation (as to which see sections 14 and 15).

(3) The Articles are set out in Schedule 1.

(4) The Secretary of State may by order make such amendments to this Act as he considers appropriate to reflect the effect, in relation to the United Kingdom, of a protocol.

(5) In subsection (4) "protocol" means a protocol to the Convention-

    (a) which the United Kingdom has ratified; or

    (b) which the United Kingdom has signed with a view to ratification.

(6) No amendment may be made by an order under subsection (4) so as to come into force before the protocol concerned is in force in relation to the United Kingdom.

Interpretation of Convention rights.
   2.–(1) A court or tribunal determining a question which has arisen in connection with a Convention right must take into account any-

    (a) judgment, decision, declaration or advisory opinion of the European Court of Human Rights,

    (b) opinion of the Commission given in a report adopted under Article 31 of the Convention,

    (c) decision of the Commission in connection with Article 26 or 27(2) of the Convention, or

    (d) decision of the Committee of Ministers taken under Article 46 of the Convention,

whenever made or given, so far as, in the opinion of the court or tribunal, it is relevant to the proceedings in which that question has arisen.

(2) Evidence of any judgment, decision, declaration or opinion of which account may have to be taken under this section is to be given in proceedings before any court or tribunal in such manner as may be provided by rules.

(3) In this section "rules" means rules of court or, in the case of proceedings before a tribunal, rules made for the purposes of this section-

    (a) by the Lord Chancellor or the Secretary of State, in relation to any proceedings outside Scotland;

    (b) by the Secretary of State, in relation to proceedings in Scotland; or

    (c) by a Northern Ireland department, in relation to proceedings before a tribunal in Northern Ireland-

        (i) which deals with transferred matters; and
        (ii) for which no rules made under paragraph (a) are in force.

Legislation

Interpretation of legislation.
3.–(1) So far as it is possible to do so, primary legislation and subordinate legislation must be read and given effect in a way which is compatible with the Convention rights.

(2) This section-

    (a) applies to primary legislation and subordinate legislation whenever enacted;

    (b) does not affect the validity, continuing operation or enforcement of any incompatible primary legislation; and

    (c) does not affect the validity, continuing operation or enforcement of any incompatible subordinate legislation if (disregarding any possibility of revocation) primary legislation prevents removal of the incompatibility.

Declaration of incompatibility.
4.–(1) Subsection (2) applies in any proceedings in which a court determines whether a provision of primary legislation is compatible with a Convention right.

(2) If the court is satisfied that the provision is incompatible with a Convention right, it may make a declaration of that incompatibility.

(3) Subsection (4) applies in any proceedings in which a court determines whether a provision of subordinate legislation, made in the exercise of a power conferred by primary legislation, is compatible with a Convention right.

(4) If the court is satisfied-

    (a) that the provision is incompatible with a Convention right, and

    (b) that (disregarding any possibility of revocation) the primary legislation concerned prevents removal of the incompatibility,

it may make a declaration of that incompatibility.

(5) In this section "court" means-

    (a) the House of Lords;

    (b) the Judicial Committee of the Privy Council;

    (c) the Courts-Martial Appeal Court;

    (d) in Scotland, the High Court of Justiciary sitting otherwise than as a trial court or the Court of Session;

    (e) in England and Wales or Northern Ireland, the High Court or the Court of Appeal.

(6) A declaration under this section ("a declaration of incompatibility")-

    (a) does not affect the validity, continuing operation or enforcement of the provision in respect of which it is given; and

    (b) is not binding on the parties to the proceedings in which it is made.

Right of Crown to intervene.
5.–(1) Where a court is considering whether to make a declaration of incompatibility, the Crown is entitled to notice in accordance with rules of court.

(2) In any case to which subsection (1) applies-

    (a) a Minister of the Crown (or a person nominated by him),

(b) a member of the Scottish Executive,

(c) a Northern Ireland Minister,

(d) a Northern Ireland department,

is entitled, on giving notice in accordance with rules of court, to be joined as a party to the proceedings.

(3) Notice under subsection (2) may be given at any time during the proceedings.

(4) A person who has been made a party to criminal proceedings (other than in Scotland) as the result of a notice under subsection (2) may, with leave, appeal to the House of Lords against any declaration of incompatibility made in the proceedings.

(5) In subsection (4)-

"criminal proceedings" includes all proceedings before the Courts-Martial Appeal Court; and

"leave" means leave granted by the court making the declaration of incompatibility or by the House of Lords.

Public authorities

Acts of public authorities.
6.–(1) It is unlawful for a public authority to act in a way which is incompatible with a Convention right.

(2) Subsection (1) does not apply to an act if-

(a) as the result of one or more provisions of primary legislation, the authority could not have acted differently; or

(b) in the case of one or more provisions of, or made under, primary legislation which cannot be read or given effect in a way which is compatible with the Convention rights, the authority was acting so as to give effect to or enforce those provisions.

(3) In this section "public authority" includes-

(a) a court or tribunal, and

(b) any person certain of whose functions are functions of a public nature,

but does not include either House of Parliament or a person exercising functions in connection with proceedings in Parliament.

(4) In subsection (3) "Parliament" does not include the House of Lords in its judicial capacity.

(5) In relation to a particular act, a person is not a public authority by virtue only of subsection (3)(b) if the nature of the act is private.

(6) "An act" includes a failure to act but does not include a failure to-

(a) introduce in, or lay before, Parliament a proposal for legislation; or

(b) make any primary legislation or remedial order.

Proceedings.
7.–(1) A person who claims that a public authority has acted (or proposes to act) in a way which is made unlawful by section 6(1) may-

(a) bring proceedings against the authority under this Act in the appropriate court or tribunal, or

(b) rely on the Convention right or rights concerned in any legal proceedings,

but only if he is (or would be) a victim of the unlawful act.

(2) In subsection (1)(a) "appropriate court or tribunal" means such court or tribunal as may be determined in accordance with rules; and proceedings against an authority include a counterclaim or similar proceeding.

(3) If the proceedings are brought on an application for judicial review, the applicant is to be taken to have a sufficient interest in relation to the unlawful act only if he is, or would be, a victim of that act.

(4) If the proceedings are made by way of a petition for judicial review in Scotland, the applicant shall be taken to have title and interest to sue in relation to the unlawful act only if he is, or would be, a victim of that act.

(5) Proceedings under subsection (1)(a) must be brought before the end of-

(a) the period of one year beginning with the date on which the act complained of took place; or

(b) such longer period as the court or tribunal considers equitable having regard to all the circumstances,

but that is subject to any rule imposing a stricter time limit in relation to the procedure in question.

(6) In subsection (1)(b) "legal proceedings" includes-

(a) proceedings brought by or at the instigation of a public authority; and

(b) an appeal against the decision of a court or tribunal.

(7) For the purposes of this section, a person is a victim of an unlawful act only if he would be a victim for the purposes of Article 34 of the Convention if proceedings were brought in the European Court of Human Rights in respect of that act.

(8) Nothing in this Act creates a criminal offence.

(9) In this section "rules" means-

(a) in relation to proceedings before a court or tribunal outside Scotland, rules made by the Lord Chancellor or the Secretary of State for the purposes of this section or rules of court,

(b) in relation to proceedings before a court or tribunal in Scotland, rules made by the Secretary of State for those purposes,

(c) in relation to proceedings before a tribunal in Northern Ireland-

(i) which deals with transferred matters; and
(ii) for which no rules made under paragraph (a) are in force,

rules made by a Northern Ireland department for those purposes,

and includes provision made by order under section 1 of the Courts and Legal Services Act 1990.

(10) In making rules, regard must be had to section 9.

(11) The Minister who has power to make rules in relation to a particular tribunal may, to the extent he considers it necessary to ensure that the tribunal can provide an appropriate remedy in relation to an act (or proposed act) of a public authority which is (or would be) unlawful as a result of section 6(1), by order add to-

(a) the relief or remedies which the tribunal may grant; or

(b) the grounds on which it may grant any of them.

(12) An order made under subsection (11) may contain such incidental, supplemental, consequential or transitional provision as the Minister making it considers appropriate.

(13) "The Minister" includes the Northern Ireland department concerned.

Judicial remedies.

8.–(1) In relation to any act (or proposed act) of a public authority which the court finds is (or would be) unlawful, it may grant such relief or remedy, or make such order, within its powers as it considers just and appropriate.

(2) But damages may be awarded only by a court which has power to award damages, or to order the payment of compensation, in civil proceedings.

(3) No award of damages is to be made unless, taking account of all the circumstances of the case, including-

(a) any other relief or remedy granted, or order made, in relation to the act in question (by that or any other court), and

(b) the consequences of any decision (of that or any other court) in respect of that act,

the court is satisfied that the award is necessary to afford just satisfaction to the person in whose favour it is made.

(4) In determining-

(a) whether to award damages, or

(b) the amount of an award,

the court must take into account the principles applied by the European Court of Human Rights in relation to the award of compensation under Article 41 of the Convention.

(5) A public authority against which damages are awarded is to be treated-

(a) in Scotland, for the purposes of section 3 of the Law Reform (Miscellaneous Provisions) (Scotland) Act 1940 as if the award were made in an action of damages in which the authority has been found liable in respect of loss or damage to the person to whom the award is made;

(b) for the purposes of the Civil Liability (Contribution) Act 1978 as liable in respect of damage suffered by the person to whom the award is made.

(6) In this section-

"court" includes a tribunal;
"damages" means damages for an unlawful act of a public authority; and
"unlawful" means unlawful under section 6(1).

Judicial acts.

9.–(1) Proceedings under section 7(1)(a) in respect of a judicial act may be brought only-

(a) by exercising a right of appeal;

(b) on an application (in Scotland a petition) for judicial review; or

(c) in such other forum as may be prescribed by rules.

(2) That does not affect any rule of law which prevents a court from being the subject of judicial review.

(3) In proceedings under this Act in respect of a judicial act done in good faith, damages may not be awarded otherwise than to compensate a person to the extent required by Article 5(5) of the Convention.

(4) An award of damages permitted by subsection (3) is to be made against the Crown; but no award may be made unless the appropriate person, if not a party to the proceedings, is joined.

(5) In this section-

"appropriate person" means the Minister responsible for the court concerned, or a person or government department nominated by him;
"court" includes a tribunal;
"judge" includes a member of a tribunal, a justice of the peace and a clerk or other officer entitled to exercise the jurisdiction of a court;
"judicial act" means a judicial act of a court and includes an act done on the instructions, or on behalf, of a judge; and
"rules" has the same meaning as in section 7(9).

Remedial action

Power to take remedial action.
  10.–(1) This section applies if-

  (a) a provision of legislation has been declared under section 4 to be incompatible with a Convention right and, if an appeal lies-

   (i) all persons who may appeal have stated in writing that they do not intend to do so;
   (ii) the time for bringing an appeal has expired and no appeal has been brought within that time; or
   (iii) an appeal brought within that time has been determined or abandoned; or

  (b) it appears to a Minister of the Crown or Her Majesty in Council that, having regard to a finding of the European Court of Human Rights made after the coming into force of this section in proceedings against the United Kingdom, a provision of legislation is incompatible with an obligation of the United Kingdom arising from the Convention.

(2) If a Minister of the Crown considers that there are compelling reasons for proceeding under this section, he may by order make such amendments to the legislation as he considers necessary to remove the incompatibility.

(3) If, in the case of subordinate legislation, a Minister of the Crown considers-

  (a) that it is necessary to amend the primary legislation under which the subordinate legislation in question was made, in order to enable the incompatibility to be removed, and

  (b) that there are compelling reasons for proceeding under this section,

he may by order make such amendments to the primary legislation as he considers necessary.

(4) This section also applies where the provision in question is in subordinate legislation and has been quashed, or declared invalid, by reason of incompatibility with a Convention right and the Minister proposes to proceed under paragraph 2(b) of Schedule 2.

(5) If the legislation is an Order in Council, the power conferred by subsection (2) or (3) is exercisable by Her Majesty in Council.

(6) In this section "legislation" does not include a Measure of the Church Assembly or of the General Synod of the Church of England.

(7) Schedule 2 makes further provision about remedial orders.

Other rights and proceedings

Safeguard for existing human rights.
   11. A person's reliance on a Convention right does not restrict-

    (a) any other right or freedom conferred on him by or under any law having effect in any part of the United Kingdom; or

    (b) his right to make any claim or bring any proceedings which he could make or bring apart from sections 7 to 9.

Freedom of expression.
   12.–(1) This section applies if a court is considering whether to grant any relief which, if granted, might affect the exercise of the Convention right to freedom of expression.

   (2) If the person against whom the application for relief is made ("the respondent") is neither present nor represented, no such relief is to be granted unless the court is satisfied-

    (a) that the applicant has taken all practicable steps to notify the respondent; or

    (b) that there are compelling reasons why the respondent should not be notified.

   (3) No such relief is to be granted so as to restrain publication before trial unless the court is satisfied that the applicant is likely to establish that publication should not be allowed.

   (4) The court must have particular regard to the importance of the Convention right to freedom of expression and, where the proceedings relate to material which the respondent claims, or which appears to the court, to be journalistic, literary or artistic material (or to conduct connected with such material), to-

    (a) the extent to which-

       (i) the material has, or is about to, become available to the public; or
      (ii) it is, or would be, in the public interest for the material to be published;

    (b) any relevant privacy code.

   (5) In this section-

"court" includes a tribunal; and
"relief" includes any remedy or order (other than in criminal proceedings).

Freedom of thought, conscience and religion.
   13.–(1) If a court's determination of any question arising under this Act might affect the exercise by a religious organisation (itself or its members collectively) of the Convention right to freedom of thought, conscience and religion, it must have particular regard to the importance of that right.

   (2) In this section "court" includes a tribunal.

Derogations and reservations

Derogations.
   14.–(1) In this Act "designated derogation" means-

    (a) the United Kingdom's derogation from Article 5(3) of the Convention; and

    (b) any derogation by the United Kingdom from an Article of the Convention, or of any protocol to the Convention, which is designated for the purposes of this Act in an order made by the Secretary of State.

(2) The derogation referred to in subsection (1)(a) is set out in Part I of Schedule 3.

(3) If a designated derogation is amended or replaced it ceases to be a designated derogation.

(4) But subsection (3) does not prevent the Secretary of State from exercising his power under subsection (1)(b) to make a fresh designation order in respect of the Article concerned.

(5) The Secretary of State must by order make such amendments to Schedule 3 as he considers appropriate to reflect-

(a) any designation order; or

(b) the effect of subsection (3).

(6) A designation order may be made in anticipation of the making by the United Kingdom of a proposed derogation.

Reservations.
15.–(1) In this Act "designated reservation" means-

(a) the United Kingdom's reservation to Article 2 of the First Protocol to the Convention; and

(b) any other reservation by the United Kingdom to an Article of the Convention, or of any protocol to the Convention, which is designated for the purposes of this Act in an order made by the Secretary of State.

(2) The text of the reservation referred to in subsection (1)(a) is set out in Part II of Schedule 3.

(3) If a designated reservation is withdrawn wholly or in part it ceases to be a designated reservation.

(4) But subsection (3) does not prevent the Secretary of State from exercising his power under subsection (1)(b) to make a fresh designation order in respect of the Article concerned.

(5) The Secretary of State must by order make such amendments to this Act as he considers appropriate to reflect-

(a) any designation order; or

(b) the effect of subsection (3).

Period for which designated derogations have effect.
16.–(1) If it has not already been withdrawn by the United Kingdom, a designated derogation ceases to have effect for the purposes of this Act-

(a) in the case of the derogation referred to in section 14(1)(a), at the end of the period of five years beginning with the date on which section 1(2) came into force;

(b) in the case of any other derogation, at the end of the period of five years beginning with the date on which the order designating it was made.

(2) At any time before the period-

(a) fixed by subsection (1)(a) or (b), or

(b) extended by an order under this subsection,

comes to an end, the Secretary of State may by order extend it by a further period of five years.

(3) An order under section 14(1)(b) ceases to have effect at the end of the period for consideration, unless a resolution has been passed by each House approving the order.

(4) Subsection (3) does not affect-

(a) anything done in reliance on the order; or

(b) the power to make a fresh order under section 14(1)(b).

(5) In subsection (3) "period for consideration" means the period of forty days beginning with the day on which the order was made.

(6) In calculating the period for consideration, no account is to be taken of any time during which-

(a) Parliament is dissolved or prorogued; or

(b) both Houses are adjourned for more than four days.

(7) If a designated derogation is withdrawn by the United Kingdom, the Secretary of State must by order make such amendments to this Act as he considers are required to reflect that withdrawal.

Periodic review of designated reservations.
17.–(1) The appropriate Minister must review the designated reservation referred to in section 15(1)(a)-

(a) before the end of the period of five years beginning with the date on which section 1(2) came into force; and

(b) if that designation is still in force, before the end of the period of five years beginning with the date on which the last report relating to it was laid under subsection (3).

(2) The appropriate Minister must review each of the other designated reservations (if any)-

(a) before the end of the period of five years beginning with the date on which the order designating the reservation first came into force; and

(b) if the designation is still in force, before the end of the period of five years beginning with the date on which the last report relating to it was laid under subsection (3).

(3) The Minister conducting a review under this section must prepare a report on the result of the review and lay a copy of it before each House of Parliament.

Judges of the European Court of Human Rights

Appointment to European Court of Human Rights.
18.–(1) In this section "judicial office" means the office of-

(a) Lord Justice of Appeal, Justice of the High Court or Circuit judge, in England and Wales;

(b) judge of the Court of Session or sheriff, in Scotland;

(c) Lord Justice of Appeal, judge of the High Court or county court judge, in Northern Ireland.

(2) The holder of a judicial office may become a judge of the European Court of Human Rights ("the Court") without being required to relinquish his office.

(3) But he is not required to perform the duties of his judicial office while he is a judge of the Court.

(4) In respect of any period during which he is a judge of the Court-

(a) a Lord Justice of Appeal or Justice of the High Court is not to count as a judge of the relevant court for the purposes of section 2(1) or 4(1) of the Supreme Court Act 1981 (maximum number of judges) nor as a judge of the Supreme Court for the purposes of section 12(1) to (6) of that Act (salaries etc.);

(b) a judge of the Court of Session is not to count as a judge of that court for the purposes of section 1(1) of the Court of Session Act 1988 (maximum number of judges) or of section 9(1)(c) of the Administration of Justice Act 1973 ("the 1973 Act") (salaries etc.);

(c) a Lord Justice of Appeal or judge of the High Court in Northern Ireland is not to count as a judge of the relevant court for the purposes of section 2(1) or 3(1) of the Judicature (Northern Ireland) Act 1978 (maximum number of judges) nor as a judge of the Supreme Court of Northern Ireland for the purposes of section 9(1)(d) of the 1973 Act (salaries etc.);

(d) a Circuit judge is not to count as such for the purposes of section 18 of the Courts Act 1971 (salaries etc.);

(e) a sheriff is not to count as such for the purposes of section 14 of the Sheriff Courts (Scotland) Act 1907 (salaries etc.);

(f) a county court judge of Northern Ireland is not to count as such for the purposes of section 106 of the County Courts Act (Northern Ireland) 1959 (salaries etc.).

(5) If a sheriff principal is appointed a judge of the Court, section 11(1) of the Sheriff Courts (Scotland) Act 1971 (temporary appointment of sheriff principal) applies, while he holds that appointment, as if his office is vacant.

(6) Schedule 4 makes provision about judicial pensions in relation to the holder of a judicial office who serves as a judge of the Court.

(7) The Lord Chancellor or the Secretary of State may by order make such transitional provision (including, in particular, provision for a temporary increase in the maximum number of judges) as he considers appropriate in relation to any holder of a judicial office who has completed his service as a judge of the Court.

Parliamentary procedure

Statements of compatibility.
19.–(1) A Minister of the Crown in charge of a Bill in either House of Parliament must, before Second Reading of the Bill-

(a) make a statement to the effect that in his view the provisions of the Bill are compatible with the Convention rights ("a statement of compatibility"); or

(b) make a statement to the effect that although he is unable to make a statement of compatibility the government nevertheless wishes the House to proceed with the Bill.

(2) The statement must be in writing and be published in such manner as the Minister making it considers appropriate.

Supplemental

Orders etc. under this Act.
20.–(1) Any power of a Minister of the Crown to make an order under this Act is exercisable by statutory instrument.

(2) The power of the Lord Chancellor or the Secretary of State to make rules (other than rules of court) under section 2(3) or 7(9) is exercisable by statutory instrument.

(3) Any statutory instrument made under section 14, 15 or 16(7) must be laid before Parliament.

(4) No order may be made by the Lord Chancellor or the Secretary of State under section 1(4), 7(11) or 16(2) unless a draft of the order has been laid before, and approved by, each House of Parliament.

(5) Any statutory instrument made under section 18(7) or Schedule 4, or to which subsection (2) applies, shall be subject to annulment in pursuance of a resolution of either House of Parliament.

(6) The power of a Northern Ireland department to make-

(a) rules under section 2(3)(c) or 7(9)(c), or

(b) an order under section 7(11),

is exercisable by statutory rule for the purposes of the Statutory Rules (Northern Ireland) Order 1979.

(7) Any rules made under section 2(3)(c) or 7(9)(c) shall be subject to negative resolution; and section 41(6) of the Interpretation Act (Northern Ireland) 1954 (meaning of "subject to negative resolution") shall apply as if the power to make the rules were conferred by an Act of the Northern Ireland Assembly.

(8) No order may be made by a Northern Ireland department under section 7(11) unless a draft of the order has been laid before, and approved by, the Northern Ireland Assembly.

Interpretation, etc.
  21.–(1) In this Act-

"amend" includes repeal and apply (with or without modifications);
"the appropriate Minister" means the Minister of the Crown having charge of the appropriate authorised government department (within the meaning of the Crown Proceedings Act 1947);
"the Commission" means the European Commission of Human Rights;
"the Convention" means the Convention for the Protection of Human Rights and Fundamental Freedoms, agreed by the Council of Europe at Rome on 4th November 1950 as it has effect for the time being in relation to the United Kingdom;
"declaration of incompatibility" means a declaration under section 4;
"Minister of the Crown" has the same meaning as in the Ministers of the Crown Act 1975;
"Northern Ireland Minister" includes the First Minister and the deputy First Minister in Northern Ireland;
"primary legislation" means any-

(a) public general Act;

(b) local and personal Act;

(c) private Act;

(d) Measure of the Church Assembly;

(e) Measure of the General Synod of the Church of England;

(f) Order in Council-

(i) made in exercise of Her Majesty's Royal Prerogative;
(ii) made under section 38(1)(a) of the Northern Ireland Constitution Act 1973 or the corresponding provision of the Northern Ireland Act 1998; or
(iii) amending an Act of a kind mentioned in paragraph (a), (b) or (c);

and includes an order or other instrument made under primary legislation (otherwise than by the National Assembly for Wales, a member of the Scottish Executive, a Northern Ireland Minister or a Northern Ireland department) to the extent to which it operates to bring one or more provisions of that legislation into force or amends any primary legislation;

"the First Protocol" means the protocol to the Convention agreed at Paris on 20th March 1952;

"the Sixth Protocol" means the protocol to the Convention agreed at Strasbourg on 28th
   April 1983;
"the Eleventh Protocol" means the protocol to the Convention (restructuring the control
   machinery established by the Convention) agreed at Strasbourg on 11th May 1994;
"remedial order" means an order under section 10;
"subordinate legislation" means any-

    (a) Order in Council other than one-
        (i) made in exercise of Her Majesty's Royal Prerogative;
        (ii) made under section 38(1)(a) of the Northern Ireland Constitution Act 1973
            or the corresponding provision of the Northern Ireland Act 1998; or
        (iii) amending an Act of a kind mentioned in the definition of primary legislation;
    (b) Act of the Scottish Parliament;
    (c) Act of the Parliament of Northern Ireland;
    (d) Measure of the Assembly established under section 1 of the Northern Ireland
        Assembly Act 1973;
    (e) Act of the Northern Ireland Assembly;
    (f) order, rules, regulations, scheme, warrant, byelaw or other instrument made under
        primary legislation (except to the extent to which it operates to bring one or more
        provisions of that legislation into force or amends any primary legislation);
    (g) order, rules, regulations, scheme, warrant, byelaw or other instrument made under
        legislation mentioned in paragraph (b), (c), (d) or (e) or made under an Order in
        Council applying only to Northern Ireland;
    (h) order, rules, regulations, scheme, warrant, byelaw or other instrument made by a
        member of the Scottish Executive, a Northern Ireland Minister or a Northern
        Ireland department in exercise of prerogative or other executive functions of Her
        Majesty which are exercisable by such a person on behalf of Her Majesty;

        "transferred matters" has the same meaning as in the Northern Ireland Act 1998;
        and
        "tribunal" means any tribunal in which legal proceedings may be brought.

(2) The references in paragraphs (b) and (c) of section 2(1) to Articles are to Articles of the
Convention as they had effect immediately before the coming into force of the Eleventh
Protocol.

(3) The reference in paragraph (d) of section 2(1) to Article 46 includes a reference to
Articles 32 and 54 of the Convention as they had effect immediately before the coming into
force of the Eleventh Protocol.

(4) The references in section 2(1) to a report or decision of the Commission or a decision
of the Committee of Ministers include references to a report or decision made as provided by
paragraphs 3, 4 and 6 of Article 5 of the Eleventh Protocol (transitional provisions).

(5) Any liability under the Army Act 1955, the Air Force Act 1955 or the Naval Discipline
Act 1957 to suffer death for an offence is replaced by a liability to imprisonment for life or
any less punishment authorised by those Acts; and those Acts shall accordingly have effect
with the necessary modifications.

Short title, commencement, application and extent.
    22.–(1) This Act may be cited as the Human Rights Act 1998.

(2) Sections 18, 20 and 21(5) and this section come into force on the passing of this Act.

  (3) The other provisions of this Act come into force on such day as the Secretary of State
may by order appoint; and different days may be appointed for different purposes.

(4) Paragraph (b) of subsection (1) of section 7 applies to proceedings brought by or at the
instigation of a public authority whenever the act in question took place; but otherwise that
subsection does not apply to an act taking place before the coming into force of that section.

(5) This Act binds the Crown.

(6) This Act extends to Northern Ireland.

(7) Section 21(5), so far as it relates to any provision contained in the Army Act 1955, the
Air Force Act 1955 or the Naval Discipline Act 1957, extends to any place to which that
provision extends.

SCHEDULES

SCHEDULE 1

Part I

The Convention

Rights and Freedoms

Article 2

Right to life

1. Everyone's right to life shall be protected by law. No one shall be deprived of his life intentionally save in the execution of a sentence of a court following his conviction of a crime for which this penalty is provided by law.

2. Deprivation of life shall not be regarded as inflicted in contravention of this Article when it results from the use of force which is no more than absolutely necessary:

(a) in defence of any person from unlawful violence;

(b) in order to effect a lawful arrest or to prevent the escape of a person lawfully detained;

(c) in action lawfully taken for the purpose of quelling a riot or insurrection.

Article 3

Prohibition of torture

No one shall be subjected to torture or to inhuman or degrading treatment or punishment.

Article 4

Prohibition of slavery and forced labour

1. No one shall be held in slavery or servitude.

2. No one shall be required to perform forced or compulsory labour.

3. For the purpose of this Article the term "forced or compulsory labour" shall not include:

(a) any work required to be done in the ordinary course of detention imposed according to the provisions of Article 5 of this Convention or during conditional release from such detention;

(b) any service of a military character or, in case of conscientious objectors in countries where they are recognised, service exacted instead of compulsory military service;

(c) any service exacted in case of an emergency or calamity threatening the life or well-being of the community;

(d) any work or service which forms part of normal civic obligations.

Article 5

Right to liberty and security

1. Everyone has the right to liberty and security of person. No one shall be deprived of his liberty save in the following cases and in accordance with a procedure prescribed by law:

(a) the lawful detention of a person after conviction by a competent court;

(b) the lawful arrest or detention of a person for non-compliance with the lawful order of a court or in order to secure the fulfilment of any obligation prescribed by law;

(c) the lawful arrest or detention of a person effected for the purpose of bringing him before the competent legal authority on reasonable suspicion of having committed an offence or when it is reasonably considered necessary to prevent his committing an offence or fleeing after having done so;

(d) the detention of a minor by lawful order for the purpose of educational supervision or his lawful detention for the purpose of bringing him before the competent legal authority;

(e) the lawful detention of persons for the prevention of the spreading of infectious diseases, of persons of unsound mind, alcoholics or drug addicts or vagrants;

(f) the lawful arrest or detention of a person to prevent his effecting an unauthorised entry into the country or of a person against whom action is being taken with a view to deportation or extradition.

2. Everyone who is arrested shall be informed promptly, in a language which he understands, of the reasons for his arrest and of any charge against him.

3. Everyone arrested or detained in accordance with the provisions of paragraph 1(c) of this Article shall be brought promptly before a judge or other officer authorised by law to exercise judicial power and shall be entitled to trial within a reasonable time or to release pending trial. Release may be conditioned by guarantees to appear for trial.

4. Everyone who is deprived of his liberty by arrest or detention shall be entitled to take proceedings by which the lawfulness of his detention shall be decided speedily by a court and his release ordered if the detention is not lawful.

5. Everyone who has been the victim of arrest or detention in contravention of the provisions of this Article shall have an enforceable right to compensation.

Article 6

Right to a fair trial

1. In the determination of his civil rights and obligations or of any criminal charge against him, everyone is entitled to a fair and public hearing within a reasonable time by an independent and impartial tribunal established by law. Judgment shall be pronounced publicly but the press and public may be excluded from all or part of the trial in the interest of morals, public order or national security in a democratic society, where the interests of juveniles or the protection of the private life of the parties so require, or to the extent strictly necessary in the opinion of the court in special circumstances where publicity would prejudice the interests of justice.

2. Everyone charged with a criminal offence shall be presumed innocent until proved guilty according to law.

3. Everyone charged with a criminal offence has the following minimum rights:

(a) to be informed promptly, in a language which he understands and in detail, of the nature and cause of the accusation against him;

(b) to have adequate time and facilities for the preparation of his defence;

(c) to defend himself in person or through legal assistance of his own choosing or, if he has not sufficient means to pay for legal assistance, to be given it free when the interests of justice so require;

(d) to examine or have examined witnesses against him and to obtain the attendance and examination of witnesses on his behalf under the same conditions as witnesses against him;

(e) to have the free assistance of an interpreter if he cannot understand or speak the language used in court.

Article 7

No punishment without law

1. No one shall be held guilty of any criminal offence on account of any act or omission which did not constitute a criminal offence under national or international law at the time when it was committed. Nor shall a heavier penalty be imposed than the one that was applicable at the time the criminal offence was committed.

2. This Article shall not prejudice the trial and punishment of any person for any act or omission which, at the time when it was committed, was criminal according to the general principles of law recognised by civilised nations.

Article 8

Right to respect for private and family life

1. Everyone has the right to respect for his private and family life, his home and his correspondence.

2. There shall be no interference by a public authority with the exercise of this right except such as is in accordance with the law and is necessary in a democratic society in the interests of national security, public safety or the economic well-being of the country, for the prevention of disorder or crime, for the protection of health or morals, or for the protection of the rights and freedoms of others.

Article 9

Freedom of thought, conscience and religion

1. Everyone has the right to freedom of thought, conscience and religion; this right includes freedom to change his religion or belief and freedom, either alone or in community with others and in public or private, to manifest his religion or belief, in worship, teaching, practice and observance.

2. Freedom to manifest one's religion or beliefs shall be subject only to such limitations as are prescribed by law and are necessary in a democratic society in the interests of public safety, for the protection of public order, health or morals, or for the protection of the rights and freedoms of others.

Article 10

Freedom of expression

1. Everyone has the right to freedom of expression. This right shall include freedom to hold opinions and to receive and impart information and ideas without interference by public authority and regardless of frontiers. This Article shall not prevent States from requiring the licensing of broadcasting, television or cinema enterprises.

2. The exercise of these freedoms, since it carries with it duties and responsibilities, may be subject to such formalities, conditions, restrictions or penalties as are prescribed by law and are necessary in a democratic society, in the interests of national security, territorial integrity or public safety, for the prevention of disorder or crime, for the protection of health or morals, for the protection of the reputation or rights of others, for preventing the disclosure of information received in confidence, or for maintaining the authority and impartiality of the judiciary.

Article 11

Freedom of assembly and association

1. Everyone has the right to freedom of peaceful assembly and to freedom of association with others, including the right to form and to join trade unions for the protection of his interests.

2. No restrictions shall be placed on the exercise of these rights other than such as are prescribed by law and are necessary in a democratic society in the interests of national security or public safety, for the prevention of disorder or crime, for the protection of health or morals or for the protection of the rights and freedoms of others. This Article shall not

prevent the imposition of lawful restrictions on the exercise of these rights by members of the armed forces, of the police or of the administration of the State.

ARTICLE 12

RIGHT TO MARRY

Men and women of marriageable age have the right to marry and to found a family, according to the national laws governing the exercise of this right.

ARTICLE 14

PROHIBITION OF DISCRIMINATION

The enjoyment of the rights and freedoms set forth in this Convention shall be secured without discrimination on any ground such as sex, race, colour, language, religion, political or other opinion, national or social origin, association with a national minority, property, birth or other status.

ARTICLE 16

RESTRICTIONS ON POLITICAL ACTIVITY OF ALIENS

Nothing in Articles 10, 11 and 14 shall be regarded as preventing the High Contracting Parties from imposing restrictions on the political activity of aliens.

ARTICLE 17

PROHIBITION OF ABUSE OF RIGHTS

Nothing in this Convention may be interpreted as implying for any State, group or person any right to engage in any activity or perform any act aimed at the destruction of any of the rights and freedoms set forth herein or at their limitation to a greater extent than is provided for in the Convention.

ARTICLE 18

LIMITATION ON USE OF RESTRICTIONS ON RIGHTS

The restrictions permitted under this Convention to the said rights and freedoms shall not be applied for any purpose other than those for which they have been prescribed.

PART II

FIRST PROTOCOL

ARTICLE 1

PROTECTION OF PROPERTY

Every natural or legal person is entitled to the peaceful enjoyment of his possessions. No one shall be deprived of his possessions except in the public interest and subject to the conditions provided for by law and by the general principles of international law.

The preceding provisions shall not, however, in any way impair the right of a State to enforce such laws as it deems necessary to control the use of property in accordance with the general interest or to secure the payment of taxes or other contributions or penalties.

ARTICLE 2

RIGHT TO EDUCATION

No person shall be denied the right to education. In the exercise of any functions which it assumes in relation to education and to teaching, the State shall respect the right of parents to ensure such education and teaching in conformity with their own religious and philosophical convictions.

ARTICLE 3

RIGHT TO FREE ELECTIONS

The High Contracting Parties undertake to hold free elections at reasonable intervals by secret ballot, under conditions which will ensure the free expression of the opinion of the people in the choice of the legislature.

PART III

Sixth Protocol

Article 1

Abolition of the death penalty

The death penalty shall be abolished. No one shall be condemned to such penalty or executed.

Article 2

Death penalty in time of war

A State may make provision in its law for the death penalty in respect of acts committed in time of war or of imminent threat of war; such penalty shall be applied only in the instances laid down in the law and in accordance with its provisions. The State shall communicate to the Secretary General of the Council of Europe the relevant provisions of that law.

SCHEDULE 2

Remedial Orders

Orders

1.–(1) A remedial order may-

   (a) contain such incidental, supplemental, consequential or transitional provision as the person making it considers appropriate;

   (b) be made so as to have effect from a date earlier than that on which it is made;

   (c) make provision for the delegation of specific functions;

   (d) make different provision for different cases.

(2) The power conferred by sub-paragraph (1)(a) includes-

   (a) power to amend primary legislation (including primary legislation other than that which contains the incompatible provision); and

   (b) power to amend or revoke subordinate legislation (including subordinate legislation other than that which contains the incompatible provision).

(3) A remedial order may be made so as to have the same extent as the legislation which it affects.

(4) No person is to be guilty of an offence solely as a result of the retrospective effect of a remedial order.

Procedure

2. No remedial order may be made unless-

   (a) a draft of the order has been approved by a resolution of each House of Parliament made after the end of the period of 60 days beginning with the day on which the draft was laid; or

   (b) it is declared in the order that it appears to the person making it that, because of the urgency of the matter, it is necessary to make the order without a draft being so approved.

Orders laid in draft

3.–(1) No draft may be laid under paragraph 2(a) unless-

(a) the person proposing to make the order has laid before Parliament a document which contains a draft of the proposed order and the required information; and

(b) the period of 60 days, beginning with the day on which the document required by this sub-paragraph was laid, has ended.

(2) If representations have been made during that period, the draft laid under paragraph 2(a) must be accompanied by a statement containing-

(a) a summary of the representations; and

(b) if, as a result of the representations, the proposed order has been changed, details of the changes.

Urgent cases

4.–(1) If a remedial order ("the original order") is made without being approved in draft, the person making it must lay it before Parliament, accompanied by the required information, after it is made.

(2) If representations have been made during the period of 60 days beginning with the day on which the original order was made, the person making it must (after the end of that period) lay before Parliament a statement containing-

(a) a summary of the representations; and

(b) if, as a result of the representations, he considers it appropriate to make changes to the original order, details of the changes.

(3) If sub-paragraph (2)(b) applies, the person making the statement must-

(a) make a further remedial order replacing the original order; and

(b) lay the replacement order before Parliament.

(4) If, at the end of the period of 120 days beginning with the day on which the original order was made, a resolution has not been passed by each House approving the original or replacement order, the order ceases to have effect (but without that affecting anything previously done under either order or the power to make a fresh remedial order).

Definitions

5. In this Schedule-

"representations" means representations about a remedial order (or proposed remedial order) made to the person making (or proposing to make) it and includes any relevant Parliamentary report or resolution; and
"required information" means-

(a) an explanation of the incompatibility which the order (or proposed order) seeks to remove, including particulars of the relevant declaration, finding or order; and

(b) a statement of the reasons for proceeding under section 10 and for making an order in those terms.

Calculating periods

6. In calculating any period for the purposes of this Schedule, no account is to be taken of any time during which-

(a) Parliament is dissolved or prorogued; or

(b) both Houses are adjourned for more than four days.

SCHEDULE 3

DEROGATION AND RESERVATION

PART I

DEROGATION

The 1988 notification

The United Kingdom Permanent Representative to the Council of Europe presents his compliments to the Secretary General of the Council, and has the honour to convey the following information in order to ensure compliance with the obligations of Her Majesty's Government in the United Kingdom under Article 15(3) of the Convention for the Protection of Human Rights and Fundamental Freedoms signed at Rome on 4 November 1950.

There have been in the United Kingdom in recent years campaigns of organised terrorism connected with the affairs of Northern Ireland which have manifested themselves in activities which have included repeated murder, attempted murder, maiming, intimidation and violent civil disturbance and in bombing and fire raising which have resulted in death, injury and widespread destruction of property. As a result, a public emergency within the meaning of Article 15(1) of the Convention exists in the United Kingdom.

The Government found it necessary in 1974 to introduce and since then, in cases concerning persons reasonably suspected of involvement in terrorism connected with the affairs of Northern Ireland, or of certain offences under the legislation, who have been detained for 48 hours, to exercise powers enabling further detention without charge, for periods of up to five days, on the authority of the Secretary of State. These powers are at present to be found in Section 12 of the Prevention of Terrorism (Temporary Provisions) Act 1984, Article 9 of the Prevention of Terrorism (Supplemental Temporary Provisions) Order 1984 and Article 10 of the Prevention of Terrorism (Supplemental Temporary Provisions) (Northern Ireland) Order 1984.

Section 12 of the Prevention of Terrorism (Temporary Provisions) Act 1984 provides for a person whom a constable has arrested on reasonable grounds of suspecting him to be guilty of an offence under Section 1, 9 or 10 of the Act, or to be or to have been involved in terrorism connected with the affairs of Northern Ireland, to be detained in right of the arrest for up to 48 hours and thereafter, where the Secretary of State extends the detention period, for up to a further five days. Section 12 substantially re-enacted Section 12 of the Prevention of Terrorism (Temporary Provisions) Act 1976 which, in turn, substantially re-enacted Section 7 of the Prevention of Terrorism (Temporary Provisions) Act 1974.

Article 10 of the Prevention of Terrorism (Supplemental Temporary Provisions) (Northern Ireland) Order 1984 (SI 1984/417) and Article 9 of the Prevention of Terrorism (Supplemental Temporary Provisions) Order 1984 (SI 1984/418) were both made under Sections 13 and 14 of and Schedule 3 to the 1984 Act and substantially re-enacted powers of detention in Orders made under the 1974 and 1976 Acts. A person who is being examined under Article 4 of either Order on his arrival in, or on seeking to leave, Northern Ireland or Great Britain for the purpose of determining whether he is or has been involved in terrorism connected with the affairs of Northern Ireland, or whether there are grounds for suspecting that he has committed an offence under Section 9 of the 1984 Act, may be detained under Article 9 or 10, as appropriate, pending the conclusion of his examination. The period of this examination may exceed 12 hours if an examining officer has reasonable grounds for suspecting him to be or to have been involved in acts of terrorism connected with the affairs of Northern Ireland.

Where such a person is detained under the said Article 9 or 10 he may be detained for up to 48 hours on the authority of an examining officer and thereafter, where the Secretary of State extends the detention period, for up to a further five days.

In its judgment of 29 November 1988 in the Case of *Brogan and Others*, the European Court of Human Rights held that there had been a violation of Article 5(3) in respect of each of the applicants, all of whom had been detained under Section 12 of the 1984 Act. The Court held that even the shortest of the four periods of detention concerned, namely four days and six hours, fell outside the constraints as to time permitted by the first part of Article 5(3). In addition, the Court held that there had been a violation of Article 5(5) in the case of each applicant.

Following this judgment, the Secretary of State for the Home Department informed Parliament on 6 December 1988 that, against the background of the terrorist campaign, and the over-riding need to bring terrorists to justice, the Government did not believe that the maximum period of detention should be reduced. He informed Parliament that the Government were examining the matter with a view to responding to the judgment. On 22 December 1988, the Secretary of State further informed Parliament that it remained the Government's wish, if it could be achieved, to find a judicial process under which extended detention might be reviewed and where appropriate authorised by a judge or other judicial officer. But a further period of reflection and consultation was necessary before the Government could bring forward a firm and final view.

Since the judgment of 29 November 1988 as well as previously, the Government have found it necessary to continue to exercise, in relation to terrorism connected with the affairs of Northern Ireland, the powers described above enabling further detention without charge for periods of up to 5 days, on the authority of the Secretary of State, to the extent strictly required by the exigencies of the situation to enable necessary enquiries and investigations properly to be completed in order to decide whether criminal proceedings should be instituted. To the extent that the exercise of these powers may be inconsistent with the obligations imposed by the Convention the Government has availed itself of the right of derogation conferred by Article 15(1) of the Convention and will continue to do so until further notice.

Dated 23 December 1988.

The 1989 notification

The United Kingdom Permanent Representative to the Council of Europe presents his compliments to the Secretary General of the Council, and has the honour to convey the following information.

In his communication to the Secretary General of 23 December 1988, reference was made to the introduction and exercise of certain powers under section 12 of the Prevention of Terrorism (Temporary Provisions) Act 1984, Article 9 of the Prevention of Terrorism (Supplemental Temporary Provisions) Order 1984 and Article 10 of the Prevention of Terrorism (Supplemental Temporary Provisions) (Northern Ireland) Order 1984.

These provisions have been replaced by section 14 of and paragraph 6 of Schedule 5 to the Prevention of Terrorism (Temporary Provisions) Act 1989, which make comparable provision. They came into force on 22 March 1989. A copy of these provisions is enclosed.

The United Kingdom Permanent Representative avails himself of this opportunity to renew to the Secretary General the assurance of his highest consideration.

23 March 1989.

PART II

RESERVATION

At the time of signing the present (First) Protocol, I declare that, in view of certain provisions of the Education Acts in the United Kingdom, the principle affirmed in the second sentence of Article 2 is accepted by the United Kingdom only so far as it is compatible with the provision of efficient instruction and training, and the avoidance of unreasonable public expenditure.

Dated 20 March 1952

Made by the United Kingdom Permanent Representative to the Council of Europe.

SCHEDULE 4

JUDICIAL PENSIONS

Duty to make orders about pensions

1.—(1) The appropriate Minister must by order make provision with respect to pensions payable to or in respect of any holder of a judicial office who serves as an ECHR judge.

(2) A pensions order must include such provision as the Minister making it considers is necessary to secure that-

(a) an ECHR judge who was, immediately before his appointment as an ECHR judge, a member of a judicial pension scheme is entitled to remain as a member of that scheme;

(b) the terms on which he remains a member of the scheme are those which would have been applicable had he not been appointed as an ECHR judge; and

(c) entitlement to benefits payable in accordance with the scheme continues to be determined as if, while serving as an ECHR judge, his salary was that which would (but for section 18(4)) have been payable to him in respect of his continuing service as the holder of his judicial office.

Contributions

2.A pensions order may, in particular, make provision-

(a) for any contributions which are payable by a person who remains a member of a scheme as a result of the order, and which would otherwise be payable by deduction from his salary, to be made otherwise than by deduction from his salary as an ECHR judge; and

(b) for such contributions to be collected in such manner as may be determined by the administrators of the scheme.

Amendments of other enactments

3.A pensions order may amend any provision of, or made under, a pensions Act in such manner and to such extent as the Minister making the order considers necessary or expedient to ensure the proper administration of any scheme to which it relates.

Definitions

4.In this Schedule-

"appropriate Minister" means-

(a) in relation to any judicial office whose jurisdiction is exercisable exclusively in relation to Scotland, the Secretary of State; and

(b) otherwise, the Lord Chancellor;

"ECHR judge" means the holder of a judicial office who is serving as a judge of the Court;
"judicial pension scheme" means a scheme established by and in accordance with a pensions Act;
"pensions Act" means-

(a) the County Courts Act (Northern Ireland) 1959;
(b) the Sheriffs' Pensions (Scotland) Act 1961;
(c) the Judicial Pensions Act 1981; or
(d) the Judicial Pensions and Retirement Act 1993; and

"pensions order" means an order made under paragraph 1.

Appendix 2

Council of Europe

European Treaties

ETS No. 5

Convention for the Protection of Human Rights and Fundamental Freedoms

Rome, 4.XI.1950

"The text of the Convention had been amended according to the provisions of Protocol No. 3 (ETS No. 45), which entered into force on 21 September 1970, of Protocol No. 5 (ETS No. 55), which entered into force on 20 December 1971 and of Protocol No. 8 (ETS No. 118), which entered into force on 1 January 1990, and comprised also the text of Protocol No. 2 (ETS No. 44) which, in accordance with Article 5, paragraph 3 thereof, had been an integral part of the Convention since its entry into force on 21 September 1970. All provisions which had been amended or added by these Protocols are replaced by Protocol No. 11 (ETS No. 155), as from the date of its entry into force on 1 November 1998. As from that date, Protocol n° 9 (ETS No. 140), which entered into force on 1 October 1994, is repealed and Protocol n° 10 (ETS No. 146), which has not entered into force, has lost its purpose."

The governments signatory hereto, being members of the Council of Europe,

Considering the Universal Declaration of Human Rights proclaimed by the General Assembly of the United Nations on 10th December 1948;

Considering that this Declaration aims at securing the universal and effective recognition and observance of the Rights therein declared;

Considering that the aim of the Council of Europe is the achievement of greater unity between its members and that one of the methods by which that aim is to be pursued is the maintenance and further realisation of human rights and fundamental freedoms;

Reaffirming their profound belief in those fundamental freedoms which are the foundation of justice and peace in the world and are best maintained on the one hand by an effective political democracy and on the other by a common understanding and observance of the human rights upon which they depend;

Being resolved, as the governments of European countries which are like-minded and have a common heritage of political traditions, ideals, freedom and the rule of law, to take the first steps for the collective enforcement of certain of the rights stated in the Universal Declaration,

Have agreed as follows:

Article 1–Obligation to respect human rights

The High Contracting Parties shall secure to everyone within their jurisdiction the rights and freedoms defined in Section I of this Convention.

Section I–Rights and freedoms

Article 2–Right to life

1 Everyone's right to life shall be protected by law. No one shall be deprived of his life intentionally save in the execution of a sentence of a court following his conviction of a crime for which this penalty is provided by law.

2 Deprivation of life shall not be regarded as inflicted in contravention of this article when it results from the use of force which is no more than absolutely necessary:

a in defence of any person from unlawful violence;

b in order to effect a lawful arrest or to prevent the escape of a person lawfully detained;

c in action lawfully taken for the purpose of quelling a riot or insurrection.

Article 3–Prohibition of torture
No one shall be subjected to torture or to inhuman or degrading treatment or punishment.

Article 4–Prohibition of slavery and forced labour
1 No one shall be held in slavery or servitude.

2 No one shall be required to perform forced or compulsory labour.

3 For the purpose of this article the term "forced or compulsory labour" shall not include:

a any work required to be done in the ordinary course of detention imposed according to the provisions of Article 5 of this Convention or during conditional release from such detention;

b any service of a military character or, in case of conscientious objectors in countries where they are recognised, service exacted instead of compulsory military service;

c any service exacted in case of an emergency or calamity threatening the life or well-being of the community;

d any work or service which forms part of normal civic obligations.

Article 5–Right to liberty and security
1 Everyone has the right to liberty and security of person. No one shall be deprived of his liberty save in the following cases and in accordance with a procedure prescribed by law:

a the lawful detention of a person after conviction by a competent court;

b the lawful arrest or detention of a person for non-compliance with the lawful order of a court or in order to secure the fulfilment of any obligation prescribed by law;

c the lawful arrest or detention of a person effected for the purpose of bringing him before the competent legal authority on reasonable suspicion of having committed an offence or when it is reasonably considered necessary to prevent his committing an offence or fleeing after having done so;

d the detention of a minor by lawful order for the purpose of educational supervision or his lawful detention for the purpose of bringing him before the competent legal authority;

e the lawful detention of persons for the prevention of the spreading of infectious diseases, of persons of unsound mind, alcoholics or drug addicts or vagrants;

f the lawful arrest or detention of a person to prevent his effecting an unauthorised entry into the country or of a person against whom action is being taken with a view to deportation or extradition.

2 Everyone who is arrested shall be informed promptly, in a language which he understands, of the reasons for his arrest and of any charge against him.

3 Everyone arrested or detained in accordance with the provisions of paragraph 1.c of this article shall be brought promptly before a judge or other officer authorised by law to exercise judicial power and shall be entitled to trial within a reasonable time or to release pending trial. Release may be conditioned by guarantees to appear for trial.

4 Everyone who is deprived of his liberty by arrest or detention shall be entitled to take proceedings by which the lawfulness of his detention shall be decided speedily by a court and his release ordered if the detention is not lawful.

5 Everyone who has been the victim of arrest or detention in contravention of the provisions of this article shall have an enforceable right to compensation.

Article 6–Right to a fair trial

1 In the determination of his civil rights and obligations or of any criminal charge against him, everyone is entitled to a fair and public hearing within a reasonable time by an independent and impartial tribunal established by law. Judgment shall be pronounced publicly but the press and public may be excluded from all or part of the trial in the interests of morals, public order or national security in a democratic society, where the interests of juveniles or the protection of the private life of the parties so require, or to the extent strictly necessary in the opinion of the court in special circumstances where publicity would prejudice the interests of justice.

2 Everyone charged with a criminal offence shall be presumed innocent until proved guilty according to law.

3 Everyone charged with a criminal offence has the following minimum rights:

a to be informed promptly, in a language which he understands and in detail, of the nature and cause of the accusation against him;

b to have adequate time and facilities for the preparation of his defence;

c to defend himself in person or through legal assistance of his own choosing or, if he has not sufficient means to pay for legal assistance, to be given it free when the interests of justice so require;

d to examine or have examined witnesses against him and to obtain the attendance and examination of witnesses on his behalf under the same conditions as witnesses against him;

e to have the free assistance of an interpreter if he cannot understand or speak the language used in court.

Article 7–No punishment without law

1 No one shall be held guilty of any criminal offence on account of any act or omission which did not constitute a criminal offence under national or international law at the time when it was committed. Nor shall a heavier penalty be imposed than the one that was applicable at the time the criminal offence was committed.

2 This article shall not prejudice the trial and punishment of any person for any act or omission which, at the time when it was committed, was criminal according to the general principles of law recognised by civilised nations.

Article 8–Right to respect for private and family life

1 Everyone has the right to respect for his private and family life, his home and his correspondence.

2 There shall be no interference by a public authority with the exercise of this right except such as is in accordance with the law and is necessary in a democratic society in the interests of national security, public safety or the economic well-being of the country, for the prevention of disorder or crime, for the protection of health or morals, or for the protection of the rights and freedoms of others.

Article 9–Freedom of thought, conscience and religion

1 Everyone has the right to freedom of thought, conscience and religion; this right includes freedom to change his religion or belief and freedom, either alone or in community with others and in public or private, to manifest his religion or belief, in worship, teaching, practice and observance.

2 Freedom to manifest one's religion or beliefs shall be subject only to such limitations as are prescribed by law and are necessary in a democratic society in the interests of public safety, for the protection of public order, health or morals, or for the protection of the rights and freedoms of others.

Article 10—Freedom of expression
    1 Everyone has the right to freedom of expression. This right shall include freedom to hold opinions and to receive and impart information and ideas without interference by public authority and regardless of frontiers. This article shall not prevent States from requiring the licensing of broadcasting, television or cinema enterprises.

    2 The exercise of these freedoms, since it carries with it duties and responsibilities, may be subject to such formalities, conditions, restrictions or penalties as are prescribed by law and are necessary in a democratic society, in the interests of national security, territorial integrity or public safety, for the prevention of disorder or crime, for the protection of health or morals, for the protection of the reputation or rights of others, for preventing the disclosure of information received in confidence, or for maintaining the authority and impartiality of the judiciary.

Article 11–Freedom of assembly and association
    1 Everyone has the right to freedom of peaceful assembly and to freedom of association with others, including the right to form and to join trade unions for the protection of his interests.

    2 No restrictions shall be placed on the exercise of these rights other than such as are prescribed by law and are necessary in a democratic society in the interests of national security or public safety, for the prevention of disorder or crime, for the protection of health or morals or for the protection of the rights and freedoms of others. This article shall not prevent the imposition of lawful restrictions on the exercise of these rights by members of the armed forces, of the police or of the administration of the State.

Article 12—Right to marry
Men and women of marriageable age have the right to marry and to found a family, according to the national laws governing the exercise of this right.

Article 13–Right to an effective remedy
Everyone whose rights and freedoms as set forth in this Convention are violated shall have an effective remedy before a national authority notwithstanding that the violation has been committed by persons acting in an official capacity.

Article 14–Prohibition of discrimination
The enjoyment of the rights and freedoms set forth in this Convention shall be secured without discrimination on any ground such as sex, race, colour, language, religion, political or other opinion, national or social origin, association with a national minority, property, birth or other status.

Article 15–Derogation in time of emergency
    1 In time of war or other public emergency threatening the life of the nation any High Contracting Party may take measures derogating from its obligations under this Convention to the extent strictly required by the exigencies of the situation, provided that such measures are not inconsistent with its other obligations under international law.

    2 No derogation from Article 2, except in respect of deaths resulting from lawful acts of war, or from Articles 3, 4 (paragraph 1) and 7 shall be made under this provision.

    3 Any High Contracting Party availing itself of this right of derogation shall keep the Secretary General of the Council of Europe fully informed of the measures which it has taken and the reasons therefor. It shall also inform the Secretary General of the Council of Europe when such measures have ceased to operate and the provisions of the Convention are again being fully executed.

Article 16—Restrictions on political activity of aliens
Nothing in Articles 10, 11 and 14 shall be regarded as preventing the High Contracting Parties from imposing restrictions on the political activity of aliens.

Article 17–Prohibition of abuse of rights
Nothing in this Convention may be interpreted as implying for any State, group or person any right to engage in any activity or perform any act aimed at the destruction of any of the rights and freedoms set forth herein or at their limitation to a greater extent than is provided for in the Convention.

Article 18–Limitation on use of restrictions on rights
The restrictions permitted under this Convention to the said rights and freedoms shall not be applied for any purpose other than those for which they have been prescribed.

Section II–European Court of Human Rights

Article 19–Establishment of the Court
To ensure the observance of the engagements undertaken by the High Contracting Parties in the Convention and the Protocols thereto, there shall be set up a European Court of Human Rights, hereinafter referred to as "the Court". It shall function on a permanent basis.

Article 20–Number of judges
The Court shall consist of a number of judges equal to that of the High Contracting Parties.

Article 21–Criteria for office
1 The judges shall be of high moral character and must either possess the qualifications required for appointment to high judicial office or be jurisconsults of recognised competence.

2 The judges shall sit on the Court in their individual capacity.

3 During their term of office the judges shall not engage in any activity which is incompatible with their independence, impartiality or with the demands of a full-time office; all questions arising from the application of this paragraph shall be decided by the Court.

Article 22–Election of judges
1 The judges shall be elected by the Parliamentary Assembly with respect to each High Contracting Party by a majority of votes cast from a list of three candidates nominated by the High Contracting Party.

2 The same procedure shall be followed to complete the Court in the event of the accession of new High Contracting Parties and in filling casual vacancies.

Article 23–Terms of office
1 The judges shall be elected for a period of six years. They may be re-elected. However, the terms of office of one-half of the judges elected at the first election shall expire at the end of three years.

2 The judges whose terms of office are to expire at the end of the initial period of three years shall be chosen by lot by the Secretary General of the Council of Europe immediately after their election.

3 In order to ensure that, as far as possible, the terms of office of one-half of the judges are renewed every three years, the Parliamentary Assembly may decide, before proceeding to any subsequent election, that the term or terms of office of one or more judges to be elected shall be for a period other than six years but not more than nine and not less than three years.

4 In cases where more than one term of office is involved and where the Parliamentary Assembly applies the preceding paragraph, the allocation of the terms of office shall be effected by a drawing of lots by the Secretary General of the Council of Europe immediately after the election.

5 A judge elected to replace a judge whose term of office has not expired shall hold office for the remainder of his predecessor's term.

6 The terms of office of judges shall expire when they reach the age of 70.

7 The judges shall hold office until replaced. They shall, however, continue to deal with such cases as they already have under consideration.

Article 24–Dismissal
No judge may be dismissed from his office unless the other judges decide by a majority of two-thirds that he has ceased to fulfil the required conditions.

Article 25–Registry and legal secretaries
The Court shall have a registry, the functions and organisation of which shall be laid down in the rules of the Court. The Court shall be assisted by legal secretaries.

Article 26–Plenary Court
The plenary Court shall

a elect its President and one or two Vice-Presidents for a period of three years; they may be re-elected;

b set up Chambers, constituted for a fixed period of time;

c elect the Presidents of the Chambers of the Court; they may be re-elected;

d adopt the rules of the Court, and

e elect the Registrar and one or more Deputy Registrars.

Article 27–Committees, Chambers and Grand Chamber
1 To consider cases brought before it, the Court shall sit in committees of three judges, in Chambers of seven judges and in a Grand Chamber of seventeen judges. The Court's Chambers shall set up committees for a fixed period of time.

2 There shall sit as an *ex officio* member of the Chamber and the Grand Chamber the judge elected in respect of the State Party concerned or, if there is none or if he is unable to sit, a person of its choice who shall sit in the capacity of judge.

3 The Grand Chamber shall also include the President of the Court, the Vice-Presidents, the Presidents of the Chambers and other judges chosen in accordance with the rules of the Court. When a case is referred to the Grand Chamber under Article 43, no judge from the Chamber which rendered the judgment shall sit in the Grand Chamber, with the exception of the President of the Chamber and the judge who sat in respect of the State Party concerned.

Article 28–Declarations of inadmissibility by committees
A committee may, by a unanimous vote, declare inadmissible or strike out of its list of cases an application submitted under Article 34 where such a decision can be taken without further examination. The decision shall be final.

Article 29–Decisions by Chambers on admissibility and merits
1 If no decision is taken under Article 28, a Chamber shall decide on the admissibility and merits of individual applications submitted under Article 34.

2 A Chamber shall decide on the admissibility and merits of inter-State applications submitted under Article 33.

3 The decision on admissibility shall be taken separately unless the Court, in exceptional cases, decides otherwise.

Article 30–Relinquishment of jurisdiction to the Grand Chamber
Where a case pending before a Chamber raises a serious question affecting the interpretation of the Convention or the protocols thereto, or where the resolution of a question before the Chamber might have a result inconsistent with a judgment previously delivered by the Court, the Chamber may, at any time before it has rendered its judgment, relinquish jurisdiction in favour of the Grand Chamber, unless one of the parties to the case objects.

Article 31–Powers of the Grand Chamber
The Grand Chamber shall

a determine applications submitted either under Article 33 or Article 34 when a Chamber has relinquished jurisdiction under Article 30 or when the case has been referred to it under Article 43; and

b consider requests for advisory opinions submitted under Article 47.

Article 32–Jurisdiction of the Court
    1 The jurisdiction of the Court shall extend to all matters concerning the interpretation and application of the Convention and the protocols thereto which are referred to it as provided in Articles 33, 34 and 47.

    2 In the event of dispute as to whether the Court has jurisdiction, the Court shall decide.

Article 33–Inter-State cases
    Any High Contracting Party may refer to the Court any alleged breach of the provisions of the Convention and the protocols thereto by another High Contracting Party.

Article 34–Individual applications
    The Court may receive applications from any person, non-governmental organisation or group of individuals claiming to be the victim of a violation by one of the High Contracting Parties of the rights set forth in the Convention or the protocols thereto. The High Contracting Parties undertake not to hinder in any way the effective exercise of this right.

Article 35–Admissibility criteria
    1 The Court may only deal with the matter after all domestic remedies have been exhausted, according to the generally recognised rules of international law, and within a period of six months from the date on which the final decision was taken.

    2 The Court shall not deal with any application submitted under Article 34 that

    a is anonymous; or

    b is substantially the same as a matter that has already been examined by the Court or has already been submitted to another procedure of international investigation or settlement and contains no relevant new information.

    3 The Court shall declare inadmissible any individual application submitted under Article 34 which it considers incompatible with the provisions of the Convention or the protocols thereto, manifestly ill-founded, or an abuse of the right of application.

    4 The Court shall reject any application which it considers inadmissible under this Article. It may do so at any stage of the proceedings.

Article 36–Third party intervention
    1 In all cases before a Chamber or the Grand Chamber, a High Contracting Party one of whose nationals is an applicant shall have the right to submit written comments and to take part in hearings.

    2 The President of the Court may, in the interest of the proper administration of justice, invite any High Contracting Party which is not a party to the proceedings or any person concerned who is not the applicant to submit written comments or take part in hearings.

Article 37–Striking out applications
    1 The Court may at any stage of the proceedings decide to strike an application out of its list of cases where the circumstances lead to the conclusion that

    a the applicant does not intend to pursue his application; or

    b the matter has been resolved; or

    c for any other reason established by the Court, it is no longer justified to continue the examination of the application.

    However, the Court shall continue the examination of the application if respect for human rights as defined in the Convention and the protocols thereto so requires.

    2 The Court may decide to restore an application to its list of cases if it considers that the circumstances justify such a course.

Article 38–Examination of the case and friendly settlement proceedings
　1　If the Court declares the application admissible, it shall

　　a　pursue the examination of the case, together with the representatives of the parties, and if need be, undertake an investigation, for the effective conduct of which the States concerned shall furnish all necessary facilities;

　　b　place itself at the disposal of the parties concerned with a view to securing a friendly settlement of the matter on the basis of respect for human rights as defined in the Convention and the protocols thereto.

　2　Proceedings conducted under paragraph 1.b shall be confidential.

Article 39–Finding of a friendly settlement
　If a friendly settlement is effected, the Court shall strike the case out of its list by means of a decision which shall be confined to a brief statement of the facts and of the solution reached.

Article 40–Public hearings and access to documents
　1　Hearings shall be in public unless the Court in exceptional circumstances decides otherwise.

　2　Documents deposited with the Registrar shall be accessible to the public unless the President of the Court decides otherwise.

Article 41–Just satisfaction
　If the Court finds that there has been a violation of the Convention or the protocols thereto, and if the internal law of the High Contracting Party concerned allows only partial reparation to be made, the Court shall, if necessary, afford just satisfaction to the injured party.

Article 42–Judgments of Chambers
　Judgments of Chambers shall become final in accordance with the provisions of Article 44, paragraph 2.

Article 43–Referral to the Grand Chamber
　1　Within a period of three months from the date of the judgment of the Chamber, any party to the case may, in exceptional cases, request that the case be referred to the Grand Chamber.

　2　A panel of five judges of the Grand Chamber shall accept the request if the case raises a serious question affecting the interpretation or application of the Convention or the protocols thereto, or a serious issue of general importance.

　3　If the panel accepts the request, the Grand Chamber shall decide the case by means of a judgment.

Article 44–Final judgments
　1　The judgment of the Grand Chamber shall be final.

　2　The judgment of a Chamber shall become final

　　a　when the parties declare that they will not request that the case be referred to the Grand Chamber; or

　　b　three months after the date of the judgment, if reference of the case to the Grand Chamber has not been requested; or

　　c　when the panel of the Grand Chamber rejects the request to refer under Article 43.

　3　The final judgment shall be published.

Article 45–Reasons for judgments and decisions
　1　Reasons shall be given for judgments as well as for decisions declaring applications admissible or inadmissible.

　2　If a judgment does not represent, in whole or in part, the unanimous opinion of the judges, any judge shall be entitled to deliver a separate opinion.

Article 46–Binding force and execution of judgments

    1 The High Contracting Parties undertake to abide by the final judgment of the Court in any case to which they are parties.

    2 The final judgment of the Court shall be transmitted to the Committee of Ministers, which shall supervise its execution.

Article 47–Advisory opinions

    1 The Court may, at the request of the Committee of Ministers, give advisory opinions on legal questions concerning the interpretation of the Convention and the protocols thereto.

    2 Such opinions shall not deal with any question relating to the content or scope of the rights or freedoms defined in Section I of the Convention and the protocols thereto, or with any other question which the Court or the Committee of Ministers might have to consider in consequence of any such proceedings as could be instituted in accordance with the Convention.

    3 Decisions of the Committee of Ministers to request an advisory opinion of the Court shall require a majority vote of the representatives entitled to sit on the Committee.

Article 48–Advisory jurisdiction of the Court

The Court shall decide whether a request for an advisory opinion submitted by the Committee of Ministers is within its competence as defined in Article 47.

Article 49–Reasons for advisory opinions

    1 Reasons shall be given for advisory opinions of the Court.

    2 If the advisory opinion does not represent, in whole or in part, the unanimous opinion of the judges, any judge shall be entitled to deliver a separate opinion.

    3 Advisory opinions of the Court shall be communicated to the Committee of Ministers.

Article 50–Expenditure on the Court

The expenditure on the Court shall be borne by the Council of Europe.

Article 51–Privileges and immunities of judges

The judges shall be entitled, during the exercise of their functions, to the privileges and immunities provided for in Article 40 of the Statute of the Council of Europe and in the agreements made thereunder.

Section III–Miscellaneous provisions

Article 52–Inquiries by the Secretary General

On receipt of a request from the Secretary General of the Council of Europe any High Contracting Party shall furnish an explanation of the manner in which its internal law ensures the effective implementation of any of the provisions of the Convention.

Article 53–Safeguard for existing human rights

Nothing in this Convention shall be construed as limiting or derogating from any of the human rights and fundamental freedoms which may be ensured under the laws of any High Contracting Party or under any other agreement to which it is a Party.

Article 54–Powers of the Committee of Ministers

Nothing in this Convention shall prejudice the powers conferred on the Committee of Ministers by the Statute of the Council of Europe.

Article 55–Exclusion of other means of dispute settlement

The High Contracting Parties agree that, except by special agreement, they will not avail themselves of treaties, conventions or declarations in force between them for the purpose of submitting, by way of petition, a dispute arising out of the interpretation or application of this Convention to a means of settlement other than those provided for in this Convention.

Article 56–Territorial application

    1 Any State may at the time of its ratification or at any time thereafter declare by notification addressed to the Secretary General of the Council of Europe that the

present Convention shall, subject to paragraph 4 of this Article, extend to all or any of the territories for whose international relations it is responsible.

2 The Convention shall extend to the territory or territories named in the notification as from the thirtieth day after the receipt of this notification by the Secretary General of the Council of Europe.

3 The provisions of this Convention shall be applied in such territories with due regard, however, to local requirements.

4 Any State which has made a declaration in accordance with paragraph 1 of this article may at any time thereafter declare on behalf of one or more of the territories to which the declaration relates that it accepts the competence of the Court to receive applications from individuals, non-governmental organisations or groups of individuals as provided by Article 34 of the Convention.

Article 57–Reservations

1 Any State may, when signing this Convention or when depositing its instrument of ratification, make a reservation in respect of any particular provision of the Convention to the extent that any law then in force in its territory is not in conformity with the provision. Reservations of a general character shall not be permitted under this article.

2 Any reservation made under this article shall contain a brief statement of the law concerned.

Article 58–Denunciation

1 A High Contracting Party may denounce the present Convention only after the expiry of five years from the date on which it became a party to it and after six months' notice contained in a notification addressed to the Secretary General of the Council of Europe, who shall inform the other High Contracting Parties.

2 Such a denunciation shall not have the effect of releasing the High Contracting Party concerned from its obligations under this Convention in respect of any act which, being capable of constituting a violation of such obligations, may have been performed by it before the date at which the denunciation became effective.

3 Any High Contracting Party which shall cease to be a member of the Council of Europe shall cease to be a Party to this Convention under the same conditions.

4 The Convention may be denounced in accordance with the provisions of the preceding paragraphs in respect of any territory to which it has been declared to extend under the terms of Article 56.

Article 59–Signature and ratification

1 This Convention shall be open to the signature of the members of the Council of Europe. It shall be ratified. Ratifications shall be deposited with the Secretary General of the Council of Europe.

2 The present Convention shall come into force after the deposit of ten instruments of ratification.

3 As regards any signatory ratifying subsequently, the Convention shall come into force at the date of the deposit of its instrument of ratification.

4 The Secretary General of the Council of Europe shall notify all the members of the Council of Europe of the entry into force of the Convention, the names of the High Contracting Parties who have ratified it, and the deposit of all instruments of ratification which may be effected subsequently.

Done at Rome this 4th day of November 1950, in English and French, both texts being equally authentic, in a single copy which shall remain deposited in the archives of the Council of Europe. The Secretary General shall transmit certified copies to each of the signatories.

Where to find Convention case law

An explanation of the different kinds decision emanating from Strasbourg is given in Chapter 2 of Part 1. This Appendix indicates where the law is reported.

(i) Law Reports

Series A[1] represents the official report of every judgment of the Strasbourg Court up to and including 1995, together with the Commission's Report. Series B of the official reports contains arguments and documents submitted by the parties. Earlier judgments were published with no headnotes, while a summary headnote was included. The series has no indexing. From 1996 onwards, official reports of cases decided by the Court have been published[2] in a series entitled "Reports of Judgments and Decisions" ("RJD").

Admissibility decisions of the Commission made before 1975 were published in roneo form in a series entitled "**Collection of Decisions**" ("Coll." or "CD") (now out of print). Early decisions are also found in the **Yearbook of the European Convention on Human Rights** ("Ybk" or "YB"), which also contains extracts from Reports and judgments of the Court. The early Commission decisions are unlikely to be of significance today.[3] **Decisions and Reports** ("D&R" or "DR"), published by the Commission since 1975, contain selected admissibility decisions of the Commission, Reports of Friendly Settlements and Merits Reports of the Commission in cases decided by the Committee of Ministers, i.e. not referred to the Court. Consolidated index volumes of D&R exist (1–20, 21–40, 41–60 and 61 to 75 and in 83 for 76–83); these index volumes are easy to use and list cases by name, number and subject-matter. Together with one of the standard works on the Convention,[4] the D&R indexes facilitate efficient research into Commission case law.

European Human Rights Reports ("E.H.R.R."), published[5] since 1979, contain nearly all judgments of the Strasbourg Court, with traditional headnotes and case references. Indexes list cases by ECHR provision, name and subject-matter. Volume 1 (1978–79) contains all judgments of the Strasbourg Court which were delivered before the E.H.R.R. started. From Volume 3 (1981 onwards), selected Commission decisions on admissibility, and selected Reports, are included with indexing, occasionally in the main pages of E.H.R.R., mostly in the supplement entitled "Summaries and Extracts", which is printed at the end of each bound volume. From the later part of Volume 13 (1991), the Commission's Opinion, extracted from its Report. is included in the report of the judgment after the statement of facts and before the Court's own ruling on the law.

Butterworths Human Rights Cases ("B.H.R.C."), published since 1997, contain reports of human rights cases decided by international tribunals and by courts from all over the world. Headnotes are included, as are indexes by subject-matter.

The main periodical on Convention law is European Human Rights Law Review ("E.H.R.L.R."). In addition to articles and commentaries. it contains summaries of recent judgments and decisions.

Commonwealth cases are reported in the usual law reports for each jurisdiction. Most judgments can be obtained through the Internet. Useful web-sites include:

---

[1] Published by the German publishers, Carl Heymanns Verlag KG (Luxemburger Straße 449, D-50939 Köln).
[2] By Carl Heymanns.
[3] See above paras 2–04 and C0–08.
[4] See bibliography, below, p. 413.
[5] By Sweet & Maxwell.

The Constitutional Court of South Africa *http://www.law.wits.ac.za/court/courtpam.html*
The Supreme Court of Canada *http://www.droit.umontreal.ca/doc/csc-scc/en/index.html*
Foundation Law, giving access to Australian, New Zealand and international legal materials
http://www.fl.asn.au/
The Supreme Court of the USA *http:/ /www.findlaw.com/casecode/supreme.html*
International Human Rights Reports ("IHRR"), published by the Human Rights Law Centre
University of Nottingham since 1994, report decisions of other major human rights treaty
monitoring bodies such as the Human Rights Committee (established under the International
Covenant on Civil and Political Rights) and the Inter-American Court of Human Rights.

(ii)   European Commission and Court of Human Rights Information
   Human Rights Information Centre, The Council of Europe, 67006, Strasbourg Cedex
France;   Telephone: 00–333–88–41–2024;   Fax: 00–333–88–41–2704.   E-mail:
hricdoc@hric.coe.fr
The Court's web-site is at *http://www.coe.fr/dhcour/*; this contains general information,
judgments, lists of pending cases, rules of procedure and press releases. It also provides a link
to HUDOC, the searchable database for the Strasbourg case law, at *http://www.coe.fr/dhcour/*
hudoc. After initial teething problems, HUDOC now works well and provides access to cases
through name and application number. Advanced searches also enable the researcher to
identify case law by Article, by country, by a number of key words and by the manner in
which the case was disposed of. Case law can be sorted by title, respondent, application
number date (oldest or newest first) or relevance. Cases can be viewed in HTM format or,
for more recent cases, downloaded in Word format.
Since the beginning of 1999 the Court's Registry has produced a very useful monthly
Information Note on the case law of the Court. All judgments and decisions referred to in
the note can be consulted in HUDOC.

(iii)   Commentaries on the Convention
   A number of texts have recently been published, or are about to be published, on the
Human Rights Act. Most prominent among them are *Human Rights Law and Practice*
(Butterworths, 1999) edited by Lord Lester of Herne Hill Q.C. and David Pannick Q.C. and
European Human Rights Law (Legal Action Group, 1999) by Keir Starmer. A good
introductory text is *Blackstone's Guide to the Human Rights Act 1998* (Blackstone Press,
1999) by John Wadham and Helen Mountfield. The following works, which deal with the
Convention rather than the Act, are particularly worth consulting.
Law of the European Convention on Human Rights (Butterworths, 1995) by D.J. Harris, M.
O'Boyle and C. Warbrick is a comprehensive and reliable commentary on the ECHR. It is
concisely written and contains a wealth of information. The book is well footnoted and
indexed.
A Practitioner's Guide to the European Convention of Human Rights (Sweet & Maxwell,
1998) by Karen Reid, a member of the Court Registry. is an excellent summary of the
Strasbourg case law dealt with by problem area (*e.g.* mental health abortion, prisoners' rights,
surveillance and secret files etc.). It also contains a very useful section setting out the Court's
awards of just satisfaction.
Constitutional Law and Human rights (Butterworths, 1996) by Lord Lester of Herne Hill
Q.C. and Professor Dawn Oliver and others. This is a stand-alone text of the re-issue volume
8(2) of *Halsbury Laws*; it provides a commentary on the ECHR and constitutional matters
with references to Commonwealth cases as well as ECHR Commission and Court case law.
The European Convention on Human Rights (OUP, 1996) by Advocate General Francis
Jacobs Q.C. and Professor Robin White is also a very good text. The foreword notes that the
coverage focuses principally on the Court's case law.
*Law and Practice of the European Convention on Human Rights and the European Social
Charter* (Council of Europe Publishing, 1996) by Donna Gomien, David Harris and Leo
Zwaak, is also a very readable, accurate statement of the case law. The book was
commissioned by the Council of Europe to provide a readable guide to the ECHR and the
Council of Europe Social Charter.
In addition to the above commentaries on the ECHR, attention should be drawn to three
studies of judicial technique and practice:

   (a)   *The development of international law by the European Court of Human Rights*
         (1993, 2nd ed., Manchester University Press) by Professor John Merrills of
         Sheffield University. This is a readable and accurate guide to the Convention

principles of construction. Topics covered include methods of interpretation, the effectiveness principle, margin of appreciation and general principles of law. The book is some 250 pages and is suitable to be read as a whole or to be used as a convenient reference tool on the topics studied.

(b) *Using Human Rights Law in English Courts*(Hart Publishing, 1997) by Murray Hunt. This is the most comprehensive and carefully considered guide to issues faced by English courts using the Convention prior to incorporation. Although some of the issues will change when the Human Rights Act takes effect, the work will remain a valuable study of judicial approaches and techniques.

(c) *The Future of Human Rights in the United Kingdom* (Hart Publishing, 1997) by Rabinder Singh. This is a well-written, thoughtful collection of essays on human rights issues produced shortly before publication of the Human Rights Bill and the White Paper.

Appendix 4

The White Paper

Rights Brought Home: the Human Rights Bill

Presented to Parliament by the Secretary of State for
The Home Department

By Command of Her Majesty

October 1997

CM 3782

Preface by the Prime Minister

The Government is pledged to modernise British politics. We are committed to a comprehensive programme of constitutional reform. We believe it is right to increase individual rights, to decentralise power, to open up government and to reform Parliament. The elements are well-known:

- a Scottish Parliament and a Welsh Assembly giving the people of Scotland and Wales more control over their own affairs within the United Kingdom;

- new rights, based on bringing the European Convention on Human Rights into United Kingdom law;

- an elected Mayor and new strategic authority for London with more accountability in the regions of England;

- freedom of information;

- a referendum on the voting system for the House of Commons; and

- reform of the House of Lords.

This White Paper explains the proposals contained in the Human Rights Bill which we are introducing into Parliament. The Bill marks a major step forward in the achievement of our programme of reform. It will give people in the United Kingdom opportunities to enforce their rights under the European Convention in British courts rather than having to incur the cost and delay of taking a case to the European Human Rights Commission and Court in Strasbourg. It will enhance the awareness of human rights in our society. And it stands alongside our decision to put the promotion of human rights at the forefront of our foreign policy.

I warmly commend these proposals to Parliament and to the people of this country.

TONY BLAIR

Introduction and Summary

The Government has a Manifesto commitment to introduce legislation to incorporate the European Convention on Human Rights into United Kingdom law. The Queen's Speech at the opening of the new Parliament announced that the Government would bring forward a Bill for this purpose in the current Session. We are now introducing the Human Rights Bill into Parliament. This White Paper explains what the Bill does, and why.

Before the General Election the Labour Party published a consultation document, *Bringing Rights Home*, setting out in some detail the case for incorporation, and its preliminary proposals for the way this should be done. A number of individuals and organisations responded helpfully with a range of comments on the paper, and have continued to make their knowledge and advice available to the Government. The Government's proposals for the Bill take full account of the responses to *Bringing Rights Home*. Any further comments in response to this White Paper or on the Bill should be sent to:

Human Rights Unit
Home Office
50 Queen Anne's Gate
London
SW1H 9AT.

We may make any comments we receive publicly available. Respondents who would prefer their comments to be treated in confidence are invited to indicate this expressly.

Chapter 1 of this White Paper explains the content and status of the European Convention on Human Rights and why the Government considers it desirable to give people in this country easier access to their Convention rights.

The United Kingdom is bound in international law to observe the Convention, which it ratified in 1951, and is answerable for any violation. In some limited circumstances, the United Kingdom courts can already take the Convention into account in domestic proceedings. But public authorities in the United Kingdom are not required as a matter of domestic law to comply with the Convention and, generally speaking, there is no means of having the application of the Convention rights tested in the United Kingdom courts. The Government believes that these arrangements are no longer adequate, given the importance which it attaches to the maintenance of basic human rights in this country, and that the time has come to "bring rights home".

Chapter 2 explains the Government's proposals to make the Convention rights enforceable directly in this country. The Bill makes it unlawful for public authorities to act in a way which is incompatible with the Convention rights. This will make it possible for people to invoke their rights in any proceedings–criminal or civil–brought against them by a public authority, or in proceedings which they may bring against a public authority. The Government prefers a system in which Convention rights can be called upon as they arise, in normal court proceedings, rather than confining their consideration to some kind of constitutional court. Courts and tribunals will be able to award whatever remedy, within their normal powers, is appropriate in the circumstances.

Although the courts will not, under the proposals in the Bill, be able to set aside Acts of the United Kingdom Parliament, the Bill requires them to interpret legislation as far as possible in accordance with the Convention. If this is not possible, the higher courts will be able to issue a formal declaration to the effect that the legislative provisions in question are incompatible with the Convention rights. It will then be up to the Government and

Parliament to put matters right. The Bill makes a "fast-track" procedure available for the purpose of amending the law so as to bring it into conformity with the Convention.

Chapter 3 sets out the other measures which the Government intends to take to ensure that the Convention rights are taken more fully into account in the development of new policies and of legislation. It also suggests that Parliament should itself establish a new Human Rights Committee. Amongst the matters on which the Government would welcome advice from a Parliamentary Committee is the possible establishment of a Human Rights Commission, but for the time being the Government has concluded that a new Commission should not be set up by means of this Bill.

Chapter 4 reviews the position on the derogation and reservation which the United Kingdom currently has in place in respect of the Convention and its First Protocol. The Government has concluded that these must remain for the time being, but the Bill requires any derogation to be subject to periodic renewal by Parliament and reservations to be subject to periodic review.

Chapter 4 also reviews the position in respect of those Protocols to the Convention which guarantee other rights (Protocols 4, 6 and 7) and which the United Kingdom has not so far accepted. The Government does not propose that the United Kingdom should ratify at present Protocol 4 or Protocol 6, but it does propose to sign and ratify Protocol 7 once some existing legislation has been amended.

The **Annex** sets out the text of the Convention rights themselves.

Chapter 1–The Case for Change

The European Convention on Human Rights

1.1 The European Convention for the Protection of Human Rights and Fundamental Freedoms is a treaty of the Council of Europe. This institution was established at the end of the Second World War, as part of the Allies' programme to reconstruct durable civilisation on the mainland of Europe. The Council was established before the European Union and, although many nations are members of both, the two bodies are quite separate.

1.2 The United Kingdom played a major part in drafting the Convention, and there was a broad agreement between the major political parties about the need for it (one of its draftsmen later became, as Lord Kilmuir, Lord Chancellor in the Conservative Administration from 1954 to 1962). The United Kingdom was among the first group of countries to sign the Convention. It was the very first country to ratify it, in March 1951. In 1966 the United Kingdom accepted that an individual person, and not merely another State, could bring a case against the United Kingdom in Strasbourg (the home of the European Commission of Human Rights and Court of Human Rights, which were established by the Convention). Successive administrations in the United Kingdom have maintained these arrangements.

1.3 The European Convention is not the only international human rights agreement to which the United Kingdom and other like-minded countries are party, but over the years it has become one of the premier agreements defining standards of behaviour across Europe. It was also for many years unique because of the system which it put in place for people from signatory countries to take complaints to Strasbourg and for those complaints to be judicially determined. These arrangements are by now well tried and tested. The rights and freedoms which are guaranteed under the Convention are ones with which the people of this country are plainly comfortable. They therefore afford an excellent basis for the Human Rights Bill which we are now introducing.

1.4 The constitutional arrangements in most continental European countries have meant that their acceptance of the Convention went hand in hand with its incorporation into their domestic law. In this country it was long believed that the rights and freedoms guaranteed by the Convention could be delivered under our common law. In the last two decades, however, there has been a growing awareness that it is not sufficient to rely on the common law and that incorporation is necessary.

1.5 The Liberal Democrat Peer, Lord Lester of Herne Hill QC, recently introduced two Bills on incorporation into the House of Lords (in 1994 and 1996). Before that, the then

Conservative MP Sir Edward Gardner QC introduced a Private Member's Bill on incorporation into the House of Commons in 1987. At the time of introducing his Bill he commented on the language of the Articles in the Convention, saying: "It is language which echoes right down the corridors of history. It goes deep into our history and as far back as Magna Carta." (Hansard, 6 February 1987, col.1224). In preparing this White Paper the Government has paid close attention to earlier debates and proposals for incorporation.

Convention rights

1.6 The Convention contains Articles which guarantee a number of basic human rights. They deal with the right to life (Article 2); torture or inhuman or degrading treatment or punishment (Article 3); slavery and forced labour (Article 4); liberty and security of person (Article 5); fair trial (Article 6); retrospective criminal laws (Article 7); respect for private and family life, home and correspondence (Article 8); freedom of thought, conscience and religion (Article 9); freedom of expression (Article 10); freedom of peaceful assembly and freedom of association, including the right to join a trade union (Article 11); the right to marry and to found a family (Article 12); and discrimination in the enjoyment of these rights and freedoms (Article 14).

1.7 The United Kingdom is also a party to the First Protocol to the Convention, which guarantees the right to the peaceful enjoyment of possessions (Article 1), the right to education (Article 2) and the right to free elections (Article 3).

1.8 The rights in the Convention are set out in general terms, and they are subject in the Convention to a number of qualifications which are also of a general character. Some of these qualifications are set out in the substantive Articles themselves (see, for example, Article 10, concerning freedom of expression); others are set out in Articles 16 to 18 of the Convention. Sometimes too the rights guaranteed under the Convention need to be balanced against each other (for example, those guaranteed by Article 8 and Article 10).

Applications under the Convention

1.9 Anyone within the United Kingdom jurisdiction who is aggrieved by an action of the executive or by the effect of the existing law and who believes it is contrary to the European Convention can submit a petition to the European Commission of Human Rights. The Commission will first consider whether the petition is admissible. One of the conditions of admissibility is that the applicant must have gone through all the steps available to him or her at home for challenging the decision which he or she is complaining about. If the Commission decides that a complaint is admissible, and if a friendly settlement cannot be secured, it will send a confidential report to the Committee of Ministers of the Council of Europe, stating its opinion on whether there has been a violation. The matter may end there, with a decision by the Committee (which in practice always adopts the opinion of the Commission), or the case may be referred on to the European Court of Human Rights[1] for consideration. If the Court finds that there has been a violation it may itself "afford just satisfaction" to the injured party by an award of damages or an award of costs and expenses. The court may also find that a formal finding of a violation is sufficient. There is no appeal from the Court.

Effect of a Court judgment

1.10 A finding by the European Court of Human Rights of a violation of a Convention right does not have the effect of automatically changing United Kingdom law and practice: that is a matter for the United Kingdom Government and Parliament. But the United Kingdom, like all other States who are parties to the Convention, has agreed to abide by the decisions of the Court or (where the case has not been referred to the Court) the Committee of Ministers. It follows that, in cases where a violation has been found, the State concerned must ensure that any deficiency in its internal laws is rectified so as to bring them into line with the Convention. The State is responsible for deciding what changes are needed, but it must satisfy the Committee of Ministers that the steps taken are sufficient. Successive United Kingdom administrations have accepted these obligations in full.

Relationship to current law in the United Kingdom

1.11 When the United Kingdom ratified the Convention the view was taken that the rights and freedoms which the Convention guarantees were already, in substance, fully protected in

---

[1] Protocol 11 to the Convention, which will come into force on 1 November 1998, will replace the existing part-time European Commission and Court of Human Rights with a single full-time Court.

British law. It was not considered necessary to write the Convention itself into British law, or to introduce any new laws in the United Kingdom in order to be sure of being able to comply with the Convention.

1.12 From the point of view of the **international** obligation which the United Kingdom was undertaking when it signed and ratified the Convention, this was understandable. Moreover, the European Court of Human Rights explicitly confirmed that it was not a necessary part of proper observance of the Convention that it should be incorporated into the laws of the States concerned.

1.13 However, since its drafting nearly 50 years ago, almost all the States which are party to the European Convention on Human Rights have gradually incorporated it into their domestic law in one way or another. Ireland and Norway have not done so, but Ireland has a Bill of Rights which guarantees rights similar to those guaranteed by the Convention and Norway is also in the process of incorporating the Convention. Several other countries with which we have close links and which share the common law tradition, such as Canada and New Zealand, have provided similar protection for human rights in their own legal systems.

The case for incorporation

1.14 The effect of non-incorporation on the British people is a very practical one. The rights, originally developed with major help from the United Kingdom Government, are no longer actually seen as British rights. And enforcing them takes too long and costs too much. It takes on average five years to get an action into the European Court of Human Rights once all domestic remedies have been exhausted; and it costs an average of £30,000. Bringing these rights home will mean that the British people will be able to argue for their rights in the British courts–without this inordinate delay and cost. It will also mean that the rights will be brought much more fully into the jurisprudence of the courts throughout the United Kingdom, and their interpretation will thus be far more subtly and powerfully woven into our law. And there will be another distinct benefit. British judges will be enabled to make a distinctively British contribution to the development of the jurisprudence of human rights in Europe.

1.15 Moreover, in the Government's view, the approach which the United Kingdom has so far adopted towards the Convention does not sufficiently reflect its importance and has not stood the test of time.

1.16 The most obvious proof of this lies in the number of cases in which the European Commission and Court have found that there have been violations of the Convention rights in the United Kingdom. The causes vary. The Government recognises that interpretations of the rights guaranteed under the Convention have developed over the years, reflecting changes in society and attitudes. Sometimes United Kingdom laws have proved to be inherently at odds with the Convention rights. On other occasions, although the law has been satisfactory, something has been done which our courts have held to be lawful by United Kingdom standards but which breaches the Convention. In other cases again, there has simply been no framework within which the compatibility with the Convention rights of an executive act or decision can be tested in the British courts: these courts can of course review the exercise of executive discretion, but they can do so only on the basis of what is lawful or unlawful according to the law in the United Kingdom as it stands. It is plainly unsatisfactory that someone should be the victim of a breach of the Convention standards by the State yet cannot bring any case at all in the British courts, simply because British law does not recognise the right in the same terms as one contained in the Convention.

1.17 For individuals, and for those advising them, the road to Strasbourg is long and hard. Even when they get there, the Convention enforcement machinery is subject to long delays. This might be convenient for a government which was half-hearted about the Convention and the right of individuals to apply under it, since it postpones the moment at which changes in domestic law or practice must be made. But it is not in keeping with the importance which this Government attaches to the observance of basic human rights.

Bringing Rights Home

1.18 We therefore believe that the time has come to enable people to enforce their Convention rights against the State in the British courts, rather than having to incur the delays and expense which are involved in taking a case to the European Human Rights Commission and Court in Strasbourg and which may altogether deter some people from pursuing their rights. Enabling courts in the United Kingdom to rule on the application of the Convention will also help to influence the development of case law on the Convention by the European Court of Human Rights on the basis of familiarity with our laws and customs and of sensitivity to practices and procedures in the United Kingdom. Our courts' decisions will provide the European Court with a useful source of information and reasoning for its own decisions. United Kingdom judges have a very high reputation internationally, but the fact that they do not deal in the same concepts as the European Court of Human Rights limits the extent to which their judgments can be drawn upon and followed. Enabling the Convention rights to be judged by British courts will also lead to closer scrutiny of the human rights implications of new legislation and new policies. If legislation is enacted which is incompatible with the Convention, a ruling by the domestic courts to that effect will be much more direct and immediate than a ruling from the European Court of Human Rights. The Government of the day, and Parliament, will want to minimise the risk of that happening.

1.19 Our aim is a straightforward one. It is to make more directly accessible the rights which the British people already enjoy under the Convention. In other words, to bring those rights home.

Chapter 2–The Government's Proposals for Enforcing the Convention Rights

2.1 The essential feature of the Human Rights Bill is that the United Kingdom will not be bound to give effect to the Convention rights merely as a matter of international law, but will also give them further effect directly in our domestic law. But there is more than one way of achieving this. This Chapter explains the choices which the Government has made for the Bill.

A new requirement on public authorities

2.2 Although the United Kingdom has an international obligation to comply with the Convention, there at present is no requirement in our domestic law on central and local government, or others exercising similar executive powers, to exercise those powers in a way which is compatible with the Convention. This Bill will change that by making it unlawful for public authorities to act in a way which is incompatible with the Convention rights. The definition of what constitutes a public authority is in wide terms. Examples of persons or organisations whose acts or omissions it is intended should be able to be challenged include central government (including executive agencies); local government; the police; immigration officers; prisons; courts and tribunals themselves; and, to the extent that they are exercising public functions, companies responsible for areas of activity which were previously within the public sector, such as the privatised utilities. The actions of Parliament, however, are excluded.

2.3 A person who is aggrieved by an act or omission on the part of a public authority which is incompatible with the Convention rights will be able to challenge the act or omission in the courts. The effects will be wide-ranging. They will extend both to legal actions which a public authority pursues against individuals (for example, where a criminal prosecution is brought or where an administrative decision is being enforced through legal proceedings) and to cases which individuals pursue against a public authority (for example, for judicial review of an executive decision). Convention points will normally be taken in the context of proceedings instituted against individuals or already open to them, but, if none is available, it will be possible for people to bring cases on Convention grounds alone. Individuals or organisations seeking judicial review of decisions by public authorities on Convention grounds will need to show that they have been directly affected, as they must if they take a case to Strasbourg.

2.4 It is our intention that people or organisations should be able to argue that their Convention rights have been infringed by a public authority in our courts at any level. This will enable the Convention rights to be applied from the outset against the facts and background of a particular case, and the people concerned to obtain their remedy at the earliest possible moment. We think this is preferable to allowing cases to run their ordinary course but then referring them to some kind of separate constitutional court which, like the European Court of Human Rights, would simply review cases which had already passed through the regular legal machinery. In considering Convention points, our courts will be required to take account of relevant decisions of the European Commission and Court of Human Rights (although these will not be binding).

2.5 The Convention is often described as a "living instrument" because it is interpreted by the European Court in the light of present day conditions and therefore reflects changing social attitudes and the changes in the circumstances of society. In future our judges will be able to contribute to this dynamic and evolving interpretation of the Convention. In particular, our courts will be required to balance the protection of individuals' fundamental rights against the demands of the general interest of the community, particularly in relation to Articles 8–11 where a State may restrict the protected right to the extent that this is "necessary in a democratic society".

Remedies for a failure to comply with the Convention

2.6 A public authority which is found to have acted unlawfully by failing to comply with the Convention will not be exposed to criminal penalties. But the court or tribunal will be able to grant the injured person any remedy which is within its normal powers to grant and which it considers appropriate and just in the circumstances. What remedy is appropriate will of course depend both on the facts of the case and on a proper balance between the rights of the individual and the public interest. In some cases, the right course may be for the decision of the public authority in the particular case to be quashed. In other cases, the only appropriate remedy may be an award of damages. The Bill provides that, in considering an award of damages on Convention grounds, the courts are to take into account the principles applied by the European Court of Human Rights in awarding compensation, so that people will be able to receive compensation from a domestic court equivalent to what they would have received in Strasbourg.

Interpretation of legislation

2.7 The Bill provides for legislation–both Acts of Parliament and secondary legislation–to be interpreted so far as possible so as to be compatible with the Convention. This goes far beyond the present rule which enables the courts to take the Convention into account in resolving any ambiguity in a legislative provision. The courts will be required to interpret legislation so as to uphold the Convention rights unless the legislation itself is so clearly incompatible with the Convention that it is impossible to do so.

2.8 This "rule of construction" is to apply to past as well as to future legislation. To the extent that it affects the meaning of a legislative provision, the courts will not be bound by previous interpretations. They will be able to build a new body of case law, taking into account the Convention rights.

A declaration of incompatibility with the Convention rights

2.9 If the courts decide in any case that it is impossible to interpret an Act of Parliament in a way which is compatible with the Convention, the Bill enables a formal declaration to be made that its provisions are incompatible with the Convention. A declaration of incompatibility will be an important statement to make, and the power to make it will be reserved to the higher courts. They will be able to make a declaration in any proceedings before them, whether the case originated with them (as, in the High Court, on judicial review of an executive act) or in considering an appeal from a lower court or tribunal. The Government will have the right to intervene in any proceedings where such a declaration is a possible outcome. A decision by the High Court or Court of Appeal, determining whether or not such a declaration should be made, will itself be appealable.

Effect of court decisions on legislation

2.10 A declaration that legislation is incompatible with the Convention rights will not of itself have the effect of changing the law, which will continue to apply. But it will almost certainly prompt the Government and Parliament to change the law.

2.11 The Government has considered very carefully whether it would be right for the Bill to go further, and give to courts in the United Kingdom the power to set aside an Act of Parliament which they believe is incompatible with the Convention rights. In considering this question, we have looked at a number of models. The Canadian Charter of Rights and Freedoms 1982 enables the courts to strike down any legislation which is inconsistent with the Charter, unless the legislation contains an explicit statement that it is to apply "notwithstanding" the provisions of the Charter. But legislation which has been struck down may be re-enacted with a "notwithstanding" clause. In New Zealand, on the other hand, although there was an earlier proposal for legislation on lines similar to the Canadian Charter, the human rights legislation which was eventually enacted after wide consultation took a different form. The New Zealand Bill of Rights Act 1990 is an "interpretative" statute which requires past and future legislation to be interpreted consistently with the rights contained in the Act as far as possible but provides that legislation stands if that is impossible. In Hong Kong, a middle course was adopted. The Hong Kong Bill of Rights Ordinance 1991 distinguishes between legislation enacted before and after the Ordinance took effect: previous legislation is subordinated to the provisions of the Ordinance, but subsequent legislation takes precedence over it.

2.12 The Government has also considered the European Communities Act 1972 which provides for European law, in cases where that law has "direct effect", to take precedence over domestic law. There is, however, an essential difference between European Community law and the European Convention on Human Rights, because it is a requirement of membership of the European Union that member States give priority to directly effective E.C. law in their own legal systems. There is no such requirement in the Convention.

2.13 The Government has reached the conclusion that courts should not have the power to set aside primary legislation, past or future, on the ground of incompatibility with the Convention. This conclusion arises from the importance which the Government attaches to Parliamentary sovereignty. In this context, Parliamentary sovereignty means that Parliament is competent to make any law on any matter of its choosing and no court may question the validity of any Act that it passes. In enacting legislation, Parliament is making decisions about important matters of public policy. The authority to make those decisions derives from a democratic mandate. Members of Parliament in the House of Commons possess such a mandate because they are elected, accountable and representative. To make provision in the Bill for the courts to set aside Acts of Parliament would confer on the judiciary a general power over the decisions of Parliament which under our present constitutional arrangements they do not possess, and would be likely on occasions to draw the judiciary into serious conflict with Parliament. There is no evidence to suggest that they desire this power, nor that the public wish them to have it. Certainly, this Government has no mandate for any such change.

2.14 It has been suggested that the courts should be able to uphold the rights in the Human Rights Bill in preference to any provisions of earlier legislation which are incompatible with those rights. This is on the basis that a later Act of Parliament takes precedence over an earlier Act if there is a conflict. But the Human Rights Bill is intended to provide a new basis for judicial interpretation of all legislation, not a basis for striking down any part of it.

2.15 The courts will, however, be able to strike down or set aside secondary legislation which is incompatible with the Convention, unless the terms of the parent statute make this impossible. The courts can already strike down or set aside secondary legislation when they consider it to be outside the powers conferred by the statute under which it is made, and it is right that they should be able to do so when it is incompatible with the Convention rights and could have been framed differently.

Entrenchment

2.16 On one view, human rights legislation is so important that it should be given added protection from subsequent amendment or repeal. The Constitution of the United States of America, for example, guarantees rights which can be amended or repealed only by securing qualified majorities in both the House of Representatives and the Senate, and among the States themselves. But an arrangement of this kind could not be reconciled with our own constitutional traditions, which allow any Act of Parliament to be amended or repealed by a subsequent Act of Parliament. We do not believe that it is necessary or would be desirable to attempt to devise such a special arrangement for this Bill.

Amending legislation

2.17 Although the Bill does not allow the courts to set aside Acts of Parliament, it will nevertheless have a profound impact on the way that legislation is interpreted and applied, and it will have the effect of putting the issues squarely to the Government and Parliament for further consideration. It is important to ensure that the Government and Parliament, for their part, can respond quickly. In the normal way, primary legislation can be amended only by further primary legislation, and this can take a long time. Given the volume of Government business, an early opportunity to legislate may not arise; and the process of legislating is itself protracted. Emergency legislation can be enacted very quickly indeed, but it is introduced only in the most exceptional circumstances.

2.18 The Bill provides for a fast-track procedure for changing legislation in response either to a declaration of incompatibility by our own higher courts or to a finding of a violation of the Convention in Strasbourg. The appropriate Government Minister will be able to amend the legislation by Order so as to make it compatible with the Convention. The Order will be subject to approval by both Houses of Parliament before taking effect, except where the need to amend the legislation is particularly urgent, when the Order will take effect immediately but will expire after a short period if not approved by Parliament.

2.19 There are already precedents for using secondary legislation to amend primary legislation in some circumstances, and we think the use of such a procedure is acceptable in this context and would be welcome as a means of improving the observance of human rights. Plainly the Minister would have to exercise this power only in relation to the provisions which contravene the Convention, together with any necessary consequential amendments. In other words, Ministers would not have carte blanche to amend unrelated parts of the Act in which the breach is discovered.

Scotland

2.20 In Scotland, the position with regard to Acts of the Westminster Parliament will be the same as in England and Wales. All courts will be required to interpret the legislation in a way which is compatible with the Convention so far as possible. If a provision is found to be incompatible with the Convention, the Court of Session or the High Court will be able to make a declarator to that effect, but this will not affect the validity or continuing operation of the provision.

2.21 The position will be different, however, in relation to Acts of the Scottish Parliament when it is established. The Government has decided that the Scottish Parliament will have no power to legislate in a way which is incompatible with the Convention; and similarly that the Scottish Executive will have no power to make subordinate legislation or to take executive action which is incompatible with the Convention. It will accordingly be possible to challenge such legislation and actions in the Scottish courts on the ground that the Scottish Parliament or Executive has incorrectly applied its powers. If the challenge is successful then the legislation or action would be held to be unlawful. As with other issues concerning the powers of the Scottish Parliament, there will be a procedure for inferior courts to refer such issues to the superior Scottish courts; and those courts in turn will be able to refer the matter to the Judicial Committee of the Privy Council. If such issues are decided by the superior Scottish courts, an appeal from their decision will be to the Judicial Committee. These arrangements are in line with the Government's general approach to devolution.

Wales

2.22 Similarly, the Welsh Assembly will not have power to make subordinate legislation or take executive action which is incompatible with the Convention. It will be possible to challenge such legislation and action in the courts, and for them to be quashed, on the ground that the Assembly has exceeded its powers.

Northern Ireland

2.23 Acts of the Westminster Parliament will be treated in the same way in Northern Ireland as in the rest of the United Kingdom. But Orders in Council and other related legislation will be treated as subordinate legislation. In other words, they will be struck down by the courts if they are incompatible with the Convention. Most such legislation is a temporary means of enacting legislation which would otherwise be done by measures of a devolved Northern Ireland legislature.

Chapter 3–Improving Compliance with the Convention Rights

3.1 The enforcement of Convention rights will be a matter for the courts, whilst the Government and Parliament will have the different but equally important responsibility of revising legislation where necessary. But it is also highly desirable for the Government to ensure as far as possible that legislation which it places before Parliament in the normal way is compatible with the Convention rights, and for Parliament to ensure that the human rights implications of legislation are subject to proper consideration before the legislation is enacted.

Government legislation

3.2 The Human Rights Bill introduces a new procedure to make the human rights implications of proposed Government legislation more transparent. The responsible Minister will be required to provide a statement that in his or her view the proposed Bill is compatible with the Convention. The Government intends to include this statement alongside the Explanatory and Financial Memorandum which accompanies a Bill when it is introduced into each House of Parliament.

3.3 There may be occasions where such a statement cannot be provided, for example because it is essential to legislate on a particular issue but the policy in question requires a risk to be taken in relation to the Convention, or because the arguments in relation to the Convention issues raised are not clear-cut. In such cases, the Minister will indicate that he or she cannot provide a positive statement but that the Government nevertheless wishes Parliament to proceed to consider the Bill. Parliament would expect the Minister to explain his or her reasons during the normal course of the proceedings on the Bill. This will ensure that the human rights implications are debated at the earliest opportunity.

Consideration of draft legislation within Government

3.4 The new requirement to make a statement about the compliance of draft legislation with the Convention will have a significant and beneficial impact on the preparation of draft legislation within Government before its introduction into Parliament. It will ensure that all Ministers, their departments and officials are fully seized of the gravity of the Convention's obligations in respect of human rights. But we also intend to strengthen collective Government procedures so as to ensure that a proper assessment is made of the human rights implications when collective approval is sought for a new policy, as well as when any draft Bill is considered by Ministers. Revised guidance to Departments on these procedures will, like the existing guidance, be publicly available.

3.5 Some central co-ordination will also be extremely desirable in considering the approach to be taken to Convention points in criminal or civil proceedings, or in proceedings for judicial review, to which a Government department is a party. This is likely to require an inter-departmental group of lawyers and administrators meeting on a regular basis to ensure that a consistent approach is taken and to ensure that developments in case law are well understood by all those in Government who are involved in proceedings on Convention points. We do not, however, see any need to make a particular Minister responsible for promoting human rights across Government, or to set up a separate new Unit for this purpose. The responsibility for complying with human rights requirements rests on the Government as a whole.

A Parliamentary Committee on Human Rights

3.6 *Bringing Rights Home* suggested that "Parliament itself should play a leading role in protecting the rights which are at the heart of a parliamentary democracy". How this is achieved is a matter for Parliament to decide, but in the Government's view the best course would be to establish a new Parliamentary Committee with functions relating to human rights. This would not require legislation or any change in Parliamentary procedure. There could be a Joint Committee of both Houses of Parliament or each House could have its own Committee; or there could be a Committee which met jointly for some purposes and separately for others.

3.7 The new Committee might conduct enquiries on a range of human rights issues relating to the Convention, and produce reports so as to assist the Government and Parliament in deciding what action to take. It might also want to range more widely, and examine issues relating to the other international obligations of the United Kingdom such as proposals to accept new rights under other human rights treaties.

Should there be a Human Rights Commission?

3.8 *Bringing Rights Home* canvassed views on the establishment of a Human Rights Commission, and this possibility has received a good deal of attention. No commitment to establish a Commission was, however, made in the Manifesto on which the Government was elected. The Government's priority is implementation of its Manifesto commitment to give further effect to the Convention rights in domestic law so that people can enforce those rights in United Kingdom courts. Establishment of a new Human Rights Commission is not central to that objective and does not need to form part of the current Bill.

3.9 Moreover, the idea of setting up a new human rights body is not universally acclaimed. Some reservations have been expressed, particularly from the point of view of the impact on existing bodies concerned with particular aspects of human rights, such as the Commission for Racial Equality and the Equal Opportunities Commission, whose primary concern is to protect the rights for which they were established. A quinquennial review is currently being conducted of the Equal Opportunities Commission, and the Government has also decided to establish a new Disability Rights Commission.

3.10 The Government's conclusion is that, before a Human Rights Commission could be established by legislation, more consideration needs to be given to how it would work in relation to such bodies, and to the new arrangements to be established for Parliamentary and Government scrutiny of human rights issues. This is necessary not only for the purposes of framing the legislation but also to justify the additional public expenditure needed to establish and run a new Commission. A range of organisational issues need more detailed consideration before the legislative and financial case for a new Commission is made, and there needs to be a greater degree of consensus on an appropriate model among existing human rights bodies.

3.11 However, the Government has not closed its mind to the idea of a new Human Rights Commission at some stage in the future in the light of practical experience of the working of the new legislation. If Parliament establishes a Committee on Human Rights, one of its main tasks might be to conduct an inquiry into whether a Human Rights Commission is needed and how it should operate. The Government would want to give full weight to the Committee's report in considering whether to create a statutory Human Rights Commission in future.

3.12 It has been suggested that a new Commission might be funded from non-Government sources. The Government would not wish to deter a move towards a non-statutory, privately-financed body if its role was limited to functions such as public education and advice to individuals. However, a non-statutory body could not absorb any of the functions of the existing statutory bodies concerned with aspects of human rights.

Chapter 4–Derogations, Reservations and other Protocols

Derogations

4.1 Article 15 of the Convention permits a State to derogate from certain Articles of the Convention in time of war or other public emergency threatening the life of the nation. The United Kingdom has one derogation in place, in respect of Article 5(3) of the Convention.

4.2 The derogation arose from a case in 1988 in which the European Court of Human Rights held that the detention of the applicants in the case before it under the Prevention of

Terrorism (Temporary Provisions) Act 1984 for more than four days constituted a breach of Article 5(3) of the Convention, because they had not been brought promptly before a judicial authority. The Government of the day entered a derogation following the judgment in order to preserve the Secretary of State's power under the Act to extend the period of detention of persons suspected of terrorism connected with the affairs of Northern Ireland for a total of up to seven days. The validity of the derogation was subsequently upheld by the European Court of Human Rights in another case in 1993.

4.3 We are considering what change might be made to the arrangements under the prevention of terrorism legislation. Substituting judicial for executive authority for extensions, which would mean that the derogation could be withdrawn, would require primary legislation. In the meantime, however, the derogation remains necessary. The Bill sets out the text of the derogation, and Article 5(3) will have effect in domestic law for the time being subject to its terms.

4.4 Given our commitment to promoting human rights, however, we would not want the derogation to remain in place indefinitely without good reasons. Accordingly its effect in domestic law will be time-limited. If not withdrawn earlier, it will expire five years after the Bill comes into force unless both Houses of Parliament agree that it should be renewed, and similarly thereafter. The Bill contains similar provision in respect of any new derogation which may be entered in future.

Reservations

4.5 Article 64 of the Convention allows a state to enter a reservation when a law in force is not in conformity with a Convention provision. The United Kingdom is a party to the First Protocol to the Convention, but has a reservation in place in respect of Article 2 of the Protocol. Article 2 sets out two principles. The first states that no person shall be denied the right to education. The second is that, in exercising any functions in relation to education and teaching, the State shall respect the right of parents to ensure that such education and teaching is in conformity with their own religious and philosophical convictions. The reservation makes it clear that the United Kingdom accepts this second principle only so far as it is compatible with the provision of efficient instruction and training, and the avoidance of unreasonable public expenditure.

4.6 The reservation reflects the fundamental principle originally enacted in the Education Act 1944, and now contained in section 9 of the Education Act 1996, "that pupils are to be educated in accordance with the wishes of their parents so far as that is compatible with the provision of efficient instruction and training and the avoidance of unreasonable public expenditure". There is similar provision in Scottish legislation. The reservation does not affect the right to education in Article 2. Nor does it deny parents the right to have account taken of their religious or philosophical convictions. Its purpose is to recognise that in the provision of State-funded education a balance must be struck in some cases between the convictions of parents and what is educationally sound and affordable.

4.7 Having carefully considered this, the Government has concluded that the reservation should be kept in place. Its text is included in the Bill, and Article 2 of the First Protocol will have effect in domestic law subject to its terms.

4.8 Whilst derogations are permitted under the Convention only in times of war or other public emergency, and so are clearly temporary, there is no such limitation in respect of reservations. We do not therefore propose to make the effect of the reservation in domestic law subject to periodic renewal by Parliament, but the Bill requires the Secretary of State (the Secretary of State for Education and Employment) to review the reservation every five years and to lay a report before Parliament.

Other Protocols

4.9 Protocols 4, 6 and 7 guarantee a number of rights additional to those in the original Convention itself and its First Protocol. These further rights have been added largely to reflect the wider range of rights subsequently included under the International Covenant on Civil and Political Rights. There is no obligation upon States who are party to the original Convention to accept these additional Protocols, but the Government has taken the opportunity to review the position of the United Kingdom on Protocols 4, 6 and 7.

4.10 **Protocol 4** contains a prohibition on the deprivation of liberty on grounds of inability to fulfil contractual obligations; a right to liberty of movement; a right to non-expulsion from the home State; a right of entry to the State of which a person is a national; and a prohibition on the collective expulsion of aliens. These provisions largely reflect similar (but not identical) rights provided under the International Covenant on Civil and Political Rights.

Protocol 4 was signed by the United Kingdom in 1963 but not subsequently ratified because of concerns about what is the exact extent of the obligation regarding a right of entry.

4.11 These are important rights, and we would like to see them given formal recognition in our law. But we also believe that existing laws in relation to different categories of British nationals must be maintained. It will be possible to ratify Protocol 4 only if the potential conflicts with our domestic laws can be resolved. This remains under consideration but we do not propose to ratify Protocol 4 at present.

4.12 **Protocol 6** requires the complete abolition of the death penalty other than in time of war or imminent threat of war. It does not permit any derogation or reservation. The Protocol largely parallels the Second Optional Protocol to the International Covenant on Civil and Political Rights, which the United Kingdom has not accepted.

4.13 The death penalty was abolished as a sentence for murder in 1965 following a free vote in the House of Commons. It remains as a penalty for treason, piracy with violence, and certain armed forces offences. No execution for these offences has taken place since 1946, when the war-time Nazi propagandist William Joyce (known as Lord Haw-Haw) was hanged at Wandsworth prison. The last recorded execution for piracy was in 1830. Thus there might appear to be little difficulty in our ratifying Protocol 6. This would, however, make it impossible for a United Kingdom Parliament to re-introduce the death penalty for murder, short of denouncing the European Convention. The view taken so far is that the issue is not one of basic constitutional principle but is a matter of judgement and conscience to be decided by Members of Parliament as they see fit. For these reasons, we do not propose to ratify Protocol 6 at present.

4.14 **Protocol 7** contains a prohibition on the expulsion of aliens without a decision in accordance with the law or opportunities for review; a right to a review of conviction or sentence after criminal conviction; a right to compensation following a miscarriage of justice; a prohibition on double jeopardy in criminal cases; and a right to equality between spouses. These rights reflect similar rights protected under the International Covenant on Civil and Political Rights.

4.15 In general, the provisions of Protocol 7 reflect principles already inherent in our law. In view of concerns in some of these areas in recent years, the Government believes that it would be particularly helpful to give these important principles the same legal status as other rights in the Convention by ratifying and incorporating Protocol 7. There is, however, a difficulty with this because a few provisions of our domestic law, for example in relation to the property rights of spouses, could not be interpreted in a way which is compatible with Protocol 7. The Government intends to legislate to remove these inconsistencies, when a suitable opportunity occurs, and then to sign and ratify the Protocol.

4.16 The Secretary of State will be able to amend the Human Rights Act by Order so as to insert into it the rights contained in any Protocols to the Convention which the United Kingdom ratifies in future. The Order will be subject to approval by both Houses of Parliament. The Bill also enables any reservation to a Protocol to be added, but as with the existing reservation it will have to be reviewed every five years if not withdrawn earlier.

INDEX